The Law of the Future and The Future of Law

Sam Muller, Stavros Zouridis, Morly Frishman and Laura Kistemaker (editors)

2011
Torkel Opsahl Academic EPublisher
Oslo

This and other books in the FICHL Publication Series may be openly accessed and downloaded through the Forum website (www.fichl.org). This site uses Persistent URLs (PURL) for all publications it makes available. The URLs of these publications will not be changed. Printed copies may be ordered at www.amazon.co.uk. This book was first published on 1 July 2011.

ISBN 978-82-93081-27-2

PUBLICATION SERIES PREFACE

The Torkel Opsahl Academic EPublisher is pleased to publish *The Law of the Future and the Future of Law* in this Publication Series. The book brings together a variety of perspectives and starts a process of reflection in a manner that resonates well with our open access publication policy. Broadening the discourse communities on questions of international law and policy and the internationalisation of law is becoming increasingly important.

The Forum for International Criminal and Humanitarian Law started the Torkel Opsahl Academic EPublisher and this Publication Series. The Forum is a department of the Centre for International Law Research and Policy, whose focus is not limited to international criminal and humanitarian law and transitional justice. The publication of this anthology signals a will to address a wider range of international law issues.

As with earlier volumes in the Publication Series, this book can be freely read, printed or downloaded from www.fichl.org/toaep. It can also be purchased through online distributors such as www.amazon.co.uk as a regular printed book. Firmly committed to open access, neither the Torkel Opsahl Academic EPublisher nor the Hague Institute for the Internationalisation of Law charges for this anthology.

Morten Bergsmo
Publication Series Co-Editor

Alf Butenschøn Skre
Senior Editorial Assistant

THE LAW OF THE FUTURE JOINT ACTION PROGRAMME

In 2010, the Hague Institute for the Internationalisation of Law (HiiL) embarked on a unique forward-looking exercise in the field of law: the Law of the Future Joint Action Programme. Taking the question 'how will law evolve in the next twenty years?' as the focal point, the Joint Action Programme is designed as a long-term process of broad consultation and exchange of views, comprised of various elements, including academic research, scenario-planning and meetings where a range of stakeholders are brought together.

At an early stage, we invited key thinkers from around the globe to contribute what we described as 'think pieces' – short, essay-like, contributions designed for a knowledgeable but not specialised audience. When disbursing these invitations, the primary purpose we had in mind was to collect input for the scenario-work we carry out in the context of the same initiative, which will lead to the *Law Scenarios to 2030*.[1] Given the insights provided by the 'think pieces', we expanded the project to disseminate the products of these pieces in an edited volume, which now lies before you.

At the same time, the think pieces have indeed served as a basis for drafting the *Law Scenarios to 2030*. Scenario thinking is a common strategy tool in business and academic disciplines such as economy and security studies, but quite uncommon in the field of law. By using scenarios on the future of law, politicians, corporate executives and societal leaders can judge how they can best respond to (legal) challenges posed by global developments. The *Law Scenarios to 2030* have been refined during a series of Scenario Building Workshops and Feedback Sessions through which a large variety of stakeholders have been consulted. The process will reach a culmination point during the Law of the Future Conference, taking place in The Hague on 23 and 24 June 2011. At this conference, the *Law Scenarios to 2030* will be further discussed and developed.

---

1 Follow www.lawofthefuture.org for updates.

The Law of the Future Joint Action Programme is a longer term process. After the Conference we will go back to the drawing board to improve the *Law Scenarios to 2030*, and revisions of the scenarios are planned every few years. In addition, ways to monitor which scenarios are unfolding will be developed. We will continue to join creative thinkers from academia and practice to reflect on alternative futures for law and legal systems. Therefore, this book is only a first edition. A second edition will be complemented with think pieces on legal issues not covered in this edition and with views from an even broader variety of experts.

The editors would like to thank Dessy Velikova and Matthew Simon and the interns at HiiL, Mellatra Tamrat, Lilly Brenna, and Shanu Teysing, for their help in the demanding process of preparing this book for publication in a rather short time. Special thanks go to Alexander Orona for his great support during the last editorial phase. His dedication, professionalism, hard work and guidance of the team of interns have been crucial to the successful completion of the book.

The Hague, April 2011

Sam Muller
Stavros Zouridis
Morly Frishman
Laura Kistemaker

SUMMARY TABLE OF CONTENTS

PART II:
THE FUTURE OF LAW

TABLE OF CONTENTS

PART I:
THE LAW OF THE FUTURE

PART II:
THE FUTURE OF LAW

Introduction

Sam Muller, Stavros Zouridis, Morly Frishman and Laura Kistemaker[*]

According to an old saying (which was recalled by one of the authors in this book), "predictions are always difficult, especially when they concern the future".[1] This truism can hardly be contested but the scope of the challenge may prove even greater when we take into account the particular aspect of the future at which this volume looks: that of law. For lawyers (as reminded by yet another of the authors herein) "are bad at predicting the future; they have enough work on their hands with the present".[2] Moreover, law, as a discipline and practice generally considered reactive to social conditions, is particularly problematic, for if law is – as Mark Osiel has noted[3] – a dependent variable in the calculus of society, then predicting its future requires first predicting the conditions of our world as a whole.

---

* **Sam Muller** is Director of the Hague Institute for the Internationalisation of Law (HiiL).
Stavros Zouridis is connected to Tilburg Law School as Professor of Public Administration.
Morly Frishman is Research and Programme Officer at HiiL.
Laura Kistemaker is External Relations Officer at HiiL.

1 Jan Klabbers, "The Idea(s) of International Law", in Sam Muller, Stavros Zouridis, Morly Frishman and Laura Kistemaker (eds.), *The Law of the Future and the Future of Law*, Torkel Opsahl Academic Epublisher, 2011. Klabbers attributes this saying to "a famous futurist". Funnily enough, this phrase has been attributed to more than 20 different people, without counting non-specific attributions such as "a famous basketball coach", "a famous philosopher" or a "wise Chinese sage". See http://www.larry.denenberg .com/predictions.html.

2 See Ralf Michaels, "Global Problems in Domestic Courts", in Sam Muller, Stavros Zouridis, Morly Frishman and Laura Kistemaker (eds.), *The Law of the Future and the Future of Law*, Torkel Opsahl Academic Epublisher, 2011.

3 See Mark Osiel, "After International Law: Non-Juridical Responses to Mass Atrocity", in Sam Muller, Stavros Zouridis, Morly Frishman and Laura Kistemaker (eds.), *The Law of the Future and the Future of Law*, Torkel Opsahl Academic Epublisher, 2011.

Against this background, it may be wise to clarify, at the outset, the objectives of the book and where the limits of this ambitious endeavour are drawn. As explained in the Preface, the book forms part of a broader initiative to encourage prospective thinking in the legal sphere. The basic premise of this initiative is quite straight forward: while prospective thinking in the realm of law is not quite common, we consider such thinking to be not only desirable but in fact necessary. Such an approach is required in order to ensure that legal systems and institutions will not constantly lag behind the ever accelerating pace of change and that law, as means for change but also for protection, will not become obsolete. Contemporary law and legal institutions are apt to undergo significant changes as our world transforms. The book thus aims to explore a range of challenges that law and legal systems are facing today and some of the challenges that lie ahead and to examine to what extent the present institutional design and the global legal universe – if such a thing exists – are apt to successfully cope with such challenges and problems.

This is already a tall order to face and what the book *does not* purport to do is to present a comprehensive set of predictions, the validity of which could later be tested as a matter of whether or not the future has unfolded in line with such assessments. The editors of this book, unfortunately, do not posses a time machine with which one can travel to the future (and to the best of our knowledge, nor do any of the authors who contributed to this book). Indeed, we have no pretention to predict the future in the manner of a fortune teller. Rather, the intent is to discuss critically the possibilities we can see today and what these trends suggest about our collective future. Therefore, the value of this book is in presenting visionary, innovative and at times bold observations and insights that attempt to look at the law of the future and the future of law; thus initiating further discussion on how to prepare for the future or, better yet, what do we need to do now to reach a desirable future. Unless one opts for an entirely deterministic perspective, the future, of course, is not merely something to look at, rather, something to *shape*. The decisions we make now will direct our collective future.

Thus, understanding the possibilities of the law of the future is relevant and important. It is relevant because the projected transnationalisation and internationalisation of law will affect an ever-widening sphere of subjects. It is important because the new processes of rule-making, adjudication and enforcement entailed in such changes are likely to dramatically alter many traditional relationships between actors and orders in our legal universe.

The authors who contributed to this book were all presented with an identical set of questions, as follows:

> What do you see as the most significant challenges for the development of the law? What developments are we likely to see in the coming two to three decades? What do those developments mean for national legal systems in the international legal order as a whole?

Unsurprisingly, the answers to this question differ from author to author, and not merely in the sense that each responded within the context of a particular specialisation. Differences are also seen in the sense that authors related their think pieces to different aspects of the law of the future and the problems of the present (from impunity in the commission of international crimes, to the future of positive legal theory in academic discussion, to the role of megacities as international actors, to name just a few examples, reflecting the great variety of issues addressed herein). Furthermore, authors took different approaches in terms of *how* their think pieces are formed. Some suffice with pointing out certain present and future challenges. Others highlight areas and contexts where it can be seen that law has so far failed to adequately respond to societal needs. Yet others attempt to think about specific problems that may not even be fully acknowledged by many, as of yet. Some authors focus on the content of various fields of law, while others take a more holistic look at the impact of developments on legal systems and on how they interact.

The outcome is thus an eclectic book featuring a plurality of perspectives and approaches; its inherent strength is the diversity of each author's unique perspective, as well as the complex mosaic that is the result of juxtaposing these perspectives. The book thus provides a particularly rich compilation of insights, observations, points of critique and suggestions for improvement, the common thread being the authors' willingness to think critically about the possibilities of their field, at least as far as the appropriateness of law and legal systems is concerned.

Substantially, there is another common thread that connects (in one way or another) virtually all the think pieces: globalisation and the internationalisation of law. Conceptually, both 'globalisation' and 'law' are the kind of elusive terms that seem to evade a precise definition (as is the 'internationalisation of law', a concept which relates to the impact of globalisation on law). The meaning of globalisation is subject to much theoretical and academic debate. Undoubtedly, it is a complex phenomenon of multiple dimensions. Many attempts to define it have been made by scholars from a range of disciplines, but no single definition can be found that neatly captures the great scope and complexity of globalisation as a matter of a consensus understanding. Literature about globalisation fills entire shelves in many libraries across the globe as well as thousands of web pages (the Internet itself being a global platform, of course).

Irrespective of globalisation, legal theoreticians have long attempted to define what 'law' is and yet a single, clear definition is not quite available. The deeper one goes into it the more difficult it may become to understand exactly what law is. The definition of law also depends on competing perceptions as to what the *role* of law is (or *should* be) and what objectives law is serving (or *should* serve). Moreover, law may be seen as one academic and professional discipline, but it may be very difficult to find a uniform definition of law's essence, role and purpose cutting across the various fields of law (criminal law, constitutional law, administrative law, private law, commercial law, etc.) and kinds of law (municipal law, national law, international law and so forth).

The legal aspects of globalisation, the role of law in this process and the consequences for legal systems are relatively under-researched, compared, for example, to the economic, political, social and cultural aspects of globalisation. A useful concept in this respect is the 'internationalisation of law', denoting the process of the accommodation by a legal system of elements of other legal systems. This process can be observed at the national level, as well as at the international, regional and global levels. The internationalisation of law is driven by vertical and horizontal processes. Vertical processes consist of top-down and bottom-up pressures on legal systems, and this is particularly applicable in respect of national legal systems. Horizontal processes involve transnational interactions between individuals, states and organisations. While recent years have shown an increasing interest in globalisation and law and in the internationalisation of law, quite clearly there is still a long way to go. Meanwhile, new challenges in this respect keep appearing.

In any event, it is hardly surprising that, in a book about the law of the future and the future of law, the phenomena of globalisation and the internationalisation of law will feature so prominently. Quite simply, so many of the problems and challenges of today and tomorrow are (directly or indirectly) an outcome of globalisation, or are otherwise related to it. The conditions of economic and social interaction generate problems and challenges at the local level. Importantly, however, an increasing number of problems and challenges are not only the result of globalisation, they are *global problems*. In his think piece, Ralf Michaels[4] provides a basic yet very helpful typology of global problems, by distinguishing between three types: problems that are global *by nature* (*e.g.*, climate change); problems that are global *by design* (*i.e.*, the global character of the problem is a consequence of design, as is the case with legal issues pertaining to the globally accessible Internet); and problems that are global *by definition* (*i.e.*, because that is how we choose to frame them, *e.g.*, crimes against humanity). Though the book's structure does not explicitly build upon such a typology, readers may be well advised to keep it in mind. The important point is that global problems, as such, are generally not the kind of problems that *national* legal systems and laws were designed to deal with. The myriad international organisations that were set up in the twentieth century reflect an attempt to compensate for that structural problem by globally dealing with global problems. For a variety of reasons, however, few would disagree that the international system in its present form suffers from a range of imperfections that frustrate its capability to successfully deal with the challenge.

In the present era, the conditions of isolation under which human cultures and societies operated for many centuries no longer exist. Spurred by growth in human technologies which enable rapid communication and transportation, our geographical remoteness has given way to complex inter-societal exchanges, the final fruits of which remain unknown. Never in the history of our species have we shared as much as we do now, and for that reason, the future which we create today is not the future of a particular political community, but in fact the future of all.

In terms of the organisation of this book, we divided the volume into two 'parts'. Part I, entitled 'The Law of the Future', contains contributions that in our view deal primarily with factors relating to how law, as well as legal systems and institutions, will or should look in the future. Part II, entitled 'The Future of Law', features contributions on

4 Michaels, 2011, see *supra* note 2.

issues that relate to factors pertaining to how law will evolve and what future role it will have. This is a rough distinction made for convenience only, and a decision taken by the editors. Each of the book's two parts contains several sections, organised around different themes. It should be noted that individual contributions are of a variable nature, such that many could be placed within either part and in different sections. However, the overall division arises from considering each piece as a whole.

Part I contains three sections: Globalisation, the International System, International Law and a Global Constitutional Framework: Towards a New Global New Deal? (Section 1); Changing State Institutions (Section 2); and: Private Actors, International Commerce and Private Legal Regimes (Section 3). Part II contains four sections: Law and its Evolution – Theoretical Perspectives (Section 4); Divergence and Convergence of Legal Systems (Section 5); New Legal Challenges Posed by Technological Development (Section 6); and: The Emerging International Criminal Justice System (Section 7).

We have opted for a thematic structure, rather than, for example, a more traditional division in accordance with the field of doctrinal law. We believe such a thematic division offers a more interesting read, as it is better suited to help exploring issues 'out of the box', thereby promoting critical thinking about the inter-linkages of different areas of law with each other and with society as a whole. Readers are invited to explore for themselves such connections and synergies and we most certainly invite feedback, which will be taken into account for the purpose of future editions of this book. The remainder of this Introduction provides readers with a roadmap as to what can be found in each of these sections.

1. Part I: The Law of the Future

1.1. Globalisation, the International System, International Law and a Global Constitutional Framework: Towards a New Global New Deal?

The first section of the book concerns the 'big questions': those problems and dilemmas that result from or go hand in hand with the process of globalisation and relate primarily to the international system of law and governance. Whereas Section 2 contains think pieces that discuss how different state institutions are changing as a result of globalisation, this section deals with the design of the international system and international institutions, rather than national law and national institutions. Legal pluralism, a multi-polar world and multi-level governance are key concepts here.

Within this section, a great deal of attention is paid to international law. Somewhat paradoxically, international law is the object of (at least) two sorts of 'attacks'. On the one hand, it is accused of being an immature or incomplete form of law: the argument that it is not even 'really law' is well-known and is echoed here as well, for example in David Koepsell's chapter, stating that "one might well argue that there is no such thing as international law ... yet".[5] On the other hand, it is criticised for being based on old, perhaps outdated, concepts, and on a power balance that no longer exists, a fact that prevents it from offering a meaningful, appropriate and adequate response to the challenges of globalisation (for an argument roughly built along these lines, see for instance Jan Klabbers' chapter in this section of the book, further described below). Yet other authors point out new directions that international law has started taking and how it is expected to continue to develop in coming decades (see, *e.g.*, André Nollkaemper's think piece on new models of international rule of law and Joost Pauwelyn's chapter on the rise of *informal* international law-making).

While we do not know what course globalisation will take in the future, it seems highly unlikely that it will disappear altogether. This assessment is shared, explicitly or implicitly, by the vast majority of the contributors to this volume, and certainly those that appear in this section. They also seem to share the conviction that law and legal systems and institutions have so far proved capable of dealing with global problems and challenges only to a very limited extent. What is even worse, globalisation has drawbacks and the role of (international) law in this respect may have not always been positive, a fact on which many authors expound. Before we present these explicit and normative points of critique, perhaps the most appropriate starting point for this book is with the call for a 'Global New Deal'.

---

5 David Koepsell, "International Law and Legal Positivism", in Sam Muller, Stavros Zouridis, Morly Frishman and Laura Kistemaker (eds.), *The Law of the Future and the Future of Law*, Torkel Opsahl Academic Epublisher, 2011.

Randall Peerenboom departs from the statement that now is an opportune time to reflect on the law of the future. Several factors come together to justify that, including the continuing sagas in Iraq and Afghanistan, the demise of the Washington Consensus, the global financial crisis, the decline of Neo Liberalism and the rise of the BRICs. According to Peerenboom, we are undergoing a major shift in the global economic order, which will undeniably have consequences for the geopolitical balance of power and for the international legal order. The new multi-polar world in the making is marked by diversity and legal plurality. Western economic, cultural and political hegemony will have to give way to other influences. At the same time, more and more problems are global problems, and these will necessitate close collaboration to resolve. All this means that the new world order will require redistribution of power, in the sense of adapting the way existing international institutions and organisations are formed, how they operate, and how they are created. The limits of the self-proclaimed universalism of the Western-conceptualised international law will be further exposed. Beyond such institutional changes, Peerenboom calls for a change of tone and approach, suggesting that diversity and plurality will be taken seriously, rather than merely being paid hortatory lip service. Peerenboom also suggests that the way forward may be inspired by the traditional Confucian approach, emphasising harmony among diverging views and interest, rather than identity. The ASEAN Way, as a modern reflection of this traditional approach, may become ever more important and useful, characterised by tolerance and informality. Formal law-based institutions and mechanisms for conflict resolution will not disappear and may remain the most appropriate avenue for resolving some issues, but the international stage will feature more and more informal mechanisms, international mediations, negotiations and compromise, which de-emphasise formal international law and judicial institutions. Peerenboom does not disregard the potential for (armed) conflict that changes in the global balance may entail, but he is nonetheless optimistic that this is not inevitable, due to various characteristics of our era, including the great extent of inter-dependence. To ensure a relatively smooth transition, a Global New Deal is urgently needed, providing for a more equitable sharing of global resources and responsibilities.

To better appreciate the proposition of a Global New Deal, we may look at the think pieces by Thomas Pogge and by Jan Klabbers, both of which offer sharp and explicit critique regarding what has gone wrong with globalisation. Furthermore, they take a normative stance against the role (international) law has played in this process. In doing so, they also sketch the future that we may wish to avert.

Amongst all the contributions included in this book, the think piece by **Thomas Pogge** provides the most outspoken criticism of globalisation. His starting point is that globalisation – which in the domain of law leads to the emergence of complex bodies of supranational law that constrain and shape national legal systems – will certainly continue into the coming decades. The problem he points out is that supranational rules, which increase in number and scope together with the spread of globalisation, are subject to much less democratic control compared to national rule-making and are far more susceptible to regulatory caption by a minority of powerful actors. The essence of the problem is that the Achilles heel of every competitive system, so he argues, is that there is always an incentive for those who are able to influence rule-making to manipulate the rules in their favour. Globalisation, however, makes the problems and the dangers much worse: if a coterie of elite individuals enjoy a favourable position of influence in domestic systems, globalisation enhances their position as the ability to influence rule-making at the international or supranational level requires such vast resources that only a few possess. Furthermore, in the global context, the temptation to corrupt the rules is enormous, since so much is at stake. Moreover, whereas in other contexts the tendency of powerful players to manipulate the rules in their favour as much as they can may be mitigated through certain shared morality and values, on the global plane it is very difficult to argue that such a strong commitment to morality and shared values exists. Thus, Pogge argues, law as moulded by powerful global actors has led (and will continue to lead) to polarisation between the rich and the poor, both *between* states and *within* states. How can this spiral effect be avoided? The little room that Pogge leaves for optimism relates to his argument that manipulative behaviour of powerful actors, in the long run, will lead to an incoherent system that would be highly vulnerable to crises and, as such, will be detrimental also to these actors themselves. Accordingly, once they realise that this is the risk they are running, they might be more willing to accept a systemic solution that reduces lobbying opportunities and thus ensures fairer competition.

Jan Klabbers seems to agree with much of this critique. His explicit concern however is with the intellectual apparatus of international law, nowadays still based on roughly the same conceptions from the late nineteenth century that were used as its foundations, and are not likely to drastically change anytime soon. Like Pogge, Klabbers is of the conviction that "to the extent that international law covers the global economy, it does so in support of the major players rather than the poor and dispossessed". But what Klabbers is emphasising is that much of the problem relates to the fact that many issues related to the global economy have been cast aside by international law. Thus, while international trade law and investment protection law have become highly developed in recent years (protecting, needless to say, the interests of investors and businesses), topics like development, taxation, migration, competition, labour rights and, finally, economic, social and cultural rights, have either been wholly ignored by the discipline of international law, or have been comparatively marginalised. Thus, on the whole, international law has been facilitating rather than regulating global capitalism, in many cases allowing for, if not actually stimulating, a race to the bottom. Another great source of concern for Klabbers is the further instrumentalisation and even commodification of international law which, he assesses, is bound to continue in the foreseeable future. This problem relates to Klabber's well known critique of soft law and its increasing popularity among policy-makers and some international lawyers. Arguing that there is a possibility to undertake commitments which nevertheless stop short of being legally binding only helps, according to Klabbers, to turn the law into just one element among other possibilities, to be utilised if and only if convenient for those in positions of power, thus leading to erosion in the power of law itself. If we were to save the future of international law as a discipline, several things need to happen. In the first place, the very fact that international law, even if it largely remains an inter-state system, impacts the lives of individuals makes it important. The negative role of international law in leading to unequal development and distribution of wealth must be acknowledged. And then, topics that were left largely untouched by international law can be brought into the discipline, even if this will come at the expense of uniformity: "the best way to combat fragmentation may be not so much the desperate search for uniformity, but rather to ensure that all aspects of life are part of the same broader fabric – only in this way can the fabric itself survive".

The question of uniformity and fragmentation in international law is the point of departure in **André Nollkaemper's** think piece. While also addressing the future of international law as a discipline, his approach and focus, however, are quite different from those of Klabbers, and seem more optimistic. Nollkaemper views the cracks in the unitary system of international law through the prism of the rule of law quality of international law. From this perspective, he identifies two models of international rule of law that will exist side by side. In the first model, the international rule of law will remain confined to the international level. Here progress can be expected to be slow, and to vary between regimes. In the second model, on the other hand, the international rule of law mingles with the domestic rule of law. The prime example here is international human rights law as well as several other specialised functional regimes. Interestingly, whereas Klabbers doubts the usefulness of the increasingly popular accountability mechanisms in such contexts (asking whether they are not leading us to an 'audit society' where trusts ends up being eroded) and is particularly suspicious towards compliance regimes (seeing them as eroding the power of law, since breaches of obligations are no longer perceived as such, rather as 'compliance problems'), for Nollkaemper these developments signify a step forward towards strengthening the rule of law quality of international law. In any event, Nollkaemper predicts that the development of this second model will be uneven across the world, as it depends on varying degrees of national legal empowerment. Moreover, it is not a blessing without a risk. In fact it creates fundamental dilemmas, since the very international law that seeks to impose itself on the national legal order remains rooted in the international legal order, with its relatively limited rule of law quality. Therefore, the two futures for the international rule of law are intrinsically connected: the international rule of law will be able to strengthen the national rule of law (see next paragraph, below), and it will benefit from the superiority of domestic enforcement mechanisms, to the extent that the rule of law at the international level will be strengthened.

Rule of law is the main concern of the think piece by **Stavros Zouridis**. He departs from the statement that during the past decades, the rule of law as a legal concept has spread all over the world, but this statement is followed by highlighting the shortcomings of our understanding of the rule of law and the ability to measure it. Most importantly, Zouridis calls attention to the durable gap between the rule of law 'on paper' (as reflected in many declarations, constitutions and legal infrastructures) and the rule of law in practice. "Has the rule of law really become a cornerstone of everyday government practices?" he asks, and the answer he provides is that the indications thus far do not justify a jubilant mood. While in-depth research in traditional rule of law countries demonstrates serious discrepancies between the law on the books and the everyday realities within public authorities, countries where the rule of law is a relatively new focus have an even longer way to go. As part of his assessment of the current situation, Zouridis also touches upon the darker side of globalisation, although pointing to different problems than those highlighted by the critics of globalisation mentioned above. While globalisation is the process that allowed for the significant spread of the rule of law in the last decades, globalisation also brought with it negative phenomena such as transnational organised crime, illicit trade and terrorism networks. These criminal activities may seriously undermine the rule of law (especially when they involve large scale corruption on various levels) but, importantly, fighting them within the confines of the rule of law is also a serious challenge. Failing to meet this challenge will result in further undermining the rule of law. Zouridis suggests that the key for the success of the rule of law is its perceived legitimacy, and in turn the rule of law will only be perceived as legitimate if it proves to be effective in coping with real social problems.

Michel Rosenfeld undertakes in his think piece the daunting task of exploring what kind of constitutional ordering would likely be both workable and normatively attractive in a legal universe characterised as increasingly layered and fragmented. For him, the most important two trends that lead to such a legal realm are globalisation (adding as it does layers of international, supranational and global legal regimes) and privatisation (adding a transnational dimension and increasing fragmentation). The most distinctive feature of nation-state constitution ordering, the hierarchical ordering and overall unity, is inapt to describe the complex multilayered and segmented legal universe nor will it be possible in the foreseeable future to create such an order on a the global realm which is ever more complex, diverse and legally pluralistic. These regimes interact constantly and combine to structure the legal universe into an aggregated multilevel edifice. Rosenfeld describes the fascinating, rather complex and at times surprising dynamics of divergence and convergence taking place in such a legal universe. On the one hand, divergences occur not only among levels but also *within* levels, as is the case for example with proponents of 'Asian values' contesting the Western conceptions of human rights (a point which reminds Peerenboom's sceptical remarks concerning the self-proclaimed universalism of fundamental rights). This would seem to make the need for increased convergence ever more crucial. On the other hand, in some contexts we see that the loss of formal convergence can be compensated for by new points of material convergence. Then again, Rosenfeld also points out that, paradoxically, attempts to create (formal) convergence sometimes, in fact, result in new (material) divergences (human rights regime once again being a case in point). Rosenfeld suggests that, contrary to constitutional frameworks at the national level, on the global scale future harmony and legitimacy can perhaps best be achieved by de-centralised and pluralistic constitutional ordering. While there is no single prescription for such ordering, Rosenfeld points towards certain possibilities and notes, in this context, a few specific constitutional tools. One is federalism (transformed to 'transnational federalism') which can achieve simultaneously both decoupling and unification. Another is the principle of subsidiarity. Other suggested tools include devolution and constitutionalising a right to secession.

The final piece in this section, by **Joost Pauwelyn**, focuses attention on 'informal international law-making'. The phenomenon he denotes with this term is generally what others have sometimes referred to as international network governance. Anne-Marie Slaughter famously warned about certain dangers embodied in such activities insofar as they are lacking transparency and are far removed from political accountability. In this volume, this criticism is echoed by Klabbers, while Rosenfeld also mentions intergovernmental networks, though in a much more neutral fashion, simply as one of the many facts that make out our complex legal universe. Pauwelyn investigates these activities more thoroughly, in an attempt to see whether they indeed give rise to grave concerns, as it is often assumed. The informality of these activities can take the form of process informality, actor informality, output informality, or any combination of the above. It is a phenomenon on the rise. Very few formal multilateral treaties have been concluded in recent years, while informal law-making is found in abundance, in many areas of life. In presenting reasons for this, Pauwelyn states that some reasons are perfectly benign and legitimate. For example, some of these activities can be attributed to the increasingly multi-polar and diverse world, with 'new powers' preferring informal arrangements (a point that echoes the approach of Peerenboom and possibly Rosenfeld as well). Other reasons are more worrisome, and give rise to legitimate concerns regarding accountability and even legality. Pauwelyn discusses how various forms of accountability (towards external or internal stakeholders, at the international or national level) can be of use, and he concludes that what is needed is not *more* accountability, but better accountability (a point which Klabbers would be likely to agree to).

1.2. Changing State Institutions

Section Two deals with changing state institutions, one of the key uncertainties of the *Law Scenarios to 2030*. A number of aspects feature: the role of constitutions, especially in the interplay between national and international law; the role of democracy and accountability mechanisms; the role of the state as provider of public goods; and the emergence of new actors beside the state. It builds on the challenges elucidated in Section 1, which looks at changes in international law – changes which, it should come as no surprise, reflect on the state.

Tom Ginsburg argues that future developments in national constitutions will be determined by the interaction of domestic and transnational actors. Current trends – including the integration of international human rights norms, constitutions' increasingly lengthy and statutory nature, and the import of provisions from similarly situated nations – are likely to continue over the long-term. Constitutions are likely to serve less as embodiments of a nation's common aspirations and highest norms than as deals between competing national and international groups. Rapid social and technological change will also contribute to the destabilisation of constitutions, and amendment procedures may become more flexible in response to these pressures. Additionally, the frequency of expansive judicial interpretation may increase in order to harmonise constitutional law with new social realities generated by globalisation. In general, constitutions and constitutional legal practice will be subject to more external influences than in the past.

Philipp Kiiver looks at parliamentary accountability in the EU, but his think piece can perhaps serve as an interesting case study on how one can deal with accountability challenges that a globalising, supranationally developing international legal order presents. His point of departure is that European governance defies classical notions of linear principal-agent relations between legislature and executive or between Member States and the EU. In his view the legislative process of the EU is relatively straightforward, but the executive functions of the EU are spread over a wide range of European and national actors, and hybrids and networks between them. In addition, treaty reform and inter-institutional agreements continue to add to both the scope and the complexity of EU action. Lastly, he observes that national parliaments are more peripheral in EU matters than they are on the domestic scene, while the European Parliament is not neatly substituting their functions. He examines parliamentary responses to this, including the development of other means of oversight, like developing alternative or supplementary concepts or mechanisms such as output legitimacy, transparency, and accountability relations with multiple principals and forums of various, not necessarily democratic, kinds. His conclusion is that the European Parliament will probably continue to strengthen its clout, such as its growing influence in the Commission, in standing up to the Council and in monitoring European agencies, however without leading to any detectable reduction of the democratic deficit. He also assumes that national parliamentary behaviour in European scrutiny has reached a steady state – after intensification of oversight in the 1990s this might be 'as good as it gets'. Actors other than national parliaments may be the most relevant actors for change from now on. European institutions themselves (providing stimulus for active engagement via, *e.g.*, the subsidiarity early warning system); upper rather than lower chambers of parliament; and (constitutional) courts insisting on greater formalisation of parliamentary oversight (as, *e.g.*, the German Constitutional Court did in the Lisbon ruling).

Global problems in domestic courts are the topic of **Ralf Michaels**' think piece. He opens with the recognition that the challenge for law lies is the fact that more and more problems are global, while our institutions are not. He argues that coping with the increasing number of global problems will require a paradigmatic change. Three kinds of global problems are distinguished one from the other: problems that are global *by nature* (*e.g.*, climate change); problems that are global *by design* (*i.e.*, the global character of the problem is a consequence of design, as is the case with legal issues pertaining to the globally accessible Internet); and problems that are global *by definition* (*i.e.*, because that is how we choose to frame them, *e.g.*, crimes against humanity). Domestic courts, even though they were not designed to be able to cope with global problems, have been forced to handle just such problems, and will continue to do so in the foreseeable future where we lack a better alternative. This places domestic courts in a difficult, and certainly challenging, position. When dealing with global problems they are not occupying familiar legal grounds. Moreover, there is a natural reluctance to what may be deemed the unilateral exercise of extraterritorial jurisdiction, which explains, according to Michaels, while domestic courts frequently present an artificial analysis so as to deny that they are handling a global problem to begin with, even when it is quite clear that that is exactly what they are doing.[6] Interestingly, Michaels suggests that even if domestic courts are not international or global in any constitutional sense (they form part of national legal systems and they are constituted and operate under national laws), as far as the scope of application is concerned, we must acknowledge that domestic courts increasingly act as international courts. Michael points to the increase in the use of comparative law by courts as an indication of increasing global awareness on the part of judges, but clarifies that more far reaching steps will be needed, including the development of new doctrines that "detach the judicial task from the furthering of domestic political interests".

Based on an analysis of global challenges and responses to them, **Hans Corell** looks at the role that domestic institutions can effectively play in realising multilateral rules-based international society. He does so by focussing on one issue: the need to develop a system in which the quality and the consistence of the norms can be ascertained. The

6 On this point compare to Klabbers who points out that domestic courts have sometimes responded in a lukewarm fashion to calls for the greater involvement of domestic courts in applying international law. Also compare to Nollkaemper, who argues that the increasing involvement of domestic courts in areas that were traditionally out of their reach can remedy a fundamental weakness in the international rule of law (the absence of independent courts that can review the use and abuse of public power) and also discusses the prospects of more and more states allowing their courts to distance themselves from the political branches of the state and become effective agents of the international legal order. Klabbers, 2011, *supra* note 1; and Andre Nollkaemper, "The Bifurcation of International Law: Two Futures for the International Rule of Law", in Sam Muller, Stavros Zouridis, Morly Frishman and Laura Kistemaker (eds.), *The Law of the Future and the Future of Law*, Torkel Opsahl Academic Epublisher, 2011.

conclusions of the International Law Commission's Study group on the fragmentation of international law and the inevitability of clashes between legal rules and principles are his point of departure. National laws can easily conflict with international norms, especially in view of the fact that the sources of those international norms are so diverse. He also addresses the issues of norms that have become, in effect, obsolete and the need for some kind of test for determining whether new laws or new international instruments are really required. Article 38 of the Statute of the International Court of Justice provides a hierarchy of sorts for rules at the international level. The Vienna Convention on the Law of Treaties also provides some guidance in this respect. The author sees this as an urgent issue that must be addressed in the law of the future. A pragmatic solution he suggests as a more immediate way forward is to give the legal advisers of ministries of foreign affairs a role in dealing with some of these concerns.

John Bell reflects on challenges for the public-private divide. The basic issue he focuses on is that public law functions on the premise that decisions of public interest are made and implemented at a national level within the constraints of democratic decision-making and democratic accountability to the domestic political community. In this, public law is distinct from private law. The concern of the paper is that this is increasingly not the case, and that a different paradigm is needed. In particular, the use of transnational providers of public services poses particular problems for the traditional conception of public law. It no longer holds true that decisions about the public interest are and can be taken simply in a nationally specific context, especially in the area of public services. The role of the central state then becomes one of regulation and purchase, and public service is an area where services are designed and purchased, typically by contract by a public body, but they may also operate by way of the free market, licensed and regulated by a public body. The state-model he sees is of the 'negotiator state' – a state which is less concerned with providing services (and thus employing people to provide them on often advantageous terms) and more about procuring the services from others, not necessarily within domestic jurisdiction.

Jean-Bernard Auby looks at a rather new, emerging actor for the future: big cities. It is predicted by some that almost two-thirds of the world's population will live in cities by 2030. His point of departure is the notion of 'glocalisation', the complex interplay between international and local realities. He foresees that this interplay will be an important factor in the law of the future. He discusses the position of cities and local realities in the process of globalisation and some legal consequences of this position that are already visible, from which he formulates some hypotheses regarding its future influence on law, both institutionally and normatively. Institutionally, big cities (in all their varieties) are becoming actors on the international stage in their own right as part of global networks – public and private – which work on specific issues. Normatively, he sees challenges to democracy and rule of law.

Janne Nijman also looks at cities and the manner in which they interact through non-governmental organisations and intergovernmental organisations. She observes that many, if not most, of the challenges of globalisation come to the fore in cities: environmental pollution, crime, inequality, migration, cultural diversity, and unemployment, to name a few. She distinguishes between the private city (its collective of private economic interests) and the public city, the city governments who increasingly act as global actors. In her think piece, she presents six propositions on how the public city will affect international law. She sees that direct links between cities and global institutions will intensify. This is already very visible in the area of environmental law with NGOs, which facilitate these links. Cities will also be implementers of international law of their own accord, thus bypassing the state. Connected with this, she also sees that the international law of the future will 'de-formalise'; local judges will simply apply it as persuasive authority and cities will become part of international rule-making. They will be significant influencers of international negotiations. Nijman even asks the question whether cities will, in the future, acquire the status of an international legal person, alongside that of states. With that, the state-centric system of today will change and become more multifarious.

1.3. Private Actors, International Commerce and Private Legal Regimes

Section Three changes the focus from the public government side to that of private actors. Challenges that emerge in this field are the phenomenon of the transnationalisation of commercial law, emerging accountability mechanisms for transnationally operating market actors, and the development of other trust building mechanisms besides law. Another aspect that is discussed in this section relates to the public-private divide and the challenge of anchoring public goods in what has, to date, been seen as essentially private, non-state, behaviour. Regulation in the financial sector, where 'private' regulation is deemed to have been less than successful, is discussed. In addition, the authors address the role of corporate social responsibility and the possible alteration of company law to accommodate new values.

Gralf-Peter Calliess outlines the challenges that national legal systems face and are likely to face in the field of commercial law. He singles out the transnationalisation of commercial law as a key development for the law of the future. He observes that, if one thinks of contract enforcement as a normative good produced on a market, the legal needs of law consumers have shifted towards institutions that provide legal certainty in cross-border situations. Meanwhile, the offer of national legal systems remains focused on domestic commerce. Private governance mechanisms such as soft law, alternative dispute resolution, and private enforcement mechanisms are increasingly relevant. Using this trend as a spring board, Calliess then points to a number of dilemmas which this development raises and he does so in relation to four core values that are embodied in the rule of law in the commercial field: access to justice, equity, legal certainty, and the public good. In order to deal with challenges which the transnationalisation of commercial law poses in respect of these values, the policy options appear to be (i) to allow privatisation to continue but to constitutionalise the values listed above through self-regulation, or (ii) to bring the state back by modernising the national legal system.

Jan Smits focuses on two interrelated trends, and does so from the perspective of private law. The first is the replacement of law by other types of trust building relationships in the global economy. If we assume that national law is becoming less and less important and will not be replaced by a similar type of law at an international level, this means that (private) parties have to look for other types of trust-building. The second trend is the increasing role of (private) parties in choosing their own law: 'legal tourism' has emerged over recent decades, and it is likely that this trend will continue. The emergence of optional regimes is only one important example of this. At the same time, states will have to be much more precise about what they can still allow as a choice for a foreign or optional legal system. Both trends are likely to reshape the entire outlook of law.

Deborah Hensler also looks at the transnationalisation of commercial law and the construction of the private, transnational legal order. She sees a trend of holding multi-national market actors to the highest standards of accountability and affording injured populations more generous compensation for losses in a wider variety of circumstances. The adoption of procedures for collective litigation, class actions, group litigation orders, and other forms of mass litigation in ever increasing numbers and in more and more countries provides new opportunities for building a transnational private order. There are, however, challenges. Increased forum shopping and the subsequent rise in the cost of litigation, divergent substantive law and an unwillingness of domestic courts to harmonise can all lead to situations in which multinational corporations craft class and mass procedures within international arbitration that remove both outcomes and processes from the public eye.

Thorsten Beck looks at cross-border banking and, in doing so, raises interesting issues about the strengths and limits of international, global supervisory mechanisms. Well-developed financial systems are critical for economic development, and growth and banks constitute one of the core segments of the financial system. Banks, however, are also at the centre of boom-and-bust periods that many capitalist economies have regularly experienced, most recently in 2008 and 2009. The susceptibility to bank runs, interlinkages of banks through interbank market and payment systems, and the critical role of banks in creating information (and thus helping overcome market frictions), generate external costs from bank failure, which have resulted in the banking system being one of the most regulated sectors of the economy. The globalisation of the financial system, illustrated by globalising markets and banks, has created new opportunities and benefits, but also significant additional risks. Regulating global banks at the national level undermines the benefits that global banks can bring to economies by exacerbating their risks. Future regulatory frameworks have to be matched to the challenges presented by global banking. He argues that bank regulation is an area where more than convergence, we need supra-national frameworks to harness global banking markets for the benefits of host economies. This does not necessarily require the construction of new supra-national institutions, but rather incentive-compatible frameworks that can be built around existing institutions. Rather than seeing this as a debate about national sovereignty, this debate should be framed as designing an optimal regulatory framework to minimise losses from bank fragility while maximizing the benefits of banking for everyone.

Tineke Lambooy asks whether legal systems support the emerging requirements of corporate social responsibility (CSR). Does corporate law, annual accounting law, environmental law, labour law, tort law, etc. anchor and promote CSR? She defines the requirements of CSR as: (i) adopting responsible corporate governance strategies; (ii) creating transparency of corporate conduct and providing information with regard to products; (iii) allowing participation of stakeholders in the decision-making process; (iv) developing innovative business approaches towards global issues, the resolution of which needs private actor support (*e.g.*, to address the ecological crises); (v) organising accountability, which amongst other things translates into effectively addressing complaints and not obstructing access to justice; and, if possible, (vi) employing mediation to achieve endurable solutions for problems related to business activities, in the design of which stakeholders participate. As a challenge for the future, she reflects on designing a new governance approach with regard to multinational corporations (MNCs). This approach covers both values and procedural matters – a framework or constitution – for MNCs that includes principles and more detailed guidelines for governing an MNC and its economic activities – in a broad sense, *i.e.*, so far as they, *de facto*, can be considered within its sphere of influence.

Jan Eijsbouts also focuses on regulating CSR, and in particular the law on and regulation of international corporate governance and CSR. He approaches the issue from two angles: the substantive angle and the form (regulatory) angle. Substantively, he deals with the alignment in the global market of corporate control, the shareholder and the stakeholder models. On the form angle he looks at the ways in which these normative approaches are being shaped; hard law, soft law, self-regulation (collective and individual) and uncodified (the societal expectations, to be judged by the courts of public opinion). Key dilemmas he sees for the future are: corporations as subjects of international law; an increasing unequal playing field by more application of the extraterritorial effect of parent company's law on foreign operations; multinational enterprise liability; different national treatment of international soft law norms;

different treatment of corporations in national criminal laws; and, finally, how to ensure that investment protection in foreign jurisdictions, on the one hand, and responsible business, on the other hand, are treated as two sides of the same coin.

Levinus Timmerman, Matthijs de Jongh, and Alexander Schild look at the phenomenon of social entrepreneurship. They see a rise of this phenomenon, both at the national and at the international level, and look at the significance of this development for company law. With government budgets being cut and the rising costs of the welfare state, the possibilities of social enterprises have gained attention. A 'third way', between the government providing public goods and the private sector catering for private needs emerges. Social enterprises are set up to create external community benefits by exploiting an enterprise. These enterprises face two key challenges, which are described as the 'dual purpose problem': (i) attracting investors/capital, and (ii) at the same time, keeping an eye on the public purpose for which the enterprise is created. The private limited company solution is not always suited to deal with this challenge. Sector regulation or permit conditions are other methods mentioned. The authors suggest a number of possible solutions to deal with the dual-purpose problem by making changes to the company law of the future.

2. Part II: The Future of Law

2.1. Law and Its Evolution – Theoretical Perspectives

Reflecting on the law of the future goes along with reflecting on legal thinking and legal theory. How should we understand law in the future? What kind of concepts and theories can and should we use to conceptualise the law of the future and the manner in which it will evolve?

Peer Zumbansen argues that a perspective on the future of law should take into account the political, social, and economic context of law. According to him, "law's extreme functionalisation is a necessary and, as such, inevitable by-product of an increasingly differentiated, complex and pluralist society". But this is both "its promise and its Achilles heel". Because of functionalisation, law has been able to become deeply embedded in society's nervous system. However, it also made law vulnerable to the needs and pressures from society. Two strands of legal theory compete for law's future. On the one hand, the economic theorists of law promote self-governing markets and law as a formal framework for "otherwise autonomous market action".[7] But at the same time politically progressive theories connect the future of law with theories of cosmopolitanism and global governance. The latter still cling to a global and juridified welfare state. Zumbansen concludes that it does not suffice to "sniff at the supposedly crude definition of law as the 'formal' counterpart to the otherwise 'informal' institution of market self-regulation". Legal theory will have to lay out its particular qualities and criteria in making the distinction between formal and informal, between law and non-law.

Jo Ritzen and Aalt-Willem Heringa also focus on the interplay between law and its social, economic, and political contexts. Instead of building trust and providing predictability, the explosion of legislation, accelerated by the internationalisation of law, threatens social trust and predictability. The exponential growth of legislation is caused by social risk aversion in combination "with a political system which is bound to over-compromise in order to gain political support". A major challenge for both international and national legislators therefore is to exercise restraint with the creation of new legislation. Ritzen and Heringa propose "to take a substantial minimum period before the adopted new legislation is implemented or even made".

Boundaries and distinctions are at the core of **Hans Lindahl**'s approach to the future of law. He convincingly argues that although cosmopolitanism and globalisation promise a single legal order without boundaries, such an order cannot exist. Boundaries join by separating, and therefore joining legal orders also implies separating legal orders. The promise of an all-inclusive legal order is a theoretically false promise, which hides the new boundaries that will evolve in an era of postnationalism. Lindahl argues that pluralism in the 'strong sense of the term' will be predominant. Pluralism will pose two major challenges to

[7] Several authors in this volume offer, in passing, very critical views regarding the economic analysis of law. See for example the think pieces by Gordley and by Klabbers: James Gordley, "The Future of Private Law", in Sam Muller, Stavros Zouridis, Morly Frishman and Laura Kistemaker (eds.), *The Law of the Future and the Future of Law*, Torkel Opsahl Academic Epublisher, 2011; and Klabbers, 2011, see *supra* note 1.

legal theory and legal practice. First, we have to address the issue of making normative sense of freedom, justice, and security if we cannot rely on a bounded community in which these concepts will be defined or on a cosmopolitan and all-inclusive legal order. Second, we have to invent institutional arrangements to foster boundary negotiations built upon the recognition that we cannot separate legal orders anymore and the impossibility of an all-inclusive and all-encompassing legal order.

Describing the law of the future assumes that law has a future at all. **James Gordley** doubts that our understanding of the core doctrines of private law will improve in the foreseeable future. At present, the basic doctrines that concern matters such as property, tort, contract and unjust enrichment are in disarray. In the nineteenth century, jurists founded these doctrines on positivism, which sought answers through the exegesis of authoritative texts, and conceptualism, which sought answers through the definition of concepts such as contract or property. These doctrines were thrown into disarray when, beginning in the late nineteenth century, jurists successfully discredited these approaches without providing a viable alternative. After over a century of failure, Gordley concludes, it is hard to think that, in the foreseeable future, we will make sense of the core doctrines of private law. The doctrines will not go away. But we will be applying law that we do not understand.

Legal positivism is at the centre of **David Koepsell**'s think piece, which examines it critically in the context of the evolution of international law. Koepsell first provides an abridged history of legal theory, from the philosophies of Hobbes, Locke and Rousseau, through the works of the main legal positivists such as Bentham, Austin, Kelsen and Hart, to later criticism, in particular by Rawls. He thus sketches the background against which legal positivism emerged, the main claims of this doctrine and the critique for which it is susceptible from any perspective that refuses to dismiss the concept of justice in legal theory. All this, he does in order to examine the consequences of viewing international law from a positivist perspective and whether better alternatives exist. International law has been formed largely in the era of legal positivism, which, according to Koepsell, also appears to be the dominant paradigm in international law today. Yet in his view "positivism must fail to give credence to international law". Keeping in mind the three prongs of positivism as phrased by Austin, (law is the commands of the ultimate sovereign, the sovereign is the one obeyed by the majority, and the sovereign's commands must be backed by a threat of sanctions), it is very difficult to explain the phenomena of international law, as it fails these tests. Koepsell proceeds to present criticism that goes to the very core of positivism itself and calls for a resurgence of natural law theory, which, in its recognition that there is such a thing as 'justice', is "more promising for the possibility of international law than the last 100 or so years of legal positivism".

Predicting the future from a modernist perspective usually implies taking some form of linear projection as a point of departure. **H. Patrick Glenn** argues that typical modernist predictions are arrow-like and assume a clean slate. Instead of being a clean slate, the present is grounded in existing laws and institutions. Based on a more realist view on the future Glenn explores some "broad themes which may underlie efforts at legal change and reform". Among these are the evolving private international law regime and the convergence of civil procedure in the common law and civil law, but also corruption and the role of the legal profession.

Any prospect of what the law of the future will look like requires a theory on legal evolution. **Marc Amstutz** suggests a circular evolutionary approach to legal change which "seeks to identify those generative impulses within society which can make possible the emergence of a new legal system". In this approach the interplay of law and society continuously moves between chaos and variation on the one hand and order and self-organisation on the other. From the perspective of a growing global society, we may expect that "in reaction to the heightened relevance of cognitive expectations in global society, existing national and supranational systems, on the one hand, and global norm clusters, on the other, interpenetrate each other genetically".

As **Pierre Larouche** argues, the future of law and the future of the legal sciences are related. The key to assess their future can be found in the connection of the factual and the normative. The main challenge for law will be to avoid becoming 'the sole repository of normativity in our societies'. Citizens and companies have outsourced too much their norms to law enacted by public authorities. Normativity should be brought back to the private sphere of business and civil society. Legal science on the other hand has to find ways to connect the analytical findings of social sciences to normative statements about law. While social sciences encounter difficulties incorporating normativity, it is at least as difficult to incorporate empirical evidence in legal science.

In his think piece **Ewoud Hondius** also advocates an interdisciplinary approach to the future of law. According to him "the discipline of law will probably not be amongst the disciplines with a large impact on the agenda". Therefore legal scholars should try to hang on to proposals from other disciplines as much as possible, before trying to convince our non legal colleagues what is 'scientific' about our research and why it is of interest for the world at large.

2.2. Divergence and Convergence of Legal Systems

What will be the impact of the internationalisation of our economies and societies on national law and specific national legal areas? And what will be the mechanisms by which economic, social, and political internationalisation will affect law? These issues are dealt with in the analyses of David Nelken, Larry Catá Backer, Hugh Collins, Stefan Grundmann, Ruth Sefton-Green, and Benedict Kingsbury.

Harmonisation seems to go along with internationalisation and globalisation, but the kind of harmonisation is itself variable. The rise of comparative law enabled horizontal harmonisation between states, such as within the European integration process. After World War II vertical harmonisation expanded, and political and legal entities were created which were superior to nation states. However, according to **Larry Catá Backer,** the twenty-first century "has witnessed the emergence of governance polycentricism, of the potential broadening of the mechanics of law beyond the memorialisation of the commands of territorially bounded states, of the rise of private law with public functions and public entities as private actors". Governance polycentricism has gone along with a functional detachment of private law from the state. Therefore states are confronted with a new harmonisation challenge, which Backer calls 'inter-systemic harmonisation', or "harmonisation of public and private governance systems and by public and private actors". Instead of adhering exclusively to the traditional public-private division, states should embrace these new forms of governance and connect them with the more familiar patterns of law-making.

David Nelken asks what will happen to the field of criminal justice if globalisation continues. It appears that to simply assume convergence is too easy. There may be real convergence, but legal systems may also copy or collaborate. And convergence may produce similarities or homogenisation, but at the same time it may produce new variety. Sometimes even "the question of diversity between cultures overlaps with that of respecting diversity in a society". Nelken provokingly poses whether "as diasporic communities grow larger and more confident the question arises as to what extent nation-states should explicitly delegate powers of conflict-processing to them". Even if globalisation produces homogeneity the question should be asked whether we should consider it as a blessing or as a matter for concern. Nelken argues that we should be cautious because many practices that work locally will not "travel well".

Hugh Collins uses European labour law to illustrate the complexity of legal convergence at an international level. Because of the strong embeddedness of labour law in national cultures and national legal systems, European law provides only limited possibilities for vertical harmonisation. At the same time, the need for a level playing field from a competition perspective forces member states to harmonise many working conditions in order to prevent regulatory competition and a race to the bottom. In the field of labour law Collins thus predicts a difficult but necessary process of European harmonisation. He concludes that conceptually there are three ways out of this paradox. First, a strategy of negative integration and deregulation can be pursued which will "dismantle" national labour law. Second, by using soft law, the contradictory demands of labour law and free competition can be bridged. A third strategy would be a European constitutionalisation of labour law. Although Collins' analysis is limited to the field of labour law, these strategies may well prove to be more general mechanisms towards convergence.

The harmonisation of contract law in Europe provides an interesting example of a nuanced approach. As **Stefan Grundmann** argues, the question is not if contract law in Europe will be harmonised but rather which form it will take. Grundmann distinguishes two possible scenarios. In one scenario, a newly created European contract law will displace national law, while in the other scenario there will be a co-existence of "an optional instrument with relatively 'free' national laws". The latter would be preferable according to Grundmann, but this requires a "well prepared codification" at the European level. Such a codification should take into account the oxymoron that tightening protective standards actually strengthens the freedom of the contracting parties. For example, "mandatory information rules … are designed to enable both parties to take their decision in as meaningful a way as possible, to enable them to understand the implications of the contract, thus creating the best conditions for material freedom in the choices to be taken". Grundmann foresees a contract law in Europe that is 'more international, more interdisciplinary, more oriented towards a comparison of solutions and to practical consequences (outcome related interpretation) and also more oriented towards the process of rule setting ('governance').

Ruth Sefton-Green's think piece on the same issue of harmonisation of contract law in Europe triggers some skepticism concerning Grundmann's answer to the question whether contract law will be harmonised in Europe the next decades. Even if an explicit harmonisation strategy is adopted by European law-making institutions, this does not mean that harmonisation will be the result. According to Sefton-Green 'there is a certain amount of empirical evidence to suggest that harmonisation does not lead to convergence, but to more fragmentation triggered by "legal irritants". Using the Common Frame of Reference as an optional instrument does not guarantee real harmonisation either, nor will any combination of these two strategies. In the end, harmonisation presupposes a European legal culture. Sefton-Green argues that it "will be necessary to radically alter the way we teach law, by removing our mental barriers. This will require de-nationalising or internationalising our training programmes from their domestic national context and putting rigorous continuous training programmes for lawyers and judges into effect. This means thinking and teaching law trans-nationally, or trans-systemically".

Benedict Kingsbury looks at one instance of such trans-systematic thinking in the context of how indicators are used more and more in both private and public governance. He considers this in the context of the law of the future. While in formal terms it may often be correct that indicators are hortatory and purport to be factual whereas law is binding and expressly normative, the similarities and relations between law and indicators are in reality much greater than a formal differentiation suggests. These similarities and relations will become increasingly important as the overlaps between law and governance become greater.[8] The phenomenon is most marked for law and governance beyond the state, but its significance within states for national and sub-national law is also growing. His paper argues that the law of the future will have to engage much more deeply than heretofore, at the levels of fundamental theory and quotidian practice, with the increasing role of indicators and other quantitative measures, while defining and maintaining a core role for law and legal principles in the whole enterprise of governance by information.

2.3. New Legal Challenges Posed by Technological Development

When thinking about the future of law, it is not only new theories of law or issues of convergence or divergence that come to mind. Exciting developments in fields such as communication technology and biotechnology very clearly force us to contemplate existing legal notions. They make clear that law as it stands is not ready for what may lie ahead. This section features five think pieces on technological developments and the role of law. They deal with new cognitive enhancement medications that are about to become available, with advancements in biotechnology that challenge the conventional notion of what it means to be 'human', with the continuous development in space technology, with data protection and privacy in a world in which more information is shared through communication technology every day, and with identity in a world where the real and the virtual are less and less distinguishable.

Some of these developments are taking shape right now. Others might seem more futuristic. But even if the future will turn out to bring different realities than sketched in some of these think pieces, it is a worthwhile exercise to think through what will need to happen in order for law to deal properly with new technologies. The overall notion is clear: technology will generate new concerns.

Certainly, these think pieces do not capture all recent let alone all future technological developments. They do, however, shed light on the complexity of problems that arise from a number of technological developments. And, as one of the authors states, they show that "technology is not just an inert tool that we might use for our own

---

8 Klabbers discusses indicators incidentally and makes a similar point: Klabbers, 2011, see *supra* note 1.

purposes, or that we might choose to ignore, if that is where our whim takes us, because the mere introduction of some technologies into society also challenges and changes our moral and legal presuppositions".

Nicole Vincent draws attention to the challenges posed to private law if certain psychopharmacological medications would make it possible to enhance cognitive performance without negative side effects. Such medications are already currently in development. Two incompatible, but intuitively plausible stances arise. Should people be expected to take these drugs when something important is at stake in the performance of their jobs, or should nobody be forced to modify their own brains for another person's benefit? According to Vincent, what makes this a novel challenge is the fact that we have never had to deal with human mental capacities being intentionally 'upgraded'. In law, especially 'neurolaw', responsibility tracks mental capacity. But so far only super-heroes in science fiction need to deal with the responsibilities that accompany above average capacities. Does responsibility in this case also track 'hypercapacity'?

The law imposes an objective standard of care on people; when loss or injury occur as a consequence of breaching this standard, the person in question is responsible. However, this objective standard is not fixed in time; it is affected by the progress of science and technology. From this reasoning, it follows that people could be legitimately expected to cognitively enhance themselves and to observe a higher standard of care than their non-enhanced counterparts. But on the other hand, an important difference between previous capacity-extending technologies and cognitive enhancement drugs is that the latter involves the modification of our own brains through the use of drugs to make ourselves into better tools. Legal policy-makers should be pro-active in deciding how this technology should be regulated. And this should be done not only in a multilateral discussion among a range of different experts, but also by taking the lay interests and lay opinions into account.

Efthimios Parasidis highlights not just one, but several developments in science, such as stem cell research, cloning, end-of-life care, neurosciences, synthetic biology and genomics. While affecting our thinking about what it means to be human, these new technologies have not lead to a comprehensive definition of who is properly classified as a human. Quite the opposite, by shedding light on, for example, the processes that underlie fertilisation of human eggs, the discussion when human life comes into existence has been complicated. After looking at findings from anthropology, comparative genomics, embryology, and medicine Parasidis suggest a way to reconcile these finding with normative theories to come to a legal definition of the essence of being human, which can help policy-makers in structuring appropriate regulations and to advance the international dialogue.

Parasidis poses two questions. What distinguishes humans from other organisms and how precisely do we define the life or death of an individual human being? The first question has been answered from an anthropological angle and from a comparative genomics angle, but it is the combination of the two that points towards the delineation of the contours of modern humans. Similarly, Parasidis approaches the second question from a holistic approach combining knowledge about embryological development with the idea of 'organism-as-a-whole', by which is meant that although the loss of one vital function may inevitably bring about death, it does not by itself constitute death, though interruption of any vital system for a period of time can result in the destruction of the organism-as-a-whole". He argues that this is a more accurate way to assess whether someone is dead than using the brain death criterion. The conclusion then is that an individual's life commences when the being begins to function as an organism-as-a-whole, and ends when the being stops functioning as an organism-as-a-whole.

Yan Ling discusses four issues related to the presence of humans or human made items in space, which may be more consequential in the near future. She points towards the lack of an up-to-date international space law. The first issue that is highlighted is the weaponisation of outer space. While a current treaty only prohibits nuclear weapons or other kinds of weapons of mass destruction in outer space and on celestial bodies, there are at least 11 categories of anti-satellite weapons. Ling provides suggestions about how to fill this gap. A second area that is not covered well in contemporary law, while becoming more and more urgent, is the likelihood of collisions between satellites and damage to satellites caused by debris. Collisions create more debris, so it will exacerbate the problem even without new space object being placed into orbit. By establishing clearer international rules on liability for damage caused by debris and on mitigating space debris, this problem could be tackled. Thirdly, the number of private enterprises and individuals involved in space activities is increasing and space tourism, private space travel, commercial space hotels and commercial space settlement are envisaged. Here too, gaps in law need to be filled pertaining to issues such as the status of space tourists, claiming private property rights to lunar land or celestial bodies, and transferrable ownership of satellites in orbit. Lastly, plans to return to the moon for exploration and exploitation purposes have been renewed, probably leading to human settlement, mining of Helium-3, and the establishment of lunar bases on the Moon for further space travel. This calls for a review of the existing Moon Agreement and for an international regime governing the exploitation of the moon. Ling points out that these are just several space related issues that need more legal attention, and that the future is likely to bring even more issues with the advancement of more sophisticated space technology.

The fourth think piece in this section – by **Peter Hustinx** – deals with the protection of personal data and privacy as a counterbalance to advancement in information technology. Two developments are closely linked with innovation: increasing complexity and globalisation. This complexity – not only because of the technology itself, but also because of the fact that companies work globally and outsource tasks – makes allocating responsibility for data protection more difficult. The lack of clear responsibility allocation, however, becomes more pressing as the capacity for information-processing evolves. At the same time, responsibilities should not cause undue burdens and jeopardise technology and innovation. Moreover, determining responsibilities is not enough. The responsible parties should be held accountable for complying with legal obligations. Hustinx mentions several mechanisms that support accountability and that could be laid down in law. Globalisation in particular and the Internet specifically, put pressure on the territoriality principle underlying law. The discussion on how to determine which law applies when data processes take place distributed over several states continues to generate controversy. According to Hustinx, "harmonisation of data protection laws remains an attractive goal in order to minimise the above problems". Development of global standards always lags behind technological development in our information society. Stimulating mutual recognition of national regulatory agencies might be a more realistic approach, but in the end, more common, binding standards of data protection and international cooperation in practical terms, going beyond mutual recognition, are necessary. Hustinx concludes that many of the challenges to data protection are similar to those in other areas: "[T]he experiences and discussions regarding data protection are … worth analysing for other areas of law".

The final think piece in this section addresses legal issues with regard to 'ambient intelligence' environments. Specifically, **Norberto Andrade** focuses on issues of regulation of personal identity and of attribution of legal personality. Ambient intelligence, or AmI, is the vision of a future in which the Internet will become integrated with the physical environment; very small computing devices will be incorporated into everyday objects –furniture, clothes, utensils, etc. – embedded with some kind of intelligence and forming a communicative, sensitive, responsive, interactive and functional network. In creating AmI, a wide array of different emerging technologies will be combined. AmI will be invisible, discrete and unobtrusive, and sensitive, interactive and responsive at the same time.

Andrade continues by addressing the question of what this might mean for personal identity. AmI will change the way a person's identity is captured, represented and disseminated because of a number of developments. First, there is a radical increase in the production, creation, circulation and exchange of personal information. Second, AmI technologies will blur the distinction between the physical and the digital worlds; the online and offline worlds will merge. Third, multiple identities of one person will arise for different purposes. Identity then becomes a complex phenomenon, inherently multifaceted and mutable. From a legal point of view, according to Andrade, this development should be accompanied by developing a right to multiple – partial – identities. Finally, Andrade describes the emergence of a new form of agent: automated and intelligent software agents, or 'AIvatars'. AmI will provide every individual with a tailor-made technological reality, deeply informed about one's characteristics and respondent to one's necessities. A sort of 'digital clone' of each individual, reflecting his personality and emulating, autonomously, what would be the user's own behaviour in a given context, will come into being, and all of this in a world where the current Internet is dispersed to the outer world. But for these 'AIvatars' to be successfully implemented and to function, they need to become generally accepted and such acceptance needs trust from the user. For that, a legal framework regulating these agents needs to be constructed. Very important in that regard is the transposition of legal institutes and theories of legal personality, representation and agency to the actions performed by the 'AIvatar'. And, the 'AIvatar' will need legal instruments and rights in order to act on behalf of the user. Whether this is feasible and appropriate needs to be discussed.

2.4. The Emerging International Criminal Justice System

The think pieces in this section show that the internationalisation of law has also touched criminal law in at least three different ways. First, some crimes have been explicitly defined by international law, like war crimes, crimes against humanity, genocide, and aggression. Although the deployment of criminal procedure in order to punish these crimes is not an exclusive matter of international organisations, these organisations (like the ICC) do play an important role. Whether international crimes should be criminalised or juridified or not, is seriously debated in some think pieces. **Mark Osiel's** think piece aims at understanding some non-legal responses to mass atrocity which seem to be effective. For example, "fearing the opprobrium of global opinion, military leaders in democratic states are impelled to unprecedented efforts at reducing innocent civilian casualties in war, in ways that the international law of war crimes does not itself require". How do we understand responses to mass atrocity like these? Should we consider norms and enforcement systems like these to be soft law, 'proto-law', or alternatives to law? Do these responses "hint at serious and even inherent limits to the process of juridification, suggesting places where it cannot and will never successfully go?" Both the limited effectiveness of an international judicial response and the democratic potential of these non-legal responses provoke some serious questions concerning the future of international criminal law.

The effectiveness of the ICC to deal with crimes defined by international law seems to be a major future contingency. But the ICC cannot be isolated from the context in which it has to operate. **Richard Goldstone** argues in his think piece that "the future success of the ICC depends entirely upon the cooperation of the governments of states that have become parties to the Rome Statue. The coming years will witness whether that cooperation will be forthcoming or not". Like other authors, he uses the arrest warrant issued against Sudanese President al-Bashir as an example of the interdependence of the ICC and its States Parties. But according to Goldstone the enforcement issue is not the only future contingency for international humanitarian law. His analysis demonstrates that it remains to be seen whether the current norms and rules of international humanitarian law can cope with the realities of modern warfare.

To improve the effectiveness of the ICC and a well-functioning complementarity principle, some unconventional solutions should be considered. **Göran Sluiter** suggests at least four possible improvements in his think piece. First, trials in absentia allow the ICC to overcome problems like the enforcement of its arrest warrants. Second, the larger the number of state parties to the Rome Statute, the fewer the number of 'safe havens' and jurisdictional gaps for accused persons. Third, the law on cooperation with the ICC can be improved. For example, an effective cooperation regime in the case of referrals from the Security Council could have prevented the Darfur problems. Finally, cooperation should be enforced. The ICC could benefit from the full-hearted support of the UN Security Council and the United States.

The enforcement problems pose real challenges for the future of international criminal law. While Goldstone and Sluiter aim at improving the implementation of the Rome Statute, Osiel considers serious non-legal alternatives. Their think pieces also have something in common. They share concern and scepticism about whether international criminal law is really the adequate answer to problems like mass atrocity and aggression. In contrast, **Sébastien Jodoin's** think piece is not sceptical. Rather, he proposes a new category of international crime. This crime he calls the 'crime against present and future generations'. It includes acts in 'any sphere of human activity', such as "forcing members of any identifiable group or collectivity to work or live in conditions that seriously endanger their health or safety, including forced labour, enforced prostitution and human trafficking" and "causing widespread, long-term and severe damage to the natural environment, including by destroying an entire species or ecosystem". According to Jodoin, these crimes can already be derived from international human rights law or other international conventions. Introducing crimes against present and future generations would address the 'governance gaps' which pose a serious challenge to national and international law.

With or without expanding the scope of international criminal law, the experiences with Europeanisation of criminal law may provide some useful lessons for international criminal law. **Filippo Spiezia's** think piece is grounded in Eurojust's experiences with transnational enforcement and criminal justice administration. It appears that both legal and extra-legal factors determine the success of transnational criminal justice. Without common values and trust at the operational, policy, and political levels, a transnational criminal justice system will not be able to function. But trust requires "a certain degree of approximation and harmonisation of national laws". Even though the EU-strategy of mutual recognition provides an alternative to harmonisation, effective enforcement demands that both national criminal law and criminal procedure also have some similarities. The experiences with Eurojust, therefore, cannot be easily transplanted to the global level. Rather, Spiezia foresees "a pluralistic model of international prosecutors, disseminated at crucial point on the planet".

Whatever the exact model, none of the think piece authors question further internationalisation of criminal law. **André Klip's** glimpse into a possible European and global future only reveals linear progress towards international criminal law and internationalisation of criminal justice systems. His 'journey into the future' allows only one conclusion: "national criminal law will increasingly give way to non-domestic law. The European and international criminal justice systems will more and more determine the rules and structures of all criminal law, regardless of whether it concerns international or local crime". He concludes that "gradually, the principle of globality replaces the principle of territoriality".

Globalisation of criminal law and criminal procedure is not a value-neutral process. Ideas on crime, punishment, and legal protection of the accused are deeply embedded in religious and cultural belief systems. We may thus expect that globalisation will reveal fundamental value-conflicts with regard to criminal law doctrine. **Maíra Rocha Machado's** think piece introduces a useful paradigm for the analysis of these value-conflicts. Her critique of 'modern penal rationality' brings together the constitutive elements of modern theories on punishment: deterrence, retribution, rehabilitation in prison, and denunciation. Machado demonstrates that this paradigm of modern penal rationality "functions as a cognitive obstacle to the acceptance of non-prosecutorial forms of justice, to the reception and enforcement of non-prison sanctions and also to the reduction of the length of prison sentences and of the frequency of their use". We may therefore expect the paradigm of modern penal rationality to be seriously challenged by further internationalisation of criminal law. Whether prisons will survive further internationalisation, also remains to be seen.

Sohail Inayatullah's think piece explores some scenarios for the future of prisons. Because of technological developments and new ideas on the causes of crime, new types of punishments are under consideration before legislatures throughout the world. Prevention and transformation of prisons may become more plausible punishments in the future. Second, crime and criminal organisations increasingly cross national borders. In order to tackle transnational crime, criminal law and criminal procedure have to be concentrated on an international level. With the internationalisation of criminal law and criminal procedure the criminal justice systems and administration also become more international.

Having presented the book's structure and the sort of discussions one can expect to find in each of the sections, a few words about the style, structure and the ordering of this book are called for.

Unlike many other book projects, which start with an envisaged table of contents, with authors subsequently been asked to write the planned chapters, this book is almost a spontaneous outcome, rather than the result of detailed planning and programming. As already indicated above, the book forms part of a broader initiative to encourage prospective thinking in the legal sphere. When we first invited key thinkers from around the globe to contribute what we described as 'think pieces' – short, essay-like, contributions designed for a knowledgeable but not specialised audience – the primary purpose we had in mind was in this way to collect input for the scenario-work we carry out in the context of the same initiative, which will lead to the *Law Scenarios to 2030*.[9] Given the insights provided by the 'think pieces', we expanded the project to disseminate the products of these pieces in an edited volume.

This history, however, has consequences for the book's style and structure, as well as for the ordering of the various contributions. It is a sampling of diverse perspectives, each presented succinctly. As such, the format does not allow extensive discussion as may be typical of a usual academic anthology. The explanation for this lies in the nature of this book as explained above, as an exercise in exploring new ground, rather than attempting to present a full analysis of any given or imaginable issue.

[9] See the Preface for more information, and follow www.lawofthefuture.org for updates.

Second, with respect to the structure, online publication permits leeway. Given the intellectual and professional achievement of the authors, we have provided them with general guidelines. In doing so, each author is able to briefly address issues within the purvey of their specialisation, but within a loose framework. We decided this to be appropriate when accounting for the diversity represented among the authors, including philosophers, judges, lawyers, academics, and policy-makers; therefore, we have left many issues of structure and content at the discretion of contributors, as per their field and background. We consider this diversity a strength.

As to the overall structure of the book and the ordering of think pieces within it, they reflect the editors' attempt to organise in a sensible manner the various contributions (which vary considerably, as already stated, both in term of their respective approaches as well as in the issues they address). Other editors may have opted for a different structure and perhaps they would have achieved a more compelling result. When preparing the (already planned) second edition of the book, its structure and ordering will both be reconsidered, and this introduction, revised.

3. Future of *The Law of the Future and the Future of Law*

This book constitutes the first of our efforts at compiling an innovative, forward-thinking monograph. As we stated at the onset of this introduction, contemplating the law of the future is of great importance. Since dialogue about future trajectories informs contemporary decision-making, we hope that by providing an opening for discourse, we can positively affect the direction of law. We anticipate that the second edition will be released in late 2011 or early 2012. We invite criticism of our first edition, and we look forward to providing a forum for critical discussion of law and its possible future.

PART I:
THE LAW OF THE FUTURE

1. Globalisation, the International System, International Law and a Global Constitutional Framework: Towards a New Global New Deal?

1.1

The Future of Law in a Multi-Polar World: Toward a Global New Deal

Randall Peerenboom*

We are currently undergoing a fundamental shift in the global economic order. These changes in the global economic order will produce a new multi-polar world with more mid-level powers from various regions. One of the dominant features of the new multi-polar world will be a dramatic increase in the diversity of cultures, religions, worldviews, economies, political regimes and legal systems. The new order will require, and be reflected in, a change in existing institutions and how they operate, as well as the creation of new institutions. Although the rise of new powers has often resulted in war in the past, there are some grounds to hope that this time will be different. But even if military conflict between old and new powers is avoided, a New Global Deal – a new vision for a more equitable world, combined with feasible development agendas – is urgently needed to ensure a more just world in which global resources and burdens are more fairly shared by all.

1. Introduction

This is an opportune time to reflect on the law of the future. The relentlessly hyped globalisation of the last two decades, the anxiously anticipated convergence of legal systems, and the fervent faith in 'international best practices' have all come under critical scrutiny. As a result, the irrational exuberance attached to the hope that all countries would quickly establish rule of law and good governance has (once again) abated. The disappointing performance of many Third Wave democracies has (once again) raised questions about the preconditions for democratic consolidation, and whether promoting democratisation before economic development is to put the cart before the horse, while the depressing sagas in Iraq and Afghanistan have (once again) undermined support for

* **Randall Peerenboom** is Director of the Foundation for Law, Justice and Society's Rule of Law in China programme, an Associate Fellow of the Oxford Centre for Socio-Legal Studies, and a Professor of Law at La Trobe University, Melbourne.

aggressive intervention in troubled states and ambitious nation-building efforts. The demise of the Washington Consensus and the fallout from the economic crisis, including the fall from grace of neo-liberalism and the 'American model' of (non-)regulation and the emperor-has-no-clothes moment when the absurdity of the rational market hypothesis became all too readily apparent, have accelerated the shift toward Asia and the BRICs, demonstrating unequivocally the need for a new international economic architecture to supplement, if not replace, the creaky Bretton Woods edifice. Meanwhile, global warming, a rash of potentially devastating global pandemics from SARS to bird and swine flu, and rapidly depleting oil reserves have all contributed to the current critical juncture where business as usual just isn't good enough.

2. The Substructure: The New Economic Order

We are currently undergoing a fundamental shift in the global economic pecking order, which will inevitably have geopolitical repercussions and consequences for the international legal order. The US is likely to remain the largest economy, however the gap between the size of the US economy and other economies, and the difference in relative living standards will continue to narrow, even if the US is able to overcome the morass of partisan politics and shift from an economy driven by financial shenanigans and leveraged consumerism to a more sustainable path fuelled by returns from higher education and investment in innovative technologies. And unless dramatic steps are taken to redistribute wealth more equitably in the US, the hollowing out of the middle class and the rising disparity between the small percentage of economic elite and the vast majority of the rest of the populace will continue to grow, fuelling protectionist pressures.

Meanwhile, Old Europe, Japan and some other high income countries (HICs) will lose power and status, living standards will deteriorate, and some may slip back into the ranks of middle income counties (MICs). The EU and Japan face severe demographic challenges with a dramatic decrease in the number of workers supporting the aged and retired. This will challenge longstanding social welfare policies in Europe, and increase political instability. While increased immigration could mitigate the crisis, immigration is politically unpopular in both Europe and Japan, and plays into the hands of right-wing nationalist parties. Australia is living beyond its geological means, and increasingly reliant on the export of natural resources to maintain the current standard of living. Absent major technological breakthroughs and/or a shift in its economic model, it is poised for a fall as resources are depleted or demand tapers in China and other emerging economies in the region. HICs that have relied on oil sales for growth may enjoy the ride for a few more years, however many are likely to suffer once the oil runs out or if the global push to go green leads to commercially viable alternative energy sources sooner than anticipated. Finally, the HIC status of small knowledge-economy countries such as Singapore or some of the island nations that have relied on tourism and their tax-haven status will remain precarious. Changes in the global economy, pressure to curb tax loopholes to force multinational corporations (MNCs) to incorporate in Euro-America, improvements in the regulatory environments and a narrowing of the education gap in emerging states all threaten to erode their economic advantages.

Among the most likely winners, the BRICs have garnered the most attention. China is likely to rise the fastest and grow the largest, though that is by no means certain. Many MICs have had their day in the sun, only to succumb to reform fatigue, corruption, collective action problems and other political economy woes that have prevented them from continuing their ascent. China has more than its share of problems, and is showing signs of the middle-income blues. Future progress will require the political will to press ahead with deeper economic, social, legal, and political reforms. India may not be far behind, although infrastructure bottlenecks, ethnic unrest and regional conflicts may hinder growth. Brazil is likely to emerge as a regional leader, though it seems destined to trail China in both growth and geopolitical importance. The jury remains out on Russia, which will have to diversify its economy to sustain growth. A number of other MICs are also likely to continue to prosper, including a handful in Latin America, several in Eastern Europe (particularly those within the EU umbrella) and Asia (including South Korea, Thailand and Vietnam), some of the more well governed Middle Eastern states that invest their oil revenues resources wisely in human capital, growth-oriented infrastructure and institutions, as well as some of the non-core Islamic countries such as Turkey and Indonesia.

That leaves a number of low income countries (LICs) – the so-called bottom billion – for whom prospects are decidedly less promising. While most are in Africa, several former Soviet republics and South

Asian countries are also underperforming LICs. Despite the occasional temporary success story, most LICs are likely to fall farther behind in relative terms, and some in absolute terms. Many are failed states, torn by war and ethnic strife. Institutions are weak. Political leaders are often incompetent, corrupt or simply overwhelmed. Few LICs are on track to meet their Millennium Development Goals. With the population expected to continue to rise sharply in LICs, poverty reduction will remain a serious challenge, with hopes for higher living standards and GDP/capita convergence a distant dream.

3. The Superstructure: Geopolitical Consequences of the New Economic Order in a Multi-Polar World Marked by Diversity

The changes in the global economic order will produce a new multi-polar world with more mid-level powers from various regions, though the US and perhaps one day China will exert a disproportionate influence on global affairs. There have been multi-polar periods in the past, but one of the dominant features of the new multi-polar world will be a dramatic increase in the diversity of cultures, religions, worldviews, economies, political regimes and legal systems, in a world where all are linked by modern telecommunication and increasingly face issues of global reach that bind everyone together and require close collaboration to resolve.

The new order will require, and be reflected in, a change in existing institutions and how they operate, as well as the creation of new institutions. Rising powers are already clamouring for greater representation and voice in the UN Security Council, IMF, World Bank and other international bodies, and the G7 has given way to the G20, if not the G77. Among the new organisations, the China-Russia led Shanghai Cooperation Organisation may one day play a larger role than NATO, whose influence will most likely continue to decline.

The redistribution of power, the expanded list of players, and the proliferation of new institutions will further expose the limits of the self-declared universalism of contemporary international law and the human rights movement, and undermine consensus-based decision making of the kind found in the UN Security Council. Accordingly, regional leaders and organisations are likely to play a greater role, including ASEAN, the South American Community of Nations, the Organisation of American States and the African Union. In the absence of a global consensus, key economic and geopolitical decisions will be made by regional leaders who will at times join other regional leaders in issue-specific shifting alliances of coalitions of the willing.[1]

However, beyond the change in institutions and voting requirements, perhaps the biggest difference will be one of tone or approach. A few short years since the breakup of the Soviet Union that led to self-congratulatory proclamations of the end of history and the victory of Euro-American secular liberal democracy, we now seem to be approaching the end of Euro-American hegemony of thought and life forms. In the new era, policy makers will need to take pluralism seriously, and their decisions will need to reflect and show respect for the wide diversity of their constituents, be they Chinese, Indian, or African; Muslims, Confucians or Buddhists; modern or traditional; urban or rural; rich or poor. To give just one example, every year the US, in a jarring unilateral act of hubris, issues human rights reports that invariably criticise other countries based on a set of human rights that we in the US consider to be the most important (although national interests dictate that strategically important allies are treated gingerly). Less if any attention is paid to other rights that citizens in other countries may consider more important given their particular circumstances, traditions and values. Yet different countries (and different dominant and minority groups within countries) will rank or prioritise rights differently. More sensitivity to such differences will be required in a world where the US is at best first among equals.

The traditional Confucian approach that emphasises harmony rather than identity or a modified form of the 'ASEAN Way' may be more

[1] Kawai and Petri propose a global federalism consisting of functional area hierarchies of global and regional organizations with overlapping membership structures, akin to the World Banks' relationships to regional development banks like the Asian Development Bank, and suggest "Asia could contribute to this transformation by building effective institutions to promote macroeconomic and financial stability and deepen regional trade and investment integration". See Masahiro Kawai and Peter Petri, "Asia's Role in the Global Economic Architecture", ADBI Working Paper No. 235, 2010, available at http://ssrn.com/abstract=1658346, last accessed 28 March 2011; also Michel Rosenfeld's think piece in this volume suggests a variety of approaches, techniques and principles that could be used to establish a new global constitutional order, including federalism, subsidiarity, devolution, decentralization, and the margin of appreciation. To this list could be added the Confucian pragmatic approach focused on harmony and the ASEAN Way.

useful and effective. The Chinese approach begins by searching for similarities and common interests while setting aside differences. Rather than treating each person as an instantiation of some universally applicable principle, it takes their particularity seriously. The goal is to find a creative context-specific solution that best suits the interests of all parties concerned rather than simply imposing a top-down solution based on some preordained standard chosen by an elite minority of powerbrokers.

The ASEAN Way is a modern statement of this traditional approach. The ASEAN Way reflects the fundamental principles for international law in The Treaty of Amity and Cooperation (TAC) in Southeast Asia (1976):

- Mutual respect for the independence, sovereignty, equality, territorial integrity and national identity of all nations;
- The right of every State to lead its national existence free from external interference, subversion or coercion;
- Non-interference in the internal affairs of one another;
- Settlement of differences or disputes by peaceful means;
- Renunciation of the threat or use of force; and
- Effective cooperation among themselves.

Disputes are to be settled in a flexible, informal way. The emphasis is on tolerance, compromise and cooperation in finding a pragmatic solution amenable to all parties. Parties will often have to agree to disagree on some points to find a mutually acceptable solution. Although ASEAN has formal mechanisms for dispute resolution, they are not often used. Mediation based on the actual interests, concerns and circumstances of the parties is preferred to dispute resolution based on formal law and compulsory enforcement.

To be sure, the new global order will require a variety of informal and formal mechanisms for addressing problems and resolving disputes. Formal law-based dispute resolution backed up by compulsory enforcement powers is no doubt more suitable to some issue areas than others. Nevertheless, the new order is likely to be characterised by and benefit from a greater emphasis on informal negotiations, political agreements and compromise – the ASEAN Way's 'diplomacy of accommodation'[2] – with a de-emphasis on international law and decisions by judicial-like bodies with coercive enforcement powers.[3]

4. War and Peace

Will a change in institutions and how they operate be enough to ensure peace and stability? The rise of new economic powers has often resulted in (and from) wars. The transition from a unipolar world to a multi-polar one is inevitably dangerous, as the reigning hegemon struggles to maintain power, up-and-comers are eager to flex their muscles and reshape global affairs in their interests, and the rest jockey for position as new alliances replace old ones. Moreover, the first half of the twenty-first century presents even more daunting challenges than the first of half of the twentieth century, when the previous round of globalisation gave way to two world wars and a global depression. While the US emerged as the undisputed leader of the 'Free World', and capitalism eventually prevailed over Marxism-Leninism, for the US to replace England as the dominant power was akin to Chico Marx replacing Harpo Marx, rather than the much more fundamental transition from a unipolar world led by the latest Western power espousing Enlighten-era inspired secular liberalism to a multi-polar world where Mohammed, Deng and Chavez are as familiar, and hold as much sway, as Locke, Madison and Montesquieu. The US and England shared similar cultures and worldviews. The rise of China, India, Brazil, Chile, Iran, Russia, Indonesia, Vietnam and other states with more diverse cultures, histories and institutions is more likely to lead to conflict.

Global security is already threatened by nuclear proliferation in Iran and North Korea, domestic and regional wars, terrorism, asymmetrical

---

2 Mely Caballero-Anthony, "Mechanisms of Dispute Settlement: the ASEAN Experience", in *Contemporary Southeast Asia*, 1998, vol. 20, no. 1, pp. 51-64.

3 To illustrate the growing importance of soft and informal law, Joost Pauwelyn cites in his think piece for this volume both long-standing examples such as transatlantic networks on competition policy, financial cooperation at the Basel Committee and standard-setting in the field of food safety, product regulations, pharmaceuticals, veterinary medicines and cosmetics, as well as informal cooperation on issues previously dealt with by treaty, including the Kimberley Scheme on conflict diamonds, regulation of the internet and cyber-security (*e.g.*, ICANN), the Proliferation Security Initiative (allowing for security check on the high seas), and the Financial Action Task Force's issuing of black and grey lists of tax heavens.

warfare, conflicts over resources, climate change, transnational crime, global infectious diseases, and the growing imbalance between wealthier countries and the bottom billion. Meanwhile, the US and China are sparring over the South China Seas, control of real and cyber space, and a host of commercial issues from currency exchange rates to intellectual property protection to standards setting.

Nevertheless, there are grounds for hope. A knock-down, drag-out battle with China for world supremacy is not inevitable. Much will depend on whether China democratises, when it does so, and what type of democracy it becomes, though democratisation alone will not be enough to ensure peace.[4] More importantly, this is a different era. There is less emphasis on territory as a source of power. Chinese exports require US consumers, and US profligacy requires Chinese purchases of US treasuries. A more developed international trade regime has clarified many of the rules of the game, and the WTO is available to resolve disputes peacefully, even if many of the most significant decisions about the global economy are made in other, more political, venues. And thanks to the global media, the world is better informed about what is happening.

Most fundamentally, for better or worse, we now live in an age of co-dependence, where we will all live or die, or at least flourish and suffer, together. Cooperation is essential to solve many of the most pressing problems from greenhouse gas emissions to deforestation and loss of biodiversity; to depletion of fisheries and fossil fuels to water and food shortages; to transnational crime and global terrorism.

5. Toward a Global New Deal

Yet a willingness to cooperate, a change in the tone of international relations and new and improved international institutions will not be sufficient to ensure peace and stability in the coming years. What is needed is a Global New Deal – a new vision for a more equitable world, combined with feasible development agendas.

The good news is that the political economy of the Existing Raw Deal for most of the world is creating the incentives for a more equitable

[4] I consider how the outcomes might differ, for better or worse, on a range of issues from rights to war, if China becomes democratic, in: Randy Peerenboom, *China Modernizes: Threat to the West or Model for the Rest?*, Oxford University Press, Oxford, 2007.

Global New Deal in both developed and developing countries, albeit mainly because the increasingly seductive alternative path of beggar-thy-neighbour protectionism has been tried and proved wanting.

Within developed countries, middle class workers, who have lost out in the latest round of globalisation, will push for protectionist measures to maintain their current cushy standards of living. The purchase of prized assets in Euro-America by state-owned enterprises or sovereign wealth funds from up and coming MICs will further exacerbate tensions and fan the flames of protectionism.

Conversely, while China, India and other developing countries may become major economic powers, they will still lag far behind Euro-America on a GDP per capita basis, which means in real terms considerably lower standards of living for the majority of the population for decades to come. Most citizens in developing countries are already aware that rich countries did not get rich by following the policies they now recommend for others, including open economies and respect for IP laws, as well as early democratisation and the protection of a wide range of civil and political rights for all citizens. They also resent the hypocrisy of rich states that preach free trade yet continue to impose unfair trade conditions on developing countries in the form of agricultural subsidies; tariffs, discriminatory quotas and anti-surge restrictions on textiles and other products for which developing countries enjoy a competitive advantage; and the large transfer of wealth from poor countries to a handful of wealthy countries under the Agreement on Trade-Related Aspects of Intellectual Property Rights (TRIPs), imposed on developing countries as one of the prices for admission to the WTO. Accordingly, LICs and MICs are likely to continue with their own mercantilist policies: a depressed currency to bolster exports, market access barriers, support for infant industries, IP violations and so on.

Meanwhile, the life-threatening problems of the bottom billion will fuel emigration and may lead to terrorism and wars that spill over into other regions or disrupt increasingly important supply lines of oil and natural resources heading to MICs and HICs.

In short, despite their different interests and perspectives, most people in developed and developing countries can appreciate the need for a Global New Deal that provides a more equitable sharing of global resources both within and between states, and policymakers with any sense of history will appreciate the dangers of another round of global protectionism, trade wars and world wars. The Global New Deal will require a redistribution of the bounty in wealthy countries, including reinvigorated welfare systems, to ensure the continued support of those who have lost out in the latest round of globalisation; modification of the international trade regime along the lines sought in the Doha round to level the playing field and better reflect the needs and interests of developing countries; compensation to developing countries for preserving forests and biodiversity; disproportionate reductions in gas emissions in developed countries combined with growth-impairing reductions in developing countries; IP-challenging cost-effective sharing of the latest and most valuable technologies and medicines; and a host of other measures. It will also require a new approach to law and development.

6. Law and Development for the 21st Century: New Development Agendas

Neither the 1960s 'old' or the more recent 'new' law and development movements have been very successful. Rather than blindly plunge ahead with a new law and development agenda, it is time to stop and take stock about what went wrong. There is no shortage of problems on the part of the international community or within the target countries. Nevertheless, among the more salient shortcomings are the excessive attention to law, in particular clear property rights enforced by an independent judiciary; the misplaced emphasis on international best practices modelled on the latest rules and institutions in developed countries; and the fruitless quest for a magic cure and one-size-fits-all solutions.

The growth of East Asian states demonstrates that the emphasis on law and the judicial enforcement of property rights is too narrow. Much more important to economic growth and investors are solid macroeconomic policies and the quality of the business environment. Lest there be any doubt about what drives business decisions, foreign investors in China recently cited as the major risks: a slowdown of the Chinese (58%) and global (44%) economies, followed by labour costs, global financial market instability, increased protectionism, RMB appreciation and Chinese financial market instability. Only after listing all of these economic/business risks did they mention 'increased bureaucracy'. Moreover, for all their complaints, over 80% of respondents have been profitable since the surveys began in 2003, with two-thirds enjoying profitability rates that meet or exceed their company's global rate. In most years over 90% of respondents have been bullish about their companies' future in China, with more than 80% bullish about their five-year outlook even in 2009 despite the global economic crisis.[5]

Developing states are regularly advised to adopt 'international best practices'. These practices are often succinctly captured in rule of law 'toolkits' or international documents such as the 22-article UN Basic Principles on the Independence of the Judiciary or IFES's 18 'judicial integrity principles' – although Eastern European countries were required to comply with more than 80,000 pages of highly specific technical requirements to join the EU! Unfortunately, LICs and MICs cannot simply mimic legal systems in Western liberal democracies. Exhorting developing countries to adopt international best practices is like telling a 10 year-old with a stick in his hand for a golf club and rock for a ball that if he wants to win the Masters he should watch Tiger Woods videos. More attention must be paid to the particular circumstances of developing countries, with reform policies genuinely 'country-owned and country-led', as opposed to the current practice where the reform agenda is designed abroad and then submitted to local government officials for ratification. For instance, LICs and MICs face different challenges, and require different reforms. Even within these broad categories, there is considerable diversity, ensuring that one-size-fits-all reform packages will not suffice. Failed LICs destroyed by war and torn by ethnic strife are different from poor but politically stable LICs in which institutions are weak but law and order prevails.

7. Neither the Washington Consensus nor the Beijing Consensus: From the Futile Quest for a Universal Model of Development to a More Diversified Context-Specific Approach

The law and development industry has sought universal solutions to diverse local problems, often adopting a reductive 'magic-bullet' approach. With the Washington Consensus largely discredited, many developing countries are now pinning their hopes on the 'Beijing

[5] American Chamber of Commerce, "The Business Climate for U.S. Firms in China", 2009, available at http://web.resource.amchamchina.org/Podcasts/WhitePaper2009.pdf , last accessed 2 March 2011.

Consensus' and the 'China Model'. Just as there never was a consensus in Washington or developing states about the Washington Consensus, neither has there been a consensus in Beijing about the principles for development for China, much less for the rest of the world. That said, China has followed a similar development path as other successful East Asian states. The 'China Model' is a variant of the East Asian Model (EAM) of state-led development, adapted for the realities of the twenty-first century.[6]

There are aspects of China's experience and the experiences of successful East Asian states in general that may be useful for other countries. However, that the EAM has proven to be a successful model for some countries in some circumstances does not mean that it is the model for all countries everywhere regardless of their circumstances. For a variety of practical and normative reasons, the EAM does not provide a detailed blueprint that other developing countries can easily follow. Although the general economic approach appears sound – or at least seemed to work in an era where American leveraged consumerism was able to support Asian export-led growth – the model is stated at a level of abstractness that still requires policymakers to make wise choices in light of the particular circumstances. East Asian countries have diverged on specific policy issues, and other countries that follow the model will as well. A non-ideological pragmatic approach to reforms has been essential to the East Asian success.

Moreover, other countries may not be able, or may not want, to follow the East Asian Model. Unlike China and many other East Asian states, most developing states that have democratised will not be able to restrict civil and political rights in the name of social stability and economic growth. Citizens of other developing countries may also object that the trade-off is unnecessary in their case or not worth it. In addition, other countries may not have the political or economic power that China has to resist external pressures to open the domestic economy to foreign competition. China is certainly different than many developing countries in terms of size, political power, the nature of its political system, and the degree to which it can control its own economic destiny.

---

6 For a discussion of the key elements of the East Asian Model, see Peerenboom, 2007, see *supra* note 4.

More fundamentally, each country faces unique challenges and opportunities. Along the way, particular choices are made. Some institutions gain power, some lose power; some segments of society are improved as a result of reforms, while others are made worse. Accordingly, the story of modernisation or law and development in any given country is inevitably a story of politics – and largely one of local politics. Thus, it is not likely that any single model will apply everywhere.

Rather, different regions, and countries within particular regions, are likely to pursue different paths to development. In Europe, EU accession requirements will ensure that states continue to follow the Euro-America model of democracy + markets + liberal civil and political rights. In Arab states and Russia, where resource dependent growth has stymied political reforms by allowing leaders to buy off the populace in exchange for rising living standards, escaping the 'natural resources curse' will require a more diversified economy, with broader investment in human capital and institutions, and deep political reforms. Turkey and Indonesia may become modern democracies in which Islam, rather than secular liberalism, shapes the national identity. In Latin America, some states are likely to continue to embrace populism because of ethnic and demographic patterns, widespread inequality and the temptation of quick fixes made possible by the availability of revenues from the sale of oil and other natural resources. The vast majority of Latin American states, however, are likely to continue on their winding path to become consolidated democracies, led in many cases by pragmatic, moderate or centre-left parties. In any event, most Latin America countries must overcome the historical legacies of colonialism, slavery and commodity-dependent economies that have led to a high concentration of economic and political power and some of the world's highest levels of inequality, while hindering state investment in poverty reduction, education, infrastructure and institutions that provided the foundation for more sustainable growth in East Asia.

8. Multiple Modernities and Post-Modernities

In sum, the emergence of China and other countries with their own distinct cultures will remake the existing international order. Yet as these countries grow and take their place in the new international order, there will be further convergence of the institutions and practices found in other wealthy modern societies. As these new arrivals negotiate modernity, and indeed post-modernity, they may very well give rise to one or more novel varieties of capitalism, rule of law, democracy, and human rights. Capitalism, rule of law, democracy, and human rights – the hallmarks of modernity – are sufficiently contested in theory and varied in practice that the final outcome in emerging countries cannot be specified at this point, much to the chagrin of those who would press their own version on them. Yet there is enough minimal determinate content to each of these four aspects to provide a teleological orientation to the process that is likely to survive into the next decades, barring extraordinary catastrophes that radically change the nature of contemporary society. Rather than lamenting the end of a false universalism built on the historically-contingent cosmopolitan values of Euro-America, we should welcome the arrival of a more pluralistic, truly global order, and work to ensure that it is a more just world in which global resources and burdens are more fairly shared by all.

1.2

A Future to Avert: Law as Contributor to Instability and Polarisation

Thomas Pogge[*]

The next decades are very likely to bring a continuation of globalisation, involving a shift of law and regulation from the national to the global level. Supranational law and regulation will increasingly pre-empt, constrain, and shape national legislation. Barring a concerted effort to achieve deep structural reform, this aspect of globalisation will drive two undesirable trends. First, the increasing prominence of supranational rule making, which is undemocratic and mostly intransparent, continually enhances the rule-shaping powers of the most affluent individuals and organisations (relative to the vast majority of ordinary citizens). This is so because only these elite players have the resources and incentives, and can acquire the requisite expertise, successfully to lobby those stronger governments that dominate supranational rule-making. Bending supranational and national law to their will, a tiny global elite will continue to grow its share of global income, twisting law away from justice in the process and also gaining even more influence. This polarisation spiral will corrupt law and its application and will ensure, despite global economic growth, the massive persistence of poverty and disease. Second, regulatory capture will happen piecemeal. Any powerful player or coalition of such players will make concessions in areas where it has relatively less at stake in exchange for other such players making reciprocal concessions in other areas where it has relatively more at stake. Such trades are collectively rational insofar as they get all powerful players more of what they want. However, such trades are also dangerous. An elite coalition 'buying' control of some piece of supranational regulation will tend to disregard the needs of the rest of humankind and of future generations because it lacks assurances that other elite players practice analogous self-restraint. Moreover, insofar as various pieces of supranational regulation are shaped by different sets of players with diverse special interests, the whole

[*] **Thomas Pogge** is Leitner Professor of Philosophy and International Affairs at Yale University and Professorial Fellow at the ANU Centre for Applied Philosophy and Public Ethics.

international rule system will become incoherent and therefore vulnerable to crises that will continue to become increasingly severe.

A very clear existing trend likely to continue into the next decades is globalisation. In the domain of law, globalisation involves the emergence of complex and ever more comprehensive and influential bodies of supranational law and regulations that increasingly pre-empt, constrain, and shape national legislation. Supranational rules are not formulated through the kind of transparent, democratic procedures that characterise national law-making in the countries that have reached a basic level of domestic justice. Rather, supranational rules largely emerge through intergovernmental negotiations from which the general public and even the majority of weaker governments are effectively excluded. Only an unusually small number of 'players' exert real influence on supranational rule-making. These are powerful organisations, including large multinational corporations, banks, and associations representing very rich individuals, that have the resources and incentives, and can acquire the requisite expertise, to successfully lobby those stronger governments that dominate supranational rule-making. Globalisation greatly enhances the rule-shaping powers of these elite players relative to the vast majority of ordinary citizens. But it is not, as we shall see, an unmixed blessing even for these elite players. The problems I point to are familiar from domestic politics, especially in the United States which has more, and more blatant, buying and selling of legislation than most other democratic states. Let me begin, then, with a more general analysis.

In the modern world, competitive and adversarial systems are omnipresent. The real economy and our financial markets are based on competition: firms and banks are competing over customers, investors, and employees. The exercise of political power is based on competition among political parties for votes and campaign contributions. Internationally, states compete for military and economic power as supported by access to natural resources, advanced technologies, and the most talented people. The interpretation and application of rules is settled by courts that function as adversarial systems driven by two parties seeking to make their own proposed application of the rules seem compelling and to discredit their opponent's proposal. There is fierce competition among the media over stories, advertisers and consumers and similarly dogged competition among NGOs over donations and success stories. And in the academy, as well, there is competition over teachers and researchers, students, donations, and the rewards of success such as grants, prizes, and media recognition. Organised competition is pervasive in modern life.

Competition can be a very powerful motivator of performance. In a competitive system, agents tend to receive greater rewards the better they perform. This much is also true of non-competitive systems; but there agents have incentives to play up the difficulties of their task, and to downplay their own capacities, in order to influence in their favour the judges or the designers of the relevant reward algorithms. By making others believe that they are working harder than they really are, agents can boost the rate at which they get rewarded. Competition avoids this problem by motivating agents to reveal their full capacities. To reap maximal rewards, agents must put in a good performance not relative to their own presumed capacities but relative to the actual performance of other agents. It is a great virtue of competitive systems that they incentivise agents to reveal their own capacities and then to give their best.

This virtue enables competitive systems to be highly effective at promoting desired outcomes. Such effectiveness depends, however, on a competitive or adversarial system being properly framed. This means that the rules of the game must be designed so as to ensure that the self-interested pursuits of the players are closely correlated with their contributions to desired outcomes and that these rules are administered in a transparent and impartial way so that the competing agents know that they will be rewarded for superior performance and only for superior performance.

The Achilles heel of competitive or adversarial systems is related to this need for proper framing. Competitive/adversarial systems contain the seeds of their own demise by providing powerful incentives to reward-focused players to attempt to manipulate the rules, or to interfere with their impartial application. Here the rules and the regulators, supposedly in charge of organising and constraining the competition, become themselves potential objects of the competition. To the extent that efforts by players to influence the design or application of the rules in their own favour (in order to corrupt the competition) succeed, these efforts diminish the effectiveness of the competitive or adversarial system. This happens in two distinct ways: first, player resources diverted toward corruption are no longer available to boost performance; and second, the incentives to work hard toward superior performance are weakened insofar as such rewards fail to track superior performance.

As an example, suppose the military needs to replace its ageing fleet of refuelling planes. It puts out a tender for a large contract for designing and supplying a new model of refuelling planes. Competing firms can now throw all their best efforts at the task of designing a plane that reaches a high level of performance at a relatively low unit cost. But a firm can make other efforts as well. It can try to influence the formulation of the call – by trying to affect who gets to write the call and/or by trying to affect how it is formulated by its authors – so that this call emphasizes features of refuelling planes in which the firm has a comparative advantage over its competitors and deemphasises features in which the firm is at a relative disadvantage. And the firm can also try to influence the judgement made pursuant to the call – again, by trying to influence the composition of the judging panel and/or by trying to influence the appointed judges. Euphemistically referred to as 'lobbying', such efforts to corrupt the rules of the competition or their impartial application are costly. When such efforts have no effect, then they merely produce a cost to the firm as well as a social cost in those cases where this firm, had it concentrated its effort on delivering a better bid, would have beaten the actual winner. Insofar as such corruption efforts succeed, they cause additional social costs: the formulation of the call for tenders, and the plane it eventually leads to, may not match the real needs of the military; a plane that is superior according to the terms of the call may be beaten by an inferior one; and, for the future, potential defence contractors may be encouraged to divert more of their resources toward corruption efforts, which in practice will result in the military receiving less suitable equipment for the money it spends.

In cases like our example, the corruption efforts typically take advantage of a principal-agent problem which arises from the fact that the people formulating the call for tenders, and those who decide which firm's design best meets the call, are not focused solely on the country's interest in an effective military but also have strong private interests, for example in positioning themselves for a lucrative future consultancy (the 'revolving door' phenomenon). But efforts to corrupt can make sense even in cases where there is no principal-agent duality. Thus take a family choosing among competing architects, car dealers, dentists or investment advisors. Here individual competitors can try to win the contract by invoking their expertise to influence their potential customer's or client's decision procedure. One can try to coax one's potential customer or client into valuing more highly those features of the relevant product or service with regard to which one has a potential advantage over one's competitors or one can try to divert the potential customer or client from a sober assessment of her options. These skills are omnipresent in the modern world and matter greatly not merely for the success of professional lobbyists, but also for that of salespeople, attorneys, politicians, corporate executives and basically everyone filling a social role with competitive or adversarial aspects.

Corruption problems of the sort I have described can be greatly reduced through protective rules that deter corruption efforts, such as rules governing the conduct of military contractors and military procurement personnel in their interactions with each other. Such rules can be helpful, but as rules they are vulnerable to these same sorts of corruption efforts as the primary rules they are supposed to protect. The application of such secondary rules will often be corrupted, or proposed secondary rules will never be adopted in the first place. Lobbyists and political incumbents benefit from a wide-ranging freedom to lobby, and it is therefore hardly surprising that lobbyists will lobby against proposed restrictions on their activities and legislators will be inclined to vote down proposed such restrictions.

An obvious antidote against the corrosive effects of corruption as defined is a shared morality, involving a shared religion or common social purpose, for example, or common moral values, goals, principles, or norms. When there is, for instance, a strong and universally shared sense of patriotism in a country, supported perhaps by a manifest threat from a powerful and expansionist neighbouring state, then corruption is likely to be kept at bay. However, outside such special situations, a strong commitment to a widely shared morality is difficult to sustain in the modern world. There are various important reasons for this. One reason is the global spread of an economic mindset that is closely associated with the omnipresence of adversarial and competitive systems. Pursuant to this mindset, controversies over ends and values, including moral ones, are not subject to rational reflection, discussion and resolution; only controversies over effective means to given ends can be rationally resolved. Accordingly, the theory and design of a modern economic system is guided by two principles: (1) there are no ultimate shared purposes that the system as a whole is meant to serve. (2) the rules of the system can and should be designed so that the diverse purposes of its participants are optimally served even while each participant is focused only on rationally advancing his or her own interests under the system's rules (including sanctions). The second principle cannot adjudicate among the many Pareto-efficient designs of the system; and since disagreement over such alternative designs is also presumed to be irresolvable by appeal to authoritative moral values or principles, such disagreement will then be settled on the basis of bargaining in which each participant will exert pressure on behalf of its own values and interests.

Here it is possible of course that these participants have important values in common and are willing to prioritise these shared values over most of their private interests. But such a fortunate coincidence is unlikely in the domain of supranational rule making. Moral values could play a substantial role in intergovernmental negotiations only if they were shared and also known to be genuinely shared among most of the parties involved. This is generally not the case because such negotiators have learned that others' appeals to moral contents are not always trustworthy and rarely explore such moral contents in any significant depth. Negotiations are then typically driven by bargaining in which each negotiator seeks to promote the interests or values of its own country or organisation (or even those of her or himself). This trend is amplified by what one may call the 'sucker exemption': it is a near-universal feature of human moralities that they regard conduct that would be immoral under conditions of full compliance as less wrong or not wrong at all when compliance by others cannot be counted upon. In other words, moralities do not require their adherents to be 'the sucker', that is, someone who can easily be taken advantage of because she continues to comply with her morality even while others are not complying with theirs.

The sucker exemption renders fragile the moral solution to the corruption problem. When much is at stake, competing agents will not willingly refrain from efforts to influence the formulation or application of rules in their own favour when they have reason to suspect that at least some of their competitors are making exactly such efforts. When even a small minority of the competing agents shows a disposition to get ahead by influencing the design or application of the rules organising the competition, then most of the remaining competitors will also shed their inhibitions; they will be frustrated by competing at a disadvantage and will attach much diminished weight to their obligation to protect the integrity of the rules and of their application.

When there is no common morality that supports a shared commitment to respect and preserve the integrity of the rules and of their application, moral language may still be prominent. But it will be used by participants strategically, for the sake of promoting their own interests and values. Participants will invoke a shared moral vocabulary in their efforts to revise some rules and to protect others from revision. Because the rules structuring a competitive system are harder to change when they are widely regarded as moralised, competitors will spend resources on 'moralising' rules they are interested in entrenching and on 'de-moralising' rules they are interested in revising. Such efforts produce a degeneration of moral discourse and undermine its standing in the wider culture.

Let me recapitulate how, according to these explanatory hypotheses, the noted Achilles heel of competitive systems becomes more dangerous with globalisation, that is, with the emergence of an increasingly dense and influential network of supranational rules. This is so for two reasons. First, as noted, our world is very far from a strong commitment to a morality that is widely shared across continents. And the agents able to affect the formulation or application of those supranational rules do not understand one another's moral outlooks well enough to be sure that most others are complying at least with their own moralities. Second, the temptations toward corruption are enormous. This is so for the obvious reason that so much is at stake in the formulation and application of supranational rules, and it is so also for the less obvious reason that only an unusually small number of agents (namely those corporations and individuals who can successfully lobby the more powerful governments that are shaping these rules with little democratic oversight) have the incentives, expertise, and power to partake in the contest over the formulation and application of supranational rules. A serious lobbying effort by a powerful company or industry can make a huge difference to its fortunes. For a very large profit-oriented multinational firm there is hardly any more lucrative investment than that in influencing the emerging global rules that structure the space in which it will operate.

One systemic problem 'predicted' by the foregoing analysis is polarisation: increasing inequality involving a small minority gaining ground at the expense of all the rest. In a globalised world, especially, the richest and most powerful agents are best positioned to engage in cost-effective lobbying: they have much to gain from favourable rules and therefore can spend a lot on acquiring the necessary expertise, on forming alliances with one another, and on lobbying the relevant political decision makers. Ordinary citizens, by contrast, each have too little at stake to make it worth their while to acquire the necessary expertise and to form alliances that are large enough to engage in effective lobbying that could rival corporate influence. And so the players that are already the richest and most powerful typically get their way and thereby increase their own relative wealth and power within the system. This in turn further increases their capacity to influence the design and application of the rules in their own favour. In the absence of global democratic institutions or other mechanisms through which ordinary people can influence the formulation and application of supranational rules, we can expect regulatory capture with a spiral of increasing polarisation that benefits a small minority at the top and, unintentionally but no less inexorably, keeps the bottom half of humankind down.

One important example of global regulatory capture is the TRIPS Agreement (trade-related aspects of intellectual property rights). This Agreement was achieved by large corporations that stood to make a lot of money from licensing their intellectual property. In the early 1990s, firms, mainly from the pharmaceutical, software, entertainment, and agricultural industries overcame their differences in order to lobby jointly for a global expansion and strengthening of intellectual property rights which was then incorporated into the WTO Treaty. Thanks to this mighty lobbying effort, any country that wants to participate in the WTO trading regime (and remaining outside this regime is a substantial handicap for any country) must now enact and enforce very strong intellectual property protections and thereby, in effect, collect massive economic rents for well-capitalised innovators in the aforementioned industries.[1] The richest have shaped the new global rules in their own favour and thereby further polarised the distribution of global household income. In this case, the impact on the world's poor majority was especially detrimental as they essentially lost access to advanced medicines. Before 2005, clever Indian

[1] For some more background, see Thomas Pogge, "Access to Medicines", in Thomas Pogge (ed.), *Public Health Ethics*, 2008, pp. 73-82.

manufacturers typically managed to bypass process patents (which were all that pharmaceutical innovators could obtain in India) by developing a different way of making the relevant molecule. After 2004, Indian law became TRIPS-compliant by entitling pharmaceutical innovators to 20-year product patents which allow them to suppress unlicensed copies regardless of how they were produced.

We can observe the effect of the polarisation spiral in the following table (figures supplied by Branko Milanovic, World Bank), which shows a remarkably rapid shift of income share toward the top five percent of the human population.

Segment of World Population	Share of Global Household Income 1988	Share of Global Household Income 2005	Absolute Change in Income Share	Relative Change in Income Share
Richest Ventile	42.87	46.36	+3.49	+8.1%
Second Ventile	21.80	22.18	+0.38	+1.7%
Next Three Ventiles	24.83	21.80	-3.03	-12.2%
Second Quarter	6.97	6.74	-0.23	-3.3%
Third Quarter	2.37	2.14	-0.23	-9.7%
Poorest Quarter	1.16	0.78	-0.38	-32.8%

We find a similar polarisation also *within* countries that have been heavily involved in globalisation. In the last US economic expansion (2002-07), average per capita household income grew by 16 percent. But this growth was very unevenly distributed. The top one percent of US households registered a gain of 62 percent; the remaining 99 percent of households registered a gain of 7 percent. The top percentile captured 65 percent of the real per capita growth of the US economy during these years. This phenomenon is not confined to the Bush Administration or Republican governments. During the 1993-2000 Clinton expansion, the top percentile did similarly well, capturing 45 percent of the real per capita growth of the US economy.[2] In fact, the trend is consistent for the entire 30-year globalisation period. During 1978-2007, the share of the bottom half of US citizens in national household income declined from 18 to 12.8 percent. In the same period, the share of the top one percent rose 2.6-fold, from 8.95 to 23.50 percent; the share of the top tenth percent rose 4.6-fold, from 2.65 to 12.28 percent; and the share of the top hundredth percent even rose 7-fold, from 0.86 to 6.04 percent of national household income.[3] The top hundredth percent of US households (30,000 people, 14,400 tax returns) now have nearly half as much income as the bottom half (150 million people) of US households – and about two-thirds as much as the bottom half (3.4 billion) of the world's population.[4] This trend is dramatically at odds with the still widely propagated Kuznets curve which depicts the evolution of inequality as a curve in the shape of an inverted U: rising in the early period of industrialisation and then falling off as a national economy matures.[5]

The same sort of phenomenon can be observed in China, another country heavily influenced by globalisation. Here the available data are spottier, presenting only deciles and only going back to 1990. But the trend is unmistakable: in the period of 1990-2004, the income share of the bottom half declined from 27 to 18 percent – while that of the top tenth rose from 25 to 35 percent.[6]

---

2 Emmanuel Saez and Thomas Piketty, "Income Inequality in the United States, 1913–1998", in *Quarterly Journal of Economics,* vol. 118, 2003, pp. 1–39, as updated in "Tables and Figures Updated to 2007 in Excel Format", August 2009, available at elsa.berkeley.edu/~saez/, Table 1 (based on data from the US Internal Revenue Service).

3 Saez and Piketty, 2009, Table A3, see *supra* note 2.

4 Saez and Piketty, 2009, see *supra* note 2; World Bank, *World Development Report 2007*, World Bank Publications, Washington DC, 2006, p. 289; David Leonhardt and Geraldine Fabrikant, "Rise of the Super-Rich Hits a Sobering Wall", available at http://finance.yahoo.com/banking-budgeting/article/107575/rise-of-the-super-rich-hits-a-sobering-wall.html, last accessed on 7 March 2011.

5 See, for example, "Kuznets Curve", *Wikipedia*, available at http://en.wikipedia.org/wiki/Kuznets_curve, last accessed on 7 March 2011.

6 Camelia Minoiu and Sanjay G. Reddy. "Chinese Poverty: Assessing the Impact of Alternative Assumptions", in *Review of Income and Wealth*, vol. 54, no. 4, 2008, pp. 572-96; and World Bank, *World Development Indicators 2008*, World Bank Publications, Washington DC, 2008, p. 68.

There is a second systemic problem emerging from the foregoing analysis of collective rule shaping under conditions of globalisation. Relatively few in number, the organisations capable of influencing supranational rule-making through the lobbying of major governments will strategically adjust their efforts to one another. One such phenomenon we have already discussed: such organisations will seek to overcome their differences in order to form alliances devoted to lobbying for a mutually desired outcome (such as the TRIPS Agreement). Another, related phenomenon is that such a powerful player (or coalition of players) will make concessions in areas where it has relatively less at stake in exchange for other such players making reciprocal concessions in other areas where it has relatively more at stake. Such trades are collectively rational insofar as they get all powerful players more of what they want. But such trades are also dangerous in the long term, in two ways. First, when an elite coalition buys control of some system rules or their application, it will tend to disregard the needs of the rest of humankind and of future generations because it lacks assurances that other elite players practice analogous self-restraint. Second, insofar as various pieces of supranational regulation are shaped by different sets of players with diverse special interests, the whole international rule system will become incoherent and therefore vulnerable to crises of increasing severity. Both phenomena exemplify the structure of 'collective action problems' (as paradigmatically exemplified by the prisoners' dilemma): The strongest players are impelled, by their self-regarding interests, to seek influence in ways that are detrimental and dangerous even to themselves collectively (and even more so, of course, to weaker players). Even the strongest are worse off in the long run than they would be if they abandoned their competitive efforts to corrupt the rules and their application in their own favour. In the long run, they must expect more risk and loss from the incoherence of an institutional order shaped by lobbying than opportunity and gain from their own lobbying efforts.

This second systemic problem of competitive and adversarial systems, especially prominent at the supranational level where special interests can lobby under unusually favourable conditions, constitutes a serious danger as exemplified by the recent global financial crisis. But it also exposes a great opportunity to overcome both systemic problems together. If the strongest corporations can be shown that their opportunities to influence the design of supranational rules are collectively detrimental to themselves (each does better with this opportunity than without, but each does worse with several having it than with none having it), they may be willing to support a systemic solution that reduces lobbying opportunities and thereby presumably also the great concentration of wealth and lobbying power at the very top. They may also be willing then to work toward the formulation of a basic moral consensus that could guide supranational rule making toward greater coherence and act as a constraint on corporate lobbying.

Such a basic moral consensus might well form around an agreement on the great scourges that all have a shared interest in banishing: the risk of major wars involving weapons of mass destruction, the degradation of our natural environment including resource depletion and catastrophic climate change, and the still very high prevalence of severe poverty and disease among the bottom half of the human population.[7] Paradoxical as it sounds, a moralisation of supranational rule making may be in the interest of the most powerful corporations precisely because they now have such unusually large power to shape supranational rules. Insofar as such corporations are taking an intelligent long-term view of their own interests, many of them will find that they have reason on balance to support such a moralisation (which is not to say that their top executives have such an interest). There is a great task and opportunity here for those trained in moral theorising and reflection: we should specify the first steps of such a moralisation in detail and seek to show how they help overcome especially the second systemic problem. I have tried to make a small contribution to this task by helping to develop, specify and propagate the Health Impact Fund proposal.[8] If we fail in this effort, or fail to make it, we can expect the law of the future increasingly to become a contributor to polarisation and serious instability.

---

[7] The scourge of overpopulation is closely related to that of poverty in that overpopulation aggravates poverty and reductions in poverty entail large reductions in total fertility rates. See Thomas Pogge, *Politics As Usual,* Polity Press, 2010, Cambridge, pp. 108-109 and note 172.

[8] See for example Thomas Pogge, "The Health Impact Fund: better pharmaceutical innovations at much lower prices", in Thomas Pogge, Matt Rimmer, and Kim Rubenstein (eds.), *Incentives for Global Public Health: Patent Law and Access to Essential Medicines*, Cambridge University Press, Cambridge, 2010, pp. 135-154. Additional information can be found at www.healthimpactfund.org.

1.3

The Idea(s) of International Law

Jan Klabbers[*]

This think piece addresses international law not so much on the level of practice, but rather on the level of ideas. It discusses the inherent biases contained in international law in favour of the powerful, arguing that some of the topics ignored by international law (taxation, migration, labour) should come to be included, since international law is, or ought to be, about improving the lives of people. The piece also discusses the ways international law is becoming instrumentalised, or even commodified, through such notions as non-legal but binding agreements, or the creation of so-called compliance procedures. Finally, the author expresses some concerns about the ever-increasing creation of accountability mechanisms and accountability techniques. These not only tend to re-conceptualise the world, but also hide from view the circumstance that action is always – at least to some extent – the work of agents, and that thus the individual virtues of those agents may be of relevance.

1. Introduction

"Predicting things is always difficult, especially when they concern the future", a famous futurologist once quipped. With that in mind, what follows should be taken tongue in cheek: while all of us make our everyday plans on the basis of some expectation of what tomorrow will bring, nonetheless actually predicting what will happen, and doing so with any degree of accuracy, is by no means an easy task. Likewise, the following should be read with some sceptical distance because it will prove hard to resist the temptation to paint a doomsday scenario: there resides a Spengler in all of us, tempted to yet again produce a *Decline of the West*.

And no wonder – the trends identified by perusing future scenarios do indeed suggest that difficult times lie ahead. A rapid population

[*] **Jan Klabbers** is Professor of International Law at University of Helsinki and Director of the Academy of Finland Centre of Excellence in Global Governance Research.

increase of near-Malthusian proportions is expected, crime will become ever more rampant, the environment is spinning out of control and, if the last three decades are anything to go by, public solutions are frowned upon and lightly replaced by confidence in the market, with performances being monitored by means of the hard currency of indicators. Those markets themselves, however, prove uncontrollable. Crisis is the global keyword, and goes hand in hand with privatisation even to the extent that yesterday's citizen is being replaced by today's consumer, whose political affiliations are being replaced by brand loyalties. Those brands, in turn, are just that – labels placed on products produced anonymously by others, sometimes even in sweatshops by children who should be out playing. The politics of symbolism takes over, and the leading symbol is that of greed. In such a setting, it is all too easy to paint the decline of the West, and the decline of the rest.

This is no coincidence. The futurologist who will publicly present the expectation that things will improve will be branded as naïve at best, and perhaps even as irresponsible. Should they be proven wrong, they will be ridiculed, and perhaps even blamed for misdirection. Moreover, they will have a hard time receiving research funding: while everyone loves an optimistic message, our scientists are supposed to be gatekeepers between the public and disaster. The alcoholism researcher who feels alcoholism is not a problem will be outcast; the social scientist who predicts a sunny future will be stifled, and the sceptical environmentalist is simply disbelieved.

All this suggests that predicting the future in international law is a troublesome activity, biased in favour of doomsday scenarios. What follows will be no different. I will address a few things which, to my mind, will have to be developed by international law as an intellectual project. I will not argue for a convention on climate change, or a treaty on global banking, or a World Human Rights Court. All these may be desirable, even necessary, in their own right, but are not my immediate concern. Instead, my concern is with the intellectual apparatus of international law. That alone will provide enough grounds for doomsday scenarios…

2. Classic or Outdated?

Intellectually, international law is still based on late nineteenth century conceptions, which were necessary at the time to facilitate an emerging global capitalist economy. It is still taught as a system of law that applies between states (with the occasional nod to individual human rights, or to international organisations and some tut-tutting about terrorist groups); as a system made up of rules expressly consented to or, alternatively, rules that happen to be to the teacher's liking, dressed up in Latin garb; and as a system devoid of sanctions. This picture is not likely to change anytime soon. Today's teachers tend to reproduce their own teachers' thoughts, and today's politicians have shown a marked desire to treat international law as purely instrumental (and are all too often supported in doing so by academic international lawyers). International law, in such an instrumentalised version, is to be used when considered advantageous (regardless of its precise contents), and to be brushed aside when something else is more useful to the immediate goal at hand – legitimacy, morality, culture, or just brute force. Globalisation seems to have bypassed the discipline of international law completely, and to the extent that international law covers the global economy, it does so in support of the major players rather than the poor and dispossessed. International law, in other words, is strongly biased, favouring the rich over the poor, and facilitating rather than regulating global capitalism.

3. The Global Economy

Much of international law relates to economic issues. Sometimes it does so directly, for instance in the form of rules on trade between states, or rules on investment protection. Much of it is less visible though. The emergence of the legal concept of the continental shelf, *e.g.*, owes much to economic incentives: as soon as oil and gas were to be found, states recognised an interest in acquiring such a shelf, and developed the law to facilitate it. Much the same applies to the time-honoured freedom of the seas, or the far younger rules on air traffic.

Over the last couple of decades, moreover, within the international legal framework two sub-disciplines have emerged which both address the protection of capital. International trade law already arose in the 1970s, but came to full blossom with the creation of the WTO and in particular its strong dispute settlement mechanism. More recently, investment protection law has established itself as an important branch of international law, characterised by a multitude of treaties and the mushrooming of arbitration and similar proceedings.

And yet, amidst all this attention for the global economy and the protection of investments and market access, it is useful to note that some topics have been cast aside or are still mostly left to domestic law. There is, for example, little or no attention for development in international law – how to overcome the structural causes of poverty – unless one would regard foreign investment as the road to development (this, however, is plausible only within a neo-liberal political philosophy). Likewise, economic, social and cultural rights are still the stepchildren of the human rights revolution, if only because they involve the sort of political choices that insistence on civil and political rights manages deftly to avoid. Global finance is by and large unregulated, as the recent banking crisis underlined yet again. Alternatively, to the extent that it is regulated, it is done on the legally subliminal level through standards established by the leading participants themselves, far from the public view.

The domestication of international affairs applies to taxation. Despite the existence of many, many treaties to avoid double taxation, international law has been reluctant to embrace international taxation as part of international law. All the same, the possibility of an international tax to protect the global commons is sometimes floated but remains utopian. The results are twofold. To the extent that companies are taxed, they can pick and choose in the absence of a harmonised regime which jurisdictions serve their interests best. Here, the absence of global regulation facilitates free movement and free choice. Starkly though, the opposite happens when individuals are concerned: they cannot normally relocate to places of low taxation (also because this will immediately affect the level of public services) but, instead, can count themselves lucky if they don't have to pay taxes twice. Either way, trying to make sense of taxation issues involved in a move abroad, or a temporary relocation, can be immensely complicated. Here then, the absence of a global regime tends to affect free movement negatively.

This is hardly a coincidence, as somehow the free movement of persons is considered anathema in a global economy which otherwise puts a premium on free movement of goods, services and capital. It is not just taxation which is left to national regulation – the same applies to migration. Migration law is typically absent from the textbooks on international law and left to domestic law, which again means that states are at liberty to erect barriers for foreigners to enter, and can exclude people at will.

Labour law too is not often treated as part of international law. Much is left to the International Labour Organisation which, as Robert Cox has reminded us, is essentially a device to facilitate global corporatism.[1] Universal rules concerning labour standards or working hours or the acceptable age for children and the elderly to start and stop working are few and far between, not to mention anything about acceptable minimum wages. Again then, as with taxation and migration issues, the system allows for, and even stimulates, a race to the bottom.

Tellingly, international law has not even occupied itself with competition other than between states. The behaviour of private companies is left without regulation, and any form of control is left to domestic authorities (these include the EU, for present purposes) and their own ideas on what would constitute a proper market, and reasonable company size and company behaviour. Tellingly, the WTO has no powers in the field of competition law, allowing companies to move freely and even affect each other's markets.

The problem with all these issues is not so much that there is no regulation on the international level, as regulation as such is no guarantee for good and desirable rules. The problem is rather that there is not even much recognition that it could be useful or desirable for international law to address these issues. And this applies *a fortiori* to global poverty. It may be the case that poverty cannot be tackled by any direct legal measures, in that typically it results not from agents' activities but from economic structures, but at the very least international law could and should recognize that it helps create those structures and helps keep them intact.

4. All Things Soft and Mushy

One thing that is bound to continue over the next few decades is, alas, the further instrumentalisation and even commodification of international law. The tendency has been, since the 1950s, to no longer regard

1 Robert W. Cox, *Production, Power, and World Order: Social Forces in the Making of History*, Columbia University Press, 1987.

agreements between states as automatically giving rise to legal rights and obligations, but, instead, to posit law as one option among many options. Along this line of thought, states can enter into legally binding agreements if they so wish, but can also conclude agreements that are considered to give rise to non-legal 'rights' and 'obligations'. This helps turn the law from the full menu into just an element on a smorgasbord of possibilities – to be utilised whenever it is deemed convenient, and to be left aside when considered inconvenient. The obvious question is then: "convenient or inconvenient for whom?" And the equally obvious answer is: "for those in positions of power". This is further stimulated by Anne-Marie Slaughter's worrying observation that much policy-making takes place in networks of civil servants, far from the public view, and far removed from any systems of political accountability, never mind legal accountability.[2]

The net effects of such activities are, at minimum, twofold. First, it means that domestic procedures with respect to treaty-making have eroded. Parliaments have often fought long and hard to receive some influence on the making of foreign policy, if only to prevent their position from being eroded by means of the conclusion of treaties. As a result, many parliaments have some formal role to play when it comes to the conclusion of treaties. However, they have no formal role to play when it comes to the conclusion of other kinds of instruments. Hence, the possibility of concluding a non-legally binding agreement will often involve the circumvention of a domestic parliament, and thereby undermine democracy.

Second, it means that the power of law (the culture of law, if one so wishes) is also being eroded. The seeming possibility of choosing which norm system or normative order is most suitable for the circumstances at hand means that law has become, and will increasingly become, an option among options. Where earlier generations still respected, or even celebrated, the law as a human artefact in its own right, the law now has to compete with politics, morality, and even brute and untrammelled force for its place in the sun.

This trend is visible not just in the conclusion of agreements. In more recent decades, states have also seen fit to establish soft tribunals,

2 Anne-Marie Slaughter, *A New World Order: Government Networks and the Disaggregated State*, Princeton University Press, 2004.

euphemistically referred to as 'compliance procedures', which aim to take the sting out of obligation. A breach of an obligation is no longer a breach, but rather a 'compliance problem'; and the most fitting approach is not to present the violating states with sanctions, but rather with assistance.

All this stems from the (understandable) desire to have law reflect existing political or moral configurations and sentiments as closely as possible, but this is deplorable, for two reasons. One is that existing political configurations tend to be those in vogue among the power holders, not the powerless. Second, it discards the function of law which, in all plausibility, is precisely to simplify those existing political configurations and turn them into workable mechanisms, where behaviour is either legal or it is not, and one is either in breach of an obligation or one is not.

All this is further exacerbated by academic trends and vogues, none more detrimental than the rising popularity of social science approaches to study, analyze and discuss the law. Some have tried to argue, in recent years, that law is only law if states actually behave in accordance with it (the behaviouralist perspective).[3] The obvious result then is that illegality is no longer a possibility, for any violation must mean that the norm was not legal to begin with. Others have even subjected international law to economic analysis, usually with terrifying results, ignoring altogether that the behaviour of states hardly fits the presumption of rationality underlying such methods and, moreover, that the number of actors is too small to draw many meaningful conclusions.[4] Together, however, such methods further confirm the idea that law is a tool among others.

Of course, there is no action without reaction, no thesis without its antithesis, and here too reactions are visible. One such response is to press for stronger sanctions elsewhere in the system. Many have advocated a bigger role for the International Criminal Court. Surprisingly, while states are increasingly left off the hook, individuals are increasingly thought suitable subjects for punishment, even those (or especially those, perhaps) who exercise little or no political power. In much the same way that water

[3] José E. Alvarez, *International Organizations as Law-makers*, Oxford University Press, 2005.

[4] Jack L. Goldsmith and Eric O. Posner, *The Limits of International Law*, Oxford University Press, 2005.

flows wherever it can, so too is responsibility assigned where the chances of actually holding someone responsible are greatest, rather than on the basis of their perceived guilt.

While non-compliance procedures have mushroomed, so too have calls for greater involvement of domestic courts in the application of international law. Those domestic courts themselves have responded in a lukewarm fashion, sometimes creating sophisticated but untenable distinctions between the existence of an international obligation and the authoritative interpretation thereof (as the US Supreme Court did in *Medellin*), and sometimes simply ignoring the international setting altogether (like the ECJ in *Kadi*).

5. Controlling Public Power

The increasing looseness or softness of international law has also been met with a response when it comes to the activities of international organisations. Ever since the demise of the International Tin Council in the 1980s and the UN Security Council found itself brought back to life in the early 1990s, the international legal community has aimed to come to terms with the exercise of public power by entities that, until then, were thought to never do wrong. The *Institut de Droit International*, the International Law Association, and the International Law Commission have been or are engaged in projects aiming to establish a regime relating to the responsibility (or, broader, accountability) of international organisations. Individual academics have devoted a lot of attention to this as well, and have borrowed notions, concepts and principles from constitutional law ('constitutionalisation') and administrative law ('Global Administrative Law') in order to curtail the activities of international organisations.

Much of this comes as no surprise: for decades organisations were allowed to run wild, without there being any controls other than fairly blunt political mechanisms (withdrawal, withholding funding). Yet ironically, those same organisations were not overly active, carefully making sure not to step on the sovereign toes of their member states. Since the early 1990s the level and scope of their activities has increased dramatically: the Security Council has started to impose sanctions on non-state actors and even individuals, and the UN at large has seen fit to demarcate boundaries, decide on war compensation claims, and even administer territory. It is no wonder then that an increased level of activity has been followed by increased calls for control.

Typically, the control takes on two related guises. The first, and so far dominant of these, is to create all sorts of standards to which organisations are supposed to adhere. These may be standards associated with constitutionalist thought (to respect fundamental rights, *e.g.*), or more often perhaps standards borrowed from administrative law: proportionality, transparency, and the like. Some posit that organisations are bound by all sorts of rules of customary international law (however unsettled these may be by themselves), and organisations themselves have taken up the gauntlet and have started to create or upgrade departments of internal oversight and so-called compliance officers, whose task is to control the organisation from the inside.

Second, the creation of standards also, almost by definition, implies the desire to see bodies created to test whether the organisations meet those standards. Those compliance officers are an example of such an accountability mechanism, as are such bodies as the World Bank Inspection Panel and *ad hoc* mechanisms such as the Volcker commission, set-up to apportion blame after the UN's Oil for Food Program turned out to be less than fortuitous. Likewise, the member states may set up *ad hoc* bodies to study events or, as happened after the Dutch military embarrassed itself in Srebrenica, award the task of finding accountability to an existing institution.

While the growing relevance of standards and accountability mechanisms (also in domestic settings) is meant to inspire public trust in public authorities, critics have noted that the effect may be well the reverse. Such trends create what Michael Power has felicitously referred to as 'the audit society',[5] where everyone eventually controls everyone else but trust ends up being eroded. The reason is, eventually, obvious: creating standards for behaviour invites actions that conform to these standards. Actors are no longer forced to ask themselves whether behaviour is right or wrong, just or unjust, honest or dishonest, but simply whether it meets with the standard concerned. Since standards are by their very nature open to different interpretations, may need to leave some discretion in order to be workable, and will never be able to capture all

[5] Michael Power, *The Audit Society: Rituals of Verification*, Oxford University Press, 1997.

possible contingencies, it follows that such standards exercise the simulacrum of control, rather than control itself. In the meantime, trust and confidence in public authorities, including international organisations, seeps away; the authority may act in perfect conformity with some standard or other, and yet not do the right thing, or act unjustly.

In addition to standards of behaviour, which are expected to single out right from wrong, a growing trend is to employ indicators of performance to monitor the exercise of public power. These do not separate right from wrong but, instead, single out effective from ineffective. In the field of human rights, this trend has already been visible for a number of years: states' human rights records are monitored with the help of indicators such as the number of incidents, the number of prosecutions, et cetera. The same is also visible elsewhere, *e.g.*, in relation to environmental protection. In principle, there is nothing wrong with this, but two dangers loom large.

The first of these is, of course, that the use of indicators is itself an exercise of public power. Monitoring agencies should not remain above scrutiny, and the choice for certain indicators over others is a political choice *par excellence*. Second, and perhaps more disturbing because less obvious, is the circumstance that indicators may come to affect the world as such: they do not only measure performance, but mould the world to accord with the indicator. Indicators may be chosen not just because they are substantially relevant, but also because they make for easy measurement or make comparisons possible. Those in positions of public power may no longer strive to fulfil their mandates as best as they can, but instead to score as well as possible on the indicators used. And this, in turn, would come to mean that we re-construct the world around us so as to coincide with our indicators, rather than the other way around. Moreover, there is enormous scope for conflict between standards of behaviour and indicators of performance – they do not necessarily go hand in hand.

6. Some Prescriptive Conclusions

What now is the discipline of international law to do? First, it should come to the realisation that international law ultimately, and in particular by regulating the global economy, affects the life of people, not just of states and other actors. That does not mean (as is often supposed) that individuals should be considered as subjects of international law; it might be perfectly possible to respect each and every individual without giving them a formal status, in much the same way that the US can respect the lives of people in other countries without pronouncing them subjects of US law. International lawyers should realise that world poverty and malnutrition are a product (or at least a side-effect) of international law, as is unequal development. To the extent that the domestication of tax law, migration law and labour law help sustain a 'race to the bottom', it would be useful for international lawyers to make sure that those fields do not remain as neglected as they now are, if only for the discipline's own sake: the fragmentation of international law may entail that the discipline as such will end up shattered, replaced by fragmented specialists in, say, maritime law, or trade law, or indeed tax law. The best way to combat fragmentation may be not so much the desperate search for uniformity, but rather to ensure that all aspects of life are part of the same broader fabric – only in this way can the fabric itself survive.

International lawyers (at least those working as independent academics) should stop providing states with the arguments to kill off their very discipline. Arguments that agreements can be binding yet remain non-legal rest on very flimsy, and eventually untenable, theoretical assumptions and, what is more, only produce similar orders devoid of the guarantees that come with law. As Michel Virally once demonstrated (without drawing the obvious conclusion), if one takes the idea of non-legally binding agreements seriously, one would need to develop a set of rules to deal with the creation of such agreements, their effects, implementation and application, and their termination.[6] Such a system of rules can only mirror the law of treaties, so, in the end, there is no real difference, except for democracy and legal protection being eroded. Much the same applies to the creation of compliance procedures: if taken seriously, these will come to look like courts in all but name. The big loser here is the idea of law, to be replaced by some kind of unclear, un-transparent functionality that only serves the interests of those in positions of power.

6 Michel Virally, "La Distinction Entre Textes Internationaux de Portée Juridique et Textes Internationaux Dépourvus de Portée Juridique (à L'exception des Textes Emanant des Organisations Internationales)", in *Annuaire de l'Institut de Droit International*, vol. 60, pp. 166-257.

Finally, one lesson to learn is that while the law is a great invention, not everything can be captured in terms of standards and tribunals. Deontology begets deontology. Increased sets of standards will lead to increased accountability mechanisms, but not necessarily to greater accountability of public power. Instead, there is every reason to believe that this will lead to increased distrust. The only remedy may well reside in a new faith in the classic Aristotelian insight that what matters is not just the standards applicable to our political leaders, but also their individual character traits.

1.4

The Bifurcation of International Law: Two Futures for the International Rule of Law

André Nollkaemper[*]

The continuing quest for the international rule of law will not develop along a uniform path. The main divergence will be between two models. In the first model, the international rule of law is confined to the international level. Here, progress can be expected to be slow, and to vary between regimes. In the second model, the international rule of law mingles with the domestic rule of law. Here it will be much more powerful, as it can profit from national institutions. However, the development of this second model will be uneven across the world, as it depends on varying degrees of national legal empowerment. Moreover, it creates fundamental dilemmas, as the very international law which seeks to impose itself on the national legal order remains rooted in the international legal order with its relatively limited rule of law quality. Therefore, the two futures for the international rule of law are intrinsically connected. The international rule of law will be able to strengthen the national rule of law, and profit from its superior enforcement mechanisms, to the extent that the rule of law at the international level will be strengthened.

Traditionally, international law is understood to constitute a unified system. It is based on a common set of sources that define which norms are part of the international legal system. General principles define the basic foundations of the relations between subjects. Unity is further supported by secondary rules that govern matters such as rules of change, interpretation and the consequences of wrongful acts. Moreover, a number of global institutions, most notably the United Nations, constitute the institutional manifestation of a unitary international legal order.

In the past few years we have seen cracks in this unitary system, often examined through the conceptual lens of fragmentation. In the coming twenty years, it is likely that these cracks will magnify and we

[*] **André Nollkaemper** is Professor of Public International Law at the Amsterdam Center for International Law (ACIL), Faculty of Law, University of Amsterdam.

may see the system divide into separate parts. These will still be connected through all of the common elements identified above. However, the distinctions between the separate parts are likely to become gradually more important.

One of the many criteria that will differentiate subsystems is the rule of law quality of international law. While the quest for the rule of law beyond the nation-state (or: the international rule of law) is as old as international law itself, there is ample evidence that this quest will continue be strengthened in the next few decades. International affairs are simply too important, and affect too many people's daily lives, to leave it to the uncontrolled arbitrary whims of politics. However, it is unlikely that the international rule of law will develop itself along a uniform path. Rather, it is likely that we will see multiple variations in the rule of law quality within the international legal system, which will affect the very foundations of international law as a uniform system applying to all states in the world.

The main dividing line is likely to be between two, coexisting, models for the international rule of law (though, as will be elucidated below, within each model there will be further variation). In the first model, the international rule of law is confined to the international level. In the second model, the international rule of law will connect with the domestic rule of law and profit from, but sometimes also undermine, the rule of law at national level. We can call this model the internationalised rule of law – 'internationalised', because a previously domestic system for the protection of the rule of law is infiltrated by international law.

In the first model, the international rule of law will be a continuity of traditional international law. It will be based on the very foundations of international law, including the core principles of sovereignty, sovereign equality, dualism, non-intervention and the prohibition of the use of force. It is not at all impossible to think about this type of international law in terms of the rule of law. Indeed, the quest for the rule of law is inherent in the existence of international law. International law is an instrument of power, but at the same time seeks to control power. From this perspective the entire system of international law can be seen in rule of law terms, as it seeks to limit the use and abuse of power by states. Thus, the rule of law at the international level, in large part, is defined though the protection of sovereignty, non-intervention and the peaceful settlement of disputes, as intervention and use of force are the most obvious violations of any rule of law system.

Precisely because of the dominant role of sovereignty, this rule of law at the international level is fundamentally different from the rule of law at the national level. Partially as a result, compared to the rule of law that exists at the national level of some (but obviously not all) states, the international rule of law remains primitive and weak, in particular in its enforcement, dispute settlement and adjudication functions. Enforcement remains largely in the hands of the very actors whose acts are to be controlled. Self-help and countermeasures are the next best option. Adjudication remains incidental and it is impossible to conceive adjudication as a systematic force in the enforcement of international law or in the settlement of disputes. It is this feature that will continue to raise the question of whether international law is truly law.

Yet, this rule of law at the international level will remain an important model, shared across the world. Much of the modern international law scholarship may underestimate the power of continuity in normative, as well as empirical terms. Indeed, much of traditional international law is utterly modern in its emphasis on the protection of distinct groups and communities that define their own social, economic and political order and their relationship with other communities and legal orders.

In particular areas of international law, the rule of law at the international level has been significantly strengthened and may even start to share qualities with the domestic rule of law, notably in its increasing reliance on independent forums for accountability. The reliance on auto-determination and self-help is gradually being replaced with international adjudication organisations and their softer counterparts of international non-compliance procedures. The next twenty years will see an extension of international adjudication currently exemplified by the World Trade Organization, investment arbitration, human rights litigation in international courts, and litigation in international and internationalised criminal tribunals for individuals. It will also see a continuation of the review of compliance by international institutions, for instance in the field of international environmental law.

It would be incorrect to consider this second type to be of marginal relevance because it would be limited to a few specialised functional regimes. We can see the strengthening of the rule of law at the international level, precisely in areas of international law that are of importance to the daily lives of many people (including fundamental rights, trade and investment and environmental protection), will be quite distinct from the traditional international rule of law.

The strengthening of the international rule of law in particular regimes and areas of international law will lead, to some extent, to a disruption of the unity of international law, in terms of its rule of law quality. Yet, in all cases, the international rule of law principle remains confined to the international level, and continues to be based on and supported by principles of sovereignty, consent and dualism that characterise traditional international law.

The second future for the international rule of law presents a radical departure from the first model. Here international law transforms itself from its international roots and interconnects and mingles with national law. In this model, the international rule of law is still based on and protected by international law, as the very concept of international law necessarily remains source-driven, and the sources are located in and recognised by the international legal order. However, unlike the first type of international law, it is not based on a duality with national law. In terms of contents and subjects, it overlaps with national law. Perhaps most importantly, it makes use of the organs of the national legal order. Thus it is not based on a separate rule of law at the international level, but rather on an integration of the international and the national rule of law. There are not two rules of law, only one, be it a particularly complex rule of law with built-in tensions and contradictions.

This second model is driven by the fact that international law is increasingly regulatory in nature, directly governing matters that are otherwise located in domestic legal orders. International law not only influences and determines the contents of the 'law that has to rule', but also determines the very foundations of the rule of law that are to apply domestically. International law, particularly international human rights law, imposes such fundamental limitations on the power of government that it has, in fact, become difficult to think of a rule of law or a relationship between a state and its citizens that does not have some connection with international law.

This increasing normative space creates opportunities for and can strengthen both the traditionally domestic rule of law and the international rule of law. As to the former, international (human rights) law strengthens and supports the domestic rule of law, for instance in protecting the autonomy of domestic courts *vis-à-vis* the political branches, and in protecting citizens against retrospective laws. As for the latter, this mingling of international and national spheres allows international law to profit from the rule of law quality of national institutions. A key institutional consequence is that national courts, which were always the natural first port of call for adjudicating rights and obligations of private parties, also become the first port of call for international claims by private parties. The effect of the allocation of rights to individuals on the power of national courts extends to issue-areas that traditionally have been removed from the power of domestic courts, including armed conflict. This can remedy, to a significant extent, a fundamental weakness in the international rule of law: the absence of independent courts which can review the use and abuse of public power.

In the coming decades, the two types of international law will coexist. One might call this a situation of legal pluralism within the international legal order. They will each occupy a separate normative space. However the second model will probably not overtake the first. The development of the second type of the international rule of law and the relative size that it will occupy in relation to the rule of law at international level, will be highly uneven and indeed raises some fundamental dilemmas.

As to the uneven development of this type of international rule of law, two considerations are critical. First, within international law there are significant variations in the degree in which particular parts of international law indeed, penetrate the national legal order. It is in particular international law that creates individual rights which circumvent the shield of the state. Kelsen correctly observed that as direct authorisation or obligation of individuals by international law replaces the traditional model of indirect authorisation and obligation, the boundary between international and domestic law evaporates.[1] While such direct regulation provides the power of international law to pierce the legal order of the

[1] Hans Kelsen, *Law and Peace in International Relations: The Oliver Wendell Holmes Lectures, 1940-41*, Harvard University Press, Cambridge, 1942, p. 96.

state, it also presents its limitation. Although there are ample examples of states that make international law part and parcel of domestic law, even irrespective of individual rights, the overwhelming trend in practice is to limit the insertion of international law in the national legal order to those rules of international law that create international rights. There is indeed a systematic connection between, on the one hand, international law that creates individual rights that protect individuals against the exercise of public power (and thus substantively are at the core of the rule of law), and, on the other hand, the power of such rules to pierce the veil of the legal order of the state. But that connection is representative of only a relatively small part of international law.

Second, the trend towards the internationalised rule of law will be a highly uneven development throughout the world. In contrast to the first two types of international law, it is only driven in part by international law alone, but depends strongly on national law. It would be simplistic to contend, as is sometimes done, that the influence of international law on national law, and the national rule of law, would *only* be a matter of national law. International rules contain fundamental principles, including the principle of effectiveness, which have direct consequences for and require effective domestic implementation. However, the actual legal effect of all international rules, including those that create individual rights and obligations, in the national legal order necessarily remains driven by a complementary role of national law. International law can mix with national law to the extent that national law supports this.

It is here that we are likely to see fundamental separations in the international legal order in the next twenty years. The number of states that allow international law to mix with national law, and allow their courts to distance themselves from the political branches of the state, thus becoming effective agents of the international legal order is increasing, however they remain fairly limited. Based on current trends, in particular as evidenced by the practice of constitutional change and the practice of national courts, it may be estimated that by 2030-2040 that number may increase to about half of the states in the world. The trend will be strongest in the European states, giving an entirely new dimension to the old concept of European international law. Somewhat paradoxically, the old notion of European international law, which was predominantly based on the European power politics, transforms itself largely (but it should be re-emphasised, not exclusively) into a European rule of law based system that incorporates part of international law. To a lesser extent, patterns supporting this third type of international law can be found in states in (South-East) Asia, Africa and Latin-America, such as Japan, India, Pakistan, Australia, South-Africa and Argentina. The group of states that by 2040 will not have moved in the direction of this second model of the international rule of law will decline, but is likely to still include powers such as China, Indonesia, Venezuela, Saudi-Arabia and Iran. A varied middle category will contain such diverse states as the Russian Federation and the United States.

The uneven nature in which the model of the internationalised rule of law will spread itself throughout the world will be based on a wide variety of political, social, economic and cultural considerations which will differ between states. However, critically, it also will be based on a structural condition of international law itself. Here we reach the fundamental dilemma that will be posed by this second model for the international rule of law. International law, as it imposes itself on national legal orders, intrinsically has a dual nature. On one hand, it prescribes national law and practice and, in cases of individual rights, directly regulates the legal position of individuals. By doing so, it will become part of the very foundations of the rule of law that are to apply domestically. But on the other hand, the very international law that seeks to impose itself on national law remains part of the international legal order where the rule of law remains in a much weaker state. While international law may benefit from mixing with national law to strengthen the character of its rule of law, its own weaknesses, in particular with regard to decisions of international institutions, may endanger the rule of law. The dilemma posed then, is to what extent and how, national law should set up controls, filters and limits to mitigate these dangers without undermining the substantive values that international law seeks. States have perceived, and coped with this dilemma in widely different ways, which in itself further contributes to the pluralism within the international rule of law.

The technical legal answer to this dilemma from the perspective of international law is simple. The principle of supremacy does not allow for states to prioritise national considerations beyond the room that international obligations leave for such considerations (which, incidentally, by no means is insignificant – international law does not come from out of the blue but is made by the same states that wish to preserve particular national interests, and that generally will know how to create room for lawfully preserving such interests).

But from a more general perspective, it may not be obvious that full performance of international obligations, whatever their substantive or procedural deficiencies, is necessarily conducive to the rule of law. The deficiencies will generate a continuous contestation between the international rule of law and the rule of law at the national level. National decisions to decline full and unconditional reception of international law, which are based on these very rule of law deficiencies, may well protect and indeed strengthen the rule of law at the international level. In this respect, national organs can contribute not only to the review of the exercise of power of national organs on the basis of international law, but can also do so in regard to international institutions. With regards to those areas where international law seeks to determine the content of national law, international law should only be allowed to do so if it meets the same qualitative standards as those that have been applied domestically. A sensible approach that deserves following was the Kadi judgment of the ECJ.[2] In this respect, the two futures for the international rule of law are intrinsically connected: the international rule of law will be able to strengthen the national rule of law, and profit from its superior enforcement mechanisms, to the extent that the rule of law at the international level will be strengthened.

2 Court of Justice of the European Union, *Yassin Abdullah Kadi and Al Barakaat International Foundation v. Council of European Union and Commission of European Communities*, Joined Cases C-402/05 P and C-415/05 P, Judgment, 3 September 2008, ECR I-06351.

1.5

The Rule of Law in the 21st Century: Bridging the Compliance Deficit

Stavros Zouridis*

During the past decades the rule of law as a legal institution has spread all over the world. It has become part and parcel of many constitutions and legal infrastructures. But has the rule of law also become a cornerstone of everyday government practices? Even though we lack an empirical body of knowledge on the actual impact of the rule of law, the indications thus far do not justify a jubilant mood. While in-depth research in traditional rule of law countries demonstrates serious discrepancies between the law of the books and the everyday realities within public authorities, new rule of law countries have an even longer way to go. Although, on the surface enforcement seems to be the key to compliance with the rule of law enforcement only works if the rule of law is perceived as legitimate. In turn the rule of law will only be perceived as legitimate if it proves to be an effective governance approach to real social problems like transnational crime, pollution, and economic growth. The roadmap towards global compliance with the rule of law therefore includes enforcement, legitimacy, and governance.

1. The Rule of Law as a Socio-Political Institution

A government bound by its laws – a *rechtsstaat* – greatly contributes to a society's prosperity, stability, and well-being. The *rechtsstaat* as a socio-political institution is a historical achievement that took hundreds of years to develop in the context of Western civlisation. However, its growth and maturity have never been a matter of course, despite the widespread belief that it constitutes a timeless and universal principle. The rule of law has evolved as an answer to a reoccurring historical problem. The caprice of powerful rulers who increasingly depended on a taxpaying class of merchants caused revolutions which in turn forced rulers to accept the rule of law. The rule of law has not followed deterministically from

* **Stavros Zouridis** is Full Professor of Public Administration at Tilburg University, The Netherlands.

historical conditions, nor shall it in the future. Rather, it canalises collective political action is a way that is at odds with its nature.

Even if the rule of law is laid down as a legal principle in constitutions and international law, it does not therefore guarantee compliance. Independent courts can be corrupted, powerful governments are very well able to operate in the shadow of the law, and fundamental rights can easily be violated and justified with an appeal to maintaining public order, fighting crime or terrorism. The separation of powers may be an attractive theory underlying the rule of law, but it has nowhere been realised to an extent that it guarantees the total adherence of public authorities to law in practice. The rule of law has always been contested and there is no reason to believe that this will change in the near future. Even in countries where rule of law has a long tradition, research demonstrates serious discrepancies between the rule of law in the books and the rule of law as government practice.

This 'think piece' argues that the major challenge the rule of law will face in the next decades is the movement from the rule of law as an abstract doctrine to the rule of law as real governmental practice. Increasingly governments throughout the world have adopted the rule of law as a leading principle, but they fail to enact corresponding practices. At the same time, countries with histories of the rule of law tout their own achievements while research shows many discrepancies between their words and actions. In order to move from the books to practice, the rule of law will face a two-part challenge. First, to the concept must be conceptually redefined and extended in order to allow an empirical assessment beyond constitutions, legislation, and legal institutions. Second, the rule of law must be enforced and respected. Both challenges are addressed in this 'think piece'.

2. The Rule of Law?

Although the rule of law is frequently cited in legal and political debate, it is a complex and problematic concept to use for scholarly purposes. Its core meaning is not contested. The rule of law means that law rules, not the whims or a ruler (*e.g.*, Neumann, 1986). Even though the Anglo-Saxon concept of the rule of law differs from its German counterpart (a *rechtsstaat*, or, literally, a state of law) both in a legal and a historical sense these concepts share a core meaning. In the realm of the state, the rule of law means that governments and public authorities are bound by law. But this core meaning raises some serious questions: what do we mean by the law that binds governments and public authorities? And what do we mean if we say that governments and public authorities are ruled by law?

2.1. The Rule of What?

Any scholarly claim beyond this core meaning is inevitably subject to contestation. The concept of law has triggered age-old debates that have not been satisfactorily settled. Law may refer to legislation and court orders (a positivist conception), but it may also refer to principles of justice, human dignity or fundamental rights (a natural law conception), fair trial and fair procedure (a formalist conception) or legal and social order (an institutional conception). Both the positivist and the formalist conceptions have been attacked by scholars because they allow for totalitarian governments and public authorities infringing on human dignity. The natural law conception addresses this concern, but only if human dignity is actually laid down in a constitution or in legislation.[1] If it remained exclusively a natural law principle, it would allow governments to surpass law so as to achieve a higher ideal. If human dignity or fundamental rights is in fact laid down in law, the rule of law blends with culture. Western Europeans or Americans will not necessarily adopt the same definition of human dignity as Chinese, Indians, Nigerians or Bolivians, for example. Bringing in natural law also means bringing in a culturally subjective element which complicates an objective rule of law standard.

If we wish to empirically establish and compare the rule of law as a real-life institution we thus need an objective standard. The doctrine of the *rechtsstaat* as a state or government bound by its own laws provides such an objective standard. This basic doctrine has been defined in Article 2 of the Code of Good Administration, an appendix to the Recommendation on Good Governance of the Committee of Ministers of

1 For example, Article 1, section 1 of the German constitution states that human dignity is inviolable and that all state powers have the legal obligation to uphold and protect it. See Grundgesetz für die Bundesrepublik Deutschland, 23 May 1949, Article 1 (1): Die Würde des Menschen ist unantastbar. Sie zu achten und zu schützen ist Verpflichtung aller staatlichen Gewalt.

the Council of Europe to Member States (Recommendation CM/Rec(2007)/7). Article 2 states:

> Article 2 – principle of lawfulness
>
> 1. Public authorities shall act in accordance with the law. They shall not take arbitrary measures, even when exercising their discretion.
> 2. They shall comply with domestic law, international law and the general principles of law governing their organisation, functioning and activities.
> 3. They shall act in accordance with rules defining their powers and procedures laid down in their governing rules.
> 4. They shall exercise their powers only if the established facts and the applicable law entitle them to do so and solely for the purpose for which they have been conferred.

Even though this approach is objective, it will still often be difficult to legally decide whether or not public authorities act in accordance with the law. Almost any rule, principle, and section of national and international law cannot be unequivocally interpreted.

2.2. What Does Law Rule?

Using the concept of rule also reveals some serious difficulties. The main problem is how to approach the relationship between law and the ruler or the sovereign within a state. If sovereigns are bound by law, how can they be considered 'sovereign' in the proper sense with respect to a political order? The rule of law sometimes seems to be a contradiction, as Neumann has argued:

> Both sovereignty and the Rule of Law are constitutive elements of the modern state. Both however are irreconcilable with each other, for highest might and highest right cannot be at one and the same time realised in a common sphere. So far as the sovereignty of the state extends there is no place for the Rule of Law. Wherever an attempt at reconciliation is made we come up against insoluble contradictions.[2]

Even if we solve this contradiction by using existing legislation, court orders, and treaties, it remains unclear how these relate to the

---

[2] Franz Neumann, *The Rule of Law: Political Theory and the Legal System in Modern Society*, Berg Publishing Ltd., Leamington Spa, 1986, p.4.

sovereign in a state (*e.g.*, the constitutional legislator). For example, to what extent does this conundrum imply that the state cannot change the law? And if the sovereign is entitled to alter the law, to what extent can it do so? Should the sovereign respect certain legal principles, fundamental rights or procedures that mark the boundaries within which he has to act? Or does the rule of law only demand that a ruler has to rule by law? And even if we limit the meaning of the rule of law to rule by law, what are the consequences for the actual functioning of public authorities? Do public authorities have to apply all law in all cases, even if law demands contradictory actions? What if environmental law requires the refusal of a permit and the principle of legal certainty requires that it should be granted? What if the police do not completely observe insignificant criminal procedure guidelines while successfully solving a major crime? Finally, does the rule of law only apply to the actions of the state, or should the rule of law also be taken into account if the state decides not to act? Should courts only assess how public authorities use their power to enforce law, or should the courts also assess the omissions of public authorities in order to detect possible non-compliance and arbitrariness? If courts do not take omissions into account, how can they ever assess possible arbitrariness on the part of public authorities?

For the purposes of this paper it is not necessary to fully consider these problems of legal change and legislative, administrative, and judicial discretion. The rule of law has been defined as a principle of lawfulness. A ruler is always entitled to change the existing laws, but only if the changes comply with higher law and if the appropriate procedures have been followed. Therefore, the rule of law obliges governments and public authorities to obey their own laws while governing, making decisions, and acting within the sphere of governance. But this definition of the rule of law requires we take all actions and omissions of public authorities as our focus instead of the actions that coincidently are brought before a judge or picked up by the media or by researchers.

3. The Current State of the Rule of Law: A Rough Sketch

3.1. Measuring the Rule of Law

Any attempt to sketch the current state of the rule of law seems *a priori* destined to end in tragedy. Besides the vast literature on institutional design, the implementation and the enforcement of law, judicial review and so on, a comparative diagnosis of the rule of law requires a stable measuring tool across time and place. For the time being we lack a worldwide survey on the principle of lawfulness and the extent to which governments and public authorities actually comply with their own laws and their international obligations. We therefore have to look for alternatives.

A group of researchers working within the scope of the World Justice Project attempted to develop such a tool. They created the Rule of Law Index 3.0, which encompasses 10 factors which are divided into 49 sub-factors.[3] At first glance many scholars will adhere to these principles and institutions and the 3.0 version is a much better attempt than earlier versions of the Rule of Law Index. But the Rule of Law Index as defined in the World Justice Project is too problematic to use for research purposes. First, some factors are too abstract and too general to refer to any reality outside law. For example, sub-factor 1.2 requires that government powers are effectively limited by the legislature. The institutional embodiment of the rule of law in the context of legal and public administration practice may differ substantially. The Rule of Law Index is therefore too indeterminate to discriminate between different designs. Second, the Rule of Law index 3.0 is not only too abstract and too general, in some respects it is also too concrete. Among the sub-factors listed, there are many sub-factors that embody a specifically Western approach to institutionalising the rule of law. For example, the index requires a guarantee of freedom from arbitrary interference with respect to privacy. As such, a number of these factors denote the individualistic and liberal orientation of Western Europe and the United States. Third, we lack reliable data on the actual state of the practice of the rule of law in almost every country. Finally, looking at the rule of law in this way conceals both the real and everyday dilemmas within the *rechtsstaat*. For example, efficient administration does not always go hand in hand with independent audits and a system of checks and balances. And fundamental rights like the fundamental labor rights can hardly be directly related to the rule of law. Sometimes fundamental rights may even force governments to violate the rule of law. This broad

---

3 Mark David Agrast, Juan Carlos Botero, Alejandro Ponce, "The World Justice Project: Rule of Law Index 2010", World Justice Project, available at http://www.worldjusticeproject.org/sites/default/files/WJP%20Rule%20of%20Law%20Index%202010_2_0.pdf, last accessed 23 March 2011.

interpretation of the rule of law thus masks dilemmas, tensions, and trade-offs between different theories of the rule of law.

The World Bank's Governance Indicators also attempt to grasp the comparative complexity by means of a standardised tool. These indicators aim to internationally compare governance on six dimensions:

- Voice and accountability: the extent to which a country's citizens are able to participate in selecting their government, as well as freedom of expression, association, and the press;
- Political stability and absence of violence: the likelihood that the government will be destabilised by unconstitutional or violent means, including terrorism;
- Government effectiveness: the quality of public services, the capacity of the civil service and its independence from political pressures; the quality of policy formulation;
- Regulatory quality: the ability of the government to provide sound policies and regulations that enable and promote private sector development;
- Rule of law: the extent to which agents have confidence in and abide by the rules of society, including the quality of property rights, the police, and the courts, as well as the risk of crime;
- Control of corruption: the extent to which public power is exercised for private gain, including both petty and grand forms of corruption, as well as an elite 'capture' of the state.

Several dimensions directly relate to the principle of lawfulness. Regulatory quality, rule of law, and control of corruption are directly connected with the principle of lawfulness, while government effectiveness and accountability are only indirectly connected with this principle. Therefore, these governance indicators may provide some partial knowledge on the current state of the rule of law throughout the world. We should be cautious when interpreting these indicators because of the different sources used in different countries and because the indicators use (expert and citizen) opinion polls instead of facts.[4]

4 See, for example, the World Bank Group, "The Worldwide Governance Indicators (WGI) Project", available at http://info.worldbank.org/governance/wgi/index.asp, last accessed 23 March 2011.

4. The Need for a Public Administration and Public Governance Perspective

In order to assess whether governments and public authorities are also ruled by law in practice we need a multidisciplinary, objective, and standardised tool based upon the principle of lawfulness. Such a tool must comprise a set of operational indicators and the application of these indicators to all public authorities at all levels of government. These indicators should not be limited to what is legally required in order to establish a rule of law. A legal perspective does not suffice to assess whether law really rules. A legal perspective only establishes whether the rule of law is laid down in legislation and whether the corpus of law incorporates the necessary legal institutions. This does not necessarily relate to real government. For example, besides Germany, the United States and the United Kingdom are perhaps, on paper, the most fully developed contemporary rule of law jurisdictions. But most in-depth studies on the actual practices of real-life implementation agencies, enforcement agencies, police and justice organisations and even courts in the United States and the United Kingdom demonstrate serious discrepancies between the rule of law in the books and the rule of law in real life government and judicial practices.[5]

A legal perspective on the rule of law may thus be useful to describe the legal preconditions of the rule of law, but it will not guarantee a rule of law in the real practices within public authorities. First, it does not include the public authorities' state of compliance with law. Second, it does not include the use of law by public authorities. Public authorities usually possess substantial discretionary powers, and

[5] For example, see Patrick O'Hara, *Why Law Enforcement Organizations Fail: Mapping the Organizational Fault Lines in Policing*, Carolina Academic Press, Durham (N.C.), 2005; Keith Hawkins, *Law as Last Resort: Prosecution Decision-Making in a Regulatory Agency*, Oxford University Press Inc., New York, 2002; Gregory Alain Huber, *The Craft of Bureaucratic Neutrality: Interests and Influence in Governmental Regulation of Occupational Safety*, Cambridge University Press, New York, 2007; Jerry L. Mashaw, *Bureaucratic Justice: Managing Social Security Disability Claims*, Yale University Press, New Haven, 1983; Eugene Bardach and Robert A. Kagan, *Going by the Book: The Problem of Regulatory Unreasonableness*, Transaction Publishers, New Brunswick, 2010; George Weissinger, *Law Enforcement and the INS: A Participant Observation Study of Control Agents*, University Press of America, Inc., Lanham, 2005; Richard A. Posner, *How Judges Think*, Harvard University Press, Cambridge Mass., 2008.

the use of these powers usually remains under the radar of legal scholars. Third, the legal perspective does not shed any light on the mechanisms that empirically guarantee the enforcement of the rule of law. To what extent does adversarial criminal procedure better guarantee the rule of law than inquisitorial criminal procedure? Do judicial institutions better guarantee the rule of law than political and democratic institutions? Do legal rules better guarantee compliance by public authorities than legal principles? In order to detect these regulatory, organisational, political, and administrative design issues, we need a broader public administration perspective on the rule of law. Moreover, to empirically measure and compare the rule of law on an international level, such a perspective must encompass three kinds of indicators:

a) *Legality indicators*: to what extent do public authorities in nation states really act in accordance with the domestic and international substantive and formal regulation (*i.e.*, treaties, constitutions, national legislation and the legislation of international organisations, the rulings of international courts and so on)? Compliance can be measured by systematically looking at decisions of governments and public authorities, the reception of international agreements in national legislation, the orders of administrative and constitutional courts, international courts, and compliance surveys.
b) *Rules of the game indicators*: to what extent do public authorities act in accordance with rules defining their powers and procedures? Do public authorities respect the international, constitutional, and administrative distribution and demarcation of powers? Compliance can be measured by looking at the decisions and acts of governments and public authorities.
c) *Arbitrariness indicators*: to what extent do public authorities take arbitrary measures, both when applying given powers and when not applying given powers? Arbitrariness can also be measured by looking at whether there are policies in a governance sector and the levels of compliance with these policies.

Besides these primary indicators, we should use secondary indicators that indirectly measure whether a state is ruled by law in practice. As we have seen the Rule of Law Index 3.0 is too biased from a Western liberal-democratic perspective. We need a more neutral tool that focuses on the principle of lawfulness while at the same time taking into account the different legal and political traditions throughout the world.[6] In theory, only three secondary indicators are needed which ensure the principle of lawfulness in the daily practices of public authorities:

i) *Clear, known and determinate laws*: a state needs laws that can be used to assess which government acts are lawful and which are not. Without such laws, there can be no *Rechtsstaat*. These laws must be clear, known, and determinate. It must be possible to define the meaning of these laws *independent of any interpretation by the state*.

ii) *A hierarchy of laws*: there must be a hierarchy of laws in order to decide which public authorities have to follow which law and which laws can be changed by which public authority. A written constitution is one expression of such a hierarchy. Some constitutions also contain a nucleus of provisions that cannot be changed.

iii) *Enforcement mechanisms*: in order to secure the principle of lawfulness, there must be mechanisms in place to enforce the law and to keep governments and public authorities within legal boundaries. At least two kinds of mechanisms are necessary:

   a. *Structural mechanisms* with real power: these might include institutions like an independent court system, but also an ombudsman, internal regulations, and auditing committees.

   b. *Cultural mechanisms*: a government must have a spirit or ethos that embraces the rule of law. Without such an ethos, the laws will not be upheld and the structural mechanisms to keep governments within the boundaries of law will not work.

Using these primary and secondary indicators allows us to establish whether governments and public authorities comply with the rule of law in practice. Up to now we have not been able to systematically gather in-depth data on these primary and secondary indicators. It is therefore nearly impossible to make any scholarly claim on the current state of the rule of law throughout the world. It is also impossible to make any comparison beyond the coincidental institutionalisation of some legal institutions like independent courts. Any claim beyond the law on the

[6] H. Patrick Glenn, *Legal Traditions of the World*, Oxford University Press Inc., New York, 2007.

books is hazardous. Even on a European level such a comparison is not possible, let alone on a world-wide scale with its manifold complexities. Hence a first challenge for the rule of law in the twenty-first century will be to build such a systematic and comparative objective body of knowledge on the rule of law in the everyday reality of government and governance.

5. The Spread of Law-Bounded Government

Even though we lack a systematic comparative body of knowledge on global compliance with the principle of lawfulness and its development over time, there exists fragmented and superficial knowledge at our disposal. We know that the rule of law ideology spread throughout the world together with the globalisation process initiated by the fall of the Eastern bloc at the start of the 1990s. In the past decades nation states increasingly adopted the rule of law formally as a guiding principle (for example, the former Eastern bloc, some African states, some of the Asian states and some states in Middle and South America). A linear progress towards a universal and global rule of law cannot yet be discerned. For example, the Governance Indicators of the World Bank paint a rather diffuse picture of the development of states between 1996 and 2008. Some nation states show substantial progress on these indicators and some of these nation states even overtook 'Western' countries. For example, Chile, Botswana and Hungary show impressive progress. Some countries show a decline on these indicators, such as Zimbabwe and Venezuela. The World Bank researchers conclude that the world-wide development is too diffuse to come to aggregate conclusions.

Some other indicators are connected with the rule of law. These also indicate an ambiguous trend. According to the Democracy Index of The Economist the number of democratic countries in the world increased from 69 to 118 during the nineties. The past couple of years the growth of democracy seems to have stagnated such that the number of autocratic regimes remains high. In 2010, the Democracy Index counted 26 full democracies (12,3 per cent of the world's population), 53 flawed democracies (37,2 per cent of the world's population), 33 hybrid regimes

(14 per cent of the world's population) and 55 authoritarian regimes (36,5 per cent of the world's population).[7]

Freedom House measures the percentage of the world's population that is considered to be free which means that the people have political rights and civil freedoms. Since 1992 the percentage of the world's population that is considered free has increased steadily. In 1992, only 24,83 per cent of the world's population was considered to be free, while in 2007 45,85 per cent of the world population was considered to be free. During this period the percentage of the world population that was considered to be partially free declined from 44,11 per cent to 17,9 per cent. The relative number of un-free people in the world also increased from 31,06 per cent in 1992 to 36,21 per cent in 2007. Ever since 2007, Freedom House observed a decline of the number of people considered to be free. One fifth of all countries demonstrated a development towards less freedom, including politically important countries such as Russia, Pakistan, Kenya, Egypt, Nigeria, and Venezuela.[8] The most recent measurement (2009) demonstrates a continuous decline of freedom throughout the world.[9]

The Global Corruption Barometer developed by Transparency International demonstrates substantial improvement during 2004 to 2007. The level of perceived corruption of political institutions (political parties, members of parliament) as well as the level of corruption of enforcement institutions (the police, the justice system, but also tax authorities) declined during this period. Contrary to the decline of perceived corruption, a majority of both Asians and Northern Americans then expected that the level of corruption in their own countries will increase in the future.[10] The most recent measurement (2010) by Transparency

---

[7] Economist Intelligence Unit, "Democracy Index 2010: Democracy in Retreat", available at http://graphics.eiu.com/PDF/Democracy_Index_2010_web.pdf, last accessed 23 March 2011.

[8] Freedom House, "Freedom in the World 2008", available at http://www.freedomhouse.org/uploads/fiw08launch/FIW08Tables.pdf, last accessed 23 March 2011.

[9] Freedom House, "Freedom in the World 2010", available at http://www.freedomhouse.org/template.cfm?page=505, last accessed 23 March 2011.

[10] Transparency International, "Report on the Transparency International Global Corruption Barometer 2007", available at http://www.ethicsworld.org/publicsectorgovernance/PDF links/BAROMETER.pdf, last accessed 23 March 2011.

International proves they are right. It signals an increasing level of corruption throughout the world.[11]

Besides the spread of the rule of law among countries (states), a large number of international institutions has been established to develop and enforce the rule of law on an international level.[12] Together with globalisation processes, a large number of regional and functional, legal and quasi-legal, legislative and judicial institutions have grown next to, within and outside the framework of the United Nations.

5.1. The Current Situation

During the past decades we have thus witnessed a world-wide spread of the rule of law. Many nation states have adapted their legal systems and their institutions in order to implement and enforce the rule of law. For example, systems for legal protection against public authorities, administrative review systems and audit systems, court systems to guarantee fundamental rights, administrative and constitutional legislation that legally institutionalises the rule of law, penal systems that are based upon the principle of fair trials, and so on. International institutions increasingly guarantee fundamental rights and the enforcement of law among nation states. We have to take these revolutionary developments into account to assess the challenges for the rule of law in the twenty-first century. But we should not be misguided by the jubilant mood of the nineties. Even though the development towards a global and world-wide rule of law seems to follow a linear pattern, the indicators point at a *sûr place* or even a decline. Less people are free, and corruption is growing. How should we understand this *sûr place*? Has the global rule of law revolution stagnated?

---

11 Transparency International, "Global Corruption Barometer 2010", available at http://www.transparency.org/policy_research/surveys_indices/gcb/2010, last accessed 23 March 2011.

12 Anne-Marie Slaughter, *A New World Order*, Princeton University Press, Princeton, 2004; Robert Owen Keohane, *Power and Governance in a Partially Globalized World*, Routledge, New York, 2002; Judith L. Goldstein *et al.*, *Legalization and World Politics*, the MIT Press, Cambridge Mass., 2001.

5.2. Rule of Law on the Books and Rule of Law in Action

In order to assess the current situation at least three considerations should be taken into account. First, the question should be posed whether the rule of law has only been institutionalised formally or whether it also exists in action and in decisions and omissions of states, governments, and public authorities throughout the world. It is definitely easier to adjust legislation or even a constitution than it is to fundamentally change the daily practices of governments and public authorities. Besides, even states that may be considered textbook examples of the rule of law have difficulty living by the principle of lawfulness. For example, the United States increasingly attracts criticism with regard to its fight against organised crime and terrorism. Recently, the Washington Post launched a huge project on top secret and intelligence agencies 'running out of control'.[13] And ever since Robert Kagan's famous study in 1978, many of the in-depth studies on implementation and enforcement agencies in Europe and the United States note substantial discrepancies between the law in the books and the law in actual government practice.[14]

5.3. Eroding Public and Political Support for the Rule of Law?

Second, some observers point at political developments that may lead nation states away from the rule of law. These do not only occur in peripheral countries with autocratic regimes. For example, according to some scholars, the political instrumentalisation of law that occurs in many European countries and the United States threatens the rule of law.[15] Others regard our contemporary democracies are also believed to threaten the rule of law.[16] In Europe, some fear that the rise of (right-wing)

---

[13] Dana Priest and William M. Arkin, "Monitoring America", available at http://projects.washingtonpost.com/top-secret-america/articles/, last accessed 23 March 2011.

[14] For example, with regard to the United States: Patrick O'Hara, *Why Law Enforcement Organizations Fail: Mapping the Organizational Fault Lines in Policing*, Carolina Academic Press, Durham (N.C.), 2005; George Weissinger, *Law Enforcement and the INS: A Participant Observation Study of Control Agents*, University Press of America, Inc., Lanham, 2005.

[15] Brian Z. Tamanaha, *Law as a Means to an End: Threat to the Rule of Law*, Cambridge University Press, New York, 2006.

[16] Fareed Zakaria, *The Future of Freedom: Illiberal Democracy at Home and Abroad*, W.W. Norton, New York, 2003

populist parties will threaten the rule of law.[17] Although some of the evidence does not substantiate these claims, there appears to be some erosion of the legitimacy of the rule of law in Western countries both among citizens and politicians.[18] On a global scale, some commentators also witness declining legitimacy of the rule of law.[19] Kagan argues that an increasing number of countries have a highly developed market economy, but these countries do not evolve towards democracy and the rule of law. The taken-for-granted status of the rule of law as an ideal is increasingly replaced by self-consciously presented alternatives. Kagan cites Russia and China as powerful examples.[20] Of course, there are multiple perspectives from which to assess these examples. Seen from a historical perspective, both Russia and China may have achieved unprecedented levels of compliance with the rule of law with respect to their own history. Even if we take the positive account of what is actually happening, the public and political support for the rule of law ideology in its modern-day (Western) shape is undeniably under attack.

5.4. The Dark Sides of Globalisation

A third consideration concerns the globalisation process that may have triggered or at least enabled the global spread of the rule of law. We do not understand the empirical connection between globalisation and the spread of the rule of law, but from a longitudinal perspective these phenomena seem to correlate. Evolving global markets, global companies, global communication, global networks, and a global mindset among citizens and politicians ever since the 1990s went along with the global spread of the rule of law and global institutions to implement and enforce

---

[17] For example, in the Netherlands scholars like Frissen (See P.H.A. Frissen, *Gevaar Verplicht: Over de Noodzaak van Aristocratische Politiek*, Gennep B.V., Uitgeverij Van, Amsterdam, 2009) and lawyers like Böhler (See Britta Böhler, *Crisis in de Rechtstaat: Spraakmakende Zaken, Verborgen Processen*, Arbeiderspers, Amsterdam, 2004) have thus argued.

[18] Stavros Zouridis, *De Dynamiek van Bestuur en Recht: Over de Rechtsstaat als Bestuurswetenschappelijk Fenomeen*, Boom Lemma, Den Haag, 2009.

[19] Fareed Zakaria, *The Post-American World*, W.W. Norton & Co., New York, 2008; Robert Kagan, *The Return of History and the End of Dreams*, Knopf, New York, 2008.

[20] Robert Kagan, *The Return of History and the End of Dreams*, Knopf, New York, 2008.

international law. However, we are also confronted with the dark sides of the globalisation process. Especially transnational organised crime, illicit trade (of people, weapons, money, drugs, and so on), and terrorism increasingly attract political and scholarly attention. Both Glenny and Naïm have intensively studied transnational organised crime and both are quite pessimistic about the possibilities of tackling these phenomena.[21] Illicit trade and transnational crime may seriously undermine the rule of law, as may, for example, be observed in Mexico. Whether transnational organised crime, illicit trade and terrorism can be tackled by public authorities in accordance with the rule of law remains to be seen. If it appears that these problems can only be addressed by violating the rule of law, we may increasingly expect further erosion of the rule of law throughout the world.

6. Future Challenges

A real life perspective on the rule of law should take into account compliance with the rule of law by public authorities and governments, but it should not be limited to a descriptive approach that merely maps the levels of compliance by public authorities and governments. We need sound and proven theories on the political, public administration, and governance institutions that hamper or improve compliance. Because of the lack of proven theories, a first challenge to a practice approach to the rule of law is to develop them. We urgently need a multidisciplinary perspective on the rule of law built with a combined body of knowledge of constitutional and administrative law and public administration theory. Such an approach includes an international comparison of the actual state of the rule of law within countries, knowledge on the discrepancies between the rule of law in the books and the daily practices of public authorities and governments, and the mechanisms that explain these discrepancies. Which regulatory, organisational, political, and cultural designs minimise the discrepancies between the rule of law in the books and the real practice of the rule of law? Which designs increase these discrepancies? What are the mechanisms underlying these processes?

[21] Misha Glenny, *McMafia: A Journey Through the Global Criminal Underworld*, Knopf Books, New York, 2008; Moisés Naím, *Illicit: How Smugglers, Traffickers and Copycats are Hijacking the Global Economy*, Doubleday, New York, 2005.

Such a research agenda will not be enough to lead the rule of law as a principle of lawfulness through the twenty-first century. Even though our knowledge on actual compliance with the rule of law by public authorities and governments is limited, we do have some clues that should cause concern. There appears to be a growing deficit between actual compliance to the rule of law and the legally defined principle of lawfulness. Logically, compliance to the rule of law will only be improved by forces which guarantee such compliance. The rule of law needs to be equipped with real power to fulfill its promise. A first point on the action agenda therefore should be enforcement. Strengthening enforcement mechanisms on every level of government, from the local level to the United Nations, should be on top of each government's and international institution's agenda. But how can we strengthen enforcement? The traditional answer is to strengthen the organisations responsible for enforcement. Thus, we observe an enforcement deficit which requires huge investments in organisations responsible for implementing international law and the rule of law throughout the world. Strengthening enforcement organisations will not be enough though. With regard to the rule of law we do not only have a lack of enforcement organisations and enforcement powers. Certainly, we should take care of the compliance deficit. Enforcement only works if it is limitedly needed. If compliance levels fall below a certain level, even strong and big enforcement organisations will not be able to guarantee compliance.

Paradoxically we therefore need more compliance and more enforcement. Compliance to the rule of law and the principle of lawfulness primarily rest on perceived legitimacy. Only if the legitimacy of the rule of law and the principle of lawfulness increases will we be able to expect higher levels of compliance. If the levels of compliance increase, the effectiveness of enforcement will also increase. Enforcement organisations are only effective if the burden of enforcement is limited. The key to a solution of the compliance deficit therefore is to strengthen the legitimacy of the rule of law and the principle of lawfulness. But how can the legitimacy of the rule of law and the principle of lawfulness be strengthened? Of course, serious and conscientious enforcement does play a limited role. Badly functioning enforcement organisations destroy the legitimacy of the rule of law. The rule of law will have to be executed conscientiously in order to generate legitimacy.[22]

But merely implementing the rule of law will not be enough to strengthen its legitimacy. To increase support for the rule of law and the principle of lawfulness, the socio-political institution of the *rechtsstaat* should be able to provide an adequate answer to real problems within real societies. The *rechtsstaat* must be equipped to tackle illicit trade and transnational organised crime, to fight crime and poverty, to reduce the pollution of our oceans, to combat deforestation and overfishing, to provide peace and stability, and to guarantee natural resources. The rule of law therefore faces a serious governance challenge. If the *rechtsstaat* is not suited to cope with these governance challenges, it will not survive the twenty-first century.

Even with limited knowledge, we are thus able to put forward three challenges that the rule of law will probably face in the upcoming decades:

i) *The enforcement challenge*: in the past decades, the rule of law has spread throughout the world. Many nation states (the former Eastern bloc, among African countries, some Asian countries and those in the Americas) have legally institutionalised the rule of law by adapting their legal systems. The major challenge for the next decades will be implementing and enforcing the rule of law in the practice of the (micro-)cosmos of governments and public authorities. Even text book examples of the rule of law like Western European states and the United States of America continue to face challenges to enforcing and complying with the rule of law. Research on the implementation and the enforcement of the rule of law in European governments and the United States of America reveals major discrepancies between the rule of law on the books and the rule of law in action. Compliance with the rule of law does not appear to be self-evident, even if a nation state has a long rule of law tradition. Therefore, a first and predominant challenge to the rule of law will be its enforcement.

ii) *The legitimacy challenge*: the global spread of the rule of law during the past decades was at least partially supported by the

[22] Tom R. Tyler, *Why People Obey the Law*, Princeton University Press, Princeton, 2006.

power of the 'Western World' (the United States and Europe). Many observers expect that the new distribution of power will dramatically change during the twenty-first century.[23] The asymmetry will gradually disappear. Having new powerful players on the world stage also implies that new ideas on the rule of law will emerge. This redistribution of power already started with economic power, but political and cultural power will soon follow, and in the end even military power will probably be more evenly distributed. If this global shift takes place, the future of the rule of law will depend on its global legitimacy. Hence the rule of law faces a legitimacy challenge. We have to prove that a government with the rule of law is better for a society's prosperity, happiness, and stability than government without the rule of law. And we have to prove that governments and public authorities that comply with the rule of law are better than governments and public authorities that do not comply with the rule of law. Although these questions may seem too trivial and self-evident for many lawyers and legal scholars, it will be a real challenge to convince others. A convincing answer should also be accompanied with empirical evidence. Besides, the legitimacy challenge is not limited to 'new rule of law countries'. Both in Western Europe and the United States, scholars observe an erosion of the legitimacy of the rule of law. A growing part of the population is increasingly alienated from the rule of law, and even contemporary polarising political elites publicly dispute the rule of law.

iii) *The governance challenge*: to a certain extent the rule of law is a luxury. If a society is too poor (for example, some African nations), if governments do not have any real power (for example, Somalia) or if governments are unable to adequately tackle social problems, the rule of law will be useless. The global increase of both wealth and government power means that the rule of law is of ever greater importance, but only to the extent that it enables governments to tackle major economic, social, environmental and other problems. If the rule of law prevents governments and public authorities from

[23] Robert Kagan, *The Return of History and the End of Dreams*, Knopf, New York, 2008; Fareed Zakaria, *The Post-American World*, W.W. Norton & Co., New York, 2008; Kishore Mahbubani, *The New Asian Hemisphere: The Irresistable Shift of Global Power to the East*, Public Affairs, New York, 2008.

addressing major problems, it will not only lose its legitimacy but it may be sidelined by rulers. Therefore, the rule of law must be adjusted to deal with major problems such as transnational organised crime, illicit trade, global terrorism, and environmental problems like overfishing and deforestation. On these issues, the rule of law should contribute to real global governmentability. This will probably imply that governments have to limit their policy ambitions because of the current overload with which implementing and enforcing agencies are confronted.

These challenges are connected. Without improving governmentability and enabling governments to adequately tackle major social and environmental problems, the legitimacy of the rule of law cannot be strengthened. And without the necessary legitimacy the implementation and enforcement of the rule of law cannot be improved. In turn, without improving the implementation and the enforcement of the rule of law, it will not be able to reinforce governance. And so on.

If these challenges make up a vicious circle, where should governments start? How can they disentangle the jumble of challenges? First of all, it might matter more to start than to aim for a perfect and comprehensive strategy. Second, why not start with implementation and enforcement? Without real enforcement of the rule of law, all other efforts are pointless. Although it may be the least politically sexy thing to do, implementation and enforcement of the rule of law will benefit the rule of law in the long run.

1.6

The Challenges of Constitutional Ordering in a Multilevel Legally Pluralistic and Ideologically Divided Globalised Polity

Michel Rosenfeld*

We live in an increasingly pluralistic legal and ideological universe. Moreover, as globalisation is complemented by balkanisation and the proliferation of supranational regimes is accompanied by a trend towards greater sub-national legal and political autonomy, constitutional ordering becomes more problematic. The formal hierarchy and unity of traditional nation-state constitutions gives way to competing constitutional frameworks that confront the law abiding person with inconsistent and even, at times, contradictory legal obligations. How may these difficulties be resolved in the future? Can a new hierarchy and unity be constructed trough search of universal formal and/or substantive norms? Or, is the best hope adaptation to plurality with some dissonance and inconsistencies? The paper will explore the possibility of non-hierarchical, non-unified pluralistic constitutional ordering, and spell out the future conditions that would have to materialise for such an ordering to become both viable and desirable.

1. Introduction

As the grip of the nation-state loosens on the path toward globalisation, legal actors are increasingly confronted with a plurality of legal regimes. On the one hand, national legal orders are supplemented by other legal orders both supranational and global. For example, in Europe, a citizen of a state that is a member of the European Union (EU) is subject to her own nation-state's legal order, to that of the EU, and to that issuing from the European Convention on Human Rights (ECHR) as elaborated by the European Court of Human Rights in Strasbourg (ECtHR) as well as to certain worldwide legal regimes, such as that emanating from the World Trade Organisation (WTO). On the other hand, legal regulation in a

* **Michel Rosenfeld** is the Justice Sydney L. Robins Professor of Human Rights, Benjamin N. Cardozo School of Law, New York.

variety of particular fields, such as the Internet or the commercial dealings among multinational corporations, which are subject to the precepts of a non-state-based *lex mercatoria*, veer toward privatisation. These fields seemingly achieve an increasing independence from governmental regulation or control, whether on a national or a transnational scale.

These plural regimes are, at times, at odds with one another, lacking, as they do, an established hierarchy to resolve inevitable conflicts. Thus, several constitutional courts of Member States of the EU have proclaimed the right to deny supremacy to EU law that is contrary to their country's constitution.[1] Without prospect for a world government, traditional solutions modelled on the Westphalian nation-state no longer seem viable.

With no apparent structural solution in sight, it is tempting to turn to ideological alternatives. Impasses, impervious to structural resolution, may be overcome through the global adoption of relevant shared or convergent norms. Along these lines, Jürgen Habermas proposes recourse to the concept of 'constitutional patriotism'.[2] Habermas' idea is that 'patriotism', which traditionally denotes a profound attachment to one's nation, can be redirected to produce a steadfast intellectual and existential commitment to the ideal of constitutionalism. The appeal to constitutional patriotism, however, is no more likely to lead to success than an appeal to traditional structural orderings. This is because contemporary legal pluralism is matched by an equally diverse and often fractious ideological pluralism.

Taken together, legal and ideological pluralism compound the problem confronting constitutional ordering. In this paper, I explore possible ways out of the conundrum posed by the convergence of the above mentioned trends of globalisation and privatisation. Assuming current trends continue or accelerate over the next generation, what kind of constitutional ordering would likely be both workable and normatively attractive?

---

1 See, for example, Bundesverfassungsgericht (BVerfG) (Federal Constitutional Court), *Solange I*, Judgment, 29 May 1974, 37 BVerFGE 271, para.24; Corte costituzionale della Repubblica Italiana (Constitutional Court of Italy), Case *Frontini* v. *Ministero delle Finanze*, 1974, C.M.L.R. 372, para.21.

2 Jürgen Habermas, *Between Facts and Norms: Contributions to a Discourse Theory of Law and Democracy*, MIT Press, 1996, pp. 491-515 and pp. 566-567.

2. Legal Pluralism in Context: A Dynamic of Convergences and Divergences

What is most distinct about the traditional nation-state constitutional order is its hierarchical nature and overall unity. In every working constitutional democracy, deployed on the scale of the nation-state, there is a hierarchically situated institutional mechanism to guarantee order and unity. This is consistent with Kelsen's account of the constitution as the basic norm structuring and legitimating the entire national legal order over which it presides.[3]

In stark contrast, in more recent transnational orderings, external norms can be binding within the nation-state without domestic constitution-based mediation or reprocessing. Thus, EU regulations can have direct effect within EU Member States without prior action by the latter.[4] Furthermore, certain legal obligations originating beyond the nation-state can clash with other obligations and, at the same time, be at odds with those generated by the nation-state. For example, obligations imposed by the EU on its Member States may conflict with obligations the latter have under the ECHR.[5]

Multilayered legal pluralism, such as that prevailing within the EU, creates divergences and, at the same time, gives rise to convergences. Thus, the greatest actual and potential challenges to the authoritativeness of EU law, has been from Member State constitutional courts.[6] To defuse such challenges, the EU's European Court of Justice (ECJ) went out of its way to incorporate the principles of constitutionalism and respect for fundamental rights in its interpretations of EU law, stressing its adherence

---

3 Hans Kelsen, *General Theory of Law and State*, Russell & Russell, New York, 1961.

4 See Court of Justice of the European Union, *The Case of Van Gend en Loos* (NV Algemene Transport- en Expeditie Onderneming van Gend & Loos v. Netherlands Inland Revenue Administration), Case 26/62, Judgment, 5 February 1963.

5 Lech Garlicki, "Cooperation of Courts: The Role of Supranational Jurisdictions in Europe", in *International Journal of Constitutional Law*, 2008, vol. 6, no. 3-4 and pp. 509-530.

6 Michel Rosenfeld, "Comparing Constitutional Review by the European Court of Justice and the U.S. Supreme Court", in *International Journal of Constitutional Law*, 2006, vol. 4, no. 4, p. 618 and pp. 633-634.

to the 'rule of law', to 'fundamental principles', and to 'the common constitutional traditions of the EU's Member States'.[7]

Constitutional courts within the EU have not abandoned the principle that a Member State's constitution prevails in case of conflict with EU law.[8] In spite of this, however, actual conflicts have been avoided, thus far, largely through judicial interpretations that have found ways to harmonise EU law and domestic constitutional requirements.

The dynamic manifest within the legal space carved out by the EU also operates in other contexts in which legal regimes overlap. Viewed systemically, the totality of different legal regimes interacting constantly, combine to structure the legal universe into an aggregated multilevel edifice. This structure comprises global, supranational, regional, and national norms, as well as a broad array of largely separate and self-contained, segmented limited-purpose fields, such as *lex mercatoria* and self-regulation of the Internet. Moreover, the possible combinations and permutations among multilevel-based orderings and segmented differentiated fields seem almost endless. If, as some have claimed, the UN Charter functions as a world constitution,[9] then it stands at the apex of a multilevel constitutional ordering that encompasses the entire globe and, presumably, all the existing legal regimes within it. In contrast, the legal regime framed by the WTO also purports to be global, although it remains segmentary, since it singles out trade from all other human activity that can be made subject to law.[10]

Multilevel and segmentary orderings can overlap and intersect. They can also cause mutual interference. A legal obligation deriving from the WTO, for example, may conflict with a proscription imposed by a nation state's constitution. More generally, the plurality of distinct

---

[7] Rosenfeld, 2006, pp. 623-624, see *supra* note 6.

[8] See, for example, Bundesverfassungsgericht (BVerfG) (Federal Constitutional Court), *Maastricht*, Judgment, 12 October 1993, 89 BVerFGE 155; Bundesverfassungsgericht (BVerfG) (Federal Constitutional Court), *Lisbon Treaty*, Judgment, 30 June 2009, 2 BvE 2/08, 2 BvE 5/08, 2 BvR 1010/08, 2 BvR 1022/08, 2 BvR 1259/08, 2 BvR 182/09.

[9] Bardo Fassbender, "The United Nations Charter as Constitution of the International Community", in *Columbia Journal of Transnational Law*, 1998, vol.36, p. 529.

[10] See Marrakesh Agreement Establishing the World Trade Organization, 15 April 1994, available at http://www.wto.org/english/docs_e/legal_e/legal_e.htm#wtoagreement, last accessed 29 March 2011.

coexisting and competing legal regimes seems to be on the rise, constantly multiplying the opportunities for divergences. These divergences, moreover, are not limited to those among levels of regulation or among different segmented fields of regulation or among clashing levels and segments. They are also bound to occur *within the same level*, particularly if the latter is broadly encompassing. Thus, universal human rights as they emerge from the 1948 UN Universal Declaration of Human Rights[11] and numerous subsequent international instruments[12] are meant to be truly worldwide in their scope and application and are accepted, as such, by the vast majority of polities.[13] Nonetheless, strong disagreements have emerged over which human rights should be enforced and how. For example, proponents of 'Asian values' have contested Western individualistic conceptions of international human rights, arguing that they are culturally and ideologically biased.[14] Accordingly, there are divergences within the most broadly encompassing levels of fundamental human rights protection.

All these divergences and many others that seem bound to arise make the need for increased convergences crucial. Without a centripetal movement to counter the strong centrifugal tendencies associated with globalisation and particularisation, the world may be headed for a war among legal regimes that could culminate in an erosion of the rule of law itself.

What is required in this context is some combination of formal and material points of convergence. The formal would reflect an acceptance of the function of the prevailing constitutional and legal order as a means to settle issues over which no material agreement among the plurality of

[11] Universal Declaration of Human Rights, 10 December 1948, United Nations General Assembly Resolution 217A (III), U.N. Doc A/810, available at http://www.udhr.org /udhr/default.htm, last accessed 29 March 2011.

[12] See, for example, International Covenant on Civil and Political Rights, 16 December 1966, General Assembly Resolution 2200A (XXI); International Covenant on Economic, Social and Cultural Rights, 16 December 1966, GA Res. 2200A (XXI).

[13] As of 2008, 161 Nations had ratified the ICCPR and 158 had ratified the ICESCR. See Office of the United Nations High Commissioner for Human Rights, "Ratifications and Reservations", available at http://www2.ohchr.org/english/bodies/ratification, last accessed 29 March 2011.

[14] See generally Joanne R. Bauer and Daniel A. Bell, *The East Asian Challenge for Human Rights*, Cambridge University Press, Cambridge, 1999.

competing views within the polity seems possible. The material points of convergence, on the other hand, would result from a normative commonality or overlap that spreads across a vast majority of competing normative outlooks within the polity.

Upon closer examination, the centrifugal tendencies unleashed by globalisation and privatisation are not as threatening to the rule of law as they might initially appear. The principal reason for this is the forces that push for globalisation and privatisation do not seek to operate in a legal vacuum. Thus, it may be advantageous for a multinational corporation to escape from legal regulation by its country of original incorporation as much as possible. The last thing it would wish for, however, is having to operate without legal protection. Instead, it may prefer segmentary regulation by a *lex mercatoria* fitted to its needs and to those of like-minded multinational corporations.

To a certain extent, the loss of points of formal convergence can be compensated by forging new points of material convergence. Although there is no legal hierarchy or overarching unity that can settle the underlying potential conflict between certain Member States' constitutions and EU law, the more the two share the same fundamental norms and values, the more unlikely it becomes that a truly disruptive actual conflict will occur.

In a post-Westphalian world, the legal realm seems to become, at once, increasingly layered and fragmented. It becomes layered, along the vertical axis – the German constitutional polity cannot be seamlessly integrated into the EU in the same way California is into the U.S. – and fragmented, through the proliferation of single, segmented, self-enclosed and self-referential legal regimes stacked alongside one another in a horizontal sequence. Within this new ordering scheme, points of convergence can be both formal and material, as already stated above; and they can be either independent of one another or mutually dependent. Within a layer, there can be agreement on formal mechanisms even in the absence of a means of integration and harmonisation among layers. For example, formal EU legal decision making may be fully legitimated from an EU perspective even if this is not the case from certain individual Member State's perspectives. Furthermore, within a self-enclosed, effectively delimited, segmented legal regime there is likely to be a high level of material convergence, often much higher than in the context of the typically pluralist contemporary nation-state. Thus, the businesses that promote a privatised legal regime based on *lex mercatoria* would seem to share many more interests and values in common than the various legal actors who interact within the precincts of their own nation-state.

The key unanswered question is whether and how it would be possible to reconcile the various new points of convergence and divergence into a workable and coherent legal universe that would encompass all the domains of contemporary legal interaction. Layering may mitigate the effects of the collapse of hierarchy; however, it is not apparent whether or how it could help the necessary reconciliation or harmonisation among layers. Similarly, separate segment-fitted legal regimes may strengthen internal material bonds, but segmentation itself, as well as the degree of separation among the segments it produces, must be legitimated. Thus, for example, multinational corporations may strongly agree among themselves and share a common culture, although they would still have to deal with employees and customers who would resist being drawn into a self-enclosed, segmented legal regime that seems stacked against their interests.

The contemporary multilayered and segmented pluralist legal universe is extremely complex. For example, the layers of international law, transnational law, and national law may be impervious to any possible unification or harmonisation. Nonetheless, they may be linked by strong patterns of convergence, as in the case of the EU and its Member State constitutions, as discussed above. More generally, if we add the claims that international law has become constitutionalised and constitutional law internationalised;[15] that private or nongovernmental networks, carving out distinct spheres of segmented self-regulation, have generated their own internal constitutional framework;[16] that these various individually adopted frameworks have much in common;[17] and that formal and informal international networks among professionals in the same field, be it private (such as physicians or climate experts) or governmental (such as ministers of the economy or of the environment of

15 Norman Dorsen *et al.*, *Comparative Constitutionalism: Cases and Materials*, West, 2010.

16 Helene Ruiz Fabri and Andrea Hamann, "Transnational Networks and Constitutionalism", in *International Journal of Constitutional Law*, 2008, vol. 6, no. 3-4, pp. 481-508.

17 Ruiz Fabri and Hamann, 2008, see *supra* note 16.

various nation-states or, even more importantly, judges across the world), share many values and objectives based on common professional interests, then it seems inevitable that these developments will lead to the consolidation of important paths of convergence.

Paradoxically, the attempts to consolidate and spread newly minted clusters of convergence may also lead to new divergences. The most dramatic example of this latter trend is to be found in the spread of international and transnational human rights norms. There are disputes concerning the legitimate content of universally applicable human rights not only at the global level, but also in more homogeneous cultural settings, such as those of the forty-seven European nations bound by the ECHR. For example, the United Kingdom banned and branded as indecent the same book that Nordic countries clearly considered to be protected speech.[18] What is more, the ECtHR institutionalised this divergence by holding that individual countries are entitled to a 'margin of appreciation' in the implementation of ECHR rights such as freedom of expression.

3. De-Centred and Pluralistic Constitutional Ordering as the Means to Future Harmony and Legitimacy

The proliferation of layering and segmentation has consequences for the integrity of every single, distinct self. This issue confronts both individual and collective selves. A typical contemporary individual forms a complex identity made up of an aggregation of links to a number of collective selves with which the individual in question has bonds of varying intensity. These links may well include ethnic, religious, linguistic, cultural, national, professional, transnational (for example, the EU), global (for example, global warming), and ideological affiliations. These will inevitably produce certain conflicts within the individual, such as, for example, where one's feminism clashes with some of the dogmas of one's religion.

There seem to be two principal ways to cope with such conflicts when one cannot resolve or avoid them: either to relativise them (per issue or context), or to learn to live with a fair, yet tolerable, degree of dissonance. As an illustration of relativisation, a French citizen may feel

[18] See European Court of Human Rights, *Handyside v. United Kingdom*, Judgment, 7 December 1976, Series A, No. 5493/72, para. 24.

alienated from the EU with regard to a dispute between the latter and France and yet, at the same time, identify with the EU concerning economic competition between the latter and the United States. Accordingly, contradiction is avoided by making each of the identifications involved context specific. In some other circumstances, however, this is not possible. Thus, if one's feminism clashes with one's religion, and both form an important part of one's identity, it is very unlikely that relativisation will work. In this latter situation, one must either give up one's membership in one of the two conflicting communities, or one has to learn how to live with the contradiction one confronts. If the conflict is all-encompassing, for example, if the religion involved considers (core values of) feminism a mortal sin, then one would be forced to choose one allegiance to the exclusion of the other. But if there is enough of an overlap between the two conflicting communities, assuming, let's say, the religion preaches love and equality among all human beings but also bars women from the priesthood; then the best available course may be to accept the dissonance resulting from the partial contradiction and to remain an active and committed member of both communities.

Whereas constitutional ordering tailored to the nation-state essentially concerns a single sphere, post-Westphalian constitutional ordering must extend over several distinct spheres. Therefore, the main challenge confronting post-Westphalian constitutional ordering is that each sphere encompasses its own distinct pluralities and that the spheres involved must cater to different constitutional needs depending on whether they encompass all-purpose or limited-purpose selves; an 'all-purpose self' being one that as a whole is deeply embedded (as is traditionally the individual citizen in her own community and nation-state), and a 'limited purpose self' being one that is typically partially engaged (as is one who partakes in a global environmental movement). In the case of a 'limited purpose self', constitutional ordering may need to be broader, yet shallower, since a self adhering to a sphere for a limited purpose presumably can turn to other spheres to more fully sustain her overall quest for self-realisation and self-fulfilment.

There is no single prescription for a pluralist constitutional ordering of post-Westphalian polities, but it is possible to suggest certain directions in which such an ordering could evolve in the future. The new constitutional ordering should revolve around two overriding objectives.

The first is to allow for greater difference and plurality within constitutionally relevant intra-communal settings; the second, to forge a sufficient number of links of identity or convergence among separate spheres of interaction to ensure that inter-communal dealings as seen from a constitutional standpoint do not lead to insurmountable incompatibilities.

A number of existing constitutional tools, alone and in combination, seem particularly well suited to reshaping the transnational constitutional order so as to better serve these two objectives. Chief among these is federalism, understood in its broadest functional sense, as a means to achieve both decoupling and unification. In the best of cases, the process of federalisation could simultaneously forge concurrent paths toward unification and toward decoupling, all within the same constitutional arena. Like federalism operating within the nation-state, transnational federalism would also simultaneously segment or subdivide and bind together, but with one crucial difference: whereas federalism within the nation-state must always impose a hierarchy or unity, on a transnational scale its very success would depend on preserving plurality and on steering away from straightforward hierarchy.

Another constitutional tool that could play a useful role in the post-Westphalian arenas (especially when combined with federalisation and adjusted for transnational use) is the principle of subsidiarity. This principle holds that regulation of a matter ought to be entrusted to the most local level of government at which it might be regulated effectively. The principle of Subsidiarity has played a prominent role in promoting the policy that the EU refrain from regulating matters that could be handled equally or more effectively by the Member States.[19] More generally, subsidiarity, if understood not only in terms of efficiency but also in terms of its appropriateness for dealing with all implicated interests fairly and when combined with a properly tailored system of federalisation, could optimise the combination of binding together and decoupling consistent with the demands of the pluralist ethos. Efficiency may not always be correlated to fairness directly, as local regulation may naturally be most

[19] See generally George A. Bermann, "Taking Subsidiarity Seriously: Federalism in the European Community and the United States", in *Columbia Law Review*, 1994, vol. 94, p. 332.

efficient in certain cases in which remotely located interests nonetheless have a legitimate stake.[20]

Other relevant constitutional tools include: devolution; use of the 'millet system', which originated in the Ottoman Empire;[21] and constitutionalising a right to secession. These instruments provide the means to manage conflicts and tensions that set intra-communal pursuits on a collision course with inter-communal ones. Moreover, all three possess great potential for constitutional ordering, particularly where there appears to exist otherwise insoluble mutual incompatibilities among competing conceptions of the good. Finally, devolution and secession as means of decoupling seem much more genuine as tools of constitutional ordering within a transnational setting than within that of a traditional nation-state. Indeed, an agreed-upon breakup, such as that of the former Czechoslovakia, perhaps can be best characterised as a 'constitutional divorce'. By contrast, breaking up a federated entity into two states within a federal republic or creating a member state within a larger constitutionalised transnational polity, such as the EU, results not in cutting off constitutional links but, rather, in the creation of a new, different constitutional ordering among the resulting units.

The millet system, devised to grant religious communities autonomy over their spiritual and communal affairs, can serve as a model in situations where the members of the particular community are not geographically concentrated. Under this system, religious communities remain within the larger polity and enjoy only partial autonomy. This autonomy, which extends to religious affairs and personal communal relationships that are closely tied to religious practice such as marriage and divorce, is, nonetheless, crucial from a pluralist perspective. It allows each religious community to pursue norms it deems of the highest importance that would otherwise remain constantly at odds with those of other religions or of the polity as a whole. On the other hand, and this seems highly compatible with the pluralist ethos, the system allows for

[20] For example, regulation of fishing in local waters may be left more efficiently to municipal than to national governments and yet members of the polity located well beyond the municipality in question may have interests as consumers or advocates of preservation that ought fairly to be taken into account.

[21] Talip Kucukcan, "State, Islam, and Religious Liberty in Modern Turkey: Reconfiguration of Religion in the Public Sphere", in *Brigham Young University Law Review*, 2003, p. 475 and pp. 480-485.

certain norms that are of lesser importance to the religion in question to be subordinated to norms that rank high in the normative spheres framed by the polity as a whole.

In spite of all their potential virtues, devolution, the millet system, and secession all share the same vice: under certain circumstances, instead of solving or significantly decreasing the conflicts that arise from profound clashes between intra-communal and inter-communal dealings, they merely displace them and reproduce them at different levels. For example, if Quebec were to secede, its Anglophone minority and its indigenous population would find themselves in a position much like that of Quebec's current position within the existing Canadian federation.

Under the millet system, on the other hand, the solution to problems among religions and between the latter and the polity as a whole seem bound to raise new, equally serious issues. These new problems are likely to involve dissident individuals or groups within a particular religion, those who do not belong to any of the enfranchised religions, and those who seek to engage in certain interdenominational activities.

These problems can be greatly mitigated in the layered and segmented post-Westphalian universe. Indeed, in a transnational constitutional setting, not only can secession preserve constitutional links between the newly separated entities, devolution may end up being less fractious because the spread of power among three levels; the subnational, the national, and the transnational can diffuse potentially explosive confrontations between a subnational unit and the nation-state in which it is embedded. Also, in such a setting, new alliances can be forged, both within and among levels, thus allowing for interlocking constructive relationships. For example, direct tensions between the U.K. and Scotland and between Spain and Catalonia could be productively diffused by institutionalising certain relationships among sub-national units within the EU.[22] This offers the possibility of overcoming a deadlock occurring on two levels, by opening paths to new horizons on a third level without requiring strict hierarchy or unity.

The problems stemming from millet-system arrangements may also be better handled by way of the greater and more varied means available in the expanded, layered, and segmented post-Westphalian constitutional

[22] Kucukcan, 2003, pp. 480-485, see *supra* note 21.

space. From a pluralist standpoint, a millet-based religious communitarianism should be harmonised as much as possible with, and if necessary limited by, (liberal) individual rights regarding freedom of and from religion. The availability of an international human rights regime and of a concentrated, segmented, and concerted pursuit of such rights, vastly increases the chances of better approximating an optimal pluralist equilibrium.

Proportionality analysis and judicial balancing, which are widely used both at the national and transnational levels,[23] are additional constitutional interpretive tools that seem adaptable to the goal of harmonisation within a multilayered and highly segmented legal and political universe. Proportionality and judicial balancing require the ranking of competing interests in terms of their relative 'weights' and the pursuits of legitimate objectives in ways that least intrude upon the pursuit of other such objectives. Accordingly, proportionality and judicial balancing seem particularly well suited to advancing the constitutional implementation of the pluralist ethos. Proportionality analysis and judicial balancing tests boil down to two essential requirements: that there be a 'fit' between means and ends, and that there be a 'balancing' of the relevant competing interests at play.[24]

As tools, proportionality and balancing can contribute to harmonizing as well as to adapting to convergences and divergences. By using the same test within different layers and segments, proportionality is likely to create parallels and greater congruity. Thus, if the conditions and practical considerations attached to a particular issue, which has arisen in a substantial number of constitutional units, are essentially similar, then subjecting this issue to a proportionality test should result in a general congruence of results across the numerous constitutional systems involved. For example, if a large number of constitutional adjudicators determine that the current 'war on terror' does not justify recourse to

[23] See, for example, Court of Justice of the European Union, *Liselotte Hauer v. Land Rheinland-Pfalz*, Case C-44/79, Judgment, 13 December 1979, E.C.R. 3727; Bundesverfassungsgericht (BVerfG) (Federal Constitutional Court), *Pharmacy Case*, Judgment, 11 June 1958, 7 BVerFGE 377; Supreme Court of Canada, *Regina v. Oakes*, Judgment, 28 February 1986, 1 S.C.R. 103.

[24] Michel Rosenfeld, "Judicial Balancing in Times of Stress: Comparing the American, British and Israeli Approaches to the War on Terror", in *Cardozo Law Review*, 2006, vol. 27, pp. 2079, 2094.

emergency powers, then other adjudicators should be led, presumably, to the same conclusion, and the constitutional standard should be similar for most constitutional jurisdictions.[25]

The ubiquity of the proportionality principle ensures the circulation of a common procedural currency throughout the vast majority of contemporary constitutional systems. Finally, the actual outcome resulting from subjecting a contested law to a process of measuring for 'fit' and weighing for 'balance' is bound to depend on substantive variables external to the proportionality standard itself. For example, in subjecting an issue such as abortion to a constitutional proportionality standard, the ultimate outcome undoubtedly would differ according to whether one operates in a country like Ireland, with deep religious objections to abortion engraved on the nation's conscience, or like Japan, with an apparent lack of major normative concern over the issue. By subjecting these substantive variables to the same constitutional test, the proportionality standard highlights both similarities and differences, as well as the relative importance of particular differences within and across constitutional systems.

4. Concluding Remarks: A Non-Hierarchical Convergence between Ideological and Legal Pluralism?

The preceding analysis, based on both the assumption of the attractiveness of a pluralist *nomos* and on an indication of the pragmatic benefits of harnessing rather than combating legal pluralism, has revealed that a pluralist constitutional ordering for the post-Westphalian polity is not only desirable but, in principle, also plausible. Such constitutional ordering must deal with daunting complexities resulting from layering and segmenting on a global scale. Is it likely that all the necessary changes will actually materialise in the foreseeable future?

Although the vast proliferation of layering and segmenting affords multiple new spheres and arenas of mutual accommodation, ultimate success depends on luck, as one can imagine many potential scenarios in which the enterprise would be doomed to failure. One such scenario

[25] Note that the U.K. was the only country among the then forty-six parties to the ECHR to have derogated from its obligations thereunder. See House of Lords, *Cf. Secretary of State of the Home Department v. AF*, 2004, Judgment, UKHL 56, (2005) 2 A.C.68, 99–101 (appeal taken from Eng.) (U.K.).

would be a polarisation of the global political arena into an unyielding struggle between fanatical jihadists and champions of an aggressively instituted globalised free market. This would pit radical libertarians against believers in an all-pervasive political theocracy, with no room for accommodation or plurality. To be sure, this scenario is extreme. But even in less extreme scenarios, the multitude of ideologies and interests, which any legitimate constitutional ordering would have to take into account, might not yield the requisite minimum degree of congruence.

Even with luck, there may be other obstacles to the success of a pluralist post-Westphalian constitutional scheme. Constitutionalism cannot succeed without democracy, and there is little doubt that, in the vastly expanded post-Westphalian universe, democracy must be rethought, reset, and redeployed. All this involves manifold risks and dangers. Suffice it for now, that in spite of numerous dangers and risks and odds of success, the best hope for the future appears to be the non-hierarchical non-unified pluralist type of constitutional ordering outlined above.

1.7

The Rise and Challenges of 'Informal' International Law-Making*

Joost Pauwelyn**

Whereas the second half of the twentieth century saw a move toward international law and international organisations, the first part of the twenty-first century is marked by a move away from law and international organisations, toward more informal cooperation.

This is not to say that international cooperation does not materialise. Only that it occurs in less formal channels (G-groups or networks rather than IOs), with soft law as output and as between new actors (including regulators, central banks, judiciaries, parliaments as well as businesses, private actors and NGOs), often crossing the lines between domestic and international legal systems.

The challenge for 'law' is how law will maintain its independent and regulating force (rule of law which is to legitimise any form of coercion or limitation on freedom) in the face of this trend towards informality. In some way, informality and law are opposites. Law can adjust and reduce its formality requirements (both in terms of subjects of law and sources of law) so as to remain sociologically relevant. Or, law can insist on its formalities, be increasingly marginalised but do so in the hope that the tides will turn again and actors will realise that cooperating under law is more sustainable and power-neutral.

1. Introduction

A core distinguishing element of law is its formal character, or so holds the conventional view. If we look carefully around us, however, 'informal' norm development is everywhere. Especially since the late

* This contribution builds on a project sponsored by HiiL on Informal International Lawmaking (IN-LAW). Papers and case studies are available at www.informal law.org. To obtain the access code, please e-mail joost.pauwelyn@graduateinsti tute.ch. This paper is the result of a collective effort by, amongst other people, Ayelet Berman, Shwawn Donnelly, Sanderijn Duquet, Ramses Wessel and Jan Wouters.

** **Joost Pauwelyn** is Professor of International Law at the Graduate Institute of International and Development Studies in Geneva.

1990s, 'informal' law-making is on the rise both domestically and internationally. Though often enhancing effectiveness, 'informal' law-making challenges traditional mechanisms of democratic accountability. With 'informal' international law-making, we refer to three distinct features, often combined into one:[1]

1. *Process*-informality: norms developed not in treaty-based international organisations but in networks, fora or G-groups often without international legal personality.
2. *Actor*-informality: amongst or involving not formal state representatives or diplomats but regulators, agencies, sub-federal entities or other elements of the 'disaggregated' state often including also private actors, industry associations, civil society and other international organisations or networks.
3. *Output*-informality: leading to norms that are not formal treaties or traditional sources of international law but standards, non-binding guidelines or indicators most of which are strictly speaking outside of the remit of public international law.

Informal international law-making so defined (hereinafter 'IN-LAW') not only crosses the boundaries between what is formal and informal, or what is law or merely has legal effect. It also blurs the traditional lines between international law and domestic law, and between private law and public law.

2. The Rise and Possible Explanations for 'Informal' International Law-Making

As José Alvarez and others have documented, the second half of the twentieth century has witnessed a move toward more formalised international cooperation, starting, in the 1940s, with the creation of the UN and its specialised agencies and culminating, in the 1990s, with the creation of the Kyoto Protocol, the WTO and the International Criminal Court. More recently, however, this trend has reversed. Whereas IN-LAW is certainly not new – the debate on soft law, for example, is much older

1 Joost Pauwelyn, *Informal International Law-making: Mapping the Action and Testing Concepts of Accountability and Effectiveness*, Project Framing Paper, February 2011, available at http://www.nilproject.org/assets/1378/INLAW_Framing%20_Paper_Pauwelyn_Feb_2011.doc, last accessed 29 March 2011.

(the ISO dates back to 1947, the Codex Alimentarius to 1963) – more IN-LAW has emerged especially in the last two decades. Anne-Marie Slaughter was among the first to describe this trend, focusing especially on international cooperation amongst regulators. Think only of the International Organization of Securities Commissions (established in 1983), the Basel Capital Accord (1988, updated twice since), the Financial Action Task Force (1989), the International Conference on Harmonization in respect of pharmaceuticals (ICH, 1990), the G-20 (1999, upgraded in 2008), the Kimberley Process to combat conflict diamonds (2000), the International Competition Network (2002), the Proliferation Security Initiative (2003), the Internet Governance Forum (2006) or the Financial Stability Board (2009). There are many other examples.

In contrast, notwithstanding the explosion of issues that require international cooperation in the face of globalisation, can you think of when the last major international organisation or formal multilateral treaty was concluded? Seen from this perspective, globalisation has bypassed the discipline of international law completely. In the face of IN-LAW, international law is struggling to remain sociologically relevant.

The argument is clearly not that international cooperation will no longer materialise. The point is only that it will occur in greater variety and, more often than not, through less formal, less traditional channels, such as G-groups or issue-specific coalitions or networks rather than IOs. It will have soft law or flexible coordination as its output, and cooperation will take place between new actors such as telecom regulators, food safety agencies or competition authorities often complemented by private actors and NGOs. These systems of cooperation will often cross the lines between domestic and international legal systems and transcend the traditional spheres of private and public law.

In terms of the participating countries, recent instances show that informal cooperation has moved beyond cooperation between like-minded states to also cover broader networks traditionally reserved for regulation by treaty (think of the Kimberley Scheme). Even when it comes to climate change, the prospects of a formal treaty are dim and what may emerge is a package of domestic initiatives informally accepted and monitored as 'equivalent' by participating countries, following the already less formal 2009 Copenhagen Accord.

Some of the reasons for IN-LAW are novel or recently on the rise. Domestically, reference can be made to the emergence of the administrative or disaggregated state. Regulators under growing domestic demands yet with limited resources and information seek to share the workload with other (public or private) parties, at home and abroad. Internationally, some of IN-LAW can be attributed to an increasingly multi-polar world (higher diversity of interests) and power shifting to countries less wedded to formal law-making mechanisms, as well as to private actors. In other cases IN-LAW models were simply copied and pasted from the European network experience and 'internationalised'. This may explain the growing number of IN-LAW mechanisms especially in the last 10-20 years. Other reasons for IN-LAW have been around for much longer, in particular, circumventing the formalities linked to formal law-making (such as, internationally, state consent and, domestically, congressional ratification) or the uncertainty inherent in specific fields of cooperation (be it science-related or technical fields or 'high politics' stakes centered on national security).

Some of the reasons for IN-LAW are perfectly benign. They portray IN-LAW as a complement or alternative to formal law (*e.g.*, in areas that would otherwise not be occupied by formal law) or even as the first-best option to deal with a cooperation problem, more appropriate or effective, or less costly than formal law (think of internet regulation or ISO standards). These reasons would not seem to raise concern or call for major reforms or changes.

Other reasons for IN-LAW are more worrisome. The goal of circumventing formalities, for example, has raised questions of accountability and even legality. Concerns also arise when countries are excluded from IN-LAW 'clubs' of selected and often more developed nations, clubs which, nonetheless, end up having a serious impact on external stakeholders in the rest of the world (think of the Basel Accords, ICH, Proliferation Security Initiative or G-20). Those reasons for IN-LAW could lead to calls for reforming, regulating or limiting IN-LAW activity. Other reasons for IN-LAW, in contrast, relate to arguably outdated features of international law itself: who can make it, how can it be made, changed and implemented, and how does it score on the scales of legitimacy and effectiveness. This raises the question of not so much how to reform or adjust IN-LAW but how to reform or adjust traditional international law to modern realities.

There are, in any event, multiple reasons for actors to opt for IN-LAW, some of which may even be in tension or outright contradictory. One way to classify those reasons is in two broad categories. First, those that, in one way or another, portray IN-LAW as a 'second-best' option that could possibly be problematic (not least in terms of accountability) as compared to the perceived 'superior' route of formal law-making. Think of IN-LAW because formal law-making is 'too burdensome' (*e.g.*, because of international or domestic formalities of notice and comment, consultation and publication or consent and super-majority ratification), 'un-attainable' (parties cannot agree to something more formal due to high uncertainty or high diversity of interests) or 'technically impossible' (*e.g.*, domestic agencies have no mandate to bind the state and international law does not normally recognise them as legal persons); IN-LAW as norm-making that 'favors the powerful' (as in coalitions of the willing or like-minded clubs that impose their views on outsiders) or IN-LAW to 'counter formal law' in the exercise of forum-shopping where powerful actors or constituencies disagree (and move debates on, for example, GMOs or intellectual property away from the WTO and into more informal fora). Those reasons are what we could call the more conventional explanations for the rise of IN-LAW which also inspired the HiiL tender that led to the IN-LAW project.

Second, less conventional or less noticed reasons for IN-LAW can be detected which set up IN-LAW not as a second-best, fall-back choice but as a 'first-best' option which may be, rather than problematic, the progressive way forward, putting into question not so much IN-LAW itself but formal law-making practices. For example, IN-LAW can simply be a 'cheaper' alternative to achieve the same goal (where countries agree and there are few incentives for defection, why go through the long-winded process of setting up a treaty or IO?). IN-LAW can also be a cultural or social practice or trend that comes hand in hand with the rise of Asian powers or as an adoption of EU network models. Most importantly, IN-LAW and, in particular, what is emerging as something of a 'Code of Good Practice' in setting standards has features that can be procedurally and substantially superior to 'outdated' formal law-making practices (*e.g.*, more inclusive 'rough consensus' as compared to individual state consent; inclusion of non-members as observers; ongoing processes of consultation and implementation rather than one-off negotiation and ratification;

flexibility to adapt to new developments; clarity, effectiveness and consistency of norms themselves).

From this perspective, the growth of informal cooperation has to do with the inadequacy of the traditional, formal system of international state-to-state cooperation to efficiently cope with modern challenges. This system has remained unchanged for a long time, centred on the consent of sovereign states (no state can be bound by a rule it did not agree to; subjects of international law beyond states remain controversial) and domestic ratification of output (in the United States, for example, few treaties are concluded since they require adoption in the US Senate by 2/3 majority before incorporation into US law). To avoid these formal strictures and obstacles both internationally and domestically, IN-LAW (output, actor and process informality) has emerged as an attractive complement, alternative or antagonist to formal law-making.

3. The Challenges and Accountability of 'Informal' International Law-Making

A note of caution is in place. Although there is a trend in favour of IN-LAW at the beginning of the twenty-first century, the balance between formal and informal law-making can easily shift. There is a risk of too much IN-LAW including IN-LAW that limits the freedom of individuals without appropriate, formal controls. Similarly, as beneficial and advanced as IN-LAW can be, certain cooperation will only materialise and stick through more formal, binding instruments (as recent experience in the financial field has underscored; similarly, within the EU, a second reversal is in play away from EU networks toward more formal EU agencies with more autonomy from both EU member states and the EU commission). The challenge is, in other words, to know when formal or informal modes are more appropriate and, either way, to keep norm-making activity accountable albeit with novel mechanisms and at different levels.

The question of democratic accountability of IN-LAW only really arises to the extent public authority or power is being wielded under IN-LAW, more specifically, action by public entities which (either *de jure* or *de facto*) unilaterally 'determines' or 'reduces the freedom of' others.[2] The accountability of IN-LAW raises questions and offers possible solutions both at the international level (where national actors and other IN-LAW participants meet and set norms) and the domestic level (where the actors involved obtain their mandate, are subject to oversight and control, and must eventually implement IN-LAW).

A broad and a narrow definition or approach to accountability can be identified. In its broadest sense, accountability has been equated with 'responsiveness' to stakeholders (as opposed to 'disregard'), with both a substantive component (output legitimacy) and a procedural component (input legitimacy). In its narrow sense, accountability has been limited to *ex post* and sufficiently institutionalised mechanisms between an 'actor' to be held accountable and a 'forum' holding the actor accountable (under, more specifically, electoral, hierarchical, supervisory, fiscal or legal accountability mechanisms).[3] A clear tension exists in this respect between, on the one hand, informal networks or IN-LAW (focusing on its process-informality axis) and, on the other hand, *ex post* institutionalised or formalised accountability mechanisms: if it is the very nature of IN-LAW to be informal, how could it include formal, institutionalised accountability mechanisms? That said, a lot of formal rules do apply in IN-LAW (process-informality contrasts IN-LAW to traditional IOs; it does not preclude the existence of formal rules and procedures). In addition, even to the extent that certain *ex post*, institutionalised accountability mechanisms may be absent (*e.g.*, legal accountability for

---

2 Armin von Bogdandy, Philipp Dann and Matthias Goldmann, "Developing the Publicness of Public International Law: Towards a Legal Framework for Global Governance Activities", in *German Law Journal*, 2008, vol. 9, no. 11, p. 1375 and p. 1376.

3 Adapting Bovens' definition to the peculiarities of IN-LAW, the framing paper offers the following, narrow definition of accountability: "Accountability is a relationship *[at the domestic or international level]* between an actor [*exercising public authority in the context of IN-LAW]* and a forum [*internal to the IN-LAW process or an external stakeholder]*, in which the actor has an obligation [*in particular, but not exclusively, expressed in legal rules or procedures]* to explain and to justify his or her conduct [*ex ante leading up to a decision or ex post in the implementation of a decision]*, the forum can pose questions and pass judgment, and the actor may face consequences [*in particular, but not exclusively, so as to enhance the democratic legitimacy of IN-LAW]*. See Mark Bovens, "Analysing and Assessing Accountability: A Conceptual Framework", in *European Law Journal*, 2007, vol. 13, no. 4, p. 447, 450, available at http://www.css.edu.pl/sns/pliki/Wierzba/M_Bovens_Analysing.pdf, last accessed 29 March 2011. See also Pauwelyn, *supra* n. 1, p. 20.

lack of legal personality of the IN-LAW network as such), these can be compensated by other control mechanisms at both the international and domestic level (and are, in any event, not normally available either for formal IOs).

Besides such accountability mechanisms in the strict sense, one can also identify (1) preconditions that enable accountability (mandate/benchmark setting, transparency, disclosure of information) and (2) other responsiveness-promoting measures (such as *ex ante* control over appointments and mandate, ongoing control in decision-making or non-institutionalised *ex post* mechanisms such as market or peer pressure).[4] Finally, a crucial distinction exists between (1) 'internal' accountability or accountability to IN-LAW participants and their constituencies, and (2) 'external' accountability or accountability to actors that are not formally within the IN-LAW network but that are affected by it.

When putting together the international versus domestic and internal versus external distinctions set out above, and adding that accountability can be owed by either (1) the IN-LAW network as such, collectively or (2) individual participants in the network (be they states, domestic agencies or regulators, NGOs or private industry), the following 'IN-LAW Accountability Table' emerges. We use the particular example of the *International Conference on Harmonization of Technical Requirements for Registration of Pharmaceuticals for Human Use* (ICH), where the United States (U.S. Food and Drug Administration, US FDA) is a member, but not Brazil even though Brazil is affected by the ICH as it *de facto* adopts many ICH guidelines. Cells in grey indicate conventional lines of accountability or control; other cells need further thinking and especially in those accountability relationships novel methods should be considered. Though not reflected in the table below, for each cell (*e.g.*, keeping the IN-LAW network as such accountable to internal

4 Pauwelyn, *supra* n. 1, p. 20: "On this premise, Corthaut *et al.* … define the broader approach to accountability as: a dual relationship (operationalized through norms and procedures) between the public and a body, through which the latter 'takes account' of the interests, opinions and preferences of the former prior to making a decision (*responsiveness*), and through which it 'renders account' a posteriori of its activities and decisions, with the possibility of facing sanctions (*control*). The effectiveness of such relationship requires other meta-principles to exist, such as transparency and reason-giving (which are *enablers*, but not *components* of accountability)".

stakeholders at the *international* level) one can think of three broad types of accountability or control: (1) *ex ante* control, (2) ongoing control, and (3) *ex post* control.

	Accountability at the INTERNATIONAL Level		**Accountability at the DOMESTIC Level**	
	IN-LAW network as such	Individual participants	Individual participants	IN-LAW network as such
Toward INTERNAL stakeholders (actors/people part of IN-LAW; delegation model)	ICH towards ICH members and their constituencies (*e.g.*, internal ICH decision-making and voting procedures; ICH budget, chair and secretariat appointments; complaints procedure; non-implementation)	FDA towards the American people, other internal stakeholders New mechanism? (*e.g.*, complaints procedure or ombudsman to challenge FDA at the international level)	FDA towards the American people (hierarchical control within FDA, political control by executive, control and oversight by Congress including through FDA mandate, budget; judicial review, notice and comment procedures; elections)	ICH towards ICH members and their constituencies New mechanism? (*e.g.*, US courts or other domestic bodies reviewing ICH responsibility)
Toward EXTERNAL Stakeholders (actors/people affected by IN-LAW; participation model)	ICH towards non-members and other affected actors (transparency, allowing input and observers from *e.g.*, Brazil; complaints procedure against ICH open to all affected entities)	FDA towards Brazilian people New mechanism? (international complaints procedure or ombudsman open to affected Brazilians to challenge FDA)	FDA towards Brazilian people New mechanism? (*e.g.*, US notice and comments procedure open to foreigners; US courts reviewing FDA in way that takes account of Brazilian interests)	ICH towards non-members and other affected actors New mechanism? (Brazilian courts reviewing ICH responsibility)

Table 1: The IN-LAW Accountability Table.

3.1. Internal Versus External Accountability

As the IN-LAW accountability table above illustrates (cells in grey), it is crucial to ensure accountability towards 'internal' stakeholders at both the international level (especially, by controlling the ICH) and the domestic level (especially, by controlling the US FDA within the United States in accordance with the regular domestic oversight of agencies).

In contrast, 'external' accountability is normally operationalised only at the international level (*e.g.*, ICH allowing input by Brazil). It is very difficult to give voice to external interests within a domestic legal system (*e.g.*, US agencies, voters or courts deferring to Brazilian interests). That said, it has been the practice of the FDA (as well as the European Medicines Agency) to accept comments by foreign countries in the domestic rule or guideline development process. Still, the core problem with generating accountability under domestic mechanisms (*e.g.*, ministerial or parliamentary oversight, elections) in respect of stakeholders that are external to the country concerned (say, the US taking account of the interests of Brazilian patients or health authorities as it relates to the ICH) is that domestic accountability systems are not normally set up to respond to foreign interests.

The biggest accountability problem of IN-LAW at the international level is that of 'external' accountability of the network and its participants toward countries and other actors or sectors outside the network but that are influenced or affected by IN-LAW output. Both public and private external stakeholders can, however, be given voice and input through observership, notice and comment procedures and transparency. To avoid capture or selective (over)representation of certain private interests, there is a trend in favor of input through consultation and 'notice and comment' procedures, and a move away from actual involvement of private interests or NGOs in decision-making itself. This can be a crucial guideline to offer to (at least some) IN-LAW mechanisms (*e.g.*, the Kimberley Scheme which does, in some respects, fully involve both NGOs and the private sector as almost equal partners to public authorities): as important as it is to involve private/NGO stakeholders, it may be best to limit their input to (meaningful) 'notice and comment' procedures or advisory roles (and to open this up to all interested actors following an 'interest representation model') rather than giving (only some of) them an actual vote in the system (which adds the risk of capture and selective representation).

3.2. International Versus Domestic Accountability

In many cases, the only thing that national agencies or regulators do when engaged in IN-LAW is exercise the mandate delegated to them by national parliaments to, for example, ensure food safety or financial stability. To fulfill this mandate they act internally and cross-border. Yet, in both cases they remain subject to internal control mechanisms that ensure domestic oversight by ministers, governments and/or national parliaments.

What is the difference between enacting a rule or guideline alone without concertation with other countries (not normally seen as presenting an accountability deficit) and enacting a rule or guideline after concertation with other countries in the context of IN-LAW (too often portrayed as presenting a major accountability problem)? If anything, the question remains the same, namely, to ensure adequate domestic oversight of agencies and regulators. Moreover, from the perspective of external accountability, when an agency or regulator acts transnationally it only enhances (rather than reduces) the accountability of whatever regulation is ultimately enacted at home (through concertation with foreign or external interests, negative externalities can be internalised).

A common misperception is to look at an independent agency (say, the US FDA or European Central Bank) acting on the international scene, to note that this independent agency is not controlled by anyone and to then call for international oversight. The independence of the agency (say, a food safety regulator or central bank) is not the result of some international conspiracy. It is the result of a domestic delegation of powers from the executive or parliament to an administrative or expert agency. Domestic control mechanisms (*ex ante* and *ex post*) must apply equally whether this agency acts domestically or internationally. There may be a role for oversight or accountability mechanisms at the international (Basel Committee or ICH) level (especially *vis-à-vis* external stakeholders, as discussed earlier). Yet, the core source of internal accountability is and must remain domestic.

	(internal) **ACCOUNTABILITY** (broadly defined)		
	Ex ante Control (*e.g.*, fixed mandate, appointment, set-up, conflict of interest and transparency rules)	**Ongoing Control** (*e.g.*, veto, participation in decision-making, supervisory or hierarchical control)	**Ex post Control** (*e.g.*, sanction for underperformance, budget, electoral, legal challenge, refuse implementation, market, peer, reputation)
No network autonomy or power (*de jure* or *de facto*)	No/less need	Complete ⇩	No/less need
Full network autonomy or power (*de jure* or *de facto*)	Crucial	Non-existing	Crucial

Table 2.

The need for accountability mechanisms at the international level rises proportionally with the degree of autonomy and power exercised (*de jure* or *de facto*) by the IN-LAW network. With no autonomy or power at all for the IN-LAW network, *e.g.*, full control by participants, 'ongoing control' by participants may be enough to ensure accountability (at least internal accountability towards participants) and there may be no or less need to set-up *ex ante* and/or *ex post* mechanisms of control. In contrast, the more autonomy or power bestowed on the IN-LAW network as such (less ongoing control by participants as is the case for central banks or expert bodies deciding on scientific risk), and the more the network produces normative output that actually changes behavior, the more it becomes important to make up for the loss in ongoing control (politicians do not get involved in interest rate decisions or risk assessments) by a tightening of *ex ante* control (*e.g.*, careful definition of mandate, appointment of officers) and *ex post* control (*e.g.*, approval of budget, dismissal of officers, legal or other complaints mechanisms, sanctions for non-performance).

This way we can combine both (1) the need to give some autonomy to IN-LAW networks in order for these networks to be effective and make accurate or overall welfare enhancing decisions, with (2) the need to keep all IN-LAW activity accountable, be it through ongoing control (where there is no or little network autonomy) or *ex ante* and *ex post* control (in cases of higher network autonomy), or both.

3.3. Not More But Better Accountability

Put differently, optimal amounts and ways of keeping IN-LAW accountable will vary with the nature and functions of the particular IN-LAW network. There is no one-size-fits-all solution, nor a silver bullet that can be suggested to ensure IN-LAW accountability. What is needed is not necessarily 'more' accountability or control (raising the risk of accountability overload that may stifle the network, as has been documented in the context of certain EU networks and EU agencies), but 'better' accountability or control. Such 'better' accountability must focus, firstly, on activating the appropriate accountability mechanisms at the right time and level and in the right relationships; and, secondly, keeping the right balance between, in particular, independence (so as to achieve effective solutions) and control (so as to maintain the mechanism accountable).

4. Outlook

In sum, there are at least two core challenges presented by the phenomenon of 'informal' international law-making:

1. In the face of IN-LAW, how to maintain law's neutrality and protective force (in particular in favour of the weak), rule of law being the only justification for any form of coercion or limitation on freedom. To the extent IN-LAW limits individual freedom (and irrespective of whether it is or is not 'law'), IN-LAW must therefore by controlled 'by law'; and
2. How to balance informality, which may be needed to enable effective cooperation or to avoid traditional strictures, with the

levels of control and accountability required to sustain this cooperation in democratic societies.

In some ways, informality and law are opposites. In the face of a move toward informality, law can adjust and reduce its formal requirements, both in terms of subjects of law and the sources of law, so as to remain sociologically relevant in a very dynamic reality. Or law can insist on its formalities, risking it will be increasingly marginalised, but hoping that the tides will turn again and the actors will realise that formal cooperation under law is more sustainable and power-neutral.

This raises an interesting puzzle for the discipline of international law: Should international law give up the little formality that it now has (*e.g.*, when it comes to consent or the legal capacity of new actors) and embrace 'informal law' so as to stay sociologically relevant and put international law 'back on the map'? Or should it, instead, insist on formalism and exclude 'informal law' from its scope to maintain international law's independence and stress the point that 'informal law' may be inappropriate as a power instrument of the strong?

Both approaches may hope for a return to international law: the first, progressive approach, by completely accommodating 'informal law' as part and parcel of international law; the second, more conservative approach, by excluding 'informal law' and denying it legitimacy in the hope that actors (in particular weak players) will realise the value added by traditional international law (with its formal guarantees, however limited) and return to it.

Whether or not IN-LAW is strictly speaking 'law' and what role IN-LAW may play before courts and tribunals (be it as law or legal facts) may lead to fascinating academic debates. What is of more immediate and practical importance, however, is how the informal law-making described above, whether or not it 'is' law, can be controlled 'by' law, be it international law or domestic law or some novel legal regime, such as global administrative law. It cannot be disputed that the influence and pressure from the outside on national polities has increased. Yet, national polities (especially smaller countries or those not actively involved in the multiple informal networks at work) see their control over this outside influence and pressure wane. This sense of loss of control and direction alienates the people from domestic politics and creates a sense of helplessness and coercion when it comes to international law.

Correction is needed both at the domestic level where domestic oversight, input and voice must increase, and at the international or transnational level where new types of accountability mechanisms and checks and balances must be tested (ranging from ombudsmen and complaints procedures to internet-based input and contestation mechanisms) so as to make up for at least part of the loss of control at home. This, in turn, will require a dramatic shift in international law from being a neutral, value-free instrument enabling state-to-state cooperation, to a genuine regulatory order with minimum standards of transparency and due process and built-in checks and balances including input and control by experts, parliaments, civil society and businesses, to enable the provision of public goods (and not merely the short term protection of national interests).

The second major challenge mentioned above is how to balance effectiveness with democratic accountability when it comes to 'informal law-making'. Here, the answer might be that effectiveness and accountability need not be (or be perceived as) polar opposites: for informal cooperation to be effective in the long term, it will need to be accountable; conversely, a core goal of accountability is to increase effectiveness by learning from mistakes and feedback from stakeholders.

The crossing of lines between legal regimes, involvement of new actors and the setting up of new accountability mechanisms at the international level will force us to rethink international law and perhaps also to create or further develop new legal spheres, variably referred to as transnational law, global administrative law or self-contained regimes in the field of trade, health, the internet or sports. A resulting challenge will be to marry this legal diversity with a minimum of coherence so as to effectively solve interconnected problems.

2. Changing State Institutions

2.1

The Future of National Constitutions in a Global World

Tom Ginbsburg[*]

This paper argues that future developments in national constitutions will be determined by the interaction between domestic and transnational actors. Current trends – including the integration of international human rights norms, constitutions' increasingly lengthy and statutory nature, and the import of provisions from similarly situated nations – are likely to continue over the long-term. Constitutions are likely to serve less as embodiments of a nation's common aspirations and highest norms than as deals between competing national and international groups. Rapid social and technological change will also contribute to the destabilisation of constitutions, and amendment procedures may become more flexible in response to these pressures. Additionally, the frequency of expansive judicial interpretation may increase in order to harmonise constitutional law with new social realities generated by globalisation. In general, constitutions and constitutional legal practice will be subject to more external influences than in the past.

1. Introduction

What will be the future of constitutions in a global society? This is a crucial question to consider, as constitutions have been regarded as the highest norm governing the nation-state for the better part of two centuries. Yet, like the nation state itself, the constitutional form is likely to be impacted by global developments. This short essay considers some of the possibilities.

It is important to clarify at the outset what we mean by constitutions. The idea of the constitution, referring to fundamental norms organising society, goes back to Aristotle's notion of the *politiea*. While every society of any scale has fundamental norms, the idea of embodying these norms in a formal written document is a relatively recent one. The first written national constitution is often seen as being that of the United

* **Tom Ginsburg** is Professor of Law at the University of Chicago.

States in 1789, and it was followed closely by similar efforts in Poland and France. Spanish liberals articulated the Constitution of Cadiz in 1812, and this document had significant influence on the written constitutions of newly independent states in Latin America. Written constitutions can be seen as a technology of government, defining the fundamental organisation of the state and its relationship with its citizens.

To be sure, there were antecedents of the written constitution, namely particular statutes and decrees of a constitutional character, as found in England and Sweden. A few countries to this day, including Saudi Arabia, New Zealand and Israel, continue to embody the constitution in a set of statutes. Still, the overall trend has been toward a single unified document that is nominally the highest body of norms in the legal order. Constitution-making has become typical for new states eager to define the purposes of the state itself (see Figure 1). From the middle of the nineteenth century, when roughly half of the countries of the world had national constitutions, the practice has spread so that virtually every country has a single such document.

The written constitution has traditionally been seen as embodying *local* values. Paradigmatically, it was "we the people" who collectively authored the text, in accordance with the social contract theories that inspired written constitutions in the first place. As the collectively sovereign people gave voice to their aspirations and ideals, they distinguished themselves from other nation-states and colonial powers.

This point illustrates that constitutions naturally reflect political ideas that are dominant during the time they are written. Early nineteenth century constitutions in Latin America, for example, reflected the influence of the American constitution, featuring such institutions as federalism, bills of rights, and, at least in some countries, indirectly elected presidencies. European constitutions written during this period reflected a more evolutionary understanding of norms of parliamentary constraint on monarchs, and tended to leave some of the important norms that actually operated unwritten. In the late nineteenth and early twentieth centuries we see the rise of certain features associated with industrialisation: rights to education, rights to organise into labour unions, and in some cases rights to social welfare. After World War II, a *zeitgeist* of human rights spread around the world, and many societies included extensive bills of rights, both negative and positive. Some included provisions for constitutional review, either by designated constitutional courts or ordinary ones. Thereafter, the wave of decolonisation in the 1950s produced new experiments.

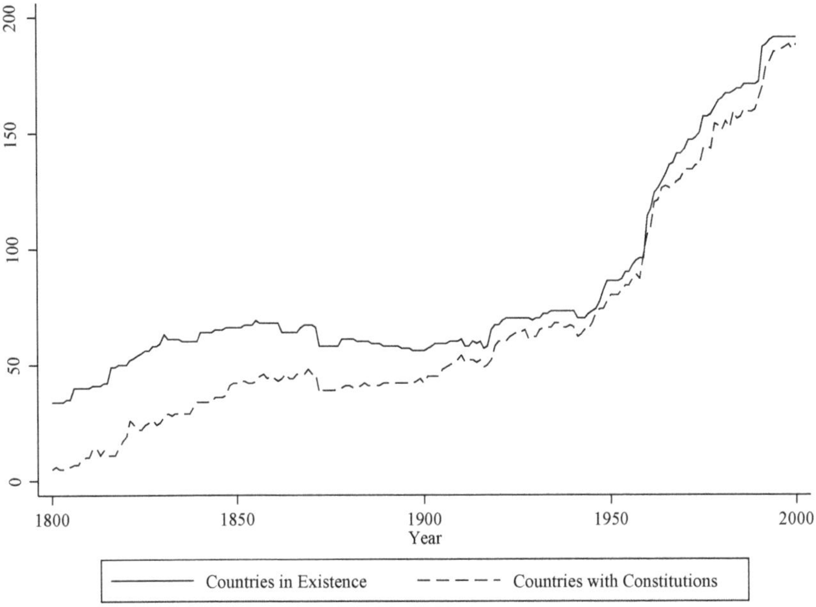

Figure 1: The Spread of the Written Constitution.[1]

The most recent wave of constitution-making occurred at the end of the Cold War and involved what I have characterised as the post-political constitution, including a distrust of political parties, institutionalised constraints on legislative power, and an extensive set of regulatory institutions. The constitutions of the 1990s also reflected neoliberal ideas of the freedom of establishment, freedom of investment and markets.

The close relationship between written constitutions and the broader social and political context is only natural. Because these contexts change, it behooves us to identify current trends and to speculate on the future of constitutions in a global era.

[1] Special thanks to James Melton and Zachary Elkins, with whom I have jointly researched many of these issues. Figure 1 is from our co-authored book. See *The Endurance of National Constitutions*, Cambridge University Press, 2009.

2. Constitutions in the Global Era

The key challenge of the global era is the general pressure on state sovereignty associated with intensified cross-border interaction in every sphere. One area in which this is much discussed is universal human rights, surely one of the areas in which traditional ideas of sovereignty have given way to a more complex reality. The machinery established by the international community after World War II articulated an extensive set of norms, nominally universal in character, and identified their furtherance as one of the main goals of international governance. Considerations of how a state treated its own citizens became an important issue for outside powers. Naturally, these efforts were more successful in articulating norms than enforcing them. But one sign of the success of the project was the instantiation of many of these norms into national constitutions. The menu of rights articulated in the international bill of rights had a significant coordinating effect on national constitution-makers, who either incorporated the international documents by reference or copied their text into the new documents. This meant that in some sense, the source of norms articulated in national documents came from outside the local context. The external source of norms was particularly apparent for non-Western countries. The image of constitutions as produced by "we the people" gathering together in some New England town hall is surely dead, if it ever had real purchase. Instead, local actors are participating in a broader global conversation, constrained and empowered by outside forces, even as they struggle to produce a nominally local document. Constitutions may no longer be embodiments of a particular people's history so much as a discrete localisation of outside norms.

One bit of evidence for this proposition is the transnational politicisation of constitution-making. Outsiders, including states, international organisations and interest groups, increasingly make their views known and play a role in constitutional design. This is clearly apparent for constitutions drafted under military occupation, as in Iraq and Afghanistan, but also occurs in lower-profile contexts. For example, in the recent drafting of the constitution of Kenya, Christian groups in the United States helped mobilise opposition to the draft on the grounds that it permitted the parliament to legalise abortion in the event of medical necessity. Their efforts were unsuccessful, but the point is that the drafting is constrained by international norms and transnational interest groups. States too, will weigh in on particular provisions in foreign texts, providing support for drafting efforts to include norms of democracy and human rights.

The same dynamic is also apparent in the design of institutions. Constitutions, like other public policies, are borrowed across borders. If rights tend to be borrowed vertically from international instruments, other constitutional institutions are sometimes borrowed horizontally from other nation states. These states can be neighbours, former colonial powers, or countries bearing certain cultural similarities, such as a common language or religion.

3. Continuation of Specific Trends

We have seen somewhat of a trend in recent decades toward constitutionalisation of various independent regulatory agencies, such as electoral commissions, counter-corruption commissions, and ombudsmen along with constitutional courts. There seems to be somewhat of a sense that politics, as practiced by popularly elected legislatures in which political parties are the dominant modes of organisation, is insufficient to guarantee good policies. Parliamentary sovereignty was in long decline in the second half of the twentieth century, and with the exception of a couple of unreconstructed socialist states and British Commonwealth societies, is mostly dead. In its place, a formally democratic system is constrained by various layers of accountability institutions. The emphasis is on accountability over efficacy of government.

Another trend is toward great specificity. The American constitution passed in 1789 was around 4500 words. The Kenyan constitution, passed by referendum in summer 2010, is more than ten times as long at nearly 50,000 words. This is clearly more representative. Two of the more successful constitutions in recent times, those of Brazil and India, are extraordinarily long. Modern constitutions seem more like statutes than fundamental unchanging texts. They often contain very detailed policies, and thus require frequent modification, again a feature thought of as more statutory than constitutional.

We also see an expansion of different types of rights-claims. Classical nineteenth century constitutions focused on first-generation rights, but constitutions were also harbingers of new kinds of second-generation rights claims that eventually became embodied in international human rights law. In turn, the international covenants served as templates for subsequent drafters. At the dawn of the twenty-first century, new forms of social and economic rights claims have become quite common, notwithstanding criticisms that they are vague and unspecified. Many of these involve collective rights, such as a right to development, or a clean environment. Some constitutional courts have proven quite effective in adjudicating claims involving these rights, further encouraging the development of new types of rights. The interaction of national and international instrumentalities and conceptions of rights is likely to continue.

In short, there are trends away from parliamentary dominance, and toward limitation of government. The content of fundamental norms is increasingly driven from outside the state, promoted by a set of transnational interest groups. This trend puts further pressure on the idea of the constitution as the embodiment of a national polity. And the language of rights serves as a kind of global constitutional discourse that continues to evolve.

4. The Future

Where will constitutions go in the next century? The fact that constitutions reflect not only the social and political circumstances of both their immediate drafting environment, but also the broader trends of their era, means that global developments will have an increasing effect.

It is clear that the trend toward international and transnational sources of constitutional norms will continue. We will see transnational mobilisation of interest groups, whether they are for human rights, abortion or freedom of establishment. Sometimes outsiders will have particular interests in, and knowledge of, the local context. In other instances, however, they will be more focused on particular issues (rather than places) and will be seeking to advance a particular policy agenda in as many contexts as possible. Once mobilised in one context, an interest group can now easily transverse the shrinking borders among states to lobby in other countries. The focus of Western Christian groups, unable to win on abortion policy or anti-gay policies in their home jurisdictions, on African constitutional drafting exercises is a harbinger of future trends. National constitutions will become international policy battlegrounds.

The global security regime will also have an impact in several ways. The challenges of 'failed states' will lead to continued efforts at state reconstruction. In recent years, we have seen that constitutional reconstruction is an important part of this effort, as outside powers seek to ensure a legal basis for the state's internal governance structure. So there will be external pressure to produce constitutions, and external involvement in the same. But this external pressure will also extend to ongoing monitoring of the implementation of certain features of the constitution. External enforcement efforts may help to ensure that such constitutions are made efficacious, at least in the areas of interest to foreigners.

Perhaps this means that future constitutions will more accurately describe the political practice of their contexts, though this relationship has always been loose at best. Even at the present juncture, we observe many countries with formally democratic institutions, embodied in a constitution, whose informal constitution operates completely differently. Yet the formal structures do constrain in ways that do not clearly track the line between democracy and dictatorship. Vladimir Putin chose to step down after his second term and take the revamped office of prime minister, while other leaders choose to amend or even tear up the constitution. The Chinese leadership takes constitutional change seriously, using the document to confirm policy movements that have already been undertaken. In short, there is a significant creativity to new forms of authoritarian pluralism, which may be embodied in constitutions. So a global constitutional era need hardly be a democratic one.

Another important factor that is likely to have an impact is that the rate of social and technological change is likely to remain high and continue to accelerate. This is likely to put great pressure on constitutional stability. Stability is at the core of the very idea of a constitution, and yet it is likely to be undercut in periods of rapid change. Rules endure as long as they are useful, and so naturally they bear some relation with the underlying conditions of society. If society changes dramatically, the rules may become brittle and out of date, leading to pressure to adopt new rules through constitutional amendment or replacement.

This observation has normative implications for constitutional design. Constitutions adjust through two primary mechanisms: formal amendment and informal interpretation. These two are substitutes for each other: as the threshold for amendment rises, courts become more empowered, and vice versa. If demand for adjustment is going to increase, it might be advisable to draft constitutions that have more flexible amendment provisions so as to allow more formal change, which usually has the advantage of involving democratic processes. We do not know if the trend toward simpler procedures is actually in operation, owing to methodological difficulties of measuring cross-nationally the ease of constitutional amendment. The implication, however, would be toward a model more like parliamentary sovereignty, in which constitutional rules are passed in a manner that looks a lot more like passing statutes than constitutions. Yet we have also observed a historical trend away from pure parliamentary sovereignty, and toward more accountability institutions.

Will the movement toward accountability and transparency continue? It seems as if there are contradictory tendencies in this regard. On the one hand, formal institutional structures of law-making are more transparent than ever before, thanks in part to technological developments. Yet some commentators have noted that there is an expanding zone of legal 'grey holes' in which the law and its institutions do not reach. The 'dual state' noted by Ernst Fraenkel many decades ago seems to be returning in an era of global (counter-) terrorism. The zone of exception has always posed conceptual challenges to constitutional government, and that is likely to continue, even as the zone of ordinary politics is effectively subjected to constitutional constraint. The relative size of these two zones is in part within the control of judges whose job is to define their own jurisdiction and to calibrate the level of scrutiny of government practices. This level rises and falls within countries and across time. It has been argued that judges are structurally unable to discipline the national security apparatus in times of emergency, but that the level of scrutiny increases as the urgency fades. There is evidence on both sides of this question, but in recent years we have observed moments of great deference as well as moments of judicial constraint of executive behaviour in wartime. It is probable that the dynamic here is a long term pattern of calibrating the pendulum, with judicial activism leading to counter-pressures on courts to back off. Either way, the very fact that courts are at the centre of this inquiry is evidence of one of the great trends of recent decades, the judicialisation of public policies. Constitutional discourse is at the centre of this trend, as judges have used constitutional jurisdiction to expand their reach and authority.

Judicialisation has had a number of causes, but is perhaps most directly related to political structure. Courts are becoming more powerful in every jurisdiction and at the international level, but their ultimate level of power is determined by their ability to remain insulated from political authority. When that authority is divided, courts tend to have a greater role; when concentrated they tend to have a lesser role. One must predict that, notwithstanding local instances of 'de-judicialisation', globalisation will force more and more use of judges as paradigmatic third party dispute resolvers. This is largely structural and so the trend toward the expansion of judicial power will continue. Constitutional adjudication is likely to be a part of this mix; but regardless, one must be bullish on the overall future of law, the theme of this project.

Judiciaries are just one example of a broader trend toward the deployment of technical expertise. We observe parallel developments in such fields as accounting, financial monitoring, and economic policy, in which knowledge and authority are sources of power. Epistemic communities and forms of knowledge are driving forces behind the secular pressures toward independent regulatory agencies, central banks, boards of audits and environmental commissions. These communities tend to communicate internally using informal channels, inaccessible to outsiders to some extent. Yet technocracy always struggles for legitimacy. There are countervailing pressures for democratic control and we will likely observe continued swings of the pendulum between democracy and technocracy for many years to come. These will accelerate as the locus of regulatory power is increasingly transnational, which is seen as presumptively illegitimate by locally entrenched actors.

5. Conclusion

In sum, the *de jure* constitution is produced, increasingly, through norms whose source is outside the nation-state, and in a process in which international actors seek to have influence. It is implemented by transnational networks of regulatory technocrats and international actors, either through a formal agreement or through entrepreneurial productions of global norms and standards. The *de jure* constitution may become a site of resistance to these transnational pressures, siding with democracy against transnational technocracy (recent decisions by the German Constitutional Court, calling into question continued European integration, may provide illustration for this). Indeed, such resistance might be used strategically by local actors to gain leverage in transnational negotiations over the content of standards. Saying that one's hands are tied by a national constitution is certainly a legitimate strategy of empowerment on the international plane. Regardless of these strategic motives, we will observe constitutional restraints on globalisation in the name of a rump sovereignty that will in fact speak to local conceptions of the good. The formal constitution is thus a site of accommodation between globally produced norms and local pressures for democratic control over policy.

One possible outcome of these developments may be that constitutions will lose their ability to serve as effective symbolic embodiments of national identity, binding diverse groups together into a new unity. If this is the case, people may look to more organic identities, such as linguistic and ethnic bonds, as their primary affiliations. This in turn would put pressure on constitutions. They will become, essentially, contractual agreements between groups that come to a kind of accommodation. But the accommodation may involve division of the political spoils rather than articulation of higher principles. In short, constitutions may become mere deals, rather than legitimating sources of authority.

We have argued that constitutions will be less enduring and more amenable to change. We have also argued that their purpose will be less noble, not so much articulating a higher set of aspirations to bring together diverse groups into a single nation, as much as serving as deals to hold them together. These features suggest a degrading of constitutional documents from their nineteenth century image as embodiments of the nation. They will instead look more like statutes or contracts, designed to achieve instrumental purposes, albeit in a global vocabulary. They will be more detailed, more flexible, and perhaps more fragile. They will be sites of a large struggle between technocracy and democracy, in which constitutional judges are likely to find themselves in a mediating role.

2.2

The Future of Parliamentary Accountability in Europe

Philipp Kiiver*

This Think Piece sketches a few perspectives for the future development of parliamentary accountability within the European Union, taking into account both the European Parliament and the national parliaments. Based on past experiences and its current interests, the European Parliament is likely to push for a further uniformisation of its own election system and to claim additional weight *vis-à-vis* the Commission and the Council but also in the oversight of executive agencies. It is, however, unlikely that any of this will lead to any enhanced connection with the citizens, especially since government-opposition dynamics are lacking and since the European Parliament's tested strategy to gain strength with respect to the other institutions is exactly the avoidance of such dynamics. The national parliaments, meanwhile, have adapted their procedures to the challenges of European integration and some new developments are likely to arise from their use of the subsidiarity review of EU legislative proposals, but chances are that by and large their adaptation process is over. It may in fact be expected that fresh impulses for the enforcement of national democratic safeguards will increasingly come from rather less obvious actors, namely senates (who are often much more active in scrutinising EU action than lower chambers) and courts (who, by insisting on parliamentary involvement in EU matters, can give parliaments an additional boost). Unexpected events, in particular financial, migration and/or environmental crises, may accelerate European integration along existing trajectories; in case of a breakup of the Union, though, national parliaments will, all else being equal, continue to be the cornerstones of democratic governance in the states that they are now, while the European Parliament will surely not be the institution that is missed most.

* **Philipp Kiiver** is Associate Professor of European and Comparative Constitutional Law at Maastricht University.

1. Introduction

We all know that European governance defies classical constitutional notions that might be inherited from nation-states and traditional international organisations. This is particularly true of linear principal-agent relations between legislature and executive, or between Member States and the EU. Thus, the familiar setup of political parties contesting parliamentary elections with a view to forming or joining a government simply does not get replicated at the European level. Neither are the dynamics of European elections shaped by the logic of government and opposition, nor is there an executive that might be sufficiently comparable with a national cabinet and its supporting bureaucracy. At the same time, it would be an illusion to believe that parliamentary representation is neatly upheld just because national governments are each accountable to their own national parliaments. Article 10(2) EU as consolidated by the Lisbon Treaty may proclaim that representative democracy is maintained directly through European and indirectly through national parliamentary elections,[1] but in the light of empirical reality, this formula appears true only in a highly formal sense. It may well be that the principles of a parliamentary system are being eroded even in the Member States, or that there may never have been anything like a golden era of parliamentarism in the first place. Yet the appeal of the parliamentary system (and its model of delegation of power) remains strong as a constitutional blueprint. Voters delegate power to parliament, which in turn delegates power to the executive, which in turn delegates power to civil servants; each principal in the chain holds his agents accountable for their actions. It is with a view to meeting this ideal that both the European Parliament and national parliaments have taken up the challenge of preserving parliamentarism in the hostile reality of European integration. Governments

[1] Consolidated version of the Treaty on European Union as amended by the Treaty of Lisbon, 1 December 2009, Article 10, para. 2: "Citizens are directly represented at Union level in the European Parliament. Member States are represented in the European Council by their Heads of State or Government and in the Council by their governments, themselves democratically accountable either to their national Parliaments, or to their citizens", available at http://eur-lex.europa.eu/LexUriServ/LexUriServ.do?uri=OJ:C:2010:083:0013:0046:EN:PDF, last accessed 29 March 2011. The Article had featured already in the Constitutional Treaty. See Treaty establishing a Constitution for Europe, 16 December 2004, Article I – 46, available at http://eur-lex.europa.eu/LexUriServ/LexUriServ.do?uri=OJ:C:2004:310:0011:0040:EN:PDF, last accessed 29 March 2011.

too are hoping to stabilise the system by introducing familiar elements of parliamentarism, or at least parliamentary involvement, for example by adopting proclamations like the Article 10 (2) EU referred to above.

2. The European Parliament

The European Parliament's strategy for democratising the EU may be summarised in the claim for a more robust status and for more powers: first the insistence on being directly elected, then greater powers of co-legislation and more recently and increasingly, of involvement in delegated legislation and of oversight over the proliferating European agencies. Also its grilling of nominees for Commission posts, especially since the 2004 appointments, seem to have become a recurring opportunity to flex some muscle. And yet it is abundantly clear that a stronger European Parliament does not directly translate into a more democratic Union; it does not even result in a higher voter turnout. That is not to say that beefed-up checks and balances are not welcome in the European institutional landscape, certainly in the opaque area of the execution of law. This only means that transnational parliamentarism is in no position to promise the same societal effects that are promised by domestic parliamentary politics. That said, if we consider the accumulation of weight with the European Parliament as a more or less linear trajectory, then it should be feasible to anticipate the next logical steps.

2.1. The Electoral System

As regards the European election system, we need to consider the two most important milestones so far. First, there was a move away from indirect elections, where the European Parliament consisted of members of national parliaments, to direct elections as introduced in the 1970s. Second, in 2002 the Council stipulated that European elections should be based on the principle of proportional representation in all Member States. The election rules nevertheless still differ per Member State, for instance between list systems and the single transferable vote systems and in the application of a minimum threshold. In the light of the above, the logical reform to aim at would be to streamline the voting process. This would mean:

- holding the elections on one day Europe-wide;

- banning Member States from announcing results prematurely; and
- pushing for a uniform model of proportional representation.

The existing overrepresentation of small Member States still shows derogation from the 'one person one vote' principle. In its 2009 Lisbon ruling, the German Constitutional Court had criticised the European elections in this respect. The establishment of the entire EU territory, however, rather than the individual Member States, as the decisive constituency, will probably still remain a distant scenario even in 20 years time. In fact, unitary nation-states do not always adhere to strict electoral equality and choose, for example, to over-represent the rural vote or to balance majoritarian democracy with an upper chamber.

2.2. Co-Legislation and Oversight

The most obvious trajectory of a strengthening of the European Parliament is the quest for co-decision across the board. Very few areas remain excluded from co-decision, and they can, under the Lisbon Treaty, actually be brought under co-decision even without an ordinary Treaty amendment. And external relations, even though they are not legislative in nature, will remain the great prize as an area where the European Parliament would seek co-equality with the Council. Success on that front will probably be a matter of practice rather than law, though, and the European Parliament's firm stance on human rights and (at least initially) on data protection does look promising. For even if we leave aside democratic properties for a moment, purely from a point of view of accountability, transparency and checks and balances, oversight by the European Parliament should remain desirable. This applies in particular to the execution of laws. Within the next decades we should seek to arrive at a common framework for oversight by the European Parliament over all European agencies, including standard rules on creation and dissolution, appointment and dismissal of board members, accountability and budgetary control.

2.3. Connecting with the Citizens

No matter how much power it accumulates, the most pressing challenge for the European Parliament is not to gain more powers as such but to connect with the citizens in the process. Perversely, success in becoming recognisable to the citizens might undermine success in gaining clout.

One issue concerns the absence of party-political competition. It is hard enough to identify one-size-fits-all issues that might galvanise voters across the continent, issues that should at the same time not polarise them into 'pro-EU' or 'anti-EU' camps. And even if that were achieved, it might still be smarter for party groups to maximise their seat numbers by catering to different Member State audiences by appealing to different, tailor-made issues. Furthermore, even though grand coalitions are known to suffocate parliamentary culture, the grand coalition between left and right that traditionally governs the European Parliament is a highly effective means to confront potentially divided governments in the Council of Ministers. Finally, the absence of a link between the European Parliament and the Commission as it exists between government party groups and the cabinet in national systems might be a crucial element in the European Parliament's strength. While it neutralises any government-opposition dynamics, it also rids MEPs of party constraints and whips, and avoids automatically turning the parliamentary majority into loyal supporters of the executive. That is, after all, something that in the Member States is known to contribute to a loss of parliamentary independence.

3. The National Parliaments

The parliaments of the Member States find themselves in a situation that is utterly schizophrenic. It is easy to depict them as legislators who have signed away their powers by ratifying European Treaties, and who have 'abdicated' their oversight functions over their governments in European affairs, thus contributing to the general democratic deficit. Yet we should also be aware that government parties in parliament are, as always, trapped between two task: a task to scrutinise the executive and a task to support the cabinet. Opposition groups, meanwhile, may find it more sensible to invest time and resources in domestic debates where results will be immediate and not subject to subsequent compromise-building in Brussels. Even where will to follow the EU policy process more closely does exist, national parliamentarians find themselves confronted with a machinery which requires vast information resources and whose pace and agenda are set externally.

In spite of these constraints, national parliaments have been adapting their institutions and procedures to the specific requirements of European oversight. Methods include scrutiny reserves, *i.e.*, rules that bar ministers from agreeing to EU measures while their national parliament is still considering the proposal; mandating procedures whereby parliament and ministers agree on negotiation tactics before Council meetings; and assent procedures whereby ministers may only vote 'yes' after parliament has explicitly agreed with the proposal. In addition, the Lisbon Treaty (in fact already the Constitutional Treaty) seeks to involve parliaments by inviting them to send objections if they find that EU legislative proposals violate the principle of subsidiarity.

It is, however, distinctly possible that this arsenal of possible parliamentary tools is now more or less complete, and that parliamentary behaviour has been adapted as far as it could be. In other words, this may be as good as it gets.[2] Some subtle developments may be expected from subsidiarity review, but we may above all expect greater relevance for rather more unconventional actors in this context: courts and senates.

3.1. Subsidiarity Review

It is very likely that the subsidiarity review mechanism, also called the 'early warning system', will be more relevant as a catalyst for national parliamentary activity than as a step in the legislative process. The reason is, first, that different parliaments and chambers find different things interesting to consider and to complain about. The Commission has been keeping track of incoming letters from national parliaments since 2006, and few EU legislative proposals receive more than three letters from national parliaments or chambers. The only cases where around 30 of them respond to the same proposal are when COSAC, an inter-parliamentary conference, has selected items for a concerted effort. And even then reactions are quite diverse, not least because it is still utterly unclear how the principle of subsidiarity should actually be defined and applied. Some parliaments or chambers consider legality and proportionality next to subsidiarity, some parliaments do not pay attention to the categories at all but submit elaborate reports proposing concrete amendments, while some parliaments choose not to participate in the dialogue over legislative proposals at all and instead focus on white papers and green papers, which is where they might still make a difference.

2 Special thanks to Tapio Raunio for bringing up this rather sobering prospect.

The actual impact of the procedure may be threefold. First, opinions from parliaments, especially lower chambers, may herald the positions to be taken by the respective governments in the Council, and are thus part of the run-up to inter-ministerial bargaining. That is either because parliament will instruct the minister to negotiate along the same lines, or because the cabinet had suggested certain points to be included in the parliamentary motion in the first place, or because the views of the cabinet and its majority in the lower chamber tend to coincide anyway. Second, subsidiarity review might galvanise parliamentary scrutiny that is not particularly subsidiarity-related, simply because it raises Euro-awareness. Third, concerted subsidiarity review via COSAC might press the Commission to prepare a more elaborate justification of its proposals. The most likely violation of subsidiarity is, after all, not a substantive breach but a formal breach, namely where insufficient reasons are stated and the principle is thus violated by default. All that is rather more subtle, and harder to detect empirically than a neatly regulated involvement of parliaments as a step in the co-decision procedure.[3]

3.2. Agents for Change: Courts

There are cases where enhanced parliamentary oversight in European affairs has actually been claimed by the affected parliaments themselves. Treaty ratification and EU accession, if it requires parliamentary approval, especially if supermajorities apply, are the most significant opportunities where additional rights may be asserted. Thus, the insertion of Article 23 of the German Basic Law, which *inter alia* lays down principles of the involvement of the federal legislature in the government's EU policy, has been secured in the context of the ratification process for the Maastricht Treaty. The Austrian rule on giving Brussels-bound ministers voting instructions has been laid down to make sure the parliament, including opposition parties, approve of accession to the EU. At the same time, we see that it is not always parliaments themselves who assert their power, and that a sharpening of oversight is demanded, stimulated or imposed from the outside. If parliamentary oversight rules and practice stay more

---

3 For a fine analysis of the early warning system see Philipp Kiiver, "The Early Warning System for the Principle of Subsidiarity: The National Parliament as a Conseil d'Etat for Europe", in *European Law Review*, 2011, vol. 36, no. 1, pp. 98-108.

or less stable, it may very well be that incidental judicial interventions will do more to promote scrutiny than parliamentary motions ever could.

An early example of a court imposing recourse to a procedure that secures national democratic (if not parliamentary) participation in a major European decision is the *Crotty* ruling of the Irish Supreme Court. In it, the Court made the Irish ratification of the Single European Act subject to a constitutional change and thus a referendum. The need for a referendum on the Treaty of Lisbon in 2008, and again in 2009, was based on *Crotty* as well.

The most famous court ruling making certain EU decisions subject to prior domestic legislative approval was the German Constitutional Court's 2009 judgment on the constitutionality of the Lisbon Treaty. The *Lisbon* judgment of course contained a lengthy lecture on the constitutional relationship between the EU and the Member States, which is what drew most academic attention. Yet the operative part of the judgment also contained concrete injunctions designed to make the application of a number of Treaty provisions dependent on legislative ratification, giving the *Bundestag* and, where appropriate, the *Bundesrat*, a veto over Germany's participation in these EU decisions.[4] Effectively, this means that it took a court to insist on rights of the legislature that the legislature should have insisted on itself. In addition, the Constitutional Court reminded parliament that it should maintain day-to-day oversight as well, something that the Court had already said in the *Maastricht* judgment.

The other Member States did not consider these clauses (notably simplified treaty amendment and the flexibility clause) to require separate ratification each time they are to be applied: one initial ratification of the Treaty as a package should legitimise the further use of all its contents. That was, in any event, the attitude taken by the French Constitutional Council and the Czech Constitutional Court. It might however also be argued that here the German judges have spotted potentially unpredictable Treaty provisions which the institutions of other Member States have failed to notice. German case-law may set a precedent, so that also in

[4] This aspect of the Lisbon judgment received far too little attention in the literature. For a refreshing exception, see Philipp Kiiver, "The Lisbon Judgment of the German Constitutional Court: A Court-Ordered Strengthening of the National Legislature in the European Union", in *European Law Journal*, 2010, vol. 16, no. 5, pp. 578-588.

other Member States, if the necessary recourse to courts is available, interested parties may challenge their government's actual or planned approval of EU measures on the ground that full parliamentary approval must first be sought. Interested parties may be opposition groups in parliament, like the Left Party in the German *Lisbon* case, but also professional complainants like Mr Brunner who challenged the Maastricht Treaty as a private citizen. In the absence of treaty amendments in the next decade, the most probable target for judicial examination is the flexibility clause of Article 352 TFEU, the beefed-up successor of Article 308 EC, which at least the German Constitutional Court considered unpredictable enough to require domestic ratification as if its exercise amounted to a treaty amendment clause. The most probable claim would then indeed be that a proposed or adopted application of Article 352 TFEU goes *ultra vires*, that the government should be barred from supporting it or that secondary legislation adopted on that basis must be rendered inapplicable in the relevant Member State.

3.3. The Rise of the Senates

The term 'national parliaments' can be deceiving in that many of the 27 EU Member States are actually bicameral.[5] We are thus confronted with upper chambers who may, on the one hand, be considered a component part of the national parliament but which, on the other hand, are quite distinct from the lower chambers. Concretely, senates tend to be in one way or another inferior to the lower chamber. The cabinet does not owe its stability to senatorial support (Italy being the exception), and in most cases senates may be overruled in the legislative process (here the Netherlands is the exception). Also, senates are often elected indirectly rather than directly (the House of Lords is the one upper chamber in Europe to be entirely unelected). The German *Bundesrat* is an inter-executive body comprising regional governments and is manifestly un-parliamentary in nature, but nevertheless it conventionally falls under the scope of being part of the national parliament, at least for EU purposes.

And yet we see that senates often tend to be much more active in the field of European scrutiny than lower chambers. In the Netherlands, the senatorial First Chamber frequently takes the lead. The most likely

5 And Belgium considers itself even multicameral as its regional and community assemblies are, in their field of competence, co-equal with the federal parliament.

reasons for this are that Dutch senators are part-time politicians, typically semi-retired, who simply have more time for in-depth scrutiny of subjects that do not promise immediate electoral gain. As they are less focused on (direct) re-election, they tend to enjoy travelling to other parliaments or to inter-parliamentary assemblies, whereas to members of the hectic lower chamber each day spent abroad is a precious day of national politics missed. Finally, the Dutch First Chamber struggles with finding legitimacy to justify its very existence, so that European scrutiny is a welcome and important cause in which it may specialise. This should be true for more senates in non-federal systems, where there is a much less self-evident need for bicameralism.

As regards European scrutiny, we see similar developments in other senates as well. Concerning opinions sent by national chambers to the Commission in response to EU legislative proposals and other documents, we observe that the House of Lords, the German *Bundesrat* and the French and Czech Senate, for instance, are much more active than the respective lower chambers.

Assuming that the trend continues, it will often be senates, rather than what we might call the parliaments proper (*i.e.*, the lower chambers) that will take upon themselves a significant role in subjecting European decision-making to parliamentary scrutiny. This should underline that parliamentary scrutiny can be, and probably should be, divorced from the notion of democratic legitimacy. If an unelected or indirectly elected upper chamber can carry out scrutiny then the added value clearly does not lie in added democratic content. It rather lies in the presence of a diligent watchdog at the national level, elected or otherwise, who may keep the European institutions on their toes and force them, for instance, to justify their actions more thoroughly than they might otherwise. Senates might be better placed to do this as they are less bound by party discipline tying them to the cabinet.

4. The Known Unknowns

What if these more or less linear extrapolations were to be disrupted by a severe crisis? The financial crisis has shown that the eurozone and the European Union as a whole can come under critical strain as it forces governments to make tough decisions about intra-European solidarity and how far they really wish to proceed with political integration. Other crises may result from environmental catastrophes and migration, such as those witnessed in the wake of the uprisings in the Arab world. Indeed, such combinations of crises sometimes appear to force a choice upon the Union between acceleration and failure. As motorcyclists can attest, acceleration is in fact often preferred over braking which seems safer but is in fact more dangerous. It is however still unlikely that acceleration in European integration would mean the hour of the European Parliament whereas a failure, such as disengagement from integration or a break-up of the Union, would restore national parliaments in their old glory. The European Parliament has not fostered significantly increased citizen engagement when it gained more power in the past, and the only scenario in which it could achieve that would arguably be a full federalisation of Europe including the core areas of sovereign statehood: coercion under criminal law, taxes and conscription. Meanwhile, national parliaments would continue to be recognisable forums in the nation-states, whether the Union breaks up or not. Since only around 20% of national laws seem to have an EU background (no, not 80%), the repatriation of competences might not even be noticed much, and parliaments are anyway not there to actually make policy – they primarily legitimise policy. What would be noticed, in case of a break-up, are the vanished benefits of European integration: potentially restored trade barriers leading to higher prices and poorer competitiveness; frustrating limitations on policy effects at national borders; and the potentially increased likelihood of introspection, provincialism, nationalism and war in Europe. National parliaments are cornerstones of national constitutions with or without an EU. The European Parliament, alas, is just another European institution, and if the Union were to disappear, the European Parliament would not be most missed part.

5. Outlook

Even in the Member States, parliamentarism is not the only feature of the constitution that keeps the political system stable and legitimate. Yet, as a democratic ingredient it is essential. The European Union will see continued efforts to replicate at least some of the features of domestic parliamentarism as well as efforts to extend the reach of national parliamentary dynamics into European affairs. At the same time, we should be realistic about the prospects of these efforts considering the incentives and institutional logic involved. Thus, it is realistic to assume that the European Parliament will continue to strengthen its clout, such as in controlling the Commission, in standing up to the Council and in monitoring European agencies. However it is also realistic to predict that this will not lead to any detectable reduction of the democratic deficit or increased voter participation. Meanwhile, it is distinctly possible that national parliamentary behaviour in European scrutiny has already reached a steady state. After intensification of oversight in the 1990s this may be 'as good as it gets'. Novel mechanisms such as the review of EU legislative proposals against the principle of subsidiarity may only have subtle effects on Euro-awareness and on the dynamics through which input to the EU policy process is generated. The good news is that if the current situation is imperfect but sustainable, it will remain imperfect but sustainable: European integration may continue to deliver positive effects without causing its own foundations to collapse.

2.3

Global Problems in Domestic Courts

Ralf Michaels[*]

We face an increasing number of problems that are essentially global in nature because they affect the world in its entirety: global cartels, climate change, crimes against humanity; to name a few. These problems require world courts, yet world courts in the institutional sense are largely lacking. Hence, domestic courts must function, effectively, as world courts. Given the unlikelihood of effective world courts in the future, our challenge is to establish under what conditions domestic courts can play this role of world courts effectively and legitimately.

1. Introduction

Lawyers are bad at predicting the future; they have enough work on their hands with the present. Despite frequent claims that law is proactive – it guides conduct – its substance is almost always reactive, a reaction to recognised social problems. The law lags. Moreover, the acceleration of all aspects of life (one of the key characteristics of globalisation) has led to a situation in which deliberative responses by lawmakers almost always come, if not too late, then at least with a considerable delay. This has long been true for legislators and courts (and has led to the turn to the executive in lawmaking). Moreover, it is true, increasingly, for executive action, too.

This inability of lawyers (and of the law) to predict the future is well-known, but it is neither trivial nor easy to overcome. It has a twofold implication for attempts to answer the question as to the biggest challenges for the law in the near future. First, although substantive problems are always new and often unpredictable, structural problems are relatively constant. We may not know what substantive questions the law will have to resolve in the future, but we can guess what structure many of these problems will have. In short, they will be global problems that transcend national boundaries (though in a particular way that I will discuss later). Second, to prepare the law for the future, we should first

[*] **Ralf Michaels** is Professor of Law at Duke University.

make sure it matches the requirements of the present. We do not know for sure what globalisation will bring in the future, but we do know that the law is structurally ill-equipped even for its present. Presuming that globalisation will continue, a law more adequately prepared for globalisation would be desirable in the future.

The biggest structural challenge for current law is well-known (and actually expressed in the background note) but not well understood: more and more problems are global, while our institutions are not. Although we have been aware of this challenge for considerable time, our responses have so far been insufficient. Supranational institutions, as one solution, will not be able to deal with all of these problems to a sufficient degree. Global legal unification will also remain incomplete. Networks are a fascinating, but at the same time slightly elusive, new concept. As a consequence, what we will be left with, for a large portion of global problems, is fragmentation, ensuring the need for domestic institutions, especially courts, to deal with these global problems. Where necessary, they have to do so in a unilateral fashion.

Fragmentation may be considered undesirable (though this is not certain), but to the extent we cannot overcome it we need to make the best of it. What we need are three things. First, we need a better understanding of what global problems actually are, how they differ from other problems that may or may not also be related to globalisation, and how they challenge current concepts of law. Second, we need a better understanding of the role that domestic institutions, in particular courts, can play in response to such problems, and thereby for the global legal system at large. Third, we need better criteria, both legal and political, for when and how domestic courts can perform these roles. In this brief position paper (based on a book I am currently working on) I will address these three aspects.

2. Global Problems

Globalisation creates a lot of new problems for the law, but many of those do not require paradigmatically new thinking because they fit in the traditional disciplines of either domestic law or international law.

Many problems are domestic in nature, which means that domestic law and institutions can deal with them in the same way as before. Recently, they have been helped more and more by comparative law –

they have realised that other countries face similar problems, and therefore may provide valuable inspiration – but this alone does not create any paradigmatic changes.

Other problems are international in nature: they concern various countries and/or their relations among each other. Much trade law is in this category. More perhaps than domestic problems, such international problems create new challenges to the law, because international law, the typical response to such problems, today covers a far broader array of issues than it did before. Again, however, what this requires is an extension of existing paradigms, not a paradigmatic change.

A paradigmatic change will be required, by contrast, for what I call global problems. Global problems are characterised by two qualities. First, they concern the world at large, not just one country or one region, or the relations between only a few countries (this does not mean that they necessarily affect everyone similarly.) Second, they cannot be separated into different sub-problems that can be solved individually. Rather, an adequate response has an effect on the whole problem.

We can distinguish different kinds of global problems, according to what makes them global (although the boundaries between these categories are not sharp, distinguishing them helps the analysis). Some problems are global by nature. Climate change may be a prime example. It is a problem that is global by nature not because the problem has been created by nature (in all likelihood it has not) but instead because the nature of our climate makes it so that solutions can never be only local. Other problems are global by design. Liability for internet defamation is a prime example here: the internet has been designed so as to be globally accessible, with the result that, without special software, content becomes accessible from anywhere. Here the global character of the problem is a consequence of the design of the internet – a redesign of the internet or its infrastructure, including software, can change the problem's character. Some problems, finally, are global by definition. Crimes against humanity, for example, are global because we decide to conceptualise them as such, as directed not against the individual victims (who may well be defined by territory or nationality) but instead against a global category par excellence, namely humanity at large.

3. A Global Problem by Nature: Global Markets

One type of global problems by nature concerns global markets. A good example from the law of antitrust is the *Empagran* decision of the US Supreme Court, rendered in 2004. Several producers of certain vitamin products, most of them European, had fixed prices worldwide and made billions of dollars in profits. The US plaintiffs sued in the US and received considerable payments under a settlement. The interesting case was brought not by US consumers but by consumers from countries like Ecuador and the Ukraine, who had also suffered injuries from inflated prices, and who sued the cartel members in a US court in a worldwide class action. Foreign plaintiffs, foreign defendants, and foreign markets – should US courts have jurisdiction?

Worldwide price fixing is a global problem by nature, because, given the current conditions of global markets, it cannot be territorially confined or split up. Where we have truly worldwide markets, participants in cartels must necessarily fix prices worldwide because if they fix them only for specific national markets, the consumers in those markets will purchase their products elsewhere, and this arbitrage will make the cartel ineffective. In this sense, the cartel participants in the *Empagran* case did not, nor in fact could they fix prices individually for individual markets; they raised prices globally because the global character of the market in vitamin products forced them to do so.

Much of the debate concerned the question whether the US had any interest, thus asking essentially whether the global cartel was a domestic problem or not. The defendants pointed out that the U.S. had no interest in regulating foreign markets. The plaintiffs on the other hand argued that US consumers would benefit from these claims by foreign plaintiffs, because these claims would enhance the deterrent effect on the cartel, which would otherwise remain undeterred. Defendants focused on the specific plaintiffs with their injuries; plaintiffs focused on the whole event of the cartel and its effects on the US economy. Both agreed, however, that the connection to the US was crucial, and both ignored the rest of the world. This was inadequate. After all, some countries such as Canada and Japan, as well as the European Commission – had levied high fines on the cartel. With regard to these countries, there was obviously additional deterrence for cartels. Other countries, by contrast, had not.

Along these lines, Europeans invoked international law and relations and submitted *amicus curiae* briefs in the litigation, arguing in essence that jurisdiction of US courts would interfere with their sovereign interests – even though all countries agree that, in substance, price fixing is illegal. They argued that each country should deal with the effects on its own local markets and that private suits to enforce antitrust laws were against European culture. The Supreme Court essentially followed these complaints (although with a twist to be mentioned later) and rejected the claim. The problem with this argument is that it presumes that the cartel can be divided into territorial subparts, and this seems doubtful. Europeans point out that the task of US antitrust law is to protect US consumers, not to regulate foreign markets. But what if the protection of US consumers requires the regulation of foreign markets? Worse, what if there is no difference between foreign and local markets at all, because we have only one global market in vitamins? Moreover, the European countries that submitted *amicus curiae* briefs argued successfully against US hegemonialism. However the result of their intervention was that plaintiffs from Ecuador and Ukraine were unable to recover their damages anywhere. One could well describe this as a different kind of hegemonialism, this time over developing countries that do not have the infrastructure to prosecute global cartels and that rely on the first world to do this for them.

In the end, both approaches appear inadequate, because they do not capture the global character of the problem. The domestic approach must fail because it ignores the degree to which the cartel has effects outside the United States. The international approach must fail because it requires separability of the cartel: the United States can leave the regulation of the European part of the cartel to Europeans, only if such a separate part exists; this however, is doubtful.

4. A Global Problem by Design: The Review of UN Security Council Resolutions

An example of global problems by design is the review of resolutions by the UN Security Council. Such problems are global by design because their global nature follows from the design of the Security Council as a global institution. Such resolutions create international law, so the Security Council can be understood as a kind of global legislator. However, judicial review of its decisions is not provided under international law. Early ideas to give review competence to the International Court of Justice (the most obvious candidate) were rejected by some of the permanent members of the Security Council.

The consequence is that such a review can only be provided, if at all, by domestic courts. This became urgent especially with resolutions that froze assets of individuals assembled on a list of presumed financiers of international terrorism. Because these resolutions did not provide these individuals with recourse, some of them appealed instead to domestic courts in various countries, and to the Court of First Instance in the European Union (*Kadi*). The *Kadi* case is an example for both the potential and the conceptual limits of domestic courts when faced with this problem (for purposes of this analysis, the Court of First Instance and the European Court of Justice as an appellate court can be understood as quasi-domestic courts). The Court of First Instance effectively denied that domestic courts were competent to review resolutions of the Security Council, except implicitly. The European Court of Justice, by contrast, presumed that it was possible to review such resolutions insofar as they had been transposed into domestic law, thereby ignoring their supranational character. Both approaches map well on a distinction between the international law and a domestic law paradigm, but both seem similarly incapable of grasping the specifically global character of these resolutions. The opinion of the Advocate General came closest to a global approach when he spoke of a situation of legal pluralism between domestic, European and international law. What is lacking from his analysis as well as from most commentary on the decisions is a proper conceptualisation of the global legal system in which domestic courts act effectively as review courts.

5. A Global Problem by Definition: Human Rights Violations

An example of global problems by definition is human rights litigation. If a Nigerian woman living in Nigeria with her Nigerian husband is stoned to death because of alleged adultery with another Nigerian, this seems to be an affair entirely internal to Nigeria. Indeed, 'internal affair' is the exact codeword governments traditionally use to oppose any intervention by foreign journalists, politicians and courts. But of course we reject such claims in the human rights realm, and we do so with an argumentative trick. We change the victim's status from (local) citizen to (global) human. We turn the perpetrator from an enemy of the victim to an enemy of the world, a *hostis humani generis*. We raise crimes from the localised crime of murder to the globalised crime against humanity. Murder would have to be prosecuted according to the territorial laws. A crime against humanity on the other hand is by definition deterritorialised, simply because humanity transcends all territoriality, except (perhaps) that of the globe. The *colère global*, to paraphrase Durkheim, the global outrage over a crime, turns a territorial event into a world event.

One of the oldest federal statutes, the so-called Alien Tort Statute, gives federal courts jurisdiction for "a tort only in violation of international law". This statute lay dormant for nearly 200 years until it was revived in 1980, and turned into a main jurisdictional basis for human rights violations. The statute gives something akin to universal jurisdiction, which means that human rights violations from all across the globe can be carried before US courts and are in fact carried there. Universal criminal jurisdiction over human rights violations is currently much discussed, and often favourably – although the International Criminal Court is often preferred as a venue, domestic courts are considered to play a role, too. The American Alien Tort Statute is special, however. First, it applies to private plaintiffs, so plaintiff lawyers rather than state attorneys decide about prosecution. Second, it has been applied not only against government officials (who are frequently immune from lawsuits), but also against corporations that collaborate with governments. Thereby, many multinational companies have been turned into potential defendants against such claims.

Not surprisingly, this basis of jurisdiction is now under severe criticism both in the U.S. and elsewhere. Human rights violations taking place elsewhere are not domestic US problems and they do not create significant US interests (beyond such secondary interests like the interest in being a good citizen of the world). It would seem easier to find international law solutions, but only *prima facie*. First, the country that is primarily interested, is often the country whose government committed or at least took part in the human rights violation. Second, and perhaps even more importantly, international law solutions tend to leave decisions over whether human rights violations are adjudicated to governments, and governments, for reasons of international relations, will often be unwilling to inquire.

6. The Role of Domestic Courts

Local events can be dealt with by domestic courts in accordance with domestic law; international events as events between nations can be dealt with by international courts, established by and under international laws. Global problems, however, cannot be dealt with adequately by domestic or international law, at least in the ways in which we traditionally understand them.

One response to global problems has been the creation of truly global courts, the International Criminal Court being a prime example. Even if we assume such institutions to be normatively desirable (and doubts exist on this, particularly in the United States), it seems clear now that, at least in the short run, we will not have a sufficient number of such institutions. International criminal law is a good example: the vast majority of cases under the jurisdiction of the ICC are dealt with (if at all) by domestic courts.

A second response has been closer cooperation – sometimes called networks – between courts. Such networks can, to some extent, substitute for true global courts by bringing everyone in. At the same time, networks face high coordination problems once the number of involved courts becomes great – as will often be the case with global problems. Moreover, networks fail where different countries differ either in their substantive perspectives or, perhaps even more often, in their desire to be active (a free-rider problem).

This suggests that much of globalisation will continue to be handled, quasi-unilaterally, by domestic institutions, in particular domestic courts. I say continue, because domestic courts already deal with such problems. Frequently, however, they feel the need to deny the global character of these problems. The Supreme Court decision in the *Empagran* case shows this clearly. In holding for the defendants, the court assumed explicitly that the cartel's effects on the US were separate from the effects on foreign markets, but we know of course that these effects are not independent from each other. The court rested its decision on facts that are demonstrably wrong, but the court had to do so in order to conceptualise the problem of global cartels. Only the fictitious compartmentalisation of global markets made it possible to reconcile global cartels with traditional approaches to jurisdiction. Obviously this does not make the problem go away, and indeed the problem may well reach the Supreme Court again.

The reason for such redefinition of the global character is our uneasiness with unilateral extraterritorial adjudication. We have long rejected unilateral action by domestic courts as illegitimate, and we still feel it to be inferior to international agreement or adjudication by supranational courts. As a consequence, the main concern in unilateral adjudication has been devoted, usually, to constraining it. Given that such unilateral adjudication will, in the foreseeable future, remain the predominant legal response to globalisation, this is unsatisfactory. We will need a better theory of when and how such adjudication is possible.

If global problems require global courts, how can domestic courts play a role? Semantically, we must distinguish two very different aspects of 'global' that are often confounded. One is the institutional, or constitutional, aspect. In this sense a global court is a court that has been set up by the world, a court of the world. Of course the world in its entirety is unable to set up the court, which is why we have recourse to international treaties or the United Nations as a kind of second best. I call these courts international courts, because they are founded on international law. But there is another aspect of 'global' in world courts, and it concerns the scope of application, the 'reach' if you will, the jurisdiction. Here, a world court is a court for the world. This aspect is analytically different from the first one, though of course both may coincide. Thus the International Court of Justice is a world court also in this second sense; its jurisdiction is worldwide. However, the reach of domestic courts on the other hand can be global, too. If it is, these courts act as world courts.

7. Challenges

How can domestic courts adequately respond to these challenges? Short of actual solutions, this paper can list the areas in which we will require rethinking.

One area concerns the discipline that will have to bear much of the burden from these problems: conflict of laws. Conflict of laws, as traditionally understood, deals with relations between different legal systems and the localisation of problems in one of these systems. It determines the competent courts and the applicable law on the basis of connecting factors that connect a set of facts more closely to one country and its laws. For global problems, however, we are frequently faced with either universal or ubiquitous jurisdiction. Universal jurisdiction is jurisdiction that, in principle, every country's courts can exercise. Ubiquitous jurisdiction can be defined as jurisdiction that is based on factors that connect a problem to every country, for example accessibility of a website. Neither universal nor ubiquitous jurisdiction fit well in the traditional criteria, and we may have to develop new approaches. One example can be found in Article 6(3)(b) of the Rome II Regulation, which allows a court, under certain conditions, to apply its own law on unfair competition even to the claims of plaintiffs who purchased on other markets. Although the provision is far from perfect, some of the criticism it has received seems unjustified: if the provision does not fit well with traditional private international law, this may be a sign less of the provision's inadequacy and instead of the discipline's inadequacy.

Notably, extraterritoriality is not a helpful criterion to assess such adjudication. If global problems could be separated into territorial components, each court could adjudicate a neatly defined territorial space, and the problem of extraterritoriality should not occur. Global problems, by contrast cannot be so separated. Global cartels are global because they transcend boundaries and territories – price changes in one country necessitate price changes in other countries. Human rights violations are global precisely because we define them as such; we emphasise the deterritorialised interests of humanity at-large over the territorially confined interests of the specific victims or their perpetrators. In short, because world events are deterritorialised, they do not involve the territorial interests which would trigger complaints that territorial sovereignty is infringed. Without territoriality there is no extraterritoriality.

Another area concerns institutional requirements. Traditionally, domestic courts are expected to deal with domestic problems, either under their own law or under foreign law – they lack a global perspective. We have made progress towards such a perspective. For example, the increased use of comparative law shows an increasingly global awareness on the part of judges. However, more will be needed. We will need doctrines that detach the judicial task from the furthering of domestic political interests. We will need courts with an understanding of the implications their decisions have for governance – not just domestic or international, but global governance. What helps courts in this regard is their relative independence. After all, the legitimacy of courts lies not in their direct accountability to the electorate but in the quality of their decisions, if necessary, against political pressure.

This last point leads to a third challenge. Accountability to the electorate prevents the other branches of government – the executive and especially the legislature – from truly globalizing; in the end they are expected to protect the interests of their voters over those of others. This suggests that democratically made law on the national level can lack legitimacy on the global sphere. The traditional response to such lack of legitimacy is for courts to limit application of domestic law to areas for which the domestic lawmaker has both jurisdiction and an actual regulatory interest. This process is inadequate – it either leads to the application of a law that is, at least potentially, equally parochial, or to the dismissal of a claim for lack of regulatory interest of any concerned government. The alternative for courts will be to develop transnational law on their own, even in deviation from domestic rules of substantive law and of private international law.

2.4

The Increased Interconnection between International and National Law and the Need to Coordinate the Legislative Process in the Future

Hans Corell*

The need for a well functioning United Nations is one of the greatest challenges that lie ahead. A particular challenge in this connection is whether the UN Security Council will be able to shoulder its responsibility for the maintenance of international peace and security. To be able to do so, the members of the Council must realise the importance of a multilateral system under the rule of law and the specific role that they must play in this respect. Seen in this perspective, one of the determining factors for the future development will be the ability of leading politicians at the national level to realise that a multilateral rules-based international society is the only way ahead and that they have a critical role to play in the work towards this common goal. The key dilemma will be whether they will be able to play this role or, with respect to some leaders, if they even want to play this role.

The focus of this think piece will, however, not be on all these challenges but on a challenge common to them all, a question of an overarching nature that must be addressed. To establish and maintain a proper rules-based system it is necessary to develop a system in which the quality and the consistence of the norms can be ascertained. Hence the title: The Increased Interconnection between International and National Law and the Need to Coordinate the Legislative Process in the Future.

This major challenge is a common denominator in all efforts in the legislative field. And it is vital that persons at the policy level are made aware of this challenge and that it is not simply a technical matter.

---

* **Hans Corell** was Under-Secretary-General for Legal Affairs and the Legal Counsel of the United Nations from 1994 to 2004.

1. Introduction

To address the topic of the challenges to legal systems in a meaningful way, it is necessary to develop different scenarios. The reason is that the law, by definition, must respond to the need to regulate different phenomena in a society at any given time.

One way of looking at the future could be to use the collective security prism employed by the United Nations High-level Panel on Threats, Challenges and Change. The Panel defined six main clusters of threats in the near future: economic and social threats, including poverty, infectious diseases and environmental degradation; inter-state conflict; internal conflict, including civil war, genocide and other large-scale atrocities; nuclear, radiological, chemical and biological weapons; terrorism; and transnational organised crime.[1]

In the past, I have focused on some of these challenges. One such challenge that could be mentioned is the need to protect human rights in an atmosphere where they will come under stress induced by climate change in combination with population pressure. This links to the empowerment of women,[2] the connection between the protection of the environment and the rule of law,[3] and the need for a world free from nuclear weapons.[4]

---

1 Untied Nations General Assembly Fifty-Ninth Session Agenda Item 55: Follow-up to the Outcome of the Millennium Summit, 2 December 2004, UN Doc. A/59/565 available at http://www.un.org/secureworld/report.pdf, last accessed 16 February 2011.

2 Hans Corell, "Protecting Human Rights: The Role of the United Nations – Major Challenges", Address at the Human Rights Week 2010, organised by Amnesty International, Law Students' Network at Oslo University, 19 February 2010, available at http://www.havc.se/res/SelectedMaterial/20100219unandhumanrights.pdf, last accessed 16 February 2011.

3 Hans Corell, "The Right Climate for the Rule of Law", in *International Bar News*, April 2008, available at http://www.havc.se/res/SelectedMaterial/20080421corellright climateforrol1.pdf, last accessed 16 February 2011.

4 Hans Corell, "Is It Possible to Outlaw Nuclear Arms?", in *NOW IS THE TIME TO PROHIBIT NUCLEAR WEAPONS!*, A special edition of the journal of the Swedish section of International Physicians for the Prevention of Nuclear War. LÄKARE MOT KÄRNVAPEN 2010 # 120, pp. 6-9, available at http://slmk.org/wordpress/wp-content/uploads/2010/03/Lakare-mot-Karnvapen-120-ENG.pdf, last accessed 16 February 2011.

In view of the tensions that will be generated by climate change and its effects on the environment, combined with a rapidly growing world population, it is necessary to have an organisation that can offer a forum for dealing effectively with these and other questions related to international peace and security. The need for a well functioning United Nations is one of the greatest challenges that lie ahead.[5] A particular challenge is whether the UN Security Council will be able to shoulder its responsibility for the maintenance of international peace and security. To be able to do so, the members of the Council must realise the importance of a multilateral system under the rule of law and fulfil the specific role that they must play in this respect.[6]

Seen in this perspective, one of the determining factors for future developments will be the ability of leading politicians at the national level to realise that a multilateral rules-based international society is the only way ahead and that they have a critical role to play in the work towards this common goal. The key dilemma will be whether they will be able to play this role or, with respect to some leaders, if they even want to play this role. For politicians in democratic societies, the challenge will be to convince the electorate that this common goal must be the primary lodestar while at the same time they must be able to retain the support of their voters. The level of vulgarity in the political debate in some quarters in recent years is a great source of concern here.

Non-democratic societies present an even greater challenge to all of us. How do we convince the leaders of such societies to work towards this common goal when they realise that they are unlikely to remain in power if international law and in particular human rights law are respected in their countries?

The focus of this think piece will, however, not be on all these challenges but on a challenge common to them all, a question of an overarching nature that must be addressed. To establish and maintain a

---

5 Hans Corell, "Who Needs Reforming the Most – the UN or its Members?", in *Nordic Journal of International Law*, 2007, vol. 76, no. 2-3, pp. 265-279, available at http://www.havc.se/res/SelectedMaterial/20071108corellwhoneedsreforming.pdf, last accessed 16 February 2011.

6 Hans Corell, "Security Council Reform: Rule of Law More Important Than Additional Members", letter dated 10 December 2008 to the Governments of the Members of the United Nations, available at http://www.havc.se/res/SelectedMaterial/20081210corellllettertounmembers.pdf, last accessed 16 February 2011.

proper rules-based system it is necessary to develop a system in which the quality and the consistency of the norms can be ascertained, hence the title: *The Increased Interconnection between International and National Law and the Need to Coordinate the Legislative Process in the Future*.

Admittedly, the title does not ring with the grandeur that may be expected from someone discussing the law of the future. But the reality is that the subject matter is a major challenge. It is a common denominator in all efforts in the legislative field, and it is vital that people at the policy level are made aware of this challenge and that it is not simply a technical matter.

2. The Challenge

The challenge is rooted in the relationship between norms adopted at the national level and norms adopted at the international level. It also concerns the interrelation between norms in the latter category. In this context reference is often made to the 'proliferation' of international norms, both binding norms and so-called soft law.

I touched briefly on the topic at a Conference in Berlin in September 2006, organised by the Federal Foreign Office of Germany and the Hertie School of Government.[7] At the time, the International Law Commission (ILC) was studying the topic from the point of departure of the fragmentation of international law.[8] In September 2006, this author suggested that irrespective of the final outcome of that work, the matter raised would present a major challenge to the international community in the future. States should therefore already discuss, preferably in the context of the report of the ILC, how to deal with the phenomenon.

[7] Hans Corell, "International Law in Flux", in *14. Forum Globale Fragen: Völkerrecht im Wandel*, Auswärtiges Amt, Berlin, Bonifacius GmBH, Paderborn, 2006, pp. 101-110, available at http://www.havc.se/res/SelectedMaterial/20060908corellintllawinfluxfinal.pdf, last accessed 16 February 2011.

[8] Study Group of the International Law Commission, "Fragmentation of International Law: Difficulties Arising from the Diversification and Expansion of International Law", 2006, finalised by Martti Koskenniemi., UN docs. A/CN/.4/L.682 and A/CN/.4/L.682/Add.1.

Later in the same year, the work of the ILC Study Group was presented in the form of a report containing 42 conclusions.[9] The ILC took note of the conclusions and commended them to the attention of the General Assembly. It also requested that the analytical study finalised by the Chairman of the Study Group, Professor Martti Koskenniemi, be made available on the website of the Commission and also be published in its Yearbook.[10] On 4 December 2006, the General Assembly took note of the 42 conclusions of the Study Group together with the analytical study on which they were based.[11] The two documents constitute an important and extremely useful contribution to the understanding of how the international legal system works. A reading of them is highly recommended.

In this context, attention should be drawn to the following two paragraphs in the analytical study:

> 481. One aspect of globalization is the emergence of technically specialized cooperation networks with a global scope: trade, environment, human rights, diplomacy, communications, medicine, crime prevention, energy production, security, indigenous cooperation and so on – spheres of life and expert cooperation that transgress national boundaries and are difficult to regulate through traditional international law. National laws seem insufficient owing to the transnational nature of the networks while international law only inadequately takes account of their specialized objectives and needs.
>
> 487. But in addressing the problems at this level – conflicts as they arise – will mean that they are addressed in a formal and open-ended way, as matters of legal technique rather

[9] International Law Commission, "Report on the Work of its Fifty-Eighth Session", 2006, UN Doc. A/61/10, paras. 233-251, available at http://untreaty.un.org/ilc/reports/2006/2006report.htm , last accessed 16 February 2011.

[10] International Law Commission, 2006, para. 239, see *supra* note 9. Also see International Law Commission, "Conclusions of the Work of the Study Group on the Fragmentation of International Law: Difficulties Arising from the Diversification and Expansion of International Law", 2006, available at http://untreaty.un.org/ilc/texts/instruments/english/draft articles/1_9_2006.pdf, last accessed 16 February 2011. The study itself is now available at http://daccess-dds-ny.un.org/doc/UNDOC/LTD/G06/610/77/PDF/G0661077.pdf?OpenElement.

[11] UNGA resolution A/RES/61/34.

> than substantive (legal-political) preference. The report has, in a way, bought its acceptability by its substantive emptiness. Yet this 'formalism' is not without its own agenda. The very effort to canvass a coherent legal-professional technique on a fragmented world expresses the conviction that conflicts between specialized regimes may be overcome by law, even as the law may not go much further than require a willingness to listen to others, take their points of view into account and to find a reasoned resolution at the end. … If international law is needed as a structure for coordination and cooperation between (sovereign) States, it is no less needed in order to coordinate and organise the cooperation of (autonomous) rule-complexes and institutions.

The following two paragraphs in the report of the ILC are also of particular interest in this respect:[12]

> 249. The justification for the Commission's work on fragmentation has been in the fact that although fragmentation is inevitable, it is desirable to have a framework through which it may be assessed and managed in a legal-professional way. That framework is provided by [the Vienna Convention on the Law of Treaties of 1969 (VCLT)]. One aspect that unites practically all of the new regimes (and certainly all of the most important ones) is that they claim binding force from and are understood by the relevant actors to be covered by the law of treaties. This means that the VCLT already provides a unifying frame for these developments. As the organ that once prepared the VCLT, the Commission is in a privileged position to analyse international law's fragmentation from that perspective.
>
> 250. In order to do that, the Commission's Study Group held it useful to have regard to the wealth of techniques in the traditional law for dealing with tensions or conflicts between legal rules and principles. What is common to these techniques is that they seek to establish meaningful relationships between such rules and principles so as to determine how they should be used in any particular dispute or conflict. The following conclusions lay out some of the principles that should be taken account of when dealing with actual or potential conflicts between legal rules and principles.

---

12 International Law Commission, 2006, see *supra* note 9.

The first conclusion among the 42 that appear in the report of the Study Group reads:

> International law is a legal system. Its rules and principles (i.e. its norms) act in relation to and should be interpreted against the background of other rules and principles. As a legal system, international law is not a random collection of such norms. There are meaningful relationships between them. Norms may thus exist at higher and lower hierarchical levels, their formulation may involve greater or lesser generality and specificity and their validity may date back to earlier or later moments in time.

The common denominator among the 42 conclusions is basically that they address situations where tensions or conflicts between legal rules and principles are at hand. It is of great importance that states and other actors concerned seek guidance in this material when such situations occur, as they inevitably will.

The question is, however, whether one should leave it at that. Even if the conclusions amply demonstrate that conflicts between legal rules and principles can be solved, such situations nevertheless represent uncertainties, frustrations and delays. It is obvious, for several reasons, that the greatest efforts must be made both at the national and the international level to avoid such situations. If nothing is done in this respect, one can foresee an increasing number of situations where it will be necessary to resort to the kind of conflict solving that is discussed in the ILC report. This may in turn have very negative effects on the respect for existing norms. It is therefore absolutely necessary to continue working in a direction towards avoiding situations of the kind that the ILC Study Group has correctly identified as problematic.

At the national level there is a natural hierarchy of norms. A constitution obviously trumps rules at a lower level in the normative hierarchy, and within this hierarchy, there may be several layers. Federal states represent a special challenge in this respect. As it appears from the analytical report of the ILC Study Group, the situation is sometimes even more complex at the international level.

A common requirement in the legislative process at the national and the international level must be to ensure that new rules are in conformity with the fundamental rules that apply. At the national level, this means that rules must be in conformity with the constitution and the legal system as a whole, including obligations flowing from international law, specifically treaties to which the state is a party. At the international level, new treaties must be in conformity with international norms of a higher standing, notably *jus cogens* or the Charter of the United Nations and the legal system in general.

Furthermore, with the increasing volume of international norms there is a corresponding need for an examination of the interrelationship between different norms at this level. At the same time the effect of the development of such norms is that the way in which national legislators can exercise their powers is gradually circumscribed. There might be either treaties or *jus cogens* norms that set the limits, or there may simply be 'political realities', in particular such that result from globalisation, that may have to be taken into consideration during the legislative process. The challenge here is therefore to establish a system of checks and balances that can be applied in a more or less seamless way, in relation to both the legislative work at the national level and the corresponding work at the international level.

3. Requirements in the Legislative Process at the National Level

As it appears from the foregoing, there are two main aspects that must be taken into consideration in the legislative process at the national level: the constitutional aspect and the consistency aspect. The borderline between the two may not always be clear, and the necessary standards require an almost seamless approach.

3.1. The Constitutional Aspect

The legislative process at the national level is of course directly dependent on the constitutional system. In some states there are elaborate constitutions, accompanied by a well-developed constitutional practice. In other states there may not even be a written constitution. Irrespective of how the system works, there has to be a method for ascertaining that proposed legislation is in conformity with the norms that apply at this level.

An important question here is how this method is implemented. If the draft legislation is prepared in a government office, there would have to be a central function that can assist the legal offices of the different ministries in this respect. This applies *mutatis mutandis* in the case where the main work is done within the elected national assembly. In some systems, an attorney general may perform this supervisory task.

Methods must also be developed to make sure that legislation proposed at other levels is subjected to a similar examination – for example, state legislation in a federal system, or rules adopted at a lower constitutional level within a nation state on the basis of delegated legislative authority, such as municipalities and local governments

One important aspect of this process is that the constitutional review must not only focus on the national constitution. Obligations flowing from important international treaties to which the state is a party must also be taken into consideration. This applies in particular to treaties in the field of human rights and humanitarian law. Even case law from international human rights courts and similar international guidance must be taken into account here.

By way of example, it could be mentioned that in legislation regarding inheritance, sale of goods, land law, customs, etc. there could be provisions that might risk conflicting with rules on fundamental human rights. Basically, such conflicts could occur in most, if not all, legal fields. In order to fully comprehend this connection, it is necessary to have an understanding of how human rights norms work and where, typically, there is a risk that human rights obligations may be violated through legislative acts. By way of example:

> A government is in the process of proposing legislation to regulate the right to purchase real estate. It is considered necessary to establish specific conditions that buyers must fulfil before they are allowed to purchase certain categories of real estate.

The obvious questions are: how are these conditions formulated? Do they entail a risk for discrimination? Who decides whether the conditions are met? Can a refusal to grant permission to purchase be appealed against before a court of law?

These examples illustrate the complexity in determining whether a proposed piece of legislation risks conflicting with obligations under international human rights law. Similar tests must be made also in other areas. To perform this task states must establish institutions or procedures with very good knowledge of how the national legal system works, and how it interacts with the international system. The key issue here is to be able to identify elements in the national legislative process that may have to be subjected to a closer examination from a constitutional viewpoint.

3.2. The Consistency Aspect

The point of departure in dealing with the consistency aspect at the national level is actually a policy question. The test described here – that the rules proposed are in conformity with the constitution in the sense understood in the present context – does not answer the initial and fundamental question in the legislative process: are the contemplated new rules really necessary?

To someone who has been involved in legislative work over many years it is obvious that a critical approach is of the essence here. In some situations it may be tempting for policy-makers to advance ideas for new legislation that may not be so well considered and perhaps conceived in a very short-term perspective. The first condition must therefore be that contemplated rules respond to a genuine need.

If the case is proven and the new rules are deemed necessary, it is extremely important not to forget the next question that must be addressed: what existing rules can be abolished at the same time? This element may seem overzealous to some. However, in my experience, this aspect cannot be over-emphasised. It is in the process of developing new legislation that those involved have to review any existing rules, in the same and in related legal fields. An expertise is developed that should also be used to assess the extent to which existing rules can be abolished or amended or maybe even amalgamated with the proposed new legislation.

If this work is not performed, there is a clear risk that the statute book will contain provisions that after some time will be completely obsolete. But their presence on the statute book leaves the prudent lawyer and others concerned no other option than to look into the matter to see whether the rules are still relevant. This creates frustration, unnecessary work and, in the long run, a risk of disrespect for the legal system.

In the case that the test is passed and a genuine need for new rules has been identified, it is necessary to develop a method for reviewing legislation to be adopted so as to ensure that it also dovetails with the national system as a whole. In the latter respect, experience shows that legislation in a particular field of law may also have profound effects for other fields of law.

A common feature in preparing proposals for legislation is to ask a commission, in some cases maybe even a standing law commission, to prepare the necessary drafts. This work may be performed on the basis of clear terms of reference laid down by the government. It is a common feature that such commissions would approach their work with great circumspection and examine the effects the proposal would have on existing legislation in other fields. Furthermore, when new legislation is introduced, the need for consequential amendments to existing legislation must also be considered. Without going into detail in this fairly technical area, suffice it to say that the process of preparing legislation at the national level must be highly dynamic with a view to creating a system that is consistent and does not generate conflict between existing norms.

4. Requirements in the Legislative Process at the International Level

At the international level, there are two main aspects that must be taken into consideration in the legislative process. They mirror the situation at the national level: the constitutional aspect and the consistency aspect. With the increasing internationalisation of law, the legislative process at the international level will gradually be more intertwined with the corresponding process at the national level.

4.1. The Constitutional Aspect

As stated by the ILC Study Group, international law is a legal system within which norms exist at higher and lower hierarchical levels. In this sense, there is a similarity with the corresponding constitutional system at the national level. However, one should be careful not to draw the analogy with the hierarchical nature of domestic legal systems too far.

The main sources of international law are set out in Article 38 of the Statute of the International Court of Justice: treaties, custom, and general principles of law. Some of these rules are more important than others and this explains why it is appropriate to speak about a hierarchy.

First and foremost among these rules are the ones recognised as superior because of their importance and content combined with the universal acceptance of their superiority. Reference is made to Article 52 of the VCLT on *jus cogens*:

> A treaty is void if, at the time of its conclusion, it conflicts with a peremptory norm of general international law. For the

> purposes of the present Convention, a peremptory norm of general international law is a norm accepted and recognized by the international community of States as a whole as a norm from which no derogation is permitted and which can be modified only by a subsequent norm of general international law having the same character.

According to the Study Group the most frequently cited examples of *jus cogens* norms are the prohibition of aggression, slavery and the slave trade, genocide, racial discrimination, apartheid and torture, as well as basic rules of international humanitarian law applicable in armed conflict, and the right to self-determination.

There are also other elements to be noted in establishing the hierarchy, notably the Charter of the United Nations and its Article 103, and rules specifying obligations owed to the international community as a whole – obligations *erga omnes*.[13]

Attention should also be paid to special regimes – *lex specialis* – that might contain requirements to be observed.

All this means that there are certain types of international rules that admit no derogation. In formulating legislation at the international level (*i.e.*, in treaty-making), it is therefore necessary to observe this distinction between different categories of norms and that there may be limits to what is permitted within a particular negotiating process.

The field of human rights law represents a special case in point. The International Covenant on Economic, Social and Cultural Rights and the International Covenant on Civil and Political Rights, both from 1966, are now ratified by 160 and 166 States, respectively.[14] At the same time, the Universal Declaration of Human Rights, adopted by the UN General Assembly in 1948, has gradually acquired the status of customary international law.

There are also the regional regimes for the protection of human rights, such as the European Convention on Human Rights 1950, the

---

13 Reference to observations 31 to 42. See Study Group of the International Law Commission, 2006, see *supra* note 8.

14 International Covenant on Economic, Social and Cultural Rights and the International Covenant on Civil and Political Rights, United Nations Treaty Collection, 27 July 2010.

American Convention on Human Rights 1969, and the African Charter on Human and Peoples' Rights 1981.

With respect to the European Convention it is clear that this treaty is not, and has not been conceived as a self-contained regime in the sense that recourse to general law would have been prevented. On the contrary, as identified by the ILC Study Group, the Court makes constant use of general international law with the presumption that the Convention rights should be read in harmony with that general law and without an *a priori* assumption that Convention rights would be overriding.[15]

It should be noted, however, that this applies to a situation where a case is before an international court. It is quite another matter what weight should be given to existing human rights norms in the international legislative process. This author believes that a keen eye should be kept on obligations under human rights law irrespective of the topic that is on the agenda in a particular treaty negotiation. There is certainly no merit in creating international norms in a particular field of law that *a priori* risk being in violation of fundamental human rights norms.

In the report of the ILC Study Group, reference is made to the technique of interpreting the European Convention on Human Rights as "an instrument of European public order (*ordre public*) for the protection of individual human beings".[16] Such an approach would no doubt also be appropriate for other bodies interpreting treaties in the field of human rights. Against this background it goes without saying that particular attention must be paid to human rights obligations irrespective of the subject matter of the negotiations at hand. This means that it is also necessary to seek advice from experts in human rights in negotiations that concern, for example, trade law, transport law or environmental law.

In sum, from a constitutional viewpoint, the legislative process at the international level presents challenges that are very similar to the corresponding challenges at the national level. For this reason it is important that there is an appropriate process for ascertaining that instructions given to national delegations that engage in negotiations at the international level are properly formulated. In the preparation of such

[15] International Law Commission, 2006, para. 164, see *supra* note 9.

[16] Particular references are made to European Court of Human Rights, *Cyprus v. Turkey*, Judgment, 10 May 2001, ECHR 2001-IV, p. 25, para. 78.

instructions the appropriate constitutional expertise at the national level should be consulted.

4.2. The Consistency Aspect

An examination of contemplated norms from the perspective of consistency is of great importance at the international level as well. An examination in the same detail as at the national level may, however, not be possible here.

First, it should be noted that every international body entrusted with a mandate to develop international agreements, in particular international conferences, believe themselves to be sovereign and might be reluctant to look at instruments adopted in other forums. This attitude is no longer tenable. To ensure consistency, there must be an attitude of openness and an understanding of the fact that there are fully legitimate rules adopted by other bodies and that there is an interest, not least from a national viewpoint, to make certain that the new rules under negotiation do not conflict with norms adopted by other bodies.

An additional problem is that, depending on the subject matter, instructions to national delegations in international negotiations often emanate from different ministries or government agencies at the national level. Therefore, the first step would be to review how this activity is performed domestically. If there is not already a centralised system for this coordination, such a system should be established.

However, the overriding problem is generated by the fact that treaties established under the auspices of the United Nations and a host of other international organisations cover such an enormous area that it is difficult to get a complete overview. However, it does not follow that matters should be allowed to develop without at least an attempt to create such an overview.

Even if this activity takes place at the international level, the control of the legislative process is basically in the hands of national delegations. It is therefore necessary that the relevant coordination expertise be developed at the national level. Since a corresponding overview function would have to be established there, with a focus on national legislation, these two activities should actually be conducted jointly, based on the same requirements.

Establishing a system of the kind outlined above is to a large extent a matter of resources. In many developing countries there is an obvious need for assistance in this respect. Such assistance is closely related to the kind of legal technical assistance that is already provided by developed states, intergovernmental organisations and non-governmental organisations and should therefore be viewed as part and parcel of the latter. The challenge here is to examine what different techniques are available and to see whether these techniques fit in a particular national legal environment. As a matter of fact it would be difficult to assist countries in developing their legislative processes in a meaningful way if the aforementioned elements are not taken into consideration.

5. How Can One Achieve Better Coordination?

The point of departure must obviously be that existing rules reflect the needs of contemporary society. Developments in international law over the past century have been tremendous, with a concentration towards the end of the period.

It is evident that new phenomena will require new rules at both the national and the international level. New rules are an inevitable consequence of the globalisation and new needs in general. To adopt new rules as necessary should be viewed as strengthening the development towards an international society under the rule of law. As emphasised by the ILC Study Group, international law covers a wide range of areas, and in some cases actors other than states develop these norms.

Against this background it is important to emphasise that states must ensure that they continue to play the lead role in developing international law. The close connection between treaty making, the most prominent method of creating international law, and national legislation is obvious. The lodestar must be the democratic society under the rule of law. In such a society an assembly elected by secret ballot makes the laws.

One particular effect of this development must however be highlighted in this context: the increasing number of international agreements entail a risk that obligations will be contradictory if the process is not well coordinated. This will, in turn, lead to difficulties when the agreements are to be implemented and applied.

It is true that the conclusions of the ILC Study Group provide useful guidance here. But as indicated above, an increasing recourse to conflict settlement in the normative area would have negative consequences. If the system becomes too inconsistent and cumbersome there is a risk that it will be disregarded and seen as irrelevant. This will have very negative effects on the respect for the norms agreed upon.

This means that the same scrutiny that ought to be applied to rules at the national level should be applied at the international level precisely because of the expansion of the body of norms at this level. Furthermore, the distinction between national and international norms will be less prominent as time passes and, as already mentioned, the freedom of the national legislator to act will be more and more circumscribed as a consequence of obligations under international law.

The question is how to achieve the necessary coordination. Admittedly, what has been said in the preceding sections is fairly elementary to someone experienced in legislative work. However, in some countries, the system may not be so well developed. Furthermore, the need for careful coordination may not be fully understood by policy-makers who are dependent on a well functioning legislative system.

It goes without saying that the reasoning above is merely a sketch, and that it is almost impossible to reflect on the particularities of different national systems. In addition, there are legislative processes that have not been considered in this brief presentation, *e.g.*, the process developed within the European Union. However, this makes it all the more important to discuss the questions raised and compare notes to see whether there are lessons learned that could be used for the common good of the whole international community.

One approach would be for the legal advisers of the Ministries of Foreign Affairs from across the world to study the question and discuss it within the framework of the informal consultations that they now conduct on a yearly basis in October on the margins of the meetings of the Sixth Committee of the United Nations General Assembly. Maybe a common understanding could be developed with a view to addressing the challenge in a systematic and coordinated manner.

6. Conclusions

The conclusions to be drawn are that legislative activity will be increasing in the future both at the national and the international level. The interrelationship between the norms established at these two levels will be even closer. In addition, it will be gradually more difficult to distinguish between the two categories. It is important to realise that this is not purely a technical matter. On a closer look it is apparent that it is the substance that is at the forefront. This requires a well managed and coordinated legislative system both at the national and the international level.

In addition, a national legal system needs maintaining through the abolition of obsolete rules. Similarly, attention must be given to identifying obsolete rules at the international level. The body of international agreements will keep growing, and eventually there will be treaties that should be abolished; their existence on the books may cause confusion or uncertainty. Therefore, the need for a systematic review of the existing body of treaties will materialise gradually. States have an interest in ensuring that the system is up-to-date and coherent.

Consequently, the system must be well managed and coordinated in the sense that the need for rules in a particular field should be constantly tested, that new rules are adopted only as and when it is necessary and that obsolete rules should be taken off the books. Even if this kind of activity seems technical, it is in fact substantive and in need of careful attention. In both cases it is a matter of maintaining the relevance and the quality of the system.

A particular challenge is to make policy-makers realise that this is a matter that must be given high priority in the immediate future. If the system becomes too unwieldy, there is a clear risk for serious consequences both at the national and the international level. A systematic approach is of the essence, and it is the duty of lawyers to take resolute action explaining the subject matter to the policy-makers they serve.

2.5

The Internationalisation of Public Services and the Character of National Public Law

John Bell[*]

"Public services" are seen traditionally as a core aspect of national public law. They are determined and organised according to national decisions of what the public interest requires, and they justify special powers on the part of public authorities. The benchmarks for which public services should be provided are increasingly international. Under privatisation, the providers are often public or private bodies from other states. It is necessary to rethink the character of state involvement in providing public services. The paper suggests that the model of the 'negotiator state', a state actively involved in brokering the provision of certain services for the general good, best fits current practice and law.

1. The Basic Issue

The basic problem is that public law works on the premise that decisions of the public interest are made and implemented at a national level within the constraints of democratic decision-making and democratic accountability to the national political community. In this, public law is distinct from private law. The concern of the paper is that this is increasingly not the case, and that a different paradigm is needed. In particular, the use of transnational providers of public services poses particular problems for the traditional conception of public law. In a sense, what is traced here has been underway for some time. But the global financial crisis is likely to accelerate it. As the amount to be raised from public taxation reduces, so the preservation of major public services will increasingly depend on counterpart funding from the private and third sectors.[1] The State's ability to dictate long-term public services will be

[*] **John Bell** is a Professor at Cambridge University.

[1] The third sector is defined as the voluntary and charitable sectors. See the OECD comment: Ian Hawkesworth, "Public-private partnerships: Making the right choice for the right reason", available at http://www.oecdobserver.org/news/fullstory.php/aid/3228/Public-private_partnerships.html, last accessed 25 March 2011.

reduced and its financial contributions will be limited. If the providers of services become increasingly global and use their scale to source resources from around the globe, then many cherished national policies on the character and source of public services will decline. This has an impact on the character of public law and its distinct place in the national legal order.

2. The Traditional Conception of Public Law

Public law is defined as the law governing a particular national state. That state draws its legitimacy and authority from the national constitution and the national democratic order. The distinctive mission of bodies governed by public law is to exercise special powers (*pouvoirs exorbitants*) in the support of public order and public services, *i.e.*, actions taken in the general or collective interest rather than for private profit. What public order and public services involve is determined by a public body subject to its accountability to the national democratic community. Within a democratic system, based on popular sovereignty (directly or indirectly), decisions require the initial approval of the community through its representative institutions.

Public law powers are basically *dominium* (property-based) and *imperium* (unilateral authority). It has always been difficult to locate and justify the *commercium* (trading, buying and selling of services) within a distinctive public law model.

There are two problems with this traditional model of public law. First, it presupposes a very national process of approval and accountability, where the polity is simply a national polity. Second, it presupposes a clear distinction between public and private law. Neither of these is true. National decision-making about public policy is increasingly determined by commitments made to other nations or by international standards, such as those developed by the OECD. As to the distinction between the public and private sectors, there are an important number of intermediate bodies which straddle the boundary and also policies have often to be determined in concertation between public and private sectors.

There continues to be a strand of doctrinal and policy writing that considers that public bodies can continue to be delivery mechanisms of public services and also involved in their design.[2] This literature presupposes that public services are governed by principles that are significantly different from private, commercial law. That is not going to be sustainable.

3. Decisions Are Not Simply National

It is simply untrue (if it ever was true) that decisions about the public interest are and can be taken simply in a nationally specific context, especially in the area of public services:

- The global conceptions of free trade (GATS: General Agreement on Trade in Services entered into force in 1995 and covers many sectors of public services): like the EU, GATS is predicated on a free trade model in which the freedom of individuals to provide services trumps national needs to protect particular services as forming part of the national interest. The regime to govern such protection is an exception to the rules, rather than of the traditional public law model of trading in services as being the exception.
- Free trade is then complemented by comparison between countries on policy issues. The OECD does provide a benchmark as well as an exchange of ideas on the way in which governments provide public services. There tends to be a bias here towards the free market, but there is also an emphasis on transparency and ethical conduct.
- Global movements in finance will mean that the funds involved in the support of public services may come from a range of sources, not all of which are within a country.
- Services are therefore going to be commodities which are purchased by a range of customers from a range of essentially commercial providers, not necessarily linked to particular states. In that free market for services, health, education, even prisons and defence will not be controlled and delivered within a single jurisdiction. Once we move into multi-national situations, then the paradigm moves much closer to commercial law.

---

2 X. Domino *et al.*, "Questions sur l'avenir de l'établissment public", in *AJDA*, 2010, 1238.

4. Public and Private Sectors Are Overlapping

The simplistic division between public law and private law in the provision of public services is increasingly under challenge. It is not simply the case that either a firm acts for its own profit or it is a concessionary working by permission of a public body and making use of publicly provided infrastructure. The provider of the service may contribute its own funding to a joint enterprise, *e.g.*, the public/private partnerships that provide schools and infrastructure in relation to a wide range of projects. In those cases, the private body is both working to provide a publicly-defined service for public service goals and to achieve private profit, and a return on its own capital investment as well. Furthermore, the provider of the service may well be a foundation (in English legal terms a charity) which has both public and private features. It has a distinct patrimony which is contributed by private individuals, investments and public bodies (including tax advantages).

This merging of public and private sectors produces a mixed economy in the definition and provision of the public service. The public interest and the private interest are merged into a project in which the aspirations of both parties and the reputation of both are engaged in a common enterprise. It is often argued that there are two distinct logics that divide public and private law. Public law is based on the public interest and the value of social solidarity. Private law is based on private interest and personal profit or fulfilment. The third sector is often described as 'not for profit' in the sense that it shares the value of solidarity with the public sector, but it also has to be focused and efficient ('business-like, but not run as a business'). In accounting terms, one has to show a stream of income (public and private, from grants and from users) that supports the activity which is deemed to be of social value. To use Stuart Etherington's analysis,[3] we would not be seeing so much of a contraction of the state to residual government, but a focus on added value where the state cannot employ all the expertise it needs itself, and has the role of mobilising resources from elsewhere. These resources mobilised might be from the voluntary sector and might be from abroad. These external sources provide a distinct added value which, in times of restrictions on public debt, will include the ability to attract funding from non-state sources.

[3] Stuart Etherington, Delivery: The Role of the Voluntary Sector, 2003, pp. 7-8.

The increasing emphasis on a 'customer focus' within public services brings their ethos closer to that of the private sector. Indeed business practices and personnel may be shared across sectors.

These developments fit the strategies of the OECD and the WTO, as well as the European Union through movement of expertise and talents across jurisdictions in the belief that competition promotes efficiency and cost-effectiveness. It is clear that in the financial crisis, bringing in private money and expertise is seen as a way in which public deficits can be managed. With public procurement as 10-15% of global GDP, this becomes a very large area to manage.

5. The Changing Character of the State

The modern state has gone well beyond the 'night-watchman state', preoccupied with policing, justice and defence. In the immediate post-1945 period, it took on the role of providing minimum social security, transport, energy, telecommunications, education, housing and health provision. But as the demands for these services expanded, these became too much for the state to manage through possible tax rises. So the provision of services has been increasingly delegated to private providers. The role of the central state then becomes one of regulation and purchase. Public service becomes an area where services are designed and purchased, typically by contract by a public body, but they may also operate by way of a free market licensed and regulated by a public body. Indeed the design of the service might be by way of an agreement with key market actors, rather than simply the product of a political process inside the public body.

6. The Place of Transnational Providers

Transnational providers of public services cause two problems for the public law model. First, within a partnership model, they are providing investment and ideas into the definition of public services. Decisions are reached by means of negotiation with the partner. This model is unlike the *imperium* and *dominium* models of authority, where all acts are subject to the control of the national polity. The *commercium* model of authority relies on very generic prior authorisation and then limited accountability. The process of negotiation leaves less scope for public participation and influence. Where the trading is with a body outside the jurisdiction and thus the polity, then the level of public involvement diminishes even further.

In many areas of activity, the cost of developing expertise to run substantial public services requires an organisation of a significant size, of which there are few. Economies of scale can be gained by providing services across a number of similar countries. So a number of transnational corporations are growing up with a portfolio of public services in a number of different countries.

The combination of the mixing of public and private partnerships in the provision of public service and the transnational diversification of enterprises creates the potential for a single enterprise to link the national interest in public services in more than one country. If the exercise of power by the private enterprise or foundation is controlled by the courts of one jurisdiction, this may well have implications for the provision of public services within another jurisdiction.

There is clearly a problem with the democratic accountability of those who provide services if the definition and provision of services is no longer part of the purely national polity's decision-making. If EDF provides electricity in France and in London (as it does) and sources its electricity from nuclear sources (as it does), then the wishes of the London polity on the sourcing of its electricity can be ignored if the demand amongst the French polity is greater.

7. Implications

The major implication of the changes sketched out here is that the state increasingly relies on its *commercium* powers in order to deliver services and regulation to control the activities of others engaged in doing similar things. Its function is as a purchaser of services from others, bulk buying on behalf of its constituent community, like a parent for a family. If that is the function of the state, then we would simply need to distinguish two processes. The first is the process by which the public body comes to make decisions (consultation, procurement, avoidance of corruption, reporting etc.) and the second is the process by which the service is agreed and delivered by the private body. It is clear that the first can be governed by special rules that reflect the public nature of the body and the process (there are particular ethics and processes involved). However, the second is increasingly like any other commercial deal. The character of the deal is essentially commercial, even if the motives for the contract are specifically public. In a world competitive market, the public body is just one body among many, competing to employ the services of a transnational company, which will use its expertise to design and negotiate a partnership in the delivery of services. To take an example, a construction firm might compete for contracts for a public project to build and manage a school and a private project to build office blocks in different countries at the same time. From their point of view, both are design, build and operate projects. Is there really anything left of the public character of the activity of commissioning, negotiating and financing services, particularly when the absence of a profit motive of the commissioning body is not essential to the definition of something as public law?

To a great extent, the model sketched is a market model for public services. The public sector is increasingly seen not as the delivery agent of services, but the procuring and monitoring agent. It is a greater departure from the French and Latin model of public law than from the Dutch, British and American models.

We are used to the idea that public authorities are able to exercise special powers (*pouvoirs exorbitants*) in order to protect the public interest. One such interest is the ability to change the service requirements, *e.g.*, because the public has elected a different party into power. A second idea is the power to require that there be a minimum service in the public interest. Both of these may make some sense in a single state situation, where the state can effectively make use of unilateral powers to which the body in question is subject. But this does not really operate as effectively in a transnational situation. The service provider has other outlets and other places to work, so the employing state is constrained. The employing state becomes much like any other substantial contracting party, exercising its contracting powers in order to achieve results. However, it is not really able to impose its will, but must negotiate a solution. In practice, this is probably not very different from some major areas of current public procurement in which there are relatively few global suppliers with whom the government has to deal on a repeated basis, *e.g.*, in pharmaceuticals and in defence industries.

The model to which this tends is of the 'negotiator state', a state which is less concerned with providing services (and thus employing people to provide them on often advantageous terms) and more about procuring the services from others, not necessarily within the jurisdiction. The state here is not simply regulating the provision of services provided by the private sector (the 'regulatory state') – it is actively engaged in brokering the provision of services and even paying (at least in part) for them. There may be some services which the state chooses to continue to provide directly (*e.g.*, hospitals and education), but the special position of the state-run services will be eroded. In addition, the provision of services not for-profit will be in competition with the general not-for-profit sector. Thus the state might run hospitals, whilst the voluntary sector provides hospice and palliative care often with state encouragement and subsidysubsidisation. Many workers move between these sectors in any case, so the future may not hold any great changes.

The major change is conceptual. Public law becomes a matter of how the public bodies govern themselves and come to decisions in the light of their responsibilities to be democratic, accountable and committed to the public sector ethos of, personal disinterestedness and social solidarity. But in the external sphere, dealing with service providers and service users, public bodies are but one actor among many in an international arena of private bodies undertaking *pro bono* acts of corporate social responsibility, third sector bodies expressing their specific mission of social solidarity and private philanthropy, and various local, regional and national governments engaged in achieving their distinctive (and often competing) conceptions of the general interest. In such a world, the values that should govern the way in which services are provided involve responsiveness, fairness, transparency and consultation. There is no necessarily privileged position for a public body. Public law processes are one way in which the voice of the community is expressed, but not the only one. As a result, public law and its privileged position need to be reduced. Transnational provisions of public services are one way in which this process will be accelerated.

2.6

Mega-Cities, Glocalisation and the Law of the Future

Jean-Bernard Auby*

In the current globalisation process, two related phenomena, both linked with 'local' realities, exercise a strong structural influence on the international governance and the evolution of public apparatuses: the rise of global cities, and that particular dialectic between international realities and local ones which is now commonly labeled 'Globalisation'. Both make corresponding local realities exist in the international legal arena, while their relations with it were previously always mediated by the state. This evolution raises various institutional and normative issues.

1. Introduction

Within the current globalisation process, two related phenomena, both linked with 'local' realities, exercise a strong structural influence on international governance and the evolution of public apparatuses: the rise of the global cities and that particular dialectic between international realities and local ones which is now commonly labelled 'glocalisation'. It is clear enough that these two phenomena will bear significant consequences on the law of the future. What they imply in terms of international emergence of local governments and mega-cities is already visible in law, and this is certainly just the first chapter of the story. In order to bring some pieces along this line into our collective debate, I will make some suggestions about the position of cities and local realities in the process of globalisation (section 2), some already visible legal consequences of this position (section 3), and hypotheses we can make about its future influence on law (section 4).

2. Cities and Local Realities in the Process of Globalisation

Certainly, one of the strongest characteristics of the world's current evolution is the impressive urban growth it entails. But, more than this

* **Jean-Bernard Auby** is Professor of Public Law at Sciences Po.

growth itself, there are accompanying phenomena which are significantly susceptible to influencing the evolution of law, among which are the rise of the mega-cities (2.1.) and the original dialectic which has taken place between the local and the global, and which is now commonly called 'glocalisation' (2.2.).

2.1. Urban Growth Around the World: The Rise of the Mega-Cities

One of the most impressive sociological features of the current development of the world is urban growth. Humanity has reached the point where more than 50% of the world population is now urban. In contrast, the rate was just 10% one century ago. However, more than this growth itself, some derived aspects of growth are of great importance to the future of law and the institutions in the world. One of them is the rise of the mega-cities – or mega-regions – whose population can reach 20 or 30 millions: 18.4 for Mexico City, 18.7 for New York City, 23.5 for Seoul, 34 for Tokyo.[1]

These mega-cities show some common characteristics.[2] Among them, their shapes are basically associated with urban sprawls and polycentricism, they combine a large number of different spaces with different uses, they juxtapose rural areas and urban ones and they entail multiple centralities. People who live in them are very mobile: they work in one part, live in another one, do their shopping in a third one, and go to a fourth one for entertainment or sport. They tend to be affected by a high degree of social and spatial polarisation, stretching, in some of them, from wealthy gated communities to large zones of slums.

Of course, mega-cities raise difficult governance issues since local government structures in general are not at the proper scale. In some cases, however, it has been possible to establish authorities situated at the level of the mega-city, either by interposing an additional layer of government, or by expanding the boundaries of existing cities.[3] Among developing big cities, some can be labelled 'global cities', in order to express the fact that they are connected to some major economic,

1 OECD, "Competitive Cities in Global Economy", OECD Publishing, 2006, p. 13.

2 OECD, 2006, pp. 43, see *supra* note 1; François Ascher, *Metropolis ou L'avenir des Villes*, Odile Jacob, 1995; Armand Colin, "V° Metropolisation", in Cynthia Ghorra-Gobin (ed.), *Dictionnaire des Mondialisations*, Paris, 2007.

3 OECD, 2006, p.22, see *supra* note 1.

political, and/or cultural networks of the globalising world. They have been described in particular by Saskia Sassen, whose analysis is mainly based on the consideration of big cities' connectivity with global financial markets.[4] Global cities are places where a lot of wealth and power are concentrated, and which are in a position to take part in very influential global networks in a state of limited but real independence *vis-à-vis* their states and national governments.

2.2. Global-Local Dialectics: 'Glocalisation'

The relations between globalisation and local economies, policies and governments are rather complex and even a bit paradoxical. The concept of glocalisation helps characterise these complexities and paradoxes. On the one hand, globalisation tends to 'erase' territorial realities since, among the evolutions it includes, many bear a trend to make territorial attachments less and less relevant, a trend to 'de-territorialise' social and economic relations. The Internet, of course, is the main example of that: a place where users' physical location – whether for fun or for an economic activity, whether sellers or buyers – does not matter very much.

Like private activities, public institutions are affected by this 'de-territorialisation' phenomenon. The social and economic realities they have to deal with become more and more transnational, so that it is more and more difficult for them to build efficiently related policies. Though on the other hand, globalisation also induces evolutions which tend to increase the importance of local realities. In the globalising world, territories compete economically, culturally, and so on; this is shown by the constant increase in the official recognition of local trade names (for wines, vegetables, fruits, honeys, and so forth).

In fact, it seems that local attachments are a way for people and institutions to counterbalance the effects of globalisation, by sticking to some roots in a world which tends to become more and more undifferentiated. Furthermore, as Yishai Blank puts it, "it has indeed become impossible to understand globalisation and its legal ordering

[4] Saskia Sassen, *The Global City: New York, London, Tokyo*, Princeton University Press, 1991; Saskia Sassen (ed.), *Global Networks, Linked Cities*, 2002; Peter Marcuse and Ronald Van Kempen (eds.), *Globalizing Cities: A New Spatial Order?*, 2000; A. Scott, *Global City-Regions: Trends, Theories, Policy*, Oxford University Press, 2002.

without considering the role of localities: they have become prime vehicles for the dissemination of global capital, goods, work force and images".[5] It is the combination of these two opposite logics which is now commonly characterised as 'glocalisation'.[6]

3. Some Already Perceptible Consequences in the Law

'Glocalisation' and the rise of mega-cities have heavily contributed to a double move which one can easily perceive in the current evolution of international relations law – the international legal emergence of local institutions (3.1.), and the international legal support these institutions receive (3.2.).

3.1. International Legal Emergence of Local Institutions

Traditionally, local entities have no legal existence in the international ambit, except, to some extent, when they are compounding states of a federal system, or in the case of cities which have received international status, such as Danzig, Shanghai or Jerusalem.[7] This is changing; local institutions tend to emerge more and more in international law. This makes them targets for rules imposing constraints or creating rights.[8]

Today it is not rare that legal obligations deriving from international sources come to be imposed on local governments. A major example of this is provided by all the rules concerning public procurement contracts which have been issued in the WTO system and in the European Union, and which local entities belonging to member states must respect.[9]

---

5 Yishai Blank, "Localism in the New Global Legal Order", in *Harvard International Law Journal*, 2006, vol. 47, no. 1, p. 263.

6 Ulrich Beck, *What is Globalisation?*, Cambridge, Polity Press, 2000, p. 42; Jan Aart Scholte, *Globalisation. A Critical Introduction*, London, Mac Millan and New York, St Partin Press Inc., 2000, p. 59.

7 Yishai Blank, "The City and the World", in *Columbia Journal of Transnational Law*, vol. 44, no. 3, 2006, p. 875.

8 Gerald Frug and David Barron, "International Local Government Law", in *The Urban Lawyer*, 2006, vol. 38, p. 1; Société Française de Droit International, *Les Collectivités Territoriales Non Etatiques dans le Système Juridique International*, Paris, Pedone, 2002.

9 Bernard Hoeckman and Petros Mavroidis (eds.), *Law and Policy in Public Purchasing- The WTO Agreement on Government Procurement*, Ann Harbor, University of

Similarly, it is not uncommon that local institutions are bound by environmental constraints originating in international norms. This is rather frequent in Europe, since the EU has produced a large body of environmental rules, and most of them directly impact local utilities and local public services (waste management, water distribution, and so on).

Conversely, it is increasingly common for local governments to find rules in some international instruments which attribute rights to them, and can be used by them as a means of protecting their powers and their autonomy. Yishai Blank mentions cases before the Israeli Supreme Court in which some UN instruments were invoked in order to challenge governmental decisions affecting local autonomy.[10] In countries which are party to the Council of Europe's Charter of Local Self-Government, local bodies can refer to this instrument in general as a basis for domestic judicial actions in order to protect their autonomy against state authorities.

What is striking is that in these situations, local authorities sometimes are imposed legal constraints which may be ignored by their national law and they sometimes receive legal advantages which can prevail over their national law. This can be expressed by saying that they no longer fully belong to their national legal system (without being fully internationalised either, of course).[11]

3.2. International Legal Support for Local Institutions

In fact, local institutions are not only emerging in the international legal ambit. They also receive much support from the international sphere. There are now a significant number of more or less formal international instruments which tend to favour local governments' autonomy and development. Within the United Nations, the body now called UN – Habitat has produced various documents in that direction, especially, the World Charter of Local Self-Government, drafted in 1998 in collaboration with the World Association of Cities and Local Authorities Coordination (WACLAC).[12] The World Bank has also widely expressed its support for

Michigan Press, 1997; Sue Arrowsmith and Arwel Davies (eds.), *Public Procurement: Global Revolution*, Kluwer Law International, 1998.

10 Blank, 2006, see *supra* note 7.

11 Jean-Bernard Auby, *La Globalisation, le Droit et l'État*, Librairie Générale de Droit et de Jurisprudence, 2010, p. 150.

12 Blank, 2006, see *supra* note 7.

local self-government on various occasions, and in particular in its 2000 report *Cities in Transition*. For the Bank, local autonomy is an important factor in economic prosperity as long as it meets some criteria: liveability, competitiveness, good government and bankability.[13] In Europe, the Council of Europe's Charter of Local Self-Government conveys a demanding conception of local government's autonomy, based upon subsidiarity and the notion that local institutions are essential as schoolhouses for democracy. Not only can local institutions rest on various international instruments, but they also find themselves more and more frequently represented and defended by special bodies in international institutions: among them UN - Habitat in the United Nations, and in the European Union, the Committee of Regions, which is now a rather important player in the EU apparatus.

4. Hypotheses on the Future

The growing presence of local governments in the global sphere as autonomous actors, or at least as legal entities relatively distinct from the states, has potentially significant consequences, both in terms of institutional logics (4.1.) and in terms of normative issues (4.2.).

4.1. Institutional Logics

Some local substatal entities emerge as global actors along states and other global actors, which may be public or private such as international organisations, NGOs, multinational companies etc. This fact is important in the current evolution of the international institutional governance arrangements. However, its consequences can only be worked out by combining this consideration with some other lines of evolution in international governance, and two in particular: the development of networks and that which is commonly characterised as multilevel governance.[14]

One of the major changes in the pattern of institutional governance nowadays is the development of various networks which link together governmental, administrative and even judicial actors, and which sometimes also include private entities. These networks take charge of

---

[13] Blank, 2006, see *supra* note 7.

[14] Auby, 2010, p. 149, see *supra* note 11.

managing some international public tasks in which diplomatic entities are normally involved.[15] Networks of big cities and of their local governments are among these networks. They have a particular weight stemming from the fact that they represent large numbers of people, and that they operate at the level where day-to-day public management issues have to be solved.[16]

The concept of multilevel or multilayered governance tries to grasp another aspect of contemporary international governance – the fact that most public affairs dealt with at the international level are conducted not just by one layer of institutions, but by two or more, which can include international in the sense of worldwide, international-regional, statal, intrastatal, international or transnational institutions of private actors.[17] It appears that local institutions play a significant role within the multilevel government frameworks that are common in the world of today; again because they are both major stages for the exercise of concrete democracy and strategic levels for responding to concrete public management issues.

The question is whether they will acquire an even higher position in international governance in the future, and even become as important as states in defining and implementing public affairs corresponding to their level. The answer is not obvious. The weight and independence of local governments varies. The way they are designed does not always place them at an optimal level for being influential. For example, some mega-cities are deprived of institutions situated at an adequate level for securing their overall governance. Moreover, in a sense, local governments are competing with states for the strategic position of governance over various public management issues. And states, which occupy the essential level in international governance, even if they are surrounded more and more by other competing actors, do not easily accept being bypassed by their local governments. This has been very well demonstrated by the evolution observed in Europe, where in the 80s and the 90s, something like a 'Europe of Regions' seemed to arise. However the states have in fact recovered their grasps and remain the unavoidable main mediators

[15] Anne-Marie Slaughter, *A New World Order*, Princeton University Press, 2004.

[16] Peter Taylor, W*orld City Networks: A Global Urban Analysis*, Routledge, 2003.

[17] Scholte, 2006, p. 143, see *supra* note 6.

between the European Union and the daily conduct of domestic public affairs.[18]

4.2. Normative Issues

One of the problems created by globalisation is that, the more it opens the door to new actors in the international ambit, the more it combines old and new actors in new arrangements like the ones that multilevel governance theory tries to describe, and the more difficult it becomes to ensure that contemporary international governance respects the basic principles of democracy and the rule of law.[19]

Are local governments and mega-cities particularly problematic in that respect? They are, in the sense that being public law entities they are normally entitled not only to implement public policies in daily administrative life, but they also possess some regulatory and even legislative competences, and therefore make particularly sensitive decisions in terms of democracy and in respect to the rule of law. On the other hand, in most of the countries, they are seats of representation and often also participatory democracy and their decisions are subject to judicial review of their legality, often including a strong verification of their respect for fundamental rights.

The challenge for the future is to keep this balance. The rise of some new global actors – notably private regulators and private networks – is sometimes criticised in itself; this is not the case for the global emergence of local institutions, which is widely, and justly, considered to be a positive development in international governance. One will only be sure that they occupy an adequate position in the latter if both the distribution of roles between them and the other major global actors (states and especially international organisations) is made clearer, and if their growing international autonomy is accompanied by a high level of

---

[18] Nicolas Levrat, *L'Europe et Ses Collectivités Territoriales: Réflexions sur l'Organisation et l'Exercice du Pouvoir Territorial dans un Monde Globalisé*, PIE, Peter Lang, 2005.

[19] Anne Peters, "The Globalisation of State Constitutions", in Janne Nijman and André Nollkaemper (eds), *New Perspectives in the Divide Between National and International Law*, Oxford University Press, 2007; Alfred Aman, *The Democracy Deficit: Taming Globalisation Through Law Reform*, New York University Press, 2004; Auby, 2010, p. 149, see *supra* note 11.

accountability and submission to democracy and the rule of law. This requires the combined efforts of international and domestic laws.

2.7

The Future of the City and the International Law of the Future

Janne Nijman*

Janne Nijman observes that globalisation is accompanied by urbanisation, and that many – if not most – of the challenges of globalisation come to the fore in cities: environmental pollution, crime, inequality, migration, cultural diversity, unemployment; to name a few. She distinguishes between the private city (the collective of private economic interests) and the public city (the city governments who increasingly operate as global actors). In her article she presents six propositions on how the public city will affect international law. She sees that direct links between cities and global institutions will intensify. This is already very visible in the area of environmental law, with NGO's facilitating these links. Cities will also be implementers of international law of their own accord, thus bypassing the state. Connected with this, Janne Nijman envisages that the international law of the future will 'de-formalise'; following local judges city governments will apply it simply by way of 'persuasive authority'. Last but not least, cities themselves will directly become part of the processes of international rule making. Given all this, cities will increasingly become actors in the making of international law and informal rules. They will be significant influencers of international negotiations. Proceeding from these phenomena, Nijman even asks the question whether cities will, in the future, acquire the status of international legal person, alongside that of states. Such a formal development would all the more change the state-centric system of today into the multi-actor system of the future.

1. Introduction: The Challenges of Global Urbanisation

The law of the future is shaped by the present and the past. It is contingent upon, and will be constructed by, interests as well as ideas. The past shows that states have not always been the pillars of global order. At

* **Janne E. Nijman** is Associate Professor of Public International Law and Senior Fellow of the Amsterdam Center for International Law (ACIL), University of Amsterdam.

various times, cities – such as Greek cities of Antiquity, the Italian republican Cities during the Renaissance, and the Free and Imperial Cities of the Holy Roman Empire – were the real commanders of (European) world power. These cities were political and commercial units conscious of a global society to which they belonged. Their legal relations developed within a system of *jus gentium et naturale* (the law of nations and nature) and in this way cities moulded, and were moulded by, a universal moral and legal order. In the light of history, the proposition that the city will shape, and be shaped by, the global (legal) order of the future is not very revolutionary at all.

Today, after centuries of state-centric international relations, cities are again developing a global consciousness: they identify themselves as entities with foreign offices and international relations, with global friends and global competitors. The self-conception of cities as global entities is not only caused by the impact of economic globalisation on the city, but also by the fact that the major global problems of our time (variations of human-political and ecological injustices) are often felt most urgently by the inhabitants of the world's cities. Again, this is not new. For centuries, social unrest and political upheaval with world changing impact have occurred in cities. In today's emerging global information society, ICTs have been instrumental to the urban societies of Tunisia and Egypt in their revolt against the human and political injustices in their countries. As Harvard Professor Edward Glaeser observes, "It's Always the Urban Pot That Boils Over".[1] These are not the only urban revolutions taking place. Globally, an urban green revolution is taking root. Cities are part of the problem of climate change, but also part of the solution. With 75% of the world's CO2 emission occurring in cities, the latter contribute heavily to global environmental problems (as well as to local health hazards). By combating environmental pollution locally, individual cities contribute significantly to solving global problems, but interesting enough cities respond to the threats of global environmental decline by seeking global inter-city cooperation on urban sustainability.

Globalisation makes cities pull people. Globalisation and urbanisation both challenge and empower the city. This is largely about

[1] Edward L. Glaeser, "It's Always the Urban Pot That Boils Over", New York Times, 1 February 2011, available at http://economix.blogs.nytimes.com/2011/02/01/its-always-the-urban-pot-that-boils-over/, last accessed 1 April 2011.

numbers and its consequences. Today, over 50% of the world's population live in in cities, that number expected to rise to 75% by 2050. The critical mass that cities offer can produce instability and human insecurity as well as all kinds of changes for the better. From an urban perspective, to put it simply, there are two contrasting scenario's for the world's future. The utopian scenario envisions an earth of 'good cities', places of the good life in both the political and the private sphere. Optimists, like Glaesar, understand the city as humanity's best hope for the future. Florida and Landry envision a prosperous influence of 'creative cities' where innovation and change will produce creative solutions to urban problems. Saunders uses the picture of successful urbanisation in *Arrival City* in which the immigrants of the megacities' slums of today are the middle classes of the future.[2] However, without adequate governance, 'failed' rather than 'successful' arrival cities will shape the world. Such a – nightmare – scenario is evoked also by Davis, who warns against an unstable urban world in *Planet of Slums*,[3] and by Kaplan in *The Coming Anarchy*,[4] which points to chaos and decay spreading from dysfunctional third world cities around the globe. The direction the world will take depends on an overwhelmingly complicated set of human choices. Cities are among the key actors to make these choices.

The city has always been a place of contrast and constitutive opposition. Political and moral philosophy is permeated with images of the 'heavenly city' setting moral-juridical standards for the government and citizens of the 'earthly city'. For many, the city is a place of opportunity, innovation, emancipation, toleration, comfortable alienation, and (historic) change. However, for most people around the world, the city is a place of capitalist hardship and social inequality, of poverty, discrimination, violence, and despair over a dead-end future lacking sufficient food, water, and work. Already today, megacities[5] – mainly in

2 Doug Saunders, *Arrival City: The Final Migration and Our Next World*, Knopf Canada, 2010

3 Mike Davis, *Planet of Slums*, Verso, New York, 2006.

4 Robert D. Kaplan, *The Coming Anarchy*, the Atlantic Monthly, 1994.

5 Megacities are cities with more than c. 8 million inhabitants. Often they lack the complexity and diversity characteristic of global cities as they are cities of endless slums rather than key hubs in the global economy. Megacities with c. 20 million people or more – for example, Tokyo or soon Lagos, Mexico City, Mumbai and Shang-

Asia and Africa – shelter approximately 1 billion slum dwellers. According to the UN, this will be doubled by 2030 despite the fact that the international community stipulated the reduction of slum-dwellers to be one of its 2015 MDGs. Even apart from the moral obligation, the *Planet of Slums* scenario has to be avoided for the purpose of preventing (social and political) unrest and instability across the globe. Governance at the urban, national and international level will have to be concerted in this effort.

The expansion of slums is however not the only challenge to which cities have to respond, nor are megacities the only cities challenged by rapid urbanisation. Other urban challenges posed by globalisation include environmental pollution, inequality, migration, and cultural diversity, access to urban public services (including access to water, sanitation and infrastructure to reach one's job). In order to respond adequately, a vibrant urban demos is needed with active urban citizens forcing city governments to develop innovative forms of governance, such as global intercity cooperation initiatives. As Feagin already pointed out decades ago, urban questions are questions of distributive justice. This is true today and in the future. Questions of global stability, global justice, and global governance will be in large part questions of urban stability, urban justice, and urban governance across the globe: "[t]he central challenge of the twenty-first century will be how to make both globalisation and urbanisation work for all the world's people, instead of benefiting only a few".[6]

In short, *how* the city deals with the challenges of globalisation and urbanisation is crucial for the future of our planet, and marks the law of the future. As the city once more becomes conscious of its global context, the urban level of governance draws closer to the global level of governance. The rest of this paper addresses the rising influence of cities as global actors, with a focus on the role which city governments take up in the global arena. I will first set apart the 'global public city' from the

hai, to name just a few - are sometimes called metacities. The metacity is a multi-centre city, a wide-spreading urban area.

6 UN-Habitat, "Cities in a Globalizing World: Global Report on Human Settlements 2001", 2001, available at http://www.unhabitat.org/content.asp?typeid=19&catid=555&cid=5374, last accessed 1 April 2011.

'global private city'. I will then explore six propositions on how the rise of the global public city shapes the future of international law.

2. The Global Private City and the Global Public City

Urban sociologists – like Feagin and more recently Sennett and Sassen, to name just a few giants in the field – have examined how globalisation constitutes global cities and *vice versa*. Sassen has coined the notion of 'global city', *i.e.*, a city defined by its dominant position in the global *economy*. Global cities are mutually connected in a global network. They are the *loci* where the global economy is controlled and commanded by the global financial-economic players. The global city is first and foremost the global *private* city. It is concerned with private economic interests. It is the urban private sector which seeks global opportunities and drives economic globalisation. A healthy urban private sector is highly significant to the urban community at-large.

However, in its efforts to secure save, equitable, healthy and sustainable urban life, cities need to be more than just globally competitive in order to attract businesses and secure economic growth. All cities – whether a hub in the global economy or not – have to develop good urban governance and sophisticated policies to distribute and sustain economic, socio-political and ecological welfare. The pursuit of the urban public good is the business of city governments, often incited by the urban public sphere. Together, the urban public sphere and the city government have a critical role to play in dealing with the challenges of urbanisation in a global context. The global *public* city in a broad sense refers to both city government and the urban public sphere. For the purposes of this essay, I use it in a slightly stricter sense, to refer to the legal notion of 'city government', which is not just part of the state structure but also a democratic representative of the urban *public* sphere and may thus operate to some extent autonomously from the state and develop external relations on a global scale to defend and promote urban values and urban public interests. The city government stands at a crucial junction between the global level of governance and the political and governmental questions of (urban) justice and (urban) public goods. With the focus on global *private* cities which is currently *en vogue*, we run the risk of missing an important determinant of the future: increasingly, city *governments* themselves become global agents. The strictly defined notion of the global public city captures the city in this role as public agent and legal entity responding to the challenges of globalisation and urbanisation. As such, it identifies and constitutes itself as an actor of the global society and within the global legal order.

The main underlying assumption of this short paper is that the global *public* city is on the rise.

Apart from globalisation and urbanisation, the rise of the global public city is furthered moreover by decentralisation. The world-wide promotion of local self-government and local autonomy through decentralisation, or as the World Bank calls it 'localisation',[7] is inspired by the aim to foster just and democratic urban societies whose local government is accountable also to their local constituencies. In these environments citizens would not lose their sense of belonging to the urban (political) society, a sense of rooted cosmopolitanism in a rapidly globalising world, by having them participate in urban public affairs. In view of the global dimensions of the urban questions for which the city is responsible, the city will reach out globally to cooperate with peers and to exchange 'best practices'. The rise of the global public city transforms the relations between the city and the state. The future of a state will be determined increasingly by the future of its cities.

As the global public city[8] takes up a significant role in global governance, it will also have a significant role in the transformation of today's international society into the global society of all societies of tomorrow. The international society of the twenty-first century will be deeply *urban*. Recognition of the rise of the public city to the global plane contributes to our understanding of the self-constitution of the global society and how in the process it replaces the old international law by new international law – the international law of the future.

3. Propositions on the Global Public City and the International Law of the Future

More and more, the global public city will be addressed directly by international law, and for its part will be a formative factor in the shaping

---

[7] The World Bank, *Entering the twenty-first century*, World Development Report 1999-2000, Oxford University Press, 2000.

[8] It is of course difficult to generalise about the future of 'the city', no two cities are the same and the differences between cities in the developed and developing countries are huge, yet here focus is on the general features of the global public city.

of international law. This relationship affects the fundamentals of traditional international law, in particular, the role of the state and its sovereignty, the role of formal consent in law-making, and the divide between the domestic and international legal order.[9] In this section I will present 6 propositions on how the rise of the global public city (hereinafter also: the city) transforms international law and thus shapes the international law of the future. Key to the rise of the global city, and thus also to this transformation, is the direct relationship developing between the global and the urban level of governance.

3.1. Direct, Institutionalised Relations between the City and Global Institutions will Intensify

The past 15 to 20 years show a clear trend. The position of cities in relation to international organisations changed considerably. While initially cities were rarely addressed directly by global institutions, they now have been fully discovered as key (f)actors in global policy implementation (see proposition 2) and as partners in new decision-making processes (see proposition 4).

The development of this trend is best visible in the field of international environment law. Agenda 21, adopted by UNCED in Rio de Janeiro in 1992, laid down a global plan of action for sustainable development in the twenty-first century. Chapter 28 of the Agenda 21 explicitly states that without the cooperation of local governments the global sustainable development objectives will not be reached.[10] Local governments are asked to engage with local communities in order to promote sustainable development at the local level and to develop Local Agenda 21 strategies. States but also the EU have followed up on Agenda 21 and stimulated regional and local sustainable development initiatives.[11] Local Agenda 21 may have been local policy yet it was at the same time part of a global policy plan. Since the early 90s when city were drawn into global

9 Janne Nijman and André Nollkaemper (eds.), *New Perspectives on the Divide between National and International Law*, Oxford University Press, 2007.

10 *Earth Summit: Agenda 21: The United Nations Programme of Action from Rio*, United Nations Conference on Environment and Development, 3-14 June 1992, Chapter 28.

11 Charter of European Cities and Towns Towards Sustainability, European Conference on Sustainability Cities and Towns, Aalborg, Denmark, 27 May 1994 ("Aalborg Charter").

environmental governance to implement global policy, the interaction between cities and international organisations has boomed. For example, relations between cities and UNEP have particularly intensified. It cooperates with *ICLEI-Local Governments for Sustainability* and other city networks, such as *C40 Large Cities Climate Leadership Group*, on climate change. The Urban Environment Unit of UNEP works together with cities and the IPCC on an *International Standard for Determining Greenhouse Gas Emissions for Cities* as an instrument to realise emission reduction in cities. Together with the Secretariat of the Convention on Biological Diversity, UN-HABITAT, ICLEI, IUCN Countdown 2010, UNITAR, UNESCO and a Steering Group of Mayors from Curitiba, Montreal, Bonn, Nagoya and Johannesburg, the UNEP launched the *Global Partnership on Cities and Biodiversity* to engage cities in the fight to reverse the loss of biodiversity by 2010. Similarly, on the issue of urban poverty reduction, the World Bank seeks cooperation with cities in the *Cities Alliance*. The alliance brings together international organisations, such as the EU, UNEP, UN-Habitat and the World Bank, NGOs, working on urban poverty and slum-dwellers, national governments and city governments, as organised in the United Cities and Local Governments, to assist cities – financially and otherwise, through sharing expertise etc. – in dealing with the impact of rapid urbanisation.

In other words, interaction between the global and local level on sustainability issues has empowered the city more generally. Important to this global trend is the organisation of cities in United Cities and Local Governments (UCLG). It is an international NGO established by city governments which aims to expand cooperation with global institutions, to strengthen the influence and formal status of local governments within these organisations (most notably within the UN and its specialised agencies and programmes), and to promote globally the political values of local autonomy and democratic self-government. UN-Habitat maintains close relations with UCLG and argues in favour of further intensification of the cities–UN relationship in order for local authorities to be better heard at the global stage. The *Agreement of Cooperation between The United Nations Human Settlements Programme and United Cities and Local Governments* (Barcelona, 2004) aims to promote local autonomy and self-governance through decentralisation played via UN-Habitat. I will come back to the *Guidelines* under proposition 4 since it illustrates well another trend: how the city has started to become involved in law-making. The Agreement – between a UN agency and an NGO – demonstrates also that global institutions such as the United Nations and World Bank indeed recognise UCLG as an important partner. UCLG develops initiatives to 'localise' global policy objectives, such as the MDGs, women's rights, and good urban governance. UCLG spares no trouble or expense in its claim to an official 'observer status' for local government within the UN General Assembly to ensure greater involvement in UN processes with quite some success, considering that the 2004 Cardoso report on relations with Civil Society proposes the UCLG to become an 'advisory body on governance matters' to the United Nations. Already, UCLG may nominate 50% of the members of the UN Advisory Committee of Local Authorities. In this vision of global governance, local governments are understood as vehicles of democracy and 'good governance'.

The growing trend that international organisations explicitly welcome the city as 'partner' and accommodate it in its new more autonomous role within the global order seems unstoppable. It is a win-win situation, driven by city governments as well as by global institutions. The incentives for global institutions lie in the effective implementation of a convention or policy. Alternatively, it fits well in its quest for legitimacy since it enables the global institution to really work with (representatives of) urban societies and thus have effect on the ground. Another indication of the future intensification of relations between the cities and international organisations is the address of former UN SG, Kofi Annan, to the mayors and other local government officials at the 2005 UCLG summit at UN Headquarters in NYC. His support of local self-governance and the inclusion of city governments in UN processes empowers the latter. Further impact of this general trend on international law besides the international institutional consequences will be dealt with when discussing the next propositions.

3.2. In the Future, International Law is Increasingly Implemented and Enforced by the City on its Own Accord

This proposition – which builds on developments described above – is based on the existing trend particularly visible in the field of human rights law and environmental law: city networks form around global norms in order to give them local effect. For example, the *Child Friendly Cities Initiative* (CFCI) is a global city network established to implement the

United Nations Convention of the Rights of the Child directly in the participating cities. The *UNESCO International Coalition of Cities against Racism and Discrimination* aims to give direct effect to anti-racism and anti-discrimination norms as included in international treaties, customary law (the prohibition of racial discrimination is *jus cogens*), and resolutions and declarations of IOs and their organs in the cities involved. These are two examples of accumulating evidence that IOs consider direct relations with city governments of quintessential importance to the implementation of global norms for which these organisations are responsible. Without direct and active involvement of the city this can hardly be done. These initiatives may, however, be explained by the conventional state-centric approach to international law. The city is under an obligation to protect its urban population against violations of human rights as well as under an obligation to respect these rights. This is not an obligation independent from the state – it is an obligation stemming from international human rights obligations of states, of which cities are a part.

Meanwhile there is a future trend in which the city directly and independently from the state can be seen to implement international law. One illustration of this trend is the initiative of the Mayor of Seattle, Greg Nickels, in the fight against environmental pollution and climate change. Unhappy with the fact that President Bush did not ratify the Kyoto Protocol, the Mayor called upon other cities in 2005 to give effect to the Protocol at the local level and implement the Kyoto emission reduction norm (7% under the 1990 level in 2012) locally. Hundreds of cities responded positively, the US Mayors Climate Protection Agreement counts more than 1000 participating cities. These cities give effect to the Kyoto norm through their local policies while the US as a state had not wishes to be bound by the protocol. International law here plays a role in the self-identification of the city as a global actor which takes account of its responsibility with respect to climate change and takes the lead in the governance of one of the most urgent global challenges.

Another way to internalise international law occurs when international law is included in local law directly. In spite of the fact that the US never ratified the UN Convention on the Eradication of Discrimination against Women (CEDAW), the city of San Francisco adopted an Ordinance in 1998 on the "Local Implementation of the UN

CEDAW".[12] For this purpose, it included the international human rights convention text in full rather in locally re-drafted form. The City's Commission on the Status of Women (COSW) develops policies on the basis of the CEDAW principles and it monitors complaints about unequal treatment of women.

These two examples point to an important development for the future: the city proceeds to implement international law directly and independently from the state. Moreover, they are also examples of local 'internalisation' of international law. This type of internalisation poses fundamental challenges to the international legal order, as it squarely by-passes the state, which withholds its consent. As such, it affects state sovereignty and challenges the basis of obligation in international law. Arguably, the city uses international law strategically, to enforce local policy backed up by international norms. If we stretch one step further, the internalisation of international law by the city may socialise the state, as its interests will gradually be reconstructed in compliance with international law.

3.3. The International Law of the Future is Less Formal

By giving effect to international norms while by-passing the state, the city acts in line with another trend: the de-formalisation of international law. Rather than applying international law because formal consent has been given by the state, the substantive or 'persuasive authority' of international law compels domestic courts or, in this case, city governments to comply with international law. Notwithstanding the fact that international law is no formal source of law in these cases – neither for the domestic judges who use international law to interpret national law nor for the city which uses international law to shape municipal law without being bound by it – international law is applied nonetheless.

The de-formalisation in international law finds further expression in the field of law-making. The trend of growing interaction between cities and international law is likely to develop from direct implementation and incorporation into cities' involvement to creation of international law. The

[12] Chapter 12K: Local Implementation of the United Nations Convention on the Elimination of all Forms of Discrimination against Women (CEDAW), San Francisco CEDAW Ordinance (No. 128-98), available at http://www.sfgov.org/site/cosw_page.asp?id=10849, last accessed 1 April 2011.

next proposition deals with the role of the city in international law-making. Here it is suffice to conclude that the various international documents produced by cities point to another trend of the future: the increasingly informal character of international law.

3.4. The City will be an (Informal) Actor in the International Law-Making of the Future

Considering the big interests at stake, the city will demand influence in the creation of international law. Mutual state consent may remain the formal source of obligation in international law but, increasingly *informal* or soft law norms are being created and both in formal and informal law making processes, the global public city seeks influence.

Formal international law-making takes place through negotiations between states and within international organisations. A trend of the future is that the city will increasingly (try to) influence such negotiations, either by specialised global city networks or organisations or by means of the UCLG which aims to represent the city in international organisations generally.

An example of the first situation are the activities of the *ICLEI-Local Governments for Sustainability* – one of the NGOs with formal 'observer status' – at COP15 in 2009, Copenhagen. During the negotiations for a new international climate change law in the UNFCCC context, the ICLEI put pressure on the negotiating states for a strong post-Kyoto climate deal which would guarantee the involvement of cities as partners in the post-2012 regime. ICLEI moreover advocated the explicit recognition of cities as key to the implementation of such a post-2012 deal. At COP15 no deal was reached. Later during COP16 in Cancun, the participating states recognised the key role of cities and local governments – the city as 'governmental stakeholder' – play in global climate change governance. This illustrates an evident trend, the city – or rather associations of cities – is rising as an informal actor in formal law-making.

An example of formal law-making within an organisation is the adoption of a resolution by the Governing Council of UN-Habitat, a subsidiary organ of the UN General Assembly, in 2007, which approved the *Guidelines on Decentralisation and the Strengthening of Local*

Authorities.[13] At an informal level, this resolution was really pushed by UCLG. Together with UN-Habitat and the Advisory Group of Experts on Decentralisation, UCLG drafted the *Guidelines*. Going beyond this, the city may become a formally recognised participant in formal law-making when the call from the WHO European Healthy Cities Network "to encourage the participation of local government representatives in Member States' delegations to meetings of WHO's governing bodies and other relevant international forums"[14] has resorted effect. In the context of the next proposition we will touch upon the possibility to delegate negotiating and treaty-making powers to the city.

Cities are involved increasingly in informal law-making. The status of agreements between cities as well as between cities and IOs is unclear. A number of these 'soft law' instruments have already been mentioned. How should we regard the status of the various founding declarations of global city networks either linked to or completely outside international organisations? What is the binding force of global city network agreements setting, *e.g.*, common targets (of GHG emission reduction or in 'going solar')? What about the sustainability cooperation agreements which some cities have concluded in the context of Agenda 21, such as the old twinning partners Utrecht and Léon? Or, what is the status of cooperation agreements between IOs and cities, such as the *Agreement of Cooperation between The United Nations Human Settlements Programme and United Cities and Local Governments,* which provides the normative framework for UN-Habitat – UCLG cooperation, also with respect to the *Cities Alliance* initiative. Being generated outside the formal mechanisms of law-making, these soft law instruments have some degree of international normativity. Chances are that with the rise of the global public city, the creation of these types of informal international norms will increase.

---

13 UN-Habitat Governing Council Resolution 21/3: Guidelines on Decentralization and Strengthening of Local Authorities, 7th Plenary Meeting, 20 April 2007.

14 World Health Organization, Zagreb Declaration for Healthy Cities, 15-18 October 2008, Article 10.

3.5. The International Law of the Future Addresses the City Directly

The international law of the future will include the now emerging 'international local government law'.[15] This body of law addresses the city directly, not as a state organ. It regulates the city and reshapes its relationship with the state. For example, the Council of Europe has adopted the *European Charter of Local Self-Government*, which stipulates that states guarantee the political, administrative and financial independence of local governments, recognise the principle of local self-government, and respect local democracy meanwhile stimulating the autonomy of cities with respect to the state-level. Inspired by the European Charter, similar norms of local self-government were adopted at the global level, the *Guidelines on Decentralisation and the Strengthening of Local Authorities*. Continuing urbanisation and global decentralisation will strengthen the call for the development of global norms of 'good urban governance', including principles of sustainable development, transparency and accountability, citizens' participation, and human rights. The nascence of such norms is taking place within the World Bank and the United Nations. To both the World Bank and UN-Habitat, good urban governance is a core value in their efforts to eradicate poverty and promote sustainability in cities. It has become a focal point of the policies of both global institutions. The objective is the "inclusive City, a place where everyone, regardless of wealth, gender, age, race or religion, is enabled to participate productively and positively in the opportunities cities have to offer".[16] In short, the international law of the future will include also standards of 'good urban governance'. As such, it deviates from a fundamental conception of traditional international law, which stipulates that the internal life of a sovereign state – including its internal organisation – is outside the reach of international law.

One can imagine 'international local government law' to develop further in a way similar to the legal framework that has been developed in

15 Cf. Gerald Frug and David Barron, "International Local Government Law", in *Urban Lawyer*, 2006, vol. 38, no. 1, pp. 1-62.

16 UN-Habitat, *Global Campaign on Urban Governance: Concept Paper*, 2002, p. 15-16, available at http://www.unhabitat.org/downloads/docs/2099_24326_concept_paper.doc, last accessed 1 April 2011.

response to cross-border cooperation between border-regions (in Europe[17] as well as, for example, the border regions of the US and Mexico and the US and Canada); such an international legal framework will develop geared to the international relations of the city. The city is then authorised by the state through a (bilateral or multilateral) treaty to employ transnational intercity relations. International law applicable to such inter-city cooperation may have a more public character aimed at the creation of a legal order within which we will find inter-city cooperation on issues such as trade, environmental protection and labour circumstances. In an attempt to protect the urban environment and the urban population against a race to the bottom, cities which have to compete in attracting businesses of the financial-economic sector can conclude binding agreements on issues of human rights and environment in order to prevent such a race to the bottom, without putting jobs in jeopardy. One can imagine 'like minded' global cities unite in a global network based on binding obligations to guarantee the same human rights and labour law standards or to reduce the urban ecological footprint. Current global networks, such as the *C40 Large Cities Climate Leadership Group* or the *ICLEI-Local Governments for Sustainability*, could become less informal, more committed, and more effective (even when such a global city network is not moulded into an independent legal person, which could also be an option). A new urban governance structure would thus emerge as well as a global law regulating it.

3.6. The City: An International Legal Person of the Future?

The trends of the future on which the previous propositions are based reshape the global society and transform international law. In the traditional state-centric model of international relations and international law, only states have been visible in "the eyes of international law".[18] Being a state organ, the city has to comply with international obligations

[17] In Europe this legal framework already partly applies to transnational cooperation between local governments not located immediately on the border.

[18] Montevideo Convention on Rights and Duties of States, 26 December 1993, Article 2, available at http://www.cosmopolitikos.com/Documents/Montevideo%20(1933).pdf, last accessed 1 April 2011.

of the state in for example areas like human rights.[19] This set-up will not change, but it may become more explicit as the global public city rises under the influence of decentralisation and thus articulates its' rights, duties and responsibilities under international law more clearly.

However, the city will seek international legal recognition of its' rising power. In the future, the global public city is a key partner of international organisations; it implements international law on its own accord, and it is involved in formal and informal processes of international law-making. Whether it will be bearer of international legal personality depends upon the approach or definition one employs.[20] Some commentators have already claimed the city has international legal personality.[21] Arguably, the city will possess 'soft international legal personality'[22] similar to the status of other international non-state actors. In any case, it seems fair to conclude that the global public city will exist in the eyes of the international law of the future.

4. The Urbanisation of International Law: Caveat and Concluding Remarks

The urbanisation of international relations is already well on its way. 'City diplomacy', urban offices for international relations, urban missions to international organisations, etc., are all well-established phenomena of the global society. Based on the previously identified trends and propositions, we may conclude that the future will show an urbanisation of international law. Naturally this conclusion comes with a major caveat – no one can be sure what the future holds. However, it is fair to

19 See European Court of Human Rights, *Tatar v. Romania*, Case 67021/01, Judgment, 27 January 2009, in which the brothers Tatar tried the city of Baia Mare for violating its positive obligations under Article 8 of ECHR.

20 Janne E. Nijman, *The Concept of International Legal Personality: An Inquiry into the History and Theory of International Law*, T.M.C. Asser Press, 2004.

21 A. Papisca, "International Law and Human Rights as a Legal Basis for the International Involvement of Local Governments", in Arne Musch (ed.), *City Diplomacy: the Role of Local Governments in Conflict Prevention, Peace-building, Post-conflict Reconstruction*, VNG International, The Hague, 2008, pp. 27-44.

22 Janne E. Nijman, "Non-State Actors and the International Rule of Law: Revisiting the 'Realist Theory' of International Legal Personality", in Math Noortmann and Cedric Ryngaert (eds.), *Non State Actors Dynamics in International Law: From Law-Takers to Law-Makers*, Ashgate, 2010.

extrapolate from the interaction between globalisation, urbanisation, and decentralisation that the rise of the global public city is underway.

The global public city challenges the conventional international institutional structures. Futhermore, it challenges state sovereignty, contributes to relative normativity, and offends the old canon of international legal persons. The rise of the global public city will reshape the global legal order. The international law of the future will be less state-centric, more complex, and it will be created more bottom-up through formal and informal processes in which global public cities are involved. The urbanisation of international law not only means an increase of international 'soft' law created by cities or city involvement. Also, the 'hard' international law of the future will be more urban than it is today, since the interests of the state will increasingly be defined by the interests of its cities. The global society of the future moreover will be deeply urban. The challenges of global justice will be challenges of urban justice. This will contribute further to the urbanisation of international law.

The global public city will have an important impact on the development of new international law, *i.e.*, law of a new international society, a society of all-humanity and all societies, including urban societies.

3. Private Actors, International Commerce and Private Legal Regimes

3.1

The Future of Commercial Law: Governing Cross-Border Commerce

Gralf-Peter Calliess*

The transnationalisation of commercial law is the key development in the field, where transnationalisation is understood as the combined internationalisation and privatisation of the governance of commercial transactions triggered by the ongoing globalisation of commerce. The key dilemmas related to this trend result from a reflection of the pros and cons of private ordering. As the main values embodied in the implementation of the rule of law by state created commercial law are access to justice, equity, legal certainty, and the public good, the privatisation of governance may put these values into question, where there is no level playing field for the competition of public and private governance regimes. It is likely that some national legal systems will increase their competitiveness in the future, while innovation is continued to be created outside of the established legal systems.

1. Introduction

This think piece will outline the challenges that national legal systems face today and are likely to face in the next decades in the field of commercial law. Since the future is always contingent, it is tenuous to write on the future developments of law. However, it seems to be feasible to, first of all, point at some recent societal trends which have influenced and will continue to influence the context in which the national legal systems operate from a scientific perspective, and, secondly, to draw on historical examples of how legal systems adapted to comparable changes in the social environment.

2. Key Development: Transnationalisation of Commercial Law

Commerce, comprising business to business (b2b) as well as business to consumer (b2c) transactions, is dependent on efficacious institutions for

* **Gralf Peter Calliess** is Professor of Civil Law, International Trade Law, and Legal Theory at Universität Bremen.

the enforcement of contracts, which might be provided by public or private actors. Such institutions comprise not only substantive norms, but include procedural arrangements for dispute resolution and enforcement. The table below shows public and private governance mechanisms employed in commercial transactions categorised by the three classical state powers of legislating, adjudicating, and enforcing.

Regulator \ Dimension	Legislation	Adjudication	Enforcement
Public	Parliamentary Act	Courts	Legal Sanctions
Private Trilateral	Social Norms	Arbitration	Social Sanctions
Private Bilateral	Relational Norms	Negotiation	Exit/Hostages
Private Unified	Corporate Norms	Board Decision	Hierarchy

Table 1: Public and Private Governance Mechanisms in International Commerce.

During the nineteenth century the rising nation-states nationalised commercial law and, thus, took over the responsibility for the provision of legal certainty in an attempt to foster commerce and thereby national wealth. However, this endeavour was successful for domestic commerce only, while cross-border commerce by and large remained unregulated. A branch of domestic law for private international law (or the conflict of laws) became part of the problem it was intended to solve.

While cross-border commerce was once regarded to be the exclusive domain of highly specialised international merchants who organised their trade by different means of self-help and private regulation, in modern times of economic globalisation, cross-border transactions have become abundant. Triggered by new trends in information and communication technologies (ICT) such as the Internet, e-commerce, and the digitisation of products, small and medium sized enterprises (SMEs) and consumers are becoming increasingly involved in cross-border commerce during the last decade. Thus, globalisation of commerce is a process which is deepening and which will continue to affect an increasing number of aspects of everyday life.

If one thinks of contract enforcement institutions as a normative good produced on a market, the legal needs of law consumers have shifted towards institutions that provide legal certainty in cross-border situations, while the offer of the national legal systems remains focused on domestic commerce. The growing gap between public offer and (private) demand is filled by service providers that offer private governance mechanisms such as soft law (private codifications, codes of conduct, standard form contracts), alternative dispute resolution (arbitral courts, conciliation and mediation services), and private enforcement mechanisms (reputation systems, escrow, credit security, and payment services). Occasionally, different governance mechanisms from the three dimensions of legislation, adjudication, and enforcement are bundled into effective private regimes.

Such private regimes, which are discussed under the catch phrases of the New *Lex Mercatoria* (b2b) or Transnational Consumer Contract Law (b2c), take advantage of the fact that private governance, as opposed to a national legal system, is not territorially limited. The combined processes of the internationalisation and privatisation of governance, which result in transnational commercial law, are reinforced by nation-states, which on the one hand refrain from adapting their national legal systems to the changed legal needs, and on the other hand lend their monopoly in the legitimate use of force to private governance mechanisms, *e.g.*, by recognising and enforcing arbitral awards.

Coming back to table 1 above, the transnationalisation of commercial law translates into a top-down shift from public governance to trilateral and bilateral private governance. In addition, many cross-border transactions are subject to unified governance, where recent estimates suggest that intrafirm-trade within transnational corporations account for one-third of world exports. The upshot is that transnationalisation is an established trend in the institutional organisation of cross-border commerce, which in the ambit of ongoing economic and cultural globalisation, as well as by virtue of path dependency, is likely to continue to characterise the field in the coming decades.

3. Key Dilemmas: Privatisation and the Rule of Law

With regard to the key problems that relate to this trend, one is tempted to think there are none. At least this seems to follow from the current reluctance of the national political systems to intervene, and from the positive appraisal of private actors and co-regulation between states, industry and civil society, which is prevalent in most international organisations. So why care?

As the main feature of the transnationalisation of law is the privatisation of governance, potential dilemmas may result from a reflection of the pros and cons of private ordering. On this point, it is advisable to remind ourselves of the reasons why commercial law was nationalised in the first place. The main values embodied in the implementation of the rule of law in the field of commercial law are access to justice, equity, legal certainty, and the public good.

4. Access to Justice

The fundamental right to access to justice flows directly from the enlightenment idea of a social contract, by which the individuals transfers their natural right to self-help with regard to the protection of their rights and interests to the state, thereby conferring a monopoly in the legitimate use of force. However, they do so only in exchange for a right to effective access to justice as provided by Article 6(1) of the European Convention of Human Rights (ECHR): "In the determination of his civil rights and obligations … everyone is entitled to a fair and public hearing within a reasonable time by an independent and impartial tribunal established by law …".[1] As the prohibition of a denial of justice with regard to aliens is a principle of international customary law, this right historically is a human right which includes foreigners and extends to cross-border situations as well.

Article 6(1) of ECHR does not prohibit alternative dispute resolution (ADR). However, where the state denies access to courts by recognising and enforcing arbitration agreements, such obligation to arbitrate shall be freely assumed by the parties. One might question if the choice to arbitrate can be regarded as free where litigation is in fact not a viable option, because state courts are slow (*e.g.*, stages of appeal), inflexible (*e.g.*, with regard to language), partial (so-called home-state bias vis à vis foreigners), too expensive (*e.g.*, with regard to small claims), unreliable (*e.g.*, regarding the enforcement of foreign judgments), or even corrupt (*e.g.*, in low developed countries). Statistically, even in highly developed legal systems such as Germany there is a clear trend of flight

[1] The European Convention on Human Rights, 4 November 1950, Article 6, para 1.

from commercial litigation to arbitration, especially when it comes to cross-border commerce ('the vanishing commercial trial').

This might not be a problem for high value disputes, where the employment of high quality private dispute resolution services is cost-efficient. However, since in the private dispute resolution market small claims are not subsidised by big claims, such high quality services might effectively be unavailable to claims raised by SMEs or consumers. But even where consumer ADR is subsidised by businesses, the impartiality of the dispute resolution process might be put into question. As discussed, for instance, in the context of cross-border consumer disputes in e-commerce, there should be a public framework for private (online) dispute resolution in place, which guarantees access to justice and procedural fairness. This is to say that where the state is unable or unwilling to provide effective access to justice through public institutions, the state has to guarantee at least the availability of fair private services at a reasonable cost.

5. Equity

While the state legal system of the nineteenth century is perceived as having been oriented towards a formal paradigm of justice, the mega-trend of the social-democratic twentieth century is said to have been the reorientation towards a substantive paradigm of justice. This is to say that judges were taking notice of the social reality of inequalities in the distribution of bargaining power and, as a counter move, exercised judicial control over contract terms, which were perceived as unjust in substance. The legislators also enacted protective laws which increasingly limited private autonomy with a view to securing social justice (*e.g.*, the EU private law *acquis*, which is predominantly protecting consumers, but also SMEs like commercial agents).

Against this background the transnationalisation of commercial law, which entails both the privatisation of legislation (*e.g.*, Unidroit Principles of International Commercial Contracts or codes of conduct for b2c-e-commerce) and the privatisation of adjudication (arbitration courts or online dispute resolution providers), seems to put the very idea of the political nature of private law into question. Do private norm entrepreneurs and private judges care about social justice, or do they simply follow the motto "he who pays the piper calls the tune"?

The answer to these questions is less obvious than it might seem. Where a private legal regime is established by a third party, which as a market maker between the transaction partners is interested in creating a safe harbour where both buyers and sellers feel comfortable (*e.g.*, eBay), the answer might be different from the situation where one transaction partner unilaterally dictates contract terms to the detriment of the weaker party (*e.g.*, Amazon). Where there is competition between different providers of private governance services, the decisive question centres around which transaction party makes the choice, since offer is driven by demand. This is to say that, if we conceive of contract enforcement institutions as being provided on a law market, the remaining role for the state might be to provide for 'legal consumer protection', which again relates to the idea of a public framework for private ordering.

With regard to substantive justice for the participants in cross-border commerce a national political perception of justice (*e.g.*, the question if a cooling-off period is 10 working days or two weeks) is far less important than the provision of reliable, impartial, and fair contract enforcement institutions at a reasonable cost. Generally speaking, it is necessary to substitute the national political perception of justice with a transnational concept of equity.

6. Legal Certainty

Access to justice and equity are services a legal system provides to individual participants in a commercial transaction. The function that a legal system performs for society as a whole, however, is to prevent future disputes by providing legal certainty. Rather than by legislation this function is performed as a by-product of the litigation process. While norms become real only by being cited and applied, the published *ratio decidendi* of each individual judgment is the added value, which the legal system contributes to the public good of legal certainty.

Insofar as the transnationalisation of commercial law implies a privatisation of dispute resolution, this surplus value of public litigation is at stake, where the results of ADR procedures are kept private. Thus, like the above described trend of the 'vanishing commercial trial', this movement in some branches of law has already led to a situation, where little or no precedent is available. This is reported, for instance, for the law of mergers and acquisitions in Germany, but it also holds true for consumer contract law in the US, where pre-dispute shrink-wrap or click-wrap arbitration agreements in consumer contracts are enforceable and have become mundane.

One possible solution to this problem is to publish arbitral awards or other ADR decisions as well. Sometimes it is held that this would interfere with the very idea of private dispute resolution, but in fact arbitral awards of the Court of International Arbitration of the International Chamber of Commerce, for instance, are increasingly published. From the standpoint of legal certainty it suffices to publish the *ratio decidendi* of a decision, while the names of the parties, their business secrets as well as other individual facts of the case may as a compromise remain a very well kept secret.

Another solution could be to modernise the state court system in order to adapt it to the legal needs of modern cross-border commerce. The State of New York, for instance, established a commercial division during the 1990s, which successfully brought a substantive share of commercial disputes back from arbitration. Furthermore, the Law Society of England and Wales published a marketing brochure in 2007 entitled 'The Jurisdiction of Choice', which is intended to bring the business of international commercial dispute resolution to London. The German answer 'Law – Made in Germany" was published in 2008, and a bill is currently under discussion in the German Bundestag, which suggests introducing special chambers for international commerce at German courts, where litigation may be conducted in English as it is the language of international commerce.

To sum up, 'bringing the state back in' with regard to international commercial dispute resolution is currently a much discussed option. There are other reforms suggested, such as pre-dispute agreements on limitation or exclusion of stages of appeals, or the implementation of the 2005 Hague Convention on Choice of Court Agreements, which within the next decades shall create a level playing field between international litigation and arbitration. The modernisation and adaptation of the court system to the changed legal needs of globalised commerce will be an important trend within the next decades. Thus, the global market for commercial dispute resolution is likely to be transformed by the advent of state courts as new competitors to arbitration courts.

7. Public Good

7.1. Preservation of the Public Order

One important reason for the solution of private commercial disputes by public institutions is that only state courts are perceived as being in a position to prevent the external effects of private disputes, *i.e.*, to guarantee that private disputes are not solved to the detriment of the public good. This function of state courts in private international law is traditionally associated with the application of internationally mandatory norms and with the public order control in the process of the application of foreign law as well as in the recognition and enforcement of foreign judgments. Typical examples of such public values are fundamental rights, laws against corruption, or competition policy issues.

Conventional wisdom will have it that private judges are not in a proper position to take care of the public good. Thus, the transnationalisation of commercial law challenges the traditional role of state courts in preserving the public good, since arbitral awards may be reviewed by state courts only for very limited reasons. One of those reasons is the *ordre public*, but since each state has its own public order, in an international commercial dispute it is quite difficult to come to terms with that issue. The position taken by the German Bundesgerichtshof, for instance, is that only a neglect of the truly international public order, that is values that are common to all civilised nations, may prevent the enforcement of an arbitral award. The European Court of Justice ruled, for instance, that the European competition rules, in that case Article 101 FEU-Treaty, belong to the European public order. A recent empirical survey of arbitral awards has shown, however, that international arbitral tribunals have successfully developed some core rules of a transnational public order, even where they were not forced to do so by state courts. According to that study, the same holds true for the fundamental right to free speech, which is applied by private panels under the ICANN Uniform Dispute Resolution Policy. Therefore, the public order might be less endangered than expected by the privatisation of dispute resolution. Rather private judges seem to make a valuable contribution to the creation of a global public order.

7.2. Vertical Integration and Competition Policy

But public values are not only endangered by the privatisation of dispute resolution. The transnationalisation of commercial governance may affect public values in a more indirect way as well. This can be made visible through the following line of argumentation: The possible reactions of commercial actors with respect to the lack of legal certainty provided by the state legal systems for cross-border commerce are not limited to the flight to private governance mechanisms such as arbitration courts. Another option is to take the transaction out of the market by means of vertical integration. Multinational enterprises organise at least one third of world exports in the form of intra-firm trade, where there is no need for third party contract enforcement, but potential conflicts are mitigated in the hierarchy of the firm. Vertical integration in this context is called private unified governance of transactions.

Conventional wisdom will have it that the so-called make-or-buy decision is determined by certain attributes of a transaction, namely frequency and asset specificity. However, this so-called transaction cost theory operates under the condition of 'lawfulness' that is a workable system of contract enforcement for market transactions created by the legal system. In a situation of 'lawlessness', in turn, transactions that in domestic trade in an OECD country would be conducted over the market may be vertically integrated in order to substitute for the lack of legal certainty on the market. This fact is well established for transformation economies with a weak legal system. However, it equally applies to the state of legal uncertainty with which international commerce is faced between OECD countries (except for the EU internal market, where cooperation in civil and commercial matters is quite well regulated).

It follows that the legal vacuum which the national legal systems leave when it comes to cross-border commerce beyond Europe leads to an increased amount of vertical integration on world markets, which from a purely economic standpoint is inefficient, because within a domestic market with a workable legal system such transactions would be conducted on the market. Unnecessary vertical integration, however, also runs counter to competition policy. Thus, the transnationalisation of the institutional organisation of commerce hampers free competition by producing over-integration in world markets. This might become a strong argument in favour of enhanced international cooperation in the area of international commercial law.

8. Resume and Outlook

Commerce defined as the marketing of goods and services comprises business to business (b2b) as well as business to consumer (b2c) transactions. Commerce is dependent on a tremendously complex set of institutions among which efficacious institutions for the enforcement of contracts figure most prominently, since they enable at-arm's-length market exchange as a basic prerequisite of the modern competitive economy. Where a contract cannot be enforced effectively at reasonable cost, the potential risks will be priced out and/or parties refrain from conducting exchange to the detriment of economic growth and national wealth. "The inability of societies to develop effective, low-cost enforcement of contracts is the most important source of both historical stagnation and contemporary underdevelopment …", as Nobel Laureate Douglass C. North has put it so aptly.

Where both the welfare of modern societies and the capacity of the nation-state to intervene with society are based on economic growth, there is a public interest in fostering commerce by providing efficient institutions for contract enforcement. In other words, legal certainty for commercial transactions is a public good, at least in the market economies of OECD countries. However, this does not necessarily imply that the state takes over the sole responsibility for the provision of legal certainty. Institutions that support contractual commitments may also be provided without the state by means of private ordering. Different private governance mechanisms, namely social norms, alternative dispute resolution, and social sanctions may eventually be bundled into effective private regimes.

During the eighteenth and nineteenth century the nation-state took over the fully fledged responsibility for the provision of legal certainty for commercial transactions. Due to its territorially limited jurisdiction, however, the state fulfilled this promise with regard to domestic commerce only, while the endeavour to create efficacious public institutions for the enforcement of cross-border commercial transactions by means of international cooperation between states failed.

Since then, the extent to which commerce is conducted across borders has risen substantially. Economic globalisation has thus led to a shift in the demand structure for institutions that support commerce. Over the past forty years, the need for institutions adapted to international commerce has increased. The normative vacuum left by nation-states was filled by all kinds of private governance mechanisms and private legal services for international commerce. The trend towards the internationalisation and privatisation of the provision of legal certainty, combine to what is called the transnationalisation of commercial law. Economic globalisation leads to a decrease in the relative weight of public institutions and to a corresponding increase in the overall importance of private ordering with regard to the provision of legal certainty for commerce.

The transnationalisation of commercial law thus described the challenges faced by the main values embodied in the rule of law as implemented in the field of commercial law. These are access to justice, equity, legal certainty, and the public good. In all four areas the policy options are basically either 1) to foster the ongoing privatisation of legal services while at the same time trying to constitutionalise them by different means of regulated self-regulation, *i.e.*, creating a public framework for private ordering, or 2) to bring the state back in by modernising the national legal system in an attempt to adapt it to the legal needs of globalised commerce. As the analysis of the questions related to the four different values has shown, these strategies are not exclusive, but may be combined in an endeavour to create a level playing field in the competition of public and private regimes.

Finally, what we can learn from comparable challenges in history is that private international legal policy in the international domain as well as in Europe is far too concerned with the harmonisation of substantive laws, which is a reason why there was so little success. But norms do come naturally as a by-product of the dispute resolution process, where effective access to justice and dispute resolution is based on equity rather than formalised rules. To give some brief examples, when Roman trade extended over the Mediterranean Sea, the Romans did not try to extend their *ius civile* to foreigners but in an innovative way developed the *ius gentium*. Equally, during the medieval revival of European trade, French merchants who complained for denial of justice at Common Law were granted by the King the right to institute staple courts, where merchants from both countries dispensed justice in an informal and equitable way. The legal innovations that were developed in the practice of this ancient Law Merchant were integrated into the national legal systems throughout Europe during the nineteenth century. Moreover, the legal innovations necessary for coping with the ongoing processes of globalisation seem to be developed by and large outside of the established national legal systems in different forms of private regimes, *i.e.*, by virtue of external competition which at the end of the day may force the national legal systems to adapt to social evolution.

3.2

Private Law in a Postnational Society

Jan Smits*

I intend to focus on two interrelated trends. The first is the replacement of law by other types of trust building relationships in the global economy. If we assume that national law is becoming less and less important and will not be replaced by a similar type of law at an international level, (private) parties have to look for other types of trust-building. The second trend is the increased role of (private) parties in choosing their own law. Many forms of 'legal tourism' have emerged over recent decades and it is likely that this trend will continue. The emergence of optional regimes is only one important example of this. At the same time, states will have to be much more precise about what they can still allow as a choice for a foreign or optional legal system. Both trends are likely to reshape the entire outlook of law.

1. Introduction

I have been asked what I regard to be the most significant challenge for the development of law in the coming three decades. This question presupposes that we have some idea of what developments are likely to occur: once we know what *will* happen, not only in the legal field, but in society in general, we will be able to say to what extent this development challenges our prevailing ideas about law. It is clear that some speculation is inherent in this type of exercise. My focus in this brief paper is on private law, although I should add that I believe it is impossible to separate this field from other areas of law. I will distinguish between substantive developments and changes in the ways in which we think about private law.

* **Jan M. Smits** is Professor of European Private Law at Maastricht University and 2010-2011 Maastricht University-HiiL Visiting Chair on the Internationalisation of Law.

2. Substantive Developments

At a substantive level, I identify three main developments, all related to the increasing de-nationalisation of law and society. For me, this de-nationalisation is a term that describes any process (such as Europeanisation and globalisation, but not limited to these) through which national law becomes less important. This de-nationalisation is in my view the most important development in the coming decades, and one that will substantially challenge our existing ideas about law. One need not be a visionary to see why this is the case. Law increasingly stems from entities other than the State, such as the European Union, supranational organisations or local legislative bodies. This development is well known and even though it raises important questions of legitimacy, the replacement of the authority of the state by other entities takes place in an explicit and transparent way. The main challenge lies somewhere else. The de-nationalisation of law also means that the authority of the national state *vis-à-vis* its own citizens becomes decreasingly important. We can identify two reasons for this.

First, de-nationalisation of law means that the law in a party's 'own' state is no longer necessarily applicable to the conduct of that party. Parties have a greater choice of which jurisdiction to use, which has led to many forms of 'legal tourism'. In various fields of law, parties can opt-out of using their national legal system and choose another jurisdiction. There is also an alternative trend which is likely to continue. Parties can increasingly choose a non-national regime, such as a European '28th' jurisdiction. This leads to a decoupling of law from the national state in the sense that citizens come to play a more prominent role in deciding which law will be applicable to the things they do. This has far-reaching consequences for how we perceive law: from law being imposed upon the citizens in a process of democratic representation, it becomes a product that citizens can choose, reminiscent of certain forms of direct democracy. Different communities will compete with each other in their efforts to apply a certain set of norms to an act or an actor.

Secondly, de-nationalisation means that the law itself is being replaced by other types of trust-building relationships. With the surpassing of national law, we should not try to replace it with a similar type of law at the international law (this is impossible at a global level), but give full recognition to alternative mechanisms. In commercial law, this means that we have to develop new forms of creating legal certainty. In consumer law, it means that, *e.g.*, labelling schemes will partly take over the function that national law plays at the moment. This does not mean that there is no longer a place for national law, bit it does mean that this place will necessarily be more limited. It also means that a fundamental discussion should take place about what states regard to be at the core of their society, leading to clear mandatory rules that citizens cannot deviate from, yet leaving scope for freedom in other fields.

3. Changes in Our Inherited Ways of Thinking

Apart from substantive developments, it may be useful to look at how legal thinking in the field of private law will be changing as a result of de-nationalisation. If we assume that private law has to meet certain requirements, one can try to identify how these requirements were met in the past (in particular in the last 200 years in which private law was highly national in nature) and how these requirements will be met in a different way in a postnational society. Here, I like to focus on three interrelated aspects: the accessibility and predictability of private law, the legitimacy of private law and private law as a way to bind people to a state.

The first function is the accessibility and predictability of private law. This function is closely related to the prevailing theory of sources: by keeping the amount of sources out of which private law originates fairly limited, private law remains manageable, thus offering the legal certainty that parties need. In civil law countries, this function has long been fulfilled by the adoption of a civil code by the national legislature and by a continuing systematisation of new case law by academics (and the use of this legal system by the courts). Codification was thus an important tool to create stability and rationality in law. In common law countries, the highest court carried out the same function by creating precedents that were binding on the lower courts and indeed, on the highest court itself.

Clearly the accessibility and predictability of law will not be ensured in the same way in the future. Already, private law is characterised by a plurality of sources and this will only increase in the future: different (or even similar) parts of private law are dealt with by different 'lawgivers', who will not have the responsibility for coherence and unity which inherently lies with an overarching institution. Multiple 'systems' of private law thus overlap with each other, as they deal with the same issues in different ways. This emerging pluralism leads to two challenges for traditional private law thinking. First, it would lead to a fundamental discussion about optimal levels of regulation: can we find the criteria to decide whether certain topics are better dealt with at the local, national, European or supranational level? Second, even if we are able to find such criteria, we still have to see how accessibility and predictability of private law are best guaranteed in a multilevel system of private law.

The second function is the legitimacy of private law. In civil law countries this function is traditionally also satisfied through a civil code and other pieces of legislation that pass through the democratic process at the national level. Again, the multiplication of sources has put an end to this. The many authoritative rules, norms and policies from sites of governance beyond the nation-state prompt us to find new ways to legitimise private law.

Finally, private law has long had the function of binding citizens to a particular country, especially in civil law jurisdictions, where the making of a civil code was an essential element of the nation-building exercise. But it is not only the idea that each country has its own unique law that ties law to a specific country. As we have seen before, citizens are in practice tied to the law of their country simply because of their place of residence. However, this is no longer true either: people today have many different affiliations and can often choose the jurisdiction they like best for different aspects of their life. In a postnational legal order, these voluntary associations with different legal orders will become increasingly important. This raises the question to what extent national states can accept this turn away from their own law.

3.3

How Economic Globalisation is Helping to Construct a Private Transnational Legal Order

Deborah Hensler[*]

Around the world, public legal orders are struggling to respond to the consequences of economic globalisation. The absence of international civil tribunals to deal with trans-national harms creates a gap that private lawyers are rushing to fill. Although the substantive legal outcomes are highly uncertain, recent events suggest convergence toward holding multi-national market actors to higher standards of accountability and affording injured populations more generous compensation for losses, in a wider variety of circumstances. The emergence of this 'collective redress' norm is powered by trans-national coalitions of private entrepreneurial lawyers and publicly-interested NGOs, with the latter incentivised by frustrations over the success of multi-national corporations in subverting public regulation through agency capture, legislative lobbying and media control. The adoption of procedures for collective litigation – class actions, group litigation orders, and other forms of aggregated mass litigation – in an ever increasing number of countries provides new opportunities for building a trans-national private order. But the piecemeal and uncoordinated nature of such developments also creates new opportunities for forum shopping that increase direct and indirect costs of litigation and frustrate attempts to regulate lawyer behavior. Absent more pro-active efforts by domestic courts to coordinate procedures and harmonise substantive law, multi-national corporations may attempt to craft class- and mass procedures within international arbitration that will remove both outcomes and process from public view.

1. Introduction

Around the world, public legal orders are struggling to respond to the consequences of economic globalisation. The absence of international civil tribunals to deal with transnational harm creates a gap that private

[*] **Deborah R. Hensler** is Judge John W. Ford Professor of Dispute Resolution and Associate Dean for Graduate Studies at Stanford University.

lawyers are rushing to fill. Although the substantive legal outcomes are highly uncertain, recent events suggest convergence toward holding multi-national market actors to higher standards of accountability and affording injured populations more generous compensation for losses, in a wider variety of circumstances. The emergence of this type of collective redress is powered by transnational coalitions of private entrepreneurial lawyers and publicly-interested NGOs, with the latter incentivised by frustrations over the success of multi-national corporations in subverting public regulation through agency capture, legislative lobbying and media control. The adoption of procedures for collective litigation – class actions, group litigation orders and other forms of aggregated mass litigation in an ever increasing number of countries provides new opportunities for building a transnational private order. However the piecemeal and uncoordinated nature of such developments also creates new opportunities for forum shopping that increase direct and indirect costs of litigation and frustrate attempts to regulate lawyers' behaviour. In the absence of more pro-active efforts by domestic courts to coordinate procedures and harmonise substantive law, multi-national corporations may attempt to craft class- and mass procedures within international arbitration that will remove both outcomes and process from public view.

2. Economic, Cultural, Political and Technological Factors Promoting Mass Private Litigation

It is well understood that economic production yields negative as well as positive social outcomes. With economic activity comes the possibility of personal injuries (*e.g.*, from unsafe products), environmental damage (*e.g.*, from toxic contamination and destruction of natural resources), financial loss (*e.g.*, from violation of securities, competition and consumer protection law), and even human rights abuse (*e.g.*, if market actors accede to or join in exploitation of indigenous populations). As the economic scale increases, the scale of potential injuries resulting from single acts (*e.g.*, product design, an oil spill, failure to accurately disclose corporate assets) increases accordingly. Whereas previously most injuries affected one or a few individuals at a time and were a direct result of individual acts (*e.g.*, a car accident involving a driver and a pedestrian victim), mass injuries become increasingly common (*e.g.*, a train derailment causing large numbers of injuries and fatalities) and the causal chain lengthens and becomes more ambiguous (*e.g.*, increased risk of heart attack and stroke accompanying the use of an anti-inflammatory drug). As capturing ever-larger market share defines economic success, the potential scale of mass injuries increases likewise. When economic activity transcends national borders, so too do mass harms (*e.g.*, financial losses associated with the collapse of US-based Lehman Brothers).

Many cultures are characterised by fatalism in the face of harm or loss (*e.g.*, "it was God's will") and acceptance of impoverishment or impairment as a fact of ordinary life. People within these cultures ask little of their leaders in the way of protection from injury or loss, except perhaps defence against attacks from others. Clear intentionality is required to activate the Hammurabian code of justice ('an eye for an eye'). In less clear-cut situations, cultural norms may discourage the seeking of compensation from members of one's own society.

Modern society members seem less inclined to accept losses incurred through no fault of their own. With fewer children and longer life expectancies, workers, consumers and investors have higher expectations of protection from harm, in comparison to earlier generations. In ordinary circumstances of injury, modern society members may respond much as their more traditional predecessors did, attributing accidents to bad luck or their own misbehaviour. However, when injured workers, consumers and investors perceive others to be at fault, they are quicker to demand accountability and compensation. The modern media provide information, of varying degrees of accuracy, which enables and encourages people to link their injuries and losses to the negligent or intentional acts of others. By reporting on compensation received by similarly situated individuals, the media promote a rising sense of entitlement on the part of others injured in the same or similar circumstances, by the same or similar entities. These feelings may be exacerbated when the entities to which fault is attributed are perceived as outside the victim's community, *e.g.*, multi-national corporations. Although such trends may be associated with modernity, national cultures will always vary depending on their historical experiences, social structure and other factors.

As the external costs of economic productivity have mounted and cultural acceptance of danger and harm has diminished, modern democratic societies have turned to public law to regulate market behaviour. Market actors who perceive the costs of such regulation to be unacceptable have resisted by lobbying legislatures for less strict rules and less rigid implementation, by capturing the regulators themselves, and by attempting to shape the public discourse. The recent de-regulatory fervour that marked the rise of neo-liberalism reflected the success of such acts of corporate resistance. In some countries, most notably the United States, private civil litigation has emerged as an alternative to public law. Particularly in the case of mass injuries associated (correctly or not) with the actions of large corporations, in this way civil dispute resolution has been re-purposed as a regulatory tool, either explicitly or as an implicit consequence of collective redress. This use of private civil litigation has been highly controversial wherever it has emerged; perhaps because its decentralised bottom-up character makes it difficult for market actors to control except by directly confronting the cultural trends that fuel it. The nature of this difficulty is vividly illustrated by the circumstances British Petroleum found itself in after the April 2010 oil rig explosion in the Gulf of Mexico. Although formally protected from liability by a $75 million cap enacted in 1990 by the US Congress after the Exxon Valdez oil spill, British Petroleum has felt compelled to accede to President Obama's demand that it establish a $20 billion escrow fund to compensate Gulf property owners and business enterprises for damages. What, if any, effect the compensation fund will have on litigation against BP is highly unclear. According to recent media reports, at least 300 lawsuits arising out of the oil spill have been filed against BP.

Innovations in the field of IT have facilitated and accelerated many of the trends identified above. Electronic technology facilitates access to and sharing of data, making it available to public regulators. Furthermore, where legal rules permit electronic technology gives private lawyers vast quantities of information on market actors' decisions, more easily and at less cost than was previously possible. When high profile incidents, such as oil spills, product recalls and corporate restatements occur the mass media quickly join the corps of public investigators, helping to recycle data from legislature to courtroom to political arena. The Internet connects citizens of countries with less-developed private law regimes to entrepreneurial lawyers in the US and elsewhere, facilitates coordination among lawyers worldwide and speeds the diffusion of new collective redress norms. The consequences of technological innovation will be exacerbated by the new 'social media' that provide vehicles for the almost immediate sharing of information (and misinformation) and promote quick development of consensual social judgments on harm, responsibility and wrong-doing.

3. The Response of National Legal Systems to Mass Harm

Until recently, modern legal systems have been characterised by cases of a single plaintiff pursuing a legal claim against one or a few defendants. The key differences among legal systems centred on the questions of who had standing to bring what sort of claim, and for what sort of remedy. Until the 1990s, class actions and representative litigation brought by one or a few parties on behalf of a large number of similarly situated persons, were only found in the USA and in one province in Canada. Today, at least twenty countries have adopted some form of representative class action and several others have adopted a non-representative (*i.e.*, aggregated) form of group proceeding. The countries that have adopted class actions are remarkably diverse; they include common and civil law regimes, democratic and authoritarian regimes, countries with strong and weak public law cultures, and countries on every continent with the exception of Antarctica. The countries include leading national economies, such as Brazil, Canada, China, Germany, and Italy, and the seats of national headquarters of multi-national corporations, such as the Netherlands. Most of the procedures have been adopted since 2000. I argue that the emergence of representative and other forms of collective litigation are a response to the trends outlined above and are intimately connected with the changes set off by the spread of neo-liberal ideology and economic globalisation. Proposals for collective litigation have been challenged in some quarters by those who view such procedures as antithetical to principles of individual autonomy and rights as espoused, for example, in the European Convention on Human Rights. However, access to justice advocates are in support of allowing claimants to join forces in seeking redress against a common wrong-doer. These advocates argue that in some circumstances collective litigation is the only practical way to open the courthouse doors.

Only a minority of the class action procedures that have been adopted in the past decade follow the American model characterised by its relaxed standing for a party to sue on behalf of a class in virtually all substantive legal domains, with access to the remedy of financial damages and an opt- out rule as a default provision, which effectively increases the scope of a class. However, recent developments suggest that over time restrictive class action procedures tend to be extended across substantive legal domains and that there is pressure to extend remedies to include money damages at least in some circumstances. Support for re-regulation in response to the global financial crisis may quell agitation for adopting or extending class actions in some countries, however I think this is unlikely. Now that the class action horse is out of the barn, it will prove difficult to herd it back behind the barn doors.

Formal law is one matter, legal practice however is another. In a majority of the countries that have adopted class action, lawyers and claimant-advocates have found it difficult to pursue collective litigation as a result of legal financing regimes, which have rarely been adjusted to suit this new form of litigation. If representative claimants face the risk of adverse costs, which are likely to be very large when defendants face potentially enormous liability, it is unlikely that any individual claimant will come forward on behalf of the class. Where any form of 'success fee' is prohibited, lawyers are unlikely to invest in prosecuting class actions, which require an unusual investment of resources and often exceptional risk. Although opt-out provisions are fiercely fought by corporate opponents of class actions, such provisions impede contractual arrangements that can secure legal representation for class members by making it feasible for each to contract individually with the class' lawyer. By enhancing the risk to plaintiffs and restricting the benefits to plaintiff lawyers of successful representation, cost-shifting and prohibitions on success fees also impede the successful use of non-representative group litigation proceedings. Failure to adjust financing rules to match the realities of collective litigation is likely to explain the small numbers of cases that have proceeded under the new procedural rules in many countries. Recently however, barriers to financing collective litigation have begun to fall. Third-party financing has emerged as an alternative to contingency fee lawyers, 'after-the-event' insurance is available in some jurisdictions and proposals have been put forward to limit cost shifting or to allow limited contingency fees to facilitate class or non-class mass litigation. Ironically, the global financial crisis appears to have fuelled interest in third-party litigation financing, which is viewed as an attractive non-correlated investment.

The existence of collective litigation procedures in a significant number of economically important jurisdictions, most of which have strong independent judiciaries, raises difficult jurisdictional questions. Can a class action brought in the US against a non-US defendant include class members who are not US residents and whose connection with the defendant is not connected with the US? The US Supreme Court recently answered no to this question with regard to securities litigation. Should a court in the Netherlands recognise the resolution in the US of claims by Dutch citizens? An Amsterdam court recently answered yes to this question in a different securities case. Would a French court enforce the outcome of a US class action? A French defendant argued in front of a US judge that France would not do so. Viewed from one perspective, these questions are not new: the issue of enforcement of a judgment reached in one court by another court is long-standing and governed by both domestic law and international conventions. However, collective proceedings add several layers of complexity: Does the enforcing jurisdiction recognise the legitimacy of collective litigation, wherever it is brought? Does it recognise collective litigation only within its own boundaries, but not if it is brought elsewhere? Does it recognise collective litigation if brought elsewhere, but only if certain conditions are met, *e.g.*, notice having been given to class members, the inclusion of opt-in requirements? What happens when the scope of classes in class actions pursued in multiple jurisdictions, in parallel, overlap?

History suggests that such issues will eventually be worked out in time and in each domestic jurisdiction and most likely in a fashion that gives priority to stakeholders that have an interest in preserving the authority of their institutions. We might also expect that domestic economic actors will resist efforts to conform their national procedures to foreign procedural rules that comparatively afford more power to likely plaintiffs than their own jurisdictions do. In sum, in the near future, the law for mass claims might be one that establishes and supports a variety of collective litigation procedures, each operating in its own jurisdictional domain and only occasionally rubbing up against each other. However comfortable this scenario might be for national courts, national bars and nationally-based domestic and multi-national corporations, I think this is unlikely. Transnational investment and its attendant risks has already created a transnational network of private entrepreneurial lawyers who cooperate in devising and implementing litigation strategies to obtain maximum leverage against defendants and maximum benefits to themselves and their clients. These networks are creating a transnational latticework that operates in the shadow of domestic court decisions and constitutes a new private international legal system.

4. The Rise of a Transnational Private Legal Order for Mass Claims

The weakness of the scenario that predicts that national courts will dominate the collective litigation domain as they dominate the individual civil litigation domain is that it assumes that private lawyers will ignore the opportunities for forum selection and coordination created by the availability of class action and other group litigation procedures in a significant number of jurisdictions. This assumption ignores the financial incentives attendant upon successfully representing plaintiffs and the variations in these incentives across jurisdictions that derive from different legal financing regimes. The current landscape of collective litigation opens the opportunity for lawyers to pursue cases in one jurisdiction that offers attractive process and outcomes (*e.g.*, the Netherlands Collective Settlement regime) while playing by the legal fee rules of another jurisdiction (*e.g.*, the United States, where there are no prohibitions on contingency fees). While long experience with class actions in the US has led to heightened scrutiny of settlements and fees to guard against self-dealing by plaintiff lawyers and collusion between plaintiff lawyers and defendants, the much more recent adoption of class actions and other group litigation procedures elsewhere may not yet have led to such heightened scrutiny. Hence, the spread of collective litigation procedures has created, at least temporarily, a less strictly regulated global private litigation process than the domestic process that has evolved to date within the US and still attracts substantial criticism as too weak.

The new global private legal order is likely to sharply increase the costs of litigation for multi-national corporations who find themselves defending their actions in multiple fora, with different substantive legal doctrines and procedural rules. The risk of failure increases as the number of jurisdictions in which a matter is being litigated increases; even if the defendant succeeds in nine out of ten courts, a plaintiff success in the tenth court, if it is the one that claims jurisdiction over global or near-global classes, may lead to huge damages. And the fact that this risk exists can be leveraged by class counsel in multiple jurisdictions to obtain jurisdiction-specific damages without shouldering the risk that a global settlement will not be enforced elsewhere. Although corporations may successfully oppose the adoption of a class action regime with broad jurisdiction in one or more countries, it is not certain that they can successfully oppose such an adoption in all jurisdictions. Hence the risk may remain, notwithstanding concerted corporate opposition to class actions around the globe.

A potentially attractive response by corporations would be to move as many private civil disputes as possible out of the public courts and into private fora, particularly international arbitration that allow parties to devise their own decisional norms and procedural rules, perhaps even including prohibitions against collective proceedings. This strategy has been adopted by US corporations for domestic civil disputes in multiple domains. During the 1990s as the number and scope of class actions expanded, corporations began inserting mandatory arbitration provisions in employment, securities and consumer contracts of all types. Health care providers and some other professional service providers followed suit. In response to challenges by labour, investor and consumer advocates, state courts in the US began to void provisions of these contracts that forbade those who entered into the contracts from joining in any collective proceedings, either in court or in arbitration. This past year, the US Supreme Court appeared to endorse the use of arbitration provisions to eliminate class proceedings. However, the courts' decisions do not prohibit a corporation from including contractual language facilitating collective arbitration proceedings.

How disputes in the form of collective actions would fare in international private arbitration is unclear. There is a long history of compensating mass claims between states and individual foreign nationals but for the most part such claims have been administered through specially-instituted commissions rather than traditional arbitration forums, as a result of political settlements between states or decisions by international institutions. United Nations Commission on International Trade Law (UNCITRAL) guidelines for adapting UNCITRAL procedural rules to multi-party contractual disputes do not seem to contemplate a very large number of parties. International Chamber of Commerce (ICC) arbitration rules include a provision for multi-party proceedings but its application to large-scale disputes is similarly unclear. Moreover the interpretation of rules defining parties to a dispute varies across national jurisdictions, meaning that ICC rules may be implemented differently in London, Paris or Geneva. The International Centre for the Settlement of Investor Disputes has some experience with mass investor claims but apparently it does not have specialised procedures for dealing with mass claims. Whether and how such processes can be incorporated in contract-based dispute resolution of claims by individuals against multi-national corporations is an open question. Substantive doctrine pertaining to the inclusion of mandatory arbitration clauses in contracts of adhesion (*i.e.*, "form" contracts) such as employment and consumer contracts varies across jurisdictions; in the US such clauses have been endorsed by the courts, but in the EU consumer protection law deems such clauses unfair and hence unenforceable. Where the relationship between the alleged victims and the alleged tortfeasor is not contractually-based, recourse to arbitration would require consent. Obtaining consent in a mass claim context would be a formidable task. Even assuming that mass claims brought by individual parties of diverse nationalities could be resolved in a single arbitral forum, the question of whether such resolution could be had in a representative class proceeding would remain. It seems unlikely that jurisdictions that are still struggling with the issue of enforcing class action litigation judgments would be more comfortable enforcing class action arbitration outcomes arrived at in private and outside their own jurisdiction. In summation, while in principle shifting transnational mass claims to arbitration might appear attractive to multinational corporations; in practice it may prove unfeasible.

In the absence of clear public law guidelines for contractual arbitration of transnational mass claims, NGOs may attempt to establish voluntary schemes for resolving transnational disputes, perhaps by articulating due process norms for ad hoc circumstance-specific procedures or by establishing dispute resolution facilities for domain-specific disputes. While such schemes might attract and resolve large numbers of claims efficiently, they would not offer the certainty of closure that is currently offered to parties by international arbitration of claims between commercial entities.

Both in the near- and medium-term, national court judges hold the keys to efficient and fair resolution of transnational mass claims. Exercising their authority wisely will require judges to look beyond their own borders to discern the international implications of decisions that formally apply only to matters within their own jurisdiction but as a practical matter will reverberate through the transnational lattice created by private entrepreneurial lawyers. Substantive, procedural and even scheduling decisions in one of these jurisdictions may affect decisions to settle (or not) within other jurisdictions, the scope of such settlements and the quantity of damages. Transnational communication among judges could identify these consequences. Transnational coordination of pre-trial – for example, consolidating cases for pre-disposition purposes only – might mitigate unintended consequences. Domestic models for such consolidation include the USA multidistrict litigation (MDL) procedure and the English Group Litigation Order (GLO). However, no formal mechanism for pre-trial consolidation of civil suits across national borders currently exists and differences in norms (as well as formal legal rules) regarding the exchange of information, judicial management of the pre-trial process and other aspects of civil litigation present significant barriers even to more informal cooperation. As a result, I suspect that national courts will be slow to embrace the notion of transnational coordination of mass claims. Multi-national corporations might play an important role in this context, by nudging domestic courts towards cooperation and consolidation. However, in this respect, as with other aspects of transnational litigation, multi-national corporations face a dilemma: unregulated transnational litigation increases uncertainty regarding norms and increases litigation costs, but embracing transnational proceedings means abandoning domestic courts that may offer more immediate protection of their interests, particularly in their home countries. For all these reasons, the evolution of public policy in response to mass transnational claims is highly uncertain. But the evolution of mass claims is not: the global economy will continue to breed mass injuries and mass losses, social media will facilitate the diffusion of collective redress norms, and private lawyers will respond to the opportunities to serve clients in new, more effective and more lucrative ways, worldwide.

5. Bibliography

On Economic Productivity and Torts:

Guido Calabresi, *The Cost of Accidents: A Legal and Economic Analysis*, Yale University Press, 1970; William M. Landes and Richard A. Posner, *The Economic Structure of Tort Law*, Harvard University Press, 1987; Peter W. Huber and Robert E. Litan (ed.), *The Liability Maze: The Impact of Liability Law on Safety and Innovation*, Brookings Institution Press, Washington D.C., 1991; George L. Priest, "The Modern Expansion of Tort Liability: Its Sources, Its Effects and Its Reform", in *The Journal of Economic Perspectives*, 1991, vol. 5, no. 3, pp. 31-50; Peter Schuck, *Tort Law and the Public Interest: Competition, Innovation, and Consumer Welfare*, W. W. Norton & Company, New York, 1991; Steven Shavell, *Economic Analysis of Accident Law*, Harvard University Press, 1987.

On Claiming and Compensation Cultures

John C. Burnham, "Why Did the Infants and Toddlers Die? Shifts in Americans' Ideas of Responsibility for Accidents – from Blaming Mom to Engineering", in *Journal of Social History*, 1996, vol. 29; John C. Burnham, *Accident Prone: A History of Technology, Psychology and Misfits of the Machine Age*, University of Chicago Press, Chicago, 2009; David Engle, "The Oven Bird's Song: Insiders, Outsiders, and Personal Injuries in an American Community", in *Law and Society Review*, 1984, vol. 18, no. 4, pp. 551-582; Lawrence M. Friedman, *Total Justice*, Russell Sage Foundation Publications, 1994; Hazel Genn, *Paths to Justice: What People Do and Think About Going to Law*, Hart Publishing, 1999; Carol J. Greenhouse, *Praying for Justice: Faith, Order, and Community in an American Town*, Cornell University Press, 1986; Donald Harris (ed.), *Compensation and Support for Illness and Injury*, Clarendon Press, Oxford, 1984; Deborah R. Hensler, *Compensation for Accidental Injuries in the United States*, RAND, Santa Monica, CA, 1991; Herbert M. Kritzer, W. A. Bogart and Neil Vidmar, "The Aftermath of Injury: Cultural Factors in Compensation Seeking in Canada and the United States", in *Law and Society Review*, 1991, vol. 25, no. 3, pp. 500-543; Herbert M. Kritzer, "Examining the Real Demand for Legal Services", Working Paper presented at the ABA Litigation Section Access to Justice Symposium, 2008, available at http://ssrn.com/abstract=1289828, last accessed 28 April 2011; Masayuki Murayama, "Experiences of Problems and Disputing Behaviour in Japan", in *Meiji Law Journal*, 2007, vol. 14; Sally Engle Merry, *Getting Justice and Getting Even: Legal Consciousness among Working-Class Americans*, Chicago Series in Law and Society, 1990; Takao Tanase, "Theory of Litigation as a Reflection of Modernisation", in *New Constructions in Civil Procedure Law Theory*, 2001, vol. 1. [Translation provided by Tom Ginsburg].

On the Evolution of Class Actions and Mass Torts in the United States:

Deborah Hensler and Mark Peterson, "Understanding Mass Personal Injury Litigation: A Socio-legal Analysis", in *Brooklyn Law Review*, 1993, vol. 59, pp. 961-1063; Deborah Hensler, et al., *Class Action Dilemmas: Pursuing Public Goals for Private Gain*, Rand, Santa Monica, CA, 2000; Deborah Hensler, "Revisiting the Monster: New Myths and

Realities of Class Action and Other Large Scale Litigation", in *Duke Journal of Comparative and International Law*, 2001, vol. 11, pp. 179-213; Arthur Miller, "Of Frankenstein Monsters and Shining Knights: Myth, Reality and the Class Action Problem", in *Harvard Law Review*, 1979, vol. 92, pp. 664.

On the Development of Procedures for Group and Representative Litigation Outside the United States:

George Bermann, "US Class Actions and the 'Global Class'", in *Kansas Journal of Law and Public Policy*, 2009, vol. 19, pp 91; Stephen Choi and Linda Silberman, "Transnational Litigation and Global Securities Class-Action Lawsuits", in *Wisconsin Law Review*, 2009, vol. 2009, pp. 465; Deborah Hensler, Christopher Hodges and Magdalena Tulibacka (eds.), *The Globalisation of Class Actions*, Sage Publications, Inc., 2009; Deborah Hensler, "The Globalisation of Class Actions", in Deborah Hensler, Christopher Hodges and Magdalena Tulibacka (eds.), *The Globalisation of Class Actions*, Sage Publications, Inc., 2009, pp. 7-29; Deborah Hensler, "The Future of Mass Torts: Global Class Actions and Third-Party Financing", George Washington University Law Review, forthcoming; Christopher Hodges, *Multiparty Actions*, Oxford University Press, 2001; Nathan Verdi, "Patent Pirates, Hedge Funds and Institutional Investors are Financing the Latest Wave of IP Lawsuits", Forbes, 7 May 2007.

On International Arbitration of Mass and Class Claims:

Alexander Blumrosen, "The Globalisation of American Class Actions: International Enforcement of Class Action Arbitral Awards", in Permanent Court of Arbitration, Multiple Party Claims in International Arbitration, 2009; Veijo Heiskanen, "Arbitrating Mass Investor Claims: Lessons of International Claims Commission", in Permanent Court of Arbitration, Multiple Party Claims in International Arbitration, 2009; S. I. Strong, "The Sounds of Silence: Are U.S. Arbitrators Creating Internationally Enforceable Awards When Ordering Class Arbitration in Cases of Contractual Silence of Ambiguity?", in *Michigan Journal of International Law*, 2009, vol. 30, pp 1017-1094.

On Lawyers Role in Building a Transnational Legal Order:

Yves Dezelay and Bryant G. Garth, *Asian Legal Revivals: Lawyers in the Shadow of Empire*, Chicago Series in Law and Society, 2010; Yves Dezelay and Bryant G. Garth, Dealing in Virtue: International Commercial Arbitration and the Construction of a Transnational Legal Order, in *Chicago Series in Law and Society*, 1998.

3.4

Matching Global Banks with Global Regulation

Thorsten Beck[*]

This paper looks at cross-border banking and, in doing so, raises interesting issues about the strengths and limits of international, global supervisory mechanisms. Well-developed financial systems are critical for economic development, and growth and banks constitute one of the core segments of the financial system. Banks, however, are also at the centre of boom-and-bust periods that many capitalist economies have regularly experienced, most recently in 2008 and 2009. The susceptibility to bank runs, interlinkages of banks through interbank market and payment systems, and the critical role of banks in creating information (and thus helping overcome market frictions) generate external costs from bank failure, which have resulted in the banking system being one of the most regulated sectors of the economy. The globalisation of the financial system, illustrated by globalising markets and banks, has created new opportunities and benefits, but also significant additional risks. Regulating global banks at the national level undermines the benefits that global banks can bring to economies by exacerbating their risks. Future regulatory frameworks have to be matched to the challenges presented by global banking. He argues that bank regulation is an area where more than convergence, we need supra-national frameworks to harness global banking markets for the benefits of host economies. This does not necessarily require the construction of new supra-national institutions, but rather incentive-compatible frameworks that can be built around existing institutions. Rather than seeing this as a debate about national sovereignty, this debate should be framed as designing an optimal regulatory framework to minimise losses from bank fragility while maximizing the benefits of banking for everyone.

1. Introduction

For better or worse, the fate of modern market economies rises and falls with their banks. Well developed financial systems are critical for

[*] **Thorsten Beck** is Professor of Economics and Chairman of the European Banking Center at Tilburg University, as well CEPR fellow.

economic development and growth and banks constitute one of the core segments of the financial system. Banks, however, are also at the core of boom-and-bust periods that many capitalist economies have regularly experienced, most recently in 2008 and 2009. The same mechanism that generates the positive effects of banks on economic development also makes banks susceptible to fragility, in particular transformation of short-term liabilities into long-term assets. The susceptibility to bank runs, the interlinkages of banks through interbank market and payment systems, and the critical role of banks in creating information (and thus helping overcome market frictions) generate external costs from bank failure, that is, costs that fall on stakeholders not related to the bank, such as other banks and the economy at-large. This, in turn, has resulted in the banking system being one of the most regulated sectors of the economy. The globalisation of the financial system, illustrated by globalizing markets and banks, has created new opportunities and benefits, but also significant additional risks. Regulating global banks on the national level undermines the benefits that global banks can bring to economies by exacerbating their risks. Future regulatory frameworks have to be matched to the challenges presented by global banking.

In the following, I will argue that bank regulation is an area where more than convergence, we need supra-national frameworks to harness global banking markets for the benefits of host economies. This does not necessarily require the construction of new supra-national institutions, but rather incentive-compatible frameworks that can be built around existing institutions. Rather than seeing this as a debate about national sovereignty, this debate should be framed as designing an optimal regulatory framework to minimise losses from bank fragility while maximizing the benefits of banking for everyone.

2. The *Status Quo* of National Regulation

The current regulatory framework for banking is basically a national one. Banks are licensed, regulated, supervised and resolved on the national level.[1] It is mostly national supervisors or ministries of finance that

[1] Resolution of banks refers to the process of addressing the failure of a bank. Resolution techniques encompass liquidation, bail-out by the tax-payer, merger and acquisition with another bank, as well as other techniques that transfer parts of the assets and/or liabilities to a different entity.

provide banking licenses. Banks are subject to national regulatory frameworks, as set out in national legislation and regulation. The responsibility for supervising banks lies primarily with national supervisors, and decisions to intervene and resolve failing banks lies again with these national authorities. Deposit insurance schemes are mostly funded and managed at the national level, and it is domestic taxpayers' resources that are used for the bail-out of banks, as has happened again and again throughout the history of crises, including the most recent one.

In the past, concerns about the stability of large international banks and unfair competition gave rise to concerted efforts among industrialised countries to establish minimum requirements in terms of capital-asset ratios (Basel 1) and supervisory standards (Basel Core Principles for Effective Supervision). The increase in cross-border activity, starting in the 1990s, has led to more supervised cooperation in the form of Memoranda of Understanding and Colleges of Supervisors. In Europe, the establishment of a Unified Market for Financial Services provided for a passport that allowed financial institutions to expand throughout the European Union with branches rather than subsidiaries. At the same time, the European Union reinforced the principle of national responsibility for bank regulation and resolution, with that responsibility linked to home countries in the case of for branches of Pan-European banks. This opened a geographic gap between activity and regulatory responsibility. While discussed among academics for many years, it was not until the Global Financial Crisis that the problem became obvious to policy makers.

3. Cross-Border Banking – Opportunities and Risks

The past 20 years have seen an enormous increase in cross-border banking activity, although there have been significant differences across regions.[2] While developing countries in Latin America and Africa have a long history of foreign banks, Western Europe has seen this trend only

---

[2] For cross-regional comparisons, see Robert Cull and Maria Soledad Martinez Peria "Foreign Bank Participation in Developing Countries: What do We Know about the Drivers and Consequences of this Phenomenon", in Gerard Caprio (ed.), *Encyclopedia of Financial Globalization*, forthcoming 2011. For a more in-depth discussion on the development of cross-border banking in Europe, see Franklin Allen, Thorsten Beck, Elena Carletti, Phil Lane, Dirk Schoenmaker and Wolf Wagner, *Cross-Border Banking in Europe after the Crisis*, CEPR-DSF-EBC Policy Report, forthcoming 2011.

over the past 20 years or so. The trend towards cross-border banking has also initiated a vigorous debate among academics and policy makers on the benefits and risks of cross-border banks, mostly focusing on the host countries of such banks.

Perhaps the most clear case of cross-border banking's constructive role can be found in former transition economies where foreign bank entry has served as a commitment tool for domestic policy makers to break the links between banks and incumbent enterprises, and thus the cycle of non-performing loans, bank recapitalisation and inflation. The countries that finalised the ownership transformation process the fastest were also the first ones to successfully emerge out of the systemic banking crises of the 1990s. Foreign banks entered mostly with long-term strategic goals and had a stabilizing impact on their host countries' financial systems and economies. While foreign firms initially focused on large and foreign-owned enterprises, improvements in the contractual and information framework pushed them towards small and medium-sized enterprises. Foreign banks did not necessarily cut lending relationships with existing customers when taking over domestic institutions and there seems to have been a positive spill-over effect on overall access to external finance by all enterprises even if foreign-owned banks did not lend to them directly. Foreign-owned banks were both more efficient than domestic banks – including government and privately-owned – and offered better services. But perhaps the most important impact of foreign bank entry was on cutting entrenched relationships between politically connected enterprises and the banking system. Foreign bank entry was thus a critical element of the disciplining framework that countries in Central Europe put in place in the mid to late 1990s and set them on a path to financial deepening.

The experience in other regions of the world has been somewhat more mixed. Overall, the effect on efficiency of financial intermediation has been positive, while the impact on competition has been less clear, especially in countries where new foreign entrants have taken over existing domestic players, without accompanying institutional reforms. Similarly, the effect of foreign bank entry on stability has been beneficial while on the other hand, the effect of foreign bank entry on access to financial services has been somewhat more muted.

There have always been concerns about the spill-over of home country shocks to host countries through global banks. Evidence leading up to the global crisis has suggested that global banks have helped expand financing opportunities and smooth business cycles in host countries. During the recent global crisis, however, financial shocks in home countries, such as the U.S. and Western Europe, were transmitted through subsidiaries to host countries as well as through global financial markets, with negative repercussions for lending and economic growth. While the jury is still out on the overall effect of cross-border banking for these economies, the Global Financial Crisis has clearly shown the risk associated with cross-border banking. Beyond these risks, the crisis and the failure of several large global financial institutions – in some cases, actual insolvency or near failure if not for government bailouts – have put the regulation and resolution framework for global banks on policy makers' agendas.

There has always been the concern that international banks are 'global in life and national in death'. In spite of international cooperation, resolution was always seen as national. It is national supervisors who make the decision to intervene into failing banks; it is national supervisors and politicians who decide to put taxpayer money into failing banks. The geographic mismatch of international banks' activities and resolution creates severe incentives problems as we will discuss in the following.

4. Cross-Border Bank Regulation and Resolution – Misaligned Incentives

To understand the incentive problems of national supervisors, let us analyze the case of a bank that uses deposits and equity to invest in a two-period project in period 0, with an uncertain outcome.[3] In period 2, the project yields a positive net return with a certain probability or fails completely. The probability of success and failures will become only known in the intermediate period when the regulator can decide to intervene and recover the face value of the investment and thus compensate both depositors and equity (minus resolution costs) or allow the bank to continue into the last period. A regulator maximizing return to domestic stakeholders, including depositors and equity holders, will maximise the expected return to the bank's project, taking into account success probability and return in case of success. The decision process

[3] For more detail, see Thorsten Beck, Radomir Todorov and Wolf Wagner, *Bank Supervision Going Global? A Cost-Benefit Analysis*, Tilburg, mimeo (2010).

changes, however, when the bank finances itself with foreign deposits and equity and invests at least part of its resources abroad. Now, the domestic regulator will be more reluctant to intervene the higher the share of foreign deposits and assets and more likely to intervene the higher the share of foreign equity. The intuition for these opposing effects is that the cost of not intervening (failure of the bank) are largely reflected in a reduction in bank asset values and pay-offs to depositors, while the benefits from regulatory leniency accrue to the equity holders of the bank (the option value of equity).

Can Memoranda of Understanding and Colleges of Supervisors overcome this incentive problem? As the recent crisis has shown this is unlikely. Memoranda of Understanding are legally not binding documents. Even if Colleges of Supervisors are supposed to exchange information, only the exchange of hard information can be legally enforced. Finally, in spite of all the cooperation, it is the home supervisor who ultimately makes the intervention decision.

Bank interventions in the recent crisis have revealed the incentive conflicts of supervisors and the limited usefulness of current cooperation arrangements. Take the example of Icelandic banks – domestically owned but with large shares of foreign deposits and assets. It was not until very late that the Icelandic supervisors acknowledged the dire conditions of several of their banks. The situation was exacerbated by the fact that the Icelandic banks were collecting many of their foreign deposits in branches rather than subsidiaries, over which host country supervisors did not have any control. Even in the case of subsidiaries, however, which are under the responsibility of host country supervisors, banks can shift resources relatively fast between parent bank and subsidiary.

Another example is Fortis Bank in which regulators also intervened relatively late: likely the case of a captured supervisor (since this was only shortly after the take-over of the Dutch ABN Amro by the Belgian Fortis Bank at a time when the latter was already in a weak position). While there was supposedly exchange of information and close cooperation between supervisors in Belgium, the supra-national cooperation broke down as intervention and bailout with national tax payer money became necessary.

Would a supranational supervisor be a solution? A supervisor that internalises the externalities caused by cross-border banking can be more efficient. However, there are certainly concerns regarding a supervisor that is further removed from the regulated bank as supervising the bank might be more costly and resolution techniques might be less efficient. Critically, such a supra-national regulator would need access to the necessary resources to resolve failing supra-national banks, a politically sensitive issue as we will discuss below. Another major concern is matching the geographic area of activity of a bank to the geographic perimeter of the regulator. Oversight of European banks by a European regulator whose cross-border activity is mostly outside Europe will not solve the incentive problems discussed above. Overall, a supra-national regulator can improve on national regulation, but is not a panacea.

Initial talks on global regulation of global banks in the context of the G20 reform discussions have not gone very far. More promising are discussions within areas with a history of policy cooperation. First attempts at creating a European-level resolution framework have fallen short, however. Yes, there are new joint supervisory structures, but ultimately, the resolution power remains at the national level, and taxpayer money can only be used in agreement with national governments. However, creating a new supervisory structure is only one out of many options. Alternatives, such as allowing large Pan-European banks to opt into supervision by the ECB or deposit insurance mechanisms at the pan-European level can achieve such objectives as well. It is important to stress that creating market-based mechanisms that complement supervision with market discipline can be very helpful in this context, although taxpayers ultimately always have to provide the insurance and resolution mechanism of last resort.

If cross-border bank regulation can help reduce agency problems and fragility, why is it politically so difficult to move towards such a system? Two main explanations can be put forward. First, and consistent, with the subsidiary principle of the European Union, regulation of banks is seen as a national policy area, especially and foremost because it might and has – in the recent crisis – involved national taxpayer money. Second, the banking industry is in many countries still seen as a strategic sector, worthy of the special attention of policy makers and the political support of national champions. This is consistent with a century-old history of government intervention in the financial system, exploiting its critical role in supporting and shaping the structure of the real economy.

One important intermediate step, however, is less controversial, and that is the convergence of bank resolution frameworks across countries. As the recent crisis has made clear, most countries do not have the necessary legal and regulatory frameworks or supervisory capacities to deal with failing banks beyond bailing them out, thus creating perverse incentives for banks to take aggressive risks, or liquidating them like non-financial corporations, thus creating spill-over risks for the rest of the financial system and the economy at-large. Creating resolution frameworks and capacities that allow dealing with failing banks in a manner that does not create perverse risk incentives while minimizing the negative repercussions for the rest of the financial system and the economy should be an important lesson from the recent crisis and an important item on the reform agenda. Such options can include merger and acquisition, purchase and assumption and bridge bank techniques. Such reforms can be a first step towards a more incentive compatible regulation of global banks, avoiding, for instance, regulatory arbitrage where global banks look to establish their home base in the country where they see the highest bailout options.

Such options, however, are less feasible for large banks, often considered too-big or too-complex to fail, where the spillover effects and external costs of failure are larger. Recent suggestions regarding automatic debt-equity trigger mechanisms or living wills can help the system move towards a more incentive compatible resolution scheme for such banks, while also inviting more cross-border regulatory cooperation. Critically, however, this again involves a certain convergence in regulatory and resolution frameworks to enable such mechanisms. Finally, planning *ex-ante* for the possible resolution of large global banks can force these banks to take on simpler organisational forms, thus easing both supervisory and market monitoring, as well as sending a clear message to the market that such banks are not necessarily 'too-complex-too-fail', ultimately reducing the size and complexity benefits these banks are enjoying in the market in the form of lower interest rates.

5. Conclusions

Cross-border banking has brought benefits but also risks to economies around the world. Exploiting the benefits of global finance while minimizing the risks requires not only a convergence in resolution frameworks across countries, but also creating frameworks on the supranational level to regulate and resolve global banks. Overcoming political resistance to such frameworks is a key challenge. Recent developments within the European Union towards a common fiscal policy can facilitate a move towards such structures.

Matching the geographic perimeter of regulation and resolution with the geographic area of banks' activities is critical for re-establishing much needed market and supervisory discipline. It does imply a move towards supra-national legal and regulatory frameworks, though not necessarily new institutional structures. This is not a question of national sovereignty, but rather re-establishing the balance between different stakeholders in the financial system, while maximizing the benefits of well-functioning financial markets for all economies.

3.5

Corporate Law and CSR: Will There Be a Constitution for Multinational Companies in 2030?

Tineke Lambooy[*]

In the think piece, the Law of the Future is explored in the context of corporate social responsibility (CSR). The approach includes the perspectives of corporate governance, corporate law and international public law. The central presumption of CSR is that private and public actors together take care of the world's treasures and people. The author first examines CSR as it stands today and whether it is already developed enough to generate socially responsible conduct on the part of multinational companies on a worldwide basis. Considering various current innovative approaches advocated by scholars, including the 'World Court of Human Rights' as proposed by Martin Scheinin, she sees as the Law of the Future the development of a Multinational Company Constitution. For discussion purposes, she mentions factors that could be used in defining the type of companies and their size to which the Constitution would apply and she makes suggestions for the possible content of the Constitution. The Constitution would govern all subjects that could be considered part of CSR, *i.e.*, besides human rights issues, the content would also include guidance on, *e.g.*, global governance, direct participation of stakeholders, and conflict resolution. The essay ends with some interesting research questions in this context, especially on the application of the Constitution.

1. The Ideal CSR Scenario

The central presumption of Corporate Social Responsibility (CSR) is that private actors and public actors together take care of the world's treasures and people. CSR therefore entails that companies demonstrate

[*] **Tineke Lambooy** is an Associate Professor at Utrecht University and the Private Actors Theme Coordinator at the Hague Institute for the Internationalisation of Law.

complementary governance hand-in-hand with national governments and international multilateral institutions.[1]

In an ideal future scenario, a socially responsible company has formulated responsible, clear, concrete and measureable ambitions and goals concerning its aspirations to realise a value increase in respect of people, planet and profit (PPP). The company has effective corporate governance strategies in place that ensure the realisation of its ambitions. A socially responsible company reports on an almost daily basis to society about its business conduct and impacts as well as about the results achieved in the three PPP dimensions.

A company that acts in accordance with the CSR model takes pride in being accountable for its strategy, business models and business operations towards its stakeholders. It will under all circumstances cooperate with stakeholders in confirming this accountability. This amongst other things translates into effectively addressing complaints of stakeholders, sharing all relevant information so that they can help to find mutually acceptable solutions, not obstructing access to justice, and if possible, employing mediation to achieve endurable solutions for problems related to the business activities, in the design of which stakeholders directly participate.

A responsible company not only allows direct participation of stakeholders in the decision-making process – it will actively stimulate this by encouraging them to participate in consultation processes regarding new business ideas and solutions, actual business development plans and the execution thereof. All results of Human Rights Impact Assessments (HRIA) and Environmental Impact Assessments (EIA), which will be conducted before any new business operation starts, will be shared with the stakeholders. It will be likely that stakeholders will participate in the governance structures and/or in the ownership of projects. The implementation of projects will involve companies, communities, civil society representatives and public representatives. CSR also presumes that companies operate in a 'corruption-free' *modus operandi*. This connects with another key aspect of CSR: to create transparency in corporate conduct.

1 T.E. Lambooy, *Corporate Social Responsibility. Legal and Semi-legal Frameworks Supporting CSR*, Kluwer, Deventer, 2010, Chapter 1; R. Lubbers, W. van Genugten and T.E. Lambooy, *Inspiration for Global Governance*, Kluwer, Deventer, 2008.

Transparency pertains to the production methods employed by the company and the results achieved in each of the PPP dimensions. The transparency notion also applies to all financial streams. The company discloses detailed information on revenues and payments, and on any profit-sharing models that it may have concluded with local governments, communities and other business partners. The information reported reflects reality, *i.e.*, it is true and complete and periodically has been verified by an independent and neutral third party. The presentation of the information follows reporting guidelines that assure that the information is standardised and comparable with earlier information presented by the same company and with the information presented by other companies. Moreover, the information is clear and understandable and with a sufficient level of detail to really constitute a meaningful disclosure for civil society, governments, financiers and investors.

Additionally, a company that abides by CSR makes its communication strategies transparent. This concerns the way in which the company disseminates information about itself and its products as well as about the needs for its products. The information will shed light on the company's advertising and sponsor strategies, but it will also divulge detailed information on the sponsoring of the research in scientific fields relevant for its business and reveal which messages are being circulated through movies or other means. Furthermore, total transparency is a precondition concerning any political engagement or lobby activities with public actors, in particular with those public actors who legislate, issue licences and are responsible for the enforcement and implementation of laws and regulations including tax. Providing transparency is also relevant in regard of products: a responsible company is able and willing to provide consumers and its employees with complete information as to the contents of a product, its technical qualities and the way in which it was produced and the impact its production process and the use of that product has, respectively will have, on nature and people (CSR qualities).

Another key area of CSR is that the company develops innovative business approaches towards global issues, the resolution of which require private actor support, including approaches that address the ecological crises and ensure a clean and healthy environment in which improving people's health will be considered most important. An example of such an approach would be that the company makes substantial investments in the conservation of biodiversity, and that it uses water and other natural resources in such a way that it can be considered sustainable according to the most advanced technologies and insights. In that context, the company would employ the cradle-to-cradle approach meaning that it has all sorts of recycling strategies in place to collect products and materials for re-use. A healthy life for people and their animals will be guaranteed by assuring clean production processes and by the implementation of healthy and responsible agricultural methods that do not damage biodiversity and that in all respects pursue the precautionary principle. Another example of innovative business approaches towards global issues would be that the company takes part in ensuring proper education or in the preservation of cultures and cultural objects, and that it supports public actors in fulfilling first, second and third generation human rights. Establishing public-private partnerships that contribute to achieving the Millennium Development Goals (MDG), *i.e.*, the UN goals for 2015 aiming at reducing poverty and promoting sustainable development, could serve that purpose.

2. The Role of Law in Supporting the Ideal CSR Scenario

Considering the ideal future CSR scenario sketched in the first paragraph, the first thought that comes to mind is: yes, that is what companies (should) do and the law should support this. A second thought would be: do the legal systems of 2011 not already support this, as we have corporate law, annual accounting law, labour law and co-determination law, environmental and administrative law, water law, energy law, tort law, consumer law, human rights law, tax law, anti-corruption and anti-fraud laws, corporate governance regulation and CSR?

The answer is yes, most of those national laws aim to regulate corporate conduct in order to direct companies to act in a socially and environmentally responsible manner. Considering current business organisations, we can observe that they indeed create wealth and jobs, provide goods and services to meet basic needs, and help us to meet our expectations and aspirations for an improved quality of life. Yet, there are other aspects to be taken into account. Corporate activity is not just about providing products, economic progress and financial performance. It also has wider impacts on society and the environment. And in an increasingly complex and globalised world, those impacts, good and bad, extend ever farther beyond national borders.

3. Examples of Current Debate About Multinational Conduct

In today's globalised world, reality can be different from the ideal picture sketched in the introduction of this think piece. The Business and Human Rights Resource Centre, an independent non-profit resource centre, disseminates on a weekly basis news and reports about the human rights and environmental impacts of 5000 companies worldwide: company by company, country by country, issue by issue, positive and negative.[2] The Centre tries to balance the coverage of issues by seeking responses from companies to allegations of misconduct.

Some examples of multinational conduct, which have caused a lot of debate, will be discussed from the perspective of CSR.

First, it is interesting to reflect on the sentence of an Ecuador court against US oil company Chevron to pay a USD 9.5 billion fine, and especially the Chevron response. The fine is to compensate the environmental pollution in the country's Amazon region. The oil firm Texaco, which merged with Chevron in 2001, was accused of dumping billions of gallons of toxic materials into unlined pits and rivers. Chevron has launched a legal appeal against the judgment in Ecuador and has issued negative public communication about the Ecuador court and legal system.[3] Besides that, Chevron has commenced international arbitration under the UNCITRAL rules of arbitration and also asserted a claim before a US court to prevent the Ecuador ruling from being enforced.[4] Keeping

---

2 See "Business and Human Rights Resource Centre – A Brief Description", available at http://business-humanrights.org/Aboutus/Briefdescription, last accessed 30 March 2011.

3 See Chevron Appeals against Ecuador Amazon Pollution Fine, BBC News, 13 March 2011, available at http://www.bbc.co.uk/news/world-latin-america-12725490, last accessed 30 March 2011: "Chevron accused lawyers and supporters of the indigenous groups who brought the case of 'corrupting' the trial". It said the judgment contained "numerous legal and factual defects".

4 No payment can be made during the appeals process, which could take years. See: *Chevron Corporation and Texaco Petroleum Company v. the Republic of Ecuador: Claimants' Notice of Arbitration*, available at http://www.chevron.com/Documents/Pdf/Ecuadorbiten.Pdf, last accessed 30 March 2011; United States Court Of Appeals For The Second Circuit, *Republic Of Ecuador v. Chevron Corporation and Texaco Petroleum Company*, Docket Nos. 10–1020–Cv (L) 10–1026 (Con), Argued: 5 August 2010, Decided: 17 March 2011, available at http://ita.law.uvic.ca/documents/ChevronTexacoVEcuador_USAppealSecondCircuit_17Mar2011.pdf, last accessed 30 March 2011.

in mind the ideal CSR framework, one could pose the question whether Chevron's response to the Ecuadorian ruling represents the best way to solve the problems of the environmental pollution in Ecuador and to address the resentment of the local population against Chevron.

The second case concerns another question which draws a lot of debate: how can victims obtain redress from a powerful company? The Lapindo case in Indonesia concerns mining operations that had caused a severe mud flow which has covered 16 villages south of Surabaya in Indonesia. Apparently, victims face many difficulties in being heard. They started a movement called Justice for Lumpur Lapindo Victims Movement.[5]

A third issue regards decision-making processes. In particular, the question has emerged to what extent direct stakeholders can exert influence. An interesting example of where things seemingly have gone wrong for the direct stakeholders is the decision to build a new dam in Brazil's Amazonia to generate hydropower. This decision has been taken despite the persistent objections of the indigenous people living in the Amazon.[6] This case raises questions as to the current processes of taking stakeholder concerns, such as those of indigenous people, sufficiently into consideration when deciding on new economic projects.

A fourth and widely debated subject concerns the oil disaster of BP in the Mexican Gulf in 2010. Numerous questions have emerged regarding BP's corporate responsibility and the way it provides transparency. The company has been criticised that it did not employ the precautionary principle concerning preservation of nature and ecosystem services. Moreover, on the topic of agreeing to be held accountable for

---

5 For an overview of information about this case, see: Confidential reports on Lapindo mudflow leaked to wiki, Mining Reporter, 4 August 2010, available at http://www.mining-reporter.com/index.php/component/content/article/40-presse-allgemein/4650-confidential-reports-on-lapindo-mudflow-leaked-to-wiki, last accessed 30 March 2011; see also The Handling of Lapindo Case Suppress Women Problems, JATAM Mining Advocacy Network, 27 May 2009, available at http://english.jatam.org/content/view/67/17/, last accessed 30 March 2011.

6 See, for example, Amazon Watch, "Stop the Belo Monte Monster Dam", available at http://amazonwatch.org/work/belo-monte-dam, last accessed 30 March 2011.

things that go wrong, it can be noted that BP commenced by pointing at other companies being responsible.[7]

When a holding company is sued, it typically first points at local subsidiaries, claiming that they were the 'wrongdoers'. Those local companies are usually subject to another jurisdiction and the holding company will argue that the case needs to be tried at that level and that local laws need to be applied to the case. This was for instance Shell's first line of defence in the current case submitted by the Dutch NGO Milieudefensie against Shell and some subsidiary companies before a Dutch court.[8] As a result of these defences, victims cannot readily find remedy. It is difficult for victims to precisely indicate which legal entity can be blamed. This is due to the complex legal and organisational international structures of a multinational company (MNC). Additionally, questions of international private law arise when examining the question of applicable law.

As a last example of current debate about the conduct of large companies, two cases commenced by companies under Bilateral Investment Treaties (BIT) will be mentioned. In one case, a claim has been filed by tobacco company Philip Morris against the state of Uruguay. The company complains about new anti-smoking legislation, because that can damage its economic interests. Another case concerns complaints asserted by Western banks against the state of South Africa, because it had introduced legislation intended to positively discriminate in favour of blacks on the employment market. It is argued that this legislation does not serve their economic interests.[9]

7 The BP report of 8 September 2010, which contains the results of BP's own investigation of what caused the oil spill disaster, states that "no single factor caused the Macondo well tragedy". BP heavily laid blame on its contractors, particularly Halliburton and Transocean. See BP Internal Investigation Points Finger at Other Companies in Oil Spill Disaster, The Take Away, 8 September 2010, available at http://www.thetakeaway.org/2010/sep/08/bp/, last accessed 30 March 2011; BP Spill Report Hints at Legal Defense, The New York Times, 8 September 2010, available at http://www.nytimes.com/2010/09/09/us/09spill.html?hp, last accessed 30 March 2011.

8 See, for example, the court documents posted at: http://www.jongbloedonline.nl/zoeken/public/uitspraak.php?uitspraakID=173610&ljn=BM1469, accessed at 20 March 2011.

9 *Philip Morris v. Uruguay* was filed on 19 February 2010 under a BIT between Uruguay and Switzerland. US-based Philip Morris has its operations center in Lausanne,

4. Discussion on the Emergence and Present Functioning of CSR

One of the views, which seeks an explanation for the current gaps in global governance, is that the Westphalian legal system of state sovereignty based on territory is not adequately equipped to direct and control the conduct of MNCs.

First of all, MNCs are often more powerful than states. They can influence economies and politics.[10] As companies can conduct business all over the world, and can have subsidiaries and joint ventures in many jurisdictions, they can grow and have indeed grown into very large organisations. Out of the world's 100 largest economies, approximately half of them are MNCs. For instance, the annual revenue of Shell in 2009 was roughly USD 278 billion, which is almost the same as the GDP of South Africa – the most developed country in Africa ranking the 32nd on the list of countries by GDP (nominal) in 2010.[11]

Secondly, as explicated by Jennifer Zerk, MNCs are comprised of a parent company, located in a 'home state' and linked to many foreign subsidiaries, affiliates and partnerships through a relationship of control. Consequently, MNCs have defied national boundaries, thereby limiting the ability of one national law system to regulate their worldwide activities.[12]

CSR as a concept has been developed in the period 2000-2010. It gained wide support in the business and political community. Besides international institutions, civil society stakeholders also collaborate with business actors with a focus on raising their sustainability. Many new

---

Switzerland. See further: Piero Foresti, *Laura de Carli and others v. Republic of South Africa*, ICSID Case No. ARB(AF)/07/1; at http://icsid.worldbank.org/ICSID/FrontServlet?requestType=CasesRH&reqFrom=ListCases&caseId=C90&actionVal=viewCase, accessed 27 March 2011.

10 *E.g.*, see the revelations through WikiLeaks regarding Shell in Nigeria: David Smith, "WikiLeaks Cables: Shell's Grip on Nigerian State Revealed", *Guardian Online*, 8 December 2011, available at http://www.guardian.co.uk/business/2010/dec/08/wikileaks-cables-shell-nigeria-spying, last accessed on 1 April 2011.

11 According to three different versions of the list made by International Monetary Fund, World Bank and CIA World Factbook, the GDP of South Africa is about USD 280 billion.

12 Jennifer A. Zerk, *Multinationals and Corporate Social Responsibility: Limitations and Opportunities in International Law* Cambridge University Press, Cambridge, 2006, p. 369.

standards and best practices have indeed been developed during the last decade. They have been laid down in international CSR codes of conduct, principles and industry codes, *e.g.*, the UN Global Compact Principles, the OECD Guidelines for Multinational Enterprises, and the OECD Risk Awareness Tool for Multinational Enterprises in Weak Governance Zones. In most cases, the content of a CSR code has been developed in a multi-stakeholder process in which business parties participated alongside NGOs and government representatives. These forms of private regulation provide guidance to companies on how to conduct their worldwide business activities. What we see is that MNCs push these types of private regulation through their international supply chains. As a result, they impact business everywhere in the world,[13] which can indirectly lead to harmonisation of corporate conduct in value chains tending towards CSR. 'Value chains' regard a product as part of a chain or cycle: from the raw materials and resources needed to produce the product upto the end-user and the waste or rest products.

CSR is a phenomenon that has commenced and is being pursued at different levels within an organisation: the board of an MNC can design socially responsible strategies and policies; shareholders can push a board to do so;[14] works councils can utilise their co-determination role to insert the CSR element into the company's strategy and into any other decisions the content of which they can influence.[15] Employees, consumers and NGOs can push an MNC for more CSR. We have seen numerous examples of public campaigns driving an MNC towards a more socially responsible strategy.[16]

---

13 *E.g.*, Ikea, Wal-Mart, Nike. These examples have been discussed in Lambooy, 2010, Chapter 6, see *supra* note 1.

14 See on shareholder communications with instructions to boards: Anita Halvorssen, "Using the Norwegian Sovereign Wealth Fund's Ethical Guidelines as a Model for Investors", in *European Company Law*, 2011, vol. 8, no. 2. See also the various shareholder resolutions, submitted to the general meetings of Shell and BP, which direct the board to adopt and implement more responsible environmental business policies: http://www.eccr.org.uk, last visited on 20 March 2011.

15 T.E. Lambooy, "A Model Code on Co-Determination and CSR – The Netherlands: A Bottom-Up Approach", in *European Community Law*, 2011, vol. 8, no. 2.

16 A. Van der Zwart and R. van Tulder, *International Business-Society Management: Linking Corporate Responsibility and Globalization*, Routledge, 2006.

However, there are other forces that press on MNCs in a different direction, *i.e.*, to act with a very short-term focus or to only consider shareholder value as a yard stick against which to test decisions. The pressure exerted by hedge funds in the first decade of 2000 has not stimulated boards to fully go for sustainability. From another perspective, the trend in the capital markets to over-emphasise index-tracking also restrains boards from implementing long-term strategies, CSR being one of them. Consequently, the current economic model and situation pressures MNCs to act for short-term financial profit and to generate cash. Shareholders demand instant profit and growth; banks and employees need to be paid; competitors need to be defeated and supply sources need to be secured.

As per 2011, the author agrees with Peer Zumhansen's observation that there are many aspects of corporate governance which must be considered before a balance between shareholder and stakeholder responsibility can be struck, not the least being the organisational design of companies.[17] The question however is how to adapt the organisational design of companies in order to have them adopt a long-term stakeholder all-inclusive perspective.

Michael Porter concentrates on business models and processes.[18] He contends that business organisations should systematically reform their models and structures in order to facilitate and effectuate the transition to a sustainable world. Hence, CSR should be methodically incorporated in business processes. 'Corporate Social Values' could be a means thereto. Charlotte Villiers rather relies on law. She points out that there is currently no consistency of responsible behaviour and she takes the position that it is only through law, possibly a combination of soft law

[17] Peer Zumhansen, "Varieties of Capitalism and the Learning Firm: Corporate Governance and Labor in the Context of Contemporary Developments and European and German Company Law", in Nina Boeger, Rachel Murray and Charlotte Villiers (eds.), *Perspectives on Corporate Social Responsibility*, Edward Elgar Publishing, 2008.

[18] See the discussion on Porter's view in Lambooy, 2010, see *supra* note 1, Chapter 1. See further his views evolving in: M. Porter, "Creating Shared Value", in *Harvard Business Review*, January-February 2011, pp. 62-76.

and hard law, that the PPP business model of CSR will be made a reality.[19]

The author has researched legal frameworks in the context of CSR. Her research focuses on those legal and semi-legal frameworks that are most important for business operations. She has examined whether and in which way they can support CSR.[20] The frameworks that have been the subject of my research included: corporate governance, financial and extra-financial accounting and reporting, management information and risk systems, corporate anti-corruption programmes, private regulation, due diligence investigations, consumer information channels, dispute resolution mechanisms amongst which mediation, public-private partnerships supporting the MDG, corporate water management, institutional investment-decision models, and mechanisms that can prompt long-term private sector participation in conservation of biodiversity and ecosystem services. The research provided evidence that indeed many of these legal and semi-legal frameworks have been stretched over the last decade to encompass CSR elements. I conclude that all of them could be further developed by legal and non-legal means to support CSR to the fullest extent possible.

The legal frameworks referred to above mainly focus on national private law, financial law and criminal law. In the absence of an all encompassing international legal model that can direct MNCs towards CSR, practices are framed in the Westphalian perspective that national legal systems govern corporate conduct.

5. International Law and MNCs

As international treaties are basically drafted by and between states and are to be executed and implemented by states, MNCs as private organisations so far cannot become a party thereto. This chapter will not discuss the concept of international legal personality as Nicola Jägers, Peter Muchlinsky, Malcolm Shaw and Andrew Clapham elaborated on this subject extensively.[21] Simplifying their very interesting elaborations,

---

19 Nina Boeger, Rachel Murray and Charlotte Villiers (eds.), *Perspectives on Corporate Social Responsibility*, Edward Elgar Publishing, 2008.

20 Lambooy, 2010, see *supra* note 1.

21 Nicola Jägers, *Corporate Human Rights Obligations: In Search of Accountability*, Antwerp, Intersentia, 2002; Peter Muchlinski, *Human Rights and Multinational En-*

all of them with different arguments move in the direction that MNCs should have international legal personality. Currently, MNCs do not have this, except that MNCs can be considered subjects of procedural rights under international law, *i.e.*, companies can bring a claim to enforce certain substantive rights under the Convention establishing the International Centre for the Settlement of Investment Disputes (ICSID), drawn up under auspices of the World Bank.[22] In ICSID arbitration, MNCs can litigate against states on the basis of BITs. These BITs however pose the dilemma that they have been designed to protect the business interests of an investor headquartered in the home state against host state measures unfavourable to the MNC, *e.g.*, expropriation of assets and other amendments of local laws. They are investment treaties, so they do not place much weight on people and planet concerns. As can be concluded from the current BIT cases mentioned in the third paragraph of this chapter, BITs presently do not offer the right approach as an international legal framework that can direct MNCs towards CSR, nor can they become a party to such treaties. The Law of the Future will probably develop in such a way that BITs include CSR elements. We can see the contours of this process developing in new BIT models. For example, South Africa, Canada and the US have developed or are in the process of developing a BIT model that includes some CSR values. However, BITs will still remain an investment law framework with a primary focus on protecting the interests of home state business organisations.

The question of how to deal with human rights, social and environmental issues, has been the subject of many international treaties. For example, the various human rights treaties, the Convention on Biological Diversity, the Ramsar Convention on Wetlands, the UN Framework Convention on Climate Change, and the Conventions and Declarations of the International Labour Organisation, all provide clear substantive norms on how we want our society, and the environment in which we live, to be and to develop. However, as has been pointed out above, in relation to international law, the position of MNCs has remained ambiguous. MNCs are often viewed as falling outside the sphere of

terprises, Oxford, Oxford University Press, 2007; Andrew Clapham, *Human Rights Obligations of Non-State Actors,* Oxford, Oxford University Press, 2006; M.N. Shaw, *International Law*, 5th ed., Cambridge, Cambridge University Press, 2003.

22 Convention on the Settlement of Investment Disputes between States and Nationals of Other States, 1966, Articles 25(1) and (2)b.

international law,[23] as this primarily addresses states and other international public actors.

6. MNCs and CSR

Obviously, MNCs can take notice of and even decide to follow the norms set out in international treaties. In fact, as international CSR codes of conduct reiterate the same norms for MNCs as have been specified in international treaties, these codes almost function as 'international treaties' between MNCs. That is: MNCs are part of the drafting process, they can decide to endorse one or more of such codes and sometimes they can even become part of a network as is the case with the UN Global Compact. MNCs also report in voluntary CSR reports about their level of compliance with for example the Global Compact Principles, the OECD Guidelines and/or the Earth Charter.[24]

As discussed above, at an international level, MNCs are the main actors of CSR, and they are very powerful for driving sustainable development. We need them alongside public actors, *i.e.*, states and international organisations, to realise global governance. Is it reasonable to expect this from MNCs?

The author is of the opinion that it is. Firstly, many MNCs already – in 2011 – suggest in their corporate and consumer communications that they are part of the solution to conquer the problems that the world is encountering.[25] They proudly communicate that their core business activities contribute to sustainable development, to MDG achievement and to providing solutions regarding climate change, the water, energy, biodiversity loss and financial crises. Secondly, being in such a powerful position, economically, politically, socially, ecologically, *etc.*, MNCs have to take up this complementary role in global governance. In any case, society expects this from MNCs. Thirdly, there are economic reasons to transform a business model into a sustainable one. According to the World Economic Forum survey of CEOs and leaders in 2004, corporate brand reputation outranks financial performance as the most important measure of success. Several studies have emerged which show

[23] Zerk, 2006, p. 369, see *supra* note 12.

[24] The GRI indicators offer a functional connection with those codes.

[25] See for example the MNCs' advertisements in the Economist in 2010/2011.

that companies practicing CSR do better financially and have a better image than companies that do not.[26] Furthermore, investors are more attracted to companies that practice CSR.[27] Research has also made clear that potential employees take an interest in the CSR policies of a potential employer. A company with a good record for social responsibility will therefore attract and retain the best employees.[28]

7. Future Scenario's Regarding MNCs and International Legal Framework(s)

As explained, MNCs operate within the gaps of many global legal instruments due to their lack of legal personality under public international law. In the last part of this chapter, the author will reflect on establishing an international legal framework for MNCs.

Many roads lead to Rome. Various legal and political science scholars have addressed the questions of the global governance gaps, which were brought up in the first paragraphs of this chapter, from a

---

26 See, *e.g.*: Simon Webley and Elise More, *Does Business Ethics Pay? Ethics and Financial Performance*, Institute of Business Ethics, 2003. CSR-oriented companies realise significant higher profits (a figure of 18 per cent on average was mentioned). Another study found that companies that practice CSR show four times the sales growth and eight times the employment growth than companies focused only on shareholders. See Arthur D. Little Inc., "The Business Case for Corporate Citizenship", available at http://www.csrwire.com/pdf/Business-Case-for-Corporate-Citzenship.pdf, last accessed 1 April 2011.

27 Halvorssen, 2011, see *supra* note 14. In addition, the growing number of sustainability indices demonstrate the interest of the capital markets in sustainable companies, as does the PRI (www.unpri.org). Interestingly, Goldman Sachs also intends to launch an index in which sustainability will play an important role. See further McKinsey and Company, "Global Investor Opinion Survey", 2002, available at http://www.mckinsey.com/clientservice/organizationleadership/service/corpgovernance/pdf/globalinvestoropinionsurvey2002.pdf, last accessed 1 April 2011. Focusing mostly on developed countries, the survey indicates that institutional investors are prepared to pay a premium of more than 20 per cent for shares of companies that demonstrate good corporate governance.

28 A study carried out by the Stanford Graduate School of Business in June 2008 found that more 97 per cent of MBA graduates would be willing to forego 14 per cent of their salary in order to work for a socially responsible business. David B. Montgomery, "Challenging Work and Corporate Responsibility Will Lure MBA Grads", 2008, available at http://www.gsb.stanford.edu/news/research/montgomery_mba.html, last accessed 28 March 2011.

positive law perspective. They have searched for ways in the contemporary legal system to address the concerns discussed. For example, in her dissertation, the author has made suggestions as to how annual reporting laws can be extended to include extra-financial information, how corporate governance models can include CSR, how works councils can participate in the decision-making process regarding the company's CSR strategy, how business due diligence investigations can integrate the subject of human rights, and in which way consumers can be assisted in obtaining CSR information on the products that they buy.

Some authors have gone beyond the present legal situation, and proposed new roads. For example, Desislava Stoitchkova's PhD research shows that the International Criminal Court (ICC) has unique possibilities to introduce a sanctioning system regarding human rights violations by companies.[29]

Sorcha MacLeod challenges the traditional concept that the nation-state is the only subject of international law and makes a plea for reinventing the same. She argues that CSR undermines the classic Westphalian concept of the international legal order.[30] MacLeod seeks support for her view in Philip Allott's observation that international law is the creation of the human mind, and that it therefore can be recreated.[31] MacLeod points at the International Criminal Court and the UN-led Global Compact initiative and contends that they evidence that private actors are becoming increasingly responsible on an international level. In her view, these developments are paving the way for future international accountability for transnational corporations and the transition from soft to hard law in the area of CSR.

---

29 Desislava Stoitchkova, *Towards Corporate Liability In International Criminal Law*, Intersentia, Antwerpen, 2010, p.

30 S. MacLeod, "The United Nations, Human Rights and Transnational Corporations: Challenging the International Legal Order", in Nina Boeger, Rachel Murray and Charlotte Villiers (eds.), *Perspectives on Corporate Social Responsibility*, Edward Elgar Publishing, 2008. See Review by Kasey Lowe of MacLeod's chapter, accessible at http://webjcli.ncl.ac.uk/2009/issue4/lowe4.html, last accessed 28 March 2011.

31 Philip Allot, *Eunomia: New Order for a New World*, Oxford University Press, Oxford, 2001, p. xxvii; see also Philip Allott, *The Health of Nations: Society and Law Beyond the State,* Cambridge University Press, Cambridge, 2002, p. x.

Martin Scheinin submitted an interesting research paper, "Towards a World Human Rights Court", within the framework of the Swiss initiative to commemorate the 60th anniversary of the Universal Declaration of Human Rights.[32] He proposes to establish a World Court of Human Rights (World Court). For the normative framework, he advocates that human rights norms should be the central element (in particular, *jus cogens* and customary norms of international law). With regard to the procedural and institutional modalities, he sets out the roles of national courts and regional human rights mechanisms in relation this World Court and he states that its competence would include complaints against private actors:

> In addition to states and intergovernmental organisations that may become actual parties to the Charter, also other entities but states, including multinational corporations, religious communities, and indigenous or minority groups may by unilateral declaration recognise the binding jurisdiction of the Court. Such a declaration must specify a) a set of human rights norms contained in existing human rights instruments to which the entity considers itself bound, and b) what internal remedies of the entity, or generally available external remedies, need to be exhausted before a complaint may be submitted to the Court. This extension of the possibility of international human rights scrutiny to cover the exercise of power by private actors is one of the main ideas in the proposal as a whole.

Lastly, John Ruggie, Special Representative of the Secretary-General on the issue of human rights and transnational corporations and other business enterprises, introduced a 'global governance framework' regarding human rights, accompanied by so-called Guiding Principles (GP). The framework rests on three pillars: (i) the state duty to protect against human rights abuses by third parties, including business enterprises, through appropriate policies, regulation, and adjudication; (ii) the corporate responsibility to respect human rights, which means that business enterprises should act with due diligence to avoid infringing on the rights of others and to address adverse impacts with which they are involved; and (iii) the need for greater access by victims to effective

32 Martin Scheinin, "Towards a World Human Rights Court", available at http://www.udhr60.ch/report/hrCourt_scheinin.pdf, last accessed 28 March 2011.

remedy, both judicial and non-judicial. Each pillar is an essential component in an inter-related and dynamic system of preventative and remedial measures: the state duty to protect because it lies at the very core of the international human rights regime; the corporate responsibility to respect because it is the basic expectation society has of business in relation to human rights; and access to remedy because even the most concerted efforts cannot prevent all abuse. According to GP 14, the responsibility of business enterprises to respect human rights applies to *all* enterprises regardless of their size, sector, operational context, ownership and structure. The GP's normative contribution lies not in the creation of new international law obligations but in elaborating the implications of existing standards and practices for states and businesses, integrating them within a single, logically coherent and comprehensive template.[33]

8. A Possible Future Scenario: An 'MNC Constitution'

The author's suggestion for a new *Via Appia* to reach Rome in the twenty-first century would be to design a new governance approach with regard to MNCs, which covers both values and procedural matters in respect of all subjects relevant for CSR. One could consider designing a 'constitution for MNCs (MNC Constitution), which includes principles and more detailed guidelines for the governance of an MNC and its economic activities. In this section, It will be explored: (i) how to determine for which MNCs the MNC Constitution would be developed, (ii) the possible content of the MNC Constitution, and (iii) its application and use.

Since it seems unnecessary to require all MNCs in the world to abide by the MNC Constitution, firstly, it has to be established to which groups of companies the MNC Constitution should apply. The idea would be that the scope would primarily include those MNCs that really have an impact on the world. Some MNCs have an impact because they shape the physical environment (*e.g.*, infrastructural or mining enterprises, timber companies, companies that need water basins and dams or power plants to

[33] See Human Rights Council, "Guiding Principles on Business and Human Rights: Implementing the United Nations 'Protect, Respect and Remedy' Framework", UN Doc. A/HRC/17/31, 21 March 2011, para. 6 and 14 and GP 14, available at http://www.business-humanrights.org/media/documents/ruggie/ruggie-guiding-principles-21-mar-2011.pdf, last accessed 1 April 2011.

produce energy). Other companies have an impact because they source (the ingredients for) their products in such large quantities that (i) the production thereof changes the landscape (*e.g.*, from forests to palm oil plantations or glass houses in Ethiopia for growing roses), or that (ii) their activities substantially impact rivers, lakes or seas (*e.g.*, fishery firms and firms that supply the fish feeding materials). Then, there are companies that have a significant impact because they influence consumer conduct or because they produce (certain types of) weapons. Some MNCs have world-scale power because they manage large amounts of capital market funds and hence can decide which economic activities or countries will be supported (*e.g.*, pension funds and banks). The question is how to determine whether an MNC is a powerful company with a considerable impact?

An attempt to define which MNCs would be 'eligible' for the MNC Constitution could be to use concepts developed in American anti-trust and European competition law. Pursuant to these laws, it sometimes has to be determined whether a company becomes too powerful and hence should split up its operations. Another question that comes up in this context is whether a company should be allowed to merge with another company, *i.e.*, will the merger result in a concentration of market power?[34] Elements used to answer these types of questions are, amongst others: turn-over volumes, market share, the degree of control over group companies or companies in a 'network organisation', vertical and horizontal power in the supply chain respectively the sector, and the number of (EU member) states in which the MNC operates and/or maintains assets. This approach could be combined with elements drawn from corporate tax law and civil law regimes in which special rules apply to large companies. For example, Dutch corporate law stipulates that so-called 'large companies' should have a two-tier board in order to institutionalise a better supervision model (*structuurregime*). Aspects such as worldwide turn-over, total assets and the number of employees are taken into account to determine whether a company is a large company. For finding the largest MNCs in the world, use could also be made of rankings such as Fortune Global 500, The Inc. 500,

[34] Council Regulation defines a concentration with an 'EU community dimension'. See Council Regulation (EC) No 139/2004 of 20 January 2004 on the Control of Concentrations between Undertakings, Article 1.

IndustryWeek 1000, etc.[35] A large number of employees all over the world could also be an important factor to take into account, although not the only factor. Due to the development of new technology, some enterprises generate very high revenues with a small staff.[36]

Regarding the possible contents of the MNC Constitution, it will encompass both a substantive framework and procedural elements. They could include:

1. A substantive ethical part (similar to the values and norms included in the OECD Guidelines, the Global Compact, the Earth Charter and maybe CSR sector codes of conduct;
2. Transparency concerning accounting and activities (applicability of one international standard for reporting and assessment that integrates financial, environmental and social information on the MNC's worldwide operations);[37]
3. Institutionalisation of direct stakeholder participation in decision-making;
4. Accountability;
5. Complaints treatment (fact finding, mediation, alternative dispute resolution, jurisdiction issues, access to justice, legal fees);
6. Litigation – International Court of Law for MNCs (or arbitration) similar to Scheinin's World Court, however with a broader scope, *i.e.*, covering all CSR subjects mentioned in the introduction of this chapter;

[35] The Fortune Global 500 is a ranking of the top 500 corporations worldwide as measured by revenue. The list is compiled and published annually by Fortune magazine. See: http://money.cnn.com/magazines/fortune/global500/, last accessed 20 March 2011. The Inc 500 includes only private companies. The ranking is based on the percentage of growth in the company's net sales over a five-year period. The IndustryWeek 1000 is IndustryWeek's report on the 1000 largest publicly held manufacturing companies based on revenue. See http://www.industryweek.com/research/iw1000/2009/iw1000rank.asp, last accessed 20 March 2011.

[36] For example, Google, an internet search engine company with around 20,000 full-time employees worldwide generated more than USD 20 billion in revenues in 2009.

[37] GRI and Accounting for Sustainability (A4S) have announced the formation of the International Integrated Reporting Committee (IIRC).

7. Finance structures – transparency, capital requirements, equitable distribution of profits (division among local tax authorities, employees, shareholders, financiers);
8. Third party rights in respect of MNC's operations;
9. Methodology on how to perform Environmental Impact Assessments and Human Rights Impact Assessments, and on how to share the results. Standards for setting up and maintaining anti-corruption programmes;
10. Democratic process and procedure (*e.g.*, board member (s)election by stakeholders, responsibility and accountability of individual board members, and of the board as a whole; suspension/dismissals; equality requirements);
11. MDG contribution (in the context of the 'right to development': how to ascertain that the present generation everywhere benefits from the economic development);
12. Sustaining biodiversity and ecosystem services (how to ascertain that the next generation will also be able to use them);
13. Attitude towards politics (*e.g.*, guidelines in respect of lobbying, sponsoring of research, and any related activities);
14. Attitude towards consumers (*e.g.*, guidelines in respect of advertisements and dissemination of information, social media policies); and
15. Educational duties.

Concerning the possible use of the MNC Constitution, the following should noted: clearly, some of the elements above are derived from CSR and corporate governance codes of conduct (*e.g.*, OECD Guidelines), European Directives (*e.g.*, EIA), the Dutch Works Councils Act, accountancy laws and regulations and international human rights treaties. So what's new? The idea is to include all elements in one document, the MNC Constitution, and to require MNCs to model their organisation and activities on that basis. Various questions come up in respect of the applicability of the MNC Constitution.

A first question is whether the MNC Constitution should be a single document which has to be followed by all eligible MNCs or, alternatively, should every eligible MNC draft its own constitution in accordance with certain basic principles or the framework laid down in the MNC Constitution?

A second question is: should the MNC Constitution contain strict rules to comply with, or alternatively, should it contain more open norms and should eligible MNCs indicate on their website and in their reporting to what extent they abide ('comply or explain')?

As to applicability, one thought could be to have MNCs voluntarily decide to 'sign up' as eligible MNC, like the proposal of the World Court. Alternatively, the idea could be developed that the MNC Constitution will be mandatory for eligible MNC. If that would be the case, the next question is how to impose it? Through national laws? This could for instance be done by making endorsement a precondition for any eligible MNCs that wishes to register in a certain state or obtain a licence to operate its business. If that were the case, states should collaborate and all act consistently in respect of an MNC.

As regards compliance by the MNC with the content of the MNC Constitution, possibly Scheinin's World Court could play a role and/or existing international instruments and courts. Complaints could be filed against an MNC by states (a 'reversed BIT'), stakeholders and/or other MNCs.

Certainly, the involvement of economists and political science scholars would help in setting up such a framework. At least, the idea offers ample possibilities for further research avenues. And it will hopefully always continue to be pleasant to end up in Rome.

3.6

International Market Regulation, Corporate Governance, CSR and Multinationals

Jan Eijsbouts*

This contribution focuses on regulating Corporate Social Responsibility, and in particular the regulation of international corporate governance and CSR. The world is facing challenges in the twenty-first century to condition the market economy system in such a way that the main drivers of wealth, business organisations, will adhere to a well organised and consistent set of norms, representing the licence to operate for business, are manifold. While markets are global and market players have a global span of organisation and activity, the main regulators are still organised nationally and diverging national claims and interests prevent global coordination and consistency. The piece addresses the substantive and the form (regulatory) angles. On the substantive angle it deals with the alignment in the global market of approaches in corporate control, the shareholder models and the stakeholder models aiming at a well balanced approach of the differing interests in the corporation. On the form it looks at the ways in which these substantive norms are being shaped; will society leave these CSR norms up to the judgment of business itself or require for certain norms regulation ranging from "imposed" self-regulation via soft law to hard law. Key dilemma's identified for the future are: acknowledgment of corporations as subjects in international law; risk of inconsistency in competitive conditions by extraterritorial effect of parent company's substantive tort law on foreign operations; adoption of a multinational enterprise liability concept to acknowledge central group management as required by corporate governance; harmonisation of national treatment of international soft law norms; harmonisation of the treatment of corporations in national criminal laws; and, finally, how to organise that investment protection on the one hand and responsible business on the other hand in foreign jurisdictions are treated as the two sides of the same coin.

* **Jan Eijsbouts** is Extraordinary Professor of Corporate Social Responsibility at Maastricht University and former General Counsel of Akzo Nobel. Member of Gaemo Group.

1. Introduction

From my background as an international corporate lawyer, I am particularly fascinated by and interested in the development of the regulation of business and business organisations in a globalising world. The challenges the world is facing in the twenty-first century to condition the predominant market economy system in such a way that the main drivers of wealth, business organisations, will adhere to a well organised and consistent set of norms, representing the licence to operate for business, are manifold. While markets are global and market players have a global span of organisation and activity, the main regulators are still organised nationally, and diverging national claims and interests prevent the much needed international if not global coordination and consistency. An expressive characterisation of contemporary globalisation is given by Stiglitz: a system of global governance without global government.[1] The joint responsibilities of both political and business leaders to organise the global markets such that limited resources are used in a responsible way for the benefit not only of the current generation but also of the future generations (Brundlandt Commission, 1987) are tremendous, but as the proceedings at the Copenhagen and Cancun Global Climate Summits have shown, we are still far from such much needed responsible politics. By the same token, the BP oil spill in the Mexican Gulf has shown that we are also far from much needed responsible business management. The challenge of law, both national law and international law, will be to operate in combination in such a way that it provides the basis for responsible and reliable global governance. This will require harmonisation amongst the national legal systems based on unified substantive concepts in the main legal fields for the regulation of business across borders and a dove-tailing of these harmonised national legal systems with international law. In this think piece I will deal with a couple of challenges for business regulation from both a substantive norms angle and a form angle and I will highlight a number of key dilemmas in the context of business regulation.

[1] Joseph Eugene Stiglitz, *Globalization and its Discontents*, W.W. Norton, New York, 2002.

2. The Substance

On the substantive norms angle, my main theme is the need for alignment in the global market approaches to corporate control: the shareholder models, on the one hand and the stakeholder models, on the other. In the modern jargon of corporate governance the still not unambiguously answered question is: whether the primary role of corporations is to provide adequate long term returns for the shareholders or to provide long term benefits for the stakeholders and thereby for society as a whole. Although the Chicago law and economics approach of short term maximisation of shareholder value, which must be held responsible for much of the current economic crisis, is no longer considered adequate to address the global challenges, there are still considerable differences among the various schools of thought as well as legal and market approaches by regulators and business relating to corporate objectives. There are still diverging views on the relation between corporate governance and corporate social responsibility, although signs can be noticed on the regulatory front that corporate social responsibility is more and more considered to be an integral part of a broadening notion of corporate governance (*e.g.*, the sometimes heated discussions leading to the new Section 172 of the UK Companies Act 2006 and Principle II.1 of the Dutch Corporate Governance Code 2009, which both refer to stakeholder interests as relevant in corporate decision-making). The recognition by an increasing number of players in the financial markets that corporations that pursue sustainable long term business strategies will be better positioned to yield long term benefits is also encouraging. Nevertheless, the predominant model remains the one focusing primarily or even exclusively on pure financial return maximisation. Externalisations of social and environmental costs, facilitated by the concept of the limited liability of corporations are still omnipresent. As recent discussions at the EU and Member State levels have shown, this is particularly true in the case of the legal compartmentisation of operations by the continued recognition of the legal independence of the often many subsidiaries within multinationals. This does not reflect modern corporate governance and CSR based requirements regarding parent company control over group activities. As Harvard's Michael Porter submits, corporations need healthy societies in order to become and stay healthy themselves. And that, he emphasises, can only be achieved if business and societies pursue strategies of shared values.[2] But at the same time it must be noted, that in practice an overall awareness of this fact, both among politicians and business leaders, is still lacking to a significant extent. The financial crisis has shown that banks have pursued short-sighted policies to maximise profits at the expense of the goose with the golden eggs. It is an alarming fact that after the collapse of quite a few banks, a smaller number of banks, mainly surviving at the expense of the general public, have grown in size and have been able to pursue the old banking business model thereby generating profits even beyond the pre-crisis levels. Examples are the high profits declared by Goldman Sachs and Morgan Stanley over 2009, the year when societies and businesses were still heavily suffering from the economic crisis. The Basel III discussions about new capital requirements for banks, aimed at a more solid banking system that protects society against the risks of another collapse of the financial system and the lack of uniformity or even divergence in views of and approaches to financial regulation among the leading economic blocks are disappointing. The approach by the US, which amounts to a return to the separation of retail and savings banks on the one hand and investment banks on the other hand, a system introduced in the 1930s, but abandoned in the 1990s with the catastrophic results known, is not followed by the EU. Competing national interests and ambitions are the major stumbling block here. There is already serious doubt whether the Basel III requirements will not be too little and too late.

In this context the need for greater consistency on a global scale in the regulation of companies and corporate groups, not only in the financial sector, must be recognised and the stakeholder model together with multinational enterprise liability must become the global standard. This will require a real paradigmatic change in the conceptual approach of the organisation of business in a market oriented economy as proclaimed by several think tanks (*e.g.*, Corporation 2020). There is, however, no global governance model to implement this and the slow progress in the discussions at the G20 on a global charter is not encouraging. Protracted discussions between the US and Europe on such technical issues as

[2] See the articles by Michael Porter and Mark Kramer: "Strategy and Society. The Link Between Competitive Advantage and Corporate Social Responsibility", in *Harvard Business Review*, December 2006; and "Creating Shared Value. How to Reinvent Capitalism – and Unleash a Wave of Innovation and Growth", in *Harvard Business Review*, January – February 2011.

financial reporting standards show that we still have to travel a long way to adopt more converging basic notions and concepts in corporate law and, broader, corporate governance and CSR on a global scale.

A reassuring development is the broad acceptance of the 2008 Framework Protect, Respect and Remedy presented by Professor John Ruggie,[3] the UN Secretary General's Special Representative on the issue of human rights and transnational corporations and other business enterprises. The unanimous acceptance by the UN Council on Human Rights in 2008 was unprecedented.[4] It means that important players in a globalising economy realise and accept that protection by states and respect by corporations of human rights are of vital importance. Ruggie's open definition of human rights and his inventory of alleged violations by corporations also show the connection between human rights, labour and the environment. The philosophic underpinning of this development is Nobel laureate Amartya Sen's characterisation, which dismisses Bentham's rejection of the concept of human rights as "nonsense on stilts" and supports Hart's characterisation of human rights as the "parents of law", motivating specific legislation, rather than Bentham's characterisation of a right as "a child of law".[5] Sen's vision should be more widely shared among and accepted by politicians, regulators and market players as leading principles. Ruggie's team has also looked at possibilities to adopt the fundamental principle of corporate responsibility to respect human rights, the second pillar of his framework, as component of the fiduciary duties of corporate directors in corporate law (the Corporate Law Project, a study of human rights and corporate law and governance in 40 major jurisdictions).

---

[3] John Ruggie is Berthold Beitz Professor in Human Rights and International Affairs at Harvard Kennedy School of Government.

[4] Upon the unanimous adoption of the 2008 Framework (see *Protect, Respect and Remedy: A Framework for Business and Human Rights*, United Nations Human Rights Council, 7 April 2008, available at http://www.reports-and-materials.org/Ruggie-report-7-Apr-2008.pdf, last accessed 30 March 2011), the UN Human Rights Council prolonged Prof. Ruggie's mandate with another three years, tasking him with proposals for the operationalization of his Framework. In the meantime draft Guiding Principles have been issued, which will be followed by a definitive proposal to the UN Council on Human Rights to be decided on in June 2011.

[5] Amartya Sen, *The Idea of Justice*, Penguin, paperback ed. 2010, p. 361-364.

3. The Form

The form angle focuses on the ways in which the substantive normative approaches towards corporate governance (and corporate social responsibility as a particular subdivision thereof) are shaped. This is a container of a regulatory mix consisting of hard law, soft law, self-regulation (collective and individual) and uncodified societal norms (the societal expectations, to be judged by the courts of public opinion).

The relevant points of attention in selecting and shaping the preferred form will be: the nature of the substantive norm, its sources, national or international, and desired and possible binding effect of regulation, hard law and alternative regulation. This is already complex on a national level, but exponentially more complex on an international level.

As a starting point, however, I submit that the still ongoing debate on whether or not CSR is voluntary or mandatory is futile. From the point of view that CSR is a set of dynamic ethical societal norms on the substantive 'Triple P' fields (people, planet and profit), which by the way may differ both time-wise and region-wise, the relevant ethical norm can take several forms: no codification at all or codification ranging from (individual or collective) self-regulation, via soft law to hard law (civil, administrative and even criminal law). In this view CSR is a set of norms which is either voluntary or mandatory depending on the chosen form, so these qualifications are not mutually exclusive. The voluntary or mandatory debate is of another nature: it relates to the practical question whether CSR should be regulated or not, which is only a matter of efficiency and not of principle.[6] There are two schools of thought: those who claim that CSR should not be regulated since regulation will provide less of an incentive for business to walk the extra mile and those who doubt that business will walk the extra mile without regulation. This debate abstracts from the factual situation of a given CSR norm and defines CSR as those norms which have not been regulated and are thus voluntary. This approach, in which a CSR norm as soon as it has been regulated cannot be called CSR any longer, disregards the fact that the ethical nature of the norm is not lost once it has been regulated. So this

---

6 See also Adele Lebano, "The Concept of Corporate Social Responsibility: A Philosophical Approach", in *ISS Working Papers – General Series*, no. 508, available at http://repub.eur.nl/res/pub/21243/, last accessed 30 March 2011.

debate should end and the above proclaimed set of criteria on the best way to address the relevant norm should also answer the basic question of whether or not a CSR norm should be regulated at all and, in the affirmative case, in what form.

Most contemporaneous national legal systems are open in character, implying that so called open norms are adopted which offer the courts to interpret them on the basis of unwritten legal norms or societal expectations. The uncertainty of whether alternative regulation (self-regulation or soft law) will be considered unwritten legal norms by the courts is a complicating matter for corporations on a national basis. The matter becomes even more complicated when international norms or practice will be considered in national law. Looking at regulation and recognising that from the perspective of business there is a need for further international and ideally even global convergence and harmonisation of substantive norms, we must realise that the way in which national law treats international law is of great importance for multinational corporations. For multinationals, which as legal persons are not (yet) acknowledged as subjects in international law, it is important to know in what ways international norms are treated in national law. First there is the preliminary question of whether the national legal system takes the monist or dualist approach. If the latter is the case, the way in which international law is implemented in the concerned national jurisdiction may be different from the international norm itself (which in a monist system applies directly in national law). This results in different legal norms for similar factual situations. Moreover, the treatment of international customary law by national law and national courts may be of even greater importance. The question of acknowledgement and interpretation of international customary law by national courts gains importance from the viewpoint of certainty of compliance and from the need to create a more level playing field. In this latter context, it should be noted that for the Western multinationals, which are subject to increasing corporate governance regulation, the lack of a level playing field with smaller corporations, particularly those in the developing world, is already a major concern.

To summarise, the nature and the aims of the substantive norm will determine the possibilities of regulation. Each form of regulation has its limitations in terms of effectiveness and it would be useful and important to establish a set of criteria for the ideal form of regulation for the various types of substantive norms. These criteria should also provide guidance as to whether or not regulation is needed or desirable at all. This guidance should also explain the interdependence and mutual influence of the interpretation and application of the distinct forms of regulation to business.

4. Conclusion

In conclusion, I submit that the following aspects deserve specific attention with a view to the relation of business and society in a globalising market economy:

- The first aspect is the need for a paradigmatic change from the shareholder value model to a global stakeholder model and, more aspirationally, the development of a new business organisation. Inspiration can be drawn from the Corporation 2020 project.
- The debate on the voluntary or mandatory nature of CSR should be concluded by the assessment that it doesn't touch on the nature of any substantive CSR norm under the Triple P scope (people, planet and profit) but only on whether, and if so in which way, the relevant substantive CSR norm should be regulated best. Related to this endeavour might be the development of a set of criteria for the best form of regulation of ethical norms including CSR norms.
- An international consensus should be reached for legal persons (namely corporations) to be acknowledged as subjects in international law, with rights and obligations, particularly in field of investment protection and the accompanying duties to observe CSR obligations and responsibilities in the host countries.
- Initiatives should be taken for the adoption of a world wide treaty establishing norms for the protection of fundamental rights by all corporations coupled with a multinational enterprise liability model for violations of universal human rights. The latter would prevent the defence by multinationals that their subsidiaries did act on their own initiative, so that the parent company cannot be held liable. This liability for corporate groups should not be based on strict liability, but on a reversed burden of proof at the side of the parent company, rather than based on the burden of proof at the side of the plaintiffs, unless the suit would appear to be clearly frivolous.

- A final concern relates to the possible different national treatments of international soft law norms, which will also potentially increase the lack of a level playing field for corporations active on world markets.

3.7

The Rise of the Social Enterprise: How Social Enterprises Are Changing Company Law Worldwide

Levinus Timmerman, Matthijs de Jongh and Alexander Schild*

This paper explains the increasing popularity of social entrepreneurship and analyzes its company law consequences. Faced with tight budgets, governments are looking to the private sector to develop businesses that serve the interests of the public. Social entrepreneurship is gaining momentum as it enables people to make a living while pursuing an objective that adds meaning to their lives. Social enterprises are confronting two key challenges. First is the need for funding. The emergence of a social investment sector requires a long-term commitment from government agencies. Second, social enterprises must balance the interests of investors with the social mission.

Legislators in many countries are creating specific legal entities to cater to the need of legal entities in which the dual purpose of social enterprises is regulated. A worldwide trend is for company law to provide a means of addressing problems relating to the dual purpose by defining the rights and obligations of directors and shareholders. Furthermore, a sufficiently flexible 'new company-law product' offering a pre-negotiated set of rules tailored for social enterprises can reduce incorporation costs for entrepreneurs structuring their businesses. A special legal entity for social enterprises also enables entrepreneurs to carry out their mission by giving them their own legal entity and allowing them to use their legal entity as a competitive advantage and a marketing tool. Accordingly, new legal entities improve the options open to entrepreneurs structuring their social businesses.

* **Levinus Timmerman** is Attorney-General at the Supreme Court of the Netherlands and Professor on the Foundations of Company Law.
Matthijs de Jongh and **Alexander Schild** are law clerks at the Supreme Court of the Netherlands.

1. Introduction

The classic distinction between the government providing public goods and services and the private sector catering to private needs has never been fully clear in any society. Roman entrepreneur and politician Marcus Licinius Crassus famously made his fortune by operating, among other things, a fire brigade in Rome that would rush to the scene of a fire to buy the property at a fire-sale price – before agreeing to put the fire out. Two millennia ago, Marcus Licinius Crassus proved that the private sector can be 'innovative' in addressing social needs.

In recent times, the distinction is as blurry as ever. Non-profit and low-profit organisations are acting like businesses; governments are pursuing their public goals through private channels. A fascinating example of the latter is the emergence over the last decade of 'social entrepreneurship' as a worldwide trend. Most 'social enterprises' are small and medium-sized enterprises acting in local markets. Others are operating on a larger scale, such as the micro-finance organisation Grameen Bank, founded by Nobel-prize winner Muhammad Yunus.

This paper explains the background of this phenomenon and considers the consequences for company law. First, we explain why the social enterprise is a phenomenon on the rise (Section 2). Then, we look at two key needs that social enterprises are dealing with: the need for funding and the need to balance the interests of investors with the social mission of these businesses (Section 3). Last, we analyze the introduction worldwide of new legal entities specifically designed to balance these possibly conflicting interests within social enterprises (Section 4).

2. Where the Public and the Private Sectors Meet

2.1. The Public Need for the Private Sector

Corporate law has always taken the shape required by societal demands at any particular time. During the rise of capitalism in the eighteenth and nineteenth centuries, several kinds of legal entities, including the public corporation and the private limited company, were devised in order to facilitate business needs.

In the twenty-first century, governments are struggling to make ends meet. Budgets are tight and costs are rising. With the percentage of retired people increasing and a global economy struggling to keep an even keel after the worst economic crisis since the Great Depression, many treasuries are finding themselves in dire straits. Governments are increasingly looking for opportunities in which businesses conduct certain activities, such as running a school or hospital, in the public's interest. Creativity combined with business savvy should enable a 'social entrepreneur' to do some of the things governments have traditionally done – and do it better and cheaper.[1] The distinction between the government providing public goods and services and the private sector catering to private needs still exists, but social enterprises are also operating in the middle.

2.2. The Drawbacks of the Private Sector

This is not the first time that governments around the globe have been looking at the private sector to solve public problems. In the 1980s, Ronald Reagan convinced many that it was not the Soviet Union but the public sector that was the real danger, and that the private sector would provide a clear solution.

In recent years, the side effects of unchecked capitalism have become visible in many ways. One of them is the awareness that we inhabit a planet with limited resources and a vulnerable natural environment. Economists have had to admit that free markets sometimes produce less than desirable results. A major problem with the private sector is that 'external costs' are of no interest to the market. The market prices of products and services often do not reflect their real social and environmental costs. Consequently, companies can shift these external costs to society, even though the benefits end up in the pockets of shareholders. For instance, the credit crisis has shown that faith in *laissez-faire* has ultimately had high external costs, as bankers have been able to pass on their losses to society.

The credit crisis has also shown the limits of business models relying on the assumption that humans can be reduced to *homo economicus* – the well-informed, rational-acting person seeking to maximise financial well-being. *Homo economicus* is, however, only a part of who we really are and what really guides us in life. What is needed are

[1] See for example "Social Innovation: Let's Hear Those Ideas", The Economist Online, 14 August 2010, available at http://www.economist.com/node/16789766, last accessed on 3 March 2011.

business models that seek to achieve sustainable economic growth as a means of promoting the well-being of society.

The credit crisis has proven that *laissez-faire* capitalism has its limits. A growing number of authors voice essentially the same concern about the direction in which our Western societies seem to be heading.[2] We have benefitted from capitalism, but we have now become prisoners in our own system. Richard Sennett has written eloquently about how modern capitalism has generated more anxiety in the workplace.[3] In today's world, money is a volatile commodity. Investors are seeking to maximise returns on a global scale and money travels in a constant flux around the globe. This has resulted in more demanding jobs and less secure employment.

2.3. Limiting External Costs vs. Creating External Benefits

Is it possible to have the marketplace take external costs into account? Usually it only takes a minute after this question has been raised for someone to refer to 'corporate social responsibility' (also known as 'CSR'). Many companies nowadays have commercial reasons for doing things like calculating their carbon footprints and avoiding child labour. If a company neglects to fulfil these 'duties', it puts its reputation at risk and can expect an angry reaction if its negligence becomes public.[4]

Social entrepreneurship is different from CSR. CSR refers to a process in which companies take general well-being into account while they try to maximise shareholder profit. A social enterprise does not conduct a business to maximise profits, but to advance a specific aspect that promotes the well-being of society. Social entrepreneurship aims to use the creativity, competition and efficiency of the marketplace to pursue

---

[2] For example, John Cassidy, *How Markets Fail. The Logic of Economic Calamities*, Ferrar, Straus and Giroux, New York, 2009; Joseph E. Stiglitz, *Freefall: America, Free Markets, and the Sinking of the World Economy*, New Norton & Company, York/London, 2010; Justin Fox, *The Myth of the Rational Market*, HarperCollins, New York, 2009; Will Hutton, *Them and Us*, Little and Brown, London, 2010.

[3] See, in particular, Richard Sennett, *The Corrosion of Character, The Personal Consequences of Work in the New Capitalism*, W.W. Norton, New York, 1998.

[4] On CSR, see Tineke Lambooy, *Corporate Social Responsibility*, Kluwer, Deventer, 2010.

a public goal. Unlike CSR, which is primarily aimed at limiting external costs, social enterprises attempt to create external (community) benefits.[5]

Although social enterprises plan to be financially sustainable, and may well be profitable or even very profitable, profit maximisation is not their primary purpose. First and foremost, they are set up to create external community benefits by operating a business. Social enterprises are also not charities. Unlike most charities, social enterprises operate as businesses in the marketplace. We acknowledge, however, that the border between social enterprises and CSR companies is fuzzy, as is the border between social enterprises and charities. For instance, Muhammad Yunus has convinced Danone to participate in Grameen Danone, a social enterprise which produces healthy low-cost yoghurt for the local population in India. Danone is, in turn, showing its customers that it takes its corporate social responsibilities seriously.[6]

2.4. *Homo Economicus* vs. the Social Entrepreneur

Why would a social entrepreneur support a public cause? Within an economic framework modelled on the premise of *homo economicus*, the behaviour of a social enterprise is indeed irrational. The owner of a social enterprise is attempting to make a decent living; however, he or she is also pursuing a goal that has intrinsic value. They seem to be saying, "In view of the fact that most jobs nowadays are so demanding and tend to become such an important part of one's life, why should I not do something that makes me feel worthwhile as a person?"

Social entrepreneurship enables people to make a living while pursuing an objective that, in their own view, adds meaning to their lives. This not only furthers the gross domestic product of a country, but also its gross domestic happiness. The concept of social entrepreneurship provides an opportunity for people to act in accordance with their values. It thereby creates jobs that are more than a means to an end. It helps people to pursue a certain way of life in which the desire to live a useful and meaningful life and to make a decent living are compatible.

---

5 We acknowledge that CSR policies frequently create positive externalities; CSR policies, however, remain subordinate to the purpose of profit maximization.

6 Muhammad Yunus, "Social Business Entrepreneurs are the Solution", in Heiko Spitzeck *et al.* (eds.), *Humanism in Business*, Cambridge University Press, Cambridge, 2009.

3. Two Key Challenges

3.1. Finance

Who is going to pay for the creation of external benefits? Why would an investor finance a firm whose agenda is something other than trying to give the investor as much return on the investment as possible? The fact that social enterprises have another interest on their agenda besides generating a proper return for their investors makes it more difficult for them to attract capital. Social enterprises are often partly dependent on grants, financial aid, or loans issued under favourable conditions by governments, charities or philanthropists.

Moreover, it is often difficult for a social capital market to develop because potential profitable investment funds lack track records and investors might overestimate the risks involved. Consequently, it is important to align the supply and demand of capital for social enterprises.[7] There are numerous ways to promote the supply of capital. A tax benefit for the company or its shareholders will often be a critical success factor. A tax subsidy compensates social enterprises and their shareholders for positive social externalities. It makes it more attractive to invest in social enterprises.

Most investments in social enterprises take the form of loans. Charities and philanthropists lend money below market rates to social enterprises. Some governments have tried to promote the emergence of a more mature investment sector for social enterprises. Over the last ten years, the United Kingdom has taken the lead in this field. It is currently attempting to create a social investment market.[8]

Several UK investment funds already deal with equity investing in social enterprises. To promote the emergence of a social investment sector, the UK is currently working on a 'Big Society Bank'. In this scheme the Big Society Bank will be funded by the government and by money held in dormant bank accounts. This bank should support existing

---

7 Ben Thornley *et al.*, *Impact Investing: A Framework for Policy Design and Analysis,* Rockefeller Foundation, 2011.

8 Social Investment Task Force, *Social Investment Ten Years On*, 2010.

social finance intermediaries in order to promote further initiatives in this area.[9]

Another recent British social innovation is the 'social impact bond'.[10] Social impact bonds are contracts between the public sector, social enterprises and investors. These bonds do not offer a fixed return; instead, the government promises to pay for improved social outcomes. The better the result, the higher the return. For instance, a social enterprise has been established to help prevent former prisoners from re-offending. Social investors, including charitable trusts and philanthropists, funded the enterprise. The UK Ministry of Justice promises to pay the investors an annual return of up to 13.5% if re-offending is reduced significantly. If recidivism does not decline, the investors stand to lose their money.[11] Consequently, the risk for the government is limited as it is paying only for positive social outcomes. The investors have an incentive to monitor the company so that it achieves the best social results. The intention is to develop a secondary market for social impact bonds.

Thanks to a long-term government commitment and coordinated support from various government agencies, the social-enterprise sector is now gaining momentum in Britain.[12] Various governmental and non-governmental associations are developing and exchanging best practices on measuring social progress in order to align the supply of capital with demand. These agencies are also raising awareness about the emerging social-enterprise sector and supporting owners of social enterprises in setting up a business and attracting capital.[13]

Most of the issues relating to the funding of social enterprises are not of a legal nature. Sufficient funding is crucial, however, for a social enterprise sector to emerge. As explained in the next section, the need for

9 *The Coutts Guide to Financing Social Enterprise*, 2010 Q3, p. 10.

10 For detailed information on social bonds, see www.socialfinance.org.uk.

11 Financial Times (February 10, 2011); www.bbc.co.uk (weblog M. Easton, January 19, 2011).

12 Thornley *et al.*, 2011, p. 16, see *supra* note 7; The Social Enterprise Coalition, Annual Report 2010, 2011, p. 3. available at www.socialenterprise.org.uk, last accessed on 3 March 2011.

13 See, *e.g.* www.thegiin.org; www.socialinvestmenttaskforce.org; www.socialenterprise .org.uk; www.cicregulator.gov.uk.

funding and the relationship between shareholders' interests and a social mission will indeed lead to legal consequences.

3.2. Dual Purpose

A second challenge is interconnected with the first: a social enterprise must keep one eye on its public purpose and the other on generating sufficient revenue to keep its investors happy. A social enterprise has a dual purpose. When the interests of the investors prevail, the public purpose may suffer. When the public purpose is all that counts in management decisions, investors can lose interest.

In a comparable context, Michael Jensen has argued that a dual purpose "directs corporate managers to serve 'many masters'. And, to paraphrase the old adage, when there are many masters, all end up being short-changed".[14] According to Jensen, having multiple purposes leads to managerial confusion, conflict, inefficiency, and perhaps even competitive failure. Although we acknowledge that its dual purpose is an important issue here, numerous social enterprises throughout the world have shown that this matter can be addressed and that a balance between the two purposes can be found.

There are several solutions to the 'dual purpose problem'. Most often, market parties are able to find a workable arrangement themselves, using traditional private limited companies or partnerships. The company and its shareholders set out in various corporate documents how to deal with possibly conflicting interests. For instance, the British private equity investor Bridges Ventures has set up a social entrepreneurs fund that seeks to meet the needs of the social enterprise, while also allowing the fund to make a reasonable financial return. Particularly if a company is not subsidised or funded through public money, it is often feasible to balance the possibly conflicting interests within ordinary private limited companies or partnerships.

The private regulation of the dual purpose will entail, however, certain transaction and incorporation costs. Private legal entities were not developed to further public interests. From a corporate law perspective, private legal entities are designed to function in the market place and to

[14] Michael C. Jensen, "Value Maximization, Stakeholder Theory and the Corporate Objective Function", in *Journal of Applied Corporate Finance*, vol. 14, 2001, p. 9.

maximise profits. Consequently, lawyers need to draft specific documents to frame a structure that has the goal of pursuing a public interest in a commercial way. Moreover, shareholders and their desires may shift over time. For example, they may change their opinion on the company's dividend policy or public strategy. In short, while we acknowledge that market parties may be able to regulate a hybrid structure, it may be expensive. In some jurisdictions, a hybrid structure set up by means of an ordinary private limited company may also be legally insecure.[15]

In many jurisdictions, the state plays an important role in regulating the dual purpose problem. Sector regulation, permit conditions or subsidy requirements may all be conducive to diminishing the dual-purpose problem. It is also possible to give a voice to certain interested parties whose interests are parallel to the social mission of the social enterprise. In the Netherlands, for instance, hospitals are obliged to install a clients' council in which the 'customers' may express their views on certain issues in which they have a stake.

4. Special Legal Entities for Social Enterprises

4.1. Why and How?

There are three reasons *why* lawmakers may choose to design a special legal entity for social enterprises. First, company law can regulate the dual purpose problem by defining the rights and obligations of directors and shareholders. Furthermore, a sufficiently flexible 'new company-law product' offering a pre-negotiated set of rules tailored for social enterprises may reduce transaction or incorporation costs for entrepreneurs setting up their businesses.[16] A legal entity specifically designed for social enterprises can also be used by a social entrepreneur as a way of establishing an easily recognizable identity in the market place. It would make the social enterprise stand out from other businesses in a positive way. This can provide a social entrepreneur with a

[15] Thomas Kelley, "Law and Choice of Entity on the Social Enterprise Frontier", p. 4, retrieved online at http://works.bepress.com/cgi/viewcontent.cgi?article=1001&context=thomas_kelley, last accessed 3 March 2011.

[16] Joseph McCahery, Erik Vermeulen, Masato Hisatake and Jun Saito, "The New Company Law: What Matters in an Innovative Economy", in Joseph McCahery, L. Timmerman and Erik Vermeulen (eds.), *Private Company Law Reform: International and European Perspectives*, T.M.C. Asser Press, The Hague, 2009.

competitive advantage, particularly in relation to like-minded potential customers and employees. Muhammad Yunus has stressed that it is important to "make social business entrepreneurs and social business investors visible in the marketplace".[17] A special legal entity can further this goal.

Most company-law systems provide for various options on *how* to regulate the dual purpose problem. First, in company law, a hierarchy can be established between the two objects of the social enterprise and, by doing so, the fiduciary duties of the directors of a social enterprise can be defined. For instance, it is possible to derive inspiration from the British 'enlightened shareholder value' model in ordinary company law. Under the British Company Act, a director must promote the success of the company for the benefit of its shareholders as a whole, taking into account the long-term consequences and the interests of the various stakeholders, such as employees and creditors. In the case of legal entity for social enterprises, the law could require directors to promote the community or social purpose, taking into account the interests of shareholders and other stakeholders. In some jurisdictions, it may also be possible to impose fiduciary duties on shareholders as well, and to oblige them to take into account the community purpose of the social enterprise.

Second, the dual purpose problem can be regulated by limiting certain financial rights of shareholders, such as dividend or liquidation rights. A limitation on financial rights warrants that part of the assets or profits are (re)invested in order to further the social purpose of the company. Third, some jurisdictions limit shareholders' control rights.[18] Fourth, a conflict of interest can be mitigated by disclosure requirements or, fifth, through light supervision by a public or private agency.

To be sure, if all of these regulatory tools were imposed on a legal entity, it would not be able to attract investors; rather, they are listed here merely as alternative ways of using company law as a regulatory and

17 Muhammad Yunus, "Social Business Entrepreneurs are the Solution", in Heiko Spitzeck *et al.* (eds.), *Humanism in Business*, Cambridge University Press, Cambridge, 2009, p. 406.

18 One of the reasons why a Dutch bill introducing a special legal entity for social enterprises was withdrawn was the limitations it would have placed on shareholder control rights.

facilitating instrument. Regulation by the means available in company law may even create the opportunity for deregulation elsewhere.

4.2. A Global Trend

Around the globe, legislators are creating specific legal entities to cater to the need for new legal entities in which the dual purpose of social enterprises is acknowledged. They take different forms and cover the wide spectrum between philanthropy and business. At one pole of the philanthropy-business spectrum, there is the South African non-profit company, which is based on a purely philanthropical philosophy. This type of company is allowed to issue shares, but it cannot pay out dividends to its shareholder. All profits are reinvested and, in the event of liquidation, the assets are paid out to organisations having a similar purpose. In India, Muhammad Yunus has advocated a type of social enterprise which generates enough surpluses to repay the invested capital to the investors.[19] Shareholders, however, would not receive any surpluses like dividends.

Gradually moving towards the business end of the philanthropy-business spectrum, there are several types of legal entities that provide for limited dividend payments to their shareholders. Take, for example, the Belgian non-profit company (*vennootschap met sociaal oogmerk* or VSO). The VSO has not yet emerged as a success, however, partly because of its strict dividend cap and because of a limitation on shareholder voting rights.[20]

The British Community Interest Company (CIC) has proven to be somewhat more successful. Since its introduction in 2005, more than 4650 CICs have been incorporated.[21] Like the Belgian VSO, the CIC is a

[19] Muhammad Yunus, "Social Business Entrepreneurs are the Solution", in Heiko Spitzeck *et al.* (eds.), *Humanism in Business*, Cambridge University Press, Cambridge, 2009.

[20] In addition, Belgian tax rules explain why only a few hundred VSOs have been incorporated since 1995. The VSO is rooted in the cooperative ideal, which emphasizes the importance of the involvement of employees in the decision-making process. For this reason, employees are obliged to participate in a VSO. As a result of a limitation of shareholder votes to 5% or 10%, as the case may be, employees do have an important say in the general meeting of shareholders.

[21] Community Interest Companies, Available at www.cicregulator.gov.uk, last visited on February 18, 2011.

limited company, with special additional features, created for social enterprises. CICs can be incorporated either as a non-profit company limited by guarantee or as a for-profit private limited liability company. CICs differ from these legal entities in three respects. First, CICs can only be incorporated if they pass the 'community interest test', *i.e.*, that "the purpose towards which its activities are ultimately directed is the provision of benefits for the community, or a section of the community". Second, CICs have been put under the light supervision of a public body, the CIC Regulator. Furthermore, the CIC Regulator assists social enterprises in their incorporation process and it has informative tasks. Third, like the Belgian VSO, the CIC limits the payment of dividends to shareholders. The CIC, however, provides for more dividend payments than its Belgian counterpart, whilst the dividend cap can be easily changed by the CIC Regulator if needed.[22] The yearly dividend cap is now set at 20% of the amount paid on the share. Compared to the Belgian VSO, the position of shareholders is also stronger because their voting rights are not impeded.

Since 2008, several American States have been experimenting with the Low-Profit Limited Liability Company (L3C). The L3C is modelled on the limited liability company (LLC), a legal entity known for its flexibility.[23] The aim of the L3C is to attract money from non-profits and charities that are, because of their social mission, willing to accept a limited return at a high risk. In this way these non-profits create opportunities for other investors to participate at a competitive return and acceptable risk. Unlike the legal entities mentioned above, there is no restriction on dividend distribution to shareholders. The L3C is not prohibited from making profits, even high profits, but the fiduciary duties of directors are not primarily focused on profit maximisation: it is a "for-profit entity with a non-profit soul". The fiduciary duties of directors should ensure that they do not primarily pursue profit maximisation.

Since 2008, eight states have introduced the L3C, while legislation in 21 other states is in preparation.[24] At this time, 326 L3Cs have been

---

22 CICs incorporated as private limited companies can also be organised as a purely non-profit company.

23 Dana Brakman Reiser, *Governing and Financing Blended Enterprise*, Working Paper, 2010.

24 Americans for Community Development, available at http://www.americansforcommunitydevelopment.org, last accessed on 27 January 2011.

incorporated.[25] As the L3C is only a few years old, it is too soon to draw conclusions about its success. Although the L3C legislation is specifically designed to guarantee that participating non-profit companies do not lose a federal tax benefit when they invest in a L3C, it is not yet certain whether the L3C legislation is 'waterproof'.[26] It is therefore remarkable that, according to an initial survey among L3C pioneers, L3C entrepreneurs in practice put more weight on the fact that the legal entity expresses the values of the company: "Seeing a business entity type that is a hybrid with a double bottom line, with social impact and creation of social value foremost fits me. [... The L3C] brings 'venture philanthropy' to life", according to an L3C pioneer.[27]

The above-mentioned legal entities are all specifically designed for social enterprises – companies that primarily focus on promoting a social purpose. In this respect, social enterprises differ from normal for-profit enterprise committed to the principles of CSR. For this purpose, the US 'B Corporation' (Benefit Corporation) has been created.[28] B Corporations are commercial enterprises that have the CSR principles injected into their DNA. The B Corporation started as a private certification system, rather than a special legal entity. Since 2010, however, two states in the USA have recognised the B Corporation as a legal entity and similar bills are pending in several other states. A private party, B Lab, provides the certificate when ordinary companies meet certain social and environmental standards. An important requirement for B Corporations is that directors consider the interests of all stakeholders involved, including, but not limited to, the interests of shareholders. Like the L3C, the B Corporation does not limit profit distributions to shareholders – the possible withdrawal of the B Corporation certificate is considered a sufficient safeguard against abuse of the certificate.

25 Intersector L3C, available at www.intersectorl3c.com, accessed on 11 February 2011.

26 Reiser, 2010, p. 4, see *supra* note 23.

27 Elizabeth Schmidt, *Vermont's Social Hybrid Pioneers: Early Observations and Questions to Ponder*, Working Paper 2010.

28 Certified B Corp, "About B Corp", available at www.bcorporation.net, last accessed on 3 March 2011; Reiser, 2010, see *supra* note 23.

4.3. All Roads Lead to Rome

The above mentioned legal entities have been introduced only very recently. Each of the different legal entities tries to solve the 'dual purpose problem' in a different manner. To date, no single model has emerged as the most efficient. Our preliminary hypothesis is that an assessment of which of the various legal entities is best will depend on the circumstances. Among those circumstances are the company's demand for equity and the potential supply of capital by different types of investors. For instance, the South African model could be preferable if there were many potential donors not seeking any profits. An ordinary company would be suitable if the social enterprise were able to attract sufficient equity or debt capital. An ordinary company could also suffice if the company were (fully or partly) financed through public subsidies granted under conditions where there exist sufficient safeguards for the use of public subsidies benefiting the firm's social purpose.

Legal entities specifically designed by lawmakers for social enterprises seem to be preferable in three situations. First, this option is attractive if social enterprises wish to carry out their social mission through a special legal entity. This can be used as a marketing tool. Incorporation under a socially-oriented legal entity makes the enterprise visible in the market. Second, the CIC shows that a legal entity for social enterprises is attractive to small and medium-sized social enterprises that do not have a large need for equity. Third, a special legal entity can be used as a regulatory tool in semi-public areas, for instance, housing corporations, hospitals, day care institutions and universities. The social mission, special dividend rules and special fiduciary duties for directors can be used to safeguard public money in such areas.

By designing legal entities, legislators should keep in mind that, to a large extent, the interests of shareholders and the public are parallel: both have an interest in companies being organised efficiently. Consequently, shareholder control rights should, in principle, not be reduced. Generally speaking, the reduction of shareholder rights should be kept to a minimum, as it is not easy for social enterprises to attract social investors. Normally, it should be sufficient if the dual purpose problem were mitigated by means of the fiduciary duties of directors (and, in so far as possible, of shareholders), as well as by a flexible dividend cap like, like that provided under CICs in the UK. Tougher regulation bears the risk that shareholders are no longer willing to invest. Depending on the circumstances, however, other alternatives might be preferable.

5. Conclusion

For those who know their history, it will come as no surprise that shifting needs have resulted in a demand for new business models. Voices occupying the middle ground between the private and the public sectors are demanding a new kind of legal entity suitable for their needs, one that may be dubbed 'the not-only-for-profit company' – a private company with a public heart that can market itself as a for-profit company while serving a public goal. Its for-profit nature sets it apart from foundations and charities while it is distinguished from regular companies in the sense that it does not seek to maximise shareholder revenue.

Around the globe, legislators are currently responding to this need. For years, social entrepreneurs in South Africa and Belgium have been working with legal entities that are tailored for social enterprises. Over the last few years, the United Kingdom and the US have followed suit, taking, however, a different approach. The experiences in these countries show that there is an interest in meeting the legal needs of social enterprises. Although other factors are also important for social entrepreneurship to grow, new legal entities improve the options open to social entrepreneurs structuring their businesses. One of the challenges for company-law systems in the future will be to meet the needs of the social entrepreneur.

Part II:
The Future of Law

4. Law and Its Evolution – Theoretical Perspectives

4.1

The Future of Legal Theory[*]

Peer Zumbansen[**]

The following think piece is concerned with the status of legal theory in the future evolution of law. It posits that the development of legal theory remains embedded in the dynamics of a functionally differentiated (world) society. In that context, legal thought, doctrine and rationality constitute a distinct but only one of many simultaneously evolving forms of creating and shaping understandings of the world. Law exists in uncountable forms and instantiations around the world, and legal theory sets itself the ambitious task of capturing the totality of legal instruments and processes. In this attempt, as legal theory became crucially concerned with the distinction of law and non-law, it sought out the lessons learned in legal sociology. It is in light of these insights, that the development of legal theory is unlikely to remain confined within the two poles of 'legal positivism' and 'natural law'. By contrast, legal theory will also not become a meta-theory of societal ordering. While such claims are raised predominantly by economics and law, as well as other disciplines such as religion, sociology or anthropology, overlap and intersect in their rendering of reality. As such, legal theory's future is defined both by interdisciplinarity and by legal pluralism, by the co-evolution of numerous forms of 'official' and 'unofficial', forms of legal ordering. The future of legal theory is to understand law as legal pluralism.

1. Introduction

An inquiry into the 'law of the future' unavoidably encompasses a reflection on the vantage point and perspective from which this future of law is being assessed. This reflection shapes the space in which we imagine tomorrow's law. As such, it is concerned with questions of both definition and context: What, we first ask, is law? In trying to define law, however,

* I am grateful for comments from Mielle Chandler, Alexandra Kemmerer, and Maria Panezi. All errors remain my own – the future will most certainly tell…

** **Peer Zumbansen** is Professor of Law and Canada Research Chair in Transnational Economic Governance and Legal Theory at Osgoode Hall Law School.

we inevitably encounter hermeneutic circles, prompting in turn an attempt to consciously expose and deconstruct each and every perspective as both relative and decisive. And, to the degree that this inquiry leads to an unfolding of different contexts – historical, systematic, theoretical – in which law is embedded, the ensuing question concerns the choice in identifying the vantage point, the context and the function of law. While being dependent on each other, the two questions are still distinct. It will become apparent that approaching these questions as two separate inquiries will allow us to recognise particular dynamics of legal evolution in a host of particular, evolving fields on the one hand and to reflect on the context in which this evolution takes place on the other.

As was suggested in the invitation to the 'Law of the Future' project, a specific analysis of law's likely development in a particular area be given priority over a general or blanket reflection on the future of law as such. However, such a general, birds-eye reflection is necessary in order to be able to recognise how legal fields do not simply 'exist', but instead, evolve according to particular dynamics and in specific contexts. Every lawyer in a specific field is well aware that the law as it stands today is by no means the same as the law of yesterday, and in many cases yesterday's law was plagued by a fundamental inability to express, in legal terms, what, a 'new' legal field or a new approach to legal thinking expresses in its legal analysis today. Tomorrow's law will encompass developments in existing legal fields as well as the emergence of new fields, without them necessarily being readily recognisable as such, to be sure. Illustrations of such developments can be found in environmental and internet law, but also in the much debated body of 'social norms' in commercial relations, whether national or transnational.

2. Definitions

Assessing the law of the future first prompts us to define law. As a cultural product, law must be defined contextually and historically, the product thus reflecting a combination of definitional approaches. The following lists competing definitions and concepts of law, each of which claims to exhaustingly capture law's nature and role.

1	Law as an institutionalised system of rule enforcement
2	Law as a means of stabilising expectations

3	Law as a means of oppression
4	Law as hope
5	Law as an empty shell—without (proper) method, heart or soul …?

The crux of these attempts to capture the essence of law lies in the embeddedness of the applied definition in a larger theory of society. A focus on 'society' does not provide, however, a disinterested or comfortably removed Archimedean point of departure. Rather, all efforts of describing, explaining and assessing society are embedded in and part of that society. This becomes clear in the distinction between law and justice and the perceived superiority of the latter over the former. Another closely related distinction is that between legality and legitimacy. While the former depicts the rules, formal or informal, that structure and validate the legal system, the latter captures the need to base the entire system on an overarching body of justifications. While these, in turn, can be derived from both procedural and substantive considerations, or from a focus on either output or input, they don't concern the functionality and coherence of the legal system, but whether or not it can be justified and defended against different competing value systems.

What is expressed in these distinctions is a tension between, on the one hand, existing and governing rules or standards and, on the other hand, the larger goals they are meant to serve as well as the foundations on which this legality is seen to rest. One cannot exist without the other. In other words, there can be no legal theory solely concerned with legality without making reference to the conceptual and valuative foundations and aspirations of the system in place. This tension between law and its valuative and conceptual underpinnings is its fundamental paradox. The one can be the other, but neither can be without the other, lurking in the background and below the surface. Much of the confusion among, for example, scholars in comparative legal studies or legal anthropologists experienced in their interpretations of 'foreign' legal cultures results from the difficulty of understanding a legal system 'from within' rather than through their own culturally pre-conceived notions and distinctions of law/justice and legality/legitimacy.

Against this background, the definitional approach to law as depicted in the table above becomes clearer. The first two definitions – law as an institutionalised rule-enforcement system and law as mode of stabilising expectations – point to law as residing in two distinct realms. The first definition demands a particular framework in order for something to be called 'law'. It refers to the institutionalisation of creating, implementing and interpreting law. Law is thus removed from other rules and behaviour-governing norms such as religious beliefs, ritual rules, or 'social norms'. This definition also carries with it an implicit substantive orientation: that law's origin in and association with a particular system of rule-creation is due to its distinctiveness in contrast to other norms. This can be shown, for example, with regard to the first definition, where the persisting problems of state-oriented legal theories with norms and standards not produced by actors that cannot claim traditional law-making authority lead to an exclusion of these norms as being outside of the law.

2.1. Institutionalised Lawmaking Authorities

It is important to emphasise that this allegedly 'traditional', institutional framework need not be, and historically was not always, the 'state'. It can be any form of societal organisation involved in the processes of legal rule creation, implementation, and interpretation. Again, this constitutes a crucial discovery not only by comparativists and legal anthropologists in their attempt to make sense of dramatically 'different' systems of legal rule creation, but also by legal historians tracing the nexus between the state and law. Crucial here is, again, the distinction between definition and context. As regards the former, the concept of the 'state' itself raises a formidable set of questions as what form of organisation or framework is indeed suggested or implied by the term. Depending on the level of substantive dimensions attributed to the term, the recognition of a nexus between the state and law can quickly turn into an argument against 'law without the state'. The legal pluralist observation of normative, enforceable and stable orders has had the potential to expose the manifold forms of norm-production and thus predates the more recent assertion of law in the 'postnational constellation'. The progressive intuition to scrutinise the complex distinction between law and 'non-law' by comparing state-originating rules with non-state-based modes of norm-creation and enforcement arose against the background of an ever more ambitious but arguably less effective regulatory state and its tendency towards 'juridification'. Looking now at context, however, it is easy to see how the relativisation of the state as an exclusive law-creating authority was enthusiastically embraced by those – surely within the evolution of the Western nation-state – who placed their hopes on the regulatory abilities of an allegedly unfettered market and against the 'interventionist' state. This ambivalence of legal pluralism was, however, not a child of the neoliberal surge in the recent wave of globalisation in the last decades of the twentieth century; instead, it marks the conflicts over the rule of law and the welfare state, conflicts that have only become more exacerbated in a context of globalised markets for capital, goods and services, transnational regimes and the unfamiliar contours of 'global governance'.

2.2. Stabilising Expectations

By contrast, the second definition, law as a means of stabilising expectations, appears to eliminate all references to the form in which the creation, implementation and interpretation of legal rules take place. Through this elimination of the formal infrastructure, the definition invisibilises the orientation and anchoring points used in the first definition to recognise law in the first place. The second definition places the emergence and evolution of law in social activity. The only requirement of sorts is the stabilisation of expectations. Shocking as this may sound when contrasted to the richly structured landscape of the state/law nexus with all its historical origins, institutions and organisations, the second definition is, in fact, much more contextually embedded than it would seem at first glance. If law's nature and role is to stabilise expectations, the question as to whose expectations and through which mode this stabilisation occurs necessarily arises. Here we find a considerable and surprising overlap between the first and the second definition. As in the first, the second can very well encompass highly sophisticated institutional frameworks of rule creation, implementation etc. But, unlike the first, the second points to the potentially highly amorphous, at first sight unstructured, unruly, and informal space in which such processes occur. Unlike the first definition, the second points to the radicalisation of the need to question the yardsticks with which the existence of a legal system is depicted, affirmed and analysed. And, unlike the first, this definition can take no refuge in the reference to known patterns of rule creation, etc. It is thrown back onto itself in trying to recognise structures of legal rule making.

The second definition captures, in crude form, a systems theory understanding of law. In contrast to a politically based concept of an infrastructure through which not only legality, but also, and importantly, legitimacy is produced and administered, a systems theory approach to defining law declares any such institutionalised form contingent. It can and perhaps did exist, but need not exist; while its existence in a particular place at a particular time has prompted the label 'law' to describe this constellation, its inexistence (in another place, another time) is an insufficient reason for denying a particular constellation the label 'law'.

The problems inherent in these two definitions are easy to see; while the first definition is likely to overburden the legitimacy promises of the infrastructure in question, the second runs the risk of turning all 'rules' into 'law' merely in light of their assumed role in stabilising norm-expectations. Considerable uneasiness about these two choices ensues; whereas the first definition appears to, on the one hand, overstate the historical presence of the state as generator and guarantor of legal rule-making, the latter, on the other, understates not only the historical contingency of state-based rule-making and the significant transformations of the state in light of globalisation, privatisation and pluralisation but also the progressive/conservative ambivalence of non-state based law mentioned above. The blind spot left by both definitions concerns the normative dimension of law-making, the ambiguous lurching of questions concerning affectedness, authorship and representation in between the institutional architecture suggested by the first two definitions. Correspondingly, thus, the third and the fourth definition address the anxiety that surrounds the 'who' and the 'why' of law, its purpose and function.

2.3. Law as Oppression/Law as Hope and Emancipatory Tool

Regarding definitions 3 and 4, law as a means of oppression and law as hope, promise, aspiration, 'the evolutionary processes of law' suggest constantly recurring adaptation to developments that respectively strengthen, rather than weaken, both of these definitions. A 'political' theory of law has long stressed the need to make legal rules responsive to changing circumstances. Part of the call for law's responsiveness was the insistence on making visible the violent silencing and excluding dimensions of law. From this perspective, law occupies a distinct – but not autonomous – place in the larger project of social change. Law has and in many cases does serve as vehicle and 'tool' of hope and emancipation. But the opposite is always a possibility, and frequently the case; great deeds of injustice are committed, a tight grip of oppression over society maintained and law deprived of all its sense of political inconclusiveness, openness and critique.

3. Futures

In comparing the definitions of law as an institution, a process, to those of law as a means of oppression or of emancipation we might ask which set of definitions is likely to capture the essence of law in the future. Each of the here identified four approaches appears to capture an important dimension of law, while also highlighting the limitations of reducing the whole of law to one particular aspect.

The elimination of a preconceived, 'typical' or 'traditional' institutional infrastructure to house the 'machinery of justice' that characterises the system's theoretical definition of law points to the abyss between the 'inside' and the 'outside' of the law. On the inside, the routinised reference to legal/illegal allows the system and those working within it to sharpen the lenses through which problems are identified, not only insofar as they pertain to 'law', but insofar as questions of specific, differentiated areas of law such as, say, contract, property, tort or criminal law are involved. Over time, this routine gives 'the law' a most powerful grip on basically all areas of society. Lawyers proliferate relative to the hegemonic expansion of law into every corner of society.

Legal overkill? 'Over-juridification'? Is the response: 'Kill all the lawyers'? To be sure, the flipside of this power of law and of lawyers is the nagging doubt regarding law's self-fulfilling prophecy, namely that it can serve a good purpose as opposed to, say, just an 'efficient' or otherwise politically neutralised 'functional' one. Should all that is being subjected to law's reach, in fact be subjected to it? Is law's future one of a sovereign, authoritative and definitive grasp on societal needs or one of its increased irrelevance?

3.1. The Conundrum of Functionality

While definitions 1, 3 and 4 seem to offer only ambiguous answers to these questions, the systems theory approach offers a sobering and quite revealing perspective on the future of law. Without reference to the Rule of Law, and to parliaments, bureaucracies or courts responsible for the making and applying of the law, the definition of what does and does not count as law must emerge out of the myriad workings of society itself. Echoing political theory's attempt to 'open' law to societal change, the systems theoretical concept of law stresses the particular quality of the distinction between law and non-law but rejects the claim inherent to political theory of law to elevate 'law' in contrast to non-law as something inherently higher, more dignified or of higher value. In fact, systems theory underscores the importance of understanding the question of legitimacy as basically unresolved. In contrast to a political theory of law, a systems theory concept of law does not conceive of a (contingently existing) legal institutional infrastructure as inherently legitimate. Rather, it highlights the complexity of the distinction between law and non-law as the foundational paradox of the legal operation itself. From this perspective, however, it is clear that law and legal norms can potentially be found anywhere. Crucial at this point, then, is the systems theory contention of a particular rationality and code employed by the legal system, namely its operational employment of the distinction between legal and illegal.

Considering the anxieties which have always accompanied the competing definitions of law, a theory which demarcates legal rationality from other societal systems solely through the identification of a distinct communicative code – legal/illegal – will inevitably provoke substantial scepticism. In part, the resistance emerges against the reductionism that seems inherent to this approach. Once this distinction is seen, however, as only one of many parallel perspectives (or, communicative forms) to depict societal 'problems', the embeddedness of legal communication in a rich context of distinct societal communications – in the form of economics, politics, religion, etc. – becomes apparent. The counterintuitive narrowness of law's rationality as defined by the bi-polarity of legal/illegal emerges as less troubling when seen as part of a wider set of highly differentiated societal communications, each unfolding according to a specific code/distinction.

Understanding law from a systems theory perspective as a form of communication which arises in the context of a society characterised by a high degree of functional differentiation, this approach does in fact open perspectives on law's nature, its functions and limits rather than close them. This is illustrated by the complementarity of the named definitions of law. To the degree that we are engaged in an assessment of the future of law we are likely to associate something distinctive with the concept of law, something which constantly seems to invoke understandings of order, control, enforcement, frequently coherence, and even legitimacy. Yet, the contrast already between the first two definitions illustrates the possible variations of law's definition. As we saw, both definitions are complementary. The first can very well be a case of the second, while the second highlights the historical-spatial contingency of the first. Looking beyond the tension between the first definition's focus on an institutionalised, historically identifiable system and the second definition's demarcation of law as a functionally determined process of expectations stabilisation, we catch a glimpse of the deeper motivations that drive our inquiry into the meaning and purpose of law: these are expressed in definitions three, Hope, and four, Oppression. It is here that we face the sobering historical record, or law's hallmark, which is its instrumentality. In the name of this or that (meaning, understanding, ideal or ideology of) law, in the name of law *tout court*, deeds are done, which some condemn as terrorism, others celebrate as acts of emancipation, some are freed, others incarcerated, some are aided and protected, others neglected, some empowered, others silenced. Law functions to sustain just as it helps to break down an existing order. Its availability for different purposes speaks to its multi-directionality and to the contingencies of its use.

3.2. Law as Empty Shell/Law as Parasite

This ubiquitous involvement of law in society's woes and throes stands in stark contrast to assumptions of an elevated stance of law, of law's dignity and supremacy over societal quarrels, of law not only as being ready to be called upon to intervene in instances of petty competition, inequality, and exclusion – but also as being able to 'solve the problem'. Yet, law's involvement in the creation and administration of these conditions reveals law's functionalist spirit: ubiquitous and 'on call', available to all who know how to serve themselves of it, or who can afford it. This suggests that we ought to complement and challenge the first four definitions with a fifth one, which, in reply to the first four, would posit that law has no proper method, heart or soul of its own, only to constantly draw on and take on board the whys and hows of the societal context it comes to operate in. In this definition, law is likened to a shell, an empty one. But perhaps an even stronger image might be one of law as parasite.

As a parasite, law attaches itself to distinct bodies of meaning and normative constructions. Its own functionality and survival feeds off the logic of the normative orders it attaches itself to. Law is thus bound to follow societal differentiation processes into the farthest corner of a highly complex society. Arguably, the idea of law as parasite might do injustice to the fact that law – in contrast to the parasite – often does not inhabit the weakest elements in a given environment, but instead seems to become symbiotically bound up in the dominant forces. Parasites also tend to weaken their hosts, whereas law tends to strengthen, perpetuate, and reinforce the normative orders it becomes bound up in, even when this strengthening requires a certain curtailing of oppression.

Surely, in this light, the notion of law as 'parasite' requires further qualification, in particular as regards the emerging image of law as such being a mere empty shell, or a rapacious organism feeding from the host, without giving anything in return. If that were the case, then the mere idea of law would be wanting. Why come up with a concept of institutional and normative order and call it law, if what we mean is but the result of ever-changing forms of such order produced in different host' contexts? The notion of parasite does point to two problems: one is the nature of the relation between parasite and host, where the former is always taking, the latter always giving. Such a characterisation appears unsatisfactory in light of the rich evidence of complex forms of exchange in societal processes. The other problem connected to the use of the notion of a parasite to describe how law is being shaped through its taking on board the normative content it is exposed to is that to represent law as a parasitic taker doesn't seem to do justice to the effect of law's presence on the context in which it operates. What emerges, then, is that law is a parasite in the sense that it is constantly feeding on normative impulses it receives from outside, but that at the same time, its presence affects the processes of normative and institutional development. The tension between law as hope, now, and as oppression, then, and vice versa, suggests, however, that an interpretation of law as always supporting the hegemon would not adequately capture law's inherent ambivalence as expressed in definitions in definitions three and four. This ambivalence is powerfully illustrated by the unending debates over the nature and function of 'human rights'. These can be mobilised against individual or systematic forms of oppression and exploitation just as they can serve to underscore and strengthen oppressive and exploitative conditions, as is evidenced in contemporary law and development discourses.

Despite these concerns, the privileging of an evocation of law – as system of order – over the identification merely of this or that 'interest', or of different, competing values or competing 'stakes' in a particular conflict, suggests a distinct problem solving ability on the part of law. The reference to law seems to imply that the uncertainty about 'right' and 'wrong' can be borne, that the tension between competing understandings of legitimacy is less important to be overcome than to be sustained. It is here that law's function as a parasite becomes ambivalent: it can but often does not take on board a myriad of conflicting values, interests and voices. In that sense it can give (the hope, illusion or promise of there being a chance that there is a sense to the conflict), but it can just as well reduce choice and scope of what in fact would be possible. Given law's vulnerability to instrumentalisation and its frequent abuse by those with effective 'access', the status of the fifth definition with regard to the foregoing ones becomes problematic.

We can address this dilemma by recognising that the fifth definition is intimately tied to the first four. In other words, it is the tension between the first four and the last definition that gives meaning to the definition of law as shell and as parasite. The last one 'knows' of the first four, but points to the impossibility of settling on only just one of these: instead, it makes clear, how law emerges from the practice of 'addressing', 'capturing', and 'expressing' the contingencies and paradoxes that mark all references to law (and justice) in the court room of first-instance as well as in a newly crafted constitutional preamble. Therefore, while none of the first four suffices to capture the complexity of referencing 'law' on their own, the fifth one incorporates and induces a sense of self-irony into the first four, but only to make a much bolder and even more radical claim. The contention expressed in the fifth definition is that law is but a particular way of translating or transforming societal occurrences into a particular form of communication that is proper to law. The fifth definition, then, expresses the exposed nature of law to society – in all its forms and appearances. Law emerges as a particular way of speaking about society. It is parasitic in the sense that it takes on myriad contents to which it applies the legal/illegal distinction. By engulfing and assimilating these myriad contents, law circumscribes possibilities, options, and 'freedoms' through the rigorous application of the legal/illegal distinction. In this process, does law remain an otherwise empty parasite; is its nourishment followed by growth? The functionalist, systems-theoretical lens sees law as operating and proliferating without gaining in proper content of its own. It remains fundamentally open – that is why its resourcefulness is recognised by the (political) right and the left, the radical and the conservative.

It is only from this perspective that the first four definitions make sense: law appears in highly institutionalised, but sometimes formal, sometimes informal settings. Law can dominate, silence and suffocate, but law can also emancipate, empower and give voice to claims not (yet) recognised as expressions of rights. It is through the lens of the fifth definition that the first four definitions reveal the deeply political, sociological and cultural dimensions of law.

4. Context

This last insight is crucial for our understanding of law's evolution in the future. Here, context is crucial: the context in which references to law occur, the context in which law prevails or fails, the context in which law reigns or is extinguished. It is impossible, even meaningless, to assess law as such, without considering the context in which this reference occurs. This has become an issue long before the alleged death or exhaustion of the nation state under the impact of all-encompassing globalisation processes. The 'end of the state'-image makes sense only in the context of state-oriented theories of law. Such theories are understandably troubled by the new challenges that border-crossing and de-territorialised societal activities create for state-institutionalised legal systems. However, one of the most important insights from legal sociology and legal pluralism already at the beginning of the twentieth century was the recognition of a vibrant tension between 'official' and 'unofficial' normative orders, only inadequately expressed through the already mentioned distinction between 'law' and 'non-law'. Legal pluralism radically challenged the exclusivist claim for law to be borne out of state-authority alone. The identification of numerous non-state originating normative orders paved the way for a host of critical inquiries into the structure of legal systems. But as the Western welfare state's concern with the creation of adequate legal protection was oriented towards vulnerable parts of society, its 'social' bias soon came under fire.

The conservative backlash against 'state intervention', briefly described above, and the contention of a 'retreat of the state' and the call for a revival of private autonomy and 'freedom of contract', coincided with the political left's frustration with the regulatory instruments of the welfare state. While progressive scholars highlighted the necessity for the state, and, more importantly for legal theory, to develop more context-sensitive, adaptable and 'learning' regulatory instruments, conservative scholars grasped the opportunity of the welfare state's regulation crisis to argue for the superiority of market self-regulation.

Thus: context matters! Processes of legal evolution are embedded in rich spheres of competing regulatory discourses and ideas. It is in these contexts that references to law (and justice) are made. Periodisations of different forms of state and society (for example 'rule of law' and 'industrial society', 'social'/'welfare state' and 'post-industrial society', 'enabling state' or 'risk society') remain tentative depictions of the specific context in which law's evolution occurs. The transformation of the (formal) rule of law into the (substantive) law of the social, 'interventionist' and welfare state during the larger part of the twentieth century emerges as but one possible depiction of what happened – and also only in some parts of the world. Alternatives, even within the state-obsessed analysis of law's fate in the nation-state setting of the Western hemisphere, run wild, if one only cares to look.

The ideological competition of progressive ('law and society') and conservative ('law and economics') models of a more empirically based, anthropologically and sociologically grounded legal theory speaks volumes of the contingency of models with which we can dare to speak of 'law in context'. The narrative of law's phases of formalism, functionalism, followed by welfare state progressivism and the ensuing programs of responsive/reflexive law on the one hand and law and economics on the other, since the 1980s, is fundamentally challenged by accounts from within and from outside the Western nation state. Inside, the progressive impetus of the rule of law / welfare state narrative is received with fundamental scepticism, while outside, especially legal anthropologists and law and development scholars have been emphasising the parochial mindset that distinguishes between allegedly 'advanced' legal cultures and so-called 'primitive', 'authentic' ones. Time and again, scholars of comparative law have become highly self-critical with regard to their preconceived notions of legal formality and substantive values. Complementing this critical self-inspection, scholars in the 'global South' – particularly in the area of human rights – have been pondering the structural impact that Western law, money and politics have had on the shaping of legal and power relations elsewhere. This has recently been opening up an ambitious and far-reaching engagement between the North and South on the way in which models of the state, law and the economy have been imposed by the North onto the rest of the world. As recently emerging forms of market governance and political control in countries such as India, China and Brazil are at least temporarily eclipsed or overshadowed by the revolutionary developments in economically structurally disadvantaged states in North Africa, the limits of our analytical toolkit but also of our information processing capacities have become clear to see.

5. Prospects

Where does this leave legal theory today, and what does legal theory have in store for tomorrow? Law's extreme functionalisation is a necessary, and as such, an inevitable by-product of an increasingly differentiated, complex and pluralist society. Law's breathless catch-up game to juridify yet-unchartered societal territory, be that in the area of technical developments, environmental risks or in the highly charged and increasingly important areas of morality and religion, is unlikely to give way to a more relaxed form of adapting law to changing societal circumstances. Instead, law's functionalist orientation is both its promise and its Achilles heel. It is its promise in light of the responsive and reflexive mode with which modern law has been drilling its way into highly complex areas of societal activity. What has marked the – Western – history of responsive/reflexive law since its origin in the 1970s is the vulnerability of this theoretical and conceptual opening of law to the needs and pressures of society. As noted, this is powerfully expressed in the methodological parallels between the progressive and the conservative theories of legal reform as promulgated by critical legal studies and 'law and society' on the one hand and by 'law and economics' on the other. Both purport to make law sensitive to the self-regulating potential in different stakeholder corners of society. But, while the progressive strand pursues this agenda from a critical theory perspective in the attempt to rescue the political promises of, say, the equity, empowerment and redistribution hopes of the welfare state, conservatives have been embracing the self-governing forces of the 'market' and of individual self-empowerment. While the former remain attached to a political theory of law and social theory, the latter operates with an openly a-historical conception of the market, for which references to 'law' function merely as denotations of the necessary, formal 'framework' for otherwise autonomous market action. This finds strong expression in the depiction of the role of law rendered by new institutional economics.

6. Interdisciplinarity

Theories of self-governing markets, 'social norms' and law as a formal institution appear comparably better suited to embrace the transformation of state-based political and legal structures in a globalised world. The challenges emerging from a globally integrated space of functional differentiation seem a promising testing ground for related theories of 'limited statehood' and self-regulatory markets. By contrast, political theories of law are currently seeking new alliances with sociological and political thinking on cosmopolitanism, global governance and world society. The challenge for these progressive approaches to legal thinking, above all, lies in the need to rethink the institutional framework of political and legal theory in a world where the conditions of democratic political action, operating through elections and rule enforcement subject to universal accountability, are subject to fundamental changes. The future of the law is, from this perspective, very much that of the 'state', but not of the state as we knew it. Legal theory will in the future have to be even more mindful of its often undisclosed assumptions regarding, for example, particular institutional safeguards but also value systems that have been taken for granted in the mere reference to law and its role in governing society. The law of the future does not yet exist, but its birth depends to no small degree on the confrontation with the blind spots and aberrations of law in the past. This retrospective inquiry into the evolution of law will inevitably occur as a result of law being challenged by alternative proposals of social ordering, above all by economics and religion.

To reinstate 'law' to play a role in the context of a globalised world, it will not be enough to sniff at the supposedly crude definition of law as the 'formal' counterpart to the otherwise 'informal' institutions of market self-regulation, as is sometimes expressed in scholarship in the area of 'new institutional economics'. The task, moreover, will be to lay out the particular qualities of legal thinking in making the distinction between formal and informal. For law, this distinction has never been a mere sociological one between, say, parliamentary statutes on the one hand and codes of conduct on the other. Rather, for law, at least after the French and American revolutions, the task has been to create a space in which a political deliberation can occur about why the distinction occurs in the first place between statute (associated with law, formality, bindingness) and code (non-law, informal and non-binding). While new institutional economics seems to treat this distinction as a mere sociological fact and as an efficiency test ('markets as better regulators'), legal theory cannot be satisfied with this distinction. Instead, legal theory points to the space in which the distinctions between law and non-law are being made.

4.2

An Imminent Implosion of Legal Systems?

Jo Ritzen and A.W. Heringa[*]

Ritzen and Heringa focus on two questions. The first is what might or will happen when (as seems to be the case) legal texts and judgments explode in numbers. Can it be argued or foreseen that there is a link between confidence in law and the rule of law and the exponential growth in law-making? This question is therefore related to the interplay between law and its social, economic, and political context. Instead of building trust and providing predictability, the explosion of legislation, accelerated by the internationalisation of law, might threaten social trust and predictability. The exponential growth of legislation is caused by social risk aversion in combination "with a political system which is bound to overpromise in order to gain political support". A major challenge for both international and national legislators therefore is to exercise restraint with the creation of new legislation. Ritzen and Heringa propose "to take a substantial minimum period before the adopted new legislation is implemented or even made". However, although the authors are inclined to assume that there is a link, or at least a possible turning point, where the abundance of laws could lead to a decline of trust in the legal order, they did not find concrete empirical proof or data to substantiate that present day, complex law-making societies show a decline in trust. Other factors are at play such as the budget deficit, for instance. However, the issue seems worth considering and researching further.

1. An Imminent Implosion?

Enter the waiting room of the Dutch Prime Minister and across from the visitor's bench you will notice book shelves with the volumes of new Dutch legislation passed through parliament, organised by the year in which the laws were passed. To start with, there is a 2 cm thick volume from 1840. From then-on, every year the volumes increase in thickness,

[*] **Jo Ritzen** is Chair and Founder of Empower European Universities.
A.W. Heringa is Dean of the Law Faculty at Maastricht University.

with two thin volumes per year in 1910, up to some 15 thick volumes in 2009, food for lawyers and politicians, food for thought for academics.

A simple logarithmic extrapolation would show us that 10 years from now we will need the full space of both the shelves containing the flow of legislation from the past 170 years, to store the volumes containing the laws passed in a single year. The flow of legislation is indeed increasing constantly, exploding, you may say, in most of the developed world. True, much of this new legislation replaces old legislation. Yet, in the process, there is also a constant increase in the stock of legislation. Furthermore, we have not even considered the growing number of international treaties, declarations, recommendations and resolutions; nor have we taken into account the regulations adopted by the EU; nor have we counted case law on domestic and international law, through an abundance of courts, committees, panels, appellate bodies and arbitrations; nor have we counted the growth of codes of conducts and similar 'rules of practice or behaviour' with less binding but possibly similar force, or at least relevant impact.

Legislation is supposed to help legal entities (individuals or firms) to chart their course in society and in time. In this think piece we hypothesize, however, that this process of constant and continuous increase in the stock and flow of legislation is bound to lead to a *kladderadatsch* – an implosion – because too much legislation decreases rather than increases trust (section 2). For now, we will focus predominantly on domestic legislation, knowing that the issues we will raise might multiply in complexity or relevance when we take EU and international rules and court cases into account. Legislation reduces transaction costs and provides predictability. The certainty of such constant and rapid change in legislation, however, is counterproductive, because it undermines the same predictability it wants to provide. We hypothesise that this contradiction dissolves trust in society, in institutions, in politics and in the legal system.

People and politicians ask for new legislation to try to cope with a variety of problems they encounter, but responding to this might also lead to rapid changes, flaws in the legal fabric and coherence, and growing disbelief in the relevance and effectiveness of legislation. It seems odd by the way, that complaints about the effectiveness of legislation to cope with societal issues are being remedied by changing the law or making a new law (as law, to begin with, or 'more law', is not always the best solution). We explore this from the perspective of the need for the presence of trust in society, in particular from trust as bridging social capital in section 3. Societies benefit from trust and the social cohesion it brings about. Legislation should support this process.

With so many arguments against the explosion of legislation, how on earth does this Leviathan-like corpus sustain its growth? The giant is even revered as it appears while potentially threatening the very existence of those who revere it. We hypothesise that it is social risk aversion which drives legislation in combination with a political system which is bound to overpromise in order to gain political support. Of course, not all new legislation is meant to reduce social risks. Globalisation and the consequent modernisation of the public sector and of legislation itself are also driving forces.

2. When Too Much Legislation Decreases Trust and Predictability

Bismarck established unemployment insurance in order to provide at least some predictability of income for the population even when unemployed. His concern was entirely founded on the need for flexibility in industry. Firms should be able to innovate and replace existing production processes with new ones, without the possible drag of workers who would want to hold on to their outdated jobs. More legislation creates predictability.

Predictability reinforces people's trust in government, in institutions, in politics, in each other. Trust is relevant in the sense that in its absence, or relative absence, people seek their own protective mechanisms. In the absence of trust, the making of contracts (an economic activity) becomes more restricted and when contracts are made, they require extensive negotiation and drafting instead of a simple handshake. Furthermore, obedience to rules must be enforced or supervised more strictly. All these measures add to economic transaction costs. So if we say that law makes a society function smoothly when practiced, and if trust or confidence in the fairness of the legal system leads to more participation and practice, then such trust is integral to the effective functioning of law and the legal fabric. Yet trust arrives by foot and leaves by rocket. Rapid changes in legislation decrease predictability rather than increase it. First of all, there are the risk perception costs: every piece of new legislation has to be absorbed by the legal parties, citizens, institutions and firms. They have to read it and translate it into their own behaviour. Rapid changes decrease predictability and tarnish basic trust, because citizens and companies who modelled their conduct according to an existing legal rule must change their behaviour when the rule changes. When we change the laws too frequently and without seeking to ascertain whether the need or fairness of the changes really balances the decrease in predictability, then a decrease in trust will be the result. This consideration should be an important factor in lawmaking, posing the question: does the need for change really outweigh the price paid in terms of loss of legal certainty and predictability? Might it not be better to allow the subjects of a rule more time to adapt to it and to fully grasp the need for changes? Secondly, on top of the risk perception costs there are also implementations costs. Legislation often contains incentives. A change of legislation implies a change in incentives. Behaviour has to adjust. This requires time and effort, taken away from other socially productive activities, and this is how implementation costs are generated. Furthermore, apart from (financial) costs, there are additional costs, less quantifiable perhaps yet still important, in the sense of anger and betrayal and the feeling of not being taken seriously, or even being ignored.

Let us illustrate this with an example pertaining to the financing of higher education. If the legislative system is changed, it means that all higher education institutions have to reflect on their strategies and reconsider their appropriateness. Strategies are supposed to be 'smart' with concrete goals which are chosen in such a way that they are rewarded in the legislative system of financing. Changes in the financing system should then only occur very rarely (no more than once every 10 years; we also think such changes should not be implemented prior to a long period (of 2-3 years) of pre-warning). If European Universities are not highly represented in the top league, it has a lot to do with the unpredictability of government. At a recent European University Association meeting in Palermo (October 2010),[1] an analysis of universities' strategy was presented to the participants. The overwhelming reaction of university presidents was: "you cannot trust government, so do not engage in a serious choice of a mission, because the government is capricious".

---

1 See Jo Ritzen, "Strategy is the Choice for a Mission on Which You Excel Within Your Competition Where Excellence is Rewarded", European University Association, 22 October 2010, Palermo, available at http://www.eua.be/Libraries/EUA_Annual_Meeting_Palermo_2010/Ritzen_Jo.sflb.ashx, last accessed 1 April 2011.

This is just an example. The field of economic activity is another area where government is widely distrusted.

3. Trust is a Repeated Game

Arrow has positioned trust in terms of experiences.[2] My trust in you is reinforced if your action is in line with our implicit or explicit agreement or mutual expectations. Conversely, trust is undermined if our agreement is breached by your actions. Putnam frames this notion in terms of bonding and bridging social capital: you bond in your direct circle of family and friends and you build up trust there.[3] This is common in most societies, including the less developed and less sophisticated ones. Agreements, contracts or legislation do not have to be in a written form: they can be part of the oral history of the 'clan'. Bridging social capital means trust created between anonymous parties which do not have a bond. Where such trust exists, transaction costs are minimal in dealings between anonymous partners. Legislation can be viewed as providing the explicit contracts between anonymous partners such that bridging social capital or trust can emerge and can be sustained. But such legislation needs to be stable and durable. An obvious deficit in many developing countries is the fickleness of legislation: a new government might all too easily overturn previous agreements. Under such circumstances trust disappears, transaction costs associated with economic and social action increase and the level of such action decreases.

It is remarkable that the developed world functions in a similar manner. However, it is not by upsetting government, but rather the problem is that, in such states, democracy has organised itself into opposing political parties in which the winner is the one with the largest number of proposed reforms. The perception of political parties and politicians of what the electorate expects from them is one in which the people generally want their representatives to do as much as they can: make many laws, meet all demands, and put their stamp on as many sectors in society as possible – essentially, to remedy all flaws and issues in society, quickly and immediately. Legislation has thus become a new consumer product,

---

2 Kenneth J. Arrow, "Gifts and Exchanges", in *Philosophy and Public Affairs*, 1972, vol. 1, pp. 343-362.

3 Robert D. Putnam, *Bowling Alone: The Collapse and Revival of American Community*, Simon and Schuster, New York, 2000.

with an ever shortening life span. The result is that progressiveness is clothed in legislative changes, without any consideration of their transaction costs or the trust the electorate has in stable rules and legal certainty. Aspects of transaction costs, surely, but also legal values in their own as part of why citizens trust their governments, legislature and legal system as such seem to be ignored and set aside as the (political or system) changes are considered as priority number one. And who wants to be labelled a conservative?

4. Social Risk Aversion Enforces Legislation: The Spiral Downwards

It is a common phenomenon that people look for culprits for things which go wrong in their lives (like sickness, unemployment and unrealised income expectations), while at the same time they look for safeguards which can prevent the culprits from striking. Risk aversion is part of the strong biological drive dedicated to survival: "to be or not to be" is followed by "whether to suffer the slings and arrows of outrageous fortunes". Private insurance has come about to reduce the effects of such 'outrageous fortunes'. Somewhat similarly, governments have used legislation as protection against unwanted risks. Moreover, political parties are in competition in promising protection to different groups. Left wing parties typically promise protection against poverty, while right wing parties promise protection to compete on the product market. A substantial part of new legislation is driven by the risk aversion of citizens and institutions, whether market or semi-public. Every piece of legislation will have its faults and its limitations. Thus, the flow of new legislation is driven by the desire to correct faults and reduce limitations. By its very nature, however, new legislation also brings about new faults and new limitations

There is another phenomenon in the background of the flow of new legislation which is often observed: "the juridification of society".[4] This is the tendency to bring every possible case of conflict between legal partners and government into regulation. Brenninkmeijer sees this tendency as legislation which aims to create order but leads to chaos in the process. He believes that the 'juridification of society' is closely related to the

[4] Alex Franciscus Maria Brenninkmeijer, "Op de Grens van Rechtsorde en Rechtschaos [On the Borderline between Legal Order and Legal Chaos]", *Ars Aequi*, 2005, p. 533, 539.

avoidance of social risks. An additional aspect in the background is 'modernisation'. However, in many respects this flow has essentially the same background as 'modernisation' because it means different public 'services' or different structural elements which better fulfil the risk-avoiding desire of citizens or of institutions .However, not all legislation fits the bill of more protection against risk. In particular all the new legislation which is aimed at government budget reduction or 'higher efficiency' in (semi) public services is outside our scope.

In order to have a better view on what causes the explosion of the flow of legislation, which in turn may lead to the implosion of legal systems, it would be useful to have a quantitative analysis of the flow and stock of legislation. For the Netherlands, Brenninkmeijer cites the memorandum 'Useful legal order' (*bruikbare rechtsorde*). According to this source, between 1980 and 2003 the growth in the stock of legislation (measured as legally applicable rules) was 60%. In the year 2003, the gross flow of new laws was 58, with a gross outflow of 7%.[5] The total of applicable articles (including Royal decrees and Ministerial Decisions) was announced in January 2004 to be approximately 140.000.

5. (How) Does the Implosion Occur?

An implosion would occur if the explosion of legislation leads to a combination of 'legal avoidance', or 'legal evasion' (ignoring legal rules; seeking ways to not follow the law by the letter; so many people or companies do not follow the rules that is seems to be impossible to enforce compliance), while at the same time reducing trust in legislation and the systems which generate and maintain legislation (political parties). Legal avoidance and evasion do occur but legal systems in general control the situation. In fact, legal avoidance has been formally incorporated in some instances; in this category there are rules such as codes of conducts, and negotiations between a government and stakeholders agreeing to abide by certain rules, arbitrations and mediations. If we arrive at a situation of implosion, the magnitude of avoidance and evasion of state-produced rules would surpass any control capacity. Trust in politics, in parliament and in government could also be under stress due to a flow of legislations which exceeds the absorption capacity of a country. We shall explore this in the subsequent paragraph.

[5] Brenninkmeijer, 2005, p. 538, see *supra* note 4.

A low level of trust in politics might have all kinds of consequences. One is the Chavez-like cry for 'business cabinets', which is in fact a form of light dictatorship, exercised with a parliamentary basis. There are as yet no signs that there is broad support for such a development in any developed countries. However, we might witness how (parts of the) electorate are on the lookout for easy, quick and effective solutions, as they feel that parliaments are only interested in talking and not in taking concrete action. Rather than being taken suspiciously, 'strong leadership' appears to be an asset in elections nowadays.

6. Trust in Legislation, Politics and Institutions

The exponential increase in new legislation is bound to lead to a decrease in trust in legislators (political parties), in public institutions and possibly in the legal system as a whole. The media and 'people on the street' have already observed a growing gap between the electorate and the elected. Let us examine whether available data can serve to confirm this impression.

The fact is that according to a Eurobarometer survey carried out between 1995 and 2009, the past 14 years have not shown any of what we see as a clear decrease in trust. Trust in the national parliament indeed decreased in 12 out of the 15 countries surveyed, as is depicted in Figure 1 in the annex to this think piece. Notice that in Denmark, Sweden and (less apparently in) Portugal, trust in Parliament increased, while it was already at a relatively high level (above 50%). Spain, Italy, the UK and Ireland have declining trust levels in a state where trust was already low (and is in 2009 below 30%). There appears to be a considerable overlap between countries which ran huge government deficits (the so-called PIIGS) and the low trust group. We do not have any data on the flow and stock of legislation, according to whatever quantity indicator. Hence we cannot statistically correlate this flow of stock with trust in Parliament.

Trust in national government has increased in 7 of the 15 countries, while it has been decreasing in 8 between 1995 and 2009. The EU has increased in trust in 12 of the 15 countries. Only 19% of voters have trust in political parties in the Europe out of 27 countries in 2009. Figure 2 in the annex to this think piece shows that in the period 1997-2009, 11 of the 15 countries surveyed, showed that trust in the legal system is either stable or increasing. Three of the four countries in which trust in the legal system is decreasing again belong to the highly indebted countries (the PIIGS) with the Netherlands as a remarkable addition (with the single largest decrease).

If anything, these data show a remarkable resilience against the explosion of legislation and are far from indicative of an imminent implosion. So this finding goes against our hypothesis. In the Western world, based upon the available data, the rapid increase of legislation and rapid changes of legislation have not led to a decline in trust and confidence in the legal systems.

7. Conclusion

There should be a serious concern about the exponentially increasing flow and stock of legislation. At some point, perception costs of new legislation, the transaction costs of implementation and enforcement costs start to override the benefits of legislation. And we ought to be concerned about the question of whether we should give more prominence to be 'more effective with less', rather than 'less effective with more'. We can achieve this by asking the question of whether a new or amended rule indeed outweighs the costs of absorbing the change (and always creating new problems) instead of doing nothing. Government and parliaments alike seem to be utterly oblivious to this development, presumably because they feel that there is no way out, no alternative. Moreover, they are not rudely corrected by the democratic process by disgruntled voters who invest lower levels of trust into action (of any undemocratic kind). Brakes on the growth of legislation can be found in many ways.[6] The most essential alternation is to take a substantial minimum period before the adopted new legislation is implemented or even made. But such a recipe is like asking the Baron of Munchhausen to pull himself out of the swamp by his own hair!

[6] Brenninkmeijer, 2005, p. 543, see *supra* note 4.

8. Annex

Figure 1: Trust in the National Parliament.

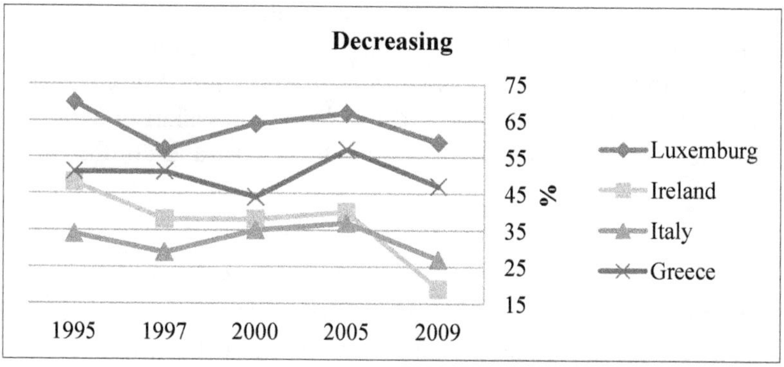

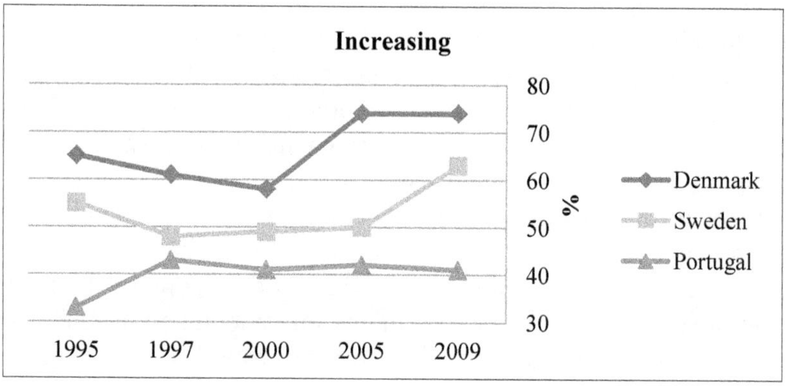

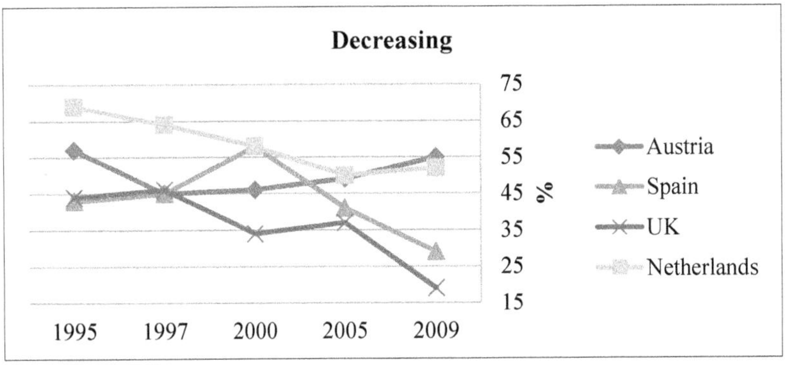
Decreasing
75
65
55
45
35
25
15
%
1995
1997
2000
2005
2009
Austria
Spain
UK
Netherlands

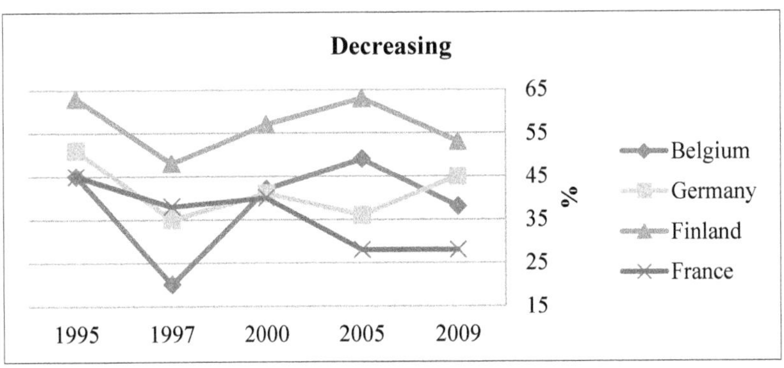
Decreasing
65
55
45
35
25
15
%
1995
1997
2000
2005
2009
Belgium
Germany
Finland
France

Figure 2: Trust in the Legal System.

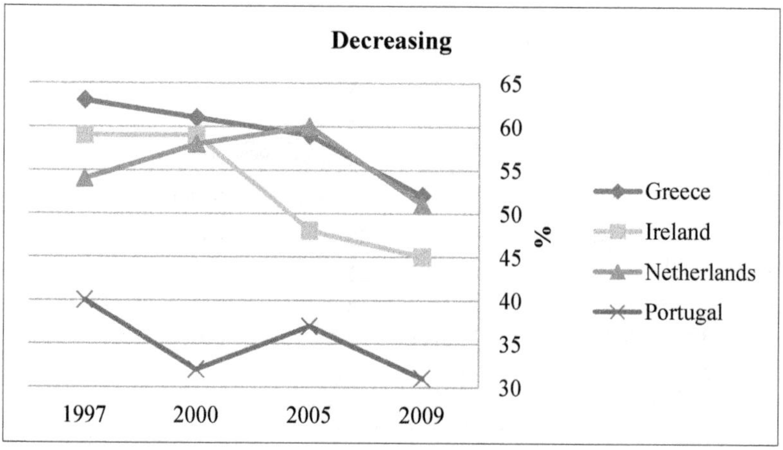

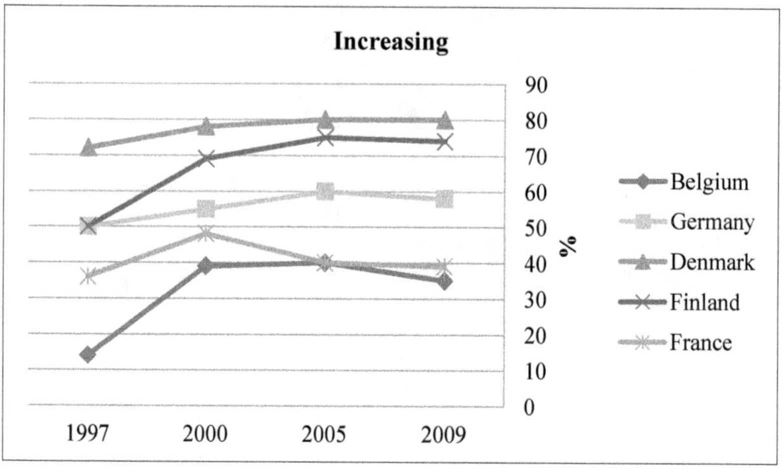

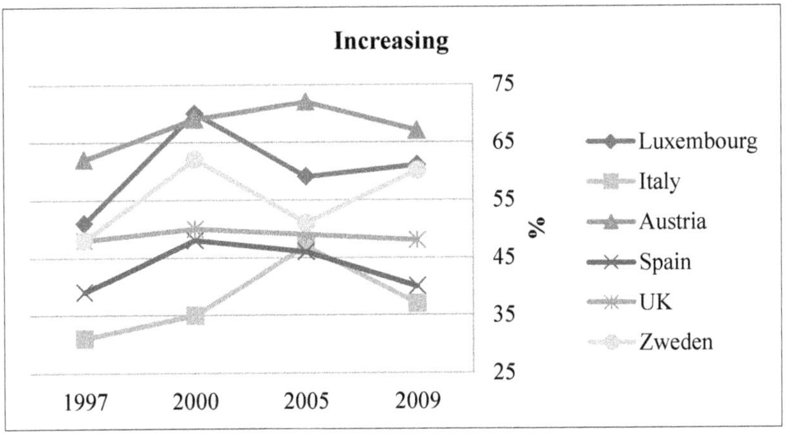
Increasing
75
65
55
45
35
25
%
1997
2000
2005
2009
Luxembourg
Italy
Austria
Spain
UK
Zweden

4.3

The Boundaries of Legal Orders in a Postnational Setting: Conceptual, Normative and Institutional Issues*

Hans Lindahl**

The boundaries of state legal orders are becoming increasingly irrelevant in the era of postnationalism. This paper argues that postnational legal orders don't overcome boundaries; instead, they set new (spatial) boundaries that include and exclude. Discussing how legal boundaries do their work of including and excluding, I argue that a central normative challenge confronting law in the future is how to make sense of freedom, justice, and security if we can neither rely on the communitarian assumption that these values can only be achieved in a bounded community, nor on the cosmopolitan assumption that these values can only be realised in an all-encompassing legal order. Institutionally, the challenge is to devise arrangements that can foster boundary negotiations between legal orders in a way that neither assumes that those negotiations should aim to join together the orders into a single, all-encompassing global order nor that they should safeguard those legal orders as simply separate and distinct units.

1. Legal Boundaries in the Postnational Era

Legal boundaries are becoming increasingly irrelevant in the era of post-nationalism – or so we are often told. This means, spatially speaking, that law has become more global, more local and more transversal than the nation-state. The World Trade Organisation, for example, purports to be global in range. In contrast, the informal legal orders of squatter settlements illustrate local forms of law that are not simply derived from, nor

* My contribution is written from the perspective of a legal philosopher, and as such, is as of much an attempt to ponder which legal developments in the coming decennia pose a renewed task for philosophical thinking, as an attempt to outline a philosophical interpretation of issues that will play an important role in legal developments into the coming two decades. The boundaries of legal orders in a postnational setting are one such theme.

** **Hans Lindahl** is a Professor at Tilburg University.

authorised by, the state order. In yet another example of the disintegration of borders, multinational corporations are governed internally by new forms of transnationally formulated rules through disparate processes of the various legal orders. A related process of fragmentation is taking place that affects the boundaries and content of such legal orders. Whereas state law and international law have largely exhausted the scope of positive law, or so it has been taken for granted, we now witness a plethora of more or less autonomous cross-border legal orders which claim to regulate specific kinds of human activity. Think of codes of professional self-regulation, *lex mercatoria*, technical standardisation and ICANN (the Internet Corporation for Assigned Names and Numbers). The temporal boundaries of the nation-state also seem to be coming under sustained pressure, as we have become acutely aware that a manifold of histories can be told about collectives. For example, the laws of indigenous peoples within and across nation states evoke histories that liberate ways of living in common; yet they are stifled by official accounts of collective time. Finally, the civic boundaries of the state are also becoming blurred. The massive distinction between citizenship and alienage cannot capture a multitude of contemporary forms of political membership and affiliation. The notion of a 'denizen' attests to the in-between status of individuals on the move around the world, a status which is not derivative or merely privative with respect to citizenship.

The fourfold legal boundaries of the nation-state – its spatial, temporal, material and subjective boundaries – are undoubtedly forfeiting at least some of their traction on human behaviour. Indeed, it has become somewhat platitudinous to assert that contemporary social relations are inadequately described and explained as taking place within – and to some extent between – sovereign states with mutually exclusive territories, populations and governments. In the same way, it is generally accepted that the doctrinal framework that took for granted a largely complementary relation between municipal and international law is incapable of affording sufficient conceptual and normative orientation in the face of globalisation. In particular, the process by which the nation-state's legal boundaries lose some of their hold on human behaviour is celebrated as marking the passage from a monistic understanding of social life to the consolidation of pluralism in law and politics. If the thought patterns that underpinned the nation-state sought to protect the integrity of its legal boundaries, often at the cost of diversity, the advent of postnationalism opens up the possibility of a pluralistic politics less mindful of securing legal boundaries and more respectful of difference – or so we are told.

Yet there is a question which has received little if any systematic and sustained attention in the legal and political theory of postnationalism, perhaps because globalisation tends to evoke the image of an unrelenting process of transcending or overcoming boundaries. The question is this: are these four kinds of boundaries as such becoming irrelevant for legal orders in a postnational setting? This question is particularly apposite with respect to spatial boundaries: does the deterritorialisation of law amount to its 'delocalisation'? More pointedly, does postnationalism offer hope of moving beyond the logic of inclusion and exclusion that animates the bounded nation-state? Or does that logic continue to hold sway, even though postnationalism perhaps transforms how it does its work?

These preliminary considerations suggest that the conceptual, normative, and institutional stakes of the question about legal boundaries are considerable, and, in my opinion, will become increasingly acute during the coming decennia:

- The central *conceptual* problem raised by the uncoupling of law and state turns on the relation between boundaries and legal order, namely whether postnational legal orders can be *orders* at all, unless they involve spatial, temporal, subjective and material boundaries of some sort. If not, and so I will argue hereinafter, then one of the main tasks for legal theory during the coming years will be to develop a notion of legal order that is sufficiently general to accommodate both the nation-state and postnational legal orders as species of a single genus, while also being flexible enough to concretely explain the differences between these kinds of legal orders.
- This set of conceptual problems is intimately linked to a circle of normative issues. In particular, the question arises whether in the future we will be able to make legal and political sense of fundamental values such as freedom, justice and security, both severally and in conjunction with each other, if it can no longer be assumed that the boundaries of nation-states will remain the sole or even primary condition for, and the object of, lawmaking. The background issue here is the more general debate concerning practical rationality as it impinges on the problem of inclusion and exclusion. Indeed, what renders the boundaries of legal orders a particularly

urgent theme is that their task is to include and to exclude. In particular, at stake is whether normative conceptions of freedom, justice and security presuppose that the realisation of an all-inclusive legal order is the cardinal injunction driving the rationality of political action. This is of course the basic stance of cosmopolitanism, a stance that sets it at loggerheads with various strands of communitarianism, which assert that freedom, security and justice are only possible within bounded communities.

- Finally, the emergence of postnationalism also brings institutional questions to the fore. In particular, the question arises whether and how postnationalism introduces new ways of institutionalising the process of drawing the boundaries of legal orders, not least in the face of their political contestation.

2. A Thought Experiment

The remainder of my contribution is dedicated to sharpening these questions, rather than attempting to resolve them. Or more precisely, I want to provide what I hope is at least a plausible, albeit highly abridged, argument for why boundaries are ingredient to any imaginable legal order and why, if this argument holds, the normative and institutional questions posed above will become particularly urgent in the coming decennia. This section lays out the core of the argument by reflecting on a thought experiment, namely, the foundation of a world polity. This case is interesting because, on the face of it, a world polity would have no boundaries, or at least no spatial boundaries (in the form of an inside and an outside), nor subjective boundaries (everyone would be included). What, then, would it take to found a world polity as a legal order, regardless of the specific mode of political organisation that were to be chosen for it?

First and foremost, it would be necessary to determine, at least minimally, a common or shared interest. In other words, it would be necessary to positively indicate at least some values and interests that are deemed to be shared, and which the legal order of the world polity is called upon to protect and foster. Needless to say, these values and interests can change through time. Closer consideration suggests that if no world polity could get off the ground without at least a minimal determination of what its members share in the way of interests, values, projects and the like, this also means that no world polity is possible that is not bounded materially (that is, in terms of the kind of behaviour that is allowed or disallowed), subjectively (that is: in terms of who is a member of the polity and, more generally, who ought to behave in the ways prescribed by the legal order), temporally (that is: in terms of a shared or collective understanding of time), and spatially (that is: in terms of the inside/outside distinction). Let's consider each of these aspects in the order I presented them.

First, in the process of articulating what is deemed to be the collective interest, it would be necessary to establish, however provisionally, who ought to do what. The key here is the reference to a determined common interest: it would be necessary to select some interests as worthy of legal protection, and discard others, usually implicitly, as legally irrelevant. See here, then, a first way in which a world polity would be bounded: it would make available a determined schedule of rights and obligations, in which certain kinds of activities are allowed and disallowed, and a host of other kinds of activities would not even be considered, as they are simply deemed irrelevant from a legal point of view.

If a world polity would have to determine, and thereby delimit, the 'what' of behaviour, it would also have to delimit the 'who' of behaviour, beginning with membership in the world polity. This may sound odd, at first sight, for by definition it seems, everyone would count as a member. But who counts as part of 'everyone'? Would membership be limited to all *humans*? If so, what about those collectives which include non-humans in the circle of law, in fact for whom the very distinction between human and non-human may not only seem unintelligible but even horrific, and which Western thinking dismisses as 'animistic' or 'primitive'? Moreover, and focusing on human beings, the possibility of identifying members of a world polity entails, as its correlate, the possibility of stripping individuals of membership if they radically contest what is deemed to be the common interest of the collective. No less than in a regional, national or sub-national community, a world polity would demand bounded membership, even if its civic boundaries remain initially latent.

The temporality of a collective would also be bounded. By this I don't mean the trivial point that a world polity would be founded on a given date that could be fixed on any of the multiple calendars in circulation. What I mean is that part of what goes into being a collective is a shared understanding of past, present and future. To be sure, this temporal arc need not be linear; nor, consequently, need the polity be temporally oriented towards the future, as we have become accustomed to taking for granted in modernity. But precisely because time can be lived through collectively in a variety of ways, the collective temporality of a world polity would be common in the twofold sense of a time that is shared by, and distinguishes the members of that collective. For this reason, a world polity would unfold a bounded temporality.

Yet would not the distinction between inside and outside disappear in a world polity? No. The spatial articulation of a common interest for the world polity would require a distribution of places determining where behaviour ought or ought not to take place. Although a world polity would have no outside in the sense of *foreign* places, or at least not initially, the inclusion and exclusion of interests articulated by the spatial boundaries that carve up the face of the earth into a distribution of places entail that the polity's foundation would give rise, at least latently, to places that do not fit in the distribution of places made available by the world polity, and which are intimated by behaviour that contests the claim to commonality raised on behalf of the global distribution of places. To the extent that a world polity, if it is to be a legal order, must in some way organise the face of the earth as a common distribution of places, any of the boundaries that mark off a single legal place from other legal places in the world polity also appears, when contested, as marking off the whole distribution of legal places as an inside *vis-à-vis* a strange outside. More precisely, a world polity would harbour an outside *within*. While the distinction between domestic and foreign places would disappear in a world polity, the inside/outside distinction would remain in the form of the distinction between the world polity's own, familiar space and places that are, in the twofold sense of the term, 'outlandish'.[1]

This is, of course, only one example. But my general claim, one that can be supported on the basis of careful empirical descriptions of a wide variety of forms of law, is that all law is bounded in these four ways. Let me summarise the upshot of this thought experiment in the following thesis: while the kinds of boundaries to which we have become accustomed in the municipal/international law paradigm are certainly contingent features of law, law would not be law unless it establishes, in one way or

[1] I have developed these ideas at greater length in my article. See Hans Lindahl, "A-Legality: Postnationalism and the Question of Legal Boundaries", in *The Modern Law Review*, 2010, vol. 73, no. 1, pp. 30-56.

another, the appropriate times and places for the appropriate subjects to engage in appropriate forms of behaviour. In this minimal sense, all law is bounded law.

I need to take a second step to complete the minimal conceptual framework that will allow me to turn and discuss the normative and institutional questions posed in section 1. This second step focuses on the two functions of boundaries: separating and joining. How do boundaries separate and join? A concrete example is far better than an abstract exposé. Consider the European Union, in particular the consideration of the Preamble to the Treaty that reappears in all later treaties, up to and including the Treaty of Lisbon: "determined to lay the foundations of an ever closer union among the peoples of Europe".[2] While the European Union has considerably widened the scope of its activities since its inception in the Treaty of Rome, the EU remains fundamentally a project of economic integration centred on the realisation of a common or internal market. As the Preamble to the Treaty of Lisbon puts it, the EU's Member States are:

> Determined to promote economic and social progress for their peoples, taking into account the principle of sustainable development and within the context of the accomplishment of the internal market and of reinforced cohesion and environmental protection, and to implement policies ensuring that advances in economic integration are accompanied by parallel progress in other fields …[3]

These two considerations, when read in conjunction, reveal how boundaries do their work of joining and separating. Notice, in effect, that the Treaties do not only distribute space by separating and opposing an inside (the European internal market) and an outside (the external market); in the same movement by which the Treaties close off the European polity from the rest of the world, they also include the EU and what it is excluded there from in an encompassing spatial unity – a world market,

[2] Consolidated Version of the Treaty on the Functioning of the European Union as amended by the Treaty of Lisbon, 1 December 2009, Recital 2 of the Preamble, available at http://eur-lex.europa.eu/LexUriServ/LexUriServ.do?uri=OJ:C:2008:115:0047:0199:EN:PDF, last accessed 25 March 2011.

[3] Consolidated Version of the Treaty on European Union as amended by the Treaty of Lisbon, 1 December 2009, Recital 10 of the Preamble, available at http://www.uchastings.edu/faculty-administration/faculty/memelink/class-website/docs/Preamble_of_The_Treaty_on_European_Union.pdf, last accessed 25 March 2011.

the denizens of which are viewed as economic actors subject to the rules of market exchange. What one might call the 'logic of boundaries' is at work here: boundaries don't simply join 'and' separate – they join by separating. Indeed, the separation of an internal and an external market also joins them together as parts of a single world market. But the work of boundaries does not stop here. Rather, the Treaties distribute space by separating Europe from itself; they split Europe, including it as a common market and excluding other possible interpretations of what constitutes Europe as a common space, such that contestation of the common market can erupt in the name of 'another Europe'. This is what occurred, for example, in the European Social Forum, which took place in Malmö, Sweden, in September 2008. The homepage of the event begins with the caption "Another Europe is possible!", and the site goes on to invite participants to submit initiatives that could flesh out the contours of an alternative to the neo-liberalism animating the European integration project.[4] The closure that gives rise to the common market cannot represent Europe as the common space of a community without folding a strange Europe into what is claimed to be the EC's own place. Whence the second leg of the logic of boundaries: boundaries don't only separate and join; they separate by joining. Concretely, boundaries join the EU's Member States into a common market by separating the latter from another Europe. Moreover, the Treaties also distribute space by separating the world from itself. In the same movement by which they split Europe, they also split the world, representing it as a market. The cry, "Another world is possible", uttered in places such as Porto Alegre, reveals that the EU cannot take its place in a world market without folding a strange world into the world it calls its own. The logic of boundaries kicks in yet a third time: the boundaries of the internal market join it to the external market by separating the world market from other worlds.

There is no space here to offer a justification of why this is a recurrent pattern in all legal orders, rather than a pattern that simply holds for the EU. Such a justification would lead to discussing the conditions that govern the genesis or emergence of legal orders. Rather than broaching this difficult topic, I content myself with advancing a second thesis:

[4] See European Social Forum, available at http://esf2008.org/, last accessed 25 March 2011.

boundaries don't simply join and separate; the crucial point is that they cannot separate without joining, nor join without separating.

3. Beyond Cosmopolitanism and Communitarianism

I would now like to consider how the two theses I have advanced about legal boundaries in the foregoing section impinge on the normative and institutional issues outlined at the outset of this paper. I will concentrate primarily on the normative aspects, reserving a few remarks for the institutional aspects in the closing remarks of the paper.

I noted that the reason for which legal boundaries are such an urgent issue is that boundaries include and exclude. This has an immediate bearing on fundamental values such as freedom, justice, and security. Indeed, the territorial nation-state has to a great extent been the locus of these values during the heydays of the municipal/international law paradigm. Succinctly, freedom has been institutionalised as a bounded freedom, justice as a bounded justice, and security as a bounded justice. This situation has been the object of extended and conflicting normative scrutiny by communitarianism and cosmopolitanism. Communitarianism has been largely sympathetic to this situation, defending the view that a bounded community is the *conditio sine qua non* of these and related values. Referring to justice, Michael Walzer, for example, argues that "the idea of distributive justice presupposes a bounded world within which distributions take place: a group of people committed to dividing, exchanging, and sharing social goods, first among themselves. That world … is the political community".[5] On this view, a right to inclusion and exclusion is ingredient to the very concept of distributive justice. This means that, subject to certain limitations, it is up to a political community to determine who and what may enter the community. As he candidly puts it, "no one on the outside has a right to be inside".[6]

The communitarian position has been strongly critiqued from a cosmopolitan perspective. There are at least two central tenets that govern cosmopolitanism's stance with respect to legal boundaries. The first is that the boundaries, especially the territorial and civic boundaries of any concrete politico-legal community, are contingent. Jürgen Habermas, for

5 Michael Walzer, *Spheres of Justice: A Defense of Pluralism and Equality*, Basic Books, New York, 1983, p. 31.

6 Walzer, 1983, p. 41, see *supra* note 5.

example, avers that "from a normative point of view, the social boundaries of an association of free and equal consociates under law are perfectly contingent".[7] As a result, there is no such thing as a 'right' to inclusion and exclusion that can be derived from the mere fact that the legal boundaries of a given community have been drawn in a certain way. To the extent that contingent boundaries determine the scope of freedom, justice and security, to that extent the normative content of freedom, justice and security are also undermined. What is the alternative to contingent boundaries? This brings us to the second tenet of cosmopolitanism. Boundaries are valid in a strong sense of the term to the extent that they are taken up in an all-inclusive legal order. And this means a legal order, the boundaries of which could obtain the consent of all those whose behaviour is limited thereby. An all-inclusive legal order, in the cosmopolitan reading, would be the order of freedom, justice and security.

The analysis I have offered of legal boundaries takes issue with both views. It shares the conviction that legal orders are bounded orders with communitarianism, albeit not necessarily in the way taken for granted by communitarianism. Whereas the latter would view a world polity as an unbounded community, my argument is that it is also bounded. But I take strong issue with communitarianism on a key point. Communitarianism takes for granted that boundaries draw a clean distinction between 'our own' community and 'alien' communities. If, as I have argued, boundaries include what they exclude, and exclude what they include, then what is strange is not simply outside – it is also within. And what is outside is not simply strange – it is also to a lesser or greater extent our own. Europe is an illustration of why communitarianism is dead-end; there is 'another Europe' that radically contests the claim to commonality raised on behalf of the European Union. Conversely, the EU is not only inside: it is also outside in that it views itself as part of a world market, in the same way that calls for 'another Europe' to go hand in hand with calls for 'another world'.

But my account of how legal boundaries do their work also takes issue with cosmopolitanism. To be sure, it shares with cosmopolitanism the conviction that boundaries are porous and amenable to transformation, such that a certain integration of what has been excluded is possible. In

7 Jürgen Habermas, *The Inclusion of the Other: Studies in Political Theory*, Ciaran Cronin and Pablo de Greiff (eds./trans.), Polity Press, Cambridge, 2005, p. 116.

other words, it shares the conviction that boundaries include what they exclude. But cosmopolitanism takes for granted that an all-inclusive legal order is possible. Although its realisation may have to be indefinitely postponed, boundaries can be overcome in a historical process in which, if all goes well, legal orders become ever more inclusive. If time, on a cosmopolitan reading, is a linear history in which the future marks the vanishing point at which humanity actualises itself as a world community, space, on that reading, manifests itself as an ever-expanding series of concentric circles. And, as we know, circles, even if they expand, have a centre and a periphery. The problem with this approach is that it overlooks the second feature of what I earlier called the 'logic of boundaries'; boundaries don't only include what they exclude – boundaries also exclude what they include. To return to the example of Europe, the EU does not only include itself and what it excludes as parts of a world market; it also excludes other Europeans and other worlds in the process of including them as parts of the world market. It would not be otherwise if the path the European integration project had taken were different. Because legal boundaries include by excluding, and exclude by including, there can be no all-inclusive legal order, not even an order of human rights.

This argument amounts to a strong defence of political pluralism. Cosmopolitanism often presents itself as a pluralistic theory of politics and law. But the plurality it envisages is, as we have seen, plurality within the unity of an all-inclusive legal order, which is highest, normatively speaking. To this extent, cosmopolitanism is thoroughly monistic. Communitarianism also presents itself as pluralistic, arguing that freedom, justice and security can only flourish in bounded communities. Yet, to the extent that communitarian defences of political pluralism rest on the assumption that boundaries include those who belong to the community and exclude the others, they defend a monistic project of politics and law. By contrast, a strong form of political pluralism emerges when one recognises that boundaries cannot exclude without including, nor include without excluding. For it entails that legal orders are neither parts of a whole nor well-demarcated units that co-exist in isolation from each other. The appropriate image here is not separate 'billiard balls', as in communitarianism, nor expanding 'concentric circles', as in cosmopolitanism, but rather variable intertwinements. My hypothesis is that the era of postnationalism into which we have entered is the era of pluralism in this strong sense of the term.

If so, then at least two issues will require considerable attention in the coming decennia. The first, what normative sense we can make of freedom, justice, and security in a postnational setting if we can neither rely on the communitarian assumption that these values can only be achieved in a bounded community, nor on the cosmopolitan assumption that these values can only be realised in an all-encompassing legal order? The second, what institutional arrangements in the postnational era could foster boundary negotiations between legal orders in a way that neither takes for granted that the task of those negotiations is to join the orders together into parts of a single, all-encompassing global order, nor that their aim is to safeguard those legal orders as separate and distinct units?

4.4

The Future of Private Law

James Gordley[*]

At the core of private law are doctrines concerning matters such as property, tort, contract and unjust enrichment. At the periphery are special rules regulating discrete problems such as pollution, housing, employment, competition, and safety. They are peripheral in the sense that they address discrete problems, although they are not of peripheral importance. As to these rules, there may be progress as we gain in experience and expertise. In the foreseeable future, however, we can expect little progress in understanding the core doctrines. They are now in a state of disarray. In the nineteenth century, jurists claimed that these doctrines could be understood in terms of two rather antithetical ideas. One was positivism: the belief that answers could be found by the exegesis of authoritative texts. The other was conceptualism: the belief that answers could be found once key concepts such as contract or property had been property defined. Beginning in the late nineteenth century, jurists succeed in discrediting positivism and conceptualism but without finding an alternative foundation on which to build. Without one, it is hard to see how we could understand the core doctrines of private law. Given our past failures, it hard to believe we will succeed in the near future.

Private law has a core of basic doctrine surrounded by a periphery of special rules, many found in special statutes. At the core are general rules that govern matters such as property, tort, contract and unjust enrichment, rules that are grounded in common law jurisdictions in case law and in most civil law jurisdictions in civil codes. At the periphery are rules regulating such matters as air and water pollution, the housing market, employment, antitrust, and safety standards for products and services. These rules are peripheral in the sense that they alter the law of property, tort, contract and unjust enrichment to address discrete problems. They are not of peripheral importance. As to these rules, there may be progress in the future as experience and expertise grow and global problems are dealt

[*] **James Gordley** is a professor of law and W.R. Irby Chair in Law at Tulane University Law School.

with internationally. This article, however, concerns the core of private law. As to the core, I believe that we have inherited problems that we cannot resolve by looking to case law or codes, and that we lack the intellectual resources to address. Although jurists in different countries face the same problems, I do not expect them to deal with them successfully in the next ten, twenty or thirty years. Over that period of time, I think the core of private law does not have a future.

The seventeeth and eighteenth centuries saw the rise of legal rationalism. In earlier centuries, jurists believed that there were principles of justice grounded in human nature which were reflected in the legal texts that they interpreted. In that sense, there was a natural law. The rationalists claimed that natural law should be understood on the model of mathematics. One can define human nature just as one can define the objects of mathematics, and then deduce the natural law from the definition by formal logic. Gottfried Wilhelm Leibnitz said that "A New Method of Learning and Teaching Jurisprudence" can be based on "demonstration", which is almost completely reducible to two rules: "no word should be used unless it is defined, and no proposition accepted unless it has been proven".[1] According to Christian Wolff, "the entire extent of natural law, which covers all human actions, can only be brought to light by following in the steps of Euclid ... that is, by explaining each term by an exact definition, and making a sufficient determination of the meaning of each proposition ...".[2] By doing so, conclusions about law can be drawn with mathematical certainty. Indeed, it would be improper to accept a normative conclusion on any other grounds. If it had not been demonstrated it was a conjecture. If it could not be demonstrated it was not true.

In the nineteenth century, jurists repudiated rationalism. They doubted that normative conclusions, or at least any definite ones, could be demonstra ted by formal logic from a definition of human nature. Indeed, for the most part they doubted that there was any way that normative propositions could be demonstrated. They turned to legal positivism. Law, as far as a jurist is concerned, is found in texts that have been promulgated

---

1 Gottfried Wilhelm Leibniz, "Nova Methodus Discendae Docendaeque Jurisprudentia", in *Philosophische Schriften Erster Band 1663-1672,* 1990, vol. 1, Akademie der Wissenschaftedn der DDR, Berlin, § 25.

2 Christian Wolff, "Institutiones Juris Naturae et Gentium", in Marcellus Thomann (ed.), *Gesammelte Werke*, 1972, vol. 26, Prefatio.

or accepted as law by those in authority. The jurist's task is to interpret them. In France, the authoritative texts were those of the French Civil Code. In Germany, they were the texts of the *Corpus Iuris Civilis* which owed their force and acceptance by authority to their long usage and which, according to some German jurists, reflected the German mind or spirit, the *Volksgeist*. In common law jurisdictions, the authoritative texts were the decided cases.

The nineteenth century jurists did not recognise the extent to which the positivism they espoused mirrored the rationalism they rejected. Positivists, like rationalists, thought that a jurist must begin from a secure starting point, one that was free from doubt. Then he must demonstrate his conclusions by a method that was neutral in the sense that it did not depend on any normative propositions extraneous to his starting point. For the rationalists, the secure starting points were definitions, and the method was logical demonstration. For the positivists, the secure starting points were texts recognised or promulgated by those in society who had authority to recognise or promulgate texts as law. These starting points were secure, not because they expressed timeless truths, or even because they were well advised, but because they were law and no one except those with the authority to do so could determine what law is. The jurist's task was to draw conclusions from these texts by a method that was neutral, in that it did not depend on any normative propositions extraneous to these texts. If he were to rely on such propositions, he would be making law, and so exercising an authority that he did not possess.

The rationalists, in pursuit of certainty, defined concepts such as property, contract, and tort abstractly, like the concepts of mathematics, without regard to the social purposes that these institutions served or might serve in different societies or under different circumstances. One can call this approach to law 'conceptualism'. Paradoxically, the nineteenth century jurists' commitment to positivism led them back to conceptualism. It is not an accident that we remember the nineteenth century as an age of positivism and conceptualism.

Sometimes, as in the case of a code, the authoritative texts contain rules framed in general terms. Sometimes the texts describe the results to be reached in particular cases. When the application of a rule to a case is clear cut, or can be made so by investigating linguistic usage or applying the techniques of philology, nothing is left for the jurist to do. Nor is there anything left for him to do if a new case is just like one described in the authoritative texts. The jurist's work begins when the application of a term is not clear cut, or a new case differs from those in his sources.

For a positivist, then, the jurist's task is to find a meaning in a rule that cannot be uncovered by the linguist or philologist, or to find a common element in the cases that prescribe a given result that allows him to go beyond the cases. The nineteenth century jurists tried to identify concepts which clarified the rule or identified the common element in the cases.

It might seem odd that they took this approach since, according to their beliefs, those in authority can make the law any which way. The rules might have no meaning except one that is arbitrary or conventional. The results prescribed in particular cases might be so random that they could have been reached by throwing dice. Yet it was hard for the jurists to think it was really so. If it were, there would be no way for a jurist to get beyond the authoritative texts. There would be no such thing as legal analysis. Instead, they turned to conceptualism. For example, when the question was to determine the rights of an owner, or the enforceability of a contract, they tried to resolve it by defining the concept of property or contract, and then drawing conclusions from those concepts.

Although French jurists were interpreting their Civil Code, Germans the Roman texts, and Anglo-Americans their cases, they arrived at similar definitions of the ideas basic to private law. For example, typically, they defined property as the exclusive right of the owner to do as he chooses with what belongs to him. They defined contract in terms of the will of the parties. Some historians have thought that the nineteenth century jurists did so because they were influenced by the economic and political liberalism of their times. The jurists themselves, however, would not have seen how else property or contract could be defined. Indeed, if one is to define such institutions in abstraction from any normative theory that explains how an owner should use his property, or on what terms parties should contract, little is left beyond the idea that the owner of property exercises his will, and that contracting parties contract on what terms they please. Consequently, one finds similar definitions among the rationalists. According to Wolff, the right "of disposing of a thing by one's own decision, indeed, as one sees fit, we call ownership".[3] He then defined con-

[3] Christian Wolff, Jus Naturae, in Marcellus Thomann (ed.), *Gesammelte Werke: II. Abteilung: Lateinishce Schriften*, 1972, vol. 17, no. I and II, § 118, § 496, § 609.

tract in terms of promise: "A promise ... is a declaration of our will to perform to another joined to the right to require the transfer of that to be performed".[4]

In the twentieth century, the conviction that conceptualism would not work became widespread. When terms such as property and contract were defined so abstractly, even when it was possible to draw conclusions from the definitions, it was not possible to square these conclusions with what a positivist himself regarded as the law in force. For example, having defined property as the exclusive right of the owner to do as he wishes with his own, the nineteenth century jurists found it difficult to explain the limitations the law imposes on his use of his property, such as those concerning disturbances among neighbours. Similarly, they found it difficult to explain circumstances in which others may make use of his property, such as their right to do so in cases of extreme necessity. Having defined contract in terms of the will of the parties, they found it difficult to explain why the parties are bound to many terms that they did not will. These terms make up most of the law of sale, lease, partnership and so forth. They also found it hard to explain why sometimes the parties are not bound to terms which they did will, as in cases of extreme unfairness.

In the twentieth century, along with the rejection of conceptualism came a rejection, in principle, of positivism. If it was true that one could not derive consequences from concepts implicit in rules or case law by a neutral method, then, it would seem, one could not, by a neutral method, derive consequences from the texts in which the rules and case law were to be found. At the turn of the century, François Gény in France and Ernst Zitelmann in Germany concluded that there must be some other way for the jurist to reach his conclusions.

The question was what this other way might be. Some jurists, such as Philip Heck in Germany, claimed that since the point of law is to set boundaries to the protection of each person's interests, the jurist should consider the interests at stake. For Heck, that did not mean neglecting the authoritative texts. It meant finding the balance the texts had struck between conflicting interests and then balancing the interests in a new situation in the same way. If that approach worked, one could draw conclusions from the authoritative texts by a method that was neutral in the sense that it replicated the normative judgments found in the texts without

[4] Wolff, 1972, no. III, § 361, see *supra* note 3.

introducing new ones. This method would be an alternative to conceptualism. The method presupposed, however, that when the law sets boundaries to the pursuit of private interest, it does so by deciding which private interests it will recognise, and what weight it will assign to them, and that these boundaries, these interests, and these weights can be discovered by examining the situations dealt with in the authoritative texts and extrapolating to other situations. It is hard to believe that the authoritative texts contain so much information about the interests to be protected and their importance. However, if instead, one cuts free from the texts and simply asks what interest outweighs another, one is making a purely normative judgment. The existence of an interest is not a fact, unless the word interest simply means that a person wants something. If so, most of us have an interest in owning diamond mines in South Africa. The weight of an interest is not a fact, unless the term means the strength of one's desire to have something. But if that were so the interests of the greedy would *ipso facto* outweigh those of others. So we are left with the idea that the law resolves conflicts among private interests. That is fine, but to speak of interest balancing does not explain how or why it does so.

Others, albeit in different ways, tried to look beyond the conflicting interests of private parties to some larger social policy which is supposed to be at stake and in terms of which the conflicts can be resolved. In France, in the 1920s and 30s, jurists such as René Demogue and Louis Josserand said it would be an 'abuse of right' for an owner, for example, to use his power to do as he sees fit in a way that defeats the social purpose of property. They left open the question of what counts as a social purpose. Other scholars tried to answer that question. In the United States, beginning in the 1940's, Harold Lasswell and Myres McDougal claimed that one had to abandon a legal analysis which seeks to interpret authoritative texts and substitute a policy science which uses the methods of disciplines other than law. They conceived of policy science as normative only in the sense that it accepted the norms accepted by those in authority. But the method itself would be neutral in that it would show, without any further normative judgment, how those norms could best be achieved. They failed to show, as most scholars today would agree, how one could move from the welter of social policies which influences a legislature to conclusions about, for example, the limits of property rights or the terms by which contracting parties should be bound. Currently, the appeal to social policy as the measure of law has taken an extreme form among members of the Law and Economics Movement such as Richard Posner. They want to resolve legal issues by looking to a single social policy, which Posner calls 'wealth maximisation', and to resolve them by using the method of economics. What an odd claim. How can it be that all that matters in law is the aggregate value of everything in which the members of society have rights? How can it be that one member of society should be entitled to less because another member of society will thereby gain more than he has lost, measured by the amount he is willing to pay? In any event, the basic question in law has always been who has what rights, the question of *meum* and *tuum*. It is odd to think that this question can be resolved simply by asking about the total value of things to which one might have rights.

Others, such as some of the *frei Juristen* in Germany, the legal realists in the United States, and more recently, members of the Critical Legal Studies movement, have said that the task is hopeless. There is no way to move by a method that is normatively neutral from authoritative texts to conclusions about what the law is. There is no neutral method for resolving legal issues even if one disregards the authoritative texts. However, if a method is not neutral, if it depends upon normative propositions not contained in the texts, one can no longer speak of the rule of law. One can only speak of people who claim to be applying the law when in fact they are imposing on others whatever normative propositions they happen to favour.

It was said earlier that the nineteenth century positivists did not recognise the extent to which they accepted the premises of the rationalism they rejected. We do not recognise the extent to which those who rejected positivism also accepted its premises. One premise is that normative propositions cannot be demonstrated. Another is that legal analysis, properly speaking, must move from authoritative texts to a conclusion by a method that is neutral in the sense that it does not depend upon any normative proposition that cannot be derived from the texts. That being so, there is a limited number of possibilities. One can look for a neutral method other than conceptualism that will allow one to move from the authoritative texts to conclusions about what the law is. One can bypass the authoritative texts and borrow a method from another discipline, a method that is neutral in that it supposedly does not depend upon normative judgments. Or one can give up.

Few jurists have given up in theory. It is often said that the Critical Legal Studies movement is dead. Yet many have given up in practice. Some do economic analyses of law. Some present their work as an exegesis of codes or case law although they have abandoned the conceptualism that the nineteenth century jurists counted on to give the doctrines of private law a structural unity and a rationale. Some have confined themselves to technical problems which they hope to resolve by a technical analysis borrowed from another discipline.

How then is there a way out? How can one resolve the problems that stumped the nineteenth century jurists, such as the proper limits to the rights of an owner, or the proper terms that belong in a contract? To go further, how can one determine the sorts of harm for which one should recover in tort, or the sorts of enrichment at another's expense that are unjust and for which one should pay compensation? There isn't any way to resolve such questions without relying on normative propositions that cannot be derived by a normatively neutral method from authoritative texts. If a normative analysis of these questions is not possible, an analysis that does not claim to be a mere exegesis of texts, then legal analysis is not possible.

Since these problems have not been resolved in the last century, it is unlikely they will be resolved in the next ten, twenty or thirty years. So I reach my conclusion: during that period, private law, in the sense of a meaningful exposition of its core doctrines, does not have a future. On a practical level, we will be dealing with the problems of the limits to an owner's rights, the terms that belong in a contract, the harms for which a plaintiff can recover, and the enrichment for which he must compensate another. But we will do so without a clear idea of what we are doing and how it should be done.

4.5

International Law and Legal Positivism

David Koepsell*

There have been two contrary forces in the developing realm of international law for the past 60 or so years. Even while international bodies and treaty organisations have attempted to bring more nations under the rubric of their influence, for more reasons (encompassing more than trade, and now enforceable now to individuals), trends in legal theory both within and among various nations threaten to undermine the moral basis of international law. If there is to be a moral basis for developing common codes of acceptable legal rules, and if we are to have morally acceptable enforcement of those rules internationally, then the legal theory of positivism must be dismissed. Legal positivism rests on the evaluation of justice as the enactment, and means of enactment, of legal rules. It rejects the notion that laws and legal systems, in order to be just, must be founded upon 'natural', immutable principles. It is clear that if we accept the tenets of legal positivism, international law rests upon a very weak foundation. Given this, we should not only resist legal positivism as a valid or workable legal theory for purposes of pedagogy or national rulemaking, but endeavour to provide a substantial basis for valid rulemaking in the realm of international law.

1. The Emergence of Positivism

In the nineteenth and early twentieth centuries, the natural foundations of law began to be challenged, especially by Anglo-Saxon legal scholarship. For more than a thousand years, legal rules were devised by sovereigns who were themselves held to be imbued with moral authority for rulemaking by deities. Of course, with the spread of the Enlightenment, and the fall of various sovereigns at the hands of liberal revolutions, the basis for valid, moral rulemaking and enforcement began to shift. With Locke, Hobbes, Rousseau, and other modern liberal political theorists, came a new vision of the basis for natural law, one that extended natural law theory beyond the simplistic, sovereign-based dogma of old, to a more consistent set of tenets. Natural law, it was argued, grounded the validity of

* **David Koepsell** is Assistant Professor of Philosophy at TU Delft.

legal rules in duties and obligations dictated by the fabric of nature (whether or not one accepted some predicate deity), and even sovereigns were subject to the dictates of nature's laws. This shift in thinking reflected a shift in scientific and theological thought, roughly reflecting the move from an involved, acting creator, to a distant, detached, clock-maker creator, who sets the world in motion and then steps back. The foundations of modern liberalism included a notion of natural law. The revolutions sparked by Locke *et al.*, were legitimised by the violation of subjects' naturally-endowed rights to life, liberty, and property, and these natural rights formed the basis for modern liberal democracies, both in their constitutions and in their laws. In a world in which just law derives from nature, there is a solid connection between law and morality. But a new trend emerges in the late Enlightenment, when philosophers and political theorists began to question the foundations of just law, as well as to reformulate approaches to ethics and justice themselves.

The British philosopher Jeremy Bentham led the love away from natural law theory in arguing against deontology as an ethical foundation. Bentham, seeking to make more scientific the study of ethics, rejected nature as a foundation of duties, and formulated the modern ethical approach we call utilitarianism. He is well known for calling natural law theory "nonsense upon stilts". His objections to natural law were epistemological, as he argued we can never rightly suppose that we know the intentions of a creator, nor can duty-based theories of ethics, like those of Immanuel Kant, ever trace back sufficiently far enough to provide a solid justification for accepting any particular duty *a priori*. Indeed, a weakness of deontology is the leap from presupposing the existence of a certain duty, and reconciling its existence with contradictory duties, or converse duties that appear to arise in exceptional situations. Utilitarianism does not presuppose the existence of categorical duties, but rather argues that the ethical compulsion lies not in intent or duty, but rather in consequences. The epistemological argument is clear: consequences can be more or less predicted, and measured *post-hoc*. Intentions can never be similarly measured. In the scientific vein of the time, Bentham sought to make the pursuit of legal and ethical theory measurable, and viewed a solid, measurable basis for judging an action only in its consequences, namely: the amount of net happiness produced. For Bentham, the good can be judged based solely upon whether it increases net happiness, and duties, intentions, or other epistemologically unapproachable matters need not be consulted. The implications for legal rulemaking are obvious, and in the absence of a natural foundation for just laws, legal theorists began to re-imagine the role and scope of legal theory.

According to John Austin, the validity of legal rules can only be judged according to the proper foundation of their enactment by a sovereign. A sovereign is one who is recognised as such by a majority, and the laws are the sovereign's enactments, backed by sanctions. No further inquiry of judgment as to the content of legal rules can be made as there is no extraneous basis by which rules can be judged to be right or wrong, morally speaking. Rule-making is valid so long as the sovereign is the majority-recognised sovereign, and has no higher sovereign, and so long as the rules are backed by the promise of sanctions in case of their violation. Even while a continental positivism of a sort was being formulated by Hans Kelsen, in which at least some solid basis for recognizing a valid sovereign is posited (a *grundnorm*), the Anglo-Saxon school of positivism becomes solidified with the work of H.L.A. Hart. Hart nicely categorises types of rules, distinguishing among primary rules (which direct action) and secondary rules (which address procedures). But in direct opposition to Kelsen, Hart rejects the theory of a *grundnorm*, and does nothing to resolve what seems now to be a significant gap in positive legal theory: reconciling rules with a notion of *justice*. As opposed to the neo-Kantian approach of the twentieth century's most prominent legal scholar outside of the positivist tradition, John Rawls, legal positivist do not see inquiring into the *just* foundations of legal rules, outside of the valid enactments of sovereigns according to established procedures, as being a coherent area of inquiry.

Legal positivism is the political extension of the ethical theory of utilitarianism. With legal positivism, we need not concern ourselves with metaphysical questions of right or wrong, just or unjust, but can focus instead on epistemologically approachable questions regarding the results of our actions, and whether they accord with our preferences. Legal positivism is the dominant theoretical paradigm in Anglo-Saxon law schools, and it is bolstered by various trends in politics, including concerns with pluralism and multi-culturalism. Natural law theory is vulnerable to critique where various cultural, religious, ethnic, or philosophical backgrounds confront problems from differing viewpoints. Adopting the natural law justification for a rule that contradicts some religious, ethnic, cultural, or philosophical viewpoint, means arguing for the error of someone else's point of view. But as we live in increasingly pluralistic societies, with ever more multicultural populations, asserting one paradigm to be correct, risks eroding what many conceive to be the foundation of liberalism: the freedom of conscience. A basic tenet of our modern liberal democracies is necessarily that people are entitled to their opinions, points of view, and to express their beliefs. Thus, states ought not to criticise the foundations of those beliefs, or force citizens to ascribe to a particular point of view. Because positive legal theory embraces the notion that a law is valid so long as it is enacted by a sovereign and backed by sanctions, then there is no further basis to question the validity of a validly-enacted rule. The freedom of conscience of those who either support or defy the rule is preserved, because no judgment about the underlying *justice* of that rule may be made. We can only classify people as rule-followers or rule-breakers, not as just or unjust, and the basis of valid rules need not be traced to something natural and immutable. Pluralism and multiculturalism are preserved both within nations and amongst them, as ethics and rules are completely divorced. A rule-breaker cannot be judged to be immoral, and rules we do not like can be changed without reflection upon metaphysical issues of justice or 'the good'. Lawmaking can be scientifically accomplished by looking at a list of projected consequences, and applying those rules that maximise the consequences we prefer.

Legal positivism is vulnerable to attacks based upon history, and our cultural, national, and international reactions to perceived injustices within sovereign states, as well as amongst them. These same attacks are consistent with criticisms of utilitarian ethical theory. Namely, if we are only guided by the consequences of an action, then on what moral basis must minorities be protected? In utilitarianism, as in legal positivism, there is no theoretical basis to necessitate the protection of a minority. In classical utilitarianism, the right thing to do is that which increases happiness (maximises utility) overall. Positive legal theorists similarly must recognise the validity of an enactment if it is enacted by a valid sovereign (supported by a majority) and backed up with sanctions. Countless examples of potential injustices can be named, both historical and hypothetical.

2. Legal Positivism and International Law

The notion of international law is historically relatively recent, emerging within the past few hundred years, and largely amorphous in practice. One might well argue that there is no such thing as international law...yet. Surely, there are attempts at creating organisation that employ something like legal systems among nations, and applicable to both nations and citizens of nations, but all of these attempts are more or less fragile, largely nascent, and rejected by numerous large, internationally-powerful sovereigns. Unlike legal systems within nations that have become mature and have developed robust systems of enactment and enforcement, international legal systems are still suffering significant growing pains. International law has been formed largely in the era of legal positivism, so it should be no surprise at all that is suffers as it does from a lack of solid foundation, or of international agreement about its justice and validity. If individual nations are facing crises in their legal foundations due to growing pluralism and multicultural sensitivity, then the vast multicultural, pluralistic world as a whole must similarly be confounded. On what basis can some international body validly criticise the actions, either internal or external, of some sovereign when there is not any world sovereign, no body or system of valid enactment of universally-applicable rules, nor methods of enforcement or sanction? Legal positivism must fail to give credence to international law in the absence of even the most basic criteria for valid legal enactments in the international sphere. Yet legal positivism appears to also be the dominant paradigm in international law. It has been centuries since Grotius first sought to enunciate a system by which international rules can be based in contractual principles, and his implicit rejection of rooting international law in natural law has grown over time as positive legal theory has spread throughout the legal profession and among legal scholars.

What is necessary in order to make legal positivism a workable paradigm for some system of international law? There must simply be some notion of a sovereign above nations. If valid enactments under positivist theory are created by sovereigns, accepted by a majority, and backed by threats of sanctions, then there is currently no framework for the general acceptance of any system of international law from a positivist perspective. There is currently no international sovereign, and although the United Nations is perhaps the closest, it fails to meet the criteria necessary to give it validity as a law-making body under positivism. Sovereigns must be accepted by a majority, but even if we accept that a majority of states back the UN (a majority of the states of the world make up the UN), even if we view UN membership as some sort of representative democracy, its member states are clearly not uniformly backed by majorities of member state citizens. Nor is memberships of the UN open to most citizens as an option for discussion, and so while the rules that the UN enacts might be applicable to states, they are clearly not applicable to citizens of those states. Furthermore, UN enactments are clearly not legal enactments. They are more akin to regulations or administrative rules if we compare them with rulemaking at the national level, rather than full-fledged laws. Finally, the UN lacks sanctions or an enforcement body of anything like the sort that a nation-state would have. As such, the UN fails all three prongs of Austin's test for valid lawmaking.

If there is ever to be an international law of the sort that passes muster under positive legal theory, then new institutions must be devised that would satisfy the generally accepted criteria. Either a new body would have to be devised that would carry the role of a sovereign, and which would stand in relation to the international community *and* its citizens as a sovereign authority with the consent of the governed, or the present systems would have to be significantly amended. Besides, the powers and role of a sovereign, the international community, and possibly the majorities of citizens of each member state, would have to consent to be governed by the sovereign, subject to its enactments and institute a binding method to enforce its commands, as well as to sanction violations, all of which assumes that, even if we were capable of creating such a system, it would somehow be *just*. But this assumption cannot be presupposed. As we have seen above, the notions of *justice* and *positive legal theory* are seemingly incommensurable.

3. A Vacuum of Justice

As with utilitarianism, or moral relativism, positive legal theory leaves open the difficult problem of determining when a particular action, or intention, is morally wrong. In fact, in none of these theories is the notion of 'moral wrongness' even comprehensible. Things may or may not be acceptable in specific contexts, or may be valued for their effect on general utility (in as much as it might be measured or measurable), but notions of right or wrong, as the terms are traditionally used in ethical theory, are not *per se* applicable. Although students of ethics are taught about utilitarianism, and ethics scholars, or applied ethicists, must resort at time to the hedonic calculus in resolving ethical dilemmas, the end result of such a calculus will always be some determination about what one should do in order to increase general utility (happiness), and not clearly an ethical judgment about what is *right* or *good* in a moral sense. This is because each decision is necessarily contingent, and hypothetical, as opposed to decisions made according to deontological theory, which are categorical and apply to every such action or intention. The weaknesses of utilitarianism in creating systems of justice are noted by John Rawls, and other modern Kantian, or neo-Kantian scholars of law and ethics. These weaknesses make it difficult to argue that positive legal theory, or utilitarianism, can lead a society to a state fairly called *just*. The term *justice* implies some accord with notions of morality. In modern constitutional parlance, there are two forms or aspects of justice: substantive and procedural. Procedural justice means simply that for every person who becomes involved in a criminal or civil judicial matter, the procedures employed are employed equally, and fairly, and their content is transparent, and their purposes are clear. Substantive justice is more complex, and the notion implies accord with some higher law. If a law fails to fulfil the requirements of substantive justice, it may justly be struck down. Substantive justice is a measure by which both constitutions and legislation may be judged, and according to which they may fail.

Given the weaknesses of positive legal theory in providing a solid context in which justice can be evaluated, or by which just legal systems and their rules could be imposed, why does it continue to thrive in legal scholarship and political theory? One explanation may be that legal and political scholars have abandoned the quaint, Kantian notions of categorical right and wrong, and have embraced a utilitarian world view. It seems to be that in so doing, and in simultaneously accepting the Rawlsian notion of *distributive* justice (as indeed some of these same scholars and theorists seem to do), they are trapped in a contradiction. Rawlsian distributive justice depends upon accepting the notion of categorical duties, including the duty to treat everyone as an end, and not merely as a means to an end. Another categorical duty under Rawls is to treat everyone with equal dignity. But Rawls accepts more or less the Kantian explanation for the existence of these duties, arguing that we would arrive at these duties in forming a society if we place ourselves in the 'original position' behind his hypothetical 'veil of ignorance' from which vantage point we have no idea of whom we might be in a society. Kant's categorical imperative is arrived at by a different heuristic, but the content is the same: we have to be able to successfully universalise an imperative without contradiction in order for the rule to be moral. Neither Rawls nor Kant judge the morality of a rule according to consequences, and Rawls is thus generally regarded to be a neo-Kantian, as he himself at times agrees.

If justice become hypothetical and contingent, as it must under a utilitarian/positivist perspective, then rulemaking will be similarly contingent, and may even fail. Just as Bentham insisted, the link between lawmaking and morality must be completely severed, and decisions about the *justice* of rulemaking or rule-makers must be limited to procedural matters. No coherent system of substantive justice could be based upon utility as a measure or standard by which just laws could be created. The barriers are epistemological (the calculus cannot be carried out to sufficient exactness, either over and across populations, or through time), as well as ontological: the calculus does not tell us what is *good* or *right*, but merely what we should do in a certain situation to maximise happiness. One blatant gap in accepting the logic of the latter statement, that somehow a coherent foundation for a just system is that it relies upon a categorical rule, one which cannot be adjudged scientifically, namely: happiness is a sound basis for moral decision-making. This itself implies a categorical, rather than hypothetical grounding which must be taken as an axiom. Because of this and similar logical gaps in utilitarianism, and unacceptable practical consequences of accepting a pure utilitarian basis for ethical decision making, legal positivism stands on similarly shaky ground. The fact is that neither rule makers nor ordinary persons function as though there is no greater grounding for just rules than utility. There are clear, historical instances both within and among nations of actors (both individuals and states) doing things that are clearly *unjust*, regardless of their effect on general utility. Evolutionary psychology may hold the key as to why we consider certain intentional states and actions to be wrong *per se*, but the fact of this acceptance is recognised in constitutions and in courts. It is the impetus behind the slow march toward greater freedom, and more perfect systems of justice. The general recognition that, despite the arguments of legal positivists, there are certain categorically *wrong* actions and intentions is what has enabled constitutional change as well as liberal revolutions, and it is what has made these historical moments *good*.

4. Progress and Justice: Embracing a Natural Basis for the Good

Even while the Austrian Kelsen was making a case for positivism with some *grundnorm*, another little-known Austrian lawyer-philosopher was arguing for a grounding of valid legal norms in natural states of affairs. Adolf Reinach's *The Apriori Foundations of the Civil Law*, explains that valid legal rules are logically dependant upon some natural state of affairs, which he calls 'grounding'. He argues that the law of contracts, for instance, is logically necessary because it is grounded in simple facts about the genesis of duties out of promises. Prior to law-making, the acts and intentions surrounding the human activity of promise generates claims and obligations. These claims and obligations disappear upon the fulfillment of the promise. Contract law is thus grounded in natural phenomena, and this he equates with the sort of logical necessity that makes the facts of mathematics true. No just enactment, he argues, could invalidate the claims and obligations that naturally arise from a promise, just as no valid enactment could make 2+2 equal 5.

Reinach and others have since extended the notion of grounding to other types of law, including property law. I and others have argued that our rights to ownership of property arise from the brute facts of possession with the same sort of logical necessity by which duties and claims arise from promises. This argument is extended by Austrian philosophers of the same vein over rights to autonomy, which is rooted in rights of self-possession. There is a revival of sorts, for Austrian philosophy of law, and other similar schools of thought that oppose positivism. Ronald Dworkin stands as an example in US legal jurisprudence. Natural law is not dead, it has been naturalised. No longer is it dependent upon any particular ideology, theology, or philosophy, and the implications it carries regarding justice, namely that there is such a thing and that it is achievable through substantive legal enactments, are more promising for the possibility of international law than the last 100 or so years of legal positivism.

In the next 40 years, there will continue to be a resurgence of natural law theory, especially as applied to the realm of international law. In order to create international systems that work, and without resorting to instituting some sort of world government, nations must continue to embrace some of the original tenets of liberalism, including the real existence of certain fundamental rights shared by all people. These rights impose duties upon nation-states, and these duties cannot justly be abrogated. Deriving from these duties are similar duties applicable to actions and intentions among states. While states do not enjoy human rights *per se*, as nations are no more persons than are corporations, there must be codes of behaviour, ethically and morally based upon natural human rights to autonomy, property, freedom of conscience and speech, etc., that are applicable among states in order to preserve the conditions, both internal and external, for the quiet enjoyment of these rights. This climate is essential for achieving justice, if we are indeed to embrace justice as something real, achievable, and desirable.

4.6

The Future of the Future

H. Patrick Glenn*

I propose to examine firstly the concept of the future, and its possible decline in the face of different concepts of time which are well-known in many legal traditions and increasingly current in scientific thought.

I then propose to speculate on the effect of a decline in the concept of the future in some different areas of law, notably private international law, civil procedure, the legal professions, and control of corruption. In point form this would yield: The concept of the future and its possible decline; Law in a world with no future; Private international law and the conciliation of laws; Reform of civil procedure; Regulation and ethics of an international legal profession; Corruption and its international regulation.

1. Introduction

It is wise to think of the future, bearing in mind that no one can tell what it will be. It has thus recently been written that "the most that one can reasonably ask of any [social science] model is predictions of a conditional kind; that is, ones that tell us what the effects of social and political changes will be if they happen".[1] The difficulties of thinking about the future are now compounded, moreover, by increasing doubt about whether there is any such thing as the future, as it has historically been understood. So some preliminary reflections seem in order on the concept of the future and its possible decline before turning to the possible role of law in a world with no future and in particular domains

2. The Concept of the Future and Its Possible Decline

We know the future in opposition to the past, and the future is therefore present as the ultimate destination in a linear progression from the (even distant or 'deep') past through the present (always with us) to the future.

* **H. Patrick Glenn** is the Peter M. Laing Chair of the Faculty of Law at McGill University.

1 Timothy Gowers, *Mathematics*, Oxford University Press, Oxford, 2002, p. 9.

We think of the future as an element in this linear concept of time because we have been taught to think so for millennia, and the primary foundation for this concept of linear time, or time as an 'arrow', is probably religious, since the ultimate goal of salvation cannot occur in our present state but must be deferred. This linear idea has now become profoundly rooted in Western language, thought and practice (time which 'goes by', 'time is money', 'billable time') but its empirical foundations are now questioned not only by non-Western legal traditions which do not subscribe to it but by Western science and Western philosophy.

Western science now challenges the notion of time as a universal, standing outside of all contexts and spaces. Time thus exists within space, in 'space-time' or in a 'block universe', and there would be no flow to it whatsoever. It is not an arrow but an envelope, or cloud, and all processes would in principle be reversible, however improbable statistically. There would be no place for something known as a future and the new scientific measure of time is B.P. (before the present), with no future measurement whatsoever.[2] In Western philosophy Charles Taylor has most recently questioned the practice of Western thought of thinking in terms of 'vertical time-slices', such as 'the eighteenth century', holding together myriad happenings both related and totally unrelated to one another.[3] A leading historian speaks of a linear concept of time as involving 'temporal structures we erect to impose order on the worlds of memories we have constructed'.[4]

If our future begins to look more and more like a kind of enlarged present or simply ongoing life, what effect might this have on our concept of law?

3. Law in a World with No Future

The thought may appear initially depressing, though this is a conditioned reflex. Life goes on; it is simply not conceptualised as extending beyond the present, into a future. We only live in the present in any event. There

---

2 H. Patrick Glenn, *Legal Traditions of the World: Sustainable Diversity of Law*, Oxford University Press, Oxford, 2010, p. 26, 88.

3 Charles Taylor, *A Secular Age*, Harvard University Press, Cambridge Mass, 2007, p. 195.

4 R. R. Davies, *The First English Empire*, Oxford University Press, Oxford, 2000, p. 4.

may be consequences of this, however, for the way in which law is thought of and used.

Stephen Toulmin has recently examined the intellectual foundations of 'modernity' over the last four centuries, finding them in what he calls 'certainty', 'systematicity', and the 'clean slate'.[5] Certainty could be brought about by systematicity and implemented on a 'clean slate'. The 'clean slate' here represents the future, an uncluttered world where contemporary rationality could implement any number of grand and lesser designs. State construction was the largest exercise of Western modernity, built on a purported clean slate amenable to national law-making. In the late twentieth century, law books were still being written with titles such as *Shaping the Future: New directions for legal services*.[6]

If the future is removed from our ways of thought, however, we are faced (only) with the present, and it is not a clean slate. It is rather filled with existing institutions and laws, which can only be improved upon and refined in the absence of any possibility of their being futuristically swept aside. Amartya Sen therefore argues that substantive justice must be the preoccupation of lawyers and political thinkers, particularly in developing countries, and that it is inadequate and fruitless to continue to think in terms of 'transcendental institutionalism', the construction of entire sets of (new) institutions which will magically solve all present problems.[7] As Toulmin puts it, "[a]ll we can be called upon to do is to take a start from where we are, at the time we are there ...".[8]

If this should be the non-utopian objective, how might it be realised in different areas of law and legal activity?

4. Private International Law

Private international law emerged as a scientific discipline only at the time of state construction, from the seventeenth century. Huber then orig-

---

5 Stephen Toulmin, *Cosmopolis: The Hidden Agenda of Modernity*, University of Chicago Press, Chicago, 1990, p. 179.

6 Roger Smith (ed.), *Shaping the Future: New directions for legal services*, Legal Action Group, London, 1995.

7 Amartya Sen, *The Idea of Justice*, Harvard University Press, Cambridge Mass, 2009.

8 Toulmin, 1990, p. 179, see *supra* note 5. See also Toulmin, 1990, p. 192: "The task is not to build new, larger, and yet more powerful powers, let alone a 'world state' having absolute, worldwide sovereignty".

inated the idea, and the name, of conflicts of laws and the idea of conflicting laws has been an essential feature of modern thinking on the relations of state laws ever since. The conflictual character of the discipline was exacerbated by Savigny's basic idea that legal relations could be geographically situated, with the result that all legal space was effectively nationalised. Conflicts of laws became inescapable and were seen as arising in all cases of difference in national expression of norms. In some countries this is taken to the point that a decision on the law applicable to the case must be taken even in the absence of allegations that choice of law makes a difference to the outcome of the case.

This conflictual way of thinking about the differences in state laws appears to be an example of Sen's transcendental institutionalism. The primary, if not the only, consideration, is that of the states which appear to be involved in the case. In this view of a utopian international world, all cases would somehow be seated in their geographical home and national sovereignty and an extended notion of territoriality would prevail even in private law cases.

There are already indications, however, that this state-dominated view of international private-law relations is breaking down. As early as 1979 Pierre Gannagé wrote that it was becoming evident that material or substantive rules of private international law were required in order to satisfy requirements of substantive justice.[9] Since then more and more national codifications and international instruments have chosen a substantive result as a means of effecting international private-law justice, whether to sustain institutions (marriage, formal validity of legal acts) or to favour a particular party in legal proceedings (children in need of support, consumers).[10]

This shift in emphasis in the choice-of-law process is beginning to be paralleled by a similar shift in emphasis in choice of jurisdiction. Again, the emphasis is towards a more collaborative approach in effecting individualised justice at the international level. This is most evident in

9 Pierre Gannagé, "La Coexistence des Droits Donfessionnels et des Droits Laïcisés dans les Relations Privées Internationales", in *Recueil des Cours*, 1979, vol. 164, no.3, p. 348.

10 See Symeon Symeonides, "Material Justice and Conflicts Justice in Choice of Law" in P. Borchers and J. Zekoll (eds.), *International Conflict of Laws for the Third Millennium: Essays in Honor of Friedrich K. Juenger*, Transnational Publishers, Ardsley, NY, 2001, p. 125-140.

international child custody cases, where the practice of direct court-to-court communication is being adopted as a means of appreciation of the best interests of the child.[11] There is also active judicial collaboration in international bankruptcy cases, in some areas of the world at least. This is likely to increase.

Private international law is thus undergoing an important change and there is likely to be increased emphasis on 'justice amongst individuals', as opposed to insistence on the 'equality of states', across the full range of private law problems.

5. Civil Procedure

Civil procedure has been with us for much longer than private international law but it too appears to be undergoing profound reform. The traditional dichotomy is between 'accusatorial' or 'inquisitorial' procedure, the language indicating a sharp distinction and inherent conflict between the two, each treated pejoratively by the adherents to the other. Behind the dichotomy however, are many complex and differentiated national models, tending towards judicial control or tending towards party control, with many efforts to effect compromise between the two. There would now be a considerable measure of convergence, with common law jurisdictions attempting to install a greater level of judicial supervision and civil law jurisdictions attempting to shift some functions to the parties and their counsel.[12] The pejorative language of the past could therefore be replaced by the more contemporary language of 'adversarial' and 'investigative' forms of procedure, while recognising that they represent a continuum of solutions as opposed to diametrically opposed opposites.

Each of these traditional types of procedure represents a utopian ideal and each, according to the dichotomy, would be incompatible with the other. In civil law jurisdictions the judge is presumed to know the law

[11] For what has become an international network of judges dealing with such cases, see W. Duncan, "Judicial Cooperation and Communication in the Context of the Hague Conventions" in Sam Muller and Sidney Richards (eds.), *Highest Courts and Globalisation*, Asser Press, The Hague, 2010, p. 59; See also Linda J. Silberman, "Cooperative Efforts in Private International Law on Behalf of Children: The Hague Children's Conventions", in *Recueil des cours*, 2006, vol. 323, pp. 261-477.

[12] See most recently the various reports in Janet Walker and Oscar G. Chase (eds), *Common Law, Civil Law and the Future of Categories*, LexisNexis, Markham, 2010

and the investigative function of the judge flows from the obligation to apply the law where it is meant to be applied. In common law jurisdictions the role of the parties is based on the historically minimal role of the judge under the writ system but is now also defended as the allegedly best means of allowing truth to be ascertained. Yet each of these types of procedure is now failing under the weight of contemporary burdens. In the common law jurisdictions, litigation has become largely impossible for natural or physical persons on financial grounds. Litigation rates in many common law jurisdictions, most notably the United Kingdom, have plummeted.[13] The trial, the hallmark of common law dispute resolution, is said to be 'vanishing' in the U.S.A.[14] There is a widespread phenomenon of parties representing themselves (*pro se* representation), in spite of the real necessity of legal counsel in adversarial proceedings. In civil jurisdictions even the large numbers of resident judges, using investigative forms of procedure, are unable to overcome the vast backlog of cases, with ensuing delays in the administration of justice.[15] In both common law and civil law jurisdictions there is now widespread resort to arbitration by sophisticated players who choose to avoid state-centred institutions, leading to claims of an autonomous international arbitral order.[16] Arbitration itself, however, may be falling victim to the same problems as civil procedure more generally.

Reform is unlikely to consist of stricter adherence to adversarial or investigative models. A third way appears indicated. Professor Cadiet has suggested that this may be found in the concept of a 'cooperative' or collaborative form of procedure, which takes as its point of departure that civil procedure belongs neither to the parties nor to the judge, since both are obliged to collaborate in bringing the case to a conclusion in a reason-

13 For the U.K., The Economist, 26 October 2002, p. 34: 60% decline in commercial cases 1996-2001; and for sharper declines thereafter, see L. West, "Woolf: Ten Years On" in *The Commonwealth Lawyer*, 2009, vol. 18, no. 2, p. 37.

14 Marc Galanter, "The Vanishing Trial: An Examination of Trials and Related Matters in Federal and State Courts" in *Journal of Empirical Legal Studies*, 2004, vol. 1, no. 3, pp. 459-570.

15 Roger Perrot, *Institutions judiciaires*, Montchrestien, Paris, 2008, p. 12.

16 Emmanuel Gaillard, *Aspects Philosophiques du Droit de l'Arbitrage International*, Martinus Nijhoff, Leiden, 2008.

able length of time, with a reasonable expenditure of resources.[17] The '*contrat judiciaire*' has appeared, and is likely to be of increasing influence. Judicial mediation has also emerged.

As in private international law, the developments in civil procedure indicate a weakening of unique institutional perspectives, increased sensitivity to private or non-state considerations of justice, and recognition of a plurality of methods.

6. The Legal Professions

The legal professions are in the difficult position of responding to the pressures of globalisation while maintaining the ethical and disciplinary standards which are those of a liberal and independent profession. In the United Kingdom and Australia the professions have been judged critically by the governments of the day, and disciplinary proceedings have been taken away from the professions and vested in state agencies. Elsewhere the challenges are equally persistent. State political boundaries are increasingly judged to be unacceptable as territorial limits on the practice of law, while technology assists lawyers in practising without regard to concepts of territorial localisation.

To the extent professional structures remain national in character, or even urban or regional, there is therefore a serious problem of professional response to trans-border cases of unethical professional conduct. There have been partial responses to this problem. There is a trans-European Code of Conduct for Lawyers in the European Community, which articulates both common rules and what can only be described as a choice of ethics rules, based on geographic factors, to deal with differences across the European professions.[18] There are non-binding codes of legal ethics in the American federations of the U.S.A. and Canada, though in all these cases there has been no creation of a trans-border disciplinary authority.

---

17 L. Cadiet, "Avenir des Categories, Catégories de l'Avenir: Perspectives", in Janet Walker and Oscar G. Chase (eds), *Common Law, Civil Law and the Future of Categories*, LexisNexis, Markham, 2010, p. 635 and p. 651.

18 Common rules are established in such matters as independence, confidentiality, personal publicity, conflicts of interest; questions of incompatibilities, regulation of fees, treatment of client funds, professional indemnity insurance are referred to home or host state regulation. See Dorothy Little, "Conseil des Barreaux de la Communauté Européenne", in *Cross Border Practice Compendium*, Law Books in Europe/Kluwer, Deventer, 1996, ch. 4, p. 15.

The situation greatly exacerbates the major disparities in the structures of the professional discipline in national jurisdictions. The 2008 Report of the Council of Europe on European Judicial Systems indicates striking differences in the rates of disciplinary proceedings against lawyers per one hundred thousand members of the national population. In Finland there are 245 such proceedings annually, in Sweden 117, in Italy 1, in Monaco, Andorra and Montenegro 0. There are certainly similar disparities within the NAFTA countries, given the diversity among U.S. states and the absence of professionally-controlled disciplinary proceedings in Mexico.

It appears the professions must develop procedures for transnational control of unethical practice. If they do not do so they will lose the control which they presently exercise. An intermediate form of solution, short of creation of transnational professional authorities, would consist in cross-border collaboration of existing national structures, such that consultation would take place on questions of jurisdiction and there would be inter-jurisdictional recognition of disciplinary judgments. The question of how to resolve substantive ethical questions is best resolved by adopting the highest standard of those which may be in present in a particular case. In any event, questions of legal ethics will occupy a larger place in bilateral or multilateral agreements on lawyer mobility. The recently concluded Quebec-France agreement on the professional mobility of lawyers provides for no testing of knowledge of substantive law but concentrates on knowledge of ethical standards.

7. Corruption

The areas of law or legal institutions discussed above are ones in which attention is increasingly given to improving the operation of existing institutions, attempting to ensure adherence to objectives and to ensure integrity and loyalty in their pursuit. The theme of corruption perhaps best demonstrates this tendency, since integrity is the primary objective of anti-corruption measures and since corruption is the most debilitating cause of the decline of law and legal institutions. It is also widespread, everywhere in the world, such that its elimination or restriction will be an ongoing priority of professional authorities, national governments and international organisations. Corruption within national states has always been illegal, either in the form of criminal corruption of public officials or in the form of civil law violation of obligations of loyalty. The most recent development is the criminalisation locally of corruption of public officials abroad, and this has involved both the enactment of the necessary legislation and the willingness to expend local resources on the prosecution of corruption which has taken place abroad. The latter now appears to be taking place. The International Bar Association, moreover, has recently announced an anti-corruption strategy for the legal profession, designed to improve internationally recognised standards and ensure the cooperation of the profession in their enforcement.[19] This will give further strength to the many recent international conventions on corruption and will usefully complement the invaluable work of Transparency International. The increasing visibility of international efforts may have a positive effect on domestic means of enforcement.

8. Conclusion

If it is difficult to predict what we designate as the future, it is still more difficult to predict specific changes to existing law and institutions. This paper has not sought to do so, but has suggested some broad themes which may underline efforts of legal change and reform. In the absence of any possibility of a clean slate, as this has been understood throughout recent centuries of 'modernity', efforts hereafter may be directed more towards the reconciliation of existing laws and existing institutional alternatives. The objectives would therefore be those of compliance and conciliation, which are among the fundamental objectives of all legal regimes.

[19] International Bar Association Global Insight online, April 2010.

4.7

Mechanisms of Evolution for a Law of the Future

Marc Amstutz[*]

The present remarks focus on the subject of how law changes over time. This is a question of particular relevance within the context of globalisation, but to which the literature has not yet provided a satisfying response. The difficulty, it is argued, lies in a widely held conception of law as developing along a linear path, adapting to change through the intervention of an external agent, the lawmaker, who acts as a 'legal planner' (legal positivisim). A more useful understanding of law, it is argued, may be found in the circular model proposed by evolutionary theory, according to which the primary mechanisms for change in the legal system are the same as those found in other natural systems: selection and spontaneous self-organisation. In this paradigm, the legal system is observed within the overall context of the society to which it belongs – and not simply as an instrument of the political system – providing a multidimensional portrayal of the synchonicity of social and legal developments. The approach here proposed has two immediate thematic objectives. The first is to work out a fully elaborated theory of legal evolution; the second is to investigate the potential for practical application of that theory as a model for the orientation of legal operations. The ultimate purpose is to enhance the ability of legal systems to adapt as circumstances change and, by that means, to raise the degree of social responsiveness with which the law is applied.

1. Introduction

The following brief essay focuses on the question of the transformation of law, a subject that has long preoccupied legal scholars, but which, given the rapidly accelerating pace of social change today, is perhaps now more relevant than ever. The question of how law changes over time has not yet found a satisfying response. The reasons for this are numerous, but at the heart of the problem lies a conception of law whose limits, particularly since the advent of globalisation, have become increasingly apparent. Law today is still widely seen as developing along a path that follows a con-

* **Marc Amstutz** is Professor of Law at University of Fribourg, Switzerland.

scious design.[1] Law is subject to change, in the modern era, almost solely through political intervention (legal positivism). To put it differently: in order for the legal system to keep up with society – so the theory goes – an external agent is required, a 'legal planner', as it were. And it is this conception that the law of the future will have to overcome. It must find a way to develop its own evolutionary capabilities, the ability to change itself 'from within', on its own impetus (without the help of a political system), if it is to be able react adequately to highly dynamic social change.[2] This proposition may be argued from a number of different standpoints.

In terms of intellectual history, the current view of law is the product of an anthropocentric bias in legal thought. There is an implicit assumption that the perpetual adaptation of law to the needs of society can only be accomplished by a conscious human effort. This conviction is accompanied by a teleological prejudice inherent in Western legal theory: the belief that there is constant progress in law, over time, based on the assumption that the knowledge of lawmakers grows continuously.[3] The truth of this assumption is, however, neither theoretically demonstrable nor empirically proven. From a sociological point of view, this conception of legal evolution only serves to obscure the nature of the relationship between the development of law and the development of society. This is so, because the alleged influence of events external to the legal system on the workings of that system is explained on the basis of (professedly causal) paradigms which ignore such factors such as coincidence, circularity and resonance.[4] Due to this, they are also blind to the most important phenomena that link social and legal systems.

Seeing the evolution of the law in this manner affects not only the way in which legal systems are described. It also has consequences for the way they operate. Traditional legal theory treats events, whether in the

---

1 Friedrich A. Hayek, *Law, Legislation and Liberty, Volume I: Rules and Order*, The University of Chicago Press, Chicago/London, 1973, pp. 9-11.

2 Marc Amstutz, "Rechtswissenschaft", in Philipp Sarasin and Marianne Sommer (eds.), *Evolution: Ein interdisziplinäres Handbuch*, J.B. Metzler, Stuttgart/Weimar, 2010, pp. 311-312.

3 Niklas Luhmann, *Law as a Social System*, Oxford University Press, Oxford, 2004, p. 298.

4 Wojciech Zaluski, *Evolutionary Theory and Legal Philosophy*, Edward Elgar, Cheltenham/Northampton, 2009, p. 75.

history of society or in the history of law, as being unique. Such events are investigated primarily in terms of the search for 'historical truth', rather than as instances of structural couplings, from which generally applicable conclusions may be drawn concerning the nature of the relationship between the social and legal systems.[5] Therefore, there is still very little known about any regularity that may characterise the channels of communication between law and society. This gap in our knowledge has important ramifications. In particular, for the study of legal doctrine, the aim of which is to articulate rules that emerge from case-law so that they can be applied to new cases without first having to be thought through ('figured out') again from scratch. Adherence to the notion of the uniqueness of historical events precludes any consideration of the implications of changing contexts for static rules, and impinges on ability of those changing contexts to effect substantive changes to the rules. It is in this approach to legal doctrine – which seeks to rationalise the application of law by establishing temporal and logical (but not social) consistency in the decision-making processes of the courts – that lies one of the principal reasons for the legal system's deficit in adapting to accelerated social change.[6]

In contrast to this conception of law, the circular model proposed by evolutionary theory would appear to be more realistic. Evolutionary theory is better suited to comprehend the reality of law in society because it provides the means for illustrating the interlocking of social and legal communications. In this paradigm, there is no decisive importance in establishing, for example, a precise and detailed account of the vicissitudes of the Napoleonic Code from the time of its original composition down to its vestigial effects on recent opinions by modern courts. Rather than tracing linear developments, evolutionary theory tries to pinpoint discontinuities within given historical contexts. It thus attempts, for example, to identify the conditions that rendered possible unexpected structural changes in the law of the Code Napoléon.[7] The transformation of law is conceived of as the intensification of deviations from an earlier state. As these deviations are themselves seen as arising in response to events that occur in

---

[5] Thomas Vesting, *Rechtstheorie: Ein Studienbuch*, C.H. Beck, München, 2007, pp. 137.

[6] Mark J. Roe, "Chaos and Evolution in Law and Economics", in *Harvard Law Review*, 1996, vol. 109, pp. 665-666.

[7] Luhmann, 2004, p. 323, see *supra* note 3.

other social systems – not only in the political and economic systems, but also in the arts, the media, religion and other subsystems of society – the evolution of the legal system is considered within the overall context of the society to which it belongs.[8] The result is a multidimensional portrayal of the synchronicity of social and legal developments. Up to a certain point, it is also possible to identify regular patterns that emerge out of the interplay between these systems. Not, of course, in the sense of blueprints for charting the future (which necessarily remains undetermined), but rather as a means of recognising the evolutionary mechanisms upon which social and legal transformations rest.[9]

The approach here proposed has two immediate thematic objectives. The first is to work out a fully elaborated theory of legal evolution; the second would be to investigate the potential for practical application of that theory as a paradigm for orienting legal operations. The ultimate purpose is to enhance the ability of legal systems to adapt as circumstances change and, by that means, to raise the degree of social responsiveness with which the law is applied. The following remarks touch on four aspects of the theory of legal evolution, for which convincing explanations have not yet been proposed in the literature: (1) the genesis of law; (2) the mechanisms of legal evolution; (3) the evolution of the concept of law (on the example of the globalisation of the legal system); and (4) the significance of legal evolution for the application of the law (evolutionary legal reasoning).

2. The Genesis of the Law

Today, the most common tactic employed in dealing with the all too perplexing question of the origins of law is to avoid it altogether. Law, it is argued, has no beginning; it starts from the middle.[10] Such arguments are symptomatic of the fact that legal theory has not yet succeeded in assimilating evolutionary categories of thought. To simply relegate an evolutionary phenomenon of such significant proportions as the origin of legal systems to the dustbin of inexplicable, and even banal, historical paradox-

---

8 Marie Theres Fögen, "Rechtsgeschichte: Geschichte der Evolution eines Sozialen Systems", in *Rechtsgeschichte*, 2002, vol. 1, p. 14.

9 Robert Boyd and Peter J. Richerson, *The Origin and Evolution of Cultures*, Oxford University Press, Oxford, 2005, p. 284.

10 Luhmann, 2004, p. 153, see *supra* note 3.

es ("law begins in the middle"), is hardly an intellectually satisfying solution.[11] In order to understand the evolutionary mechanisms of law, its origins must be elucidated. The contemporary relevance of the question lies in the fact that the highly dynamic nature of today's society leads, in numerous instances, to transitions in legal systems. A case in point is transitional justice, involving the introduction of newly valid legal norms where there is a change in the ruling regime (as has occurred in recent history, to name only a few examples, in the German Democratic Republic, in South Africa and in Chile).[12] Each such transition represents, simultaneously, the demise of one legal system and the inception of a new one. In order to understand precisely what happens when such legal transitions occur – a question that is likely to take on increasing importance in the coming years – a theoretical basis of far greater complexity than what is currently available will be required. The following paragraphs explain the basic lines along which such a theory could be constructed.

The starting point is the Hegelian notion of 'deferral' (*Aufschub*), as adapted by Jacques Derrida in the concept he called *différance*.[13] This supplies the means for overcoming the major drawback of traditional theories, namely the idea that the explanation of origins necessarily entails the discovery of a 'final cause' (in the Aristotelian sense of the final cause that is prior to all other causes). This notion, which is the product of a linear conception of causality, is replaced by a circular causal approach. Rather than attempting to name an act by which a legal system was created, *ex nihilo*, as it were, the circular approach seeks to identify those generative impulses within society which can make possible the emergence of a new legal system. With the help of such notions as the 'logos' or Derrida's *supplement*, it becomes possible to reconstruct the genesis of law without the need for any imaginary point of origin or primary cause (which, in reality, is nothing more than a founding myth, that is, a fiction treated as fact), or for any other metaphysical construction. By means of such a circular-genetic construct, it becomes possible, for the first time, to

[11] Marc Amstutz, "The Genesis of Law: On the Paradox of Law's Origin and its supplement", in Peer Zumbansen and Gralf-Peter Calliess (eds.), *Law, Economics, and Evolutionary Theory*, Edward Elgar, Cheltenham/Northampton, 2011, pp. 226-247.

[12] Jon Elster, *Closing the Books: Transitional Justice in Historical Perspective*, Cambridge University Press, Cambridge, 2004.

[13] Jacques Derrida, *Of Grammatology*, The Johns Hopkins University Press, Baltimore/London, 1997, p. 143.

arrive at thorough understanding of the way in which legal and social systems are intertwined with each other.

The hermeneutic usefulness of this new theoretical approach could be tested by applying it to various legal theoretical conundrums. An example would be the question of how it is possible for law to emerge out of newly enacted legal statutes – which, contrary to received opinion, begin their existence not as law, but as political decisions.[14] In order to test the universality of the approach proposed here, a comparative analysis would have to be attempted, using examples taken from the laws and the courtroom practice of various countries. Another useful source for the theory of legal genesis here proposed would be the study of legal change in the wake of regime transitions (against the background of war crime tribunals, for example).

3. The Mechanisms of the Evolution of Law

A common feature of the prevailing models used to explain legal evolution is that they all rely almost exclusively on the classic Darwinian mechanisms of variation, selection and retention.[15] As such, they fail to make use of a substantial part of the advances made in evolutionary theory in the century and a half since Darwin, in particular the insights of the so-called Modern Synthesis (neo-Darwinism). Moreover, the most recent advances of so-called developmental theory are also ignored.[16] In view of this situation, a new model of legal evolution is required, the possible foundations of which can here only be briefly outlined.

The theory developed by Stuart Kauffman[17] – notable for its usefulness not only in the biological disciplines, but also for the social sciences – is of particular interest here. Kauffman's thesis (supported by extensive and persuasive computer simulations) is that the ordering effects of natu-

---

[14] Marc Amstutz, "Das Gesetz", in Peter Gauch and Pascal Pichonnaz (eds.), *K(l)eine Festschrift für Pierre Tercier*, Schulthess, Zürich, 2003, pp. 155-165.

[15] Stephen Jay Gould, *The Structure of Evolutionary Theory*, The Belknap Press of Harvard University Press, Cambridge, Mass./London, 2002, pp. 12-24.

[16] Paul E. Griffiths and Russel D. Gray, "Darwinism and Developmental Systems", in Susan Oyama *et al.* (eds.), *Cycles of Contingency: Developmental Systems and Evolution*, The MIT Press, Cambridge, Mass./London, 2001, pp. 202-203.

[17] Stuart Kauffman, *The Origins of Order: Self-Organization and Selection in Evolution*, Oxford University Press, New York/Oxford, 1993.

ral evolutionary processes come about only through the interaction of two other mechanisms present in nature: selection and spontaneous self-organisation. This leads inevitably to the question of precisely how these two mechanisms interact, a matter of central importance for understanding the interdependence of legal and social systems, as hypothesised here. Kauffman argues that the mechanisms of selection are able to function only where the evolving systems are themselves capable of spontaneous self-organisation. In other words, in order for selection (and thus also evolution) to take place, the evolving organisms must themselves develop a very specific form of internal organisation. The specificity of that organisation lies in the fact that it acts to constantly propel the organism (or system) towards the edge of chaos. In this way, it assures its ability to continue evolving. As Kauffman explains, it is the increased dynamism of the system, resulting from the interaction between order and chaos, which renders a system capable of evolving. The system must be sufficiently stable to not dissolve entirely into chaos when it is disturbed, while, at the same time, maintaining a certain minimum level of instability, so as not to become fully impervious to external irritations, like an adamantine crystal. By continuing to operate in an organised manner, while remaining at all times within the reach of chaos (that is, remaining flexible due to its location "at the edge of chaos"),[18] the system develops a heightened capacity for absorbing the shocks caused by external perturbations and for adapting itself accordingly.

The evolution of legal systems, according to the theory proposed here, occurs through similar mechanisms. Taking this model of legal evolution as a basis, a comparative analysis of the common law and civil law systems could be undertaken. The working hypothesis would be that the differences between the two systems are far less fundamental than generally assumed, since the evolutionary mechanisms at work in both are largely similar. This being the case, the increasing tendency towards a convergence of the social environments in which they are embedded leads almost inevitably to convergence of the legal systems as well. Their respective orders are in constant interaction with the same disorderly events of the evolving world in which we live and, faced with similar problems, it is hypothesised, they tend to bring forth similar solutions.

[18] Kauffman, 1993, pp. 255-263, see *supra* note 17.

4. The Evolution of the Concept of Law (as a Function of the Globalisation of Law)

At issue here is no longer the evolution of a specific legal domain (as, for example, that of German corporate law, or that of family law in the United States). The focus is rather on a phenomenon that occurs at a level once removed: the evolution of the concept of law, as such. This 'meta-evolutionary' process can be studied by examining what is variously referred to as global or transnational law, that is, the legal system that appears to be emerging within the context of world society. The point of departure is a simple question: What are we talking about when we speak of a 'world society'? Taking direction from the work of Niklas Luhman,[19] the approach here proposed takes the high level of complexity that characterises this evolving phenomenon as a central fact, the ramifications of which call for a detailed investigation. In particular, it is necessary to consider the complications that arise out of the discrepancy between the predominantly cognitive expectations that result from high complexity and the normative expectations fostered by local legal systems. The principal difference between these two types of expectations lies in the reaction of those who hold them when they are not met. In the case of cognitive expectations, disappointments when expectations are not met lead to a change in future expectations; in the case of normative expectations, on the other hand, the holders maintain their original expectations even in the face of disappointment. This reaction reflects the very essence of national legal systems, whose *raison d'être* lies in the stabilisation of such normative expectations so as to maintain social stability. In the exponentially more complex system taking shape in the form of global society, such stability is neither desirable, nor even possible, given the fact that its ability to rapidly metamorphose is its most constant feature. What this means is that any legal system that may emerge in that society will, by definition, need to address the cognitive nature of the expectations that guide the conduct of its members. If one considers the gradual transition from national societies to a global society as evidence of an evolutionary leap taking place in social self-organisational systems, it is clear that legal systems will have to make this leap as well. For this to occur, the concept of law evolve in a direction in which law is seen as a process; a process by which, in reaction to the heightened relevance of cognitive expectations in

[19] Luhmann, 2004, pp. 480-490, see *supra* note 3.

global society, existing national and supranational legal systems, on the one hand, and global norm clusters, on the other, interpenetrate each other genetically.[20]

Evidence for the proposition that such an evolution in the concept of law is already taking place is available. For the purpose of the present remarks, three examples will suffice. First, certain shifts in the concept of law are intrinsic to efforts to create a pan-European private law (the so called 'Common Frame of Reference'); these conceptual shifts have thus far, however, elicited little comment.[21] Secondly, the concept of law underlying the development of codes of conduct, corporate social responsibility (CSR) and other similar initiatives by multinational enterprises and transnational organisations testifies to a gradual evolution of notions of legal normativity.[22] Lastly, the concept of law that underlies the expansion of Islamic banking (in particular in African countries) has, for some time now, become a phenomenon of global proportions which cannot fail but to have a lasting influence on any emerging system of global law.[23]

5. The Implications of Legal Evolution for the Application of Law (Evolutive Legal Reasoning)

The issues raised in the foregoing remarks focused on the positive analysis of specific aspects of legal evolution. It remains now to consider the potential implications of such an analysis for the practical application of law in the future. At issue is the role of socio-legal findings in the normative discourse. This, of course, brings us back to the time-honoured conundrum of how to bridge the divide between what 'is' and what 'ought to be'. The present remarks are, of course, not intended to provide a full solution to this question, but merely to suggest a reconsideration of the rules of legal reasoning, that is, of the rules to be applied when subsuming the facts of a case (the legal 'is') under the law in force (the normative

[20] Marc Amstutz and Vaios Karavas, "Weltrecht: Ein Derridasches Monster", in Gralf-Peter Calliess *et al.* (eds.), *Soziologische Jurisprudenz: Festschrift für Gunther Teubner zum 65. Geburtstag am 19*, De Gruyter, 2009, pp. 645-672.

[21] Marc Amstutz, "In-Between Worlds: Marleasing and the Emergence of Interlegality in Legal Reasoning", in *European Law Journal*, 2005, vol. 11, pp. 766-784.

[22] Amstutz and Karavas, 2009, pp. 657-669, see *supra* note 20.

[23] Izah Mohd Tahir and Nor Mazlina Abu Bakar, "Islamic Banking Operations: Preparing the Fit for Internationalization", in *Journal of Islamic Economics, Banking and Finance*, 2009, vol. 5, pp. 49-62.

'ought'). The point of departure here is the circumstance that the media of the legal system, the means through which law expresses itself (orally, textually, and digitally) are the same as those through which it evolves.[24] These media may thus be seen as pre-adaptive advances that enable the legal system to evolve. The primary question to be addressed then is whether the insights gained through evolutionary legal theory may allow for a 'reformatting' of legal reasoning, so as to facilitate its application in a manner better suited to the newly emergent social reality. In a nutshell: can legal evolutionary theory provide a more socially adequate method of legal reasoning?

Any attempt to respond to this question requires a more thorough investigation into the media of law than has thus far been undertaken. To take 'textuality' as an example: legal theory long accepted the Platonic notion of the text as a 'crystal', that is, as a stable medium of fixed meanings. This notion is still at the base of the prevailing theories of legal reasoning, which accordingly define the object of legal interpretation as consisting in the 'discovery' of a lawmaker's original intent (as expressed in the text). In current literary theory, largely thanks to the work of the French structuralists in recent decades, texts are now seen as more complex phenomena. It has been recognised that texts continue to develop even after they have been set down on paper. In other words, a text is not simply a physical object, but a living thing that continues to function even after it has been separated from its author. From the moment of that separation, it mutates into a kind of floating *perpetuum mobile* for the production of meanings. The original context in which it was written loses its significance. The text exists independently and can be re-embedded into new contexts. Just like every other form of communication, texts, once they have been emitted, also "take off into space", as it were, following their own autonomous trajectory, independently of the will or the original intent of their authors.[25]

Seen in this way, it is clear that legal texts are also an important medium of legal evolution. Future legal reasoning will have no choice but to adapt to this circumstance. The question is: how? A definitive response cannot be offered here. What is possible, however, is to suggest a point of

[24] Vesting, 2007, pp. 144-157, see *supra* note 5.

[25] Marc Amstutz, "Der Text des Gesetzes: Genealogie und Evolution von Art. 1 ZGB", in *Zeitschrift für Schweizerisches Recht*, 2007, vol. 126, pp. 237-286.

departure for finding the response. And my suggestion would be to start with what we have: in opinions issued by the European Court of Justice there are clear signs that elements of what may be termed 'evolutive legal reasoning' have already found their way into the Court's thinking – most remarkably in the *Marleasing* decision and those for which it has served as a precedent.[26] In these opinions the Court has demonstrated openness to legal arguments that are based in part on social realities external to the legal system itself. By analysing and comparing such written opinions, it should be possible to identify some of the ways in which legal method is attempting to enhance its evolutive capacities to match those of the world in which it is called upon to perform.

[26] Court of Justice of the European Union, *Marleasing SA,* Case C-106/89, Judgment, November 1990.

4.8

Law, Society and Normativity

Pierre Larouche[*]

Law faces two major challenges in the coming decades. On the one hand, the legal system should not become the sole repository of normativity in our societies. Legal subjects are increasingly requesting and expecting that normative issues be solved by law, thereby relieving legal subjects from having to reflect upon the courses of action open to them. This trend towards normative outsourcing should be rolled back. On the other hand, law and legal science must understand how to make the jump from the analytical findings of social sciences to normative statements about law. They are not yet equipped to deal with the normative consequences of the findings of other social sciences. Legal science must rise to the challenge by developing a model of law that is richer than what is commonly used in other social sciences (law as rules), and upon which findings from social sciences can be grafted.

1. Introduction

While some more specific developments can be anticipated within the next few years, it is very difficult to make long-term predictions on concrete topics. At the same time, a long-term perspective as is required here, which naturally lends itself to more fundamental reflections. This contribution will accordingly take a more abstract and more theoretical turn than might have been expected.

Because of the nature of my experience, this contribution mostly concerns public law, although it is not written specifically for it. The remarks made below could apply to other legal areas as well. This contribution is also written against the background of my recent experience within an inter-disciplinary research centre, the Tilburg Law and Economics Centre (TILEC). I have more experience with the interplay between law and economics, but in principle, the remarks made here (especially in the second part) can apply to other social sciences as well.

[*] **Pierre Larouche** is Full Professor at Tilburg University.

In a nutshell, I believe that law will face two related, and perhaps paradoxical, challenges in the coming decades. On the one hand, positive law must avoid becoming the sole repository of normativity in our societies. On the other hand, law, and in particular legal science, must develop and maintain its own coherent understanding of the jump from the analytical results of other social sciences to a normative viewpoint about what law should be. This contribution ends with a brief summary where the last challenge is also discussed.

2. Positive Law and Normativity

Our vision of what law is and what role it plays in our society is influenced by long-term trends in philosophical and scientific thought, however the original theory is not always entirely or accurately reflected in the actual developments that ensue.

With the postmodernist movement came the idea of moral and cultural relativism. By implying that morality is relative to the subject, relativism pushed morals out of the public sphere and into the private sphere of family and personal relationships. In the public sphere, the task of providing the necessary normative framework for human interaction is then left to the law.[1] For instance, at the most general level, human rights instruments set out the most fundamental principles for the conduct of society. It is true that human rights instruments have brought human rights to the fore and have forced them onto the agenda in situations and in places where they might not otherwise have been respected. At the same, they embody principles which have been with us for centuries yet were not couched in legal terms or enshrined in the institutional framework of the law.

In keeping with the development of systems theory, law is also presented as a self-referential (autopoietic) system, whose function is to maintain expectations, *i.e.*, provide normative guidance. According to Luhmann's theory, in a society made up of specialised self-referential systems communicating with each other, law is the system specialised in normativity. Lawyers are its specialists, and within law there are a number of sub-systems, each with its own super-specialists, from general public law, criminal law and civil law, down to further layers of specialisation.

1 A similar outcome can be reached by following positivist legal theory, whereby law must be kept strictly separate from morals, which are seen as too subjective.

Against this background, we can observe a tendency to turn to law for any and all normative questions in our modern societies and correspondingly, a tendency to expect law to provide answers to these inquiries. This is true in particular for larger organisations, including business firms, which are becoming increasingly mono-dimensional in their function (profit-seeking or other). To borrow a fashionable business term, morality and more broadly normativity are being outsourced to the legal sphere. Outsourcing is the operation whereby a firm decides to cease self-providing a function which it deems no longer a part of its core business, in order to entrust that function to an outside contractor who will be more efficient and specialised in that function.[2] I believe that the same is happening with moral issues; instead of trying to ask hard questions about the proper course of action, firms and individuals are downsizing their moral functions and outsourcing them to the law, *i.e.*, they are turning to the law for guidance without prior self-questioning.[3]

A few examples might help illustrate this trend. Firstly, in the regulation of network industries, commentators often note that the liberalisation policies pursued since the 1990s in the EU have resulted in more, not less, regulation. While this may seem contradictory on a superficial level (given that liberalisation was often portrayed as entailing deregulation), the perceived increase in regulation is explainable in practice. Throughout the liberalisation process, public policy objectives remained constant (for instance, the need to provide every citizen with access to energy, communications, etc.). Whereas these objectives were historically pursued via the internal processes of state-owned monopolies, in a liberalised context,[4] they must henceforth be externalised, since their pursuit is now incumbent on the whole sector. Such externalisation takes the form of law, namely in

2 Most commonly, outsourcing occurs in the information technology (IT) sector. For instance, a chemical firm would downsize its internal IT department and contract with a specialist outsourcing firm to take care of all its IT needs.

3 It is worth noting that in this context, the 'law' is often reduced to legislation. Guidance through case-law will often be perceived as insufficient. This is in keeping with an impoverished vision of the law-as-rules, which prevails at a more theoretical level in other social sciences. See below under the second part of this contribution.

4 And with the concomitant corporatisation and privatisation of the former state monopolist.

this case of network industries, sector-specific regulation.[5] Therefore, the perceived increase in regulation is in fact a normative shift away from internal processes towards externalised law. As such, this shift is unavoidable, and it is *prima facie* desirable considering the upheaval created by liberalisation.[6]

Yet similar shifts can be observed in other sectors as well. They are generally characterised by a request for 'legal certainty' issued by businesses and other actors.[7] While legal subjects are entitled to legal certainty under constitutional systems founded upon the rule of law, such requests go deeper. What is requested is in fact that the public authorities lay out in great detail, completely and immediately what legal subjects must or may not do. Outside of the scope of such obligations and prohibitions, legal subjects are then free to act as they wish. This goes beyond any measure of legal certainty that is warranted under applicable law.[8] When such requests are made, the mantle of legal certainty is stretched excessively in two respects. Firstly, public authorities cannot be expected to attach legal consequences to every conceivable course of action at any given point in time. This would be a massive cognitive undertaking, and a prohibitively expensive one. Secondly and more importantly from a dynamic perspective,[9] new courses of action become possible over time, or known courses of action produce different results. If public authorities consent to exaggerated requests for 'legal certainty', they are effectively

---

5 In addition to the need for regulation arising from the externalisation of processes formerly internal to the monopoly operator, regulation – this time *ex novo* – is also required to govern the relationship between the market players in a liberalised market.

6 Up to the point where regulated firms would either develop a dependency towards regulation or turn regulation into a part of their strategic interactions.

7 See also the relatively common contractual clause stating that parties "will do course of action *X* [in whatever jurisdiction they might be active] unless prohibited by the law of jurisdiction *Y*", without any further consideration as to whether course of action *X* might generally be objectionable if certain jurisdictions go as far as to prohibit it.

8 Considering that freedom to act is the guiding principle in our modern open societies.

9 The first line of argument takes a static perspective and has been around for some time. The second remark, with its dynamic perspective, takes more relevance in our era, characterised by rapid change and innovation.

taking the public policy risk upon themselves[10] and relieving legal actors from the burden of reflecting upon the consequences of their actions.[11]

In response to the above, one could point to the increasing use of self-regulation, which would indicate that legal subjects still possess a sense of normativity and are able to discern what should or should not be allowed for themselves. In practice, spontaneous self-regulation is rarely observed. More often than not, self-regulation takes place as an alternative to a clear threat of regulatory intervention.[12] In that sense, self-regulation can be seen as a situation where public authorities hand over to private actors large parts of their own power to enact and enforce the law. Nevertheless, it is quite conceivable that self-regulation would take place as part of a broader process of normative outsourcing as described above, where self-regulation would have been preceded by a request for more 'legal certainty' and would be designed to settle regulatory concerns once and for all, thus relieving legal subjects of the ongoing burden of reflecting upon their own actions.

The phenomenon of normative outsourcing is not restricted to business. It is present throughout society. Whenever society is confronted with a significant detrimental event or development, such as a perceived increase in crime, consumer fraud or an environmental disaster, there is a tendency to simply legislate away the problem. A new legal regime would be introduced, or the existing one would be strengthened. More difficult issues are left aside, such as whether the event in question was isolated or not, whether change could be effected via non-legislative means, whether sufficient resources were dedicated to crime prevention and law enforcement. The recourse to law or legislation is relatively inexpensive and creates the illusion that the event or development has been dealt with.

At the end of the day, I am worried about exaggerated expectations towards law. It is impossible for law to take care of every normative issue

---

10 *I.e.*, the risk that subsequent developments prevent public policy from being achieved, even if they might fall squarely within existing law.

11 Until the point where the consequences are so detrimental that social pressure is exerted upon them irrespective of the legal situation. For example, there is the case of BP and the oil spill off the Louisiana coast. In contrast, despite the outcry, it seems that the financial sector has not significantly altered its practices after the recent crisis.

12 Typically, it would then be a form of co-regulation, where private legal subjects self-regulate within certain parameters given to them by public authorities, in order to stave of intervention.

in our society. Some would claim that, if the law gives clear incentives and is backed by sufficient enforcement,[13] legal subjects acting in their own self-interest would naturally adopt a socially desirable course of conduct. This proposition has not yet been tested in all its generality, and my belief is that it will not be proven empirically. A mere look at the tax system suffices to realise that it would not function unless a fairly large proportion of taxpayers were paying taxes out of the conviction that taxes serve a purpose and that citizens should pay them. Law cannot work unless it rests on fertile ground. Legal subjects must also have their own normative compass in place and be willing and able to reflect upon their actions, even if the outcome of such reflections might not always be in line with what would be expected from a social perspective.

In conclusion, a major challenge for law and especially public law, in the coming years will be to ensure that it does not become the sole repository of normativity in our societies. In the past decades, legal subjects, businesses and individuals alike, have grown overly accustomed to trusting law in providing normative guidance, at the expense of their own reflections on the courses of action available to them.

3. Law and Legal Science *Vis-à-Vis* Other Social Sciences

On the issue of who produces law and on which basis, law and legal science faces the opposite challenge; it must improve its understanding of how social science can feed into the law in order to keep control of a higher-level normativity.[14]

In recent decades, we have seen a vast improvement in the analytical power of the social sciences and a strengthening of their theoretical and empirical foundations. Law and legal science greatly benefit from social science research, as it enables legal discussions to be conducted on

13 Meaning the appropriate level of enforcement which, combined with the size of the consequences for breaching the law (fines, liability, etc.), will bring legal subjects to behave in a socially optimal fashion. It must be noted that the level of concern is likely to be fairly low, *i.e.*, considerably fewer than all potential cases need to be treated for the risk of adverse consequences caused by perception of law enforcement by legal subjects.

14 Normativity plays here at a different level than under the first challenge. The first challenge concerns first-level normativity (what is the appropriate course of conduct?), whereas the second challenge concerns second-level normativity (what is the appropriate norm to govern these courses of conduct?).

the basis of harder data and better analysis, instead of relying on assumptions or generalising on the back of individual cases.

While the contribution of other social sciences is very valuable, the results achieved by these sciences are usually analytical, in the sense that they pertain to improve our understanding of society. For instance, a research project in economics will theoretically or empirically demonstrate that a given form of corporate governance is more efficient in protecting the interests of shareholders. When taken up in a legal discussion, that outcome can quickly gain a normative dimension as a statement on the desirability of that form of corporate governance over others. That jump from an analytical result in a given social science to a normative statement about the law has not yet been completely mastered.

Typically, social scientists hold reservations about the ability of their work to take a normative dimension. Sometimes they are careless or at least blind about the jump to normativity. In the case of economics, the social science that I am most familiar with, a number of analytical devices have dripped down into popular thought, in the process acquiring a normative gloss which was not intended:

- Generally, individuals (and firms) are assumed to be simply seeking to maximise their own utility ('rational behaviour'). Then economics research goes on to analyse how individuals would behave in a given context and under certain assumptions. This includes the subsequent inquiry into whether the aggregate of utility-maximising individual behaviour also maximises social welfare; this is often not the case. In its popularised version, the 'rational behaviour' assumption is interpreted as an endorsement of selfishness by economic science.[15]
- Similarly, public choice theory models public institutions along the same lines as product markets, which can be analytically interesting and often enlightening. For the sake of analysis, public authorities – and the public officials staffing them – are assumed to be seeking to maximise their own utility. Here too, economic science is distorted

[15] The influence of the 'rational behaviour' assumption in popular thought provides an underpinning to the normative outsourcing phenomenon described earlier in this essay. Indeed if one takes as a given that the selfish pursuit of utility is acceptable, it takes only a small step to infer that it is up to public authorities to notify the legal subject whenever a selfish course of conduct is undesirable in society.

in popular discourse to feed hostility towards politics and public affairs.

- Contract theory relies on a theoretical model of a 'complete contract', whereby all future eventualities are provided for. Commercial law practice turns this tool into a norm and produces ever more complex agreements in a quest to provide for every eventuality, even where the agreement becomes so intricate that it is ignored in the life of the relationship between the contracting parties.
- Financial economics posits the 'rational market' hypothesis to guide research work. Financial markets are presumed to return rational prices based on all the information available. Again, in the policy realm, the rational market hypothesis is turned into a normative standpoint – which is only now coming under question – after the last of a series of speculative bubbles brought the financial sector to its knees.

I am confident that similar examples can be found in other social sciences.

It is beyond the scope of this essay to elucidate why the jump from the analytical to the normative is problematic for social sciences. As far as the incorporation of social science results into law is concerned, however, an explanation can be ventured, albeit tentatively. In my view, social sciences might harbour too narrow a view of law, as a mere set of rules. This view would ignore both the rich texture of substantive law (from general principles, unwritten, laws, open-ended norms, all the way to detailed and specific rules) and the institutional framework of law (including procedure, institutions, discourse, heuristics and epistemology).[16] If law is merely a set of rules, then the translation of scientific results into law is a formalistic exercise and it might indeed be better to leave it to the lawyers.

Unfortunately for that view, law is more complex. Herein lies the second challenge; law and legal science are not yet equipped to deal with the normative consequences of the findings of other social sciences. Not only are those findings analytical in nature, but they are also made under a set of assumptions and a research hypothesis which typically narrows the

[16] Luckily, more recent developments – for instance the rise of new institutional economics – in social sciences point towards a more accurate understanding of law.

focus of inquiry to make it more manageable. A premium is put on the strength of the findings at the expense of complexity. In contrast, when it comes to investigating which normative content the law should take, lawyers are bound to take a broader perspective; the law must be such that it achieves the objectives it is meant to achieve (as they might have been agreed in the polity) while remaining coherent. A legal norm which would achieve efficiency while completely ignoring competing values, such as social justice, personal integrity or the coherency of the legal system, might conform to the findings of economic research, but it would not be acceptable from a legal perspective. Law must be operational within the broader context of the polity, with any and all goals and objectives which the polity might decide upon (even if these goals and objectives are not 'pure' from the analytical perspective of a given social science).

In the decades to come, legal science faces the daunting challenge of developing a better understanding of how social science feeds into law and how the jump from the analytical to the normative is made. In so doing, legal science needs to give more substance to its own analytical framework. Key principles such as justice and fairness are still relatively unarticulated, in no small part because they are both richer and more concrete than comparable notions in other social sciences.

If legal scientists fail to rise to the challenge, then there is a risk that the substance of law will be increasingly derived directly from social sciences, under conditions stemming from these sciences. As other social sciences come to espouse a more sophisticated view of the law, they will also no doubt lay stronger claims to control the normative jump. Similarly, if only because different social sciences are bound to hold different views as to what the law should be, it seems clear that the normative jump should be a legal issue, upon which law and legal science has the final say.

In the end, legal science must find its place among social sciences. The relationship between general medicine and medical specialities might provide an appropriate metaphor. General medicine connects with all specialities, without going into depth in any given speciality. However, it is concerned with the day-to-day care of patients. It deals with patients in their entirety and in their specific context. In comparison, specialists typically deal with a subset of the human body, seen with a certain measure of abstraction. Lawyers and legal scholars would then be general practitioners in social sciences, able to understand specialists, call upon them and deal with them, whilst ultimately being best placed to oversee the general operation of law in society.

4. Conclusion

I see two large challenges facing law in the coming decades. On the one hand, the legal system should not become the sole repository of normativity in our societies, in other words, normative outsourcing should be rolled back. On the other hand, law and legal science must understand how to make the jump from the analytical findings of social sciences to normative statements about law, and thereby help legal science find its place among social sciences.

As far as national legal systems are concerned, the first challenge goes to the heart of their future. If the only normative guidance is to be found in law (as enforced by legal institutions), then national legal systems might not to be able to exert sufficient influence to steer the conduct of large multinational actors. If, however, legal subjects continue to exert their own normative judgment, then it is quite conceivable that a given national legal system could interact with said judgment. As for the second challenge, it is quite conceivable that different legal regimes for feeding social science into the law can co-exist as among various national legal systems. No single best solution exists now, nor is it likely to exist in the future. At the same time, social science tends to be framed in universalist terms, so to the extent that the jump from the analytical to the normative is left to the other social sciences as opposed to law, chances are that national legal systems will be pressured into convergence. Yet as social sciences themselves improve their understanding of the law, they should be better able to cope with variations between national legal systems.

4.9

A Private Law Perspective Focusing on Procedural Aspects

Ewoud Hondius[*]

In his think piece, Ewoud Hondius analyses the research agenda for the future. He suggests that although developments outside the law, such as the internet, may be highly uncertain, legal developments on the other hand are very predictable. There is a vast literature on the latter. As for the first, he suggests to hang on to proposals from other disciplines so as to ensure the involvement of legal researchers.

1. Delimitation of the Subject

Predicting what the law of the future is going to be, even only a couple of decades from now, appears to be a daunting task. One way of dealing with such a task, is to limit one's aims from the outset. First, what the future has in stock for us may be divided into legal and non-legal developments. When looking at legal developments, we may have in mind trends such as the globalisation of law, the growing importance of non-legal disciplines, the convergence of common and civil law and the intermingling of public and private law. Non-legal developments which may have an impact on the future of the law include developments in neuroscience, DNA research, climate change, interreligious and ethnic strife, demographic developments, etc. The difference between the two kinds of development is that the first are not so difficult to analyse. Legal developments often trail developments in society by some decades, which means that the law of 2031 may reflect the society of 2011. That is now! Legal developments also have the tendency to occur incrementally. If Gaius were to teach a law course today, the structure of the course would not be all that different from that of the *Institutiones,* his well-known Roman law textbook of some 1,850 years ago.

Non-legal developments on the other hand are often difficult to predict. Who could have foreseen the communication revolution two decades

[*] **Ewoud Hondius** is Professor of European Private Law at University of Utrecht.

ago or the development of the science of DNA? Why were the predictions made two centuries ago that large city traffic would become all but impossible due to horse droppings in the streets so erroneous? And here comes the second difficulty with non-legal developments: how are trained legal researchers supposed to keep up-to-date with potentially relevant developments in so many different fields? This is not unfeasible. It is therefore useful to make a distinction between legal and non-legal developments. This paper will focus on the former category. This is not to say that this distinction is always easy to make. The growing importance of social sciences for legal science serves as an example.

A second restriction of this paper will be that it is inspired by private law. Until two or three decades ago, this would have been a serious shortcoming of international level, because at that time private law was rather parochial. Now, thanks to the impact of Europe, this has changed and private law has become one of the most internationally focused areas of the law; witness in the Netherlands the legal research assessment board's 2010 report.[1] One shortcoming of most current research is the restriction to Europe. Globalisation will surely be the next step. When in 1993 the late Gerrit Betlem defended his PhD thesis at the University of Utrecht,[2] he was a harbinger of the future for apologising to the jury that he had "limited his research to Europe" (while at the time this was a great expansion as compared with many other PhD theses). A second shortcoming of the present Europeanisation movement is that only elite academics concern themselves with the internationalisation of private law in Europe, while the large majority of legal practitioners are still blissfully unaware of the impact of Europe on private law.

A third restriction of the paper is that for reasons which will become clear in a moment, it is especially legal research which I have in mind. This is once again not at all meant to belittle the importance of legislation, case-law and customary law. It simply happens to be so that precisely in the area of research the issue is a current one.

---

1 See *Rechtswetenschappelijk onderzoek in Nederland*, Kwaliteit en Diversiteit, 2010, p. 433, available at www.vu.nl/nl/Images/Evaluatie%20onderzoek%20Rechten_tcm9-169244.pdf, last accessed 1 April 2011.

2 Gerrit Betlem, *Civil Liability for Transfrontier Pollution: Dutch Environmental Tort Law in International Cases in the Light of Community Law*, Graham and Trotman, London / M. Nijhoff, Dordrecht, 1993, p. 627.

2. Material

On a first reflection, one may presume that publications on the future of law and of the world at-large are difficult to find. Once one browses for materials on the future of the law for some time, one arrives at the conclusion that the contrary is the case. Books and other publications on the subject simply abound. In this section I will give a summary impression, thereby focussing on my own jurisdiction – that of the Netherlands. One should be well aware that 'future' is not the only relevant Google keyword: words such as 'innovation' and 'progress' will also result in substantial numbers of hits.

A well-known book on the future of society a half century ago was *Die Zukunft hat Schon Begonnen* by Robert Jungk (1952). Limiting ourselves to the law, we also find a plethora of publications speculating about the future of law. Institutional congresses seem to be a very suitable occasion to engage in this kind of exercise. Inaugural addresses have the same tendency; by way of example I mention the inaugural lecture of Michiel Scheltema, the current President of HiiL's Programmatic Steering Board, in accepting the position of the G.J. Wiarda Chair at the University of Utrecht.[3]

In the Netherlands, conferences in the recent past have been dedicated to the law of the future. In 2001, a meeting was convened by the Dutch Ministry of Justice on "Justice for Tomorrow". The meeting was attended by academics, civil servants and judges. The seven main issues targeted were internationalisation, the growing diversity of society, the decreasing willingness to accept individual risks, the decreasing authority of the state, structural immigration, the rule of law, and increasing normative quality in government.[4] Progress in the law, a very much related theme, was the subject of a small volume published at the occasion of the honorary doctorate conferred upon Jan Vranken by the University of Leiden.[5] In 2010, the University of Utrecht organised a conference on the future of restricting access to the *Hoge Raad,* the highest court in the

3 M. Scheltema, *Het Recht van de Toekomst: De Gevolgen van de Internationalisering van het Recht*, Kluwer, Deventer, 2005, p. 14.

4 Ministerie van Justitie, *Justitie over Morgen: Een Strategische Verkenning*, The Hague, 2001, p. 156.

5 J.H. Nieuwenhuis and C.J.J.M. Stolker, *Vooruit met het Recht: Wat Geldt in de Rechtswetenschap als Vooruitgang*, Boom, The Hague, 2006, p. 132.

Netherlands.[6] The future of the machinery of justice more in general seems a popular theme for conferences.[7] When it comes to individual publications, references to the future are even more plentiful, whether it be in areas like contract law,[8] copyright law,[9] jurisprudence[10] or other subdisciplines.

This is by no means a Dutch phenomenon of course. Some fame was achieved by the late Jacques Austruy's *Le Droit et le Futur*.[11] Another recent publication is one of the future of international law.[12] The notion of progress likewise is a popular theme in public international law.[13] Future scenarios are also a fruitful area for academics; witness the example of HiiL's 'think piece' contributions.

Finally, it may be of interest to look back at the past in order to find out what our ancestors had in mind as to the future of law. When modern rulers such as Gaddafi and Mubarak are depicted as dictators, it is often overlooked that in ancient Rome the *dictator* was considered an extreme but necessary solution for extreme perils which beset the Republic. In a

---

6 The conference papers were published in A.M. Hol, I. Giesen and F.G.H. Kristen (eds.), *De Hoge Raad in 2025: Contouren van de Toekomstige Cassatierechtspraak*, Boom, The Hague, 2011, p. 316.

7 Another example is Bert van Delden, Gert Jan van Muijen and Leo Stevens (eds.), *Rechtspraak in 2040: Liber Amicorum der Gelegenheid van het Afscheid van Mr G.A.M. Stevens als President van het Gerechtshof 's-Hertogenbosch*, Kluwer, Deventer, 2009, p. 694.

8 J.M. Smits and R.R.R. Hardy, *De Toekomst van het Europees Contractenrecht*, WPNR, 2002, Nr. 6513, pp. 827–833.

9 E. Huizer, *et al.*, *De Toekomst van het Auteursrecht*, DEA, Amsterdam, 2004, p. 62.

10 See, for instance, H. Ph. Visser 't Hooft, *Het Recht van de Toekomst: Over Morele Aspecten van Duurzaamheid*, Klement/Pelckmans, Kampen, 2006, p. 96.

11 Jacques Austruy, *Le Droit et le Futur*, PUF, Paris, 1985, p. 153.

12 Alejandro Alvarez, *Le Droit International de l'Avenir*, Kessinger Publishing LLC, 2010, p. 158.

13 See, for instance, Russell Miller and Rebecca Bratspies (eds.), *Progress in International Law*, Martinus Nijhoff, Leiden, 2008, p. 912 (inspired by Manley O. Hudson, *Progress in International Organisation*, Stanford University Press, Stanford, 1932); Thomas Skouteris, *The Notion of Progress in International Law Discourse*, Asser Press, The Hague, 2010, p. 276.

recent essay, Raoul Van Caenegem develops the theme that originally sound ideas may in the end lead to absurd or even nefarious results.[14]

3. Importance of the Subject

The importance of the exercise of looking into the future may be twofold. First, both for theory and practice, it is good to know what to focus on. Is climate change as great a challenge to the world as some scientists make us believe? It is obvious that an affirmative answer may greatly impact policy decisions to devote funds to help the reduction of the CO_2 levels in the world's atmosphere. Legal research in the past has often focussed on current legislation and litigation. Where litigation is mostly absent, researchers will have to look into necessary future legislation, co-regulation and self-regulation. More philosophical questions, such as the steerability of society, are bound to follow. Is that all there is?

There is another practical reason why looking into the future is of interest for law researchers, at least in the Netherlands. This year, the Royal Netherlands Academy of Sciences started work on establishing a Dutch Science Agenda.[15] The first such Agenda should be published in 2011.[16] Currently, the two Departments of the Academy, Sciences and Arts, and their various sub-divisions are preparing proposals for consideration.[17]

By the end of the fourteenth century the humanist Coluccio Salutati argued that Law should occupy the highest rank among sciences.[18] It is

---

[14] R.C. Van Caenegem, "Sound Ideas and Absurd Consequences: Reflections of a Legal Historian", in *European Review*, 2011, vol. 19, no. 1, pp. 93–104.

[15] Koninklijke Nederlandse Akademie van Wetenschappen, "Voor de Wetenschap: De Akademie in de Kennissamenleving", Strategische Agenda 2010–2015, KNAW, Amsterdam, 2010.

[16] It has only an indirect link with the Kennis en Innovatie Agenda 2011-2020. See KIA, *Kennis en Innovatie Agenda 2011-2020*, KIA, available online at www.kennisinnovatieagenda.nl/downloads/kenniseninnovatieagenda_2011-2020.pdf, last accessed 1 April 2011.

[17] I had the honour of participating – together with Corien Prins, Nico Schrijver, Arend Soeteman and Ben Vermeulen – in a small commission which pre-prepared the proposals.

[18] A.M. Hol, "Pleidooi voor een Jurisprudentia: Over Recht en Rechtswetenschap", in J.W.L. Broeksteeg and E.F. Stamhuis (eds.), *Rechtswetenschappelijk Onderzoek: Over Object en Methode*, Boom, The Hague, 2003, pp. 5–22.

not certain whether this opinion is still the prevailing one among scientists, and anyway it is certainly not among members of the academy. It even is not wholly unlikely that some non-lawyers will consider law as a non-science. Since it is not inconceivable that this opinion – utterly wrong as it may be – will gather some support, I have recommended adopting a worst case scenario. This would entail that the law subdivision tries to hang on to proposals from other disciplines as much as possible and to restrict the number of its own proposals to two or three. Some proposals from other disciplines which may be promising from a legal perspective are neurotechnology and brain research (just imagine what this may have in store for traditional will theory in the formation of contract) and climate change. Intellectual property may also find it easy to hang on to sciences, which usually show a practical interest in this area of the law.

Of the various legal options, the changes in the national/international dichotomy are an obvious choice. Theoretically this is not a very challenging item, but in practice it is. The same is true for the combination of insights from other disciplines concerning legal discourse. This does not mean the end of dogmatic science,[19] but increasingly this will be accompanied by research from other disciplines.[20] Finally, there is coherency against a pluralist society, including the public/private divide. One major problem is that many scientists consider the discipline of law non-scientific especially because of its lack of empirical studies.[21]

4. Conclusion: A Procedural Approach

It is now time to establish a research agenda for the coming decades. The discipline of law will probably not be amongst the disciplines with a significant impact on that agenda. We therefore need to fundamentally rethink law's position and contribution to new research. What we should try

---

[19] J.B.M. Vranken, "Pluriforme Rechtswetenschap", in *Alleen Samen: Opstellen Aangeboden aan Prof. mr M.A.M.C. van den Berg*, Instituut voor Bouwrecht, The Hague, 2010, pp. 445 – 467.

[20] W.H. van Boom, I. Giesen and A.J. Verheij (eds.), *Gedrag en Privaatrecht: Over Gedragspresumpties en Gedragseffecten bij Privaatrechtelijke Leerstukken*, Boom, The Hague, 2008, p. 616.

[21] According to Peter Cane and Herbert Kritzer, *The Oxford Handbook on Empirical Legal Research*, Oxford University Press, 2010, p. 4: empirical research "involves the systematic collection of information ('data') and its analysis according to some generally accepted method".

to do is develop interdisciplinary approaches to real problem before trying to convince our non-legal colleagues what is 'scientific' about our research and why it is of interest for the world at-large. Having done so, we can come back to more practical proposals at a later stage.

5. Divergence and Convergence of Legal Systems

5.1

Inter-Systemic Harmonisation and Its Challenges for the Legal State

Larry Catá Backer*

Harmonisation is currently proceeding along different lines that reflect ambiguous and multi-vector interactions between traditional and emerging governance actors and that suggest the context in which the future of legal systems, however understood, will be determined. This think piece first considers the foundations. The great nineteenth century project of horizontal harmonisation, centered on states and their domestic law systems. The twentieth century project of vertical harmonisation focused on legal internationalisation, from which the edifices of supra-national institutions and public transnational law evolve. It then turns to the current challenge of inter-systemic harmonisation. Founded on governance polycentricity, of the mechanics of law beyond the domestic legal orders of states, of the rise of private law with public functions, and of public entities as private actors, it is changing the landscape of law. The greatest challenge for law is to avoid becoming irrelevant where corporations use contracts to govern their supply chains, states become private market actors, and private enterprises regulate markets by assessment and rating.

1. Introduction

We have been asked to consider, in a summary essay form, three fundamental questions affecting the law-state in this century:

> What do you see as the most significant challenges for the development of the law? What developments are we likely to see in the coming two to three decades? What do those developments mean for national legal systems in the international legal order as a whole?

The questions put at issue, in a precise way, the fundamental understanding of the basic building blocks of twentieth century socio-economic political culture, and particularly the character of law, the state and non-

* **Larry Catá Backer** is W. Richard and Mary Eshelman Faculty Scholar and Professor of Law and International Affairs at Pennsylvania State University.

state actors. But these questions also raise issues that are dynamic and that implicate fundamental questions of institutional form, function and legitimacy. These issues revolve around communication, autonomy and interdependence in the governance activities of state and non-state actors, and the forms in which communication is undertaken, autonomy revealed and interdependence manifested. There is thus a dynamic element at the core of the questions that requires elaboration and that serves as the 'urtext' for governance actors for this century. The thesis of this essay is this: whatever the outcome in the decades to come, states and their domestic legal orders will not be able to maintain their isolation from the emerging non-national governance frameworks and they will retain a substantial relevance. To avoid irrelevance, states and their law systems must recognise governance polycentricism and more effectively communicate with the emerging extra-legal governance frameworks of public and private governance systems and by public and private actors. It is that dynamic element of *inter-systemic harmonisation and its challenges for law-states* that this essay considers, weaving this theme within the three questions initially posed.

2. The Future: Divergence, Coordination, and Contradiction in Ideologies of Convergence

At the start of the twenty-first century, governance harmonisation has become a more complicated, more desired, and yet more elusive enterprise. Even as the enterprise of harmonisation has grown, states have begun to more aggressively resist harmonisation as its ability to serve as a framework for the transfer of governance power from states to new centres has been more widely felt. However, that element of resistance has been complicated by the entry of new actors into governance circles. Harmonisation is currently proceeding simultaneously along a number of different lines—horizontal, vertical and inter-systemic—that reflects these ambiguous and multi-vector interactions and that also suggests the context in which the future of legal systems, however understood, will be determined.

Horizontal harmonisation occurs between entities (traditionally state entities) roughly similarly situated within hierarchies of authorities. For example, between the States of the United States, between the Member States of the European Union, or between two less formally connected states, for example between India and Chile or between other states in the global community. It can be as simple a project as finding a common language for communication and as complicated a project as integrating legal systems. This push toward horizontal harmonisation of laws among sovereigns describes the great project of comparative law with its origins in European nineteenth century notions of the state. Much that passes for law-making remains at this level of nineteenth century conceptions, even as the foundations for those conceptions – the superiority of the state and of the positive law produced by a sovereign *demos* – has been severely challenged. The challenges are both horizontal and vertical. Harmonisation among states unequal in power or development is sometimes understood either as a form of colonialism (a political undertaking through law) or more insidiously, as a means of imposing the ideologies and political choices of powerful states on less developed ones under the guise of simplicity, communication and other virtues of legal harmonisation. Even something as basic as the linguistics of a language, can have ideological effects when transposed, especially when words migrate from the legal cultures of developed states into those of developing states. For example, the migration of developed state notions of property imported into Brazil or Panama to protect the rights of squatters on public lands has been used as a vehicle for developers to deprive these dwellers of their properties through sale or mortgage foreclosures.

The monopoly of horizontal harmonisation was broken in the aftermath of the World Wars of the twentieth century. After 1945 the focus increasingly shifted from the state to a community of states, and from horizontal to vertical harmonisation. Vertical harmonisation, that is the harmonisation between superior and inferior political entities, is less well developed and there is no real consensus about its utility or legitimacy. Yet it is the central element of the great twentieth century project of legal internationalisation – and of the fundamental change in the understanding of the state – now deeply embedded within an increasingly managed community of states. The move towards internationalisation of standards and the communal management of certain behaviours (by individuals, enterprises or states) – corruption, human rights, and war – through positive law has become an important element of global and transnational governance. The financial crisis of 2007-08 brought this project into the foreground as the power of states, funnelled through the G-20 framework, sought to coordinate and channel state power through a supra-national entity whose consensus views would then be adopted by all states. Transnational constitutionalism represents an important form of efforts to undertake development of a customary practice of vertical harmonisation. The recent constitutional crisis in Honduras, and the critical role played by international norms in resolving that domestic constitutional crisis, provides a recent example of the development and growth of this form of harmonisation. Yet, the project of vertical harmonisation remains incomplete, and its fundamental premises continue to be challenged, even as the great edifices of supra-national institutions are created and public transnational law evolves.

However, vertical harmonisation continues to be grounded at its core in the state. Ironically, the great project of vertical harmonisation – economic globalisation – has also served to illuminate the limitations of a state centred approach to law and harmonisation. The twenty-first century has witnessed the emergence of governance polycentricism, of the potential broadening of the mechanics of law beyond the memorialisation of the commands of territorially bounded states, of the rise of private law with public functions and of public entities as private actors. This has substantially changed the landscape of law. These changes have given rise to the most controversial form of harmonisation, at once the most interesting and potentially most far reaching variant – 'inter-systemic harmonisation', or harmonisation of public and private governance systems and by public and private actors. States operating as private enterprises in economic markets and economic entities serving as substitutes for the state in weak governance zones suggests the context in which public and private governance systems remain autonomous but communicate and converge. The movement from customary and positive law to contract and the governance mechanisms of surveillance expand and change the nature and character of governance. The great projects of sovereign investing by Norway and the People's Republic of China through their sovereign wealth funds provide examples of one of the forms that inter-systemic harmonisation is already taking. Sovereign investing integrates systems of traditional state law-making, public policy, administrative mechanisms and participation in private markets to produce a comprehensive and transnational approach to governance objectives.

These changes both augment the power of states (with respect to the expansion of the palette of legitimate governance tools) and shrink the scope of its control (as other governance communities emerge with authority over actors operating within the territory of states). The management of that convergence, communication and interaction has been a great challenge for current efforts to harmonise polycentric public-private systems, existing within states and outside of the domestic legal order of any state. Projects like that of John Ruggie's business and human rights governance framework – the Three Pillar Protect-Respect-Remedy Framework – provides a contemporary application of these issues and serves as a harbinger of things to come. Indeed, within the cluster of governance issues understood as business and human rights, for example, the intersection among domestic and international public legal orders, private governance orders, the public role of private entities and the private role of public entities becomes acute.

Consequently, in place of the traditional focus on the law-state and its obsession with the division between public and private, another focus is emerging, one in which the comparative law project will need to bridge gaps between public law based state systems and private social norm based systems. Just as law-making might have become unmoored from the state, the state has itself become unmoored. And so the issue of corporate citizenship serves as a proxy for the equally important converse issues – that of the private rights of states as participants in global markets. At the international level, states and other collectives might well have to meet more as equals, even as they interact within vertical hierarchies in particular contexts. But even those localised hierarchies are now unstable. Corporations negotiate 'agreements' with small states; nations negotiate treaties. Large corporations can coerce small states in ways that mimic the ways in which larger states can do the same to smaller and more vulnerable ones. States and corporations are now capable of deploying forces in the field – sometimes states hire corporations that serve as mercenary armies for hire. The clear lines of public and private authority, and even the once clear lines of its Marxist-Leninist opposite, have become blurred.

3. The Challenge for the Development of Law: Avoiding Containment and Irrelevance

The construction and management of inter-relations between public and private governance communities and the move from law to extra-legal systems of behavioural control will serve as the great project of the twenty-first century. As a consequence, the greatest challenge for law in the twenty-first century is to avoid becoming irrelevant in an emerging global governance order in which corporations use contracts to regulate their supply chains, states reconstitute themselves as private market actors and private enterprises assert regulatory control of markets through authoritative systems of assessment and rating.

Consider for example, the conventionally understood relationship between public and private law. Private law has traditionally been understood to derive its power and legitimacy from the state. It is attached to the state. The attachment of private law to the state provides a strong ideological basis for the management of private relationships by the state apparatus and the political community it represents. That attachment also suggested a place outside of which law does not reach, but which was not considered legitimate or legal, whatever its binding effect. And that was the end of it, as far as the jurisdictional boundaries and legitimacy-dignity of law was understood to extend. Thus, for example, with respect to limits on the use of real property, the focus is on the individual common law states, whose rights and obligations are mediated by the state through an application of the law of nuisance. In China, the same limits start from the obligations of individuals to the community, memorialised in the great principles of Harmonious Society mediated through the state apparatus under the leadership of the Communist Party. In theocratic systems, the focus is on the community of the faithful whose collective obligations are mediated by a priestly institution through religious law.

Beyond the law of any of these variants lies a universe of morals, psychology, markets and religion to which law was opaque (though was not above deploying discretely from time to time through the device of 'policy' focus, for example), and which existed subject to the pre-emptive power of law. The ideology of law produced an incentive towards autarchy totalitarianism in which the highest authority is characterised as political and vested in territorially bounded states whose legitimating organs (today democracy, yesterday anything from the Kaiser to the priest) were solely vested with authority to bind all juridically recognised persons within the state. The ideology of law permitted a certain variation – sustaining the political framework of the United States, the Soviet Union, Imperial Japan, and Nationalist Socialist Germany simultaneously.

But the twenty-first century has witnessed the rise of a new institutional phenomenon – *the functional detachment of private law from the state*. This suggests a fundamental reorientation of governance, a movement away from the law-state binary to one grounded in the law-norm binary (within which the state is not necessarily present). That reorientation, in turn, suggests polycentricism, breaking the monopoly of power exercised by the state producing positive law through democratically elected institutions and reviving the autonomous force of custom. Yet this is custom of a non-traditional sort; custom is now understood as producing rules that are given force through the state apparatus (the traditional understanding of customary domestic law) but it is also now understood as producing rules that memorialise the customs of other governance communities, from multi-national corporations, to supra-national actors. Law systems, in all their traditional variation, now co-exist with the regulatory contract systems of multi-national corporations, with the governance norms of transnational law-religion systems and with supra-national organisations that produce and seek to enforce their own sets of governance norms among their consenting members.

But detachment also produces different forms of governance. Law tends to assume a simple and single dimension form – a command to be obeyed, usually in the form of an injunction to act or avoid acting in particular ways. However, the forms of governance have expanded well beyond this simple and ancient technique. The movement away from law to governance techniques has also made it easier for non-state communities to develop an institutional framework and mechanics of effective governance. Monitoring, surveillance, disclosure, standard-setting, binding principles, and objective evaluation techniques are among the methods of governance that have acquired an increasing regulatory aspect. One can govern as effectively by fine-tuning the classes of information required of an individual and providing consequences for the results of the evaluation thereof, as by the command of a statute.

This challenge to law suggests another – an institutional convergence in governance capacity. Developed states and the largest multinational corporations are closer in form and operation than either is to less developed states and smaller corporations. Larger corporations and developed states are then more likely to look to each other for governance harmonisation than either would look to developing states or smaller corporations. That, in turn, suggests a fundamental reorientation of governance chains grounded in a functional abandonment of the public-private distinction. The resulting polycentricism becomes a powerful governance force as the historical movement toward the assertion of near monopoly power by states within their territories is reversed under the operative framework of economic globalisation.

Opening borders to commerce and investment has a strong collateral effect on the extent of the empire of law as the operative instrument of the law-state. Open borders permit a disaggregation of citizenship from residence, especially among investors and their investments. It also produces a power in individuals to consent to membership in communities with its own rules and institutional structures, whose objectives and functions straddle multiple territorial borders. Law now finds itself in a competitive environment of a force unseen since the Enlightenment in Europe. On the one hand, the character of law within states in changing. On the other, new techniques of law-making and porous borders have increased the sources of governance. Law, like the state, has not so much been reduced in scope and power, as it has now come to share governance space with a host of different institutions producing distinct forms of command that may have some of the effects of traditional law but are not law (classically understood as a legitimate command sourced in the apparatus of a political state).

4. Toward a Mechanics of Relevance for National Legal Systems in the International Legal Order as a Whole

States need not embrace the passive virtues of the philosophy of *quietism*. Indeed, it is essential for each state to not merely rethink the basis of its legitimacy, form and function within its territory, but also to stake out a space for its positive contribution within emerging jurisdictional challenges posed by new governance frameworks, especially with respect to its areas of control. The great challenge for states is to find a way in which they might more actively engage in the processes of inter-systemic and vertical harmonisation without losing their fundamental character and democratic connection with their citizens. That requires a willingness to develop a domestic legal order that incorporates evolving international standards that are themselves a product of the active participation of states and other relevant stakeholders. This can work, for example, in the area of corporate governance, in standards for bribery, and in the regulation of conflict.

That task requires a number of actions. First, states must not pout. States that embrace insularity in the face of the emerging global polycentric governance orders, states that raise walls of domestic legal systems around the borders of their national territories (with the occasional extraterritorial foray) will, quite perversely, increase the ability and ease with which other regulatory actors might penetrate those barriers. The penetration would take advantage of the blindness of law-states to governance frameworks beyond the state, that is, they would take advantage of the limits inherent in the territorial borders that once served more positively as a means for asserting a monopoly of state power within them. Foreign multinational corporation regulation of host state suppliers through contract provisions with little connection to the domestic legal order of the host state, or the fidelity of host state actors to the requirements of foreign supra-national evaluation and standard setting bodies are examples of penetration that states would find difficult to prevent without foregoing those connections that are almost invariably essential to the well-being of its people.

Second, states and their domestic legal orders will have to engage polycentricism within their territories. That might require some flexibility in communicating with autonomous systems and a willingness to harmonise their domestic legal order with those of important parallel systems. This future is likely to be represented by the governance communication and harmonisation challenges faced recently by a multinational corporation in the mining business, which found itself in violation of the requirements of an autonomous international system of norms for the conduct of its subsidiary, operating a mine through a subsidiary jointly owned by it and a provincial government in the place where the mine was located, despite the fact that the highest national court had determined that the conduct at issue met all of the legal requirements imposed by the state in which that mine was located. States without sufficient points of contact with non-state governance systems will find themselves isolated and less in control of the activities that occur within their national territory.

Third, the complexities of governance, and the dispersion of governance authority pose institutional management problems for states. One of the greatest is what John Ruggie has called problems of incoherence. At the state level, incoherence denotes the failure of communication and coordination of policy and law-making among the various ministries and regulatory agencies of a state apparatus. The classic example is that of the South African Republic, whose negotiation of bi-lateral investment treaty provisions by one ministry did not take into account the requisites of human rights based policy being implemented by another ministry. The resulting conflicting obligations produced litigation to the detriment of state policy. At the international level, incoherence is more common and illustrated by the disjunction between the rules applicable within a state through domestic law and the international obligations of the state without direct domestic effect.

Fourth, states must avoid legal segmentation. In the context of nineteenth century global horizontal harmonisation, legal segmentation produced a harmonised law for elites driven by the state and a local traditionalist law/custom for everyone else. In places like Japan before 1945 this produced a tendency towards multiple domestic legal orders within a single territory. The same effects are sometimes exhibited in developing states subject to significant harmonisation pressure through their entanglements with the global financial community regulators – the International Monetary Fund and the World Bank. In the context of inter-systemic harmonisation, similar patterns produce a challenge of multiple domestic legal orders that harmonise rules applicable, at least functionally, to distinct segments of the national population. There is already evidence of this; China exhibits a tendency toward bifurcated labour markets depending on whether labour is hired for production within foreign dominated supply chains or domestic ones. Bi-lateral investment treaties create pockets of private law and rule-making with respect to which the domestic legal order may not play a decisive role.

Taken together, these strategies suggest in the briefest form, the contours of the challenges posed by inter-systemic harmonisation, and the dangers of resisting harmonisation among these governance frameworks of 'unequal' and distinctive governance organs – states, intergovernmental organisations, transnational private actors and multinational corporations and religions, to name only a few. States seek to remain effective and powerful autonomous actors. The expression of state power through law must remain vital. Yet these two objectives have become complicated in a world in which states, and law, no longer occupy the governance stage without competitors. States that can accommodate the new realities of power diffusion and governance variety – of corporations that regulate, of states that seek to project their power through traditionally private juridical persons (corporations, transnational public and private organisations, and sovereign investment funds), of functional law effectuated through survey, surveillance, disclosure, standards, conditional income support programs, supply chain relations, religious command and the like – are likely to be more effective actors within and without their territories than those who hide from these changes or resist them.

But the processes of inter-systemic harmonisation, like those of horizontal and vertical harmonisation, will neither be harmonious nor a rationally unfolding well-managed process compelled by the power of its internal coherence and its external incentives. The process will be messy and the results uneven. Vanguard states will become both more powerful internally and more influential within global governance communities; rejectionist states will seek to preserve traditional approaches in solidarity with like minded states but become, in the process, less relevant globally. An important factor determining the extent of conflict in moving to a world organised on principles of inter-systemic harmonisation, of course, and the effects of these transformations, are also largely dependent on variations in state power. The least developed and least powerful states (politically, culturally or economically) are likely to face these challenges in a more direct and consequential form than the largest or most powerful states. China and the United States can resist emerging trends longer, and reach accommodations with the products of such trends in ways which are impossible for the least developed African states. And indeed, in some ways, and though it seeks to turn the process to advance its own interests, China has already begun to move toward an inter-systemic harmonisation model more successfully than the United States. A most interesting set of challenges face states that are already deeply enmeshed in supra-national governance organisations. The Member States of the European Union have greater experience in the dynamics of cooperation within loosely bound normative structures. They also have experience in governance within diffuse governance frameworks in which power is shared among a number of stakeholders. Yet all of this diffusion remains confined to the state and its supra-national creatures. Much can be learned from the experience of Europe, though European states will have much to learn, as well, from the experiences of developing states that confront the power of transnational non-state governance. Inter-systemic harmonisation suggests the possibility that law might preserve its relevance and autonomy. But it can achieve this objective only by conceding its monopoly on governance.

5.2

Globalisation, Comparative Criminal Justice, and Diversity

David Nelken[*]

In this think piece, David Nelken examines some aspects of the likely future of national criminal justice systems as they are challenged by cross border crime and the rise of globalisation. He argues that a focus on 'common threats' and the defence of national borders too easily pushes to one side the implications of developing such a 'common' response for questions of difference and diversity between and within various criminal justice jurisdictions. Hence the need to bring together the study of comparative criminal justice and globalisation, as to have the tools to understand and try to shape the way the future unfolds.

1. Introduction

Cross-border crime is a phenomenon on the rise. At the same time, violations of human rights and international tribunals fundamentally change the way we think about the state as an isolated jurisdiction. How do legal institutions deal with the changing face of crime and criminals?

There may be some dissonance between the tasks of acting as neutral futurologists, or as prophets, seeking rather to change it. But I have the sense that many of those who try to describe the challenges in this (and perhaps many other) areas are actually seeking to change things, and often succeed in doing so, even when they present their analyses as dispassionate accounts of what is happening, or what is going to happen. My own approach to the question is to worry that this focus on a 'common threat' and the defence of national borders pushes aside the implications of developing such a 'common' response for questions of difference and diversity between and within various criminal justice jurisdictions too

[*] **David Nelken** is Distinguished Professor of Legal Institutions and Social Change at the University of Macerata in Italy and Distinguished Research Professor of Law at Cardiff University, UK.

easily.[1] Hence the need to bring the study of comparative criminal justice and globalisation together so as to have the tools to understand, and try to shape, the way the future unfolds.[2]

Certainly, the attempt to move towards a 'globalising' criminological perspective has the merit of bringing hitherto neglected crimes, including state crimes, into better focus. There are many collective problems – from those regarding the environment to those that have to do with financial security (do the threats from merchant banks constitute cross-border crimes?), that cannot be solved by states acting alone, as well as the many abuses suffered by individuals and groups which cannot safely be left to the responsible state to address. But the idea that 'a willing coalition of the good' is all that is needed to defeat these problems is overly simple. Even those seeking to fight various forms of criminal abuse may, in other relevant respects, have different (legitimate) interests and values. Thus the task is to move forward, bearing such differences in mind. It is this purpose which animates these notes.

2. Globalisation and Criminal Justice

A number of issues arise if we want to study the effects of globalisation on criminal justice. Some have to do with questions of classification – for example, the need to define globalisation in relation to trends such as late-modernity and neo-liberalism, Americanisation, Europeanisation, 'liquid modernity', the move to the 'network society' or the rise of the 'risk society'. Others are more descriptive and empirical. What is going on in the various spheres of society and criminal justice that globalisation is said to be affecting? Where are influential norms, scripts, ideas, practices and institutions coming from? Then there are explanatory questions – for example, can transnational policing be seen as part of the creation of a new world order (or of rival world orders)? Finally, there are evaluative questions, such as where should new ideas about criminal justice be taken

---

1 David Nelken, "The Globalisation of Crime and Criminal Justice: Prospects and Problems', in Michael Freeman (ed.), *Law and Opinion at the End of the twentieth century*, Oxford, Oxford University Press, 1997, pp. 251-279; David Nelken, "Criminology: Crime's Changing Boundaries", in Peter Cane and Mark Tushnet (eds.), *The Oxford Handbook of Legal Studies*, Oxford, Oxford University Press, 2003, pp. 250-270.

2 David Nelken, *Comparative Criminal Justice and Globalisation*, Ashgate, Aldershot, 2011.

from? How much should diversity be respected, why, by whom, and when?

As a consequence of the greater mobility of capital (sometimes, but not always, willingly embraced by states as a political neo-liberal choice) new forms of international interconnections grow at the expense of national or more local ones. 'Governance' increasingly replaces government, and power is increasingly shared with other transnational and private actors. Hence many key crime initiatives now link regional or local centres of power[3] or are delegated to the private sector. As globalisation increasingly blurs the differences between 'units', it also reshapes spaces, the meaning of place, and the location and significance of boundaries. It becomes increasingly difficult to distinguish the 'inside' from the 'outside'. New units emerge as objects and as agents of control; we can think for example of the internationalisation of policing or attempts by international courts of justice to enforce common minimum standards of conduct on states. The same applies to the increased blurring between war-making, peacekeeping and criminal justice. At the same time the use of cyberspace requires and generates a variety of forms of control, and may point to new (not necessarily utopian) forms of social ordering.

Globalisation's effects are not easily classified as either 'good' or 'bad' (also because globalisation can communicate the knowledge that can be used to help counteract its bad effects). In a Durkheimian view, changing forms of social and economic exchange both reflect and produce changing forms of 'moral' interdependence. Hence globalisation could contribute to a new international solidarity, as seen perhaps in the strengthening of international criminal justice and the increasing role (and rhetoric) of international human rights.[4] Even within their own national law, countries now penalise sex tourism committed by their citizens abroad as well as seeking to stop human trafficking to their own shores. On the other hand, from a neo-Marxist perspective, globalised exchange is too often itself a form of disguised exploitation; businesses and others find ways to avoid criminal penalties in the 'space between the laws'

---

3 Adam Edwards and Gordon Hughes, "Comparing the Governance of Safety in Europe", in *Theoretical Criminology*, 2005, vol. 9, no. 3, pp. 345-363.

4 David Nelken, "Corruption and Human Rights: An Afterword", in Hans Nelen and Martine Boersma (eds.), *Corruption and Human Rights,* Intersentia, Antwerp, 2010.

whilst international bodies impose financial straightjackets as the price for loans.

Some writers try to distinguish between hegemonic or counter-hegemonic globalisation (or between globalisation 'from above' or ' from below') but, in practice, it can be difficult to find fail-safe criteria for picking and choosing what is 'progressive' or not, and we must remember that intentions and outcomes often do not coincide. Any given international blueprint or 'global prescription' can have contradictory effects. The promotion of transparency as urged by Transparency International would seem to be an appropriate panacea for corruption. But closer familiarity with the phenomenon in specific contexts shows that transparency also has the effect of entrenching it – the more that is known about the use of underhand methods, the more others may feel they have to do the same.[5] The extension of human rights is a largely positive development, especially for the protection of women and other vulnerable groups. But, in the sphere of youth justice, globalisation spreads both an often-harsh insistence on greater responsibility as well as a concern to protect rights.[6]

The fight against transnational organised crime and against cross-border crime generally (which is not limited to such actors) provides a good example of these points. On the one hand, there are a variety of extremely serious harms committed by such groups. But for almost every one of their activities there are at least two narratives that can be told. One stresses the noble fight of the state and/or relevant Inter-Governmental and Non-Governmental Organisations,[7] the other the extent to which controllers selectively exploit the problems of given victim groups for their own interests.[8] The way such threats are characterised often tells us more about political and law enforcement stereotypes than it does about their fluid and changing nature. The repeated scare claim – that criminal justice

---

5 David Nelken, "Corruption as Governance", in Keebet von Benda-Beckmann and Julia Eckert Franz von Benda-Beckmann (eds.), *Rules of Law, Laws of Ruling*, Ashgate, Aldershot, 2009, pp. 275-295.

6 John Muncie, "The Globalisation of Crime Control – The Case of Youth and Juvenile Justice: Neo-liberalism, Policy Convergence and International Conventions", in *Theoretical Criminology*, 2005, vol. 9, no. 1, pp. 35-64.

7 Moses Naim, *Illicit: How Smugglers Traffickers and Copycats Are Hijacking the Global Economy*, Arrow Books, 2005.

8 Willem Van Schendel and Itty Abraham (eds.), *Illicit Flows and Criminal Things*, Indiana University Press, Bloomington, 2005.

is territorial whereas organised crime is not confined by national boundaries – tends to exaggerate the degree of collaboration between such groups and to underplay the growth of official responses. The best work on 'mafias on the move' points out how very rare it is for organised criminal groups to abandon their own localities.[9]

3. Studying the Spread of Criminal Justice Blueprints

Assuming that we are looking for a common response, where do shared recipes come from?[10] There is an increasing recognition that the globalisation of the 'local' depends on the localisation of the (supposedly) global, that it is not just a matter of impersonal macro-social forces but also involves the various agents who bring it about. But there is still little agreement on how best to study these processes. We need to study *what* is being spread – scripts, norms, institutions, technologies, fears, ways of seeing, problems, solutions, new forms of policing, punitiveness, conceptual legal innovations such as the 'the law of the enemy', mediation, restitutive or therapeutic justice. We can also ask from where to where, *e.g.*, from or to national, sub-national and supra-national levels in Europe, or more widely, or by agreement amongst signatories to conventions etc., or those subject to regulatory networks, for example. It takes little skill to discover that what purports to be global frequently comes out of the USA, but members of the European Union, amongst others, are also quite actively involved, singly and collectively.

We need to take a broad view of who is involved. The key actors may not only be legal ones such as judges, lawyers, police, probation officers and prison officers (often through meeting colleagues from abroad). They may also be representatives of businesses such as security providers or those who build and run private prisons. And they include politicians, NGOs or pressure groups, regulatory bodies, journalists, and even academics themselves. Attention needs to be given to the role of institutions, singly, collectively or in competition. In Europe, but also beyond it, the EU institutions, the Council of Europe and the EHRC system are im-

[9] Federico Varese, *Mafias on the Move*, Princeton University Press, Princeton, forthcoing.

[10] Tim Newburn and Richard Sparks, *Criminal Justice and Political Cultures: National and International Dimensions of Crime Control*, Willan, Cullhompton, 2004, pp. 80-103.

portant players. The same crime threat may call forth responses from a variety of intergovernmental and non-governmental organisations, such as the UN commissioner for rights, the International Labour Organisation, or the International Organisation for Migration, Human rights watch, Amnesty, etc.

Another set of questions has to do with the means by which criminal justice ideas and practices are being spread. Some exchanges may involve groups of 'experts'; others only concern 'virtual' conversations, as in the way judges read sentences in other jurisdictions as they seek to provide justifications of local practices such as the retention or abolition of the death penalty.[11] Why do various initiatives follow given circuits? How is it that a given practice, such as adversarial justice, can spread so well abroad even whilst it is being greatly criticised in its home countries? What are the implications of the fact that local agents and institutions often try to use their global influence locally as a source of prestige in competition with other actors. Where are certain things appealing where they are? What explains why day fines and conditional dismissals make sense only in some places in Europe? Are there some approaches that everyone wants? Tonry argues that "technology is a no-brainer" and mentions prison security equipment, credit card smart technologies, and electronic monitoring as examples.[12] However, apparently even technical approaches, such as the move to 'actuarial justice', can produce quiet revolutions within the field of criminal justice. What counts as 'only' a technical matter will also vary culturally.

Finally, we also need to reflect on what succeeds and what is meant by success. Who decides what the indicators of 'success' are, and whose claims get to be believed concerning what is supposed to happen, and what has in fact happened? Who gets to impose their sense of continuing similarity and difference, and its significance? Can a society get more

[11] Roger Hood, "The Death Penalty: A Worldwide Perspective", in *Punishment and Society*, 2001, vol. 3, pp. 331-354; Robert Macrudden, "Judicial Comparativism and Human Rights", in Esin Orucu and David Nelken (eds.), *Comparative Law: A Handbook,* Hart, Oxford, 2007, p. 371; and David Johnson and Frank Zimring, *The Next Frontier? National Development, Human Rights, and the Death Penalty in Asia*, Oxford University Press, New York, 2009.

[12] Michael Tonry, "Symbol, Substance, and Severity in Western Penal Policies", in *Punishment and Society*, 2009, vol. 3, no. 4, p. 517.

than it bargained for?[13] Discussions of the spread of criminal justice ideas and practices sometimes confuse explaining whether a certain model has spread successfully and whether this is a good thing. We are likely to be told that 'zero tolerance' ideas that have not changed practices on the ground are merely 'symbolic'.[14] On the other hand, if human rights ideas begin to change the local discourse (or add a new layer to it) as in the case of conventions dealing with violence against women even if they do not change (other) practice on the ground, this may nonetheless be counted as success.[15]

4. Towards a Common Criminal Justice?

For a long time – even within the sphere of the European Union – politicians and judges defended the distinctive features of their criminal law procedures, and only a few academics argued for a more common approach. Although there was some debate about the possibilities and merits of harmonising private law (especially within the EU) discussion of this key question in the area of criminal law was desultory. More recently, however, there has been a change of heart, largely attributable to the threat of transnational crimes – first regarding frauds against European Union finances, then terrorism and other serious crimes, as well as continuing concerns over irregular immigration. Within the European Union there has been some progress in creating shared policing and prosecuting institutions, and not only where this helps protect the European Union's own funds. The European Court of Human Rights strives to arrive at some minimal standards in penal procedures, prisoners' rights and similar matters. But the debate is still very patchy. The most heated question in current comparative criminology is why, in so many countries, prison rates have risen over a period in which crime rates have actually been falling. But those scholars who advocate a move to the adversarial system make

[13] Jim L. Nolan, *Legal Accents, Legal Borrowing: The International Problem-solving Court Movement*, Princeton University Press, Princeton, 2009.

[14] David Nelken, "Normalising Time: European Integration and Court Delays in Italy", in Hanne Petersen, Helle Krunke, Anne-Lise Kjær and Mikael Rask Madsen (eds.), *Paradoxes of European Legal Integration*, Ashgate, Aldershot, 2008, pp. 299-323.

[15] Sally E. Merry, *Human Rights and Gender Violence: Translating International Law into Local Justice*, University of Chicago Press, Chicago, 2006.

no reference to this issue[16] even though it is countries with this type of system who tend to incarcerate the highest number of offenders.

Does the spreading of ideas and practices encouraged by globalisation in fact reduce differences amongst systems of criminal justice? To examine this question, it is useful to distinguish amongst processes of convergence, copying and collaborating. Political and economic convergence can bring about similarities even where this is not the aim. Copying, by contrast, is an example of actively seeking similarity through borrowing or imitation. Collaborating, finally, involves trying to understand what others are doing so as to facilitate coordinated action, even if we do not necessarily want to copy them. Convergence has both objective and subjective aspects. Although technological and other changes can reflect and produce the need for similarity, it is also important to see (contrary to much writing on the subject) that globalisation and homogenisation do not always go together.[17] In its economic aspects, globalisation relies on and often reproduces economic and social differentiation, and neo-liberalism too is compatible with socio-cultural differences between places (these can even be marketed). Cyberspace has lent itself not only to efforts to transcend boundaries of place and tradition but it is also used by those who seek to create tightly bounded groups united by hate of those with different identities At the subjective level, the spread of globalising common sense means that distant forces penetrate local worlds and that local meanings are often dislodged. People in Germany fed on television episodes of Perry Mason assumed that they too had an adversarial system of criminal justice.

Researchers differ about how easy it is to deliberately bring about similarity. Jones and Newburn, for example, examined the outcomes of efforts in England and Wales to introduce the USA's practices regarding private prisons, 'three strikes and you're out' sentencing reform, and zero tolerance policing. The authors saw themselves as trying to reconcile "insights coming from the broad global/convergence and local divergence vantage points".[18] Although they found clear evidence of borrowing taking place, they concluded that this has made relatively little difference in

[16] Richard Vogler, *A World View of Criminal Justice*, Ashgate, Aldershot, 2005.

[17] Nelken, 1997, see *supra* note 1.

[18] Trevor Jones and Tim Newburn, "Policy Transfer and Criminal Justice", Open University Press, 2008, p. 8.

practice. By contrast, another recent description of the transplanting of US-style institutions comes to a somewhat different conclusion. In his excellent account of the introduction to American-type problem solving courts in five other common law jurisdictions, Nolan stresses how much was successfully transplanted. His concern if anything is that such borrowing will eventually bring about some penetration of wider aspects of American culture in societies that are purportedly somewhat critical of it.[19]

Many studies of collaboration in criminal justice worry about who is in charge and where it may lead. But they spend less time in discussing how it is even possible. Jacqueline Ross argues that champions of closer transnational cooperation may be too quick to envision it as occurring through a sequence of technical fixes. In a series of richly detailed analyses, she shows the considerable theoretical difficulties faced by those she interviewed when seeking to bring their own working practices into alignment with those that belong to other systems of criminal justice.[20] In particular, she focuses on the significance of cooperation in the battle against transnational crime and the fact that the United States and European nations conceptualise, legitimate and control undercover policing in substantially dissimilar ways. Ross tells us that covert operations are controversial everywhere but that this may not always be for the same reason. In comparing American and Italian ways of formulating the issue, she argues that whereas Americans primarily worry that covert agents may corrupt innocuous targets, Italians are especially concerned that covert operations may slide into state- sanctioned lawlessness.

As this suggests, comparative criminal justice comes into its own wherever the local sense of a given global initiative or script needs to be deconstructed. International human rights standards are hammered out over years of negotiation so as to find phrasings that satisfy representatives of different countries and NGOs. But diversity remerges in the way that such agreements are implemented. For example, the Palermo Protocol against human trafficking ('the new slavery' for sexual, child or labour exploitation) has been signed and ratified by a very large number of coun-

---

19 Nolan, 2009, see *supra* note 13.

20 Jaqueline E. Ross, "The Place of Covert Policing in Democratic Societies: A Comparative Study of the United States and Germany", in *American Journal of Comparative Law*, 2004, vol. 55, p. 493.

tries. The Protocol has increased the possibility of providing relief to unwilling victims of trafficking. But what is at stake in this campaign is not the same for supply, transit and demand countries (or for political elites, employers, workers and others) and the way in which individual countries use the protocol is shaped by their specific political, cultural and other differences.[21] Supply countries have a desperate need for the economic remittances of their migrants. Churches in some places in Nigeria pray for the success of those who go abroad so as to earn remittances through some form of prostitution. Amongst demand countries, Sweden is engaged in an effort to reduce prostitution and makes little or no use of the Palermo Protocol. Germany and the Netherlands are more concerned about having well regulated systems of sex work. The USA operates sanctions against countries it classifies as being reluctant to stop trafficking, but has learned to live with millions of unregistered Mexican migrants. In the economically advanced (demand) countries the needs of victims continue to be subordinated to the goal of ending illegal migration.[22]

5. Respecting and Learning from Difference

In addition to the many descriptive, explanatory and interpretive issues raised by the cross-national spread of criminal justice ideas and practices, there are also value questions of what this spreading does, could do or should do to diversity. Increasingly, the question of diversity between cultures overlaps with that of respecting diversity within a society. If units are less and less distinguishable, this is in part also because of population movements. The many young female judges in the Italian courts increasingly find themselves processing (usually by fast track procedures for those caught *en flagrante*) young Muslim offenders disproportionately to the number of such immigrants in Italy. On the wall hangs a crucifix. The legend inscribed over the bench reads that "the law is equal for all". But this may not be the way it is perceived. What aspects of this everyday situation, if any, should be treated as requiring more respect for diversity? As diasporic communities grow larger and more confident, the question arises as to what extent nation- states should explicitly delegate powers of

---

[21] Vanessa Munro, "Stopping Traffic? A Comparative Study of Responses to the Trafficking in Women for Prostitution", in *British Journal of Criminology*, 2006, vol. 46, no. 2, pp. 318-333.

[22] Nelken, 2009, see *supra* note 5.

conflict-processing to them. The periodic discussion of the wearing of veils is a distraction from this underlying dilemma.

More generally, should we see the reduction of diversity, insofar as it can be achieved, as progress or as a problem? So much of course depends on what is at issue: the decline in use of the death penalty, the elimination of torture, the setting of minimal standards for prisoners. Or are we speaking of sharing common definitions of corruption or ideas of how criminal procedures should be organised? It is important to ask how far the Strasbourg Court of Human Rights is imposing 'universal' criminal procedure principles of good practice on the signatories to the convention it enforces, and how far – as in imposing limits on acceptable court delays – it is (also) involved in a process of 'normalisation' towards a European average.[23] Why are trials that are too short in the sense that they are well below the average time devoted to trial in comparable places not also considered a breach of human rights? Is it right to threaten Italy with exclusion from the European Convention on Human Rights for conduct which follows from the fact that it is an outlier? The only other signatory treated in this way is Turkey, for its failure to comply over Cyprus and its continuing maltreatment of the Kurds. Italian court times do create suffering. Justice delayed is, too often, justice denied. But it is questionable whether excessive court delay is the same sort of breach of human rights as torture.

The author of a recent introduction to comparative criminal justice offers the following reflections by way of conclusion to his book: "Globalisation will diminish the variety of criminal justice systems. Common threats will invite common responses, which will increase the similarities in criminal justice systems around the world".[24] He goes on to say that "on the one hand, this could be seen as a loss", but on the other hand, "criminal justice systems are not like the natural world, where we should celebrate diversity for its own sake. Increased requirements for communication and harmonisation provide rewards for convergence, and criminal justice systems will, after all, be judged on their effectiveness. In any case, he concludes, 'one can remain sure that as long as cultures, lan-

[23] Nelken, 2008, pp. 299-323, see *supra* note 14.

[24] Francis Pakes, *Comparative Criminal Justice*, Willan, Cullhompton, 2004, p. 178.

guages, public opinions and social discourses differ, so will criminal justice systems and the way they operate".[25]

These remarks, thoughtful as they are, also beg a number of questions. Is there really no reason to value diversity for its own sake once we recognise that criminal justice systems are not part of the natural world? What of the benefits of maintaining a variety of forms of social experimentation? What of the need for procedure to fit society's values and its traditions? What if the greater homogeneity that emerges – through the imitation or imposition of the currently successful Anglo-American model – reflects and produces the sort of society that requires a high level of punishment? Familiarity with the differences amongst criminal justice systems should make us cautious about the claim that systems of criminal justice will "after all be judged on their effectiveness". Who will be (who should be?) the judge of effectiveness? It is not enough to say that 'the balance between fairness and effectiveness' will be worked out differently in different places – the issue is rather whether the meaning of these terms stays the same and how far the metaphor of 'balancing these ' values' is shared cross-culturally. The plea I would make is to try and learn from difference.[26] The difficulty is how to do this.

Many practices that work locally will not 'travel well'. It is hard to imagine many other places copying the Japanese in seeking to reform a rapist by telling him to write a *haiku*.[27] But the need to give attention to the local and the particular does not mean that we cannot talk about 'best practice' as evaluated according to widely shared standards. And, even if considerable caution needs to be used in interpreting cross-national ratings, some places may be doing better or worse in terms of such standards. If one in ten children in Denmark who grow up in local government care go on to further education, whereas in the UK only one in a hundred does so, then we would do well to try to learn why.

Yet comparative research should not be treated only as a means of identifying best practices to be adopted wholesale, but also as an opportunity to reflect on our own practices and values in the light of what others do. Other places' practices can be a potential resource for this without

[25] Pakes, 2004, p. 178, see *supra* note 24.

[26] David Nelken, *Comparative Criminal Justice: Making Sense of Difference*, Sage, London, 2010.

[27] David Johnson, *The Japanese Way of Justice*, Oxford University Press, Oxford, 2000.

hypothesising that the problems or solutions are necessarily universal. We can learn from what happens elsewhere so as to engage in 'internal critique' according to our own standards. Those in the common law systems could learn that paying more attention to 'due process' considerations could even help achieve the goal of 'crime control' (by increasing legitimacy, public confidence and cooperation). Conversely, strengthening the role of defence lawyers in the French system could help increase the chances of the truth emerging from the process – a key value in that system. As important, the best practice for 'us' to learn from may not always be best practice as such, but rather that which stretches our imagination about what is possible. For example, it may seem obvious to many observers of Italy (as well as to some Italians) that the Italian criminal justice system could benefit from increased pragmatism and perhaps even from some much dreaded managerialism. But vice-versa, Italy may have something important to teach more pragmatic countries about possible counter productive consequences of too much concern for 'efficiency' in their penal systems. The Italian juvenile system may seem to Anglo American eyes leisurely for our circumstances. However, in England and Wales, the government's recent stress on dealing with caseloads more expeditiously led to a substantial rise in youth custody, in contradiction with its general commitment to reduce this number. The problem, at least, is unlikely to arise in Italy's juvenile justice system. Moving a little nearer to what we would otherwise never normally think of doing may be just what we need to re-evaluate our own priorities.

5.3

The Impossible Necessity of European Labour Law

Hugh Collins*

When the EC/EU was founded, it was believed that it would be unnecessary in the common market to regulate labour relations at the federal level, and also politically very difficult because each country had established a delicate legal balance between the interests of capital, labour, and government (the taxpayer). But this arrangement is probably no longer possible because of the free market in services and the growth of the service economy. Creating an EU labour law that balances the relative interests of the groups could present the EU with its greatest challenge so far, not just because it is politically controversial (both in the sense that the rules will be disputed and in the sense that many will dispute that the EU has a role at all), but also because it is doubtful that common rules would be suitable for the variety of capitalist institutional arrangements in the different countries, particularly the divergence between the corporatists arrangements of Germany and Scandinavia, on the one hand, and the more liberal market approach in the UK. But the EU would be well advised not to go down the route of the USA and its federal labour law for a number of reasons – the uniform straightjacket has atrophied employment law, failed to adapt to a service economy, and also failed (as the recent health reform problems demonstrated) to join up labour market regulation with the development of a welfare system. So the EU needs to find some paradoxical solution which both achieves a uniform federal solution but at the same time is sensitive to local difference and capable of evolution. No easy task.

1. Introduction

What does the future hold for labour law in the European Union? What role will the European Union, as opposed to its Member States, play in regulating labour markets and employment relations? In the European Union (EU), and perhaps in other regional economic blocs, will labour

* **Hugh Collins** is Professor of English Law at the London School of Economics.

law become transnational law? If so, what will be its aims, institutions, and regulatory methods?

My exploratory answer to these questions in this paper describes labour law in the European Union as an 'impossible necessity'. A number of reasons are advanced for believing that transnational labour law will be absolutely necessary in Europe. Indeed, steps in this direction of the construction of a transnational labour law system can already be observed. At the same time, however, other reasons are advanced for believing that transnational labour law will prove impossible to achieve in Europe. The essay concludes by assessing what routes out of this paradox may be available and seem likely to occur.

2. Regulatory Competition

When the EU was founded (as the Common Market), an official report that influenced the content of the Treaty of Rome argued that it would be unnecessary and undesirable to regulate labour relations at the transnational level.[1] The removal of barriers to trade would prevent the Member States from protecting inefficient industries by customs tariffs. In the short term, this measure would lead to restructuring of businesses in the face of international competitive pressures; but in the longer term, businesses would either have to improve their productive efficiency (in the sense of cost per unit of production), or the pressure of competitive market forces would revise the international division of labour, so that countries would specialise in different goods and services according their comparative advantage based on productive efficiency. Such improvements in productivity, it was believed, would lead to higher living standards throughout the Community. On this view, natural selection, or an invisible hand, would result in a rise in average living standards for everyone, without the need for intervention at a transnational level, with the

[1] The Spaak report was largely based on the Ohlin Report of the ILO. See Paul-Henri Spaak, *Rapport des Chefs de Délégation aux Ministres des Affaires Etrangères*, Comité Intergouvernemental Créé par la Conference de Messine, 1956, ("Spaak Report"); International Labour Organization, "Social Aspects of European Economic Co-operation", in *International Labour Review*, 1956, vol. 74, p. 99-123; see also Simon Deakin, "Labour Law as Market Regulation: the Economic Foundations of European Social Policy" in P. Davies, A. Lyon-Caen, S. Sciarra, and S. Simities (eds.), in *European Community Labour Law: Principles and Perspectives*, Oxford University Press, Oxford, 1996, p. 63.

possible exception of aid to regions adversely affected during transition periods. Article 151 of the Treaty on the Functioning of the European Union (TFEU) still expresses with confidence the proposition that the improvement in living standards 'will ensue' from the operation of the internal market, though it also acknowledges the possibility of a need for harmonisation of laws.

At the time, the only significant exception to this legal abstentionism with regard to labour law was the provision in the Treaty on equal pay.[2] This exception requiring equal pay for women was justified on the ground that, in industries that were predominantly staffed by women, a major disparity in wages between the sexes might give one country a competitive advantage over another where women were paid equally. In such a case, the competitive pressures generated by the internal market might function to reinforce the sex discrimination in wages. This outcome was regarded as both a 'distortion' in competition and 'unfair' competition, which should be eliminated at the transnational level in the Treaty. Later on, of course, equal pay was repackaged by the Court of Justice, not as a rule about unfair competition, but rather as a social policy and eventually as a fundamental human right.[3]

The problem with the original acknowledgement of this exceptional case of unfair competition, however, is that, like the thin end of a wedge, the economic reasoning has the potential to undermine altogether legal abstentionism in labour law at the transnational level. For instance, if one country has a law that limits working hours to 40 per week, but another lacks any controls over working hours, the latter country might be able to survive in the bracing waters of the competitive internal market by simply making employees work for longer and longer hours each week with no increase in wages. The identical argument might be made with respect to wages – the lowering of wages can protect businesses against foreign competition. Indeed, much the same argument may be applied to all employment laws: assuming such employment protection laws impose some costs on employers, productivity can be improved by deregulation.

---

[2] Treaty on the Functioning of the European Union as amended by the Treaty of Lisbon, 1 December 2009, Article 157.

[3] See Court of Justice of the European Union, *Defrenne v. Sabena*, Case C-43/75, Judgment, 8 April 1976, ECR I-455; *Deutsche Post AG v. Sievers and Schrage*, Joined Cases C-270/97 and C-271/97, Judgment, 10 February 2000, ECR I-929.

Here we encounter the theory of regulatory competition and the hypothesis that nation states will engage in a race to lower standards in social regulation in order to enhance the international competitiveness of their national businesses.[4] Responses to the danger of the race to the bottom in regulatory standards between national legal systems could comprise either uniform laws or minimum standards at a transnational or international level. In its Directives, the European Union has so far opted for the latter – minimum standards rather than a level playing field in labour law (full harmonisation or federal pre-emption). In so far as these Directives are designed to impose similar costs on businesses, thereby diminishing the advantages derived from lighter regulation, they prevent a race to the very bottom, though the transnational standards are likely to be set at a minimal level, and there may be pressure on both courts and national legislatures to level down national laws towards the minimum. In any event, unless we are prepared to tolerate the gradual diminution of protective employment law, the dangers of regulatory competition appear to render European labour law a necessity.

3. Pluralist Settlements

Federal or transnational labour law in Europe is also very difficult to accomplish politically. During the twentieth century, each country established a delicate legal balance between the interests of capital, labour, and government (the taxpayer). Though not fixed in their details, through a mixture of legislation and collective agreements each nation established the rules and institutional mechanisms of labour law, which created settled expectations for the framework of rules surrounding the relations of production. The interests of labour, including those of trade unions, were firmly entrenched by codes, legislation, judicial decisions and conventional practices. In particular, collective bargaining between unions and employers was accepted in the twentieth century as a normal framework for setting wages and other terms and conditions of employment, either at a local firm level, or by sector, or even, in smaller countries, as part of a national economic settlement. Only bold politicians would seek to chal-

[4] Not everyone accepts the validity of the race to the bottom hypothesis. But in my view, once one moves beyond core or basic standards, such as the move from a minimum wage to a collectively agreed standard living wage, international competitive pressures do become troublesome. Brian A. Langille, "What is International Labor Law for?", in *Law and Ethics of Human Rights*, 2009, vol. 3, no. 1.

lenge these settled legal frameworks, and even then their national initiatives had more bark than bite. Reconstructing these diverse and embedded labour law systems was a task that seemed well beyond the political capabilities of the institutions of the European Union.

The highly sensitive nature of some of these labour law issues is evidenced in the TFEU. Article 153(5) excludes the legislative competence of the EU from "pay, the right of association, the right to strike or the right to impose lock-outs". This exclusion served to protect the political settlements found in national labour systems on the rules of conflict between organised labour and capital, including the processes governing recognition of trade unions, collective bargaining, and industrial action. Other significant matters may only be regulated under Article 153 where there is unanimity among the Member States: protection of workers where their employment contract is terminated; representation and collective defence of interests by workers or employers; and conditions of employment for legal non-EU migrant workers. The breadth of these exclusions from the powers of the EU has forced EU law to the periphery of national systems. It does not regulate collective bargaining, though directives require some kind of consultation with representatives of the workforce in the event of restructuring of the business involving mass dismissals or a sale of the business.[5] The majority voting system applicable to proposed laws on 'working conditions' and 'health and safety' under Article 153 enabled the EU to enact some more comprehensive individual employment rights, as in the example of the Directive on working time,[6] but even in such fields the Member States have been unwilling to agree to a comprehensive floor of rights. The path-dependency of labour law on the earlier pluralist settlements between capital and labour often renders it impossible to secure agreement upon transnational labour law standards in Europe.

Reaching an agreement on a common EU labour law that balances the demands of capital, labour, and other interests presents the EU with its

[5] Council Directive 2001/23/EC of 12 March 2001 on the approximation of the laws of the Member States relating to the safeguarding of employees' rights in the event of transfers of undertakings, businesses or parts of undertakings or businesses; Council Directive 98/59/EC of 20 July 1998 on the approximation of the laws of the Member States relating to collective redundancies.

[6] Directive 2003/88/EC of the European Parliament and of the Council of 4 November 2003 concerning certain aspects of the organisation of working time.

greatest challenge so far, not just because it is politically controversial (both in the sense that the rules will be disputed and in the sense that many will dispute that the EU has a role at all), but also because it is doubtful that common rules would be suitable for the variety of capitalist institutional arrangements in the different countries, particularly with respect to the divergence between the more corporatist arrangements of Germany and Scandinavia on the one hand, and the more liberal market approach in the UK on the other.[7] Labour law systems are embedded in formal and informal institutional patterns that constrain permissible forms of economic activity, including the type and content of transactions in the labour market. As a shorthand expression, these institutional structures, which encompass the operations of the welfare state as well as labour market regulation, can be described as aspects of the 'European Social Model'. It seems likely that those corporatist arrangements in some European countries that rely upon an extensive bundle of legal rights and obligations to achieve protections for both individual workers and trade unions have come under pressure from competitive markets to deregulate labour relations and to permit non-standard work to proliferate.[8] But even if these competitive pressures have caused a degree of convergence of the national labour law systems towards the liberal Anglo-Saxon model, this change will not necessarily lead the political representatives of those countries to welcome laws that embody more liberal market models and diminish the political and economic role of trade unions and collective bargaining. There have been many occasions in the history of legislative enactments at the EU level where agreement on a comprehensive measure is either blocked because of the radical differences between labour markets and practices, or is achieved only at the price of watering down the

7 Peter A. Hall and David Soskice (eds), *Varieties of Capitalism: the Institutional Foundations of Comparative Advantage*, Oxford University Press, Oxford, 2001; Gøsta Esping-Andersen, *The Three Worlds of Welfare Capitalism*, Princeton University Press, Princeton, 1990.

8 The empirical picture is complicated because whilst marginal and vulnerable workers may be progressively excluded from legal protections, at the same time core workers may enjoy improved benefits and better legal protections, as in the case of Italy: see Marco Michelotti and Chris Nyland, "Varieties of Capitalism and Diversity in Labour Standards Regulation: The Case of Italy" in *European Journal of Industrial Relations*, 2008, vol. 14, no. 2, pp. 177-195. See also Wolfgang Streeck, *Re-Forming Capitalism: Institutional Change in the German Political Economy*, Oxford University Press, Oxford, 2009.

measure through opt-outs and the like. If transnational labour law in the EU must rest on some degree of consensus, it seems impossible to achieve.

4. The Inevitable Accident of EU Labour Law

The above arguments explain why important aspects of labour law, especially collective bargaining and industrial action, are absent from European law. But the next point explains, paradoxically, how European labour law is inevitable and has already emerged in a tentative form. Indeed, strains on the embargo in the Treaty on addressing labour law have always been evident and appear inevitable. Within the Treaties themselves, there are two well documented tensions.

First, the Treaty prohibits cartels that affect inter-state trade, but does not mention any exception for the actions of trade unions. The Court of Justice has had to create an exception,[9] but its scope in relation to collective bargaining remains uncertain, because it will depend upon the application of a test of proportionality in which normal collective bargaining serves a legitimate purpose, but may still amount to an unnecessary and inappropriate interference with cross-border trade.

Second, the market freedoms enshrined in the Treaty, which protect free movement of goods, services, and capital, will inevitably come into conflict from time to time with the actions of organised trade unions. The union may blockade the free movement of goods by picketing;[10] or it may use industrial action to prevent an employer from entering or keeping a contract with a provider of services that does not comply with the collectively bargained rates of pay applicable to that economic sector or region;[11] or the union may use industrial action to try to prevent the em-

[9] Court of Justice of the European Union, *Albany International BV v. Stichting Bedrijfspensioenfonds Textielindustrie*, Case C-67/96, Judgment, 21 September 1999, ECR I-5751.

[10] Court of Justice of the European Union, *Eugen Schmidberger, Internationale Transporte und Planzüge v. Republik Österreich*, Case C-112/00, Judgment, 12 June 2003, ECR I-5659.

[11] Court of Justice of the European Union, *Laval un Partneri Ltd v. Svenska Byggnadsarbetareförbundet, Svenska Byggnadsarbetareförbundets avd. 1, Byggettan, Svenska Elektrikerförbundet*, Case C-341/05, Judgment, 18 December 2007, ECR I-11767; See also Court of Justice of the European Union, *Dirk Rüffert v. Land Niedersachsen*, Case C-346/06, Judgment, 3 April 2008, ECR I-01989.

ployer from relocating the seat of its business to another Member State.[12] All such forms of industrial action will interfere with the directly effective market freedoms in the Treaty. To be lawful, the union must seek to justify the industrial action by reference to an important public policy under a test of proportionality. It cannot rely on the legality of the action under national labour law as its justification for breaching a fundamental market freedom.

Owing to the growth of employment in services as opposed to industry, this problem of the accidental, but inevitable, development of EU labour law has become more apparent. In the industrial sector of the economy, any cross-border element that provokes the supervision of the EU normally concerns only the free movement of goods. Any flashpoint between EU law and national labour law is confined to the legality of blockades of goods passing between countries. Embargoes on foreign imports enforced by industrial action are likely to be unlawful under national law already, though of course the willingness of the national authorities to intervene may vary according to the political circumstances. In the services sector, in contrast, a wider range of labour law issues may arise in connection with cross-border trade. An employer and its employees can easily be located in different countries, and the workers can move from one country to another in order to provide the services of the employer's business (*e.g.*, construction), and the employer can also move the seat of its business (*e.g.*, flag of convenience for ships) in order to obtain tax benefits, corporate law advantages, or efficiency savings stemming from reduced costs arising from compliance with employment law. The growth in Europe of the service sector as a proportion of the economy necessarily augments the frequency of cross-border labour, disputes that threaten an infringement of market freedoms, which in turn increases the need for EU regulation of labour disputes.

These tensions between labour law, on the one hand, and market freedoms and competition law on the other, exist within national legal systems themselves. The national labour law systems provide rules for reconciling these conflicting objectives. Typically, a trade union will be regarded as a cartel that is permitted on grounds of public policy, provid-

---

[12] Court of Justice of the European Union, *C-438/05 International Transport Workers' Federation and Finnish Seamen's Union v Viking Line ABP and OÜ Viking Line Eesti*, Judgment, 11 December 2007 [reported at 2008], ICR 741.

ed that it acts in an approved manner, according to prescribed processes, and for approved purposes. The problem now is that EU law has rules on competition and market freedoms, but no settled rules on when and how organised labour can act within a permitted exception.[13] In the EU, the Court of Justice is left to fend for itself, relying on vague provisions in the Treaty that acknowledge the importance to be attached to the rights of organised labour, but which fail to specify in any detail the scope and application of those rights. For instance, Article 151 links the social policy of the EU to two Charters of workers' rights,[14] but 'having in mind' these Charters surely provides sparse guidance on important practical questions about when an employer must recognise and bargain with a union, when an employer must comply with collective agreements, when industrial action is lawful, and what protections strikers should receive against retaliatory action. In effect, the Court of Justice has to write EU labour law, without a clear mandate – indeed, it should be recalled that many of these issues technically fall outside the competence of the EU – and without determinate criteria. In short, EU labour law is both necessary in practice, but being outside the Treaties' definitions of the competences of the EU, it is also impossible.

5. Private International Law?

Can the application of private international law solve the above problems, thereby removing the need for transnational labour law in the EU? In principle, the employer and employee may choose the law applicable to

[13] Fritz A. Scharpf, "The Asymmetry of European Integration, or Why the EU cannot be a 'Social Market Economy'" in *Socio-Economic Review*, 2010, vol. 8, no. 2, pp. 211-250.

[14] Consolidated Version of the Treaty on the Functioning of the European Union as amended by the Treaty of Lisbon, 1 December 2009, Article 151: "The Union and the Member States, having in mind fundamental social rights such as those set out in the European Social Charter signed at Turin on 18 October 1961 and in the 1989 Community Charter of the Fundamental Social Rights of Workers, shall have as their objectives the promotion of employment, improved living and working conditions, so as to make possible their harmonisation while the improvement is being maintained, proper social protection, dialogue between management and labour, the development of human resources with a view to lasting high employment and the combating of exclusion".

the contract of employment. Under the Rome 1 Regulation,[15] Article 8, when an employee is directed to work in a foreign country, the parties may agree that either the home state law or the host state law should be applicable. However, Article 8 does not permit a choice of law that deprives the worker of mandatory employment law rights of the home state, which the worker would have enjoyed by virtue of his or her habitual residence and performance of work in the home state, but for the choice of law clause. In the absence of such a choice of law, the position is more complicated, but essentially a temporary posting of an employee abroad should not alter the applicable law from that of the home state.

Attempts by a host state to impose its own labour laws on workers who have temporary postings within that jurisdiction have been rebuffed by the Court of Justice on the ground that the Rome 1 Regulation and the Posted Workers Directive,[16] when read together, normally limit the scope of the application of mandatory labour laws by the host state to matters specified in Article 3 of the Directive, namely restrictions on working time, statutory minimum rates of pay, conditions of the hiring out of workers, health and safety, anti-discrimination legislation, and protections for pregnant workers. To this list should probably be added cases involving infringements of fundamental or constitutional rights, such as laws against slavery and servitude.[17] As a consequence of this interpretation, which promotes the purpose of this legislation to facilitate the free market in services, it is entirely possible that a foreign business may post its workers to another jurisdiction to provide a service and avoid the host state's laws on such matters as unfair dismissal and redundancy (because they are not listed in Article 3) and also avoid having to pay collectively agreed rates of pay and/or enter into negotiations with local unions. The host state cannot use its laws to prevent this outcome, and nor can a trade union seek to use industrial pressure, for such initiatives will prove unlawful under European law.

---

[15] Regulation (EC) No 593/2008 of the European Parliament and of the Council of 17 June 2008 on the law applicable to contractual obligations (Rome I).

[16] Directive 96/71/EC of the European Parliament and of the Council of 16 December 1996 concerning the posting of workers in the framework of the provision of services.

[17] Directive 96/71/EC, Article 3, para 10, see *supra* note 16. In this context, see also Catherine Barnard, "The UK and Posted Workers: The Effect of *Commission v Luxembourg* on the Territorial Application of British Labour Law" in *Industrial Law Journal*, 2009, vol. 38, no. 1, pp. 122-132.

In a nutshell, the effect of the application of private international law is that EU law renders unlawful measures taken by national governments and organised labour to vindicate national labour standards and collective norms outside the minimum standards set by the Posted Workers Directive. Thus private international law encourages regulatory competition by ceding advantages to suppliers of services from states with lower labour standards. Only transnational standards can prevent these potential deleterious effects of private international law.

6. De-Paradoxification

To summarise these points, European labour law is impossible because of the diversity of European labour law systems, which embrace divergent national political settlements and rest upon different models of the social regulation of capitalist markets. These differences provide the principal explanation for the absence of the formal competence of the EU in many aspects of labour law under the Treaties. At the same time, European labour law is necessary to counteract the potentially damaging effects of regulatory competition, to place limits on the effects of laws of competition and the market freedoms on trade union activities and national regulation, issues that will become increasingly prominent as the service economy grows. Private international law appears not to offer any solution, but rather seems to exacerbate the problem. The EU needs to find some paradoxical solution to the paradoxical problem of the impossible necessity of EU labour law that both achieves a uniform federal solution but at the same time is sensitive to local differences. Three options for this de-paradoxification will be outlined.

6.1. Negative Integration and Deregulation

One possible route is to permit negative integration around the market freedoms to run its course, with the result that much of the national labour law systems would be slowly dismantled. Federal labour law would, however, preserve those aspects of labour law that are necessary for the European Employment Strategy. These elements consist mainly of anti-discrimination laws to reduce exclusion from the labour market and to promote equal opportunity. Laws promoting employability and providing assistance to workers adversely affected by restructuring would also form part of the body of European labour law. The effect of such a strategy would be to dismantle the so-called European Social Model piece by piece, pushing Europe towards convergence in its model of capitalism to that of the United States. Such a route would be politically unpopular and in so far as it might be achieved by technocratic and judicial means, it would serve to heighten the awareness of the democratic deficit in European institutions. Even so, Claus Offe argues that this dismantling of corporatist arrangements is the most probable outcome, because, "'Embeddedness' is a condition that is more easily lost than gained, owing to its dependence upon supportive dispositions of a cognitive as well as moral kind'.[18] In other words, owing to the impossibility of securing agreement to uniform corporatist laws at a transnational level, the alternative of eliminating such laws under the pressures of negative integration and regulatory competition seems much more likely to happen. Labour law would survive in the EU only as a collection of exceptions to the market freedoms and competition laws, subject always to a test of proportionality.

6.2. Soft Law

A second route to de-paradoxification is to relegate European labour law to 'soft law'. Under this proposal, the method of co-operation between Member States known as the Open Method of Co-ordination (OMC) would be extended beyond the Employment Strategy and the Social Exclusion Strategy to include the raising of labour standards more generally. The OMC encourages innovation and dissemination of beneficial regulatory techniques, without compelling the Member States to conform to particular uniform regulations. It stresses aims rather than means, thereby permitting considerable variation in approaches. This route has the advantage that it avoids the problem of challenges to the pluralist settlements of the Member States and permits the continuation of corporatist institutional frameworks, subject to their conformity with the aims and principles of the soft laws produced by process of the OMC. Furthermore, this approach has the advantage that by foregoing uniform federal legal rules, it reduces the risk of preventing innovation and adaptation to changing circumstances by imposing substantial institutional impediments to

[18] Claus Offe, "The European Model of 'Social' Capitalism: Can It Survive European Integration?" in Max Miller (ed), *Worlds of Capitalism: Institutions, Governance, and Economic Change in the Era of Globalization*, Routledge, London, 2005, pp. 146-154.

change. The example of the ossification of American labour law around a model based upon Fordist industrial production is a salutary warning in this respect.[19] In the USA, the uniform federal straightjacket, which prevents experimentation by the states, has atrophied employment law, failed to adapt to a service economy and also failed (as the recent problems in agreeing health care reforms demonstrated) to join up labour market regulation with the development of a welfare system. The way in which this alternative soft law approach could function is to provide that national laws supported by and integrated into the approved goals for labour law standards at the European Level would provide Member States with justifiable reasons for restricting the market freedoms protected in the Treaty. In effect, national laws endorsed under the OMC would become permitted host state rules of labour law under the Posted Workers Directive and under the Rome 1 Regulation, so that the host state would be permitted to enforce those rules against foreign business and foreign workers.

6.3. Constitutionalisation of Labour Law

A third route to de-paradoxification, which may appeal to rather more to lawyers than to others, is to complicate the dilemma by inserting a further normative discourse into the debate; the application of fundamental social and economic rights. Drawing on the European Charter of the Fundamental Rights of the EU, now given indirect legal effect in the Treaty, it is possible to argue that the European Social Model can be preserved in its essential respects by the need for EU law to conform to fundamental rights. These rights include the basic elements of a labour law system, though of course these social and economic rights are only stated in fairly abstract generalities (which would require more detailed elaboration) and they contain cautious qualifications and limitations that threaten to hollow out the substance of the rights.[20] As an aid to the interpretation of the Charter, the substantial, relevant jurisprudence of the European Court of

[19] Cynthia L. Estlund, "The Ossification of American Labor Law" in *Columbia Law Review*, 2002, vol. 102, no. 6, pp.1527-1612.

[20] Since there is no applicable EU law, a literal interpretation of this right could mean that if national law does not provide the right, the worker does not have one. See Charter of Fundamental Rights of the European Union, 7 December 2000, Article 30: "Every worker has the right to protection against unjustified dismissal, in accordance with Union law and national laws and practices".

Human Rights could be added to the mix.[21] The 'rights route', of course, depoliticises the issue of the future of labour law in Europe and hands over the task of shaping EU labour law to the courts, a prospect that is unlikely to find favour in every quarter.

Even so, this third route of the 'constitutionalisation of labour law' may prove to be the only practicable legal alternative to either deregulation or soft law for the future of labour law in the EU. In its favour it can be argued that as a 'living instrument', the Charter of Fundamental Rights can adapt to changing circumstances and values. Furthermore, the adoption of social and economic rights as legal standards might encourage the broader international movement to try to create minimum standards that would be accepted by all nations. But most of all, as a document based on the ideals of individual dignity, equality and freedom, the Charter of Fundamental Rights asserts implicitly through its varied provisions, the fundamental ideal that motivates labour law: 'labour is not a commodity'.

7. Broader Lessons for the Future

This story about the impossible necessity of labour law in the European Union suggests broader implications. It indicates that in any free trade bloc between states, the issue of labour law cannot be ignored. Although the states concerned will probably prefer to retain their national sovereignty over labour law, inevitably labour law issues will arise in the course of constructing and policing the operation of the free trade area. There will be inescapable pressures to regulate employment matters at the same level as the regional free trade zone. In this context, the future of labour law will turn on how the denationalising tendencies are reconciled with the sovereign powers of states to preserve their prior political settlements. If, as has been suggested, the best mechanism for achieving such a reconciliation lies in appeal to general, abstract labour rights, work on a coherent and credible system of labour rights becomes a central task for the future of labour law.

---

[21] K.D.Ewing and John Hendy QC, "The Dramatic Implications of *Demir and Baykara*" in *Industrial Law Journal*, 2010, vol. 39, no.1, pp. 2-51; Virginia Mantouvalou, "Work and Private Life: *Sidabras and Dziautas v Lithuania*" in *European Law Review*, 2005, vol. 30, pp. 573-585.

5.4

The Future of Contract Law

Stefan Grundmann[*]

This contribution asks the question whether at the turn of our millennium, we are living similarly fundamental change as, for instance, around the French revolution with the rise of party autonomy. With this, the contribution asks the question of the future of contract law. It does so primarily for Europe. To answer this question, it is argued that both institutionally and in substance contract law is indeed undergoing fundamental change, starting only a few decades ago. Contract law has become, in its dynamics, largely European, decreasingly national, and will become over the next few decades, in substance, method and style, even primarily European. It has become a law in which party autonomy and instruments of order and protection have become similarly important and this process will continue. Standard contract terms, consumer protection, anti-discrimination are only three buzz-words; the financial crisis will trigger further thinking. The aim is an equilibrium in which the material freedom of all parties concerned is best furthered. The article then discovers that a trend towards codification comes together with a trend not to consider the code as 'universal order' any longer; that a trend towards generalisation comes together with a trend to differentiate more, even in a general part of contract law: between different types of contract partners, different types of groups of contracts (spot contracts and long-term contracts), and different types of the formation of contracts. The article concludes with examining some core areas where major steps of modernisation have been taken lately and it forecasts that contract law will be more international, interdisciplinary, more interested in the rule-setting process, more market and business oriented, in short: that a similar discussion as with corporate governance will develop for contract governance on a European level.

1. Introduction

This contribution asks the question whether at the turn of our millennium we are experiencing a fundamental change similar to, for instance, the

[*] **Stefan Grundmann** is Chair of Civil Law, German, European and Private International Law and Business Law at Humboldt University.

time around the French revolution with the rise of party autonomy. I consider the future of contract law, primarily in Europe. In doing so, I argue that both institutionally and in substance contract law has indeed undergoing fundamental change, starting only a few decades ago: contract law has become largely European in its dynamics, decreasingly national, and will over the next few decades become primarily European, in substance, method and style. Increasingly, the law is one in which both party autonomy and instruments of order and protection are on an equal footing, and this process will continue. Moreover, other aspects of standard contract terms, consumer protection and antidiscrimination are only some areas in transition, while other triggers, like the financial crisis will stimulate more thinking. The aim is an equilibrium in which the material freedom of all parties concerned is best furthered. I point out the trend towards codification which joins with a trend not to consider the code as 'universal order' any longer and. Separately, there is a trend towards generalisation which comes together with a trend to differentiate more evenly in a general part of contract law between different types of contract partners, different types of groups of contracts (spot contracts and long-term contracts), and different types of formations of contracts. The article concludes with examining some core areas where major developments of modernisation have been taken place lately and it forecasts that contract law will be more international, interdisciplinary, more interested in the rule-setting process, more market and business oriented, in short: that a similar discussion as with corporate governance will develop for contract governance at a European level.

2. Institutional Questions and Questions Concerning the Overall Framework

When asking the question of which 'future' can be envisaged for contract law and contract law thinking – and this is the question raised by this contribution – then it would seem quite obvious that, at least in Europe, it cannot be seen solely and not even primarily in national contract law. Therefore, the broader institutional setting has to be considered and prioritised. This setting, however, not only has to do with new regulators and standard setters (see below section 3.), but also with content: And these are the more 'material' standards, in particular constitutional standards (see below section 4.). 'Europeanisation' and 'materialisation' as the two single most important developments – with respect to the institutional framework and with respect to content – will be considered first.

3. Starting Point: New Levels of Legislation and New Legislatures

3.1. Supranational Level

The future of contract law in Europe will almost certainly be much less national, perhaps a bit more international, but mainly more supranational – 'European' – than today. Even today – due to the doctrine of indirect effect and to broad transposition, also beyond the ambit of application of EC Directives – the following areas of law should no longer be interpreted primarily according to methods of national law, but in conformity with the standard set in European law:

- the information regime governing the pre-contractual phase, including even at this point, publicity which is typically the first step towards a contract;
- the law of formation of contracts in distance marketing, e-commerce and in doorstep situations (including information duties and revocation rights), but not in traditional business in the presence of both parties;
- the law of standard contract terms (in which case, however, the point of reference from which parties may not deviate too much, *i.e.*, the default rule, is not harmonised yet);
- the law on anti-discrimination;
- the law on breach of contract, at least of sales contracts, but in some countries, such as Germany, of all contracts because the regime has been adopted as a general one (the exceptions with respect to damages would be largely eliminated with the adoption of the proposed EC Consumer Rights Directive);
- most banking law contracts and of large volume contracts in tourism, partly also in insurance law and for contracts concerning intellectual property (software etc.);
- important contract law phenomena from the whole area of distribution of goods and services.

While all these areas still are not really interpreted in national practice 'on the basis of the European original', such 'European' interpretation, in principle, is accepted not only by the European Court of Justice (ECJ), but also by all national courts, namely those of last instance. They accept that the interpretation given to the European standard really takes precedent over national modes of interpretation, for instance via indirect effect but also in cases of broader transposition. It is just a matter of time before enough case law by the ECJ has been built up because of preliminary references and that younger, more 'European' generations of lawyers really bring this idea to bear.

On the other hand, while the international level will still produce some material, it is highly unlikely that in the near future, there will be such broad legislation at this level like the UN Sales Law of 1980. Even as a model which is often displaced by party agreement, it is outstanding and will probably not find a 'successor' of similar importance. Moreover, there are important international legal measures which increasingly fall into decay, namely the Uniform Laws on Bills of Exchange and Cheques. The dominant level is the one in the middle, and at least in contract law. This type of a 'regionalisation of the world' may perhaps also serve as a model elsewhere.

The real question is not so much whether the European level will increasingly be the dominant, but in which form this will happen. Today, two developments would seem to be the most likely ones. It is possible that harmonisation will still increase, will become more detailed, cover the areas more densely and, because of increased recourse to the principle of full harmonisation, will more extensively displace national contract laws. It is this approach which is proposed nowadays, mainly through a new EC Consumer Rights Directive.

It is, however, also possible that, quite diversely, a European codification comes into being, as it has been most vigorously been proposed by the European Parliament, as a so-called optional instrument. All (other) EC legislative organs would seem to favour it if they pronounced themselves in favour of codification. In this second scenario, an additional question remains open, and this is whether, because of a combination of approaches or at least in the long run, such codification will not, nevertheless, in two ways lead to a very far reaching displacement of national contract laws. Firstly, will the optional instruments combined with ongoing broad harmonisation (the effect then being the one described above) or the optional instrument by itself become, in the long-run, 'exclusive'? In this way, the optional instrument remains a true alternative only. Secondly, the displacement of national contract laws could occur even if such an instrument remains optional and harmonisation is not increased or even reduced, in which case the optional instrument really is an alternative to national laws which continue to exist, perhaps becoming more independent from supranational influence than today. In the first case, the European regime largely supersedes the national one or even displaces it completely (intensive harmonising effect). In the second case it serves mainly as an alternative to national laws (and thus serves as a paradigm for national laws, but without a claim to exclusivity).

In my view, there are important arguments in favour of the second solution in the codification scenario, *i.e.*, a co-existence of an optional instrument with relatively 'free' national laws, with full freedom of choice for the parties between both alternatives, also in the purely domestic cases. An argument in favour of codification (an 'optional instrument', in whichever form) would seem to be an argument that system building for a modern contract law can be more coherent and more visibly advanced by such a codification than by mere ongoing harmonisation, even if intensified. Codification could serve as a model – perhaps even world-wide – for a modern contract law of the twenty-first century, which harmonisation, because of its piece-meal approach, would seem less appropriate. For contract law and its development – its substantial shape – a well prepared codification at European level would therefore be preferable to ongoing, progressive harmonisation.

Which of these paths of development supranational contract law will take may not be certain. It is, however, certain that those characteristics of style will be dominant with respect to the content and form of discussion which are usual for European contract law and which differ in a significant way from national law discussion. This relates in particular to the evaluation of solutions, which is more prominent, and therefore interdisciplinary approaches often concentrate on European contract law rather than on national law. Moreover there would be an additional impact on the style of discussion if indeed a European Optional Contract Law Code could also be chosen in the purely domestic case as a substitute for national contract law, and thus different sets of rules (not just standard contract terms) would compete – as is the case so far (only) in company law.

3.2. Private Ordering and Rule Setters?

Private ordering and rule setting is seen by some authors as an alternative or at least a supplement to the Europeanisation of contract law. Some authors even think that the model contracts which large law firms develop and use in practice would render a European harmonisation or codification largely superfluous.

If indeed a European codification was to be drafted largely by (groups of) legal scientists, it would still follow paths already known in state or international legislation. These paths could indeed also be followed by supranational legislation. In fact, such drafting scenarios are known from the history of the large codes in France, Austria, Switzerland or Germany.

Except for such input in drafting, genuine 'private ordering' is known today in Europe, its Member States and worldwide much more in company law than in contract law, *i.e.*, as sets of rules which stem from private standard setters, not state bodies, and which become positive law without modification, just by an act of incorporation, as can be seen in accounting law (The International Accounting Standards Board (IASB) in London), corporate governance or the law of prospectuses (International Organization of Securities Commission (IOSCO)). In contract law, the standard contracts drafted and used in practice by the large law firms are not really of comparable shape; they are not formulated in a uniform way for whole markets and published as such. These are just contract rules often used in the same way ('forms' or 'model rules'), in part standard contract terms – even though there is obviously some convergence. What comes closest to the sets of rules named for company law are standard contract terms which associations representing the different stakeholders in markets have negotiated and agreed upon, such as those applied in the German construction business. In the future, these may well be negotiated not only at the national level, but for the whole of Europe. To create a level playing field for this development, *i.e.*, to allow for free circulation of such negotiated standard contract terms in Europe, which would also be based on a consideration of the protective needs, is one of the prime questions in the further development of the EC Standard Contract Terms Directive, as well as of the application of the EC fundamental freedoms. On the other hand, beyond labour law, it seems rather unlikely that, in the near future, private sets of rules as such will be applied in the same way as objective law, as has been the case in company law over the last few decades – and this not only for particular sectors, but broadly and generally for a particular area of the law. The group of stakeholders seems not homogeneous enough and not so clearly 'organised' as in accounting law, in the law of prospectuses or in corporate governance of listed companies. And if consumer law created similar dynamics for contract law over the last few decades as capital market law did for company law, this does not imply that market forces and self-regulation were seen in a similar way as well. Indeed, they are seen here by the core decision-makers and in the public perception much more sceptically, as had traditionally been the case in the company law setting and capital market law.

4. Optimising Freedom via Tightening Protective Standards

The concept of 'optimising freedom via tightening protective standards' – which in my view is the most important substantive law development over the last few decades – would seem like a contradiction in itself. This refers to the phenomenon which some authors have described as 'materialisation' of the law or also the 'death of contract'. What is meant can best be illustrated by first describing core examples of such 'optimising freedom via tightening protective standards'. The overall tendency is to guarantee more material freedom for both partners to the contract (at least in the overall aggregate) – abandoning on the other hand increasingly a concept of (purely) formal freedom.

4.1. Core Examples Today

Cases of 'optimised freedom via tightening protective standards' can be seen today mainly in four lines of examples.

The first line is about intensification of those traditional limits which party autonomy encountered in the standard of good morals and in the case of fraud and duress. These traditional limits are largely undisputed, also from a comparative law perspective. Increasingly, however, courts and doctrinal developments go beyond these limits and apply stricter standards of protection. In Germany (and similarly in Italy and increasingly also in other European countries), this trend seems even particularly prominent given that doctrinal contract law thinking sees in it one of the major inroads of other areas into contract law – if not *the* most important one. In the most prominent decisions, fundamental rights have been instrumentalised, taking them as standards the core of which any (national) judge (or other state body) must bring to bear when adjudicating in a purely private law case between private parties (theory of a duty to protect those standards actively). The German Constitutional Court speaks in this respect of a 'structural imbalance' between the parties, in which case such a state duty to protect the standards actively is seen to exist, at least in principle, in favour of the weaker party. In its content, this is, however, by no means a development which can be found only in Germany. In other countries, if they do not follow the 'fundamental rights path' in this respect, very similar results are reached by broadening the concept of fraud ('guarantee given [only] necessary for our files', as had been said in the surety case of the German Constitutional Court) or the concept of duress ('this is the moment to show your husband your love', same case).

The second line of examples are information rules which have become dominant in contract law over the last two decades; this follows a similar development had already taken place some time before in company law with the intensification of accounting and capital market law. The theory of information economics, well developed in the 1970s, had some influence on this. Therefore, comparing the beginning and the end of this century for sales law, a transition from the *caveat emptor* principle to a *caveat praetor* principle has been sensed, and this is even true for English law which, in tendency, ranks among the less protective regimes. Two core ideas can indeed be derived from the EC Sales Directive: the seller is subject to detailed disclosure obligations if he wants to offer quality below market standards (the 'defect' has to be specified rather precisely), and the seller has to respond to any information given in public by a member of the distribution chain including the producer himself, even those contained in publicity. This is a rather 'comfortable' regime for the client which he can recognise and observe quite well, and in core respects, the seller is under a duty to deliver information. Thus, information delivered then forms part of the contract, irrespective of when it has been given, and performance can be requested. While this has been regulated directly only for sales law, the model has been or is about to be generalised at the national level in some Member States and potentially also at European level. If disclosure duties have been violated, the client's remedy to rescind the contract or to ask for expectation damages are those which typically put the heaviest burden on the supplier. On the other hand they often are the most attractive ones for the client as well, be it only for questions of proof. Yet another development which is already a bit older has, of course, much to do with information economics and an information model: this is the evolution of a generalised and more stringent substantive control standard in the case of (pre-formulated) standard contract terms.

A third line of examples should be seen in the increasing number of revocation rights. Some authors have seen them as a nucleus of more 'competitive' contract law, others have insisted on their functioning as an unconditioned right of the client to 'repent himself'. Two policy foundations would seem to exist for them which can be distinguished: insofar as revocation rights are granted because the contract has been formed in a doorstep or distance marketing situation (and also in the case of timeshare contracts), the guiding principle would seem to be that these marketing techniques differ substantially from traditional marketing in shops which gives to both parties at least the chance to inform themselves before the deal. Conversely, in these alternative marketing techniques, the client does not have the possibility to compare or inspect the product and/or his decision whether to enter into such a contract at all is – often – not a sufficiently free one. In some case patterns of distance marketing, this is more difficult to justify or even questionable. In principle, however, it would seem fair to conclude that the simple answer to the problem in these cases is to provide the chance of information (comparison of products) or the freedom of formation of will afterwards, and to do so by giving the client a right of revocation (without any need of justification) for such a (short) period of time which is typically needed for getting such information or for freely deciding the matter. It is paramount that the decision on whether to form the contract can indeed be revised without considerable disadvantages (costs), and that, on the other hand, this be only for as short a period of time as needed in order to reduce as much as possible the risk of *ex post* opportunism from the side of the client. The second case pattern in which revocation rights are granted is quite different. Here, informing is certainly possible before formation of contract, and the right to revoke without cause has to be seen as a form of protection against decisions which are taken too easily and without precaution. This is so in those contracts which (can) produce existential risks – for instance in the case of life insurance or large loans – and again a revocation right is granted. Justification is more difficult in this case, namely whether other forms of such protection would not be more suitable. This, however, does not affect the overall characterisation of the development described.

The fourth line of examples is to be seen in anti-discrimination law which, in the last decade, has been expanded beyond the frontiers of labour law, at least with respect to discrimination based on sex and race, in Germany also with respect to (old) age and ideological beliefs. In Germany in particular, this development has been seen as the 'death of contract' – *i.e.*, of party autonomy, and indeed these prohibitions are paradigmatic for the development and its characterisation.

4.2. Characterising the Two Poles and Their Interplay

All developments described – and perhaps most strikingly anti-discrimination law and the fundamental rights control of contracts, but also the development leading to an information model – have often been understood as an ever further-reaching reduction of freedom of contract (party autonomy). These developments can, however, also be understood in a different way: They can all be seen as an endeavour which is aimed at maximising the *substantive* freedom – not only a formal freedom – of *both* parties to the contract. The most important element would then be that the legislature tries to isolate those cases in which one party, in substance, has to decide in a situation of relatively reduced substantive freedom of choice or cannot act at all (anti-discrimination), and that the price for (state) intervention is to curtail the freedom of the other party, but only to a considerably lesser extent than what is gained on the other side. Whether the balance is always struck correctly, may be questionable, but that this is indeed the core motivation in all developments described would seem to be rather obvious and undoubtable.

Thus, for instance, it is characteristic for information rules that, formally, they form mandatory law, but that they produce effects which differ substantially from those of other (substantive) mandatory rules; mandatory information rules, contrary to what mandatory substantive rules do, do not fix the contents of contracts, but leave the parties leeway to decide themselves. Mandatory information rules, to the contrary, are designed to enable *both* parties to take their decision in as meaningful a way as possible – to enable them to understand the implications of the contract – thus creating the best conditions for material freedom in the choices to be taken. As far as revocation rights are designed to provide the client with the chance to inform himself after the formation of a contract (because before this was impossible), the reasoning is of course a very similar one, and this is the case in the majority of revocation rights. Even for the case law based on fundamental rights, namely in the cases on sureties, similar explanations can be given. When balancing the gain of freedom for the potential suretor on the one hand and the loss of freedom on the side of the credit institution on the other, the overall 'gain' would seem quite palpable: The suretor in the cases decided had been put under massive psychological pressure to serve as a suretor for amounts which he or she would most likely not be able to pay back and he or she had also been informed very 'optimistically' about the consequences. The credit institutions on the other hand, without such surety, would potentially have lost the chance to form this loan contract. Even anti-discrimination law, can be seen from this perspective. Its application has deliberately been restricted to 'public' contracts, in part also mass transactions, in which the aim to choose on the basis of very 'individual' criteria is typically less important. Moreover there has been intensive discussion about grounds for justification, and broad areas have totally been exempted. Finding an optimum of freedom remaining and freedom gained was quite clearly an aim. At the same time, with discrimination on the basis of sex and of race, two criteria have been chosen for which it is difficult to deny that they have massively been the grounds for actual discrimination. This, on the other side, also implied that freedom of access to quite important goods – such as housing or insurance – has been massively reduced or that persons have been massively humiliated on these grounds. Whether this has the same weight in the case of public offers of goods and services as in labour relationships may be open to discussion, but the overall scope is nevertheless quite evident: the gain of freedom on the one side tends to outweigh quite clearly the loss of freedom on the other. This at least would seem to be the intention. The scope is not to loose the chances of a gain in material freedom for *both* parties by sticking to a more formal concept of freedom of contract. Some loss of (formal) freedom of contract on the one side has to be accepted for the overall gain, *i.e.*, for the much higher gain of material freedom of contract on the other side. This would seem to be the prime scope even in anti-discrimination law although here, it may be argued, one additional scope is to change discourse in society by subjecting private parties to the duty to behave more rationally in these respects. This search for potential gains in material freedom increasingly not only refers to the phase of contract formation, but also to the phase of execution. A characteristic example would seem to be Section 490 (2) of the German Civil Code, introduced in 2002, which codified case law already existing: credit institutions should no longer be allowed to hold a client to a loan if the client was prepared to pay for the damages incurred by the credit institution because of early termination. Formerly banks had charged in addition a surplus for their consent to such termination.

If the question is asked which framework conditions seem to favour such a search for additional gains in material freedom and for increasingly refined solutions furthering this scope, the following may be characteristic. These solutions came into being in situations of rich competition: Several courts participated in the search: national Supreme Courts, national Constitutional Courts and the European Court of Justice; the latter mainly in the area of anti-discrimination and of an information model. Moreover, yardstick competition via increased comparative law research seemed to exercise its influence (see later), but also the interplay between different disciplines, in which economic theory was particularly important with respect to information rules – just as is possibly the case today and in the future with bounded rationality and with the influence of behavioural sciences. Thus, the intensive search or even the 'race for more material freedom' would be the fruit of a competition between institutions, jurisdictions and disciplines.

There is one development which accompanies this search for ever new potential material freedom via a balancing of the freedoms of all parties concerned – this is that traditional facilitative contract law is increasingly interwoven with (mandatory market) regulation. In the beginning, with antitrust law as the old paradigm of market regulation, traditional facilitative contract law seemed far removed from regulation. Today, however, both aspects – rules, typically default rules, which are primarily aimed at facilitating the use of party autonomy and rules which regulate markets and are aimed at maintaining the pre-conditions for free choices by all stakeholders – are increasingly interwoven. Contract law – just as has been the case in company law for some time already – contains in its very core a substantive amount of regulation as well. The search for more freedom for all partners (in aggregate dimensions) leads as well to a closer relationship between the parts of contract law primarily related to the use of party autonomy on the one hand and of the regulatory parts of contract law on the other. This would seem to imply that modern contract law scholarship has to enter even more into an exchange with business law, and namely company law, discussions and scholarship.

If it is convincing that today's contract law tries to optimise (aggregate) freedom of all parties concerned via a tightening of protective standards, it may well be that this is too vague a description. In other words, one might criticise the fact that this is so general a trend that it is not really concrete enough and therefore meaningful as a development. If the criticism is that similar trends can easily be found in other areas of the law, the criticism is unfounded because in this case, it would only say that the trend is characteristic for many areas of the law and therefore even more important. It might even amount to a real 'threshold criterion'. If, however, the criticism is that similar trends have always existed and are not characteristic just for the last two or three decades, the criticism would indeed be relevant for our discussion of contract law and its future. The question therefore is whether this trend differs in a significant way from what can be seen in the nineteenth and in large parts of the twentieth century. In my view, the answer is clearly positive: information rules, revocation rights and anti-discrimination rules clearly did not exist, or at least not to a considerable extent, in contract law before the 1980s. And in addition, the case law based on the fundamental rights and on the good faith principle differs considerably from the older development based on the application of the good faith principle which most resembles the modern one. This is the evolution of a case law for changed circumstances. In these cases, however, the aim was not to protect the material freedom of one party against inroads from actions taken by the other party, *i.e.*, to regulate in a mandatory way the different areas of freedom (this is the aim of the case law based on fundamental rights). Conversely, in these older cases, the aim was to re-construct the parties' intentions under fundamentally changed circumstances. Apart from this, the doctrine of changed circumstances as developed by German courts has never strongly appealed to other jurisdictions. Conversely, the case law based on fundamental rights was quite successful, namely on the supranational level (see the section below.). According to what has been said, this is likely to be the most relevant level for the future of contract law.

5. Summary and Conclusions

Contract law of the future, in the European Member States, is primarily supranational, even more so than international.

Its content is characterised by an increasing, subtle and nuanced search for an optimal equilibrium between the (contractual) freedoms of *both* parties or more generally: *all* parties concerned.

Thus, there is an increasingly inseparable combination and mix of those parts of contract law which have enabling character (facilitative law) and the regulatory parts, establishing and safeguarding (market) order.

The general part of contract law – also with respect to legislation – is more principle oriented, but more important still, is more nuanced and bi- or multi-polar in several respects, because within contract law, rules apply differently to different groups of persons, different groups of types of contracts, and different modes of formation of the contract.

A codification on the supranational level is desirable; it would be a particularly good place to render visible what may be seen as characteristic for a European social model in which the manifold interests of all stakeholders are considered. It is, however, paramount for such codification that it remains manageable, confined to contract law but at the same time encompassing all contract law, and that such codification properly depicts the current status of society and of contract law development. Just to lift the system of the German Civil Code (the *Bürgerliches Gesetzbuch*) to the supranational level, does not solve the problem that this system represents the status of 1900.

Core areas of modernisation have been named and discussed. They should encounter particular attention in discussion and in a modern codification.

The style is increasingly richer – more international, more interdisciplinary, more oriented towards a comparison of solutions and to practical consequences (outcome related interpretation) and also more oriented towards the process of rule setting ('governance'). It may be that the exchange between contract law and company law will be more intense in the future.

5.5

Transformations of European Contract Law Over the Next Two Decades

Ruth Sefton-Green[*]

This paper focuses on the future of European private law, examining how two crises of a different nature affect European contract law and its potential transformations of the legal systems of Member States. The first crisis relates to the financial and economic crisis of the global market. The second, relating to law-making, is linked to the democratic deficit in the EU. The challenge is to work out how to strengthen the single market with a democratically acceptable European contract law, while respecting the 'diversity of legal traditions among Member States'.

The present proposals for a Common Frame of Reference indicate that either maximum harmonisation or an optional instrument will be adopted to regulate European contract and/or consumer law in the near future. In relation to the latter, many questions as to its nature, scope, levels of protection, capacity to resolve obstacles linked to legal and other kinds of diversity remain unanswered. In addition, the need to create a European legal culture and a European Legal Institute, as a means of overcoming legal nationalism, is discussed.

1. Introduction

This paper focuses on the future of European private law and the implications for the diversity of legal systems in the EU. European private law, particularly European contract law, including the *acquis communautaire*, is constantly evolving as well as being the subject of much academic activity. The European Commission has been interested in European general contract law, since its Communication in 2001,[1] whereas the European

---

[*] **Ruth Sefton-Green** is Maître de conférences in Private Law and Criminal Sciences at the University of Paris 1 (Panthéon-Sorbonne).

[1] Communication from the Commission to the Council and the European Parliament on European Contract Law, Brussels, 11 July 2001, COM (2001) 398 final, OJ C 255, 13 September 2001. This was followed up by A More Coherent European Contract Law: an Action Plan, Brussels, 12 February 2003, COM (2003) final, OJ C 63, 15.3.2003 (the "Action Plan"); and then European Contract Law and the Revision of the *Acquis*:

Parliament tried to promote a European Civil Code, including contract law, as early as 1989.[2] In May 2010, following the publication of the academic Draft Common Frame of Reference (DCFR) in 2009[3] and the Council's invitation in the Stockholm Programme,[4] the European Commission set up a legal expert group to prepare a proposal for a Common Frame of Reference in European contract law.[5]

The Commission's recent policy on European contract law is closely connected to Europe 2020,[6] followed up by two reports: A New Strategy for the Single Market[7] and Project Europe 2030.[8] This paper examines how two crises of a different nature affect European contract law and its potential to transform Member States' legal systems. The first relates to externalities: the financial and economic crisis of the global market. The EU must respond with a dynamic strategy in order to strengthen the single market in the face of globalisation. The desirability and feasibility of possible solutions thus need to be discussed. The second crisis relates to internalities: I will call this a crisis about law-making, linked to the democratic deficit in the EU. The challenge presented by this second crisis involves a more reflective enquiry into the *method* and the *means* of Euro-

the Way Forward, Brussels, 11 October 2004, COM (2004) 651 final (the "Way Forward").

2 Resolution A2157/89 of the European Parliament on Action to Bring into Line the Private Law of the Member States, *OJ* 1989 C 158/400; Resolution A300329/94 on the Harmonization of Certain Sectors of Private Law *OJ 1994* C 205/518.

3 Christian von Bar, Eric Clive and Hans Schulte-Nölke (eds.), *Principles, Definitions and Model Rules of European Private Law: Draft Common Frame of Reference*, Outline Edition, Sellier, 2009 (the "DCFR").

4 The Stockholm Programme – An Open and Secure Europe Serving and Protecting Citizens, adopted by the Council of the European Union on 10-11 December 2009, Doc. 17024/09, p. 33.

5 Commission Decision of 26 April 2010 Setting up the Expert Group on a Common Frame of Reference in the Area of European Contract Law, IP/10/595, OJ 27.4.2010, L 105/109. The remand specifically mentions both consumer and business contract law.

6 Communication from the Commission: Europe 2020: A Strategy for Smart, Sustainable and Inclusive Growth, Brussels, 3 March 2010, COM (2010) 2020.

7 A New Strategy for the Single Market: At the Service of Europe's Economy and Society, Report to the European Commission by Mario Monti, 9 May 2010 (the "Monti Report").

8 *Project Europe 2030: Challenges and Opportunities: A Report to the European Council by the Reflection Group on the Future of the EU 2030*, May 2010.

pean law-making. These two strands of enquiry, though treated separately, are in fact inextricably linked.

In short, the challenge is to work out how to strengthen the single market with a democratically acceptable European contract law, while respecting the 'diversity of legal traditions among Member States'.[9]

2. The Need for Further Integration to Facilitate Cross-Border Transactions

According to the Commission, though the point has never been empirically proved, the diversity of private law rules in national legal systems creates an obstacle to the single market and entails unnecessary transaction costs. The Commission's response to this perceived need for further integration is to improve the coherence of European contract law, whatever that means, and consequently boost the confidence of consumers (and businesses?) in the single market, with the ultimate aim of facilitating cross-border trade. This is a tall order and certain scepticism about its feasibility seems justified.

This challenge can be situated in the context of further integration in the EU, a consequence of the ambitions of the Lisbon Treaty which state that the EU has to create a "highly competitive social market economy",[10] combating both economic and legal nationalism, while also maintaining a high level of consumer and social protection. From a global perspective, the EU has a role to play as an actor in a global market, to forge the characteristics of a EU market economy. This complex challenge European contract law will face in the next two decades involves reconciling and satisfying diverging interests of both businesses and consumers (and many other categories of private actors), as well as making political decisions about the social nature of the market economy in the EU.[11]

The specific challenge the EU is facing necessarily conceives European contract law as a means of regulating the relationship between indi-

---

[9] Action Plan Implementing the Stockholm Programme, Brussels, 20 April 2010, COM (2010) 171 final, p. 4.

[10] Consolidated Version of the Treaty on European Union as amended by the treaty of Lisbon, 1 December 2009, Article 3, para.3. See also Commissioner Jose-Manuel Barroso's letter contained in the Monti Report, p. 4, see *supra* note 7.

[11] Gert Brueggemeier, et.al., "Social Justice in European Contract Law: a Manifesto", in *European Law Journal*, 2004, vol. 10, no. 6, pp. 653-674.

viduals, the market and civil society,[12] thus obscuring the distinction between private and public law. Furthermore, European private law, including contract law, may have a role to play in constructing the identity of European citizens. Although the linkages are not obvious, this topic has repercussions on numerous intersecting themes of interest, including (i) internationalisation (of national private law); (ii) the changing relationship between public and private law (since European contract law blurs the dividing line and is inspired by the two different modes of reasoning); (iii) the making of rules, accountability and legitimacy, with regards to the processes of law-making; and (iv) the legal profession, teaching and research. What emerges from the above is the more general question: how can we constitute a European legal culture? These themes have further ramifications on issues of social inclusion, multiculturalism, multilingualism and fairness in general, which can be encapsulated in the idea of social justice.

2.1. The Objective: The Quest for Coherence of European Contract Law or Convergence of National Private Law Rules

It is far from clear what the need to improve the coherence of European contract law actually means. Is this a juridical concern for (conceptual) coherence or for improving the functionality or efficacy of European contract law? Is the criterion of improving coherence qualitative, relative, relational or even quantitative? Or is coherence perhaps a euphemism, in other words a synonym for convergence of national private law rules?

2.2. The Means: How to Achieve Convergence

A certain antagonism about the means to achieve the convergence, or approximation, of national private law rules exists. A rapid historic summary reveals that this is not a novelty: the developments in this field, engineered by the European Commission, with resolutions from the European Parliament, have moved through varying degrees of intensity. Such measures include: proposals by the European Parliament for unification in the form of a European Civil Code; the Commission's and the Council's strong denial and refusal of the latter;[13] steering, instead, towards further

---

[12] Hugh Collins, *Regulating Contracts*, Oxford University Press, 1999.

[13] Report from the Commission: Second Progress Report on The Common Frame of Reference, Brussels, 25 July 2007, COM (2007) 447 final; 2863rd Council Meeting:

integration through the means of maximum harmonisation; and, last but not least, the Common Frame of Reference ('CFR').

Today, two apparently contrary strategies for the CFR can be identified. First, measures for further integration can be implemented by way of harmonisation, now a classic method for achieving the approximation of laws in the Member States.[14] An example of this approach can be found in the Draft Directive on Consumers' Rights. Secondly, discussions about the CFR refer to it both as a toolbox, but also as an optional instrument for European contract law, the so called '28th system', the scope of which is unclear. The Council describes the CFR as "a non-binding set of fundamental principles, definitions and model rules".[15] Recently, the European Economic and Social Committee delivered an opinion in favour of an optional instrument.[16]

The implementation of either one of these strategies will inevitably transform both European contract law and also private law rules in national legal systems. First, the push for further top-down integration of European contract law through harmonisation has led in the past (and will continue to do so in the future) to fragmentation and transformation of sources of law, as well as legal categories that are familiar to private law in national legal systems. Second, the opposite tendency, orienting the direction of European contract law towards greater bottom-up decision-making, and giving parties greater freedom of contract will likewise result in transformations and fragmentation. In either event, but for different reasons, it is plausible that neither movement will achieve greater convergence of legal systems: on the contrary, it will create more diversity. This presents a key dilemma, not because I wish to suggest that diversity is a good or bad thing, but simply because it is the opposite of the Commission's objectives.

Justice and Home Affairs, Luxembourg, 18 April 2008, Council of the European Union, 8397/08 (Presse 96), p. 11.

14 Consolidated Version of the Treaty on the Functioning of the European Union as amended by the Treaty of Lisbon, 1 December 2009, Article 114.

15 The Stockholm Programme, p. 33, see *supra* note 4.

16 See Opinion of the European Economic and Social Committee on 'The 28th Regime - an Alternative Allowing Less Lawmaking at Community Level' (Own-initiative opinion), 26-27 May 2010, INT/499 ("The 28th Regime – Less Lawmaking"). The EESC prefers to talk about a "2nd" regime, proposing that the parties can choose either a domestic contract law or European contract law.

2.3. Uncertainty and Decision-Making

The Commission initiated the idea of the CFR, and the optional instrument, at a time when the EU institutions were striving to achieve better law-making. As a result, a process of consultation with stakeholders was implemented, in conjunction with the research activities of several expert groups. The results of this consultation process are inconclusive. On one level, this could be perceived as a total transformation from top-down to bottom-up policy-making, which has emerged as a result of the lack of consensus and criticism arising out of the former. However, the Commission's choice of strategy remains uncertain. At least two causes for this indecision can be identified. First, empirical observation suggests that periodic internal changes in the Commission constantly lead to radical changes in policy-making or simple inertia. The cause of these cyclic revolutions can be attributed to an institutional obstacle, or bureaucratic uncertainty and an incapacity for decision-making. A second cause is that the process of the decision-making is heavily reliant on expert advice. Experts, by their very nature, give advice but they do not (or should not) hold decision-making power. In this respect, in reply to the question "What might happen in the next few decades in this area?" The simple response would be "Nothing, just like in the last few decades".

Has nothing really happened in the last few decades? Legal scholars might disagree if the quantity of scholarly activity and production is considered. Though this is true, we must keep in mind that scholarly production may never be implemented (but the Commission did ask the Expert Group on the CFR to use the DCFR as a starting point).[17] Moreover, in the context of the present global economic crisis it is generally accepted that we cannot allow inertia to continue.

3. Evaluating the Options

What then are the options for such transformations to occur? The following paragraphs discuss three possibilities, as well as their respective obstacles: a) harmonisation; b) an optional instrument; and briefly c) a combination of the two.

[17] See Commission Decision of 26 April 2010, Article 2, see *supra* note 5.

3.1. Harmonisation and Fragmentation: The Risk of Backfire

Harmonisation through directives, as a means of approximating the laws of Member States, is familiar in the field of European contract law: examples abound.[18] However, the exact consequences of harmonisation are not always predictable: harmonisation transforms the face of national legal systems and it has even been suggested that "Europeanization has triggered disintegration".[19] Indeed, the integration of the single market through minimum harmonisation measures (setting a minimum threshold level, *i.e.*, allowing Member States to provide more protection) is not totally successful, as the Unfair Contract Terms Directive of 1993 demonstrates. Guenter Teubner accurately identified this outcome, by suggesting that the insertion of European concepts into national legal systems' private law rules would trigger a series of "legal irritants".[20] If a directive has produced more fragmentation,[21] one can talk of backfiring, since the aim of directives is to approximate laws of Member States towards convergence, not disintegration. The Product Liability Directive of 1985, which turned into a maximum harmonisation measure (preventing Member States from offering a higher level of protection) as a result of the intervention of the then European Court of Justice in 2002,[22] has also backfired. The perceived deficit or incapacity of minimum harmonisation directives to achieve their goals through an end-based reasoning may have sparked further overt attempts at maximum harmonisation. If the Com-

18 See for an empirical survey, Hans Schulte-Nölke, Christian Twigg-Flesner and Martin Ebers (eds.), *EC Consumer Law Compendium: Comparative Analysis*, 2007, available at http://ec.europa.eu/consumers/cons_int/safe_shop/acquis/comp_analysis_en.pdf, last accessed 1 April 2011.

19 Christian Joerges, "Europeanization as a Process: Thoughts on the Europeanization of Private Law", in *European Public Law Journal*, 2005, vol. 11, no. 1, p. 62, 63.

20 Gunther Teubner, "Legal Irritants: Good Faith in British Law or How Unifying Ends up in New Divergences", in *The Modern Law Review*, 1998, vol. 61, no. 1, pp. 11-32.

21 Thomas Wilhelmsson, "Private Law in the EU: Harmonised or Fragmented Europeanisation?", in *European Review of Private Law*, 2002, vol. 10, no. 1, pp. 77-94.

22 Court of Justice of the European Union, Case C-52/00 *Commission v. France* [2002] ECR I-3827; Case C-154/00 *Commission v. Greece* [2002] ECR I-3879; Case C-183/00 *Gonzales Sanchez v. Medicina Asturiana SA* [2002] ECR I-3901.

mission's discourse is taken at face value, harmonisation in the future will be "full and targeted",[23] though the terms are somewhat meaningless.

It is as yet too early to see the effects of maximum harmonisation measures. In sum, there is a certain amount of empirical evidence to suggest that harmonisation does not lead to convergence but to more fragmentation triggered by legal irritants.[24] It might not be appropriate to evaluate these unintended side effects from a moral standpoint, but even against the Commission's own measuring stick, the goal of levelling out national legal systems' differences has not been achieved, or not optimally so. This situation will undoubtedly be exacerbated with the enlargement of the EU, since room for fragmentation as a back-firing consequence of harmonisation will be multiplied with the diversity of the legal systems of the EU's 27 Member States.

3.2. An Optional Instrument: Choosing Between Domestic Law and the European ('28th') Regime

Let us suppose that an optional instrument for European contract law is adopted. At first glance, it is rather difficult to see how an optional instrument could increase the coherence of European contract law, since it actually increases diversity, rather than decreasing it. Will businesses or consumers actually use such an instrument? If so, will it help strengthen legal certainty and the single market in general? How? What effect, if any, would such an instrument have on non-EU contracting parties? The answers to these questions will turn on the content of the instrument (as well as its form): the degree of mandatory provisions, levels of protection for different categories of contracting parties, etc. Social dumping, though controversial, is a cause for concern. It is suggested that an optional instrument might reinforce inequality on the market, leading to social exclusion. These difficulties are highly complex: different concerns arise depending on whether the optional instrument will be used in Business-to-Business (B2B) or Business-to-Consumer (B2C) contracts. For example,

---

23 See Press Release of Commissioner Viviane Reding, Speech/10/91, 15 March 2010, available at http://europa.eu/rapid/pressReleasesAction.do?reference=SPEECH/10/91&format=HTML&aged=0&language=EN&guiLanguage=en, last accessed 1 April 2011.

24 Hans Schulte-Nölke, "EC Law on the Formation of Contract – from the Common Frame of Reference to the Blue Button", in *European Review of Contract Law*, 2007, vol. 3, no. 3, pp. 332-349.

the optional instrument must not be allowed to override national mandatory provisions protecting consumers. The partisans suggest this entails that the optional instrument will have to be more protective than the average national legislation, but the evidence that its content will be more protective is presently lacking.

Leaving aside questions of competence, three overlapping aspects of the form and scope of such an instrument will be discussed: (i) the legal form; (ii) an optional instrument for whom?, and iii) in respect of what European contract law (general, or specific contracts)? Revealing these major preliminary obstacles has implications about the probability of an optional instrument's actually being adopted.

3.2.1. The Legal Form of an Optional Instrument

An optional instrument could be contained in a future EU directive or regulation. If the former is chosen, it would be subject to transposition by Member States and thus to all the difficulties this entails. However, it seems more likely that an optional instrument will be included in a regulation. The ultimate legal form of an optional instrument is ineluctably linked to the competence question and depends on political variables, but at present a regulation looks the most probable. If a regulation is chosen as the form, there would be no national law variations as to the form or content of the optional instrument and it would be directly applicable in all Member States once adopted. Still, the instrument would remain optional, in that it will be left for the contracting parties to decide when to use it, if at all (with the strong reservation that this assumption is founded on the myth of freedom of contract). Moreover, there is a political slant to consider and the liberal or non-welfarist implications of this policy choice have already been pointed out.

3.2.2. An Optional Instrument for Whom?

One answer is that three options exist: an optional instrument for (i) B2B contracts; (ii) B2C contracts, or (iii) both. But the question can be reformulated, so as to focus not on the quality or status of the parties, but on actual impact: who will end up exercising the option?

In this context, we also need to ask whether it will be an 'opt-in' or 'opt-out' instrument. The 1980 United Nations Convention on Contracts for the International Sale of Goods (CISG) contains an opting-out measure that is considered quite successful. Behavioural economics studies suggest that people tend towards an opt-out or default option. Consequently, it is likely that the optional instrument will apply European contract law by default. The literature assumes that consumers will be asked to choose whether they want European contract law or domestic law to apply. This assumption presents a number of difficulties. First, the informational issues are crucial: it is unclear how and to what extent consumers, or even businesses, will be informed about the consequences of their decision. How many lay consumers, not law professors, read the general conditions before clicking on the button in an Internet sale? And even if they do, how many of them actually understand such conditions? Second, testing or verifying this assumption would require carrying out empirical studies. The law cannot merely rely on general standards, such as the much-criticised notion of the average European's consumer's behaviour.[25] Third, factors other than legal diversity *per se* (such as consumers' fear of the unknown, legal costs and language), may constitute greater, or at least tantamount, obstacles to the single market, as consumers would intuitively choose domestic law for its familiarity, rather than a new and unfamiliar European contract law.

Furthermore, the content of the optional instrument will be foreign to national judges during a transitional period. As with any law reform, an adaptation process of interpretation and getting acquainted with the optional instrument will be inevitable. This will have an impact on legal training and notably in the next few decades, will require rigorous continuous training for both judges and other legal professionals. Moreover, there is the difficulty of multilingualism and transaction costs: in what language(s) is the optional instrument going to be written and then offered? If it is written in English, which is highly probable, linguistic difficulties will subsist and should not be neglected. The EU will have to bear the costs of translating the instrument but in order for language not to be a factor of social exclusion from the market, businesses will also have to bear the costs of translating their contracts into the 23 languages of the EU. This is unrealistic. How many small and medium size enterprises (SMEs), for example, will be able to afford to offer their contracts in all

[25] See, for example, Thomas Wilhelmsson, "The Average European Consumer: A Legal Fiction?" in Thomas Wilhelmsson, Elina Paunio and Annika Pohjolainen (eds.), *Private Law and the Many Cultures of Europe*, Kluwer Law International, 2007, pp. 243-268.

languages? Conversely, SMEs may find themselves contracting in English, with European contract law applying by default, without the means to understand certain linguistic niceties properly. Even if one of the ideas behind an optional instrument is to lower transaction costs by allowing businesses to use the same European contract law for cross-border (and even domestic?) transactions throughout the EU, this may not suffice to facilitate cross-border trade since it will not necessarily reduce transaction costs linked to translation. In other words, linguistic diversity may turn out to be just as an important stumbling block for cross-border trade as the diversity of legal systems is perceived to be, a point rarely considered.

3.2.3. The Field of Application: General Contract Law or Specific Contracts Only?

This question is closely linked to whether the optional instrument will apply to B2B or B2C contracts and whether it will apply to cross-border transactions only. There is a considerable amount of literature promoting the idea of such an instrument being used for Internet sale contracts. This 'blue button' option[26] has already been discussed for some time and is appealing for obvious political reasons: it concerns common cross-border transactions of the type the single market wants to encourage. It fits in with the desire to develop a digital society.[27] In addition, it has been suggested that the use of the optional instrument should be dictated by the relevant market for certain types of contracts, *e.g.*, financial services or insurance contracts.

3.3. A Combination: Not One or the Other but Both?

A combination of the alternative discussed above is also conceivable. A combination would be feasible if for example, the optional instrument related to general contract law and the Commission continued to initiate vertical sector-specific or horizontal directives in European consumer law. However, it is perhaps not necessary to consider all the possible permutations in detail at this stage.

---

[26] Scholte-Nölke, 2007, pp. 348-349, see *supra* note 24.

[27] Notice that the Commission presented a digital agenda for the single market on 18 May 2010 (IP/10/581).

4. Greater Transparency in European Law-Making: Who Are the Law-Makers?

We have already seen that the presence of legal diversity in the single market is presented as an obstacle to the smooth functioning of the market. We have examined the hypothesis that an optional instrument (the form, scope and content of which is uncertain) will be adopted in the next two decades as a means to reduce legal diversity, perceived as a barrier to trade. However, this will not necessarily overcome other significant obstacles to cross-border trade, such as consumers' lack of confidence or multilingualism. Indeed it may create new obstacles, such as social exclusion from the market.

Nevertheless, extrinsic reasons may help explain why there is a certain orientation in favour of an optional instrument in the present economic and political climate of the EU. First, an optional instrument will have other potentially dramatic repercussions: it will radically change the relationship between, and the relative strength, bargaining position, etc, of private actors on the market. Second, an optional instrument may be perceived not only as a solution to the perceived problem of legal diversity, but also as a satisfactory response to the difficulties raised by the democratic deficit in the EU. The existence of an optional instrument will, conveniently, shift the responsibility and co-decision power of EU law-makers onto private actors: namely civil society, legal experts, stakeholders, etc. It will also affect Member States as law-makers, if national laws co-exist with the 28th system of European contract law. For example, if the optional instrument is actually used by contracting parties, this could mean in the long-term that national legal systems' rules of contract law will be usurped by the optional 28 system. Conversely, the optional instrument's adoption may not bring about significant changes, since in practice contracting parties will not opt-in or will opt-out, but it will nevertheless contribute to shifting and re-distributing the decision-making power of law-making to private actors. In this respect, the contribution and role of legal experts must not be underestimated. Who will be the law-makers of the EU in the future? Will legal experts take over the role of European and Member State law-makers?[28] Will an optional instrument make European law more attractive to European citizens on the basis it is

28 Cecile Robert and Antoine Vauchez, "L'académie Européenne. Savoirs, Experts et Savants dans le Gouvernement de L'Europe", in *Politix*, 2010, vol. 23, pp. 9-34.

more democratically acceptable, emerging from a civil society consensus? These issues may radically affect the nature of legal norms, if soft law prevails over hard law, and also how we think about the law. Is there not a risk that the market alone will dictate the law, to the exclusion of other important considerations? Where is the 'social' part of the 'European market economy'? How can we ensure that legal experts will include the necessary social aspects of European contract law, since they have no legitimacy for anything other than the 'technical'? If European private law is de-politicised, who will look after the social issues? What guarantee can we have that an optional instrument will be more protective than average national legal rules? Legal experts cannot be totally neutral, even if they are presented as providing technical solutions. The danger of replacing one democratic deficit for another should not be underestimated.

5. Hopes for a European Legal Culture: Wishful Thinking?

The utopia of constructing a *ius commune* of European contract law has attracted both partisans and detractors. One way to go about this is through the creation of a European legal culture or method, a plan that requires person-power, in order to construct and cultivate the concrete object or subject matter of legal culture in the EU. Plans are already in motion to create a 'European Legal Institute', an idea that has been floating around for a while. Many believe that working towards a European legal culture is a necessary complement to more formal top-down plans to create a European contract law. Many processes of emulation and reciprocal influences already exist through judicial cooperation and exchange. Major innovations in legal education are required in order to put this plan in action. It will not suffice to set up an institute with professors at the top of the Ivory Tower. It will be necessary to alter radically the way we teach law, by removing our mental barriers. This will require de-nationalising or internationalising our training programmes from their domestic national context and putting rigorous continuous training programmes for lawyers and judges into effect. This means thinking and teaching law transnationally, or trans-systemically.[29]

[29] See, for example, "Transsystemic Legal Education", Quebec Research Centre of Private and Comparative Law, McGill University, available at http://www.mcgill.ca/crdpcq/transsystemic/ , last accessed 1 April 2011.

At the same time, legal nationalism continues to rear its rather unsightly head. Examples vary from Pierre Legrand's radical writings, which suggest that the common law is an endangered species in need of protection,[30] to a French counter-proposal to the DCFR,[31] and even to the DCFR itself, criticised by many jurists (including Germans), as being intensely Germanic in form and structure.[32]

Are we (or will we be) ready for the emergence of a European legal culture over the next few decades? Legal mentalities are slow to change and conservatism in legal academia and amongst legal practitioners leads me to suspect that two decades might be too short of a time-frame to achieve this utopian objective.

[30] See, for example, Pierre Legrand, "European Legal Systems are Not Converging", in *International Comparative Law Quarterly*, 1996, vol. 45, pp. 52-81.

[31] Guillaume Wicker and Jean-Baptiste Racine (eds.), *Principes Contractuels Communs: Droit Privé Comparé et Européen*, Paris, Société de Legislation Comparée, 2008, vol. 7.

[32] See, for example, Reiner Schulze and Thomas Wilhelmsson, "From the Draft CFR Towards European Contract Rules", in *European Review of Contract Law,* 2008, vol. 2, pp. 154-168.

5.6

Indicators and Governance by Information in the Law of the Future*

Benedict Kingsbury**

Indicators are becoming ubiquitous in public and private governance. What are the implications of this for the law of the future? While in formal terms it may often be correct that indicators are hortatory and purport to be factual whereas law is binding and expressly normative, the similarities and relations between law and indicators are in reality much greater than a formal differentiation suggests. These similarities and relations will become increasingly important as the overlaps between law and governance become greater. This phenomenon is most marked for law and governance beyond the state, but its significance within states for national and sub-national law is also growing. This paper argues that the law of the future will have to engage much more deeply than heretofore, at the levels of fundamental theory and quotidian practice, with the increasing role of indicators and other quantitative measures, while defining and maintaining a core role for law and legal principles in the whole enterprise of governance by information.

1. Introduction

Indicators are becoming ubiquitous in public and private governance. What are the implications of this for 'the law of the future'? While in formal terms it may often be correct that indicators are hortatory and purport to be factual whereas law is binding and expressly normative, the similarities and relations between law and indicators are in reality much

* This paper draws on ideas from an extensive joint project on Indicators and Governance by Information with NYU Professors Kevin Davis and Sally Engle Marry, and IILJ Program Director Angelina Fisher; see www.iilj.org. That work has been initiated with support from Carnegie Corporation of New York, the Rockefeller Foundation, and the National Science Foundation, as well as NYU Law School. Thanks to all of them, to Megan Donaldson for help with this paper, and to other collaborators in the IILJ-NSF research project.

** **Benedict Kingsbury** is Murry and Ida Becker Professor of Law and Director of the Institute for International Law and Justice at New York University.

greater than formal differentiation suggests. These similarities and relations will become increasingly important as the overlaps between law and governance become greater. This phenomenon of complementarity, substitution or competition between law and indicators is most marked for law and governance beyond the state, but its significance within states for national and sub-national law is also growing. This paper argues that the law of the future will have to engage much more deeply than heretofore, at the levels of fundamental theory and quotidian practice, with the increasing role of indicators and other quantitative measures, while defining and maintaining a core role for law and legal principles in the whole enterprise of governance by information.

2. What Are Indicators?

An 'indicator' can be defined as follows:

> An indicator is a named collection of rank-ordered data that purports to represent the past or projected performance of different units. The data are generated through a process that simplifies raw data about a more complex social phenomenon. The data, in this simplified and processed form, are capable of being used to compare particular units of analysis (such as countries or institutions or corporations), synchronically or over time, and to evaluate their performance by reference to one or more standards.[1]

Many of the best-known indicators are aggregations or 'mash-up' compilations, with substantial discretion available to the compiler in choosing what specific indicators to include, with what weightings and what devices to limit double-counting or to smooth over data unavailability (examples include the Human Development Index, Consumer Price Index, and the World Governance Indicators.[2]

Five features of indicators are of particular significance for this paper: (1) the formality of naming the indicator (and the associated assertion, itself an act of power, that the indicator represents, or even defines, a

[1] Kevin E. Davis, Benedict Kingsbury, Sally Engle Merry, "Indicators as a Technology of Global Governance", IILJ Working Paper 2010-2, available at http://ssrn.com/abstract=1583431, last accessed 6 April 2011.

[2] Martin Ravallion, "Mashup Indices of Development", Policy Research Paper No. 5432, The World Bank, 2010.

phenomenon such as 'the rule of law'), (2) the ordinal structure enabling comparison and ranking and pressure for 'improvement' as measured by the indicator, (3) the simplification of complex social phenomena, (4) the 'scientific' justification through the use of social scientific methodology and the claim that the indicator reflects robust underlying data (although, in fact, missing or unreliable data may be fundamental), and (5) the potential to be used for evaluative purposes.[3]

3. Producers, Users, and Subjects of Indicators

Indicators are a social technology of power. In a simplified schematic, this technology can be modeled as operating in the triangular relations between the producers of the indicator, the users of the indicator, and those who are subjects of the indicator (the indicated).

3.1. Producers

The production of indicators may be a complex and collective process, and in many cases there will be a distinction between the main promulgator of a particular indicator and the individuals or organisations actually engaged in its production. The producers of an indicator, or its promulgators, may be concerned primarily with technical considerations of measurement, data collection and calculation, in a process dominated by statisticians and other social science experts. They may also have advocacy objectives; the appeal of rankings in popular culture and news media has made indicator production a relatively low-cost means to increase public salience of an issue or the visibility of an organisation. The production of the indicators may itself be a policy intervention: a way of articulating and framing a particular social phenomenon as a problem to be solved. Some producers have commercial objectives, such as making profits from clients requesting ratings or indicators, or from selling more specific or customised versions of information encapsulated in the indicator, or from selling publications or web site advertising, or from ancillary services (such as risk assessments) to which customers are attracted by the prominence of the indicator.

The spectrum of indicator producers is perhaps even wider than the spectrum of producers of more formal norms or rules purporting to affect

3 Davis *et al.*, 2011, see *supra* note 1.

global governance. Whereas rule-making in global governance is potentially subject to some constraints, including the application of global administrative law principles in certain circumstances, the production of indicators is often almost unconstrained. This has been true even for indicator production by some public law entities that exercise (international) public authority; although it has been argued that formalised assessment activities by such entities should be subject to international public law.[4] The types of entities producing indicators include:

- **Treaty-based intergovernmental organisations** such as the World Bank's Good Governance and Doing Business indicators, UNDP's Human Development Index, the UN's MDG indicators, WHO/UNICEF's immunisation coverage indicators, and the OECD's PISA school-student educational achievement rankings.
- **Non-treaty intergovernmental networks** such as the Financial Action Task Force, which has used a banding system to designate some countries or territories as 'non-cooperating', and works closely with associated regional network organisations.
- **Hybrid public-private international entities**, such as the Global Fund to Fight HIV/AIDS, Malaria, and Tuberculosis, and the Global Alliance for Vaccines and Immunisation (GAVI) which both use performance indicators in funding decisions.
- **National governments**, evaluating performance of different countries, such as the U.S. State Department's Trafficking in Persons index, which ranks countries in bands and places some countries on a watch list.
- **Private sector commercial entities** producing ratings for global markets such as Political Risk Services risk ratings and Moody's and Standard and Poor's credit ratings.
- **Private sector non-commercial or partly-commercial entities** ranking countries, such as Freedom House's Freedom in the World index, Transparency International's Corruption Perceptions Index, various private producers of indexes of state fragility/failure or state

4 Armin von Bogdandy and Matthias Goldmann, "The Exercise of International Public Authority through National Policy Assessment: The OECD's PISA Policy as a Paradigm for a New International Standard Instrument", in *International Organizations Law Review,* 2008, vol. 5, no. 2, pp. 241-298.

effectiveness including the US Fund for Peace, and social impact ratings of companies and funds for the information of investors (*e.g.*, the Global Investment Impact Reporting Standards).

- **Producers of intra-state indicators**, such as national governmental or non-governmental agencies producing indicators focused solely on issues within that country, but which are taken up by global governance bodies: examples include indicators of internally displaced persons in Colombia required by the Colombian Constitutional Court, indicators of maternal and early childhood mortality in Argentina, and local indicators of corruption and its meaning in Albania and India.

3.2. Users

Indicators have many different kinds of uses and users. Of obvious significance for law are uses of indicators in legal decision-making, or to allocate resources, or in certain processes of governance which may be subject to legal requirements or review structures. For example, eligibility for some World Bank funding depends on a country's score on a composite of indicators. The Heavily Indebted Poor Countries (HIPC) debt forgiveness arrangement uses indicators, such as levels of DP3 immunisation of children at age one year, as elements in the decision process. US law provides for sanctions against countries which receive scores in the lowest band in the State Department's Trafficking in Persons indicators, although these sanctions can be waived. The Office of the UN High Commissioner for Human Rights has piloted indicators which might help measure compliance with human rights, and could eventually be used in structuring remedies and perhaps even in determining violations. Many other uses of indicators also have implications for law and governance. Several of these are discussed further in this paper.

3.3. Subjects

The subjects of indicators – the countries and entities assessed and ranked by indicators – may welcome such rankings, or at least some leaders or components of the national public may do so. External rankings may be used by national groups to leverage change within the state, in much the same way as international treaties are used. High rankings can trigger benefits, including higher investment flows or lower borrowing costs that may be the result of a favourable credit rating. These benefits may be greater than, or synergise with, similar benefits flowing from legal commitments, for example such benefits (if any) as may flow from entering into bilateral investment treaties. Indicators may also be used by civil society groups to hold the government to account.

An example of a highly engaged response to indicators is the effort organised by the South Korean Government's inter-ministerial committee on indicators, which monitors Korea's rankings on approximately 20 indicators (including privately produced indicators on global competitiveness and environmental sustainability, and OECD PISA indicators on educational attainment). Efforts are made to improve Korea's performance through legal and policy reform, promoting more favourable perceptions of Korea for perceptions measures, supplying updated data to indicator producers, and on occasion contesting methodologies. Examples of using indicators include a country's citation of its World Bank Doing Business score to prospective investors (provided the score is high), and reform groups within a country using the country's low ranking on indicators to press for more resources or reforms in a particular sector, as with German states (*Lände*) seeking to raise their performance on OECD PISA educational assessments.

While the subjects of the exercise of power through indicators may influence or make use of that power, they may also seek to contest it. A notable example of a successful contestation is the challenge by the international labour movement and members of the US Congress of the World Bank's Employing Workers Indicator (EWI), on the grounds that it unduly favoured labour market deregulation and the ease of firing workers, and was in some tension with International Labour Organization conventions. The World Bank in 2009 announced it would move to develop a new EWI, and no longer use the contested EWI in its Country Policy and Institutional Assessments (CPIAs).

4. Indicators in Governance: Historical Antecedents

At least two different genealogical tracks led to the burgeoning use of indicators in global governance that has occurred in recent decades. One is the use of indicators as a technique of management within the jurisdiction of a single overarching government (or empire), associated in the twentieth century with central planning and then with new public management, and eventually extended into global governance practices. A second genealogical track has been the use of inter-country comparisons as a diagnostic tool and driver of reform, which has long been a staple activity of international organisations.

The use of statistics (*e.g.*, tabulated numerical data) as a technique of government is ancient. It includes comparative assessments of performance in the same unit over time (*e.g.*, year-on-year comparison of tax revenues from a particular province). On the other hand, systematic synchronic numerically-based performance comparison between different units subject to the broad control of a single central government seems to be predominantly a modern phenomenon, perhaps because of difficulties experienced in earlier period to obtain reliable and comparable data. One illustration is the British East India Company, which collected large volumes of data from its different posts for purposes of planning as well as accountability, but does not seem to have produced or used direct inter-unit numerical comparisons of performance. By the second half of the eighteenth century, efforts to produce such data were gaining strong intellectual support.[5] Adam Smith built several of his arguments on quantitative empirical comparisons, for example of court fees for civil litigation in different jurisdictions. Thomas Jefferson thought it persuasive to compare Europe with his America on many actual or speculated qualitative dimensions, down to differences in the average weight of pigs. The framers of the U.S. Constitution stipulated on democratic grounds that a periodic census would be used to reallocate seats in the House of Representatives. William Playfair introduced the bar graph and the pie chart, which quickly became popular for representing data on national and comparative political economy. Jeremy Bentham constructed an elaborate scheme for measuring and inter-unit comparison between 250 poor-houses to be run by a single company as productive factories; each would then adopt the management practices of the best replicable performer on each issue.[6] The field of *Statistik* began to influence German public law, including the 1750 work of Gottfried Achenwall and Johann Stephan Pütter on what became Achenwall's *Elementa Juris Naturae*, ideas from which were

5 Alain, Desrosières, *The Politics of Large Numbers: A History of Statistical Reasoning*, Harvard University Press, Cambridge, MA, 1998.

6 L.J. Hume, "The Development of Industrial Accounting: The Benthams' Contribution", in *Journal of Accounting Research*, 1970, vol. 8, no. 1, p. 23.

soon echoed by Vattel; and the monumental compilations of diplomatic and international treaty material by G.F. Martens.[7]

Central-planning governments such as the USSR, and more recently democratic governments engaged in 'new public management' (NPM), have used the familiar private-sector management technique of setting quantitatively-assessed performance targets (sometimes measuring performance by reference to indicators). In England since the 1980s these have been backed by powers of dismissal of under-performing managers and take-over of under-performing institutions, and variants of NPM are used by many governments throughout the world. Adaptation of these techniques has been pursued in the internal management of some global governance organisations. Moreover, attempts have also been made to use such techniques externally in global governance. These coercive techniques are most easily used by a single government *vis-à-vis* other states, as with US threats of sanctions triggered by poor performance in US assessments of a country's anti-trafficking legislation. Inter-governmental networks such as the Financial Action Task Force have also used this model, but the FATF's move away from seeking to impose sanctions on non-member 'non-cooperating countries and territories' is indicative of the difficulties of sustained use of such techniques even in limited membership 'coalitions of the willing'-type networks. As noted above, some inter-governmental organisations or networks set performance targets for purposes of eligibility to receive further aid or financing (sometimes structured as *ex ante* eligibility criteria to avoid problems of *ex post* enforcement of conditions in 'conditionality' regimes). Much more frequent is the use of performance measures in hortatory ways that may nevertheless exert considerable pressure directly on a government, or indirectly through their signalling function *e.g.*, to prospective foreign investors. The World Bank's Doing Business ranked indicators illustrate this. Performance measures are often combined in governmental and private governance with reporting and audit. For example, some privately-financed aid projects define targets or objectives (which may be specified and announced by an intermediate institution matching funders to recipients for small development projects), and also use anonymous or non-anonymous

---

[7] M. Koskenniemi, "G.F. von Martens (1756-1821) and the Origins of Modern International Law", NYU Institute for International Law and Justice Working Paper 2006-1, 2006, available at www.iilj.org, last accessed 4 April 2011.

reporting by people in the recipient community, partly to detect abuse, but partly also to improve policy and outcomes.

Numerical comparisons between different political entities not part of a single government, including what might now be called international comparisons, had become quite familiar by the mid-nineteenth century. The General Statistical Congress held in Brussels in 1853 addressed many such issues. One of these was statistics on crime, leading to the International Congress on the Prevention and Repression of Crime held in London in 1872. These initiatives were led principally by sociologists of crime and by statisticians working on these issues nationally, many of whom were interested in reforms. This drive for statistics, reform, comparison, learning from experiences of other countries, and discussions of best practices, also animated the formation in this period of the two major professional associations of international lawyers, the International Law Association (1873) and the more narrowly elite *Institut de Droit International* (1873).[8] The latter was originally planned as an organisation for the comparative study and improvement of national legislation, including through the use of comparative data, and indeed one of the leading journals founded by members of this group was a journal of international law and comparative legislation (*Revue de Droit International et de Legislation Comparée.*)

Collection, systematisation, and diffusion of such data has been a paradigmatic function for formal international organisations from the late nineteenth century, and one in which they have a comparative advantage, owing partly to their identities as organisations constituted by the member states collectively that are not status-rivals of (or threats to) any state and do not compete on the same plane for legitimacy. Issues concerning what information an international organisation should gather, and how this should be disseminated, can be highly contentious, and state governments are sometimes very effective at blocking specific projects (or at instigating them). Nonetheless, it is speculated that activities concerned with information are among those technocratic activities in which intergovernmental organisations are most likely to have exogenous effects (that is, where they are not simply endogenous to – a kind of pass-through for – the sum of the interests and specific objectives of the member

[8] M. Koskenniemi, *The Gentle Civilizer: The Rise and Fall of International Law 1870-1960*, Cambridge University Press, 2002.

states). These are also activities in which the organisation exercises considerable power (as governor, *vis-à-vis* the governed and the public). Within some limits imposed by the political and financial costs, the leaders and rising stars in such organisations have incentives to undertake such information projects, to exercise influence. Charismatic individuals (or individuals with a charismatic big idea) may form alliances and seek to pursue this idea through mobilisation of an international organisation's information-collecting and disseminating capabilities – this is part of the story of the UNDP's Human Development Index and the World Bank's Doing Business Indicators.

While formal international organisations have been prominent producers of indicators, the diffuse structures of contemporary global governance by information mean indicators are now readily produced by entities of many different kinds, as attested by the wide range of producers mentioned above.

5. Roles and Problems of Indicators in Contemporary Global Governance

Indicators are thus well established as tools of governance by information in two distinct forms which in some instances blur together: presentation of comparative data, and (potentially more coercive) performance measurement. The familiar problems of performance measures within national central-planning or NPM regimes experienced in governmental contexts recur also in broadly parallel ways in global governance institutions: managers aiming only to meet targets rather than greatly exceed them where they can (knowing that the government operates a ratchet so that a bumper level one year will simply become the target for the following year), managers focusing only on measured goals and ignoring things that are vitally important but unmeasured, massaging or fraud in the data, and collusion between target-setters and managers not to expose failings (*e.g.*, by deliberately leaving monitoring gaps). One important effort to avoid some of these pitfalls is through various forms of experimentalist governance, notably in different iterations of the European Union's Open Method of Coordination, in which indicators play a central role in benchmarking, learning, and revision of approaches and criteria.[9]

[9] Charles Sabel and Jonathan Zeitlin (eds.), *Experimentalist Governance in the European Union: Towards a New Architecture*, Oxford: Oxford University Press, 2010.

Indicators can also play very significant roles in governance that go beyond comparative data and performance management. Indicators frame a 'problem'. This involves deciding what the problem is – what is within its parameters, and what is marginal or only obliquely connected or lies outside and is excluded. Indicators also contain implicit theories of what is causing a problem, and of what it would mean to solve the problem – what outcomes would be ideal. When indicator designers decide what to measure and how the aggregations of what is measured are to be labelled, and when users of indicators seek to reward or censure 'good' or 'poor' performance on an indicator or a suite of indicators, the designers and users of indicators frequently are embracing theories about what causes the problem and how it can be solved or at least ameliorated. These causal connections and ideal-states may be made explicit, but often they are left implicit, and indeed they may not have been thought out very well in the design of the indicator. Design of indicators may neglect serious engagement with these matters and instead be driven by what data are available across the full range of countries or other units to be evaluated, or how expensive it is to obtain data and deal with problems of incomplete or missing data, or how clear-cut and eloquent the indicator can be made to seem for a particular policy environment. Use of indicators may be driven more by a desire to show results and satisfy particular constituencies, than by a drive to achieve slower or less measurable but more fundamental progress. Sophisticated designers of indicators may attach many cautionary notes about the data and about the claims that the indicator can and cannot support, but these cautions and caveats are very frequently ignored when the indicator is used in reductionist contexts.

In complex social problems, the behaviour of many different actors will be needed to be aligned, and some will need to make major new efforts, if outcomes are to be improved. This can be difficult for many reasons, including standard collective action problems. One compounding reason may be that many of these actors are uncertain about how to frame a particular social problem and about what its causes and likely solutions may be. Whether they are certain or uncertain, they may disagree vehemently with each other on these issues. This lack of a shared view about the nature and causes of the problem, and about who the key actors are and what they should be expected to do, can make efforts to understand and solve such problems ineffective. Indicators are increasingly used as a deliberately structured dimension of a policy intervention: not simply as a tool for diagnosis of problems and evaluation of results, but more strongly as a way of moving key actors toward a common framing of the problem and a shared sense of engagement in solving it. Conversely, an indicator which frames a problem wrongly, or omits to measure and value any contributions from some key actors, or measures quick results donors want but not long-term impacts, can undermine effectiveness.[10]

The choice about what indicators to produce and use is thus itself an intervention, going far beyond an internal commitment to basing decisions on good data. Promulgation and use of a particular indicator may be a significant component of an intervention in a complex problem. The indicator might come to define the problem and favoured approaches to it, and it might draw the key actors together into a network on the basis that they all have a stake in what the indicator measures. The indicator may help give an existing network a problem-relevant orientation and increased salience. (Davis and Kingsbury, 2010)

Work is currently in progress on the effects of indicators through networks,[11] but some conjectures may be advanced. First, indicators may have greater impact in sparse networks (where there are relatively few flows between participants, and some participants are almost isolated), than in very dense networks with vast numbers of existing flows, in which indicator-related activity will be only a small part of the volume of activity. Secondly, it is a well-established proposition in network analysis that weak ties can matter a lot to outcomes, even in strong networks. Thus an indicator could play a significant role in creating or giving content to an important if weak tie between different participants. Third, in some situations, existing networks are an obstacle to change or to solving a social problem. For example, if in a segregated society affluent people only have significant contacts with other affluent people, they may resist voting for taxes that help improve the health of poorer people in the society. If the obstacle to better outcomes is connected to social distance, new indicators might be promoted (together with other interventions) to focus on what people all have in common (*e.g.*, health effects in the whole area of long-range air pollution). Fourth, power analysis through network mapping may be useful in establishing subtle but significant hierarchies, and in

[10] Kevin Davis and Benedict Kingsbury, "Constructive Roles for Indicators in Addressing Development Problems", draft, 2011.

[11] Davis and Kingsbury, 2011, see *supra* note 10.

delineating who has what ability to control or influence outcomes. Indicators might be calibrated to align with these structures and achieve influence by flowing through them; or to work around some of these structures. Fifth, the impact of indicators may be linked to how they fit into (or alter) patterns of diffusion of ideas and innovations in the relevant sector.

6. Indicators and Law

Indicators are formally very different to legal norms, but there are many commonalities. Both aim to influence behaviour, and can be attached to sanctions and incentives. Both seek to set aspirational standards, and are addressed to a whole set of relevant actors, not isolates.

Indicators can also be a necessary complement to law; where a legal standard is framed in very general terms, indicators and other quantitative measures can be used to help give precision and content necessary for routine concrete application. Indicators may indeed be built into legal structures: for example, tax deductions may be available only for donations to charities that achieve a certain 'quality' rating in terms of social impact or other criteria such as organisational efficiency, and such ratings may be determined by indicators. Credit ratings already play a significant role in legal governance, both nationally and under the Basel capital adequacy accords.

The use of indicators in decision-making can be aligned with important rule of law values. Use of indicators can contribute to consistency and even predictability in decisions, and can be part of the reasoned basis of decisions. Use of indicators can make some decision-making more transparent. However, there are concerns from a legal standpoint about reliance on indicators. Use of indicators accords very considerable power to experts who design and understand them, and it may be difficult for others to challenge this power and the important political policy decisions that are built into the exercise of this power in some cases.

One response to this is to develop legal or regulatory controls on producers and users of indicators; such controls may also have implications for those subject to indicators, as well as for other affected groups. Potentially applicable principles of global administrative law include requirements relating to transparency, participation, reason-giving, review, and accountability.[12] Even if such requirements are not formally applicable as legal obligations for a particular entity (as will often be the case for private entities producing or using indicators), some of these principles may be followed as part of standards of good practice or in order to meet market or political demands.

Use of quantitative measures, especially in the simplified form that indicators enable, can flatten out the subtle processes of legal interpretation, law development, and discerning judgment. Indicators tend to aggregate different situations, and to be probabilistic over large numbers of cases but not necessarily discerning in individual cases. This can undermine some important features of law, including the roles of law in expressing moral and political values, and in realizing societal commitments such as those of each person as a moral and political agent. Indicators can also promote a view of behaviour as a continuous variable, rather than the binaries of violation or non violation and binding or not binding that is associated with some views of law. Indicators can produce a false sense of certainty and knowledge, and make it likely that one view of the factual becomes normative through governance processes that embody this view.

In practice, however, more and more law is concerned with, and part of, governance. Indicators are an important part of governance, and questions and problems about the production, uses, roles and limits of indicators must be specifically investigated and addressed. A much richer understanding of law that takes this reality of governance and indicators into account will be a significant dimension of the law of the future.

[12] Benedict Kingsbury, Nico Krisch, and Richard B. Stewart, "The Emergence of Global Administrative Law", in *Law and Contemporary Problems*, 2005, vol. 68.

6. New Legal Challenges Posed by Technological Development

6.1

The Challenges Posed to Private Law by Emerging Cognitive Enhancement Technologies

Nicole Vincent*

We normally think that people's responsibility diminishes when mental capacities are lost and that responsibility is restored when those capacities are regained. But how is responsibility affected when mental capacities are extended beyond their normal range through cognitive enhancement?

For instance, might some people – *e.g.*, surgeons working long shifts in hospital – have a responsibility to take cognitive enhancement drugs to boost their performance, and would they be negligent or even reckless if they failed or refused to do this? Alternatively, once enhanced, would people acquire new and possibly greater responsibilities in light being more capable? Could they be blamed for failing to discharge those greater responsibilities, and does this make them more vulnerable to liability if things go wrong?

The off-label use of prescription drugs such as Modafinil and Ritalin is on the rise, but although the current literature covers issues such as safety, effectiveness, coercion and justice, these drugs' effects on people's responsibility have not been investigated. The standards which the law currently uses to assess people's responsibility presuppose that human mental capacities are capped at a particular level. But if humans can surpass this level of mental capacity through cognitive enhancement, then this calls for a re-assessment of those standards.

1. Introduction

This 'think piece' describes a challenge posed to private law that stems from developments in the field of psychopharmacology. Here is a scenario that helps to explain the main idea and motivation behind this 'think piece':

Suppose that you are a surgeon who is about to perform a very delicate, challenging, lengthy and ultimately risky operation. For most sur-

* **Nicole Vincent** is a Research Fellow at Macquarie University and TU Delft.

geons, the chance that the operation will be a success and that the patient will walk away cured rather than damaged (or maybe even dying), is only around 30%. But a few really skilled surgeons consistently show a success rate of around 50%, which is attributed to their perceptiveness, mental clarity and superior ability to stay focussed throughout this lengthy procedure. But suppose further that you, an average surgeon, could take certain medications that would have no bad side effects, but which would increase your wakefulness, mental acuity and your ability to stay alert throughout this lengthy procedure, and which as a result could raise your own success rate to around 50%. Should you not take these 'cognitive enhancement' medications to give your patients the best chance of recovery and survival? Turning the table, suppose instead that it is your own child who is about to be operated on by another average surgeon who could also take these cognitive enhancement medications – wouldn't you want the surgeon to take these medications for your child's benefit? And if they didn't do so and the operation was a failure, wouldn't you feel aggrieved because they didn't do all that it was reasonable to expect them to do, and mightn't you even feel that this made them negligent or maybe even reckless?

The challenge that is posed to private law in the above scenario, and which is described in this 'think piece', is that such cognitive enhancement medications are now already being developed, and this creates the following tension. On the one hand, there are compelling reasons to suppose that professionals should indeed enhance themselves when something important like another person's life is at stake in the performance of their jobs, and when the costs of doing this (*e.g.*, side effects) are minimal or non-existent. However, on the other hand, it also seems right that nobody should ever be expected to modify their own brains with drugs for another person's benefit – *i.e.*, this seems like an overbearing expectation to impose on anyone – and that a person's refusal to do this should not open them up to allegations of recklessness and negligence should things go wrong. The problem however is that both of these positions seem intuitively plausible, but only one can be endorsed since each is incompatible with the other.

What makes this into a novel challenge to the private law *per se* – *i.e.*, a challenge that has never before been encountered, and which requires urgent attention – is that at present society is ill-equipped to address such questions because we have never before been in a position to seriously consider the responsibilities of people with intentionally-constructed above-average mental capacities. However, technological and scientific progress is making this a real possibility. The standards that the law currently uses to assess people's responsibility presuppose that human mental capacities are capped at a particular level. But if humans can surpass this level of mental capacity through cognitive enhancement, then this calls for a re-assessment of those standards. Although science fiction has considered the responsibilities of super-heroes with above average capacities, that is not a foundation for serious reasoning about such important matters.

2. Background Assumption – Responsibility Tracks Capacity

We normally think that the degree of a person's responsibility co-varies (among other things) with their mental capacity. This is after all why we think that children, the senile, and those suffering from certain kinds of mental illness or retardation are less than fully responsible for what they do – *i.e.*, because they have significant deficits in the mental capacities that are required for responsible moral agency – why children acquire more, and often more weighty, responsibilities as they grow up, and why people's status as responsible moral agents is re-established as they recover from mental illness. Some plausible mental capacity candidates that come to mind include the ability to perceive the world without delusion, to think clearly, to guide actions by the light of our judgments, and to resist acting on mere impulse. Or, for the legal context, H. L. A. Hart suggests that "[t]he capacities in question are those of understanding, reasoning, and control of conduct: the ability to understand what conduct legal rules or morality require, to deliberate and reach decisions concerning these requirements, and to conform to decisions when made".[1] Responsibility depends on other things too – for instance, how the particular (in)capacities came about, and on norms of reasonableness that influence what we think it is legitimate to expect of one another in a range of different situations. Mental capacities certainly play an important role.

[1] H.L.A. Hart, "Postscript: Responsibility and Retribution", in *Punishment and Responsibility*, Clarendon Press, Oxford, 1968, p. 227.

3. Neurolaw – The Assessment and Restoration of Responsibility Through Neuroscientific Techniques

Establishing people's mental capacities is a difficult task – people can pretend to have mental deficits to get a lighter sentence, and others can fail to realise that brain disorders caused their own criminal behaviour. Thus, in the pursuit of justice, the law is increasingly turning to neuroscience for help. 'Neurolaw' researchers aim to develop ways of using diagnostic neuro-imaging techniques to individually assess people's level of responsibility by revealing mental disorders that diminish relevant mental capacities. And mental capacities can also be modified with neuroscientific intervention techniques. For instance, defendants are sometimes given anti-psychotic drugs to restore their capacity to stand trial or to be punished – *i.e.*, to take responsibility for what they have done; and cyproterone acetate restores repeat sex offenders' capacity for self-control and thus to be responsible individuals by reducing their sex drive.

The above 'capacitarian' idea that responsibility tracks mental capacity is therefore also the operative assumption behind a significant portion of current 'neurolaw' research which aims to help the law to assess and to restore people's responsibility by using modern neuro-scientific techniques to discover, to detect and to treat mental disorders.

4. Cognitive Enhancers – Does Responsibility Track Hypercapacity?

But if responsibility diminishes when mental capacities are lost, and is restored when they are subsequently regained, then what would happen if a person's mental capacities were extended even further – *i.e.*, beyond the level that most humans can reasonably be expected to reach – through the use of cognitive enhancement technologies? Recent research suggests that drugs originally designed to treat mental disorders – *e.g.*, Ritalin, bromocriptine, donepezil, and modafinil – can significantly improve mental performance when taken by healthy individuals. Given this, would a person whose mental capacities have been enhanced beyond the normal range accessible to most humans through the use of such drugs become "hyper responsible", and if so then in what sense?

For instance, would cognitively enhanced people acquire new responsibilities that they otherwise wouldn't have had? Might they, as a consequence, be legitimately blamed when they fail to discharge those greater responsibilities? And would that increase the likelihood that they will subsequently be held responsible (*i.e.*, liable) when things go wrong? On a different note, if cognitive enhancers indeed improve mental performance, then might it become morally and legally obligatory for people in some situations to cognitively enhance themselves? For instance, given how much is at stake in an operating theatre, on a military battlefield, and on long-haul flights, and indeed in almost any other walk of life and profession where something important is at stake in the performance of our tasks, it could be argued that surgeons, soldiers and aeroplane pilots (and probably many other people as well) have a moral and maybe even legal duty to take cognitive enhancers to ensure the highest performance possible, and that they would be negligent or even reckless if they didn't enhance themselves.

The relatively recent development of cognitive enhancement drugs thus raises two related problems for the law, stated here in the form of two questions, to which the law as it currently stands has no clear answers. First, may some people, by virtue of what is at stake in the performance of their professional or social roles, be legitimately expected to cognitively enhance themselves, even if they would rather not do so, and would their failure to do this constitute negligence or even recklessness on their part? Second, once a person becomes cognitively enhanced, may they then be legitimately expected to observe a higher standard of care than the non-enhanced counterparts, and should their breaches of such higher standards attract regulatory, civil and criminal sanctions?

5. Theoretical Background and Historical Precedents

Legal determinations of responsibility hinge critically on assumptions about what is reasonable to expect of people in different circumstances. In general, people are expected to take sufficient care to avoid causing harm to others; so long as the amount of care that they take reaches the minimum threshold of sufficiency, then they will not usually be regarded as responsible in negligence for accidents that might eventuate. What passes for sufficiency is in turn pegged to what a reasonable person would have done. Thus, for instance, under many legal jurisdictions a driver is deemed negligent if her loss-causing behaviour does not meet the standard of the reasonable driver – *i.e.*, her actions must meet this minimum standard if she is to avoid being assessed as responsible for those losses in the event of an accident. And professionals' actions are also assessed in a similar fashion, except that the standard against which their actions are assessed is not the standard of a layperson, but rather that of a professional of their kind. Naturally, jurisdictions differ in regards to who sets this minimum standard for professionals, whether this is determined by society at large (*e.g.*, by judges and where applicable by juries), or by other professionals (*e.g.*, by professional associations through published codes of conduct). However, irrespective of who gets to set the content of this minimum standard, the point is that negligence is defined by reference to that standard.

The law imposes an objective standard of care onto people, and when a loss or injury occurs as a consequence of a breach of this standard, then the person in breach is deemed to be responsible for it. In a much-quoted passage, Oliver Wendell Holmes Jr. argued that:

> If for instance, a man is born hasty and awkward, is always having accidents and hurting himself or his neighbours, no doubt his congenital defects will be allowed for in the courts of Heaven, but his slips are no less troublesome to his neighbours than if they [had] sprang from guilty neglect. His neighbours accordingly require him, at his proper peril, to come up to their standard, and the courts which they establish decline to take his personal equation into account.[2]

But as history shows, changes in circumstances – for instance, the introduction of new technology – affect our expectations and beliefs about what a reasonable person would do. Put another way, the objective standard of care that the law imposes on everyone is itself sensitive to (*i.e.*, it tracks) people's capacities. When various medical diagnostic techniques which are common today (such as x ray imaging) were originally developed, their diagnostic value was not yet established, their risks were unknown and not easily controlled, they were available only in select research laboratories, and all of these factors coupled with their expense meant that a medical practitioner who failed to use them to diagnose what was wrong with their patient could not have been considered negligent or reckless for failing to use them. But today, now that the clinical value of these diagnostic techniques is widely recognised, and they are relatively inexpensive, largely free of risk, and ubiquitously available, a medical practitioner who fails to request that their patient be tested using these

2 Oliver Wendall Holmes, *The Common Law*, Project Gutenberg, p. 108.

techniques (where such a test could be diagnostically useful) could be deemed negligent and maybe even reckless.

As time went by, the applicable standard of care changed – it got updated – such that a medical practitioner who still only uses nineteenth century diagnostic techniques today could be justifiably accused of gross negligence, recklessness and maybe even stupidity. Put another way, what has happened in the intervening time is that as circumstances have changed, as new enabling technologies have been developed that extend our capacity to diagnose a range of previously undiagnosable conditions, so too the applicable standards of care have been updated. What was reasonable a century ago was tied to our capacities back then. But now that our capacities have been extended through the progress of science, medicine and through the introduction of new technologies, what is reasonable today is tied to our present extended capacities.

The significance of this example for the present discussion is that although Holmes' comments about the law's imposition of the same objective standard of care onto everyone may still hold true, that standard is pegged to today's capacities. But, by analogy, once the cost-benefit ratio associated with enhancing our cognitive powers is deemed to reach the right level – something that will inevitably happen as we develop safer and more effective cognitive enhancement techniques – the new objective standard may well include the expectation that under some circumstances (*e.g.*, surgeons performing mentally and physically demanding operations during long night shifts in hospital, or those who perform particularly risky and cognitively demanding operations) people should avail themselves of cognitive enhancement techniques. Furthermore, once people are expected to use these techniques in certain situations (*e.g.*, in the operating theatre, as per the above example), the new anticipated standard of care in those contexts will also be pegged to the standard that an enhanced reasonable person can be expected to attain.

Responsibility is a threshold concept, *i.e.*, to avoid being deemed negligent, a reasonable person must find our actions to be unobjectionable. But what a reasonable person will think is unobjectionable is not something that stands still over time, and it is certainly not something that is unaffected by our continually expanding capacities, often due to the progress of science and technology. Rather, capacities, both to do things and to develop the capacity to do previously unattainable but valuable things, play a crucial role in defining the objective reasonable person standard. The threshold of reasonableness is itself sensitive to capacities. Thus, the fact that responsibility is a threshold concept in no way diminishes, but rather it underscores and emphasises, the expanding effect which the development and availability of cognitive enhancement technologies seems to have on responsibility.

But on the other hand, at least on the face of it, there seems to be an important difference between previous capacity-extending technologies (*e.g.*, better medical diagnostic techniques) and cognitive enhancement drugs. Namely, the former are tools that people use to achieve better outcomes, whereas the latter involve the modification of our own brains through the use of drugs to make ourselves into better tools. And this difference raises the question of whether people should not perhaps be permitted to resist the perfectionist pressure to enhance themselves, even if a lot hinges on it in terms of other people's interests, without later risking accusations of negligence and recklessness should things go wrong.

6. Current Lack of Legal Policy on Important Questions

Once the benefits of cognitive enhancement outweigh the risks that they inevitably impose, something which is bound to happen once safer and even more effective drugs are developed, the public, professional associations, law makers and judges will face two pressing questions.

First, may some people, by virtue of what is at stake in the performance of their professional and social roles, be legitimately expected to cognitively enhance themselves, even if they would rather not do so, and would their failure to do this constitute negligence or even recklessness on their part? Second, once a person becomes cognitively enhanced, may they be then legitimately expected to observe a higher standard of care than non-cognitively enhanced counterparts, and should their breaches of such higher standards attract regulatory, civil and maybe even criminal sanctions?

These questions bear on the personal liberties of said professionals, since our answers to them determine whether they may choose to not cognitively enhance themselves, what expectations may be imposed onto them, and how they may subsequently be treated if things go wrong. However, at the same time society's interests should not be discounted either, since presumably the public also has a right to expect professionals to show reasonable (interpreted in a modern context) standards of care.

There has recently been a sharp increase in off-label use of the above-mentioned prescription medications for cognitive enhancement purposes. But although considerations of safety, effectiveness, coercion and distributive justice have been discussed in current literature, next to nothing is written about these drugs' effects on people's moral and legal responsibility despite the important practical ramifications that this may have for an individual's responsibilities and liabilities for the society at large. This leaves pharmaceutical companies, medical practitioners, professionals in socially important roles and the legal sector in a morally and legally uncertain position.

7. Conclusion

In his thought-provoking think piece titled *The Essence of Being Human* (also in this volume), Efthimios Parasidis argues that biotechnological advances have strained traditional legal views about what it means to be human and for human life to begin and end. This, on his account, has legal significance for the legal regulation of a wide range of human endeavours including "stem cell research, cultivation of human embryonic stem cells … in vitro fertilisation, proper use of discarded human embryos, … the extent of gene therapy and genetic selection that should be permitted, and the scope of intellectual property protection for human-animal chimeras ...".[3] Parasidis writes that "we find ourselves in the unique position of not only determining the genesis of our own species, but also the parameters of inclusion into our select club"[4] because of new developments in biological technologies.[5]

What emerges from Parasidis' discussion is that technology is not just an inert tool that we might use for our own purposes, or that we might choose to ignore if that is where our whim takes us, because the mere introduction of some technologies into society also challenges and changes our moral and legal presuppositions. Viewed from this angle, my own contribution in this think piece is that advances in the fields of neuroscience and psychopharmacology – specifically, those that will in the near

---

[3] Efthimios Parasidis, "The Essence of Being Human", in Sam Muller, Stavros Zouridis, Morly Frishman and Laura Kistemaker (eds.), *The Law of the Future and the Future of Law*, Torkel Opsahl Academic Epublisher, 2011, p. 539.

[4] Parasidis, 2011, p. 543, see *supra* note 3.

[5] Parasidis, 2011, p. 523, see *supra* note 3.

future enable us to enhance our mental capacities – will also directly affect the legal landscape by changing the obligations that people owe to one another and thus the rights that the law needs to protect.

When a multi-national pharmaceutical company discovers and subsequently markets cognitive enhancement medications, it is not merely providing new tools for our use or pills for our consumption, things which we are free to use or ignore as we personally see fit. Rather, just by making such drugs available they radically alter what is within the easy grasp of the citizen and thus what we can be expected to do for others. Therefore, the actions of multi-national corporations can directly alter our moral and legal standing with respect to one another by modulating our rights and obligations.

Naturally, legal policy makers can just sit back and watch how things unfold and how the introduction of these drugs into society will affect people's obligations and rights. However, the stakes in this case are arguably higher; we are no longer just talking about whether medical doctors should send their patients off to get an x ray or a blood test before deciding on a treatment, but rather whether they can be expected to sharpen-up their own brains for the sake of their patients' wellbeing by taking cognitive enhancement drugs. This provides at least one good reason for legal policy makers to take a pro-active stance and play an active role in deciding how this technology shall be regulated – *i.e.*, when it will be released, to whom, and under what legal conditions.

The issue identified in this think piece transcends the borders of any individual jurisdiction, because all legal systems must wrestle with the question of what standards of care should be applied to different populations, and whose interests should prevail when conflicts arise. Furthermore, technology transcends the borders of individual nations, and in this case cognitive enhancement medications will most likely be marketed by multi-national pharmaceutical companies across the world. Whether the particular disputes that arise will be in the context of civil litigation over (*e.g.*,) alleged medical malpractice (something which is more likely to occur in Anglo-American jurisdictions where there is a history of civil litigation), or in the context of government regulators or judges imposing greater standards of care on professionals (this would, for instance, be a more likely scenario in a country like The Netherlands), the tension between people's competing liberty and security interests will have to be settled in a way that is fair to all parties concerned.

On the one hand, this will require multi-lateral discussion among a range of different experts. For instance, while government regulators and judges might attempt to impose top-down rules for the governance of use of cognitive enhancement medications, professionals may also contribute to this process by developing their own codes of conduct that detail the expectations imposed on members of their professional associations. However, on the other hand, to the extent that the security interests involved are those of lay people – *i.e.*, the public stands to benefit from professionals' enhancement of their cognition, and of course the experts who although they may be expected to enhance themselves in a public context are also lay people in private and in other contexts – lay interests and lay opinions should also be taken into account in such discussions.

6.2

The Essence of Being Human

Efthimios Parasidis*

Recent and emerging advancements in a number of areas of research, such as genetics, stem cell technologies, assisted reproductive technologies, human-animal chimeras and the creation of a synthetic life forms, continue to challenge historical notions of what it means to be human. The ramifications of failing to keep pace with science, in terms of distinguishing human life from other forms of life, are significant. For instance, not only does defining precisely what it means to be human raise macro-issues in law, religion and public policy, it also challenges individual religious and cultural beliefs. Through arriving at a definition of human life necessarily implicates sensitive and challenging questions, these issues ought be adequately addressed so as to facilitate appropriate regulation of the biotechnology industry and the establishment of accurate legal standards for matters ranging from rights of the unborn to classification of entities eligible for patent protection. Though international harmonisation may ultimately prove to be difficult to obtain, a robust and ongoing debate will, at the very least, raise awareness of the importance of this issue and encourage public discussion of its parameters.

1. Introduction

Each generation faces the immutable struggle to adapt to new technologies while furthering the sensible goal of harmonizing man's insatiable appetite for exploration with normative conceptions of an ethically just society. One area where this endeavor is particularly challenging is research that focuses on innovations that could compromise, destroy, or augment human life. Examples of activities that are often discussed in connection with such ventures include stem cell research, genetic engineering, artificial intelligence, creating new organisms through synthetic biology, cloning, abortion, and end-of-life care.

---

* **Efthimios Parasidis** is Assistant Professor of Law at the Center for Health Law Studies, St. Louis University School of Law. This essay appears in Volume 13, Issue 1, of the *Minnesota Journal of Law, Science and Technology*.

Each of these paradigms raises important bioethical concerns. For example, is there a point at which a genetically-engineered, physically-altered, or pharmacologically-enhanced human ceases to be a human? In classifying humans, should a distinction be drawn for *in vitro* human embryos, anencephalic infants, or individuals with severe neurological impairments? Ought a synthetic living organism ever be deemed human? Often underlying these inquiries is the desire to preserve human integrity and encourage respect for individuals as autonomous entities. Though ostensibly laudable goals, beneath these assertions is the presumption that 'human' has been appropriately defined.

Legal definitions of who or what qualify as human have traditionally been based on normative positions with minimal reference to objective characteristics. Though normative assertions inform legal frameworks, the absence of objective descriptions frustrates judicious dialogue. With an eye towards assisting policymakers in structuring appropriate regulations, this 'think piece' outlines the essence of being human by synthesizing normative theories with objective findings from anthropology, comparative genomics, embryology, and medicine.

An examination into defining what it means to be human must be placed in historical context. The question has been pondered for centuries, with diverse disciplines such as philosophy, anthropology, and religion framing concepts integral to the dialogue. Despite the best efforts of numerous advocates, however, there remains significant disagreement on what characteristics are uniquely human. Importantly, the lack of discussion between disciplines has resulted in duplicated efforts and foregone opportunities to exchange relevant insights.[1]

Coupled with the lack of interdisciplinary collaboration, there is significant divergence as to how individual nations address the legal parameters of what it means to be human. These differences manifest in various areas of law and public policy, including regulations surrounding synthetic biology, stem cell research, neurological enhancement and manipulation, abortion, and end-of-life issues. Although nations have successfully limited treatment and research in these and other areas, in some instances, these limitations have stimulated an underground market and encouraged therapeutic and non-therapeutic forum shopping. Importantly, the growing ease at which individuals are able to cross national borders,

1 "A Look Within", in *Nature*, 23 October 2008, vol. 455, p. 1008.

and thus avail themselves of competing legal and public policy frameworks, complicates and jeopardises the practical reach of any individual legal standard.

Though obtaining widespread consensus on such contentious issues seems unlikely, this should not deter efforts to engage in international dialogue. By asking difficult questions and fostering meaningful debate, law and policy makers will begin down a path which ends at appropriate regulatory standards. Articulating clear legal standards for defining what it means to be human will serve as a helpful tool to oversee research and utilisation of treatments and to delineate practical limitations of treatments that are deemed to be clinically unsafe, lacking in efficacy, or morally unjustifiable. In this respect, lawmakers should strive to balance the goals of furthering the public health and respecting religious and ethical considerations of their constituents.

Defining 'human' also has significant implications in terms of intellectual property protection. For example, the use of public funds to support stem cell research has received far greater publicity than the government's encouragement of research through issuance of stem cell patents.[2] Though competing biotechnology companies often allege infringement of issued stem cell patents,[3] and scholars debate moral and economic issues surrounding stem cell research,[4] discussion of subject matter eligibility for stem cell technologies has received modest attention. This is despite the fact that, in the United States, over 1,700 stem cell patents have been issued.[5]

Following the United States Supreme Court's landmark decision in *Diamond v. Chakrabarty* and subsequent breakthroughs in stem cell technologies, commentators began to fear that the patent laws could be uti-

---

[2] Margo A. Bagley, "Patent First, Ask Questions Later: Morality and Biotechnology in Patent Law" in *William & Mary Law Review*, 2003, vol. 45, p. 469.

[3] Ann E. Mills and Patty M. Tereskerz, "Empirical Analysis of Major Stem Cell Patent Cases", in *Nature Biotechnology*, 2010, vol. 28, p. 325.

[4] John A. Robertson, "Embryo Stem Cell Research: Ten Years of Controversy", in *Journal of Law, Medicine and Ethics*, 2010, vol. 38, p. 191.

[5] Along with the issued patents, the Patent Office has published over 6,000 stem-cell related patent applications. Tao Huang, "Stem Cell Patent Landscape and Patent Strategy", in *Trends in Biopharmaceutical Industry*, 2010, vol. 6, p. 43.

lised to gain property interests in humans or human-animal chimeras.[6] In 1987, as a response to these fears, the U.S. Patent Office argued that there is a constitutional basis for precluding patent protection for property interests in 'human beings' where the 'broadest reasonable interpretation' of a patent claim could be read as encompassing a 'human being'.[7] Ironically, that same year, the Patent Office issued a patent to Johns Hopkins University titled "Human Stem Cells".[8]

The ban on 'human being' patents was expanded in 2004. Seeking additional methods of limiting research in controversial areas such as embryonic stem cell research, U.S. lawmakers passed what is now known as the Weldon Amendment.[9] Part of the appropriations bill, the Weldon Amendment requires that "none of the funds appropriated or otherwise made available by this act may be used to issue patents on claims directed to or encompassing a human organism".[10] Whereas the Patent Office receives its government funding through the appropriations bill, the Weldon Amendment seeks to preclude the office's ability to issue patents on 'human organism' claims. Although some have questioned the validity of the prohibition, the Weldon Amendment has been reinstated in the appropriations bill every year since 2004.[11]

Current laws provide little guidance in defining the phrases 'human being' or 'encompassing a human organism', and a significant number of issued patents arguably fall under these definitions. For example, the Wisconsin Alumni Research Foundation, a non-profit foundation that manages intellectual property generated by researchers at the University of Wisconsin, owns three patents that provide a property interest over a method of isolating human embryonic stem cells, as well as the resultant stem cell lines, on research derived from experiments on human blasto-

---

6 Alan Pompidou, "Research on the Human Genome and Patentability: The Ethical Consequences", in *Journal of Medical Ethics*, 1995, vol. 21, p. 70.

7 Thomas Magnani, "The Patentability of Human-Animal Chimeras", in *Berkeley Technology Law Journal*, 1999, vol. 14, p. 449.

8 U.S. Patent 4,714,680.

9 Timothy Holbrook, "The Expressive Impact of Patents", in *Washington University Law Review*, 2006, vol. 84, p. 599.

10 Consolidated Appropriations Act of 2004, Pub. L. No. 108-109, 118 Stat. 3, 101.

11 O. Carter Snead, "Public Bioethics and the Bush Presidency", in *Harvard Journal of Law and Public Policy*, 2009, vol. 32, p. 887 n.62; Consolidated Appropriations Act of 2010, Pub. L. No. 111-17, 123 Stat. 3153.

cysts.[12] During reexamination, the Patent Office initially raised an issue of non-obviousness, which the patent holders were eventually able to overcome. A subject matter objection was not discussed. Subsequent reexamination of the patents resulting in an office action that recommended invalidation; however, this invalidation was solely based on non-obviousness grounds.[13] The reexamination proceeding is still pending, and a final judgment may not come until after the patents have expired.

With these considerations in mind, this 'think piece' takes an interdisciplinary approach to examining a seemingly straightforward question – who is properly classified as a human – in order to further the academic debate and assist policy-makers in framing legislation in light of emerging biotechnologies. To begin, I argue that the question is best answered when divided into two independent inquiries: (i) at the population level, what distinguishes humans from other organisms and (ii) how precisely do we define the life and death of an individual human being?

Answering the first question requires a synthesis of the anthropological record with comparative genomics. With respect to the second question – identifying the life and death of an individual human being – I advocate a definition of human that is linked to the aforementioned population-based perspective coupled with an 'organism-as-a-whole' conception of life and death. Specifically, an individual human being is properly deemed to be alive so long as it is functioning as an organism-as-a-whole, irrespective of the functionality of any particular physiological trait. Thus, an individual's life commences when the being begins to function as an organism-as-a-whole, and ends when the being stops functioning as an organism-as-a-whole. Throughout this 'think piece', I use the words 'human', 'human being', and 'person' interchangeably.

2. Distinguishing Humans from Other Organisms

Arriving at a population-based definition of humans requires an exploration of the physical and cognitive evolution of humans as a species. This inquiry is not merely an esoteric dispute. Rather, it has significant impli-

[12] John M. Golden, "WARF's Stem Cell Patents and the Tensions between Public and Private Sector Approaches to Research", in *Journal of Law, Medicine and Ethics*, 2010, vol. 38, p. 314.

[13] BPAI decision, dated 28 April 2010, available at http://pub.bna.com/ptcj/101854Apr28.pdf.

cations for the way in which we view our lives and structure our laws.[14] For example, given the ability of researchers to create human-animal chimeras and receive patent protection for their creations, clearly defining human beings is necessary to define the contours of subject matter that is eligible for patent protection. Similarly, outlining the parameters of our species allows regulators to delineate protocols for research on human and non-human subjects. With these legal and policy issues in mind, I will turn to examining the anthropological record and comparative genomics in an effort to highlight traits that are uniquely human.

2.1. The Anthropological Record

Modern-day humans are classified as belonging to the subspecies *Homo sapiens sapiens*, which is part of the genus *Homo* and species *Homo sapiens*. Of the species *Homo sapiens*, two subspecies have been identified – the extant *Homo sapiens sapiens* and the extinct *Homo sapiens idaltu*. Anthropological data suggests that *Homo sapiens sapiens* emerged in Africa approximately 150,000-200,000 years ago, first dispersed to Arabia around 60,000 years ago, and reached Europe 20,000 years thereafter.[15] *Homo sapiens* evolved from earlier hominids, either *Homo erectus* or *Homo ergaster*, who were themselves descendents of *Australopithecus*.[16] Recent studies suggest that *Homo neanderthalensis* (commonly referred to as Neanderthal Man) co-existed with *Homo sapiens* in Europe and elsewhere for thousands of years. Although the extent to which each group interbred or exchanged ideas is unknown, it is likely that contact with other species affected the world-view of each.[17]

---

[14] David Lewis-Williams, "Of People and Pictures: The Nexus of Upper Palaeolithic Religion, Social Discrimination, and Art", in Colin Renfrew and Iain Morley (eds.), *Becoming Human*, Cambridge University Press, Cambridge 2009, p. 136.

[15] Colin Renfrew, "Becoming Human: Changing Perspectives on the Emergence of Human Values", in Colin Renfrew and Iain Morley (eds.), *Becoming Human*, Cambridge University Press, Cambridge 2009, p. 1; Christopher Henshilwood, "The Origins of Symbolism, Spirituality, and Shamans: Exploring Middle Stone Age Material Culture in South Africa", in Colin Renfrew and Iain Morley (eds.), *Becoming Human*, Cambridge University Press, Cambridge 2009, p. 30.

[16] Colin Renfrew, "Situating the Creative Explosion: Universal or Local?", in Colin Renfrew and Iain Morley (eds.), *Becoming Human*, Cambridge University Press, Cambridge 2009, p. 76.

[17] Paul S.C. Tacon, "Identifying Ancient Religious Thought and Iconography: Problems of Definition, Preservation, and Interpretation", in Colin Renfrew and Iain Morley

The anthropological record reveals that many traits that historically have been associated with modern humans are, in fact, shared by earlier hominids and other animals. For example, *Homo erectus* exhibited behaviors such as tool manufacture and the use of fire, while *Homo neanderthalensis* fed and looked after severely handicapped members of their communities. Findings also indicate that *Homo erectus* deliberately buried their dead, and that *Homo neanderthalensis* treated their dead in a varied, complex, and multidimensional manner.[18] Moreover, in recent times, gorillas have been observed to bury their dead. These traits are significant insofar as they indicate a heightened sense of respect for both the living and dead.[19] Similarly, a variety of characteristics – which include the development and use of language, the ability to teach and learn, and the establishment of intricate social groups – are found throughout the animal kingdom.[20]

Coupled with research into various species-specific traits, anthropologists often focus on cognitive differences between members of the genus *Homo*. For instance, the brain of *Homo sapiens* includes a developed frontal lobe, which is an area that is intimately involved in functions essential to symbolic thought.[21] Symbolic thought, which may be defined as the representation of reality through language, imagery or abstract concepts, has long been viewed by anthropologists as a trait that is uniquely human. In addition to *Homo sapiens*, however, recent findings suggest that *Homo neanderthalensis* also demonstrated abstract thought and symbolic behavior, and that *Homo neanderthalensis*, *Homo erectus*, and *Homo ergaster* all questioned their position in the universe. Given these and other similarities, including genomic comparisons, some anthropologists

(eds.), *Becoming Human*, Cambridge University Press, Cambridge 2009, p. 70; Lewis-Williams, 2009, p. 139, see *supra* note 14; Jane M. Renfrew, "Neanderthal Symbolic Behavior?", in Colin Renfrew and Iain Morley (eds.), *Becoming Human*, Cambridge University Press, Cambridge 2009, p. 59.

18 Renfrew, 2009, p. 3, see *supra* note 15. Renfrew, 2009, p. 54, see *supra* note 16.

19 Renfrew, 2009, pp. 51-54, see *supra* note 16.

20 A.I. Dagg, *The Social Behavior of Older Animals*, The Johns Hopkins University Press, 2009.

21 Henry de Lumley, "The Emergence of Symbolic Thought: The Principal Steps of Hominisation Leading Towards Greater Complexity", in Colin Renfrew and Iain Morley (eds.), *Becoming Human*, Cambridge University Press, Cambridge 2009, p. 10.

have argued for inclusion of *Homo neanderthalensis* under the species *Home sapiens*, defined as a subspecies *Homo sapiens neanderthalensis*.[22]

Interestingly, evidence suggests that the ability of *Homo sapiens* to interpret their own mental state began to appear approximately 75,000 years ago.[23] Insofar as the ability to think introspectively is commonly believed to be a defining characteristic of humans, the timing of the development is significant. Specifically, it appears that early *Homo sapiens* did not have the cognitive capacity for this type of mental activity, or that they did not utilise their cognitive capacity in this way. Interestingly, the earliest evidence of jewelry and bodily adornments dates back approximately 164,000 years.[24] This aspect is significant, as the notion of beautifying one's body through material objects is often cited as uniquely human.

Coupled with these findings, evidence suggests that the development of a distinct vocal cord, which is present in modern-day humans and allows for the development of language, occurred approximately 100,000 years ago, while the vocal ability found in modern-day humans has been present for less than 50,000 years ago.[25] Furthermore, until about 10,000 years ago, most *Homo sapiens* lived as hunter-gatherers. Accordingly, the advancements that modern-day humans are heralded for – which include the development of diverse disciplines in the arts and sciences, the quest for exchange of information and ideas, the ability to manipulate and alter their environment, and the creation of global systems of social networks and regulations – are recent accomplishments that are not found throughout the existence of *Home sapiens*. The extent to which these factors support the claim that today's humans ought be distinguished as a distinct species or subspecies is worthy of further analysis.[26]

---

22 This debate has existed for over a century. Bruce Bower, "Defining Neandertals", in *Science News*, 15 January 2011, p. 31.

23 Renfrew, 2009, p. 45, see *supra* note 15.

24 Renfrew, 2009, p. 77, see *supra* note 16; Bruce Bower, "Tool Finishing Technique Arose Before Humans First Left Africa", in *Science News*, 20 November 2010, p. 6.

25 L.E. Newton, "What Makes Us Human?", in *Biosciences Report*, 2007, vol. 27, p. 186.

26 Keith Ward, "Innovation in Material and Spiritual Culture: Exploring Conjectured Relationships", in Colin Renfrew and Iain Morley (eds.), *Becoming Human*, Cambridge University Press, Cambridge 2009, p. 256; J. Wentzel van Huyssteen, "Interdisciplinary Perspectives on Human Origins and Religious Awareness", in Colin Ren-

In reviewing the anthropological record, we must be mindful not to read our own ways of thinking into the enigmatic records of the past.[27] There is significant debate as to how anthropological findings ought be analyzed, and thus the findings summarised herein should not be taken as the definitive position of the discipline as a whole. Rather, the aforementioned findings are intended to highlight the difficulty that anthropologists face in arriving at a precise definition of what it means to be human. Though the work of humans has provided humans with an intricate understanding of our place in the universe, much additional work is needed to unearth new information and analyze relevant findings in an effort to gain an improved understanding of this age-old question.

2.2. Comparative Genomics

As with every organism, humans have a unique genome that is shaped by our evolutionary history. Although the Human Genome Project was 'completed' over a decade ago, no one really knows exactly how many genes make up the human genome or the genetic components necessary to make a human.[28] Other research suggests that each person not only has a unique genetic blueprint, but that each person has a different number of genes.[29] Furthermore, significant portions of a person's genome can be missing from, or added to, a person's genome, sometimes with no apparent ill effects.[30]

frew and Iain Morley (eds.), *Becoming Human*, Cambridge University Press, Cambridge 2009, p. 237.

27 Tacon, 2009, p. 61, see *supra* note 17.

28 For instance, the RefSeq database, which is maintained by the U.S. National Institutes of Health, estimates that humans have 22,333 genes that encode proteins. On the other hand, the Gencode database, maintained by the Wellcome Trust Sanger Institute in England, currently sets the number at 21,671. These figures vary drastically from earlier estimates. For instance, between 1990 and 1996, estimates placed the human gene count between 80,000 to 100,000 genes. Between 2000 and 2001, the number dropped to 30,000 to 40,000. Furthermore, the number of genes in a species' genome does not necessarily correlate with the complexity of the species. For example, grapes are estimated to have 30,434 genes, chickens 16,736 genes, and fruit flies 14,889 genes. Tina Hesman Saey, "Scientists Still Making Entries in Human Genetic Encyclopedia", in *Science News*, 6 November 2010, pp. 5-6.

29 Saey, 2010, p. 6, see *supra* note 28.

30 Saey, 2010, p. 6, see *supra* note 28.

Though limited in number and scope, genetic research supports some of the anthropological studies highlighted in the previous section.[31] In addition, the mapping of the chimpanzee genome has provided an important reference point for comparative genomic analysis. Interestingly, once the extent of the similarity between the human and chimpanzee genomes was published, some scholars advocated for the merger of the genus *Pan* (of which the chimpanzee and bonobo are species) with the genus *Homo*.[32]

Although comparative genomics reveals that humans and chimpanzees share approximately 98.8% of their genes, and that *Homo neanderthalensis* and *Homo sapiens sapiens* are approximately 99.5% equivalent, these figures provide little guidance as to the functional significance of the genetic distinctions between the species.[33] Notably, the order of magnitude of the divergence between humans and chimpanzees is less than that between mice and rats. As most would agree, however, what separates us from chimpanzees is far more profound than what separates the two rodents. In this respect, the question becomes the extent to which comparative genomics can supply helpful information in deciphering what genetic factors are uniquely human.[34]

Recent findings reveal that modern-day humans in Europe and Asia have inherited between 1% and 4% of their genes from *Homo neanderthalensis*. These genetic similarities are not found in modern-day Africans, suggesting that *Homo neanderthalensis* interbred with *Homo sapiens sapiens* in select regions of the world.[35] Genetic analysis of 40,000-year old bones found in a Siberian cave suggests a third species – neither *Homo neanderthalensis* nor *Homo sapiens sapiens* – that split from the line that led to modern-day humans over one millions years ago.[36] Called

---

[31] Renfrew, 2009, p. 76, see *supra* note 16.

[32] Newton, 2007, p. 186, see *supra* note 25.

[33] E. Pennisi, "Ancient DNA: No Sex Please, We're Neandertals", in *Science*, May 2007, vol. 316, p. 967.

[34] T.S. Mikkelsen, "What Makes us Human?", in *Genome Biology*, 2004, vol. 5, p. 238.

[35] "Reading the Neandertal Gene", in *Science*, 17 December 2010, vol. 330, p. 1605; Ann Gibbons, "Tiny Time Machines Revisit Ancient Life", in *Science*, 17 December 2010, vol. 330, p. 1616.

[36] Laura Sanders, "Genes Reveal Mysterious Group of Hominids as Neandertal Relatives", in *Science News*, 15 January 2011, p. 10; Gibbons, 2010, p. 1616, see *supra* note 35.

Denisovans (after the Denisova Cave in which the bones were found), their genome shares 4% to 6% of genes with the modern-day Melanesian population of Papua New Guinea and Bougainville Island. Interestingly, remains of *Homo neanderthalensis* and *Homo sapiens sapiens* were found along with the Denisovan bones found in the Denisova Cave. Taken together, these findings suggest that the lineage of modern-day humans is much more intertwined than originally thought.

Despite the limited information currently available, to the extent that the evolution of a species has a genetic footprint, comparative genomics provides an important framework for identifying relevant genetic differences between species. Equally as important is arriving at an understanding of how the genetic basis (genotype) relates to observable characteristics (phenotype). Given the immense complexity of an organism's phenotype, however, evolutionary changes are quite difficult to detect at this level.

The role of epigenetic factors further complicates the calculus. Epigenetic mechanisms are heritable changes in gene expression that are not coded in the DNA sequence itself.[37] Internal and external environmental factors impact epigenetic mechanisms, which in turn gradually alter gene expression. In other words, non-genetic factors cause the genes to behave differently, and this expression may be passed down to future generations. Examining the relationship between genetic and epigenetic factors has led to new concepts on disease and the heritability of traits, further complicating the process of unraveling the genomic evolution of humans.[38]

Clearly, comparative genomics provides great promise for bringing to light genetic factors that are uniquely human. Given the complexity of phenotypic plasticity and the role of epigenetic factors, however, significant research must be conducted to better understand the significance of genetic variation. Current efforts to unravel this information are often borrowed from genetic information derived from studies of human disease, mutational analysis of model organisms, and gene expression profiles. Since these methods rely on indirect inference, rather than experimental validation, they do not address the functional consequences of specific

[37] A.P. Feinberg, "Phenotypic Plasticity and the Epigenetics of Human Disease", in *Nature*, 24 May 2007, vol. 447, p. 433.

[38] G. Egger, "Epigenetics in Human Disease and Prospects for Epigenetic Therapy", in *Nature*, 27 May 2004, vol. 429, p. 457.

evolutionary changes.[39] Furthermore, intellectual property protection has hindered the use of much of this information, and thus stunted the development of the field.[40]

Although genetic research is at the forefront of many of today's emerging biotechnologies, current research strongly suggests that it takes much more than genes to make a human.[41] Arriving at an understanding of human genomic development requires additional genomic studies of humans, living primates, and extinct hominids, and an understanding of the functional evolution of both coding and non-coding sequences.[42] By combining advancements in comparative genomics with the anthropological record, our ability to delineate the contours of modern humans will be significantly enhanced.

3. Identifying the Life and Death of an Individual Human

As evident from a brief review of comparative genomics and the anthropological record, defining humans at the population-level involves a balanced analysis of numerous factors, many of which require further research. Though population-based definitions of humans are often linked to identification of specialised traits, this approach is problematic when applied at an individual level. For instance, for any one trait – be it consciousness or the ability to teach, learn, make tools, use language, empathise, etc. – there will be individuals who, due to disability, injury, or other factors, will be incapable or exhibiting the given characteristic. Further, for each of these characteristics, researchers have identified other organisms that possess the same or similar traits. Accordingly, it cannot be said in absolute terms that these traits are uniquely human, or that any given trait is a necessary condition for being human. This is not to say that identifying characteristics often found in humans is not worthwhile in framing a concept of humans. Rather, though identifying characteristics is integral to the debate, it is not dispositive of the issue.

---

[39] N. Mekel-Bobrov and B.T. Lahn, "What Makes us Human: Revisiting an Age-old Question in the Genomic Era", in *Journal of Biomedical Discovery and Collaboration*, 2006, vol. 1, p. 18.

[40] Newton, 2007, p. 186, see *supra* note 25.

[41] Elizabeth Culotta, "What Genetic Changes Made Us Uniquely Human", in *Science*, 1 July 2005, vol. 309, p. 91.

[42] Mikkelsen, 2004, p. 238, see *supra* note 34.

Whereas the fields of medicine and embryology permit a more informed theory of personhood at the individual level, drawing the line of where human life begins and ends has proven to be quite controversial. Essential to defining the existence of a particular human life is the notion of identity over time – that is, one must be able to identify the relation between a person at one time and another time, and the characteristics that make the person the same person. Various criteria for this continuity have been proposed – these include continuity of soul, bodily continuity, cognitive continuity, genetic continuity, and biological continuity.[43]

One traditional view, proposed by theologians and described by Rene Descartes, claims that the continuation of an immaterial soul is what accounts for human identity. Often referred to as a dualist perspective, dualists claim that a person could acquire a completely new body or continue to exist with no body at all. Building on the notion that human identity is linked to a soul, Saint Thomas Aquinas sets forth an alternative view, and classifies humans as 'ensouled bodies' or 'embodied souls'. Under this perspective, personal identity lies in the continuation of an ensouled body. The soul and body are inextricably linked, and the soul is what unifies and individuates a human.[44] Although an examination into defining what it means to be human is often linked to one's religious views, and it is important to be mindful of varying religious perspectives, this 'think piece' will not explore or critique religious notions in great detail.

Apart from perspectives that focus on the continuity of a soul, a number of scholars have identified humans as living beings possessing bodily continuity, cognitive continuity, or genetic continuity. Despite the intuitive appeal of these perspectives, each fails to sufficiently account for the continuity of all humans. For example, throughout the course of a lifetime, a person may lose their arms or legs, or may have a transplanted heart, liver, eye, or face. Identifying a person's life as a continuous body fails to account for these factors. Similarly, the fact that each person begins as an unthinking embryo, may enjoy a productive life, and then may

[43] Derek Parfit, "The Unimportance of Identity", in John P. Lizza (ed.), *Defining the Beginning and End of Life*, The Johns Hopkins University Press, Baltimore, 2009, p. 118.

[44] John P. Lizza, "Introduction", in John P. Lizza (ed.), *Defining the Beginning and End of Life*, The Johns Hopkins University Press, Baltimore, 2009, p. 2.

end up as an unthinking person with severe cognitive impairment, demonstrates that no sort of mental continuity is necessary.[45] Furthermore, through germline gene therapy, the genetic makeup of an individual may be altered, thus breaking any sort of life-long genetic continuity.

To the extent each of these theories fails to account for the continuity of humans over time, a more accurate barometer is preferred. I support a notion of continuity, proposed by various scholars, that is linked to a biological basis for identifying a person as an 'organism-as-a-whole'. This is a holistic approach that reflects the coherent unity of an organism, and views each person as a complex and integrated organism whose existence is dependent on the emergent functioning of many physiological components.[46] The organism-as-a-whole is not merely the whole organism – one may continue to exist as an organism-as-a-whole without continuity as a whole organism. Accordingly, during the course of one's lifetime, physical, cognitive or genetic traits may come and go, and continuity of existence may remain in tact, so long as there exists an identifiable organism-as-a-whole throughout the course of each change. Within this framework, this 'think piece' will focus on delineating the beginning and end of human life. Elucidating clear boundaries for life and death permits a more informed discussion of legal, ethical and regulatory issues related to emerging biotechnologies.

3.1. Interpreting Embryological Development

From the time of the ancient Greeks, scholars have debated the proper moment at which human life comes into existence.[47] Many argue that human life begins at conception, which occurs when a human egg becomes fertilised with human sperm and becomes a zygote. Fertilisation, however, does not occur in an instant, but rather is a process that lasts approximately twenty-four hours. Proponents of a conception-based defi-

---

45 Eric T. Olson, "An Argument for Animalism", in John P. Lizza (ed.), *Defining the Beginning and End of Life*, The Johns Hopkins University Press, Baltimore, 2009, p. 86.

46 James L. Bernat, "The Biophilosophical Basis of Whole-Brain Death", in John P. Lizza (ed.), *Defining the Beginning and End of Life*, The Johns Hopkins University Press, Baltimore, 2009, p. 420.

47 William A. Wallace, "St. Thomas on the Beginning and Ending of Human Life", in John P. Lizza (ed.), *Defining the Beginning and End of Life*, The Johns Hopkins University Press, Baltimore, 2009, p. 470.

nition must be specific as to when, precisely, a human life begins. Is it when the sperm begins to fuse with the egg, when the fertilisation process is complete, or somewhere in the middle? For those who claim that human life begins once an egg is fertilised – a position that many religious scholars adhere to – to be consistent, they must adopt the position that the completion of the fertilisation process marks the beginning of a human life. If so, then contraceptives such as the morning-after pill do not destroy a human life, so long as the pill is taken prior to the completion of the fertilisation process. Complicating this analysis is the phenomenon of parthenogenesis, where an embryo is produced without sperm. While parthenogenesis occurs naturally in various species, recent studies have used parthenogenesis to create human embryos.

Following fertilisation, the zygote begins to divide, with each division occurring approximately every 24 hours. Up to 8-cell stage, each single cell is a distinct entity in the sense that there is no fusion between the individual cells. Rather, the zygote is a loose collection of distinct cells, held together by the zona pellucida, which is the outer membrane of the egg. These early cells are totipotent, which means that they have the potential to produce an entirely new organism. Around day 14, the development of the primitive streak correlates with a loss of totipotency.

Prior to the primitive streak, identical twins can develop from a single zygote. Of course, twins may also form when two eggs are fertilised and two zygotes produced; in some instances, however, the zygotes combine, forming a chimera, and continue to develop as a single organism.[48] Under these circumstances, continuity as a distinct individual may only be traced to some period after fertilisation and prior to the primitive streak stage. Furthermore, whereas the zygote's development does not immediately differentiate the cells that form the embryo from those that form the placenta and other tissues, a zygote, in and of itself, is too indeterminate to constitute a real and ongoing human individual. For these reasons, a number of bioethicists argue that a human life cannot be said to exist prior to the primitive streak stage.[49]

---

[48] Helfa Kuhse and Peter Singer, "Individuals, Humans and Persons: The Issue of Moral Status", in John P. Lizza (ed.), *Defining the Beginning and End of Life*, The Johns Hopkins University Press, Baltimore, 2009, pp. 341-343.

[49] Germain Grisez, "When Do People Begin?", in John P. Lizza (ed.), *Defining the Beginning and End of Life*, The Johns Hopkins University Press, Baltimore, 2009, p. 303.

A recent decision by the German Supreme Court highlights further practical concerns of defining human life prior to the primitive streak stage. The German high court recently acquitted a doctor who performed pre-implantation genetic screening in his clinic.[50] Notably, the doctor reported himself to authorities in an effort to seek clarification of German law. The German court limited use of the screening for detection of serious diseases, and specifically indicated that the method could not be utilised to select for eye color, hair color or gender, noting that the law does not permit 'designer babies'. Although *in utero* genetic screening and pre-implantation genetic diagnosis often require the removal of one or more totipotent cells, the court did not discuss whether the practice kills a potential human being or whether the removed cells equate to human life. These screening methods are commonly used in a number of nations for disease-based testing, including the United States, United Kingdom and a majority of EU nations, while a number of other nations have no policy that directly prohibits use for non-disease selection factors. Do such screening methods constitute legalised eugenics or intelligent use of reproductive technologies?

In addition to conception and the primitive streak stage, viability is a stage of fetal development that is often cited as a defining line as to where human life begins. Although a viable fetus is theoretically able to survive outside the mother's womb, until it actually does so, it is not functioning as an organism-as-a-whole independent of the mother's body. Prior to that point, the organism is properly deemed to be a fetus, embryo, blastocyst, etc., and is properly identified as life or a developmental stage of human life. Human life, however, does not begin until birth, where there is biological and physiological independence, and the life is functioning as an organism-as-a-whole independent of the mother's body.

Though a developing embryo or fetus has the potential to become a human, and this potential intensifies with each passing day, the actuality of being a distinct human does not occur until birth, where the fetus moves beyond the stage of being a potential human and actually becomes one. Notably, the conception of human life that I support is consistent with Jewish principles, which hold that full title to life arises only at birth. Under Talmudic law, the fetus is considered to be part of the mother's

50 "Federal Supreme Court allows pre-implantation diagnosis", accessed on 23 July 2010, available at www.Research-in-Germany.de.

body until the birthing process begins, at which point the fetus is considered a distinct life.[51]

This is not to say that the zygote, embryo and fetus have no rights. Rather, the rights ought be linked to the relevant developmental category of life, and should not be categorised as human rights. As such, it is defensible for nations to grant fetal rights, and hold individuals liable for failing to adhere to their responsibilities. For example, such fetal rights may be structured to criminally sanction abusive fathers who harm a developing fetus or mothers who engage in illicit drug use.

Regardless of whether one agrees with the positions set forth in this 'think piece', legislators must closely examine the issue of when human life begins in order to intelligently frame public policy in light of emerging biotechnologies. Issues that are directly related to this inquiry include regulation of stem cell research, cultivation of human embryonic stem cells produced from parthenogenesis, standards for *in vitro* fertilisation, proper use of discarded human embryos, whether human embryos can be created solely for research purposes, the extent of gene therapy and genetic selection that should be permitted, and the scope of intellectual property protection for human-animal chimeras or any other manmade entity that arguably encompasses human life or a developmental stage of human life.

3.2. Cessation of the Organism-as-a-Whole

The continuing existence of a person depends on the continued functioning of the organism-as-a-whole.[52] Though many consider the brain to be the most critical system, the body is highly dependent on multiple systems. The heart pumps blood, the lungs provide intake of oxygen and output of carbon dioxide, the intestines provide nutrition and hydration, and the liver and kidneys detoxify ingested material and excrete waste. Although the loss of one vital function may inevitably bring about death, it does not by itself constitute death, though interruption of any vital system

[51] Aaron L. Mackler, "Jewish Perspectives on Abortion", in John P. Lizza (ed.), *Defining the Beginning and End of Life*, The Johns Hopkins University Press, Baltimore, 2009, p. 284.

[52] Lynne Rudder Baker, "When Does a Person Begin?", in John P. Lizza (ed.), *Defining the Beginning and End of Life*, The Johns Hopkins University Press, Baltimore, 2009, p. 397.

for a period of time can result in the destruction of the organism-as-a-whole.[53]

Historically, death has been defined as irreversible loss of circulation, respiration, or brain function. Although brain death is generally seen as providing a more reliable criteria for death than cardiopulmonary criteria, there is significant disagreement as to what justifies a diagnosis of brain death. Many patients diagnosed as brain dead have the ability to breathe spontaneously and maintain a variety of reflexes in the esophagus and other areas. In fact, it is generally accepted that the organism-as-a-whole can die though the entire body is not yet dead. This idea is essential to the notion and ability to transplant live organs from dead patients – it is an explicit recognition that something in a patient remains alive despite the death of the patient. Most startling is how bodies commonly react to incisions during organ harvesting. The heartbeat quickens and the blood pressure rises rapidly. The reactions are often so extreme that some hospitals utilise general anesthesia during organ harvesting.[54]

Some argue that these bodily reactions do not demonstrate that a person is alive. Others acknowledge that sections of the brain can remain active, but claim that these pockets of activity have no meaningful significance since the brain-as-a-whole no longer exists as a functioning organ. Doctors in some countries are legally permitted to pronounce a patient as brain dead without observing the electrical activity of the brain, while others may rely on vague cognitive diagnoses for brain death. For instance, for one to be diagnosed as being in a persistent or permanent vegetable state, there must be some irreversible loss of consciousness or other cognitive functions. Since a determination that this loss is irreversible is not absolute, but rather based on probabilities, there is intense debate regarding who qualifies for such classifications, and disagreement as to whether the specified cognitive functioning is lost temporarily or irrevers-

[53] Bernat, 2009, p. 422, see *supra* note 46; Michael B. Green and Daniel Wikler, "Brain Death and Personal Identity", in John P. Lizza (ed.), *Defining the Beginning and End of Life*, The Johns Hopkins University Press, Baltimore, 2009, p. 510.

[54] David A. Jones, "An Unfounded Diagnosis: Revisiting the Medical and Metaphysical Justifications of 'Brain Death'", in John P. Lizza (ed.), *Defining the Beginning and End of Life*, The Johns Hopkins University Press, Baltimore, 2009, p. 450.

ibly.[55] Ambiguous demarcations are problematic when one is faced with a clinical decision in an individualised circumstance.[56]

Since nearly all brain inputs and outputs pass through brain stem, and because the brain stem is the center for breathing, blood pressure control and wakefulness, some argue that the permanent cessation of its functioning equates to death. This definition, however, fails to account for individuals with locked-in syndrome. Locked-in syndrome is a state of preserved conscious awareness where paralysis is so profound that evidence of the preserved awareness may be very difficult to detect. For patients with locked-in syndrome, although the brain stem and other portions cease to function, portions of the brain responsible for cognition and consciousness remain in tact.[57] In addition to humans with locked-in syndrome, thousands of anencephalic infants are born each year. Anencephaly is a severe and uniformly fatal abnormality resulting in the congenital absence of a skull, scalp and forebrain. At the time of birth, there is no functional cortex but only a hemorrhagic mass of neurons and glia.[58] Although half of these infants are still-born and, of the other half, about 90% die within the first week, survival beyond a few weeks has been reported in a few instances.[59] A comprehensive conception of death must account for these states of existence.

The medical community generally agrees that ongoing biological activity in various cells or tissues is not sufficient to mark the presence of a living organism. For example, in some patients with total brain failure, the body still fights infections, heals wounds and maintains temperature.[60]

---

55 Multi-Society Task Force on PVS, "Medical aspects of the persistent vegetative state: Parts 1 and 2", in *New England Journal of Medicine*, 1994, vol. 330, p. 1501; Lizza, 2009, p. 15 n.2, see *supra* note 44.

56 Green and Wikler, 2009, p. 523, see *supra* note 53.

57 Jones, 2009, p. 449, see *supra* note 54; John P. Lizza, "On the Definition of Death", in John P. Lizza (ed.), *Defining the Beginning and End of Life*, The Johns Hopkins University Press, Baltimore, 2009, p. 534.

58 S. Shinnar and J. Arras, "Ethical issues in the use of anencephalic infants as organ donors", in *Neurologic Clinics*, 1989 , vol. 7, p. 730; J-M Guerit, "The Concept of Brain Death", in C. Machado and D. A. Shewmon (eds.), *Brain Death and Disorders of Consciousness*, Springer, New York, 2004, pp. 19-20.

59 Lizza, 2009, p. 16 n.3, see *supra* note 44.

60 The President's Council of Bioethics, selections from *Controversies in the Determination of Death: A White Paper*, in John P. Lizza (ed.), *Defining the Beginning and End of Life*, The Johns Hopkins University Press, Baltimore, 2009, p. 559.

Whereas parts of the organism remain alive, the organism-as-a-whole does not. Though use of technologies to support the body's vital functions may prolong life, removal of, or refusal to use, such functions is best defined as acknowledgement of the natural functioning of the organism-as-a-whole, rather than the hastening of death.

Overall, although societies have established various laws and practices surrounding dying and death, the event of death is a biological phenomenon that can be studied and described.[61] Accurately defining the moment of death is not only significant for the people close to the dying human, it has important implications for issues such as organ harvesting, when providers can stop treatment, and when payers can stop payment for treatment.

4. Conclusion

While emerging biotechnologies have significantly enhanced the human condition, they have also challenged conventional notions of how we define human life. It may be the case that humans are the only organism that can contemplate their own existence. Indeed, some have argued that the human capacity for self-definition may be viewed as one of the crowning achievements of our species.[62]

This faculty, however, comes with a price. The ability to determine who we include as part of us has an important moral dimension, and we must be mindful not to engage in ontological gerrymandering.[63] As history reveals, the capability has been frequently utilised as a tool to suppress the rights of minorities and indigenous peoples.[64] Although such historical malfeasance has often been discussed, the social, cultural and historical depth of defining personhood has been insufficiently explored, especially in the context of modern technological advancements.

The wisdom gained from the work of anthropologists, geneticists, embryologists, and physicians provides an important starting point for an interdisciplinary discussion of issues such as human origins, human na-

---

61 Bernat, 2009, p. 414, see *supra* note 46.

62 Tacon, 2009, p. 66, see *supra* note 17.

63 Van Huyssteen, 2009, p. 236, *supra* note 26; Green and Wikler, 2009, p. 515, *supra* note 53.

64 Grisez, 2009, pp. 296-297, *supra* note 49.

ture, and human uniqueness. Though policy-makers must balance competing interests that are seemingly irreconcilable, this does not imply that we are incapable of making progress towards consensus. Progress requires critical reflection of personal beliefs coupled with a thorough understanding of the relevant disciplines, each placed in historical context. Whereas some scholars argue that we can handle relevant moral issues without settling the question of personhood, I think that today's moral issues can be more appropriately addressed if we first have a comprehensive understanding of what it means to be human.

The findings discussed in this 'think piece' are intended to highlight the value and limitations of various disciplines. A review of the anthropological record reveals clues as to the origins of humans, though the record does not provide us with a definitive statement as to when modern-day humans entered this world. Genetics guides our awareness of the evolution of mankind and the differences between species, yet fails to delineate the significance of genetic variation and demarcate precisely where one species ends and another begins. Medicine provides us with a window into embryonic and fetal development, however, it fails to identify the normative status of the developing life.

And thus, we find ourselves in the unique position of not only determining the genesis of our own species, but also the parameters of inclusion into our select club. Regardless of one's individual perspective, all can agree that elucidating a clear vision of what it means to be human permits resolution of important legal, ethical and regulatory issues, and guides one's vision of life and well-being.

6.3

The Future of Space Law

Yan Ling[*]

The international space legal regime was established in the early years of the space age, primarily by five international treaties. Space technology has never stopped developing since the first satellite was successfully launched into orbit in 1959. However, international space law lags far behind and has not adapted to new situations. This think piece presents the current problems such as space debris and space weapons, which have an adverse impact on national security and space safety, have not been fully addressed by the existing space law treaties. It also foresees some future legal problems arising from active involvement of private enterprises and individuals in space activities and increased missions to explore the Moon, other celestial bodies and their natural resources. It then analyzes different approaches to address these issues such as amendment or review of current treaty provisions, conclusion of new treaties, making guidelines or code of conduct etc. It concludes that a code of conduct, though not legally binding, may be the first step towards the full prohibition of space weapons. Space debris is a problem that must be solved with political volition, technical measures and a legal framework. As to the private participation in space activities and further exploration and exploitation of the Moon and other celestial bodies, there may be a need to make legal regimes with more details to govern these space activities. It also envisages that the scope of space law will expand to be much broader and more complex in the future.

1. Introduction

The international space legal regime was established in the early years of the space age, mainly by five international treaties: the Treaty on Principles Governing the Activities of States in the Exploration and Use of Outer Space, including the Moon and Other Celestial Bodies (Outer Space Treaty), the Agreement on the Rescue of Astronauts, the Return of Astronauts and the Return of Objects Launched into Outer Space (Rescue Agreement), the Convention on International Liability for Damage

[*] **Yan Ling** is Professor of Political Science and Law at China University.

Caused by Space Objects (Liability Convention), the Convention on Registration of Objects Launched into Outer Space (Registration Convention) and the Agreement Governing the Activities of States on the Moon and Other Celestial Bodies (Moon Agreement). Space technology has never stopped developing since the first satellite was successfully launched into orbit in 1959. All mankind has benefited from satellite communication, satellite broadcasting, satellite remote sensing, satellite navigation, etc. Manned flights to outer space, lunar exploration projects and sub-orbital and space tourism will provide another way for human beings to see the universe. Meanwhile problems such as space debris and space weapons arise from space activities, which will have an adverse impact on national security and space safety. However, not a single new treaty has been concluded to tackle these problems since 1979. International space law lags far behind and has not adapted to new situations.

2. Weaponisation of Outer Space

At present, the Treaty Banning Nuclear Weapon Tests in the Atmosphere, in Outer Space and under Water (Partial Test Ban Treaty) of 1963 and the Outer Space Treaty of 1967 are the only international treaties governing space weapons. They prohibit only nuclear weapons or other kinds of weapons of mass destruction in outer space and on celestial bodies. Space law "does not prohibit the development and use of conventional space weapons that have a nuclear source" or "the use of particle-beam or laser weaponry in space".[1] A report of the U.S. Space Commission identified at least 11 categories of anti-satellite attack.[2] These weapons will threaten the existence of satellites, the security and economic development of all states. Obviously, the existing multilateral treaties did not fully address the issue of non-weaponisation of outer space and did not take into account technical advances that have taken place. Therefore there is a need to fill in these gaps.

1 Michel Bourbonnière and Ricky J. Lee, "Legality of the Deployment of Conventional Weapons in Earth Orbit Balancing Space Law and the Law of Armed Conflict", in *European Journal of International Law*, vol. 18, pp.881-882.

2 Jon Kyl, "China's Anti-Satellite Weapons and American National Security", Heritage Lecture #990, 29 January 2007, available at http://www.heritage.org/Research/NationalSecurity/hl990.cfm.

There are different approaches to solve the problem. The first approach is to amend Article 4 of the Outer Space Treaty. The proposed Article 4 will also ban "kinetic vehicles, space-based laser weapons, and ASATs".[3] However, the constant development of space technology will make it difficult to exhaustively list all space weapons. In addition, to fully address the issue, it is necessary to introduce a verification mechanism.

The second approach is to conclude a multilateral treaty on comprehensive prohibition of space weapons. China and Russia proposed a draft Treaty on Prevention of the Placement of Weapons in Outer Space and of the Threat or Use of Force against Outer Space Objects to the Conference on Disarmament on 12 February 2008.[4] The draft treaty would obligate states "not to place in orbit around the Earth any objects carrying any kinds of weapons, not to install such weapons on celestial bodies and not to place such weapons in outer space in any other manners; not to resort to the threat or use of force against outer space objects; and not to assist or induce other States, groups of States or international organisations to participate in activities prohibited by this Treaty".[5]

This proposal has been opposed by the USA government because it denies that there is a space arms race.[6] More importantly, a treaty on the prevention of space weaponisation requires an agreed definition of space weapons. However, the core conception of space weapons is vague. Many things can be used as space weapons and some space objects can be used for both civil and military purposes. Therefore, it would be difficult to negotiate a treaty on the comprehensive prohibition of the space weapons.

To avoid all difficulties in conclusion of a multilateral treaty banning space weapons, the Council of the European Union issued a Draft

---

[3] Alex B. Englehart, "Common Ground in the Sky: Extending the 1967 Outer Space Treaty to Reconcile U.S. and Chinese Security Interests", in *Pacific Rim Law & Policy Journal*, vol. 17, no. 3, p.152.

[4] CD/1839, 29 February 2008.

[5] Draft Treaty on Prevention of the Placement of Weapons in Outer Space and of the Threat or Use of Force against Outer Space Objects, Article 2.

[6] Frank M. Walsh, "Forging a Diplomatic Shield for American Satellites: The Case for Re-evaluating the 2006 National Space Policy in Light of a Chinese Anti-Satellite System", in *Journal of Air Law and Commerce*, vol. 72, 2007, p.761.

Code of Conduct for Outer Space Activities[7] to EU member states on 3 December 2008. Among other things, key activities to be covered under the code include avoiding collisions and harmful interference with other states' right to the peaceful exploration and use of outer space. Under the Draft Code of Conduct, the subscribing states are responsible for taking "all the adequate measures to prevent outer space from becoming an area of conflict".[8] They will, in conducting outer space activities, refrain from any intentional action which might cause damage or destruction of outer space objects.[9] The Draft Code of Conduct will also serve as a basis for consultations with key third countries in order to reach a text that is acceptable to more countries. This may be a flexible means to solve the problem of weaponisation of outer space. A code of conduct would serve the same purpose as a treaty does in respect of banning space weapons. Although a code of conduct is not binding, it may be the first step for the full prohibition of space weapons. Soft law may evolve into customary norms through the practice of states. It will be easier to incorporate customary rules into treaties.

3. Safety of Space Objects

Placement of more and more satellites in outer space increases the likelihood of collision between satellites and damage to satellites caused by debris. According to the cascade effect argument, the problem of debris may become more serious because increases in the amount of debris left in outer space by space activities could generate more debris through collisions, even without new space objects being placed in orbit.[10] This became more than a hypothesis when a US communication satellite collided with a defunct Russian satellite in February 2009, releasing massive debris clouds. It is well known that even tiny debris with high velocities may cause fatal damage to space objects and astronauts. Therefore, two

---

7 European External Action Service, "Council Conclusion and Draft Code of Conduct for Outer Space Activities", Brussels, 3 December 2008, available at http://www.consilium.europa.eu/showPage.aspx?id=1570&lang=EN, last accessed 20 April 2011.

8 European External Action Service, 2008, section 2, see *supra* note 7.

9 European External Action Service, 2008, section 4.2, see *supra* note 7.

10 Sethu Nandakumar Menon and V. Gopala Krishnan, "State Responsibility and Need of International Legal Consensus for Debris-Free Environment", International Astronomical Congress, 2007, IAC-07-E6.3.06.

issues need to be more carefully dealt with. One is liability for damage caused by debris. The other is a need to mitigate space debris.

With respect to the liability issue, in cases of damage occurring in outer space, the launching state of a space object that caused damage shall be liable. The problems are, first, that it is difficult to identify the launching state of tiny space debris generated from the break-up of a space object. If untraceable debris causes damage to a space object or person in outer space, the suffering party may not be able to get compensation. Second, even if the damage is caused by traceable debris, it is still difficult to determine whether the launching state is at fault. Future space law needs a legal mechanism to solve the liability problems related to damage caused by debris that occurs in outer space.

As for space debris mitigation, none of the five space law treaties foresee the problem of debris and address the issue. Efforts of the international community have resulted in two guidelines regarding space debris mitigation. The Inter-Agency Space Debris Coordination Committee (IADC) produced technical guidelines on orbital debris mitigation in 2001.[11] UNCOPUS approved space debris mitigation guidelines based on revised IADC ones in January 2007.[12] The UN General Assembly endorsed these guidelines in February 2008.[13] They are not binding. States are advised to follow them on a voluntary basis. Thus, it is desirable to address the issue of debris and related problems in international legal instruments in the future.

Firstly, international space law needs to provide legal definitions for space objects and space debris. The existing space treaty describes a space object as including component parts of a space object as well as its launching vehicle and parts thereof. The question is whether all debris is covered by the term 'space object'. For example, a glove left by an astronaut in outer space seems not to be regarded as a space object but it is space debris. IADC's guidelines distinguish space objects from debris depending on whether they are functional. The term 'space debris' in that document refers to "all man made objects including fragments and elements thereof, in Earth orbit or re-entering the atmosphere, that are non

[11] IADC-02-01, Revision 1, September 2007.

[12] Report of the Committee on the Peaceful Uses of Outer Space, General Assembly Official Records, Sixty-second session Supplement No. 20 (A/62/20)

[13] UN Doc. A/RES/62/217, 10 January 2008.

functional". The question is whether a defunct satellite should be excluded from the definition of a space object.

Secondly, there is a need to impose obligations on space faring nations to mitigate space debris. These obligations could include four major provisions. First, space faring nations shall take measures to limit debris released during the launching, operational and mission ending stages to a certain extent. It appears that the entire prohibition of debris release is not practical. There are always unexpected and exceptional circumstances. Therefore, an acceptable standard should be established to limit debris generation. Second, when there are good reasons for destruction of a defunct satellite, the satellite shall not be destroyed in a manner that will release debris or pose threats to the safety of other satellites. Third, states shall be required to retrieve defunct satellites or remove them to junk orbit. This is not only to prevent obsolete satellites from break-up in orbit, but also to clean the orbital positions that the satellites take. After all, continuous space activities for decades, hundreds or even thousands of years require satellite orbital positions. Removing non-functional satellites from operational Earth orbit will become necessary sooner or later. Fourth, when there is a probability of collision between two satellites or between a satellite and a natural celestial body, states shall take measures to avoid the collision.

Thirdly, states shall have obligations to cooperate, firstly, to establish an international debris tracking network aimed at monitoring those debris that may cause damage to space objects and astronauts in outer space and damage on the surface of the Earth or to aircraft flight. Some states already have national debris tracking systems. By joining their efforts, an international debris tracking network will be able to track debris more effectively and provide more accurate information. Second, states shall cooperate to disseminate and share information about the probability of collisions and damage. The information shall be made available to the concerned states. The collision of the US satellite and Russian satellite revealed that the US company was not aware of the probability of collision prior to the event. Therefore, situational awareness is an important factor for dealing with the debris issue. States also have an obligation to provide assistance to the concerned state in controlling and removing debris or manoeuvring satellites if necessary. In short, debris is a problem that must be solved with political volition, technical measures and a legal framework.

4. Private Participation in Outer Space Activities

Outer space activities have been long carried out by governmental organisations. According to the Outer Space Treaty, space activities carried out by private enterprises must be under the authorisation and supervision of an appropriate state. The Outer Space Treaty obligates states to ensure that private entities' space activities shall be in conformity with international law and space treaties. The launching states of the space object shall be liable for the damage caused by private-owned space objects. In short, private participants of space activities have no legal status in international space law.

However, involvement of private enterprises and individuals in space activities are increasing nowadays, especially after the USA adopted a space policy to encourage, promote and enhance private commercial space activities. Private space tourism, private space travel, commercial space hotels and commercial space settlement are envisaged. Satellite communication industries are in the process of privatisation. The following legal issues which arise from these phenomena are beyond the scope of existing treaties.

First, there is a need to clarify the status of space tourists. According to Article VIII of the Outer Space Treaty, the state of registry of an object launched into outer space retains jurisdiction and control over that object and over any personnel thereof, while in outer space or on a celestial body. Here, what does 'personnel' means? Does it refer to the persons on a mission in outer space or all persons onboard a spacecraft? Article V of the Outer Space Treaty regards astronauts as envoys of mankind in outer space. States that are party to the Rescue Agreement are required to render astronauts all possible assistance in the event of accident, distress, or emergency landing. In accordance with this provision, the Rescue Agreement has further developed a rescue of astronauts and the return of the astronauts' framework. In the Agreement, the term 'astronauts' are replaced by the term 'personnel'. The question is whether astronauts and personnel are the same? Tourists are probably not regarded as astronauts or envoys of mankind because they go to outer space purely for their own pleasure. If the term 'personnel' only refer to astronauts, tourists will be excluded from the application of the Rescue Agreement.

Second, claiming private property rights to lunar land or celestial bodies has happened in some countries in the latest decades, which has brought about debates on whether private property rights are allowable in accordance with international space law. Some space lawyers argue that both governmental and private space activities are national space activities. Since Article II of the Outer Space Treaty states that outer space, including the Moon and other celestial bodies is not subject to national appropriation by any means, private property rights to lunar land and other celestial bodies are not allowed. This view is supported by the board of directors of the International Institute of Space Law.[14] Other space lawyers argue that international space law permits private property rights because the article does not explicitly prohibit private appropriation.[15] It was understood that the purpose of the prohibition of national appropriation of outer space and celestial bodies is to ensure free access to all areas of celestial bodies. However, some space lawyers voiced their concerns that since there is no state sovereignty in outer space, domestic law relating to private property rights can not be applied in outer space and celestial bodies; therefore private investment in outer space and celestial bodies will not be protected.[16] In the view of some businessmen, current international space law does not encourage private investment in the exploration and use of outer space.[17]

Different proposals for establishing private property rights in outer space in accordance with international space law have been proposed. One proposal suggests that states create pseudo-property rights in outer space.[18] A pseudo-property right in outer space is not really a property right but it gives someone the right to exclude others from using, for ex-

---

[14] Statement by the Board of Directors of the International Institute of Space Law (IISL) On Claims to Property Rights Regarding The Moon and Other Celestial Bodies, 2004, available at http://www.iislweb.org/docs/IISL_Outer_Space_Treaty_Statement.pdf, last accessed on 16 February 2011; Statement of the Board of Directors of the International Institute of Space Law (IISL), 22 March 2009, available at http://www.iislweb.org/docs/Statement%20BoD.pdf, last accessed 16 February 2011.

[15] Wayne White Jr., "Implications of a Proposal for Real Property Rights in Outer Space", Proceedings of 42nd Colloquium on the Law of Outer Space, p.366-372.

[16] Paul Tobias, "Opening the Pandora's Box of Space Law", in *Hastings International and Comparative Law Review*, vol. 28, 2005, p.300.

[17] Henry R. Hertzfeld and Frans G. Von Der Dunk, "Bringing Space Law into Commercial World: Property Rights without Sovereignty", in *Chinese Journal of International Law*, vol. 6, 2005, p.81.

[18] Sam Dinkin, "Property Rights and Space Commercialization", *The Space Review*, 10 May 2004.

ample, a piece of real estate on a celestial body. Another proposal suggests that states confer functional property rights.[19] These rights would be based on the principle of first-come, first-serve occupation, and the prohibition against harmful interference with other states' activities. Conferral of the title would depend upon the government's control over the space objects and personnel at a location. Once conferred, these rights would be almost identical to terrestrial property rights. The rights would be limited to the area occupied by the space object, and to a reasonable safety area around the facility. The rights would terminate if the concerned activity were halted. There is also a proposal for establishing a new space law framework, under which a natural or juridical person could acquire a charter from a granting state: "The charter allowed the grantee to claim land in the name of the grantor state and entitled the grantee to certain contractual benefits and obligations pursuant to the provisions of the charter".[20] It is probably still too early to set up the rules on private space property rights because private space activities at this stage can proceed well without the said rights. International space law may need to address this issue when private space industries mature in the future.

Third, the ownership of satellites in orbit may be transferred from one company/state to another company/state by sale, bankruptcy, or some similar means. According to Article VIII of the Outer Space Treaty, the state on whose registry an object launched into outer space is carried has jurisdiction and control over such an object and over any personnel thereof, while in outer space or on a celestial body. Such an object, when it returns to the Earth and is found beyond the limit of the state of registry, shall be returned to that state. The state of registry must be a launching state of a space object. Four categories of states are qualified as a launching state: (1) a state which launches a space object; (2) a state which procures the launching of a space object; (3) a state from whose territory a space object is launched; and (4) a state from whose facility a space object

[19] Wayne White Jr, "Real Property Rights in Outer Space", in *40th Colloquium on the Law of Outer Space*, 1998, p.370.

[20] Jonathan Thomas, "Privatization of Space Ventures: Proposing A Proven Regulatory Theory for Future Extraterrestrial Appropriation", in *International Law and Management Review*, vol. 1, 2010, p.220.

is launched.[21] A state or a governmental or non governmental organisation to which the ownership of a satellite in orbit is transferred may not fall into any categories of launching states. This may cause problems of liability for the damage caused by the satellites because only the launching state(s) of a satellite is (are) liable for the damage caused by a satellite. It will also affect the application of the Rescue Convention as all the obligations are related to launching states or authorities. A state who obtains a satellite after the satellite has been launched into orbit has nothing to do with the launch of the satellite. Therefore, it is not qualified to be a launching state. However, it would be unfair if the original launching states remain liable for the damage caused by a satellite no longer owned by it. Further, according to the Registration Convention, only one of the launching states shall register the satellite they have launched. The Registration Convention does not provide guidelines specific for transfer of satellite ownership in orbit. Therefore it may cause problems concerning jurisdiction over the satellites and the personnel thereof while in outer space or on celestial bodies. Namely, the owner and/or operator of a purchased satellite does not have a legal right to exercise jurisdiction and control over the satellite.

In practice, some states have changed a satellite's state of registry concurrent with a transfer of ownership by mutual consent. Some states that have purchased a satellite in orbit have taken the obligation of a state of registry by declaration. To harmonise the practice of states and international organisations in registering space objects, the UN General Assembly adopted a resolution which recommends that following the change in supervision of a space object in orbit, the state of registry should furnish to the Secretary-General additional information about the date of change in supervision and the identification of the new owner or operator. If there is no state of registry, the appropriate state according to article VI of the Outer Space Treaty should furnish the above information to the Secretary-General.[22] Nevertheless, the UN General Assembly resolution is not binding. There is a need to fill the gap in space law.

---

[21] Convention on Registration of Objects Launched into Outer Space, 1975, Article 1; Convention on International Liability for Damage Caused by Space Objects, 1972, Article 1.

[22] Recommendations on Enhancing the Practice of States and International Intergovernmental Organisations in Registering Space Objects, A/RES/62/10110, January 2008.

5. Space Law Relating to Exploration and Exploitation of the Natural Resources of the Moon

Exploration of the Moon was initiated by USA and the then USSR soon after the beginning of space activities in 1959. By 1976, more than 50 lunar exploration missions had been launched. During these missions, human beings successfully landed on the Moon, performed a number of scientific experiments and brought lunar samples back to Earth. Presently, Japan, the ESA, China and India have joined the lunar exploration club. The USA also renewed its interests in returning to the Moon. It can be envisaged that these lunar exploration and exploitation plans will probably lead to human settlement, mining of Helium-3, and the establishment of lunar bases on the Moon for further space travel to Mars and other small celestial bodies.

The Moon Agreement set up a series of principles for the activities on the Moon and other celestial bodies. Most of them reiterate the general principles and obligations enshrined in the Outer Space Treaty. The provisions of the Moon Agreement are sufficient to support current investigations of the Moon. However, so far, only 13 countries are party to the Agreement. Most of the space faring nations have not acceded to it. The reasons could be that they do not envision that the exploitation of natural resources of the Moon is feasible in the near future and/or they are not happy with some of the principles or provisions of the Moon Agreement. The Moon Agreement needs to be reviewed to attract more countries. An international regime governing the exploitation of the natural resources of the Moon shall be established in the future, hopefully by the international community and not by only a few countries.

This paper only touches upon a few legal space issues. Some issues such as demarcation between outer-space and air-space have long been discussed without ever reaching a conclusion. The UN General Assembly resolutions on principles governing satellite remote sensing activities, satellite broadcasting and the use of nuclear sources remain as guidelines for activities in these areas. In the future, there may be a need to conclude international treaties with more details to govern these space activities. Besides, it can be envisaged that the scope of space law will expand to be much broader and more complex in the future, with the development of more sophisticated space technology, a variety of space activities and more participants. Aerospace planes and space elevators serve as examples. They may change some concepts of space law such as space objects and launch vehicles and mix some applicable laws in, if these dreams or plans become true. If the dreams or plans become true, this may lead to a change of some of the concepts of space law such as the definition of space objects and launch vehicles, and/or lead to a mixture of air and space law to apply.

6.4

Privacy and Data Protection – Legal Lessons?

Peter Hustinx[*]

This article takes stock of the present state of future thinking in the area of privacy and data protection – partially as to how the law should deal with phenomena such as growing complexity and globalisation. It builds on discussions in the context of the ongoing review of the EU legal framework for data protection and raises the question to what extent the experiences in this area could be extrapolated to other fields of law.

The growing complexity of the information society, driven by technological and organisational changes, gives rise to similar risks as have recently become evident in the financial system and our natural environment. At the same time doubts have arisen as to present systems of governance. Consequently there is a need to better define and allocate responsibilities and enhance the accountability of actors. These concepts are currently being developed in the area of data protection. This will probably lead to a combination of proactive and reactive measures, partly building on self-regulation, with interesting consequences, both internally and externally.

As a result of globalisation, the principle of territoriality, as traditional basis for public policy, is under pressure. The internet in general, and particularly the phenomenon of cloud computing, may require new criteria for applicable law and jurisdiction. At the same time, there is a growing trend towards development of global standards, both in formal and more informal ways. International cooperation at various levels is a crucial third component that is also making some good progress.

1. Introduction

Future thinking in the area of privacy and data protection is not a rare phenomenon. Privacy and personal data cannot be sufficiently protected without the ongoing consideration of changing circumstances. Data protection as a counterbalance to technological developments requires that the rules – and therefore also the rule makers – anticipate such develop-

[*] **Peter Hustinx** is European Data Protection Supervisor.

ments, and that supervisory authorities interpret those rules with a view to the future.

Challenges to data protection from the information society are enormous. Information is processed in a technologically complex environment where national borders are increasingly irrelevant. Companies operate on a worldwide basis, data flows are global and information is available via networks in multiple locations at the same time.

On 4 November 2010, Commissioner Reding presented a Communication which elaborates her intention to change the current patchwork of EU data protection rules into a modern and comprehensive legal instrument. The European Data Protection Supervisor (EDPS) is closely involved in the ongoing discussions. This 'think piece' builds on these discussions in data protection and attempts to extrapolate the experiences in this area to other fields of law where growing complexity and globalisation require a new approach.

2. Complexity

The complexity of our society is increasing. Technology is one reason, but companies themselves are becoming more complex, working on an international or global scale. Significant tasks are often outsourced and so the legal reality (legal personality) does not always coincide with how relationships are organised in practice. Given this complexity, allocating responsibility is more difficult and traditional command and control legislation will not always be effective. It is not always easy to determine which law applies, who is responsible. Furthermore, traditional sanctions under national law are not always sufficiently dissuasive.

Companies as well as governments underestimate the consequences of uncontrollable systems or chains of different actors. We have witnessed a worldwide financial crisis because the main players in the financial markets did not assume the responsibility for the market as a whole and governments did not have the means for adequate responses. Another example is the catastrophic consequence of giving a major oil company a permit for deep drilling in the ocean. Neither the government, nor the company concerned was capable of assuming its responsibility and ending the incident quickly.

In the information society we face similar risks. The recent phenomenon of cloud computing means that masses of information (including large volumes of personal information) are stored at undetermined places, without an appropriate legal regime dealing with the associated risks. The governance of the Internet itself is left with an organisation that has only indirect links to responsible governments.

Complexity has resulted in a shift of the balance of power towards the private sector, but – as the examples show – the private sector itself is not always in control of developments. If governments are not in a position to react properly to new realities in the public interest, then the systems of governance themselves are at stake. It is a core task of governments to ensure the protection of their citizens, be it against substantive economic threats (like the financial crisis), against substantive environmental threats (like the BP crisis), or against infringements of the fundamental rights of citizens, such as their rights to privacy and data protection (which are both protected under the EU Charter of Fundamental Rights). In a complex society where persuasive powers are no longer in the hands of the government alone, there is a need to better define and allocate responsibilities and enhance the accountability of actors. These concepts are currently being developed in the area of data protection. In short:

a) allocating responsibility in a complex environment;
b) accountability of responsible organisations for what happens in a chain.

2.1. Allocating Responsibility

In data protection law, the point of departure is that for each activity relating to personal data ('processing') there is someone responsible ('controller') and there may be a party ('processor') who acts on behalf of the controller, for instance in cases of outsourcing.

The legal concept of what constitutes a data controller is crucial in two connected ways: first, because it determines the entity/entities ultimately responsible for compliance with data protection rules, and second, because in doing so, it minimises the possibility for operators to evade responsibility, thus contributing to effective compliance. Increasingly data protection laws combine proactive and reactive measures to ensure compliance. The former aim at encouraging operators to take the necessary measures to ensure the protection of personal data and privacy, as the law may require. These measures can take different forms, including the participation in self-regulation initiatives. The concept of accountability described below is an example.

Reactive measures apply in situations where there has been unlawful processing of personal data. Recent data protection legal frameworks increasingly incorporate mandatory security breach notification obligations. An example at European level is the recently amended e-Privacy Directive which imposes such requirements upon internet service providers and telecom operators. This type of obligation requires organisations to notify end-users and authorities of incidents involving personal data breaches, and has been proven to encourage them to take more responsibility for the data they process, in addition to enhancing transparency for individuals. Obviously, reactive measures also involve liability and sanctions which can lead to the possibility of collective lawsuits.

However, the above is not always simple and easy, and in no way does it provide all the answers. While rules determining the responsible entities and the type of responsibilities they have are positive, in complex organisations and complex chains of activities, it is not always evident who is responsible, or more precisely, who is responsible for what part of the activities. It is also not always clear whether there are multiple, cumulative or concurrent responsible parties.

Take for example e-Government portals which act as intermediaries between the citizens and public administration units. Often the portal transfers the requests of the citizens and deposits the documents of the public administration unit until these are recalled by the citizen. Whilst each public administration unit remains controller of (and thus responsible for) the data processed for its own purposes, the responsibility of the portal itself is less obvious and may require close examination of the facts and circumstances of its involvement in the processing of the data. This is not an isolated case, but rather a common one, and explains why organisations are expected to assess the factual circumstances of a particular data collection and processing in which they are engaged in order to allocate responsibilities to the different players.

Another aspect of complexity is the role of technology and technology providers, and hence their responsibilities for the protection of personal data. For example, if information is uploaded onto a social networking service, what is the role of the provider of the social network regarding the information that users voluntarily upload to that service? Are technology providers responsible for the use of such information? Are they under any obligation to implement data protection and security features in their services?

As the capacity for information-processing evolves, the need to allocate responsibility to the providers of certain information technologies becomes more acute. There is a need to reflect on how such responsibilities could be imposed without causing undue burdens and ensuring that technology and innovation is not jeopardised.

2.2. Accountability

Determining responsibilities is a first step, but a second step is also required, to ensure that the responsible parties can be held accountable for complying with legal obligations. This may require the obligation to take proactive measures to ensure compliance, as mentioned before.

The law must provide the necessary incentives to do so and must contain effective dissuasive sanctions in case of non-compliance. In a complex environment where the position of governments is weakening, emphasis should also be put on positive incentives – 'the carrot'. Being compliant should become an asset for the private sector. In the data protection context, for instance, compliance with legal obligations should imply trustworthiness. The principle of accountability is currently further developed in the area of data protection. Accountability consists of:

a) an internal aspect requiring that organisations put in place internal mechanisms and control systems that ensure compliance;
b) an external aspect to force organisations to provide evidence – such as audit reports, annual reports – to demonstrate compliance to the general public and to external stakeholders, including regulatory authorities.

Accountability could be further enhanced by supporting mechanisms that could be laid down in law. Some examples of these supporting mechanisms are currently being discussed in the area of data protection: minimising the *ex ante* formal requirements for organisations capable of demonstrating accountability; giving strong powers to regulatory authorities; building in incentives for the design of technological products ('privacy by design'); certification *ex ante* and possibilities to verify compliance *ex post*. Obviously, an effective mix of such measures would be essential.

It goes without saying that many of these elements also work in other areas. We have recently seen many developments in the banking area – a stress test for instance is a mechanism for ensuring accountability. In the European Union another area where this type of approach has been tested is the environment field where organisations are encouraged to implement the highest levels of environmental performance and seek certification accordingly. The system is strongly backed by governments and environmental regulators.

3. Globalisation

Our society has not only become more complex but also increasingly globalised. The limitations of government power become more and more significant due to the existence of physical borders and the concept that government power is based on the principle of territoriality. Here again, examples can be found in a wide range of legal areas. The financial crisis and the difficulties for the world community in effectively addressing important environmental issues (such as CO_2 emissions) are telling of that.

3.1. Territoriality Under Pressure

The territoriality principle is under pressure. In contemporary society, territoriality raises questions as to what exactly determines the link with the territory of a given state. With regard to data protection, there are several elements which could determine which national law is applicable. One could take for instance the country, in which the data processing takes place, or the country in which the person who is responsible for the processing is established, or alternatively the country where the person concerned is situated.

The Internet in general, and particularly the aforementioned phenomenon of cloud computing, illustrates however that each of these options leaves many open questions about how to apply them. For example, the country in which the data processing takes place is a difficult criterion to apply when data processing operations are carried out on the Internet, since it is difficult to localise such data processing operations as occurring in a particular state. The application of the law of the person concerned (data subject) – usually referred to as the passive personality principle – is understandable insofar as it aims to protect individuals. However, at the same time, it entails an application of the law outside the national borders, raising relevant questions about the real possibilities of enforcing the law and the subsequent risk that the respect for the law may be low.

The evaluation of which applicable law criteria and principles should apply is on-going. Meanwhile harmonisation of data protection laws remains an attractive goal in order to minimise the above problems.

3.2. Developing Global Standards

Globalisation forces states to establish standards which ensure a satisfactory level of protection. These standards should ideally be laid down in binding legal instruments and be accompanied by an enforcement structure to make them effective. However, the reality is that such developments are much slower than the technological developments in the information society.

Since around 1970, standards on data protection have been developed mostly on a regional basis, such as within the Council of Europe, the OECD and within the European Union. Gradually, institutional structures were also created for the enforcement of these standards. In the last decade, discussions have concentrated on how to bridge the transatlantic data protection gap between the EU and the United States, resulting in a soft law instrument stating which data protection principles both parties have in common. An agreement between the EU and the US is likely to be negotiated in the near future. In November 2009, global standards on data protection were adopted by the International Conference of Data Protection and Privacy Commissioners in Madrid. These standards can be seen as the first step towards a truly globalised approach to data protection. However, we are still a long way from binding global standards, for instance, in a future agreement under the flag of the United Nations. A more realistic approach would be preserving and developing the common core and fostering synergy and interoperability of existing regional and other international instruments.

Data protection and privacy legislation has so far often regulated the movements of personal data across national borders (referred to as 'trans-border' data flows). The typical goal was to prevent the circumvention of national laws by simply transferring the information to third countries and to ensure the protection of individuals even when their data is outside national borders. However, the increasingly globalised world economy relies on the free flow of data and this is not compatible with rules on trans-border data flows. Existing and new solutions are being discussed: adequacy findings, bilateral agreements, Binding Corporate Rules (BCR), principles of accountability, etc. In the European Union there is an increasing interest in promoting the principle of mutual recognition whereby the decision of a national regulatory agency, for example to authorise a set of transfers, is recognised in other EU Member States.

Mutual recognition is being used by some data protection authorities in relation to the approval of BCR. Such authorities agree on recognising the decision given by a leading (coordinator) data protection authority of another country, stating that the BCR presented by an international corporation meet all the safeguards required. Some further analysis of how to make full and better use of this principle would be beneficial.

4. International Cooperation

It follows from the above that globalisation not only necessitates the development of more common, binding standards on data protection, but also international cooperation in practical terms, going beyond mutual recognition. Cross border data processing can only be effectively supervised if the authorities of different countries work together. This is an area where some important progress has been made, and more effective progress will be necessary in the near future.

Supervisory authorities – at national or EU level – play a crucial role in enhancing and ensuring the effectiveness of data protection rules. On 9 March 2010, the EU Court of Justice underlined that the existence of independent supervisory authorities is inherent to the right to data protection. These authorities fill the gap created by technological and political developments going beyond the average citizen's understanding and thus beyond his control. In order to fulfil their supervisory role, their independence must be assured and they should have sufficient powers and adequate means to exercise them effectively.

In a globalised world these authorities need to work together. In the context of the EU, a group was created consisting of the representatives of the national supervisory authorities of the EU Member States ('Article 29 Working Party'). The task of this Working Party is to provide the European Commission with independent advice on data protection issues. The numerous opinions that the Working Party has delivered for more than a decade have gained increasing authority as they represent the consensus of all members, and are based on the well-established experience in the different Member States. However, discussions in the Article 29 Working Party also highlight that there are still many discrepancies between how data processing is regulated in the different Member States.

In recent years, the Article 29 Working Party has acted also as the platform for coordinated action on issues affecting all Member States, such as the 'privacy invasive' features of the Internet and the activities of key players in the online environment. In this context, the Working Party has dealt with search engines, social network sites and behavioural advertising, where the most important actors are often operating from a different legal environment in the US. A very welcome development is therefore that the Working Party is developing closer relations with the Federal Trade Commission, the most relevant consumer and privacy protection agency in the US.

On a global scale, conferences are being organised, such as the one which resulted in the Madrid Resolution, but international cooperation between supervisory authorities and regulators should be developed further. Such cooperation should lead to common action, exchange of best practices and could establish fertile ground to create and develop binding global standards.

5. Concluding Remarks

This 'think piece' briefly described the main challenges that globalisation and the growing complexity of contemporary society present for the protection of personal data. Questions have been raised and some insight has been given regarding the direction in which discussions at EU level on the new legal framework for data protection are developing. EU legislation can provide answers, but it is clear that not all questions can be addressed satisfactorily. This is due to the fact that the information society is a global phenomenon which stretches far beyond the physical borders of the EU.

Many of the challenges to data protection are similar to those in other areas. Data protection has been developing since the 1970's as a counterbalance to technological developments. So there are well-established experiences of addressing new challenges. It cannot be said that all attempts to address these challenges have been successful or that certain data protection scandals would otherwise not have taken place – a recent example of this being the SWIFT affair. Data protection will always be a work in progress with an eye on the future, following a path of trial and error. However, the experiences and discussions regarding data protection are at least worth analysing for other areas of law.

6.5

Future Trends in the Regulation of Personal Identity and Legal Personification in the Context of Ambient Intelligence Environments: The Right to Multiple Identities and the Rise of the 'AIvatars'

Norberto Nuno Gomes de Andrade[*]

This think piece[1] analyses two major challenges for the development of law brought by the so-called vision of Ambient Intelligence (AmI). AmI reflects a prospective scenario where the human will be surrounded by a seamless environment of computing, advanced networking technology and specific interfaces.[2] Amidst the wide array of challenges posed by this vision of forthcoming reality,[3] I focus on the issues of regulation of

---

* **Norberto Nuno Gomes de Andrade** is a Scientific Officer at the European Commission's Joint Research Center (JRC), Institute for Prospective Technological Studies (IPTS).

1 This contribution contains parts of Norberto N.G. de Andrade, "Right to Personal Identity: The Challenges of Ambient Intelligence and the Need for a New Legal Conceptualization", in Serge Gutwirth, Yves Poullet, Paul de Hert and Ronald Leenes (eds.), *Privacy and Data Protection: An Element of Choice*, Springer, London, 2011a; Norberto N.G. de Andrade, "The Right to Privacy and the Right to Identity in the Age of Ubiquitous Computing: Friends or Foes? A Proposal towards a Legal Articulation", in Christina Akrivopoulou and Athanasios Psygkas (eds.), *Personal Data Privacy and Protection in a Surveillance Era: Technologies and Practices*, Information Science Publishing, Hershey, PA, 2011b; Norberto N.G. de Andrade, "Technology and Metaphors: from Cyberspace to Ambient Intelligence", in *Observatorio (OBS) Journal*, 2010, vol. 4, issue 1; Norberto N.G. de Andrade, "The 'A.I.vatar' – Intelligent Agents in the context of Ambient Intelligence", paper presented at the 21st International Conference on Legal Knowledge and Information Systems, Workshop on Game Theory, Agents and the Law, New Models for Legal Informatics, 2008.

2 G. Riva, F. Vatalaro, F. Davide, and M. Alcañiz (eds.), *Ambient Intelligence: The Evolution of Technology, Communication and Cognition Towards the Future of Human-Computer Interaction*, IOS Press, Amsterdam/Oxford, 2005.

personal identity and of legal personification of a particular category of non-human actors. In relation to the former, I stress the need to rethink the right to personal identity, proposing a right to multiple identities. With respect to the latter, I emphasise the need to consider the possibility of endowing automated software agents with (some sort or degree of) legal personality.

1. Introduction

The present contribution is structured in three parts. First, I succinctly describe the Ambient Intelligence scenario, summarizing its main characteristics and features. Second, I focus on the challenges that such scenario will pose to identity, elaborating on how AmI will fundamentally change the way in which our personal identities will be perceived, constructed and represented. In this section, and as a response to those foreseeable changes, I underline the need for legal systems to re-conceptualise and strengthen the right to personal identity, advancing the idea of a right to multiple identities. Third, and in light of a scenario model construction, I describe the emergence of a forthcoming generation of automated and intelligent software agents, designating those new actors by the collective term of 'AIvatars'. In this respect, I describe their main characteristics and features. In addition, I stress the need for legal systems to acknowledge and anticipate the future societal relevance of these agents, pondering the possibility of endowing them with legal personality.

2. The Vision of Ambient Intelligence

The European Union's Information Society Technologies Program Advisory Group (ISTAG), in its 1999 vision statement, coined the term 'ambient intelligence' (AmI) to portray the image where "people will be surrounded by intelligent and intuitive interfaces embedded in everyday objects around us and an environment recognising and responding to the presence of individuals in an invisible way".[4] For more than a decade since then, the AmI vision has been substantially developed and enriched

[3] For a detailed account of the various challenges posed by the vision of Ambient Intelligence, see Antoinette Rouvroy, "Privacy, Data Protection, and the Unprecedented Challenges of Ambient Intelligence", in *Studies in Ethics, Law, and Technology*, 2008, vol. 2, issue 1, pp. 51.

[4] ISTAG report 1999, in which the term 'ambient intelligence' was, for the first time, coined. See ISTAG, *Orientations for Workprogramme 2000 and Beyond*, 1999.

with studies, research initiatives, reports and analysis aimed at emphasizing the technical, social, ethical and legal implications that this upcoming technological setting will bring about.

Ambient Intelligence (AmI) represents a vision of the form and means computing will take in the forthcoming years. Denominated also by the terms 'internet of things', 'everyware', or 'ubiquitous, pervasive, proactive and autonomic computing', Ambient Intelligence constitutes a vision of a future technological ecosystem; an idea of an aspiring reality – automated, intelligent, imperceptible, and omnipresent; a foreseeable future stage in which the 'internet', as we know it – in the shape of a network of computers, will gradually envelope the physical environment, distributing the technology focus and its computing power from computers to an infinite multiplicity of everyday objects.[5] In this sense, it is "a vision of processing power so distributed throughout the environment that computers per se effectively disappear".[6] Such a technological setting underlines, in this manner, the passage from the present internet structure (which currently covers only a limited number of output devices) to a world where a wide array of miniaturised computing devices (processors, tags, tiny sensors) will be integrated into a multiplicity of everyday objects, seamlessly blending in the environment.[7] The new technological scenario will, thus, be made of items, dresses, utensils, books and any kind of physical object you can think of,[8] embedded with some kind of intelligence and forming a communicative, sensitive, responsive, interac-

5 Andrade, 2010, pp. 121-146, see *supra* note 1.

6 Adam Greenfield, *Everyware: The Dawning Age of Ubiquitous Computing*, New Riders, Berkeley, 2006, p. 1.

7 Such process "will, in the foreseeable future, result in processors and tiny sensors being integrated into more and more everyday objects, leading to the disappearance of traditional PC input and output media such as keyboards, mice, and screens". See Jürgen Bohn, Vlad Coroama, Marc Langheinrich, Friedemann Mattern, Michael Rohs, "Social, Economic, and Ethical Implications of Ambient Intelligence and Ubiquitous Computing", in Werner Weber, Jan M. Rabaey and Emilie H.L. Aarts (eds.), *Ambient Intelligence*, Springer, Berlin/New York, 2005, p. 5.

8 "This involves seamless integration of nano- and opto electronics, natural user interfaces and integration of electronics in new computing substrates like fabrics and plastic". See M. Alcañiz and M. Rey, "New Technologies for Ambient Technology", in G. Riva *et al.* (eds.), *Ambient Intelligence: The Evolution of Technology, Communication and Cognition towards the Future of Human-Computer Interaction*, IOS Press, Amsterdam/Oxford, 2005, p. 4.

tive and functional network. According to such anticipated vision, "we will communicate directly with our clothes, watches, pens, and furniture – and these objects will communicate with each other and with other people's objects".[9]

Departing from technological advances in the fields of miniaturisation, computing power, embedded intelligence and wireless connectivity, such new paradigm forms a complex technological environment, requiring little deliberate human intervention and encompassing a wide array of different emerging technologies, such as mobile sensors, radio frequency identification (RFID) tags, software agents, brain computer interfaces, ICT implants, affective computing and nanotechnology.[10] Furthermore, the ambient intelligence scenario builds upon automated profiling practices and human-centric computer interaction design, dispersing and integrating networked devices into the environment by attaching them to everyday objects. The AmI will thus be characterised, on the one hand, by its invisibility, discretion and unobtrusiveness and, on the other, by its sensitivity, interactivity and responsiveness to the human person.[11]

In sum, AmI will be "invisible, embedded in our natural surroundings, present whenever we need it, enabled by simple and effortless interactions, attuned to all our senses, adaptive to users and context and autonomously acting".[12]

---

9 Bohn, Coroama, Langheinrich, Mattern and Rohs, 2005, p. 5, see *supra* note 7.

10 For further details on the vision of Ambient Intelligence, see Emile Aarts, Rick Harwig, Martin Schuurmans, "Ambient Intelligence", in Peter J. Denning (ed.), *The Invisible Future: The Seamless Integration of Technology into Everyday Life*, New York: McGraw-Hill, New York, 2001; Emile Aarts, Stefano Marzano, *The New Everyday: Views on Ambient Intelligence,* 010 Publishers, Rotterdam, 2003. Werner Weber, Jan Rabaey, Emile Aarts, *Ambient Intelligence,* Springer, Berlin/New York, 2005; Riva *et al.,* 2005, see *supra* note 2; Hideyuki Nakashima, Hamid Aghajan, Juan Carlos Augusto, *Handbook of Ambient Intelligence and Smart Environments*, Springer, New York, 2009; Andrade, 2010, see *supra* note 1.

11 Summarising this group of features, Hildebrandt describes AmI as an adaptive, smart environment which "should always be one step ahead of the user, like a butler who unobtrusively anticipates his master's wishes even before the master becomes aware of them". See Mireille Hildebrandt, "Profiling and AmI", in Kai Rannenberg, Denis Royer and André Deuker (eds.), *The Future of Identity in the Information Society: Challenges and Opportunities*, 2009, p. 287.

12 See Menno Lindwer, Diana Marculescu, Twan Basten, *et al.*, "Ambient Intelligence Visions and Achievements: Linking Abstract Ideas to Real-World Concepts", Paper presented at the Design Automation and Test in Europe, 2003, p. 10.

3. The Challenges of AmI to Personal Identity and the Right to Multiple Identities

The incessant digitisation of information concerning the human person, derived from technological developments – especially since the creation and diffusion of the Internet towards the Ambient Intelligence environment – are challenging the legal conceptualisation and protection of different aspects of the human personality, namely our personal identities. This technological trend affects the human person so intimately that many scholars go beyond the mere digitisation of information to the outright *per se* digitisation or 'informational-isation' of the human person. In this sense, Roger Clark talks of the 'digital persona',[13] while Luciano Floridi refers to the 'inforg'[14] and Stefano Rodotá alludes to the idea of 'networked persons': "[P]ersons who are permanently on the net, configured little by little in order to transmit and receive signals that allow tracking and profiling movements, habits, contacts and thereby modify the meaning of contents of individual's autonomy",[15] and, I would add, identity. In this way, different facets of one's personality are perceived, established and projected through information and communication technologies that mediate human interaction. Different aspects of one's personality are reduced to bits and bytes, being managed, transferred and represented through algorithms and other computing processes. With the consolidation of the information revolution and the move towards full data-based societies, everything has become a question of data, information and knowledge, including the protection and definition of one's identity.

In this context, a rather silent and unnoticed revolution is changing the way we see, perceive and represent ourselves, altering in a profound manner the way we define and construct our own personal identities. While much of the legal attention and energy has been, for the past decades, dedicated to tackling the threats and dangers that Information and Communication Technologies (ICTs) pose to privacy, there has been a

[13] Roger Clarke, "The Digital Persona and Its Application to Data Surveillance", in *The Information Society*, 1994, vol. 10, issue 2, pp. 77-92.

[14] Luciano Floridi, "A Look into the Future Impact of ICT on Our Lives", in *The Information Society*, 2007, vol. 23, issue 1, pp. 59-64.

[15] Stefano Rodotá, "Data Protection as a Fundamental Right", in Serge Gutwirth, Yves Poullet, Paul de Hert, Cécile Terwangne and Sjaak Nouwt (eds.), *Reinventing Data Protection?*, Springer, London, 2009, pp. 77-82.

generalised lack of attention to the challenges that such technologies pose to identity. In this respect, I argue that one of the most significant challenges for the development of law in the coming decades concern the protection and promotion of our personal identities. As such, this section examines the fundamental challenges operated by new ambient technologies to the classical understanding, construction and concept of identity.

The AmI scenario will carry a number of important transformations to the way a person's identity is captured, represented and disseminated.[16] Such important changes will derive from a number of new characteristics and tendencies present in the future world of AmI.

In the first place, there will be a radical increase in the production, creation, circulation and exchange of personal information. The AmI scenario will increment and accentuate the continuous digitisation of personal information, generating, collecting, analysing, processing and storing massive amounts of personal data.[17] It is thus expected an explosive boost of digitisation of personal characteristics and personal information. Such fact will bear important changes on future identification processes, as well as upon the ways in which individuals' identities will be represented and used. The increase of personal information will, moreover, derive from both the embedded smart objects.[18] In this way, electronic systems, sensors and other objects distributed throughout the physical world – via the constant monitoring of our actions and behaviour – will, themselves, generate and produce massive amounts of personal data and information concerning our identity and behaviour.[19]

---

16 It is important to stress that many of these changes are already under motion (through the web 2.0. mobile applications, augmented realities and location-based services), having AmI an accelerating (and aggravating) effect.

17 The Future Group Report (2008), written by the Informal High Level Advisory Group on the Future of European Home Affairs Policy, has used the expression 'tsunami' of data to illustrate the massive amounts of data expected to be produced by RFID systems and sensor technologies. See Hildebrandt, 2009, p. 274, see *supra* note 11.

18 The boost of personal information will also originate from the users themselves, as people will be able to create, describe and define their identities through a greater number of instruments and platforms.

19 Many times, and to some extent, people will not even know about or be aware of the collection and processing of such information.

Second, AmI technologies will blur the distinction between the physical and the digital worlds.[20] In this regard, the frontiers that demarcate the physical territory from the digital one will become increasingly difficult to distinguish, as both spaces will tend to converge in "one seamless environment of computing, advanced networking technology and specific interfaces".[21] With the slow and relentless "disappearing of the frontier between the offline and the online world, the new identity that will emerge will bring in the physical world many of the characteristics present in the online worlds, such as increased transparency and massive tracking and profiling".[22]

Third, this novel and technological environment will favour the multiplication of identities. In view of that, the tendency to multiply and polarise various and distinct identities from a single one[23] will only tend to increase. Such tendency, in particular, will consist of a more intense virtualisation and multiplication of different identities, with virtual and

20 Alongside this change there will also be another important one: the blurring between private and public spaces, as both the public and the private spheres will increasingly become more entangled and intertwined. In this regard, and along the same lines, Nissenbaum has argued that the digitalisation of our environment has blurred the borders between the private and the public spheres, while also decreasing the anonymity traditionally associated with many public spaces. See Helen Nissenbaum, "Privacy as Contextual Integrity", in *Washington Law Review*, 2004, vol. 79, no. 1, pp. 119-158.

21 ISTAG. "Ambient Intelligence: From Vision to Reality", in G. Riva, F. Vatalaro, F. Davide, and M. Alcañiz (eds.), *Ambient Intelligence: The Evolution of Technology, Communication and Cognition Towards the Future of Human-Computer Interaction*, IOS Press, Amsterdam/Oxford, 2005. An illustrative example of the symbiosis between the physical and the digital world is given by emerging notions of 'virtual residence' and 'digital territories' developed by the European Commission's Institute for Prospective Technological Studies (IPTS). Regarding the concept of digital territories, "the underlying premise is that citizens should be empowered to create, shift, and sustain borders in order to develop and sustain their personal identity". See Hildebrandt, 2009, p. 302, see *supra* note 11.

22 Kai Rannenberg, Denis Royer, and André Deuker (eds.), *The Future of Identity in the Information Society: Challenges and Opportunities*, Springer, Berlin/London, 2009, p.23. As I shall point out, it is the spill-over of typical features pertaining to digital and virtual identities (such as multiplicity and permanent availability) that justifies a re-conceptualization of the right to personal identity, namely through the incorporation of the right to multiple identities and the right to be forgotten.

23 Phenomena recurrently observed in the Internet and its paraphernalia of communication and interaction platforms: social networks, virtual worlds, blogs – spaces which offer different 'lives' and 'existences'".

partial identities being created for the most different purposes and reasons, such as for security, business, convenience or entertainment. In addition, and within the AmI world, "[t]hese virtual and multiple identities and the paradigms behind them are feeding back into the 'physical' world, offering a mix of physical and virtual plural identities and processes to deal with them".[24] As a result, further to becoming increasingly profiled and networked, identity will be fragmented into different partial and virtual identities.

To sum up, the concept of identity in an AmI world will be essentially characterised by its ubiquity[25] and multiple facets.

Regarding its ubiquitous character, traces of one's identity will become dispersed, decentred and permanently registered. In the first place, ubiquitous identity presupposes that traces of our identity will be dispersed in the environment, scattered throughout smart objects, intelligent interfaces, databases and networks located everywhere. Secondly, ubiquitous identity will also mean that the traces of one's identity, further to being dispersed, will also become decentred, that is, outside one's sphere of command. With AmI, such a trend will only tend to aggravate, as our personal identity will not only be susceptible of being (mis)represented by other people, but also by machines and autonomous agents, namely through the profiles and the representations of one's identity constructed by those AmI machines and agents (namely through profiling automated processes).[26] Thirdly, the traces of one's identity, besides existing everywhere and existing outside oneself, will also tend to exist perpetually. Such traces will not only be spread out in the physical-digital world of

[24] Rannenberg *et al.*, 2009, p. 1, see *supra* note 22.

[25] Thierry Nabeth, "Identity of Identity", in Kai Rannenberg *et al.* (eds.), *The Future of Identity in the Information Society: Challenges and Opportunities*, Springer, Berlin/London, 2009, p. 53.

[26] Profiling is the "process of 'discovering' correlations between data in databases that can be used to identify or represent a human or nonhuman subject (individual or group) and/or the application of profiles (sets of correlated data) to individuate and represent an individual subject or to identify a subject as a member of a group or category". See Mireille Hildebrandt and Serge Gutwirth, *Profiling the European Citizen: Cross-Disciplinary Perspectives*, Spring, New York, 2008, p. 19.

AmI (hybrid space), but they will also be permanently stored and registered (as it already happens with the Internet).[27]

Concerning the multifaceted aspect of identity, it is worth underlining that a series of technical developments observed in the Internet[28] (which will only tend to be aggravated with the development of the AmI vision) pose a serious challenge to the traditional understanding of identity. Such understanding tends to ascribe identity to a single person, advocating a classical, strict and unequivocal identity bound to a certain person as "a one-to-one link".[29] In the AmI world, and on the contrary, the connection between 'one person – one identity' will no longer apply, as identity will be increasingly fluid, undetermined, variable and fragmented. This phenomenon can already be seen today, through different cases and examples. As such, people nowadays manage different and simultaneous identities through their email accounts and social networks, or in online forums and virtual worlds.[30]

Identity is thus becoming an increasingly complex phenomenon, inherently multifaceted and mutable. In this light, the idea of a unique and stable identity assumes pre-historical contours, as people tend to present, more and more, different identities, dissociated from one another and, many times, constructed upon profound incongruences. In this sense, "[p]eople are not only different to one another, but they are also different within themselves. They are objects of incessant variations. They have dissociated identities build upon internal contradictions and opposing

---

27 This tendentiously eternal character of one's identity elements draws our attention to the need of incorporating the so-called right to be forgotten within the umbrella of the right to personal identity. For further details on the conceptualization of the right to be forgotten, see Andrade, 2011a, see *supra* note 1.

28 People nowadays (and many times unconsciously) generate multiple identities. Besides the different identities one may have and develop in the physical world (according to the context in which one is: at work, at home, with family, etc), people are increasingly undertaking different identities (virtual and partial) through their email accounts, online forums, social networks and virtual worlds.

29 David-Oliver Jaquet-Chiffelle, Emmanuel Benoist, Rolf Haenni, Florent Wenger, Harald Zwingelberg, "Virtual Persons and Identities", in K. Rannenberg, in Kai Rannenberg, Denis Royer and André Deuker (eds.), *The Future of Identity in the Information Society: Challenges and Opportunities*, 2009, p. 76.

30 The reverse case also occurs quite frequently, with single identities being shared and managed by several persons (as it is, for example, the case of an email account of a given institution shared by its members).

forces. The person exists but is not unified and it would therefore be very problematic to encapsulate him or her in fixed screenplays that do not take into account this fluid and complex dialectic".[31] In order to account for this progressive trend, I propose a renewed conceptualisation of the right to personal identity. In the ambit of such theorisation, I advance the idea of a right to multiple identities.

3.1. The Right to Multiple Identities

With the advancement of technology and the eruption of the internet, the possibilities to invent and construct other identities have developed to unprecedented levels. Furthermore, and with the progressive implementation of the AmI scenario, several identities can now be formed across the mixed environment of physical and digital dimensions. Having previously seen how the traditional link 'one person – one identity' has become obsolete, it is important to note that technological developments in the internet and, in the future, in the AmI environments are forging "new forms of identities that have been created partially separated from the original, unique identity of the person".[32] We are thus moving towards a deep fragmentation of personal identity, shattered into multiple and different concepts of partial and virtual identities,[33] such as avatars, pseudonyms, categories, profiles, etc.

Departing from such hypothesis, and taking into account the previous considerations on the fragmentation and multiplication of identity emerging from the AmI scenario, a right to multiple identities seems absolutely fundamental in order to capture and regulate the increasingly complex and dissociated character of personal identity.

Rather than a schizophrenic exercise, the right to multiple identities addresses the need of every individual to have, according to the context in which one would act, her partial identities (both digital and physical) recognised by law. Such recognition entails, moreover, that every partial identity (that is, the sum of particular elements describing and representing that person's partial identity) would only be subject to identification

---

31 Patrick Boumard, Georges Lapassade, Michel Lobrot, *Le Mythe de l'Identité: Apologie de la Dissociation*, Economica-Anthropos, Paris, 2008, p. 14.

32 Jaquet-Chiffelle, *et al.*, 2009, p. 77, see *supra* note 29.

33 For a detailed analysis of these new forms of identity, see Jaquet-Chiffelle *et al.*, 2009, see *supra* note 29.

according to those specific elements, preventing that the latter could in anyway be linked to any other elements and, thus, to other partial identities.

This is clearly a right *in statu nascendi* and more work is needed in order to consolidate this legal figure, namely studies covering the possible connections between the right to multiple identities, on the one hand, and the rights to anonymity and the legal protection of pseudonyms, on the other. The conceptualisation of this right is, as such, an important challenge for the development of the law of the future.

4. The 'AIvatars' and the Attribution of Legal Personality

This section portrays a 'scenario within a scenario', that is, a vision of a new generation of intelligent agents, adaptive to the users' profiles, preferences and needs, operating in the AmI environment. In the following, I describe the emergence of these agents within the Ambient Intelligence scenario and propose one overarching term to denominate the new breed of intelligent agents within such context: the 'AIvatar'.[34]

4.1. The Rise of a New Breed of Intelligent Agents: The 'AIvatar'

Based upon technological advances in the fields of miniaturisation, computing power, artificial intelligence and wireless connectivity, the AmI environment will populate the earth with an almost infinite number of smart objects.[35] As such, any kind of material, thing or substance will be transformed into computing units, endowed with the capability of exploring and sensing the environment, interacting and responding to humans, as well as locating and recognising objects and people, including even the emotional status and intentions of the latter.[36] In this way, the AmI will

[34] 'AIvatars' (A.I. + Avatars) stand for avatars ruled by artificial intelligence (A.I), operating in a scenario of ambient intelligence (A.I.) and conflating the boundaries between agency and identity.

[35] The foreseeable technological developments will therefore add an additional new quality to everyday objects – these might be able not only to communicate with people and other 'smart' objects, but also to discover where they are, which other objects are in their vicinity, and what has happened to them in the past. Bohn *et al.*, 2005, p. 14, see *supra* note 7.

[36] Andrea Gaggioli, "Optimal Experience in Ambient Intelligence", in G. Riva, F. Vatalaro, F. Davide, and M. Alcañiz (eds.), *Ambient Intelligence: The Evolution of Tech-*

provide every individual with a tailored-made technological reality, deeply informed about one's characteristics and respondent to one's necessities, *i.e.*, an environment which "should be aware of the specific characteristics of human presence and personalities; adapt to the needs of users; be capable of responding intelligently to spoken or gestured indications of desire; and even result in systems that are capable of engaging in intelligent dialogue".[37] In order to achieve such a level of personalisation, the deployment of a new breed of intuitively intelligent software agents, embedded in any kind of object, assumes paramount importance. These agents will be the 'AIvatars': highly personalised, intuitive and intelligent software agents operating in the context of the AmI envisaged scenarios, meticulously shaped and programmed according to the profile, the personality and the character of the user.

4.2. Main Characteristics and Features of the 'AIvatar'

4.2.1. The Extreme Level of Personalisation That Can Be Achieved by the 'AIvatar'[38]

One of the main characteristics of the 'AIvatars', which distinguishes them from 'traditional' intelligent software agents,[39] is its degree of per-

---

nology, Communication and Cognition Towards the Future of Human-Computer Interaction, IOS Press, Amsterdam/Oxford, 2005, p. 35.

37 ISTAG, 2005, p. 45, see *supra* note 21.

38 The personalisation and intelligent profiling carried out by 'AIvatars' will be continuous, pervasive but also invisible and unobtrusive. All these characteristics combined render the personalisation of technology extremely troublesome from the privacy point of view, as data will be collected and processed not only through the consented stream of information consciously transmitted by the user, but also (and fundamentally) through an unconscious and perhaps non-consensual amount of information collected by the agents (through bio-sensors, etc). The solution will be not to prevent the aggregation of that information (which is indispensable for the implementation of the AmI vision), but to keep it confidential (giving control over that information to the user and letting the latter decide whether to maintain such information private or to allow it to be shared or disclosed). The privacy concerns implicated in the use of personalisation technologies and intelligent profiling by these agents deserve further research and study; nevertheless, this particular issue goes beyond the scope of this think piece.

39 Intelligent Software Agents, also called digital, electronic or artificial agents, are computational entities, capable of autonomous action in complex contexts. According to Wooldridge, "[a]n agent is a computer system that is situated in some environment,

sonalisation *vis-à-vis* the user, *i.e.*, the amount and detail of knowledge regarding the user that the 'AIvatar' will be able to retain and process. Amidst the many exciting AmI technological components rendering possible the launch of the 'AIvatar' (as the digital autonomous 'replica' of the user) and the personalisation of the environment according to each individual, two specific technologies assume particular relevance: machine-learning technologies and 'affective computing'. Regarding the former, the 'AIvatars' will integrate "[m]achine-learning technologies which analyse past behaviour and preferences in order to predict needs and to personalise services".[40] Agents in an AmI context will then be able to act on behalf of the user by learning about his habits, tastes and preferences. Regarding the 'affective computing', it is a term coined by Picard, who defined it as "computing that relates to, arises from or deliberately influences emotion".[41] The affective computing technology applied to intelligent agents will enable the 'AIvatars' to intuitively detect and recognise the user's mood and emotions and, on the basis of that, make judgements and take decisions.[42] As such, "[t]he recognition of the user's affective state can be done through such means as the measurement of physiological signals, the analysis of facial expressions, voice tone, gestures, the strength of keystrokes, etc., as well as by inferring what the user's affective state should normally be, from the knowledge of the user's goals, past behaviors, etc. and an evaluation of the situation, using an ap-

and that is capable of autonomous action in this environment in order to meet its design objectives". Michael Wooldridge, *An Introduction to Multiagent Systems*, John Wiley and Sons Hoboken, NJ, 2009, p. 21. The fundamental characteristic of agents, the reason for their technological and economical significance, is their capacity of decentralized and autonomous action. 'AIvatars' and 'traditional' intelligent software agents share in common a great number of important characteristics, such as autonomy, reasoning, decision, reaction and learning capability. Despite being somewhat similar, they differ substantially in terms of degree of personalization, range of proactive decisions and actions, versatility and unobtrusiveness.

40 David Wright, *Safeguards in a World of Ambient Intelligence*, Springer, London, 2008.

41 Rosalind Picard, *Affective Computing*, MIT Press, Cambridge, Mass 1997.

42 The influence and even manipulation of the user's emotions by the correspondent agent can also be conceived as a technological possibility. Nevertheless, the odds of that happening raises the intricate question of the independence and autonomy of the human *vis-à-vis* the agent, topic which goes beyond the scope of the present contribution.

praisal emotion theory".[43] In this manner, 'A.I.avatars' will be able to constantly perceive and interpret the affective state of the user, taking decisions (and, for instance, making contracts) on behalf of the user, in accordance with his state of mind and in response to his needs and wishes. In this light, 'AIvatars' will, for example, adapt to users "through sound, scent, shape, and movement",[44] making use of the large ambient space that encompasses the user and which is not utilised by conventional user interfaces like keyboards and screens. Such advanced and highly sophisticated agents will render the AmI "a world of machine learning and intelligent software, where computers monitor our activities, routines and behaviours to predict what we will do or want".[45] Such agents, attuned to the needs of the user and embedded in the physical environment (wristwatch, clothes, house, car, etc) will not be only reactive, acting under the command of the user, but also (and fundamentally) proactive, acting autonomously on behalf of the latter. Further to the capacity of recognizing individual people and their personal idiosyncrasies, these agents will also be able to sense the emotional status and (even perhaps) to read the thoughts[46] of the user. Supported by an army of sensors, tags and actuators dispersed throughout the physical environment, and equipped with powerful technologies of intelligent profiling, machine-learning, affective computing and (perhaps) mind-reading, the 'AIvatars' will capture and process unimaginable amounts of data and information, reaching the point of knowing more about the user than the user himself.[47] The 'AIvatar' will thus emerge as a sort of 'digital clone', impersonating the user, reflecting his personality and emulating, autonomously, what would be the user's own behaviour in a given context. By doing so, the 'AIvatars' will act on behalf of the latter according to his actual intentions and accurate desires.

---

43 Alcañiz and Rey, 2005, p. 14, see *supra* note 8.

44 Alcañiz and Rey, 2005, p. 4, see *supra* note 8.

45 Wright, 2008, p. 1, see *supra* note 40.

46 Recent improvements observed in the field of neuroscience (particularly in the denominated field of mind-reading machines) seem to point in that direction. For further information, see "Mind-Reading Machines: How Far Should They Go?", available at http://blog.wired.com/wiredscience/2008/03/mind-reading-ma.html, last accessed on 15 March 2011.

47 The desirability or non-desirability of this end-result is obviously highly problematic and controversial, constituting a matter for further research and debate.

4.2.2. The Scope and Sphere of Action of the 'AIvatars'

Whereas 'traditional' intelligent software agents are normally connected with the Internet,[48] operating on multiple platforms, networks and software systems located in computers and servers, the 'AIvatars' will expand their scope of activities to the physical environment. As such, and while current intelligent software agents perform their actions within the sphere of the Internet, working with data produced within that network, the 'AIvatars' will no longer be limited to the classical infrastructure of computer networks, having at their disposal an incommensurably larger pool of information: the AmI environment. This new stage of operations will be made possible by the implementation of the AmI vision which, grounded upon technological developments in the field of nanotechnology, sensors and wireless connectivity, will (as already mentioned) disperse the current Internet to the outer world. In this way, and while traditional software agents only work with information available in Internet's websites and databases, 'AIvatars' will work with an incomparable greater amount of information, captured not only through the websites we visit and clicks we make but also through the actions we make and the decisions we take in the physical world, including the conversations we have, the places we visit, the people we encounter, the things we see, smell, eat and (even perhaps) think, among many other human activities.

[48] Nevertheless, and as Murch and Johnson point out: "An agent can, of course, operate in any environment, even a mainframe with no network. In that environment, it would be limited to operating on the local but would still be extremely useful". Richard Murch and Tony Johnson, *Intelligent Software Agents*, Prentice Hall PTR, Upper Saddle River, N.J, 1999, p. 14. In this sense, agents are not necessarily limited to the Internet and can operate in any environment outside the network of the networks. Nonetheless, it is important to bear in mind that the impact, utility and potential of these agents outside the Internet will be greatly diminished. The insertion of an agent within an ever-expanding network of computers such as the Internet, with millions of hosts, acting upon an incommensurable amount of data is surely more valuable. Such networked environments will endow the agents with the possibility of operating within a greater pool of data and information, disposing of an almost endless amount of resources. The same reasoning applies to the AmI setting, which will constitute an even more important and impressive environment, generating an incomparable amount of data when compared to the current Internet. As such, one can argue that the employment and utility of agents within such an AmI setting will be even more valuable.

4.2.3. The Range of Proactive Decisions and Actions Available to the 'AIvatar'

As a consequence of the meticulous knowledge that the 'AIvatar' will hold regarding the user (personalisation) and the larger environment in which it will operate (the AmI), the range of decisions and actions available to the agent will be incommensurably wider. As such, the 'AIvatar' will have a much larger room of manoeuvre to act and operate on behalf of the user when compared with the current intelligent software agents. The 'AIvatars' will autonomously 'think' and decide ahead of the user, predicting the needs of the latter and acting in accordance. As such, the 'AIvatar' will, for example, tell the user which roads to take in order to avoid traffic and arrive at work on time, or postpone automatically the meeting in case of the user being irreparably late; buy tickets for the must-see movie for tonight's premier; store the fridge with the products needed for tomorrow's dinner; call the user's mother (or the user's mother own 'AIvatar') to plan the family trip next Sunday; respond to some trivial emails in the meantime; make phone calls using natural speech technologies; search for the best packages and deals for the upcoming summer's vacations, negotiating with the correspondent agencies; read a number of books which are of the interest of the user and prepare summaries for the latter to read, etc. The range of proactive actions which the 'AIvatars' will be able to perform is as vast as one can imagine it to be.

4.2.4. The Versatility, Continuity and Longevity of the 'AIvatars'

As the examples listed above demonstrate, the 'AIvatars' will not be limited to specific goals and purposes, assisting the individual only in particular contexts and exclusively addressing specific needs. As deeply personalised agents, the 'AIvatars' will deal with every possible need, concern and activity related to the individual. As such, the 'AIvatars' will distinguish themselves from current intelligent software agents, which tend to operate on an occasional basis and only in specific sectors of activity (entertainment, banking, shopping, etc).

The AmI agent will, moreover, grow with the user, accompanying the individual on a permanent basis, from an individual's early age (or conceivably from his birth) till his death.[49] Throughout this joint man/machine upbringing, the 'AIvatar' will constantly learn about the user (namely from the actions, conversations, judgements and attitudes taken by the individual, and monitored and recorded by the agent), perfecting its 'replica-profile' of the user and becoming his permanent lifetime 'companion'.

4.2.5. The 'Invisibility' and Unobtrusiveness of the 'AIvatars'

As the AmI environment aims at being a technological unobtrusive and discrete scenario, 'hidden' in the environment and operating in the background, the same characteristics will accompany the deployment and use of the 'AIvatars'. Contrarily to the current intelligent software agents, which demand an active role from the user (through queries and lengthy processes of selection, routing the end user to a decision), the 'AIvatars' will act in an inconspicuously manner, facilitating the user's life without the latter even noticing it. As such, the 'AIvatar' will make use of its increased autonomy to unobtrusively anticipate solutions and answers to the user's problems and needs.

4.3. Legal Personification

A wide and general acceptance of the 'AIvatars' in society will be a mandatory requirement for the successful implementation and functioning of these new breed of agents. Such acceptance requires trust from the user *vis-à-vis* the 'AIvatars', which will necessarily entail the construction of a legal framework regulating these agents and, by so doing, ensuring their reliability and exploring their full potential. As such, and among the various elements that the drafting of this new legal framework should bear in mind, one aspect assumes particular importance: the transposition of legal institutes and theories of legal personality, representation and agency to the actions performed by the 'AIvatar'.

Relevant work in this field has been developed in the framework of the European Commission's COMPANIONS project: Intelligent, per-

49 Interesting (and rather disturbing) questions on the post-mortem use and destiny of an 'AIvatar' (*i.e.*, after the decease of the correspondent user) should also be considered. An attempt to answer such questions goes, nevertheless, beyond the introductory scope of this think piece.

sistent, personalised Multimodal Interfaces to the Internet,[50] along with various studies devoted to the concept of Artificial Companions (ACs). The latter has been defined as "typically intelligent cognitive 'agents', implemented in software or a physical embodiment such as a robot. They can stay with their 'owner' for long periods of time, learning to 'know' their owner's preferences, habits and whishes. An AC could enter a close relationship with its owner by chatting to, advising, informing, entertaining, comforting, assiting with tasks and otherwise supporting her or him".[51]

In this context, authors have specifically addressed the possibility of having such entities legally representing and acting on behalf of the user, even after her or his death. As described elsewhere:

> Wilks[52] speculates that future artificial companions could act as an owner's agent: e.g. on the Internet or, further in the future, perhaps holding power of attorney in case of an owner's incapacity or, with the owner's advance permission, of being a source of conversational comfort for relatives after the owner's death. O'Hara[53] foresees the possibility of an artificial companion functioning on the owner's behalf after the bodily death of that person (e.g. for overseeing and administering trust funds and the execution of wills).[54]

Apart from these specific issues, other interesting enquiries regarding the juridical implications of the legal representation of intelligent agents on behalf of the human person have also been advanced. This is the case of the questions concerning the intervention of intelligent agents in the negotiation and formation of electronic contracts, the conclusion of

50 See the home page of COMPANIONS at http://www.companions-project.org. COMPANIONS project-related papers are available at http://www.companions-project.org/?p=res_projects, last accessed 28 April 2011.

51 Malcolm Peltu and Yorick Wilks, *Close Engagements with Artificial Companions: Key Social, Psychological, Ethical and Design Issues*, OII Forum Discussion Paper No. 14, 2008.

52 Yorick Wilks, "On Being a Victorian Companion", in Yorick Wilks (ed.), *Close engagements with artificial Companions: Key Social, Psychological, Ethical and Design Issues*, John Benjamins Publication Company, 2010, pp. 121, 128.

53 Kieron O'Hara, "Arius in Cyberspace: Digital Companions and the Limits of the Person, in Yorick Wilks (ed.), *Close engagements with artificial Companions: Key Social, Psychological, Ethical and Design Issues*, John Benjamins Publication Company, 2010, p. 35.

54 Peltu and Wilks, 2008, p. 22, see *supra* note 51.

agreements without human intervention or supervision, the issues of expression of will and of consent, and the conferral of some degree of legal personality on electronic agents.[55] Authors, in this respect, have called the attention to the "urgent need of rethinking many legal theories that we had since long ago already thought as definitively established, such as the theories of will, personality, consent and representation".[56] In this way, the 'AIvatar' will need legal instruments and rights in order to act on behalf of the user, producing legal effects in the sphere of the latter. In this light, legal systems should address the questions regarding the attribution of legal personality and the application (with obvious and necessary modifications) of legal instruments of representation and agency to the 'AIvatars', debating its feasibility and appropriateness.

The application of the notions of "legal personality" and representation to electronic agents, such as the AIvatar, constitutes an endeavouring challenge. Despite the fact that existing legal norms are not yet suitable to take this bold step, it is high time to seriously consider this possibility.

The legal personification of new juridical actors – not only electronic agents and robots, but also animals and natural ecosystems – is part of a more general trend towards the acception and the articulation of the 'non-human' in law. As Teubner stated in one of his articles, "Personifying other non-humans is a social reality today and a political necessity for the future".[57]

---

55 Regarding these various issues, see, for instance, Francisco Andrade, Paulo Novais and Jose Neves, "Divergence between Will and Declaration in Intelligent Agent Contracting", in *Proceedings of the ICAIL 2007 of the Eleventh International Conference on Artificial Intelligence and Law*, ACM Press, Stanford University, Stanford, 2007. See also Francisco Andrade *et al.*, "Contracting Agents: Legal Personality and Representation", in *Artificial Intelligence and Law*, 2007, vol. 15, no. 4,; E. M. Weitzenboeck, "Electronic Agents and the Formation of Contracts", in *International Journal of Law and Information Technology*, 2001, vol. 9, no. 3, pp. 204-234. Regarding the attribution of legal personality, arguments in favour of granting a legal right to personhood to intelligent artifacts have been recently advanced, for instance, by Patrick Hubbard. See Patrick Hubbard, "Do Androids Dream?: Person hood and Intelligent Artifacts", in *Temple Law Review*, 2010, vol. 83.

56 Francisco Andrade, Paulo Novais, Jose Neves, *Issues on Intelligent Electronic Agents and Legal Relations*, available at http://repositorium.sdum.uminho.pt/bitstream/1822/3169/1/Lea2004.pdf, last accessed 28 April 2011.

57 G. Teubner, "Rights of Non-humans? Electronic Agents and Animals as New Actors in Politics and Law", in *Journal of Law and Society*, 2006, vol. 33, no. 4.

7. The Emerging International Criminal Justice System

7.1

After International Law: Non-Juridical Responses to Mass Atrocity

Mark Osiel*

The most promising recent initiatives to restrain and redress mass atrocity either operate primarily by way of informal social norms, rather than international legal ones, or are juridifying in ways at odds with the liberal normative theory to which Western legality has been historically tethered. In either event, the ultimate judgment must be the same: with respect to these often-heartening efforts, at least, international law is of little help in advancing any recognizably liberal response to mass atrocities. Those of liberal persuasion, committed to staunching these recurrent horrors, would often be advised to look elsewhere – to possibilities ranging from traditional diplomatic intercession to the latest tactics of internet-based, social mobilisation.

1. Introduction

Some of the most prominent efforts to restrain and redress mass atrocities in our time, heartening from almost any view of global justice, are largely non-legal and extra-judicial in character. They rely scarcely at all on the application of binding international rules by international courts; they bear only the most equivocal, attenuated, often-tangential relation to international law, and in fact sometimes sit quite uneasily with it. Why is this so, and what does it mean for assessing the proper place of international law – and its alternatives – in the world's response to mass atrocity?

Consider, in this regard, the following recent initiatives:

1) Under the rubric of voluntary 'corporate social responsibility', managers of multinational corporations find themselves increasingly pressed to tread much more cautiously in countries whose rulers covertly employ forced migration and involuntary labour to assist foreigners' construction projects.

* **Mark Osiel** is Aliber Family Chair in Law at the University of Iowa, College of Law.

2) Fearing the opprobrium of global opinion, military leaders in democratic states are impelled to unprecedented efforts at reducing innocent civilian casualties in war, in ways that the international law of war crimes does not itself require.
3) Without fully affirming its legal status, diplomats everywhere earnestly proclaim their countries' 'responsibility to protect' the denizens of distant societies from mass atrocity by local despots.
4) Inspired by a growing global expectation of 'effective remedies' for mass atrocity victims, national legislators in many countries engage in anguished deliberations over how best to provide such persons with some form of civil compensation or administrative redress.
5) Heads of state in Turkey suffer worldwide chastisement in parliamentary resolutions for failing to acknowledge and apologise for their distant predecessors' policies of genocide, despite the absence of any legal duty to issue such proclamations. Similarly, Japanese leaders have increasingly become targets of official condemnation by regional neighbors, victimised by Japan's crimes of WWII.

These initiatives give rise to a number of questions. To what extent and for what reasons have they evaded or eluded juridicisation? What influence, if any, does international law nonetheless exercise upon their workings, if only at the margins? And what influence in turn have these initiatives had, or may likely have, upon law? When does the particular initiative serve to buttress the commitments of international law, to resist such law, and when does it simply stand aloof, charting a different but compatible path? If we compare and contrast the five efforts, what overall patterns emerge and can such patterns be explained by any existing or imaginable theory of international law's place in the world?

The non-juridical aspects[1] of these responses present a puzzle, if not an outright embarrassment, for anyone concerned with strengthening the response to mass atrocity by international law and international tribunals. The mainstream view within the field, and among lawyers and rights advocates more generally, is that atrocity responses should be governed by law and undertaken to a substantial degree by legal institutions, often in-

[1] The terms 'non-juridical', 'non-legal', and 'extra-legal' will be used interchangeably here.

ternational ones.[2] Yet much of the most promising and intriguing action today lies elsewhere.

To imply that there is a problem here might be to succumb to a certain 'legalism' – our professional tendency to view the delivery of justice as properly the monopoly of the state and its law, or of only those international institutions to which states formally delegate law-making authority. Such 'legalism' in responses to mass atrocity has been subject to trenchant criticism.[3] More generously, we might see the 'problem' of international law's relative absence from these initiatives as simply a legitimate expression of our desire to lend a helpful hand, with (what we consider to be) relevant expertise, to such morally salutary developments. And since the non-legal initiatives seek to coerce conduct, they necessarily raise questions about the legitimacy of limiting freedom without the accompanying protections of formality, neutrality, and accountability which law may uniquely provide.[4] International lawyers are not the only people vexed by the curious conundrum. Many of their creators and proponents view such initiatives – however successful in certain respects – as unstable, precarious, in need of support and consolidation by international law, through the forms of institutionalisation it alone can provide, they believe.

---

2 This view reaches it apogee in the contention that any genuine 'rule of law' at the international level requires a full 'constitutionalisation', by which all applicable legal sources and rule-making or enforcing bodies are arranged in a single hierarchy. See, *e.g.*, Bardo Fassbender, *The United Nations Charter as the Constitution of the International Community*, Martinus Nijhoff Publishers, 2009 (arguing that the UN charter has constitutional status); Jeffrey L. Dunoff and Joel P. Trachtman (eds.), *Ruling the World? Constitutionalism, International Law, and Global Governance*, Cambridge University Press, 2009 (collecting papers discussing world constitutionalism).

3 See, *e.g.*, Bronwyn Anne Leebaw, *Judging State-Sponsored Violence, Imagining Political Change,* Cambridge University Press, forthcoming 2011 (arguing that optimal responses to mass atrocity have in many places been distorted and misdirected due to liberal law's inherent predisposition to ascribe collective wrong and structural injustice to the intentional conduct of discrete individual persons).

4 This concern finds keen expression, for instance, in Joost Pauwelyn, "The Rise and Challenges of 'Informal Law'", in Sam Muller, Stavros Zouridis, Morly Frishman and Laura Kistemaker (eds.), *The Law of the Future and the Future of Law,* Torkel Opsahl Academic EPublisher, 2011, p. 138: pondering whether international lawyers should "insist on formalism and exclude 'informal law' from its scope to maintain international law's independence and stress the point that 'informal law' may be inappropriate as a power instrument of the strong…".

Leading advocates of a 'responsibility to protect', for instance, leave no doubt about their wish to see this normative aspiration reflected within customary international law, curtailing the U.N. Charter provisions with which armed humanitarian intervention would otherwise be incompatible.[5] In fact, all five initiatives invoke plausible moral arguments in drawing up close to the point of demanding much more of international law than has been hitherto contemplated. Why it should not accede to these emergent expectations is no longer obvious to many citizens of the world. And let us grant, without fear of strenuous dissent, that morality demands more of us in preventing and redressing mass atrocity than international law has traditionally required.[6] Our several non-juridical efforts do suggest, at the very least, that there is little danger that responses to mass atrocity will be effectively restricted to what international law currently endorses. Such law has not achieved any monopoly, in other words, over the range of relevant response. In imagining effective ways to restrain and redress mass atrocity, the undoubted influence of legal analogy and legal thinking – clear, for instance, in the language of a 'responsibility to protect' – has not been to narrow the breadth of ethical reasoning and political action, and virtually no one denies that international law has often been grossly inadequate to the task.

In their central aim and overall import, the new non-juridical initiatives sketched above at first seem congruent with the major progress of recent years in holding perpetrators of mass atrocity accountable for their crimes. That progress takes a decidedly juridical form, in the creation of several criminal tribunals (international and hybrid national-international), in the significant number of high-profile cases they have processed, and in their judicial development of legal doctrines imposing clearer, more stringent demands upon those who employ force in service of their political aims. The creation of an International Criminal Court, in particular, re-

5 Gareth Evans, *The Responsibility to Protect*, Brookings Institution Press, 2008.

6 This raises a variant of liberal jurisprudence's perennial puzzle: to what extent should law incorporate the full range of morality's claims upon us, and to what degree should we be instead content to rely upon informal public mores, diffuse sociopolitical pressures, and private conscience to ensure moral conduct. That question normally arises in connection with the most intimate and personal of behavior. Here it presents itself in a context at once global in scale, empirically complex, and likely to prove deeply disruptive of well-entrenched institutional arrangements, both national and international.

flects a great emboldening of international law's moral agenda in this area.

National courts as well, increasingly applying rules of international law, have been integral to the legalising turn.[7] The upshot has been a growing 'juridification' of the world's response to mass atrocity, in the sense of a collective insistence on extricating the terms of that response from the influence of 'politics', in a word, an influence perceived as almost invariably corrupting.[8] It should not pass without brief observation here, at least, that many millions of people throughout the world now look to these developments with great hope and yearning.

All these considerations make the conspicuously non-juridical aspect of the initiatives mentioned above that much more perplexing, and worthy of reflection. We must ask: are these concerted efforts to improve the world's response to mass atrocity likely to continue in their non-juridical form? Or do they show signs of likely assimilation to the more prominent forces of legalisation just noted? If they will persist in standing significantly apart from these forces, do they merely represent curious contingencies, anomalous outliers to deeper trends and abiding tendencies, disclosing no general significance – practical or theoretical? Or do they hint at serious and even inherent limits to the process of juridification, suggesting places where it cannot and will never successfully go? If so, then study of these conscientious initiatives should help identify the likely future contours of international juridification itself. This in turn will

7 Under the moniker of international 'legalisation', political scientists now study the frequent 'delegation' by states of policy issues to international institutions with law-making and enforcement authority. See, *e.g.*, Judith Goldstein, *et al.* (eds.), *Legalization and World Politics,* The MIT Press, 2001 (employing a definition of legalisation as involving obligation, precision, and delegation of disputes to a third-party decision-maker); Christian Brutsch and Dirk Lehmkuhl (eds.), *Law and Legalization in Transnational Relations*, Routledge, 2007. The initiatives examined here, in contrast, involve no such delegation.

8 International lawyers have also shown, to be sure, acute recognition of the need to accommodate political forces that insist upon the right to influence the functioning of international legal institutions aimed at redressing mass atrocity. These are political forces which, if not placated, could effectively nullify the operation of such legal institutions altogether. This sort of accommodation is particularly apparent in how the Rome Statute for the International Criminal Court accords the permanent members of the U.N. Security Council considerable influence over the cases and situations that the Office of the Prosecutor may investigate.

educate us lawyers about where and how we might most effectively press forward and make a valuable contribution – and where we may not.

2. The Central Argument

Despite some significant differences between them, the organised initiatives examined all find their chief inspiration and institutional footing in social forces and political processes – domestic and transnational – largely insusceptible by nature to international juridification. That these efforts have operated in ways exogenous to the field of international law is not a contingent fortuity, but an ineluctable fact. It would be misguided, even counter-productive at key points, to insist on somehow rendering them into international legal form. We international lawyers should resist the temptation to take on board these salubrious responses to mass atrocity, according them juridical recognition and endorsement, in hopes of bolstering their prospects. These efforts will and should remain mostly beyond our professional ken, notwithstanding the revealing and occasionally fruitful interactions between it and them. International law need not yoke these developments to its professional carriage "so as to remain sociologically relevant", in the telling words of one leading scholar.[9]

This conclusion may at first seem obtuse, even willfully perverse. If the extra-legal developments sketched above hold out some realistic hope for a better world, why should international law not find some way to accommodate them, at least incorporate them by reference, in the process making them formally its own? Why should this burgeoning body of law, preeminently concerned today with confronting mass atrocity, not benefit from and lend sustenance to other laudable achievements to this end now emanating from distinct sociopolitical springs? Why not then, for instance, a legal duty to protect others against mass atrocity, or to apologise after the fact for one's role in its occurrence? There is no longer any self-evident basis for a negative answer to such questions, if there ever were.

Yet differences between the legal and extra-legal responses to mass atrocity ultimately prove more salient, sometimes strikingly so, than the congruencies, limiting the scope of effective interchange and frictionless reciprocal endorsement. Our instances of response to atrocity often find effective expression, take organisational form; in ways that international

9 Pauwelyn, 2011, p. 138, see *supra* note 4.

law fails even conceptually to cognise, much less practically advance. These pragmatic and theoretical 'failures', if they may be so described, owe to reasons that no measure of good intentions and professional ingenuity on our part, as international lawyers, can hope – or should therefore seek – to overcome. What might these reasons be?

3. Reasons for Non-Juridification

Two principal hypotheses – one material, the other ideal – suggest themselves in explaining the lay of the land, the limits of law's reach in our case studies of atrocity response.

First, perhaps the limitations lie chiefly in familiar considerations of *realpolitik*, the sort highlighted by 'realist' accounts of international politics. Powerful states have no interest in, and effectively prevent, juridification from going further, on this view, since that process is a means of 'moralising' the resolution of questions which states prefer to leave to the play of power. Such considerations loom vaguely in the background within most of our case studies, to be sure.

Yet these cases also disclose other political forces at work that strengthen, rather than hamper, atrocity-response beyond what international law itself seeks. The relative weight and effect of political power – in both realist and non-realist conceptions – will necessarily concern us throughout, in making sense of where juridification does and does not occur. For instance, the increasing willingness of large, multinational corporations to submit to voluntary U.N./NGO monitoring of their labour practices surely reflects at once their power to resist a more juridicised alternative and their fear that altogether dismissing such non-juridical initiatives could ultimately lead to precisely that, whether in home or host states. It is the weakness of states and their inability to press their interests that are most apparent here, as well as the strength of non-state actors to play even the most powerful states off against one another.[10] This is not the world as depicted by state-centric, geopolitical 'realists,' even if machinations of power do figure ubiquitously within it.

[10] Multinational corporations can threaten, for instance, to relocate their headquarters to other countries, thereby potentially defeating the exercise of legislative and adjudicatory jurisdiction (including taxation authority) over them by states of initial incorporation.

A second hypothesis would be that international law's stance toward these salubrious initiatives may be limited not so much by external geopolitical constraints on its sphere of operation as by its own normative commitments, particularly its implicit liberalism, *i.e.*, the moral and political theory underlying much of Western legality. For instance, an official apology for mass atrocity (or other extensive human rights abuse), delivered on behalf of an entire national population, for the misconduct of unelected prior leaders who ruled long ago, over an altogether distinct governmental entity (*e.g.*, the Ottoman Empire vs. modern Turkey), sits uneasily with most understandings of liberalism. So does the extensive public provision of 'reparations' to beneficiaries bearing only the most indirect relation to immediate victims of atrocity. Yet mass atrocity often calls forth both such remedies today, in many countries.

In such situations, we have more reason to be concerned about the undesirability of extending international law's reach in requiring such practices than with the practical impossibility of so doing – the preoccupation of avowed 'realists' in the study of international politics. We might understandably wish to see international law take no position at all on such contentious issues, steer clear altogether. For the question of just *how* liberal a national society we truly wish to inhabit – in principled but uncompromising ways that might foreclose such 'collectivised' atrocity-responses – is likely best resolved by elected representatives more sensitive to domestic public sentiment than us international humanitarian lawyers, with our promiscuous proclivity for pronouncing and propagating (what we consider to be) universalistic moral truths.

A related possibility is that there exists a category of normative claims – Kant calls them 'imperfect duties'[11] – that properly influence our conduct in non-justifiable ways. These duties are imperfect in that they are not clear enough about whom they bind, and in which concrete ways, to warrant legal liability for infraction. The 'responsibility to protect' potential victims of mass atrocity in other countries is surely a plausible candidate, at least, for such characterisation.[12] So are, in differing measure, some of the other initiatives here examined.

---

11 Immanuel Kant, *Critique of Practical Reason*, 1788.

12 In fact, it may be that many of today's international human rights, particularly social, economic and cultural rights, may fall under the category of imperfect duties. This would mean that "there is a huge world of legitimate human rights beyond the limits

The rights corresponding to imperfect duties are best honored and protected, writes Amartya Sen, through acts – both official and unofficial, collective and individual – of "social recognition [via 'naming and shaming' of violators],[13] informational monitoring, and public agitation ...".[14] Methods of this sort involve "ethical argument" in "public reasoning",[15] but not as steps toward legislation or litigation. Our case studies of atrocity-response present much evidence of such methods vigorously in operation.

Yet this fact may simply reflect a recognition that extending the reach of international law is currently impossible as a practical matter; it offers no evidence of self-restraint by advocates, no reason for thinking that principled doubts about the desirability of limiting international law's reach into these areas actually explains the shape such limits have taken. Nor does Sen's position tell us much about how to proceed when even the best-reasoned, most urgent calls to honor non-juridical duty fall on deaf ears, as they regularly do.

In fact, there might be good reason to enshrine such imperfect duty formally into law even where there is no genuine intention to implement it coercively. At the domestic level, at least, certain norms of appropriate conduct – once legally codified – sometimes seem to have greater, salutary impact on behavior than if left to float freely, with the measure of

of law". Amartya Sen, "Human Rights and the Limits of Law", in *Cardozo Law Review*, 2006, vol. 27, pp. 2913-2927; see also Amartya Sen, "Normative Evaluation and Legal Analysis", Lecture, Wash. University, St. Louis, March 31, 2001: "Many human rights can serve as important constituents of social norms, and have their influence and effectiveness through personal reflection and public discussion, without their being necessarily diagnosed as pregnant with potential legislation". Sen is here chiefly examining the nature of human rights, but he can also be seen as implicitly seeking to "save" human rights discourse from self-professed adherents who, in claiming too much for it (*i.e.*, in legal recognition and coercive means of enforcement), threaten to call the larger enterprise into disrepute. Much the same spirit informs the present study, in its argument that our several anti-atrocity initiatives do more good by continuing to operate independently of international law than by being given a greater foothold within it. In the relation between these initiatives and international law, each side will often do better without too close a link to the other.

13 Sen, 2006, p. 2925, see *supra* note 12.

14 Sen, 2006, p. 2927, see *supra* note 12.

15 These processes, insofar as they affect the self-understanding of states, their leaders, and other relevant actors, occupy a central place in 'constructivist' theories of international relations, which will therefore play a role in the ensuing analysis.

compliance determined only by informal social sanctions. This is not because the police and courts will thereafter proceed to enforce such rules, which would often be preposterous.[16] Rather, it is simply that the inherent 'authority of law' induces greater deference in many people to the norm, *i.e.*, once it has passed through the formal procedures necessary to become binding upon members of the community of which they are members and with which they identify.[17] As citizens, after all, we can recognise domestic legal norms as the result of democratic self-determination, and hence an expression of our collective will, even when we may disagree with their content.

It is highly questionable, however, whether many people accord such deference to international law, or afford it great authority independent of its effective enforcement powers or intrinsic normative appeal – both of which are often uncertain, at best. To be sure, normative appeal does provide international prohibitions of mass atrocity with the considerable legitimacy they now enjoy. Yet international law's inherent authority, its mere status *as* law, does little work either in restraining potential perpetrators or impelling others to resist their misdeeds. The intrinsic authority of international law, as simply the expression of a genuine international community with which all members – as citizens of the world – strongly identify, is slight.[18] It seems juridificating the relevant norms here has not much enhanced their worldly impact. If so, then Sen's argument against the juridification of imperfect duties, including certain universal human rights, convincingly resists the claim that law's elemental, inner authority, and the impact of that authority on conduct, is reason enough to render all such rights into positive law.

We must also consider the possibility that obstacles to further juridification of the world's response to mass atrocity turn out to be quite different in each of our cases, disclosing no overarching pattern, belying ef-

---

[16] This is likely the case, for instance, of prohibitions against the spanking of children, conduct formally criminalised in certain Scandinavian states.

[17] On how this may occur, see Joseph Raz, *The Authority of Law: Essays on Law and Morality*, Oxford University Press, 2009, pp. 29-33 and pp. 116-117.

[18] We exclude from this generalisation, of course, the countless (but politically inconsequential) professors of international law and academic theorists of global justice who do, to be sure, often accord such intrinsic authority to international law, even when it has not been ratified by states or rendered domestically justifiable through municipal constitutional procedure.

forts at generalisation and theorisation. If so, then international law and lawyers would have to find their way case by case, discovering their possible means of assistance to such initiatives without aid of more systematic understanding, testing the value of their learning and professional tools in an *ad hoc* fashion. Call this the null hypothesis.

To answer convincingly the questions raised above would go a long way toward a general theory of the proper place of international law in confronting mass atrocity. Such a theory is as likely to emerge from this form of inquiry as by dwelling entirely – as virtually all scholarship now does – on international criminal law's 'cutting edge', *i.e.*, where it has recently made, or sought to make, its most ambitious advances. As a methodological matter, we can surely learn as much about international law's necessary and proper role by focusing on responses to mass atrocity – successful and otherwise – that little depend upon such law as by concentrating on its more glamorous moments in the sun, those fleeting occasions when it enjoys the world's enthralled attention.

A full understanding of international law's relative capacity requires that we compare not only its own successes and failures, but also the now-considerable efforts originating elsewhere and operating through quite different causal mechanisms. In fact, the key moral principles and policy aims underlying recent reforms of international criminal law, reforms greatly enlarging and empowering that enterprise, often continue to find stronger endorsement and more effective enforcement through causal pathways that treat legal doctrine and judicial institutions as marginal, if not quite inconsequential.

This is true beyond the immediate context of mass atrocity, in the usual sense.[19] A sociology of martial restraint would be concerned, more generally, with the causes of unnecessary suffering in war. It would treat limitation by belligerents in their use of force as the dependent variable (in the idiom of social science), and regard both law and non-legal considerations as alternative independent variables. The relative causal weight of such competing factors presents an empirical question, open to

[19] The usual, lay sense of the term would probably be limited to intentional wrongdoing, whereas the act of causing disproportionate civilian harm – excessive 'collateral damage', as it is sometimes informally described – can be a war crime (attributable to an individual) or a violation of the laws and customs of war (attributable to states) if the wrongful actor merely knows that excessive civilian harm will result.

investigation, permitting quite different conclusions in various historical and contemporary conflicts. Where available evidence permits, this study engages that task. We will thus ask, for instance, both how well-juridified is the proportionality norm (prohibiting excessive 'collateral damage' to civilians), and how much does that legal norm actually restrain battlefield violence, compared to non-juridical factors? Such extra-legal factors may press either in the same direction or in the opposite, *i.e.*, for lesser inhibition on armed force.

The present project might fairly be described as undertaking a charge that is essentially 'negative', identifying areas where international law cannot make much headway in enlarging its effective sphere of operation. This method carries us only so far, on its own. It would need to be combined with others' efforts to fathom international law's demonstrable strengths in atrocity-response. A full vision of international criminal justice begins to emerge, then, only from such a conjunction of complementary efforts. Still, putting international law 'in its place', one might say, is an admitted aim of the current inquiry. This is not to disparage such law's genuine achievements, past or present, merely to help identify its proper sphere. The contours of that domain may admittedly evolve and likely enlarge as non-juridical practices and the humanitarian movements spawning them begin to influence legal norms (as well as vice versa). Recognition of this dynamic, diachronic relationship between the two realms should give pause to any attempt at a temporal typology, seeking simply to identify the many ways they may interact. An adequate portrait, any comprehensive theory, would have to include some account of change, past and prospective, with all the contingencies and imponderables this entails.

It may be, in particular, that that the informality of recent non-legal regulatory initiatives at the international level, though presently necessary, proves a passing phase in their longer-term development. International law might therefore, as one leading scholar speculates, "insist on its formalities, be increasingly marginalised but do so in the hope that the tides will turn again and actors will realise that cooperating under law is more sustainable and power-neutral".[20]

One might even take this wishful prediction as something deeper, the claim to discern a latent dialectic by which the very advance of non-

[20] Pauwelyn, 2011, p. 125, see *supra* note 4.

juridical response – joined to increasing awareness of the shackles under which it continues to labour – will at some point call forth, willy-nilly, a recognizable need and irresistible demand for more law. The very challenge *to* law, in this view, would presumably elicit a well-tailored response *from* law. That scenario succumbs, alas, to the logical fallacy in all functionalist social explanation, *i.e.*, to the fact that even the most pressing of a society's 'needs' – despite accurate identification and full acknowledgement as such – never possess sufficient wherewithal to ensure their own fulfillment.[21]

We must closely attend both to achievements and disappointments of non-juridical response, asking: under what circumstances do such initiatives emerge and acquire some measure of efficacy? One might be tempted quickly to answer: when legal efforts clearly fail, and the urgent need to 'do something' becomes inescapable. Yet alas, many mass atrocities still go entirely without any organised response, belying any such functionalist account of the successes, which remain all too rare. Very often – as with the Asian 'comfort women'; of World War II and the mass rape of women in today's Congo,[22] for example – neither legal nor extra-legal efforts bear much fruit in prevention of mass atrocity, compensation of its victims, or even eliciting official acknowledgement of its occurrence.

By comparing the results of our five cases, it is possible inductively to derive some general lessons about the optimal place of international law in the world's response to mass atrocity. Our method will be to focus on those pressure points where these non-juridical responses encounter, run up against, sometimes operate almost at cross purposes *vis-à-vis*, the workings of a more stolid, conventional, international legal machinery. We will for instance wish to contrast the operation of non-juridical

21 A functionalist explanation is one that sees institutions as coming into being because of the systemic functions they serve, that is, apart from the interests, ideals, and intentions of those who might create, or resist the creation, of such institutions. On the failures of functionalism as social explanation, see Jon Elster, "Functional Explanation: Social Science", in Michael Martin and Lee McIntryre (eds.), *Readings in the Philosophy of Social Science*, The MIT Press, 1994.

22 "Approximately 500 women were raped in eastern Congo in July and August, demonstrating that both rebel militias and government troops used sexual violence as a weapon, two U.N. officials said Tuesday". See Neil MacFarquhar, "U.N. Says Congo Soldiers Carried Out Some Rapes", N.Y. Times, 7 Sept 2010.

U.N./NGO-devised mechanisms seeking greater 'corporate social responsibility' by foreign direct investors in repressive states with the fully juridicised Alien Tort Claims litigation in U.S. courts, increasingly aimed at the very same ends. The latter, lawyerly endeavors prove decidedly less promising, standing alone, than the former, non-juridicised ones. Yet it is also true that the litigation, the prospect of multi-million dollar liability it now plausibly presents, has sometimes contributed to corporate willingness to participate seriously in the U.N. initiative.

4. Democratic Opinion: The Continuing Place of Politics

In recent years international law has devoted great efforts to reduce, if not quite eliminate, the distorting influences of power politics in how the world responds to mass atrocity. This effort has not failed, exactly.[23] In fact, the aspiration for a body of international criminal law that is morally meaningful and relatively determinate has been so broadly achieved in recent years that the central and harder questions we must now ask of this field are quite different from those of the last century. The proper place of political considerations, of democratic opinion especially, in determining official response to such crimes must be reassessed and, in key respects, revalorised.

The prospect of liability before courts of law, national or international, remains and will remain far less significant than the influence of such political forces, broadly speaking, in restraining and redressing mass atrocity. There is no reason why such political pressures should necessarily find full expression through formal legal mechanisms. This is true even as the pressures at issue work to give additional effect to aims unequivocally embraced by international law as well.

[23] To observe this success in rule-creation is not to deny, of course, the frequent failure in implementing such norms, often owing to constraints of *realpolitik*. As a leading defense counsel in international prosecutions rightly observes, "international criminal justice still operates selectively within the cracks that international politics have opened up for it". See Guenael Mettraux, "Other International News", International Criminal Law Bureau, 16 May 2010, available at http://www.internationallawbureau.com/blog/?p=1457, last accessed on 14 March 2011. See also Elizabeth P. Allen, "Cowering in Fear", in *The New Republic*, 3 August 2010 (noting how Sudan's President Omar Al Bashir, though indicted by the International Criminal Court, travels officially to several other African states that have ratified the Court's Statute, which obligates them to honor the Court's extradition orders).

The political processes that make possible our non-juridical responses to mass atrocity are invariably managed by elites. Even so, they generally reflect widespread, well-considered public sentiment throughout much of the world and, in that sense, can be called 'democratic' in spirit. But in observing the inexpugnable vitality of politics in these initiatives, the aim here is not to celebrate some agonistic conception of democracy,[24] fearful of the impulse to dispel conflict through the rule of law, prizing the raw amorphousness of robust action. Rather, it is the simple fact that in our case studies we find forces of democratic opinion, national and international, frequently pressing accountable parties toward responses to mass atrocity more ethically satisfactory – and always more exigent – than anything international law within international courts has attempted or is capable of achieving, without straying perilously from its core commitments. If these innovative efforts could be trained to operate entirely within law's empire, there would be no good reason to banish them from it – certainly not, at any rate, the impulse to preserve them from disciplinary domestication.[25]

The most compelling objection to international juridification, here as in other areas, has always been its apparent 'democracy deficit', the relative unaccountability of international decision-makers to those affected by their decisions at the national level, *i.e.*, those who are asked to entrust international legal institutions with governance authority over them.[26] The initiatives here assayed offer an alluring counterpoint in this regard, for they hold out the prospect of greater accountability to the world community – for both those perpetrating mass atrocity and those

[24] For instance, Chantal Mouffe, *On the Political,* Routledge, 2005, p. 20; Wendy Brown, "'The Most We Can Hope For': Human Rights and the Politics of Fatalism", in *South Atlantic Quarterly*, 2004, vol. 103, pp. 451-456.

[25] Conversely, neither do the proponents of these atrocity-responsive projects disclose any urgent desire to resist the clutches of juridicizing encroachment, seen as some latent evolutionary process with the wind of history at its tail. To be sure, some proponents occasionally display a certain doubt about whether international law and international courts ultimately have much to offer in furtherance of their efforts. They pose to themselves, in other words, many of the same questions this inquiry also poses.

[26] Jed Rubenfeld, "Unilateralism and Constitutionalism", in *NYU Law Review*, 2004, vol. 79, p. 1971; but see Robert Keohane, Stephen Macedo and Andrew Moravscsik, "Democracy-Enhancing Multilateralism", in *International Organization*, 2009, vol. 63, p. 1.

claiming authority to redress it – through forms of normative ordering that avoid the delegation of coercive legal powers beyond the nation-state. For that reason these organised efforts may offer the provisional basis for an alternative model of international response to atrocity, or at least a necessary supplement to more juridicised approaches – where and whenever the latter give out. This is, at least, a possibility requiring investigation and reflection herein.

Though our initiatives often display genuine democratic inspiration, some readers may wonder whether a darker force lurks beneath. A common fear is that, though their apparent innocuousness now assures them wide support, their proponents actually harbor a long-term, incremental strategy which is more questionable. This begins with creating non-legalised global authority over the least controversial matters, then juridicising such response when non-legal measures fail, as they regularly will, finally advancing the law – of international human rights, in particular – into deeply contested issue-areas,[27] by which point it will become much more difficult for countries skeptical of such law's (likely illiberal) direction, to exempt themselves from its widening gyre.

Thus, mass atrocity – because of its surpassing moral exigency – will enthusiastically call forth voluntary initiatives at first requiring no complex global legal apparatus. Over time their limited efficacy will reveal, however, the unavoidable need to put the world's response to such recurrent crises on stronger institutional footing, an objective which juridification surely advances. Beginning, then, with an International Criminal Court, prosecuting only the world's most grievous wrongdoings, the empire of international law will expand willy-nilly. By demonstrating its increasing efficacy, it will move into territory where staunchly liberal societies like the U.S. may not wish to follow. Whether initiatives like those here explored seriously risk our descent along such a slippery slope to serfdom[28] is a question over which reasonable readers may differ. It will occasionally press itself upon our consideration, from an ever-present backdrop where it hovers gloweringly.

27 These would presumably include prohibition of the death penalty, the criminalisation of hate speech, even perhaps a human right to economic inequality, on some accounts.

28 The concern from this perspective is the potential capacity of unelected, life-tenured federal judges to incorporate what they take to be customary international law – on an indulgently capacious and ideologically-driven conception of such doctrine – into U.S. law by way of the notion of federal common law.

5. False Leads: An Inventory of Tantalising Missteps

Familiar notions and nostrums come quickly to mind for characterising the five initiatives. Yet none proves to fit their facts very closely. For instance, none of these efforts operates 'in the shadow' of the law, for that term refers to situations where parties negotiate in light of how they anticipate a court, applying pertinent legal rules, would decide their dispute. Here, by contrast, international legal rules are largely absent or not directly applicable, and international courts lack jurisdiction over the parties or contested subject matter.

Second, one might be tempted to say that these initiatives occupy the penumbral zone of normative ordering vaguely called 'global governance'.[29] That term, however, is not especially helpful here, because our initiatives often lack stable social organisation; they reflect more spontaneous, ephemeral outbursts of diffuse mobilisational activity.

A third way to think about these developments, because of their voluntary and extra-judicial character, might be as expressions of 'soft law'.[30] But that term implies agreement upon some norm, and there yet exists no genuinely settled norm in our cases, as with the demand to apologise for genocide. In others cases, as with the 'responsibility to protect', the emergent norm – if it may be so described – finds only very limited expression in any formal document to which states have agreed,[31] a basic element of 'soft law'. Other endeavors, like the pressure for corporate social responsibility in repressive states, do not originate with states, ei-

[29] On the emergence of global governance and its vicissitudes, as conceived by leading scholarly defenders, see, *e.g.*, Benedict Kingsbury *et al.*, "The Emergence of Global Administrative Law", in *Law and Contemporary Problems*, 2005, vol 68, p. 15; and Joshua Cohen and Charles Sabel, "Global Democracy?", in *International Law and Politics*, 2005, vol. 37, p. 763.

[30] See generally Kenneth Abbot and Duncan Snidel, "Hard and Soft Law in International Governance", in *International Organization*, 2000, vol. 54, p. 421; also Dinah Shelton (ed.), *Commitment and Compliance: The Role of Non-Binding Norms in the International Legal System*, Oxford University Press, 2000.

[31] In 2005, a U.N. General Assembly resolution endorsed the concept of a 'responsibility to protect', though the nature and terms of this duty remained ill-defined by that document. World Summit Outcome, Draft Resolution referred to the High-level Plenary Meeting of the General Assembly by the General Assembly at its fifty-ninth session, at http://www.who.int/hiv/universalaccess2010/worldsummit.pdf, last accessed 15 March 2011.

ther the states of foreign investors or those hosting such investment. This initiative presents no particular choice for states, then, between hard and soft governance, which is the question of institutional design at the center of all discussions about international 'soft law'.[32]

Fourth, we might first be inclined to see these initiatives as forms of 'law in action', as contrasted with the 'law on the books'.[33] This distinction refers, however, only to situations, unlike those here, where formal legal sources apply directly to the conduct under examination, enabling us to speak meaningfully of deviations between *de jure* rules and the *de facto* operation of practices and institutions nominally governed by them. In any event, most invocation of the 'law in action' sounds in a tragic key, because in practice much law falls short of its drafters' aspirations. Yet in all five cases we find significant advances, in the 'societal' response to mass atrocity, beyond anything required – even authorised, at times – by international law.

Finally, it is initially beguiling to see our several atrocity-aversive efforts as emanations of what is sometimes called 'living law'.[34] This term refers to convergent human behavior and norms endorsing it that spring up spontaneously, without design, almost without active human agency, within the social life of organisations and communities. There might thus be – or come into being, at some point – a living law from and for an emergent 'international community', in particular. But the concept of living or incipient law suggests greater social harmony than we find in our empirical materials, which disclose considerable contestation over

---

32 See, *e.g.*, Gregory Shaffer and Mark Pollack, "Hard vs. Soft Law: Alternatives, Complements and Antagonists in International Governance", in *Minnesota Law Review,* 2010, vol. 94, p. 706.

33 Roscoe Pound, "Law in Books and Law in Action", in *Am. L. Rev.*, 1910, vol. 44 , p. 12 and pp. 20-21.

34 See generally Mark Hertogh (ed.), *Living Law: Reconsidering Eugene Ehrlich,* Hart Publishing, 2009; Philip Selznick, "The Sociology of Law", in *International Encyclopedia. of the Social Sciences*, 1968, vol. 9, p. 50 and p. 55 (writing of "incipient law … implicit in the way in which public sentiment develops or in an increasingly stabilised pattern of organisation … a compelling claim of right or a practice so viable and so important to a functioning institution as to make legal recognition in due course highly probable.").

how best to treat atrocity, and where normative consensus over optimal response often exists only over glittering generalities.[35]

[35] Jeremy Webber, "Naturalism and Agency in the Living Law", in Mark Hertogh (ed.), *Living Law: Reconsidering Eugene Ehrlich,* Hart Publishing, 2009, p. 201 and pp. 202-203.

7.2

The Future of International Criminal Justice and Its Impact on Domestic Law

Richard Goldstone*

This think piece considers the three questions raised by HiiL in the context of international criminal law (ICL). Specifically, it will address the competition between national sovereignty and the growth of ICL, both conventional and customary. The most significant challenges for the development of ICL are i) the application of complementarity by the International Criminal Court, ii) the ability and resolve of the UN Security Council to enforce its ICL-related resolutions, and iii) the lawful use of force and individual participation in asymmetrical warfare. Despite these challenges, this think piece proposes that in the next two or three decades there will be i) developments and increased use of the principle of complementarity and customary international law, ii) diminished distinction within international humanitarian law between international and non-international armed conflicts, and iii) the development of a generally accepted legal framework regarding civilians who directly participate in hostilities. These challenges and future developments will i) require States to give greater consideration to their international legal obligations, ii) possibly increase international intervention in cases where States do not implement their international legal obligations, and iii) mandate greater use of international treaty and customary international law by national courts.

1. Introduction

This 'think piece' concerns the future of international criminal law, including International Humanitarian Law (IHL), and justice. Section 2 points out the most significant challenges for the development of the law: (2.1.) The application of the principle of complementarity; (2.2.) the resolve of the United Nations Security Council (UNSC); and (2.3.) asymmetric wars and other realities of modern warfare. Section 3 then discusses developments that are likely to occur in the coming two to three dec-

* **Richard Goldstone** is a former ICTY and ICTR Chief Prosecutor and former Justice of the Constitutional Court of South Africa.

ades: (3.1.) increased use of the principle of complementarity; (3.2.) further development and increased use of customary international law; (3.3.) diminished distinction between IHL for international and non-international armed conflicts; and (3.4.) development of the legal framework regarding civilians who directly participate in hostilities. Finally, in Section 4 I briefly suggest what such developments might mean for national legal systems. I propose to consider the topic in the context of the competition between national sovereignty and the growth of international law, both conventional and customary.

2. The Most Significant Challenges for the Development of the Law

2.1. Application of Complementarity

The mere existence of the International Criminal Court (ICC) creates potential for tension with national sovereignty. This tension is supposed to be mitigated by the principle of complementarity, the 'cornerstone' of the ICC, according to which the ICC is complementary to national criminal jurisdictions. How exactly this principle will work in practice is still evolving. It should be noted that three of the situations presently before the ICC arise from self-referrals from governments (Uganda, Democratic Republic of the Congo and the Central African Republic), and accordingly do not really demonstrate the potential pressure on national sovereignty. Then, the situation in Darfur was referred to the ICC by the UNSC (see discussion under subsection (2.2.) below). The most recent situation engaged by the ICC, that of Kenya, is most relevant for our discussion here.

The competition between national sovereignty and international law may draw more attention in the coming months in light of the ICC Prosecutor's successful application to a pre-trial chamber for authorisation to investigate, *inter alia*, the violence that erupted in relation to the national elections that were held in Kenya in 2007. That authorisation was granted in a decision delivered on 31 March 2010. This is the first case in which the Prosecutor has sought to use his *propria motu* powers to investigate any situation (such powers conferred by Article 15 of the Rome Statute). He sought that authorisation in the face of Kenya, a state party to the Rome Statute, refusing to adopt the recommendation of an official commission of inquiry to the effect that a criminal investigation should be launched into the alleged criminal conduct. The ICC has now issued warrants of arrest for Kenyan officials. At the time of writing, the Government of Kenya has reiterated its commitment to the Rome Statute but as regards the principle of complementarity, it noted that it was moving as expeditiously as possible with the implementation of reforms which would allow national proceedings to be undertaken by the Kenyan courts.[1] Moreover, the African Union has endorsed Kenya's request to the UNSC for a deferral (under Article 16 of the Rome Statute) of the ICC proceedings.[2] This situation in Kenya indeed poses a great challenge: it is the first test of the relationship between the ICC and a state party to the Rome Statute and will help demonstrate how the principle of complementarity functions in practice.

2.2. The Resolve of the United Nations Security Council

On 31 March 2005, the UNSC referred the situation in the Darfur region of Sudan to the ICC. It did so under the powers conferred on it by Chapter VII of the United Nations Charter read with Article 13 of the Rome Statute. In Darfur, President al-Bashir's government has been battling ethnic African rebels since 2003. Reports indicate that up to 300,000 people have been killed and 2.7 million have been driven from their homes. Formal investigations were instituted by the Prosecutor in June 2005. In 2007, the ICC issued warrants of arrest for Humanitarian Affairs Minister, Ahmad Harun, and alleged Janjaweed militia leader, Ali Kushayb. Then, on 4 March 2009, on the application of the Prosecutor, a pre-trial chamber of the ICC issued a warrant for the arrest of President al-Bashir for crimes against humanity and war crimes. On 12 July 2010, a pre-trial chamber issued a second arrest warrant for President al-Bashir on three counts of genocide.

Although the reference of the Darfur situation by the UNSC is binding on Sudan, the issue of the arrest warrants against Harun, and Kushayb is being flouted by its government. This has been reported by the judges

1 See "ICC Weekly Update # 63", 31 January 2011, available at http://www.icc-cpi.int/NR/rdonlyres/5586A1EB-C379-4B4D-91FD-94CF90372920/282954/Ed63Engl.pdf, last accessed on 16 February 2011.

2 BBC Online Edition, "African Union Backs Kenya Call to Delay ICC Case", 1 February 2011, available at http://www.bbc.co.uk/news/world-africa-12332563, last accessed on 16 February 2011.

of the ICC to the Security Council, most recently on 25 May 2010.[3] To date, the Security Council has taken no action pursuant to this report. The Sudan is further in breach of the 2005 UNSC resolution by ignoring the recent arrest warrants issued against President al-Bashir.

The UNSC, having itself referred the situation to the ICC, is having its authority and indeed its credibility tested by the refusal of the Government of Sudan to comply with the arrest warrants issued by the ICC. The issue now is whether the UNSC will be prepared to allow its authority to be questioned in this way or whether it is prepared to take appropriate action, under the Charter, to enforce its authority. The resolution is expressly binding on Sudan. It is also expressly stated not to be binding on states that have not ratified the Rome Statute. States that have ratified it are clearly bound by the arrest warrants issued by the ICC and this has generally been taken seriously by them.[4] Most importantly, in April 2010 the South African Government withdrew an invitation to President al-Bashir to attend the inauguration of President Zuma and Zuma himself later warned al-Bashir that if he attempted to visit South Africa for the Football World Cup in July 2010 he would be liable to be arrested.

The future success of the ICC depends entirely upon the cooperation of the governments of states that have become parties to the Rome Statute. The coming years will witness whether that cooperation will be forthcoming or not. Arguably, this might depend on the resolve of the UNSC in respect of the Darfur situation. The failure of the UNSC to take action and enforce the arrest warrants issued by the ICC against Sudanese officials might well constitute a negative incentive for individual states to cooperate with the ICC.

---

3 The same has been reconfirmed in the latest periodical report of the ICC Prosecutor to the UNSC. See "Twelfth Prosecutor's Statement to the United Nations Security Council on the Situation in Darfur", 10 December 2010, available at http://www.icc-cpi.int/NR/rdonlyres/3D32F788-15EF-4B56-9B26-55FD73458A7A/282820/12thspeechtotheUNSC.pdf, last accessed on 16 February 2011.

4 It could be argued, though, that even State Parties to the Rome Statute are not required to enforce the arrest warrant. UNSC Resolution 1593 only "urges" states not party to the conflict to cooperate. Sudan and all other parties to the conflict "shall" cooperate. This distinction read with Article 98 of the Rome Statute may be used to argue that since Sudan is not a party to the Rome Statute, states parties cannot violate the immunity of a head of state such as al-Bashir.

2.3. Asymmetric Wars and Other Realities of Modern Warfare

In some recent armed conflicts, it has been claimed by some leaders that the traditional laws of armed conflict have become outmoded and inapplicable to aspects of the new situations that have presented themselves.

Increasingly, the use of force and application of coercive measures have been applied by states fighting non-state actors or terrorist groups. The latter have frequently been accused of using civilian populations as human shields. A recent illustration is to be found with regard to Operation Cast Lead in which the Israel Defense Force launched an armed attack in Gaza in reaction to sustained rocket attacks against Israel by Gaza-based militant groups. The use of human shields has been relied upon by Israel to partly explain the high civilian casualty rate. So, too, the Sri Lankan Army launched massive attacks against the Liberation Tigers of Tamil Eelam (LTTE) rebel group and in the process killed and injured many tens of thousands of civilians. Some leaders in both Israel and Sri Lanka have called for current IHL to be updated and amended in order to facilitate measures taken in those circumstances by regular armies operating against such terrorist groups. The changes they have in mind have not been specified and it will be difficult to conceive of changes without violating the fundamental principles of IHL. The core requirement of distinction between belligerents and civilians, and the requirement of proportionality are well able to cope with any new situation that has arisen.

There are further related issues such as civilians who are 'directly participating in hostilities'. One of the core principles of IHL is that of 'distinction', *i.e.*, civilians must be distinguished from combatants and never be the intentional targets of attack. However, civilians might forfeit that protection by directly participating in hostilities. In the case of asymmetric wars, where the battle is not between two armies as such, the kind of conduct that constitutes 'direct participation' is a question of some complexity and much dispute. And, even if they have clearly and directly participated in hostilities, at what point will that participation end and allow them to revert to civilian status? These are questions on which there is much debate. Other issues relate to the use of new technology in warfare. One example is the use of unmanned aerial vehicles (UAVs) by non-military personnel (*e.g.*, US Central Intelligence Agency or private contractors). There have been targeted killings, especially with the use of UAVs. Oversight and measures of legal accountability are required regarding these practices. There are some fundamental questions such as the law that authorises (or does not authorise) the targeted killings of individuals who are not located on the battlefield or even in countries that are not direct parties to a war (*e.g.*, Pakistan). A related issue is remote war masking the true costs and tragedies of armed conflict. The number of civilian casualties occasioned by the use of UAV attacks in Pakistan is not known. Further, as described by Prof. Philip Alston in his 2010 UN report (discussed below), operators of UAVs, who undertake missions entirely through computer screens and remote audio-feed, run the risk of developing a "play-station" mentality to killing. Since operators do not face the risks of battle, they may not be instilled with the same level of respect for IHL as battlefield soldiers.

The core question is whether the current norms and rules of IHL are sufficient to cope with the foregoing and other realities of modern warfare. IHL is founded on four fundamental principles: those of distinction between military and civilians, military necessity, unnecessary suffering and proportionality. Do these fundamental principles remain effective to cope with the challenges posed by the realities of modern warfare? Is there a need to amend the law? Or is it not a question of applying these same principles to the new paradigms and realities, rather than requiring new norms and principles to be made applicable? It may be that the further development of the law should be left to constantly evolving norms of customary international law, *i.e.*, by the case-by-case application of the law. The crucial issue now and in the future is how national legal systems and especially military law regimes will respond to and address such potential inadequacies in IHL.

3. Developments Likely in the Coming Two to Three Decades

3.1. Development and Increased Use of the Principle of Complementarity

It has already been suggested above that the application of the principle of complementarity by the ICC is one of the great challenges ahead. It should also be noted, however, that this principle is gaining prominence in international law and is not limited to its application with regard to the ICC. The concept of the Responsibility to Protect that has been accepted by the UN General Assembly (GA) includes the principle of complementarity. Paragraph 139 of GA resolution (60/1 (2005)) states "In this context, we [the assembled Heads of State and Government at the GA meeting] are prepared to take collective action, in a timely and decisive manner, through the Security Council, in accordance with the Charter, including Chapter VII, on a case-by-case basis and in cooperation with relevant regional organisations as appropriate, should peaceful means be inadequate *and [if] national authorities are manifestly failing to protect their populations from genocide, war crimes, ethnic cleansing and crimes against humanity*" [emphasis added].

In the struggle between state sovereignty and enforcement of international human rights, the principle of complementarity seems to be a potential solution or a 'happy medium'. However, as already argued above, the principle of complementarity has yet to be truly tested. For example, for the purposes of the Rome Statute, what would constitute an investigation or prosecution for the purposes of Article 17 (which embodies the principle of complementarity in the form of a condition for admissibility of cases)? Would a legitimate truth and reconciliation commission be considered sufficient? And in what circumstances would the ICC decide that a state is not *genuinely* willing or able to undertake an investigation and prosecution?

In terms of the Responsibility to Protect, what type of evidence or grounds would be necessary for the Security Council (or potentially members of the international community without UN Security Council authorisation) to invoke the Responsibility to Protect concept? Given the extensive debate in the UNGA in July 2009 regarding this principle, it appears that complementarity might be useful in theory but it would certainly be difficult for an international institution (or the international community) to invoke if and when it might become necessary.

Another development is proactive or positive complementarity. This form of complementarity is essentially state capacity building that is undertaken or supported by international institutions and the international community. This approach calls for international institutions, such as the ICC, to focus some of their resources on empowering and building national legal systems in order to end impunity for perpetrators of crimes. In terms of the Responsibility to Protect concept, the state holds the primary responsibility to protect its population. The international community should assist, rather than directly intervene, in respect of states that are willing, but are financially or structurally unable to fulfil their responsibility to protect their own citizens. I would suggest that positive or proactive complementarity will become increasingly relevant as governments seek to avoid the jurisdiction of the ICC.

3.2. Development and Increased Use of Customary International Humanitarian Law

In 2005, the International Committee of the Red Cross (ICRC) published a massive volume titled Study on Customary International Humanitarian Law. Some of its findings are controversial and have not been accepted by some governments including the United States. One of the controversies relates to the appropriate sources of customary international law. For instance, the United States, in a response to the ICRC contends that military codes should not be relied upon but rather what happens in the field of battle. Another area of debate relates to the number of instances or situations necessary to justify regarding particular conduct as giving rise to a norm of customary IHL. This notwithstanding, the study has received much attention in the literature and will certainly influence future developments of the law and decisions of international and domestic war crimes tribunals as well as domestic courts.

3.3. Diminished Distinction Between IHL for International and Non-International Armed Conflicts

Traditionally, there has been a distinction between IHL for international armed conflict (IAC) and non-international armed conflict (NIAC). For example, the Geneva Conventions of 1949 and Additional Protocol I of 1977 address IAC, while Article 3 common to the four Geneva Conventions and Additional Protocol II apply to NIAC. However, the distinction between IHL for NIAC and IAC may become blurred in the future (if not already so). As indicated by the aforementioned ICRC study, there appears to be a growing number of rules of customary IHL that are identical between IAC and NIAC. Of the 161 rules in the ICRC study, 136 rules pertain to both IAC and NIAC. Further, the first amendment to the Rome Statute added three acts to the list of crimes during NIAC, which are already listed as war crimes during IAC (*i.e.*, employing poison or poisoned weapons, asphyxiating or poisonous gases, and expanding or "dum-dum" bullets). The diminishment of the distinction may be due to the phenomenon of NIACs spreading beyond the borders of one state into several other states (including non-adjoining states). As NIACs become transnational, the rules that are analogous to those in IAC may be necessary. Notwithstanding this potential, it may be appropriate to question the necessity for the distinction between IAC and NIAC, at least for a significant portion of IHL. The diminished distinction between the IHL for IAC and NIAC will increase the subject-matter jurisdiction of international criminal law in NIAC. In terms of national legal systems, rules which previously only pertained to IAC may soon have to be adopted for internal armed conflicts and appropriate domestic investigations and prosecutions will need to be undertaken.

3.4. Development of the Legal Framework Regarding Civilians Who Directly Participate in Hostilities

With regard to targeted killing and civilians who directly participate in hostilities, Prof. Philip Alston, the UN Special Rapporteur on Extra-Judicial, Summary and Arbitrary Executions has indicated in a recent report: "Such policies are often justified as a necessary and legitimate response to 'terrorism' and 'asymmetric warfare', but have had the very problematic effect of blurring and expanding the boundaries of the applicable legal frameworks".[5] It is stated further that:

> Even where the laws of war are clearly applicable, there has been a tendency to expand who may permissibly be targeted and under what conditions. Moreover, the States concerned have often failed to specify the legal justification for their policies, to disclose the safeguards in place to ensure that targeted killings are in fact legal and accurate, or to provide accountability mechanisms for violations. Most troublingly, they have refused to disclose who has been killed, for what reason, and with what collateral consequences. The result has been the displacement of clear legal standards with a vaguely defined license to kill, and the creation of a major accountability vacuum.[6]

This displacement of legal standards needs to be rectified. As suggested in Prof. Alston's report, states and organisations such as the ICRC

[5] Philip Alston, "Report of the Special Rapporteur on Extrajudicial, Summary or Arbitrary Execution" A/HRC/14/24/Add, 28 May 2010, available at http://www2.ohchr.org/english/bodies/hrcouncil/docs/14session/A.HRC.14.24.Add6.pdf, last accessed on 16 February, 2011.

[6] Alston, 2010, see *supra* note 5.

should work towards a legal framework with respect to targeting civilians who directly participate in hostilities. This framework should be universal and dissuade states from adopting their own separate version of what constitutes such direct participation. The 2009 ICRC Interpretative Guidance on civilians' direct participation in hostilities is a good starting point for negotiations, but it must be refined and gain acceptance in the international community. Further, national legal systems will have to implement measures for investigations, transparency and accountability whenever a state targets civilians who directly participate in hostilities (especially when the state employs UAVs and new technologies for remote warfare).

4. Consequences for National Systems in the International Legal Order as a Whole

4.1. Greater Consideration by States of Their International Legal Obligations

As the world contracts and as international criminal activity increases, states will be forced to give greater attention to their international legal obligations and insist on other states doing likewise. These obligations will include adherence to the norms and principles of customary international law apart from multilateral and bilateral treaties. Proactive complementarity is likely to be more widely recognised and practiced and this might well extend to the Responsibility to Protect.

These international legal obligations may also encompass enforcement measures, such as international arrest warrants with the use of national armed forces. As posited by Prof. Theodor Meron, international armed forces (*e.g.*, UN peacekeepers or NATO forces) already operating in a certain area could be called upon to enforce the arrest warrants of the ICC. This would be similar to NATO forces enforcing the arrest warrants of the International Criminal Tribunal for the former Yugoslavia (ICTY). However, a clear UNSC resolution or an agreement with the state in which the foreign armed forces operate may be necessary for the armed forces to undertake such enforcement measures. Amongst other things, respect for the sovereignty of the territorial state will have to be balanced against the legal obligations of the respective states contributing to an international armed force. The national legal systems of the territorial state as well as the 'enforcing' state will have to respond to the respective international legal obligations applicable to the parties.

4.2. Possible Increased International Intervention in Cases Where States do not Implement Their International Legal Obligations

It is a difficult and open question as to whether states will again intervene in order to protect the human rights of citizens of other states – whether failed states or those whose leaders violate on a massive scale the human rights of those people subject to their rule. A recent example of this was in 1999 when NATO armies under US leadership used military force to protect the Albanian citizens of Kosovo, a province of Serbia who were being ethnically cleansed by the forces of Slobodan Milosevic. That action was taken without the authorisation of the UNSC and was thus in violation of the Charter of the United Nations and was therefore unlawful. After the capitulation of Milosevic, a Russian resolution before the Security Council to condemn the unlawful use of military force was convincingly rejected. Nonetheless, it might turn out that the NATO intervention in Kosovo was an aberration and has not established a new practice.

One of the problems with this kind of intervention is that it will always be politically driven and certainly never used against a powerful state or a state under the protection of a powerful nation. At the same time the ICC has now been seen to act against a head of state (President al-Bashir of Sudan) and against a state that has failed to take appropriate action against its own citizens (Kenya).

4.3. Use of International Treaty and Customary International Law by National Courts

Greater recognition of international treaty and customary law in the international legal order might well have as a consequence that those norms and principles will be adopted and applied more frequently in domestic courts. In the Canadian case of *R v Hape* (2007), the Supreme Court of Canada was called upon to determine whether the Charter protection against unreasonable search and seizure applied extra-territorially to investigations conducted by Canadian officials abroad, in that case in the Turks and Caicos Islands. The Canadian police were authorised by the foreign government to investigate a case of money laundering subject to its laws. In answering the question, the Canadian Supreme Court was guided by customary international law. It expressly applied customary international law in aid of its interpretation of Canadian law and the development of the common law. Discussion and seminars in the post-*Hape* period have included the concern for the lack of awareness of customary international law by lawyers and judges, and the call for legal education to help remedy this. The South African Constitutional Court has in a number of cases similarly referred to foreign law, international law and customary international law in the interpretation of legislation and the Constitution.

5. Conclusion

Of course, the ICC may yet prove to be unsuccessful as a deterrent and as an instrument to bring justice to the victims of serious war crimes. If that occurs, the states that support it will withdraw and refuse to continue to fund it. If that were to happen, we would be back to the pre-2002 situation in which effectively international war crimes tribunals would only be established by the UNSC (as in the case of the ICTY and ICTR) or by action between individual states and the United Nations (as in the case of the Special Court for Sierra Leone or the Lebanon Tribunal). Such an eventuality would again make international criminal justice subject to the political will of powerful nations and especially the veto of the permanent members of the UNSC.

I have referred to the rapid developments in the fields of international criminal law and justice. I have raised a few of the issues that will in all probability engage the attention of international lawyers. There will no doubt be many others.

7.3

The Future of International Criminal Justice

Göran Sluiter[*]

The future of international criminal justice is hard to predict. The first vital aspect is the future occurrence of mass atrocities and their international criminalisation. It seems that there will remain much to do in international criminal justice, because system criminality continues to be committed, and the international community is still on the track of further criminalisation (*e.g.*, the crime of aggression). It is unsure where the response to international crimes takes place at the national or the international level. This piece is skeptical about the principle of complementarity and submits the thesis that the ICC is likely to remain the central factor in combating impunity for the decades to come. Regarding the functioning of the ICC, it is argued that the problems it currently faces in expeditious administration of justice are unlikely to be solved in the decades to come. There are structural (procedural) problems which make it near impossible to finish trials expeditiously. Moreover, the ICC will be facing the problem that certain (powerful) individuals may never be tried at all. It is recommended that these problems are addressed first – *i.e.*, consolidating the current legal edifice – before expanding the scope of the ICC or engaging in new experiments (*e.g.*, the crime of aggression).

1. Introduction

Below I develop a few thoughts on the future development of the international criminal justice system. A distinction will be made between the following three aspects:

a) the occurrence of mass atrocities and the question of criminalisation;
b) the response of the international community; and
c) the functioning of the ICC.

[*] **Göran Sluiter** is Professor of Law, University of Amsterdam.

After dealing with these three aspects, a few tentative conclusions in terms of the key dilemmas for the international criminal justice system will be offered.

2. The Occurrence of Mass Atrocities and Issues of Criminalisation

The international criminal justice system relates to conduct penalised by the international community, giving rise to direct individual criminal responsibility under international law. The future development of this system first and foremost depends upon the scale and level of future (mass) violence and on the processes of criminalisation. Ideally, one would like to see a decrease in the occurrence of mass violence in the future. Hopefully, the accumulated results of the international criminal justice system will lead to an increasing deterrent effect. However, it remains to be seen whether and to what degree deterrence will prove to be one of the positive aspects of the international criminal justice system. For the time being, and for the coming two decades as well, it is safe to assume that conflicts and situations of mass violence will not be exceptional in the world.

In the face of conflicts and situations of mass violence, as well as other types of 'problematic conduct' from the perspective of the international legal order, it must be decided whether further criminalisation is appropriate. It must be noted that in domestic criminal justice systems there is an equal trend towards both decriminalisation (*e.g.*, prostitution in certain countries) and criminalisation (*e.g.*, cybercrime). The reasons for trends in both directions is the ever evolving and changing morals of society and the necessity for each society to strive for a complete criminal justice system.

In contrast, the international criminal justice system does not yet know decriminalisation; since the Nuremberg trials we have witnessed more crimes occurring, rather than a disappearance of crimes. The reason for this is that the international criminal justice system is incomplete, only focusing on the most serious crimes. Any discussion on whether such crimes still merit being punishable therefore seems pointless. What matters more is whether certain acts should give rise to individual criminal responsibility under international law. It is not inconceivable that certain crimes, although very serious, would stop being considered international crimes, because it may no longer be necessary to have them as crimes against the international legal order.

Yet, such developments seem very far away. At least, I can think of no conduct being a serious candidate for decriminalisation. Rather, there is a trend of continuing criminalisation, taking place on two levels. First, there is the conspicuous practice of direct legislation: States codify and criminalise conduct in treaties. A recent addition was the crime of aggression in the ICC Statute (although it can also be said that this was a mere codification of customary international law existent since the Nuremberg Judgment). Second, judges have a tendency to expand the protection underlying international crimes in international criminal proceedings and have resorted to expansive methods of interpretation. Thereby they have supported further criminalisation.

I do not expect the trend above being reversed in the near future. Apparently, there is a sense that the edifice of substantive international criminal law is not yet finished. Among states there are proposals for inclusion of new crimes in the jurisdiction of the ICC, or other international(ised) tribunals, such as terrorism or piracy. Also, judges still display an expansive interpretation of the definition of crimes and modes of responsibility (*e.g.*, the recent decision of the ICC PTC on the scope of crimes against humanity, related to the Kenya investigation).

The vital question is, of course, whether this process of criminalisation is a positive development or whether it should be discouraged. This is one of the key dilemmas of the future. Although we still are far away from a reverse trend of decriminalisation and there may still be gaps in the international criminal justice system that need to be filled, the risks are apparent and should not be underestimated. The legitimacy of the international criminal justice system may be at stake when further criminalisation goes at the expense of legal certainty or compromises the 'acquis' of the international criminal justice system, as it has been in the last two decades. The inclusion of the crime of aggression is a good example. Some believe with some merit that the conditions of jurisdiction attached to investigating aggression politicise the ICC too much and may damage the Court's legitimacy; in addition there is a concern that a precedent now exists to install specific jurisdictional regimes for other add-ons to the Rome Statute in the future. The paradox thus is that while one attempts to strengthen international criminal justice by adding new crimes and by expansive interpretation of current crimes, the opposite of weakening the system looms on the horizon. As a result, while further criminalisation appears inevitable in the coming two decades, this must be done with the utmost caution.

The international community would be well-advised to establish certain parameters on the basis of which conduct deserves criminalisation and to justify the addition thereof to the Rome Statute. 'System criminality', meaning criminality on a widespread scale as a result of an organisational plan or policy and often involving the state, should in my view be an important guiding point in establishing these parameters. But regard must also be had to the conceptual applicability of general principles of international criminal law, as set out in part 2 of the ICC Statute, as well as in jurisdictional rules and principles to possible future expansion of the subject matter jurisdiction of the ICC. To put it simply, the crime must fit in the ICC Statute and not the other way around.

The creation of the aforementioned parameters for admission of new crimes would protect the international criminal justice system against abuse for political purposes, as an (inappropriate) response to problems that dominate the international agenda. An example here is the problem of piracy. This is clearly not conduct that should be part of the ICC Statute, or of the international criminal justice system in its sense of being reserved to the most serious international crimes.

3. Response of the International Community

There are three possible responses to international crimes, in terms of their investigation and prosecution. First, it can be undertaken by national courts, second, by internationalised courts and, third, by international courts. In the past two decades we have seen all three responses with varying degrees of success. The question is whether the law of the future will consolidate the need for all three forms. With the creation of the ICC the emphasis has come to focus more and more on national prosecution. If states have difficulty in organising this, the international community needs to assist possibly in the form of internationalised courts. But is this really a trend to be predicted – stronger attention for national investigations and prosecutions – and if so, how will the law reflect that trend?

I am not persuaded that the ideal of more and better national prosecutions will be realised in the future. There is reason to be sceptical about 'complementarity'. I do not think that the desired, and perhaps expected, shift of caseload to national courts will materialise in the next two decades. There are a number of reasons for this. First, the major international criminal tribunal, the ICC, does not seem to fully adhere to the principle of complementarity itself. In its initial practice the ICC has adopted an approach towards complementarity which optimises taking in cases at the ICC. Although this may change, it is not unlikely that the ICC will remain interested in cases, even if national prosecution is feasible. The aspiration of an inactive ICC as an effective ICC is not a reality.

Second, related to this, state parties are cognisant of the ambitions of the Court and generally glad to let them take the lead in the prosecution of international crimes. True, certain states have adopted improved legislation to prosecute international crimes more effectively. However there is no widespread, strong and convincing practice of national prosecutions. Even in the few more active states, like The Netherlands, the number and pace of prosecutions is very modest and cannot be compared with the expected output of the ICC, once it is really up and running. Third, we must thus acknowledge that national resources devoted to the prosecution of international crimes remain very limited. Absent mechanisms of accountability, it is not likely that in the continuing struggle over resources, the prosecution of international crimes will be a priority. This may be different in states where the crimes have been committed, exercising jurisdiction on the basis of territoriality. But such prosecutions may be problematic, because the state concerned is (a) not in a position to organise them (failed or partially failed state), (b) is not interested in doing so, with a view to maintaining national peace and stability, or (c) using prosecutions as a political tool against (defeated) political enemies, making truly impartial and independent justice impossible.

It is not realistic to expect that the law will play a significant role in improving the national reluctance to prosecute international crimes. In fact, the formal obligation has existed since WW II (1949 Geneva Conventions; 1948 Genocide Convention) and has largely been ignored. In addition, complementarity has been very confusing as a concept and vaguer still since the creation of the ICC in the sense that it can be interpreted in practically any direction. From a policy perspective, the ICC's Assembly of State Parties (ASP) is probably the organ where states should be encouraged to prosecute international crimes domestically. But this body seems incapable of getting its members to do that, failing a clear obligation to that end in the Statute. Furthermore, states may, with some reason, claim that their support for international criminal justice is invested by means of their financial contribution, in the ICC. In other words, they may be hesitant to pay twice for the struggle against impunity and may consider that they have 'outsourced' their commitment to the ICC. The latter does not seem to object strongly, for the simple reason that it is an ambitious institution and also because it can only demonstrate what it is really worth by processing cases.

The danger that looms on the horizon as a result of this initial practice, *i.e.*, an ambitious and ever growing ICC and reluctant/passive states, is that it is very difficult to reverse. Of course, one might argue, that the aspiration is to have both an active and ambitious ICC and states. But this cannot be achieved on the basis of the frail and utterly ineffective principle of complementarity.

I expect that without structural changes in the relationship between states and ICC, the national activity in relation to international crimes will remain modest. States may be quite happy with this. But in the interest of an efficient international criminal justice system it is wise to consider alternative mechanisms to complementarity. An interesting idea, worth further research, is whether a mechanism of referral of cases from the ICC to national jurisdictions[1] could strengthen the idea behind complementarity. Practically, one can imagine an ICC Prosecutor shaping the contours of investigations and prosecutions in a situation and identifying the cases and charges, with a view to later divide the caseload between the ICC and states. This mechanism, although it has its problems and was born out of necessity, worked quite well for the ICTY. It does not (yet) really work for the ICTR, but this is very much a jurisdictional problem[2], which is not likely to occur in the same degree with crimes committed after entry into force of the ICC. The advantages of a referral mechanism built into the ICC Statute are at least twofold. First, there is one institution which takes the lead and coordinates the prosecution of international crimes. Second, when a direct request for referral is made, this is more likely to generate national prosecutorial activity than when states are expected to develop their own strategies in this respect. Although referrals at the ICTY/ICTR

[1] Such as Rule 11bis of the ICTY. See "Rules of Procedure and Evidence", International Criminal Tribunal for the former Yugolsavia, Rule 11bis.

[2] See International Criminal Tribunal for Rwanda, *Bagaragaza*, Case No. ICTR-2005-86-11bis, Decision on Prosecutor's Request for Referral of the Indictment to the Kingdom of The Netherlands.

function in tandem with primacy, there is no reason why it couldn't also function together with complementarity. Just as in the case of the ICTY, this does not have to be a duty of cooperation for states parties. However, the mere fact of this being available as a formal cooperation framework under the ICC Statute is in my view a significant advantage over an isolated and confusing complementarity principle.

The prediction of the law of the future does not only concern the ICC and national prosecutions of international crimes, but also other mechanisms and responses to mass atrocities. In addition to the ICC and by their own national courts, states can also respond to international crimes by *ad hoc* international or internationalised courts. In the past two decades we have witnessed a unique proliferation of such institutions and undeniably they have greatly contributed to the international criminal justice edifice. However, it is uncertain whether and how many similar institutions we will see in the future. Although international(ised) criminal tribunals have been set up after the creation of the ICC, it must be noted that, with the exception of the Special Tribunal for Lebanon, all these institutions deal with crimes committed before the ICC entered into force on 1 July 2002. Using the ICC is not an option in respect of crimes committed prior to that date.

Although it cannot be excluded that *ad hoc* international(ised) tribunals continue to be created to deal with crimes committed prior to 1 July 2002, the interesting question is how the international community wishes to respond to crimes committed after 1 July 2002. It seems that after a period of significant resistance against the ICC by the US, which strongly advocated the creation of alternative *ad hoc* mechanisms, the ICC now almost seems to be the only show in town. Creation of a separate international criminal tribunal dealing with crimes over which the ICC could also exercise jurisdiction is unlikely to occur in the future. Also the UN Security Council has found its way into the ICC (Darfur situation), and there seems to be a general 'tribunal fatigue', which can – in part – be explained by the significant expenses involved in the creation of international tribunals.

Having said this, I think that in the future, the international community will continue to assist states in the domestic prosecution of international crimes. Such assistance can take a variety of forms, such as financial assistance, training, making lawyers available, and in creating a separate institution/chamber. As to the latter, this rather would go in the direction of an institution/chamber within a state's existing court structure, rather than in creating a new and separate legal entity. The biggest problem in providing assistance to national courts in the prosecution of international crimes is the matter of ownership and the corresponding issues of responsibility. When the international community, or certain of its members, support proceedings in another country where, for example, the right to a fair trial is not properly respected, it also carries some degree of responsibility, especially when there is a question of structural violations and support is being provided in the knowledge thereof. After the experiment of the politicised ECCC (Cambodia) the international community, and individual states, may be expected to be more reluctant in supporting criminal proceedings in states that do not fully adhere to human rights law.

4. Future Functioning of the ICC

It is a safe prediction to say that the ICC will increasingly be the focus of international criminal justice. As already mentioned, in the next two decades it may as well be the 'only show in town'. Obviously, the future of international criminal justice rests to a large degree upon the shoulders of the ICC. I already indicated that I do not foresee much change in the future role of the ICC; it will remain the centrepiece in international criminal justice and although functioning under the principle of complementarity in theory, in practice the ICC plays a primary and leading role in the investigation and prosecution of international crimes.

One would hope, and also expect, that in light of the fragile nature of the ICC, its state parties have a strong interest in improving the system. However, there is great reluctance to make changes to the law of the ICC. It seems that any attempt to make changes is regarded as a risk for the new system and the danger of opening 'Pandora's box' is said to loom on the horizon. The practical result is an extreme degree of passivity on the part of the states. This has been illustrated by the recent review conference in Kampala. In addition to defining aggression, and a few other matters, the exercise of stocktaking the ICC was on the agenda. Instead of being a sincere attempt to improve the Court's functioning, the stocktaking exercise proved to be a waste of time. It resulted in resolutions which are full of clichés, but do nothing to address the problems of the court.

It is my great concern that the problems the ICC is facing are not addressed seriously or expeditiously enough. States, acting through the ASP, do not seem to live up to their role as legislators. The question is whether this is problematic, and which aspects of the ICC would especially require intervention.

The problems primarily concern the procedural functioning of the ICC and are of a twofold nature. First, the trials that are currently being conducted take up too much time and have given rise to problematic procedural incidents, such as the disclosure problems in the Lubanga case. This is not the place to go into detail, but it seems that critical assessment of procedure is in order and inevitable in the coming two decades. Whether changes to the process of the confirmation hearing and victim participation are necessary must be particularly considered. In the coming two decades state parties will have to decide what in terms of output of the ICC is acceptable to them. Especially compared to the ICTY, the ICC has not been very productive up till now. Procedural problems play an important role in this respect and it is up to the legislator, the ASP, to solve such problems. This can be done, for example, by restricting victim participation and abolishing, or revising, the confirmation hearing procedure.

Secondly, an even bigger problem in the decades to come, possibly forever, for the ICC is the fact that certain trials cannot be conducted, because the arrest warrants for a significant number of individuals are not enforced. A lack of cooperation has plagued, in varying degrees, all contemporary international criminal tribunals, and will be a matter that will also dominate the agenda of the ICC in the future. At present, the problems of cooperation troubling the ICC can best be illustrated by the Al Bashir arrest warrant. It is not only problematic that for several years this arrest warrant has not been executed by states, it is also disconcerting that states fail to do so in an increasingly open and provocative way. For example, Chad recently received Al Bashir and openly refused to arrest him, among other things, because it regarded the ICC as a Court discriminating against Africans, and this is a state party!

When we consider solutions and improvements for cooperation problems, we can do so on the following levels and I suspect the discussion in the next two decades will reflect this. First, the discussion may concentrate on the question of what degree the ICC has to rely on cooperation. The progress of cases is currently 'hijacked' by forms of cooperation as a *condicio sina qua non*. The prohibition on trials *in absentia* means that no case can go forward failing the arrest of the suspect, making the ICC particularly vulnerable when this cooperation is not provided. Although trials in absentia are certainly problematic, they offer the advantage to go forward. They have recently been reinstated in the field of international criminal law by virtue of the Special Tribunal for Lebanon law of procedure, and in case of the ICC, a permanent body, a retrial is possible in case the suspect/accused is arrested. It is my estimation that the more arrest becomes a problematic form of cooperation the greater the need to re-consider the availability of trials in the absence of the accused.

Second, to gain effectiveness the ICC must continue to increase the number of states parties, thereby minimising the number of 'safe havens' and jurisdictional gaps. This is a difficult task and raises the 'cooperation or effectiveness paradox' of the ICC. This paradox means that to be effective the ICC is in need of more states parties; however, at this stage, the remaining non-states parties may only be interested in becoming a party or in cooperating with the ICC subject to many and substantial conditions. Hence, the paradox, that to be more effective and attract more state parties, the Court must first become less effective (a less powerful cooperation regime). It will not be easy to find a solution within the next two decades and we will thus continue to face the reality of a substantive number of non-state parties. The solution, for the time being, may lie in increasing the efforts to secure cooperation from non-states parties on an *ad hoc* basis.

Third, the law on cooperation of the ICC is still relatively weak compared to its predecessors the ICTY and ICTR. The provisions in the ICC Statute are at times unclear and contain a number of unfortunate compromises[3]. A particular problem, which is now very much felt in the Darfur situation, is that the Statute does not contain a separate and more effective cooperation regime in case of referrals from the Security Council. Indeed, it seems logical that when the Security Council refers a situation to the ICC, acting in the interests of international peace and security, some of the obstacles to cooperation, like complementarity, should not be applicable. It is uncertain to what degree the problems in the substantive law on cooperation will be addressed in the future by the ASP. The prob-

3 Rome Statute of the International Criminal Court, 17 July 1998, Article 99 (4) and Article 93 (7).

lem with cooperation issues is that the law tends to be overlooked and much of the energy focuses on finding political solutions.

The fourth challenge, already an issue at this early stage in the ICC's lifespan, is that it can safely be said that there are enormous problems in enforcing cooperation. This problem has also plagued the ICTY and to a lesser degree, the ICTR. The enforcement of rules of international law has been, currently is and will remain the biggest challenge to the international legal order. The problems of the ICC in this respect are thus not unique but concern international law in general. That said, within the international criminal justice system particular efforts must be made to improve enforcement and the following observations are in order. The ICC, as compared to the *ad hoc* tribunals, faces two particular problems. First, the UN Security Council is not behind it; even in the sole SC referral, Darfur, one has the impression that the support of the Council is only half-hearted. Second, there does not seem to be one or a block of truly powerful states that are in a position and willing to exert pressure on non-cooperative states. The United States has been, in many instances, the driving force behind enforcing cooperation with the ICTY and the ICTR, but this state is, regrettably not a party to the ICC. Its absence as a member is very much felt in the area of enforcing cooperation. The European Union could potentially fill the gap a bit, but is too often divided on foreign policy. It has had success when it could 'threaten' states with talks on EU membership (Serbian cooperation with ICTY), but this is hardly of any help to the ICC. In this vacuum of truly powerful allies, the ICC is very much on its own when it comes to enforcement of cooperation; this means that the ASP appears to be the only body to enforce cooperation. However, it remains uncertain to what degree it can be effective, because (a) there is no specific procedure and no sanction regime for non-cooperative states, and (b) the non-complying state or states is a member of the ASP and could try to influence the deliberations; generally speaking, this is an organ consisting of diplomats, and there is reluctance to be critical in relation to other states. In this light, the ASP is well-advised to outsource the enforcement procedure to a separate and independent body.

5. Key Dilemma: Build or Consolidate?

Based on the above, I think one can identify one big overarching key dilemma for international criminal justice. There seems to be a tendency of continuing expansion and little awareness of solving the existing problems. In other words, should we continue to build or consolidate and improve the existing edifice? Although one does not have to exclude the other, priorities have to be set. As the ICC will continue to develop as the centrepiece of international criminal justice in the next two decades, it deserves better treatment. This treatment will hopefully consist of the following main elements:

a) caution in the addition of new crimes to the ICC Statute; development of objective parameters governing such future additions, protecting the 'acquis' of the ICC;
b) qualifying the principle of complementarity, accepting and taking advantage of the ICC's leading and coordinating role in international criminal justice; and
c) making sure that shorter, and thus also more, trials can take place at the ICC, by improving (1) the Court's procedural law and (2) law.

7.4

Crimes Against Present and Future Generations: Ending Corporate Impunity for All Serious Violations of International Law

Sébastien Jodoin*

A patchwork of weak, non-existent, or inadequately enforced laws in both developed and developing states has resulted in significant gaps in the governance of transnational corporations and creates conditions conducive to serious violations of international law. Addressing these governance gaps in both national and international law is likely to be one of the most important challenges of the law of the future. In meeting this challenge, law will not only need to develop standards capable of addressing the most significant harms suffered by vulnerable populations and environments, but also mechanisms for effectively enforcing these standards. In this paper, I argue that the emerging system of international criminal justice has the potential to deliver both the standards and mechanisms of accountability that are required to correct the most harmful excesses of transnational corporate activity. I also argue that before international criminal law can fill all the gaps in the governance of corporate activities in developing countries, it will be necessary to expand its scope of application to economic, social, and cultural rights and international environmental law. One possible path forward would be to create a new category of international crime that would prohibit acts and conduct that have severe impacts on the long-term health, safety and means of survival of human groups and collectives – crimes against present and future generations.

1. Governance Gaps and Permissive Environments Conducive to Serious Violations of International Law

The expansion of the power, activities and scope of transnational corporations has significantly influenced law in the second half of the twentieth century, especially with respect to trade, investment, and cross-border

* **Sébastien Jodoin** is a Lead Counsel at the Centre for International Sustainable Development Law.

business activities. These changes in corporate regulation have done much to facilitate globalisation and have resulted in some positive benefits in terms of global and transnational economic growth. On the other hand, law has done little to address some of the challenges arising from transnational corporate activities, most notably in the areas of human rights, human health and the environment. At the level of international law, transnational corporations benefit from their lack of legal status and ambiguities in the scope of application of international legal norms to their conduct and activities.[1] While a number of voluntary codes of conduct or sets of norms applicable to corporations have been developed to fill this gap, such voluntary initiatives, lacking effective measures to monitor and sanction non-compliance, have proved to be ineffective and insufficient.[2] At the level of national law, transnational corporations take advantage of the unwillingness or inability of developed and developing states to effectively regulate their activities. Developed states, where many transnational corporations are headquartered are often reluctant to hold corporations accountable for their conduct abroad due to concerns that they may relocate elsewhere.[3] Developing states are equally disinclined to sanction abuses committed by corporations on their territories. Their governments benefit from the economic growth and resources (as well as from bribes and patronage) that come with transnational corporate activities or may be directly implicated in abuses committed by or on behalf of corporations.[4]

This patchwork of weak, non-existent, or inadequately enforced laws in both developed and developing states has resulted in gaps in the governance of transnational corporations operating in developing coun-

1 For an early account of this phenomenon, see Jonathan Charney, "Transnational Corporations and Developing Public International Law", in *Duke Law Journal*, 1983, vol. 1983, no. 4, pp. 748-788.

2 See, for example, a publication of Amnesty International which is critical of the human rights record of two participants in Voluntary Principles process, Chevron and Shell: Amnesty International, "Nigeria: Ten Years On: Injustice and Violence Haunt the Oil Delta", 3 November 2005, available at http://www.amnesty.org/en/library/asset/AFR44/022/2005/en/63b716d6-d49d-11dd-8a23-d58a49c0d652/afr440222005en.pdf, last accessed 30 March 2011.

3 Concerns over economic competitiveness and leakage have most recently been expressed by Canada over proposals to ensure greater levels of corporate social responsibility on the part of Canadian extractive companies operating abroad.

4 Irene Khan and David Petrasek, *The Unheard Truth: Poverty and Human Rights*, W.W. Norton & Company, New York, 2009, Chapter 8.

tries. These governance gaps "provide the permissive environment for wrongful acts by companies of all kinds without adequate sanctioning or reparation".[5] Addressing these governance gaps in both national and international law is likely to be one of the most important challenges of the law of the future. In meeting this challenge, law will need to not only develop standards capable of addressing the most significant harms suffered by vulnerable populations and environments, but also mechanisms for effectively enforcing these standards. In this paper, I argue that the emerging system of international criminal justice has the potential to deliver both the standards and mechanisms of accountability that are required to correct the most harmful excesses of transnational corporate activity. I also argue that before international criminal law can fill all of the gaps in the governance of corporate activities in developing countries, it will be necessary to expand its scope of application to economic, social, and cultural rights and international environmental law. This will require the creation of a new category of international crime that would prohibit acts and conduct that have severe impacts on the long-term health, safety and means of survival of human groups and collectives – crimes against present and future generations.

2. The Potential of International Criminal Justice for Addressing Corporate Impunity for Serious Violations of International Law

The potential of international criminal justice in sanctioning corporate abuses committed in developing countries rests in its established set of rules and mechanisms for holding individuals criminally accountable for serious violations of international law.[6] International criminal justice can be understood as the application of individual criminal responsibility for serious breaches of fundamental international norms. Such breaches are

5 See a report from the Special Representative of the Secretary-General on the issue of human rights and transnational corporations and other business enterprises: John Ruggie, *Protect, Respect and Remedy: A Framework for Business and Human Rights*, United Nations Human Rights Council, 7 April 2008, p. 3, para. 3, available at http://www.reports-and-materials.org/Ruggie-report-7-Apr-2008.pdf, last accessed 30 March 2011.

6 See generally International Commission of Jurists, "Corporate Complicity and Legal Acountability: Criminal Law and International Crimes", in *Report of the International Commission of Jurists Expert Legal Panel on Corporate Complicity in International Crimes*, 2008, vol. 2.

penalised through one of the following categories of international crime: war crimes, crimes against humanity, genocide and aggression. War crimes cover serious violations of the law applicable in armed conflicts, such as the torture of prisoners of war or deliberate attacks against civilians. Crimes against humanity and genocide can both be seen as penalising the most serious violations of international human rights and humanitarian law: the former are acts committed as part of widespread or systematic attacks against civilian populations; the latter are acts committed with the intent to destroy, in whole or in part, a national, ethnical, racial or religious group. Aggression covers violations of the prohibition on the use of force in international affairs committed by military or political leaders, such as ordering the invasion of another country. Of these four core international crimes, the first three are the most relevant to corporate activities in developing countries, especially in conflict and fragile states.

International criminal justice operates through both international and national mechanisms.[7] The field was effectively revived at the international level in the mid-1990s through the creation by the U.N. Security Council of two *ad hoc* international criminal tribunals to try those persons most responsible for crimes committed in conflicts in the former Yugoslavia and Rwanda. The momentum generated by the work of these tribunals led states to adopt the Rome Statute in 1998 to create a permanent International Criminal Court (ICC).[8] The ICC, which began operating in 2002, has the jurisdiction to investigate and prosecute any of the four core crimes referred to above[9] committed by a national or on the territory of a state party to the Rome Statute. The Rome Statute actually enshrines the complementary role of the ICC in responding to international crimes. The preamble to the Rome Statute affirms that the effective prosecution of international crimes "must be ensured by taking measures at the national level" and that it is therefore "the duty of every State to exercise its criminal jurisdiction over those responsible for international crimes". As a re-

7 Another set of mechanisms, hybrid mechanisms, involve the creation of a special court or the internationalisation of a national court combining national and international law, structures and judges.

8 Rome Statute of the International Criminal Court, 17 July 1998, ("Rome Statute"), available at http://www.icc-cpi.int/NR/rdonlyres/EA9AEFF7-5752-4F84-BE94-0A655EB30E16/0/Rome_Statute_English.pdf, last accessed 30 March 2011.

9 It should be noted that the ICC's jurisdiction over the crime of aggression is not activated at this time.

sult, pursuant to Article 17, the ICC will only assume jurisdiction over crimes that states are genuinely unwilling or unable to investigate or prosecute themselves. As such, national criminal investigations and prosecutions are meant to serve as the primary response to international crimes, with international mechanisms serving as fallback options when necessary. It is important to note that existing international criminal courts have jurisdiction over natural, but not legal, persons.[10] On the other hand, a number of states do provide for the criminal liability of corporations for certain international crimes.[11] In any case, whatever the advantages of corporate liability in terms of the availability of reparations, individual criminal liability is arguably just as useful, if not more, for addressing corporate involvement in international crimes – to paraphrase a famous dictum of the Nuremberg War Tribunal, international crimes are committed by individuals (such as corporate officers), rather than abstract entities (such as corporations).[12] Article 25 of the Rome Statute sets out the various ways in which individuals may held liable for the commission of international crimes.[13] Article 28 of the Rome Statute also provides for the criminal responsibility of civilian superiors if they knew or consciously disregarded that subordinates under their effective control had committed

10 Rome Statute, Article 25, para.1, see *supra* note 8: "The Court shall have jurisdiction over natural persons pursuant to this Statute". In fact, the creation of corporate liability was mooted and rejected during the negotiations that led to the adoption of the Rome Statute. See W. Cory Wanless, "Corporate Liability for International Crimes under Canada's Crimes Against Humanity and War Crimes Act", in *Journal of International Criminal Justice*, 2009, vol. 7, no. 1, pp. 201, 201-202.

11 Anita Ramasastry and Robert C. Thompson, "Commerce, Crime and Conflict: Legal Remedies for Private Sector Liability for Grave Breaches of International Law: A Survey of Sixteen Countries", Fafo, 2006, pp. 15–16, 30, available at http://www.fafo.no/pub/rapp/536/536.pdf, last accessed 30 March 2011.

12 See International Military Tribunal, Nuremberg, Trial of the Major War Criminals, 14 November 1945 – 1 October 1946, Official Documents, 1947, p. 223: "Crimes against international law are committed by men, not by abstract entities, and only by punishing individuals who commit such crimes can the provisions of international law be enforced".

13 These include: committing or attempting to commit a crime, whether as an individual, jointly with another or through another person; ordering, soliciting or inducing the commission of a crime which in fact occurs or is attempted; aiding, abetting or otherwise assisting in the commission of a crime or its attempted commission; and in any other way, intentionally contributing to the commission or attempted commission of a crime by a group of persons acting with a common purpose with the knowledge of the intention of the group to commit the crime.

or were committing crimes and failed to take all necessary and reasonable measures within their powers to prevent or repress their commission or to submit the matter to the competent authorities for investigation and prosecution.

The provisions setting out the modes by which individuals may be held liable for the commission of international crimes could thus cover many of the scenarios involving the commission of crimes by or through corporations. A number of cases before the International Criminal Tribunal for Rwanda have indeed involved prosecutions of individuals serving as company directors.[14] Additionally, in 2003, the ICC Prosecutor warned extractive companies operating in the eastern Democratic Republic of Congo that "[t]hose who direct mining operations, sell diamonds or gold extracted in these conditions, launder the dirty money or provide weapons, could also be authors of the crimes, even if they are based in other countries".[15] The prevention, investigation and prosecution of international crimes committed by corporate officers and corporations could thus play a significant role in addressing corporate impunity for certain serious violations of international law committed in developing countries. Regrettably, the current scope of international criminal law is capable of addressing the full range of serious violations of international law that are of relevance to corporate abuses. Two areas that are particularly critical are international, economic, social and cultural rights and international environmental law. Although there is some scope for using or expanding the elements of certain existing international crimes to cover serious violations of international law in these areas, these existing international crimes require the presence of elements that are largely limited to acts of direct physical violence and situations of armed conflict. Given that corporations have frequently been involved in serious violations of interna-

---

14 Accused persons before the ICTR have most notably included directors of a tea company (see International Criminal Tribunal for Rwanda [ICTR], *Prosecutor v. Michel Bagaragaza*, Case No. ICTR-05-86, Judgment, 30 August 2006), a radio station and a newspaper (see ICTR, *Prosecutor v. Ferdinand Nahimana, et al.*, Case No. ICTR-99-52, Judgment, 3 December 2003).

15 Luis Moreno–Ocampo, "Second Assembly of States Parties to the Rome Statute of the International Criminal Court: Report of the Prosecutor of the ICC", International Criminal Court, 8 September 2003, available at http://untreaty.un.org/cod/icc/asp/2ndsession/ocampo_statement_8sep(e).pdf, last accessed 30 March 2011.

tional law occurring in peace-time, a new category of international crime is required to penalise these types of violations.

3. Crimes Against Present and Future Generations

Crimes against present and future generations is a proposed new category of international crime encompassing serious violations of international law that have severe impacts on the long-term health, safety and means of survival of human groups and collectives.[16] The definition of crimes against present and future generations reads as follows:

> 1. Crimes against present and future generations means any of the following acts within any sphere of human activity, such as political, military, economic, cultural, or scientific activities, when committed with knowledge of the substantial likelihood of their severe consequences on the long-term health, safety, or means of survival of any identifiable group or collectivity:
>
> (a) Forcing members of any identifiable group or collectivity to work or live in conditions that seriously endanger their health or safety, including forced labour, enforced prostitution and human trafficking;
>
> (b) Unlawfully appropriating or acquiring the public or private resources and property of members of any identifiable group or collectivity, including the large scale embezzlement, misappropriation or other diversion of such resources or property by a public official;
>
> (c) Deliberately depriving members of any identifiable group or collectivity of objects indispensable to their survival, including by impeding access to water and food sources, destroying water and food sources, or contaminating water and food sources by harmful organisms or pollution;

[16] In 2007, the World Future Council tasked the Centre for International Sustainable Development Law to provide advice and research on the development of a new international crime to protect the rights of future generations. Through three years of research as well as workshops and consultations held with leading international judges and lawyers, this collaboration yielded the definition reproduced here. The Campaign to End Crimes against Future Generations, which I direct, seeks to fulfil the promise of this concept by working to raise awareness in public opinion about the severity of conduct amounting to crimes against present and future generations and to advance their recognition as crimes under international law. To find out more about this initiative, visit: www.crimesagainstfuturegenerations.org.

(d) Forcefully evicting members of any identifiable group or collectivity in a widespread or systematic manner;

(e) Imposing measures that seriously endanger the health of the members of any identifiable group or collectivity, including by impeding access to health services, facilities and treatments, withholding or misrepresenting information essential for the prevention or treatment of illness or disability, or subjecting them to medical or scientific experiments of any kind which are neither justified by their medical treatment, nor carried out in their interest;

(f) Preventing members of any identifiable group or collectivity from enjoying their culture, professing and practicing their religion, using their language, preserving their cultural practices and traditions, and maintaining their basic social and cultural institutions;

(g) Preventing members of any identifiable group or collectivity from accessing primary, secondary, technical, vocational and higher education;

(h) Causing widespread, long-term and severe damage to the natural environment, including by destroying an entire species or ecosystem;

(i) Unlawfully polluting air, water or soil by releasing substances or organisms that seriously endanger the health, safety or means of survival of members of any identifiable group or collectivity;

(j) Other acts of a similar character gravely imperilling the health, safety, or means of survival of members of any identifiable group or collectivity.

2. The expression "any identifiable group or collectivity" means any civilian group or collectivity defined on the basis of geographic, political, racial, national, ethnic, cultural, religious or gender grounds or other grounds that are universally recognised under international law.

As the definition makes clear, crimes against present and future generations would not be future crimes, nor crimes committed in the future. They would apply instead to acts or conduct undertaken in the present that have serious consequences in the present and that are likely to have serious consequences in the future. For all but one of the crimes, the immediate victims would be individuals alive at the time of the commission of the crime. The only exception is sub-paragraph (h), which would penalise severe environmental harm, without requiring harm to individual victims in the present. Just as crimes against humanity are not directly committed against all of humanity, crimes against present and future generations would not be directly committed against present and future generations either. Rather, they would penalise conduct that is of such gravity that it can be characterised as injuring the rights of future generations belonging to an affected group or collectivity.

Like other international crimes, crimes against present and future generations would be comprised of two parts: an introductory 'chapeau' paragraph that sets out a general legal requirement that serves to elevate certain prohibited acts to the status of an international crime and a list of prohibited acts. The establishment of a crime against present and future generations would thus require the commission of one of the prohibited acts listed at sub-paragraphs 1(a) to (j) of the definition with knowledge of "the substantial likelihood of their severe consequences on the long-term health, safety, or means of survival of any identifiable group or collectivity". This does not imply that the prohibited act must affect each and every member of the identifiable group or collectivity in question, but only that it must be committed against the members of the identifiable group or collectivity and be of such magnitude or scale that it is likely to have the prohibited consequences on this identifiable group or collectivity in the long-term. Moreover, it is clear that a crime against present and future generations could be committed before the prohibited consequences listed in the general legal requirement materialised. This is similar to the crime of genocide, which does not require that each and every member of a group be eliminated before an underlying act of genocide directed to this goal can be prosecuted. That said, in the context of crimes against present and future generations, this requirement would entail a knowledge element, as for war crimes and crimes against humanity. It is not a special intent requirement, as for genocide, in order to avoid difficulties in proving that certain activities were undertaken with the intent to cause long-term harm to an identifiable group or collectivity. The knowledge element in the general legal requirement of the crime would be met if it were shown that a perpetrator knew of the substantial likelihood of the prohibited consequences listed in the general legal requirement or if they knowingly took the risk that these prohibited consequences would occur in the ordinary course of events.[17] Moreover, knowledge could be inferred from the relevant facts and circumstances of a given case,[18] such as, *inter alia*, the perpetrator's statements and actions, their functions and responsibilities, their knowledge or awareness of other facts and circumstances, the circumstances in which the acts or consequences occurred, the links between themselves and the acts and consequences, the scope and gravity of the acts or consequences and the nature of the acts and consequences and the degree to which these are common knowledge. The language of 'substantial likelihood' is drawn from the customary international law standard for the mental element of the mode of liability of ordering. It requires that the perpetrator knew that his or her acts would be substantially likely to have the prohibited consequences listed in the general legal requirement; the perpetrator need not know therefore that his acts or conducts are likely be the *only* cause or the *sine qua non* cause of the prohibited consequences.[19]

Crimes against present and future generations would have a fairly broad scope of application. The introductory paragraph explains that they are intended to cover a wide range of acts or conduct and can be committed in peace-time and in war-time. In addition, the second paragraph adopts a broad definition of "any identifiable group or collectivity". This definition, drawing on a similar expression included in Article 7(1)(h) of the Rome Statute, means that crimes against present and future generations would apply to a wide variety of discrete or specific human populations defined on the basis of shared political, racial, national, ethnic, cultural, religious, gender or other grounds recognised under international law. It is however expanded to cover geographic grounds for identifying a group or collectivity. Although the conduct amounting to crimes against present and future generations is often undertaken with the intent to discriminate against a specific group, such intent would not be a general re-

---

17 Rome Statute, Article 30, para.3, see *supra* note 8; International Criminal Tribunal for the former Yugoslavia [ICTY], *Prosecutor v. Dragoljub Kunarac, Radomir Kovac and Zoran Vukovic*, Case no. IT–96–23 and IT–96–23/1–A, Appeal Judgement, 12 June 2002, p. 31, para.102, available at http://www.icty.org/x/cases/kunarac/acjug/en/kun-aj020612e.pdf, last accessed 30 March 2011.

18 International Criminal Court, Elements of Crimes, June 2000, General Introduction, para. 3.

19 ICTY, *Prosecutor v. Tihomir Blaskic*, Case no. IT–95–14–A, Appeal Judgement, 29 July 2004, p. 16, para. 42.

quirement for establishing the commission of crimes against present and future generations.

The following table sets out the purpose and sources for the prohibited acts listed in sub-paragraphs 1(a) to 1 (j) of the definition of crimes against present and future generations. The table shows that crimes against present and future generations would penalise conduct that is already prohibited as a violation of international human rights law[20] or other international conventions or would extend the scope of application of the conduct that is already prohibited in the context of armed conflicts or widespread or systematic attacks against civilian populations.

Sub-paragraph	Purpose	Interpretative Sources
1(a)	Penalises serious violations of the rights to liberty and security of the person and to freedom of residence and movement (ICCPR, Articles 9 and 12) and the rights to work of one's choosing and to work in safe and healthy conditions (ICESCR, Articles 6(1) and 7(1)).	Draws on the crimes of forced labour and human trafficking found in the crime against humanity of enslavement (Rome Statute, Article 7(1)(c)) and the crime against humanity of enforced prostitution (Rome Statute, Article 7(1)(g)).
1(b)	Penalises grave violations of the customary international law principle of permanent sovereignty over resources, which provides that the citizens of a state should benefit from the exploitation of resources and the resulting national development.[21]	Extends a similar war crime of pillaging to the context of peace-time (Rome Statute, Article 8(2)(b)(xvi)) and is also based on the crime of corruption as set out in Article 17 of the UN Convention against Corruption.[22]
1(c)	Penalises serious violations of the right to life, referring in particular to the rights to food and water	Extends a similar war crime to the context of peace-time (Rome Statute, Article 8(2)(v)(xxv)) and draws on

[20] The references below are to the International Covenant on Economic, Social and Cultural Rights, 16 December 1966, 993 U.N.T.S. 3 [ICESCR]; or to the International Covenant on Civil and Political Rights, 16 December 1966, 999 U.N.T.S. 171 [ICCPR].

[21] Nico Schrijver, *Sovereignty over Natural Resources: Balancing Rights and Duties*, Cambridge University Press, Cambridge, 1997, pp. 390-392.

[22] United Nations Convention against Corruption, United Nations General Assembly Resolution of 31 October 2003, 2349 U.N.T.S. 41, available at http://www.unodc.org/documents/treaties/UNCAC/Publications/Convention/08-50026_E.pdf, last accessed 30 March 2011.

	(ICESCR, Article 11).	the underlying act of genocide (Rome Statute, Article 6(c)).
1(d)	Penalises one of the most serious violations of the right to housing (ICESCR, Article 11(1)).	Draws on the general comment of the U.N. Committee on the ICESCR relating to the right to housing (General Comment no. 7).
1(e)	Penalises one of the most serious violations of the right to health (ICESCR, Article 12).	Draws on the general comment of the U.N. Committee on the ICESCR relating to the right to health (General Comment no. 12) and extends a similarly worded war crime to the peacetime context (Rome Statute, Article 8(2)(b)(x)).
1(f)	Penalises serious violations of the right to culture (ICCPR, Article 27 and ICESCR, Article 15).	Draws on the previous drafts of the Genocide Convention which included the crime of cultural genocide.[23]
1(g)	Penalises one of the most serious violations of the right to education (ICESCR, Article 13).	Draws on the general comment of the U.N. Committee on the ICESCR relating to the right to education (General Comment no. 13).
1(h)	Penalises serious violations of the customary international law duty to prevent grave environmental harm and damages.[24]	Based on a similarly worded war crime (Rome Statute, Article 8(2)(b)(iv)).
1(i)	Penalises serious violations of the right to life, particularly the rights to health, housing, food, and water (ICESCR, Articles 11 and 12).	Draws on the general comments of the UN Committee on the ICESCR relating to the rights to health, housing, food, and water (General Comments no. 12, 14 and 15).
1(j)	Penalises serious violations of the rights protected by other sub-paragraphs.	Draws on a similar catch-all provision for crimes against humanity (Rome Statute, Article 7(1)(k)).

[23] Report of the Ad Hoc Committee on Genocide, 5 April-10 May 1948 (Official Records of the Economic and Social Council, Third Year, Seventh Session, Supplement No. 5 (E/794), Article HI.

[24] See Stockholm Declaration on the Human Environment, UN Doc. A/C. 48/14 (1972), 11 ILM 1461 (1972), principle 21. See also 1991 Draft Code of Crimes against Peace and Mankind, Yearbook of the International Law Commission, 1991, Vol. II, Part Two, UN Doc. A/CN.4/SER.A/1991/Add.l (Part 2), p. 107.

4. New International Norms and Crimes

The principal advantage of creating of crimes against present and future generations would be to make the international and national mechanisms of individual criminal liability available for serious violations of economic, social and cultural rights and international environmental law. Beyond its immediate benefits in terms of potential prosecution, the creation of crimes against present and future generations would also give advocates, policy-makers, stakeholders and corporations themselves a new tool for understanding the basic obligations of corporations and corporate officers and for assessing their conduct in light of these obligations. The notion of an international crime is indeed one of the most important means through which the international community can condemn morally opprobrious behaviour. Ultimately, the recognition of crimes against present and future generations under international law is as much about punishing and deterring harmful conduct rising to the level of an international crime as it is about strengthening existing prohibitions and taboos within the international community.

There is no doubt that an effort to create a new international crime along the lines of crimes against present and future generations will have its detractors and critics. One obvious criticism that may be levelled at the idea of creating crimes against present and future generations in international criminal law is one of institutional overload. Critics are likely to ask question whether our emerging system of international criminal justice, based around a fledging and under-resourced institution like the ICC, should be given the mandate to prosecute a whole new category of international crimes, especially when it is already struggling to provide justice for existing international crimes. To be sure, the issue of institutional overload and capacity is one that must be addressed if the creation of crimes against present and future generations is going to make a difference to the victims of the serious violations of international law that it seeks to address. It also important to ensure that the creation of any new international crime does not undermine the existing system of international criminal justice in counter-productive ways – a debate that has recently emerged in the ICC regime in the wake of the adoption of an amendment creating the crime of aggression.[25] It should be stressed that an amend-

[25] See Amnesty International, Concerns at the 9th Assembly of State Parties (6-10 December 2010) Index: IOR 53/016/2010, pp. 9-12.

ment of the Rome Statute of the ICC is only one option, among others, that may be pursued for creating crimes against present and future generations, and it is moreover only an option that would be pursued after a careful consideration of its implications for the ICC. Indeed, the promise of crimes against present and future generations lies in changing the way that states, corporations, and citizens view serious breaches of international law – moving beyond the rhetoric of violations of international law and governance gaps to the powerful language of crime and accountability. Many other avenues are available for accomplishing this normative shift: the adoption of a convention authorizing or requiring states parties to exercise jurisdiction over crimes of international concern at the national level (such as treaties on the theft of nuclear material or terrorist bombings);[26] the creation of a crime at the domestic level; and integration into binding codes of corporate conduct.

Another criticism may focus instead on the seemingly bold idea of criminalizing conduct amounting to crimes against present and future generations. However, while the idea of creating this type of crime certainly seeks to move international law forward, it does so in the spirit of attaching the appropriate penal consequences for behaviour that the international community has already recognised as being reprehensible. Indeed, crimes against present and future generations would build upon international law by seeking to extend the scope of application of existing international crimes from war-time to peace-time or establish criminal liability for existing prohibitions in international law. Given the principle that all human rights should be treated equally,[27] there is little justification for restricting the scope of international criminal law to the category of serious violations of what essentially amount to basic civil and political rights only. As such, the creation of crimes against present and future generations is much more in keeping with existing international law than

[26] See Convention on the Physical Protection of Nuclear Material, 3 March 1980, 1987 U.N.T.S. 125; International Convention for the Suppression of Terrorist Bombings, 15 December 1997, 2149 U.N.T.S. 256.

[27] Vienna Declaration and Programme of Action, as adopted by the World Conference on Human Rights on 25 June 1993, U.N. Doc. A/CONF.157/23, para.5: "All human rights are universal, indivisible and interdependent and interrelated. The international community must treat human rights globally in a fair and equal manner, on the same footing, and with the same emphasis".

previous legal innovations like the creation of crimes against humanity and genocide.

For instance, crimes against humanity emerged in international law in the wake of the Second World War as a creation of the Charter of the International Military Tribunal at Nuremberg (Nuremberg Charter).[28] During the negotiations which led to the Nuremberg Charter, it became apparent that certain crimes committed by the Nazis did not fall within the purview of existing law, most notably those atrocities perpetrated by German forces against their own nationals. In order to resolve this lacuna, the Allies conceived of a third category of crimes, crimes against humanity, to fill the gap left by the provisions pertaining to crimes against peace and war crimes.[29] The creation of a crime against present and future generations would not simply fill a gap in the law, but would in fact build upon existing international law.

This is important not only from the perspective of protecting the integrity of international law – it also has important tactical advantages. Among other traits, the most effective initiatives for normative change have usually managed to graft new normative proposals on existing norms that have resonance and influence in particular constituencies. For example, the successful campaign to ban land mines eschewed the need for arms control in favour of a focus on how land mines violated existing norms in international humanitarian law regarding the protection of civilians against the indiscriminate effects of certain weapons, for which an overwhelming consensus already existed.[30]

It is also to be expected that many corporations concerned about any expansion in potential zones of liability and the governments that support their industries will likely oppose the creation of crimes against present and future generations. One need only to look at the recent attempt in Canada to adopt a bill providing relatively less significant measures for holding corporations in the extractive industry accountable for their complicity in human rights violations occurring in their opera-

[28] Antonio Cassese, *International Criminal Law,* Oxford University Press, 2003, p. 70.

[29] M. Cherif Bassiouni, *Crimes Against Humanity in International Criminal Law*, 1992, Springer, p. 17 and pp. 22-24; Cassese, 2003, pp. 68-69, see *supra* note 28.

[30] Richard Price, "Reversing the Gun Sights: Transnational Civil Society Targets Land Mines", in *International Organization*, 1998, vol 52, no. 3, p. 613.

tions abroad.[31] But overcoming objections of this sort is at the very heart of the project of creating crimes against present and future generations. Beyond moral persuasion, there is a business-friendly case that can be made for the creation of crimes against present and future generations. For one thing, a clear and international standard could create a level competitive playing field between those corporations that are subject to human rights scrutiny because of their visibility or incorporation in a developed country and those have a greater leeway to act with little cost to their reputations. In addition, crimes against present and future generations, in seeking to protect economic, social and cultural rights, would avoid the principal criticism that states and corporations have made in relation to these rights, namely that they are vague and impose positive obligations (to adopt certain conduct) rather than negative obligations (to refrain from certain conduct). By focusing on the deliberate commission of serious violations of economic, social and cultural rights, crimes against present and future generations provide a clear and 'negative' approach to respecting minimal, core aspects of these rights.

Finally, some particular criticisms may be levelled at the precise definition presented here. Although the definition of crimes against present and future generations presented here has been fine-tuned and has had many of its details fleshed out, it is expected – perhaps hoped – that this version of the definition will have a short life-span as it will have been taken up, modified, and negotiated by others. In the end, the exact phrasing of the definition does not matter as much as the overall concept of ending impunity for the underlying conduct which it captures. The idea of presenting this definition at this conference and other venues is meant to be the start – not the end – of a policy dialogue on developing innovative accountability-based solutions for addressing current challenges to human security and development and securing our common future.

Addressing the governance gaps and permissive environments generated by economic globalisation will be one of the principal challenges

[31] The bill in question, Bill C-300, would have directed the Minister of Foreign Affairs and the Minister of International Trade to issue guidelines that articulate corporate accountability standards for mining, oil and gas companies in Canada and would have enabled them to monitor compliance with these standards and to withdraw consular and export credit support in situations of non-complicance. The bill was strongly opposed by the mining industry and the Conservative government and was defeated in the House of Commons 140 to 134.

of the law of the future. This will not only require the adoption of best practices and codes of conduct, but also the prevention and repression of deleterious and morally blameworthy human behaviour. International criminal law could have an important role to play in this regard, especially if it comes to penalise all serious violations of international law that have severe impacts on the long-term health, safety and means of survival of human populations. It is time to seriously consider the need for a new crime, one that can ensure that all human rights are protected in all circumstances by international criminal law: crimes against present and future generations.

7.5

The Coordination of Investigations at International Level: Towards a World Public Prosecutor?

Filippo Spiezia[*]

Globalisation has generated not only new markets, but also new approaches to criminality which are increasingly transnational in nature. Within this framework, the article underlines the crucial importance of enhancing cooperation and coordination processes at the international level among police and judicial authorities, more and more actors of common and shared policies. Indeed, the challenges posed by modern criminality have evidently showed how states have not been capable of individually tackling new emergent forms of crime. The necessity to deal with growingly international crimes that spill over borders and implicate many legal and judicial systems, requires the adoption of concrete solutions. To solve these pressing problems, this paper points to harmonised criminal penal systems at the global level through a common shared system of values to protect, and, consequently, of crime provisions and sanctions. Additionally, the creation of several international public prosecutors operating in different areas, taking into account as a possible model the creation of the European Public Prosecutor according to Article 85 of the Lisbon Treaty, would promote the gradual convergence of the different national penal systems and enhance a coordinated approach to fighting crime.

1. Introduction

The scenario for the coming two decades, from the globalisation of the economy and the markets towards a growing organised dimension of crime and its transnational nature. Being an EU citizen, practitioner and a well experienced prosecutor in the field of organised crime and a college member of Eurojust, it does not seem to me an impossible exercise to express my views when it comes to imagining a scenario for the coming two decades. Of course my contribution will focus mainly on the area of crim-

[*] **Filippo Spiezia** is Deputy National Member for Italy at Eurojust.

inal law and of public power and punishment, even if there are some implications related to institutional and constitutional aspects that are worth considering as well. It is a reasonable expectation that the current trends will more or less continue. However, the features of these trends will intensify and have much more serious consequences. Over the last few years, we have witnessed the emergence of a new dimension of modern crime, its transnational nature, which is linked to three fundamental factors:

- The mobility of trafficked goods. If in the past, the interest of criminals was oriented towards immovable goods (in the field of agriculture, public contracts and construction). There is now an increasing criminal interest towards movable goods such as weapons, drugs, rubbish, and even human beings. The pursuit of these new criminal targets and their transfer from the country of production to their final destination is a generating factor of this new dimension of modern crime;
- Institutional and political developments, particularly the abolition of external borders among some specific areas and regions. A good example of this is the EU, where the abolishment of its internal boundaries has facilitated the free movement of people, goods and services, as well as criminals;
- Technological developments that allow and encourage swift circulation not only of people, but also of illicit money gained through crime (the proceeds of crime); for which it is vital to find a secure placement for money laundering.

The evolution of modern crime has another decisive element that enormously differentiates it from the past – the organisational dimension. Very soon criminals will become more affiliated with each other, discovering the added value of working together to carry out illegal activities. The experience of the network dimension is no longer a trait exclusive to traditional criminal groups (*e.g.*, the mafia and the Camorra groups, pervasive in the Italian experience), but, a widespread feature of modern crime and strictly connected to the internationalisation of many illegal activities.

This view can be confirmed by looking at available data provided by specialised analytical organisations. At the EU level, the 2008 and the 2009 Organised Crime Threat Assessment (OCTA) Report by Europol highlighted how much the landscape of organised crime within the EU is shaped and nourished by international criminal networks which may have their centre of gravity inside or outside of the EU as well as struggles faced by national and international authorities in dealing with them. This does not only apply to traditionally strongly internationalised fields of international crime, such as drug trafficking and money laundering, but it also applies to comparatively new but now very powerful phenomena such as the facilitation of illegal immigration, the trafficking of human beings and the counterfeiting of commodities. It is no exaggeration to say that most modern crime phenomena, rather than having an international dimension are essentially transnational in nature, with a recurrent organised crime dimension.

These two features are likely to become progressively stronger in the coming decades. As a result of the advances of modern technology (*e.g.*, the increasing use of internet communication) and the availability of enormous quantities of illegally gained money thus far, will the individual criminal who acts on his own remain a distant memory? Shall the current trends of criminality continue in the coming years? The answer is likely to be yes. In any case there is no doubt that at this stage of the analysis the more dangerous threats to the international community and the world population, will be posed by transnational and organised criminal networks

2. The Inadequacy of the Answers Provided by National States: The Tension between the Principle of State Sovereignty and the Internationalisation of Crime

The challenges posed by modern criminality brought about a reaction from the affected states to compensate for the abolition of their external borders at regional levels by fighting crime in its transnational dimension. It was very soon understood that an isolated reaction from a single state can not face the challenge posed by modern crime. This gave rise to the concept of international cooperation. It has been a long process and the construction, still in evolution, has produced new organs and new legal tools all over the world. As far as the EU area is concerned this cooperation is particularly well developed. A European criminal law emerged, and continues to develop, with its own specificity while retaining a part in cooperation in criminal law. In the last forty years, mutual criminal assistance has revealed itself in two ways.

The first emanated from the Council of Europe. As an example of this process we can refer to the Convention on Mutual Legal Assistance of 1959 and to the European Extradition Treaty of 1957. However, many other conventions have, of course, been enacted. This first way has been supplemented inside the European Union by the provisions of the European Treaties and their derived legal sources and acts (Maastricht, Amsterdam, Nice, and Lisbon). It means that, as far as the concept of judicial cooperation is concerned, a dual European legal area is emerging; one created in the framework of the Council of Europe and the other one elaborated by the European Union. The European Union represents a unique form of international cooperation. Almost all Western and Central European countries have joined together to form an intergovernmental structure, accepting some important limitations on their sovereignty. Twenty-seven countries acting together deal with important policy questions that have cross-border implications. These decisions and other European legal acts concern not only the economy, taxation, industry and agriculture, but they also affect law enforcement and criminal justice. In this framework, a new concept was set up in 1997, the European Area of Freedom, Justice and Security, as introduced formally by the Amsterdam Treaty. It is an original concept, aimed at creating and strengthening the European judicial area by combining two different elements in apparent opposition: sovereignty and integration. Judicial and police cooperation ceased to be merely a matter of 'common interest' and became the main objective of the European Union. This represents a break with the traditional concept of judicial cooperation as a defined set of acts performed by the competent legal authority of a requested state on behalf of the requesting authority of another state. For in the new concept of the judicial area, the member states accept some limitations to their sovereignty.

This new dimension forces the EU member states to reconsider their prerogative in matters of criminal justice and penal actions and to accept the idea of shared sovereignty. In order to understand this concept from a legal point of view, it is sufficient to consider that EU decisions in the area of criminal justice can also have an effect on the structure and operation of the criminal justice systems in the 27 member states, potentially affecting the lives of hundreds of millions of people. It is obvious that, inside this new concept of a common area with no national borders, of free movement of people, goods and services and for the presence of global criminality, no State is able to face the challenges of transnational crime acting on its own. The concept of common space has not only been original, but furthermore it has been dynamic. We can trace a long evolution in its interesting development, and the paths followed by European institutions and the national parliaments have not evolved in a straightforward Cartesian manner. There have been many setbacks, resumptions and accelerations. The Treaty of Amsterdam in 1997 represented a decisive step in the development of judicial and police co-operation inside the European Union's Institutions. The Amsterdam Treaty especially, gave the European Union a new objective: the area of freedom, security and justice. In this new area, important progress was made in a brief period of time: the setting up of networks (the European Justice Network, European Police College, European Judicial Training Network), of data banks (Schengen Information System), and of European bodies, (like Europol and Eurojust), the creation of innovative concepts (judicial space, mutual recognition) and new judicial instruments (common actions, decisions and framework decisions). 1999 was a particularly decisive year in the formation of this original idea of a common space: the European Union threw its weight behind mutual recognition. However, the European Union also decided that work should continue on the harmonisation of key areas of legislation, such as the prevention and control of money laundering, terrorism, human trafficking and other forms of organised and transborder crime. Towards the end of 2004, the European Union reviewed the progress it had made since 1999 and decided, by approving the so- called Hague Programme, on what further work was needed to develop the European area of freedom, security and justice. A new Constitutional Treaty was signed on 29 October 2004 that, among other things, would have led to the elimination of the distinction between the pillars. After the results of the French and Dutch referenda, said Treaty was rejected. New perspectives are now being sprung and disclosed by the Treaty of Lisbon of 2007, which entered into force in December 2009 and the rate of democracy in European institutions should now improve, with more powers granted to the European Parliament, with greater involvement of national parliaments, and also by abolishing the third pillar entirely, essentially unifying the decision-making process. The Treaty of Lisbon brought an end to several years of negotiation regarding institutional issues. It amends the EU and EC Treaties, without replacing them.

The new treaty will provide the Union with the legal framework and tools necessary to meet future challenges and to respond to citizen demands.

The objectives of the new Treaty are as follows:

- A more democratic and transparent Europe with a strengthened role of the European Parliament and national parliaments, more opportunities for citizens to have their voice heard and a clear sense of who does what at the European and national level;
- A more efficient Europe, with simplified working methods and voting rules. Streamlined and modern institutions for an EU of 27 members and an improved ability to act in areas of major priority for today's Union.
- A Europe of rights and values, freedom, solidarity and security, promoting the Union's values. Introducing the Charter of Fundamental Rights into primary European law. Providing for new solidarity mechanisms and ensuring better protection for citizens.
- Europe will achieve as an actor on the global stage by bringing together Europe's external policy tools, both in determining and developing new policies.
- More Justice, Freedom and Security. Building an area of Justice, Freedom and Security as a high priority for the European Union. The Treaty of Lisbon will have a considerable influence on the existing rules governing freedom, security and justice at EU level, and will facilitate more comprehensive, legitimate, efficient and transparent EU action in the field. Until now, important matters in the field have required decision by unanimity in the Council, with a limited role given to the European Parliament and the European Court of Justice. The Treaty of Lisbon will lead to increased democracy and transparency as a set of uniform legal acts will be adopted with a stronger role for the European Parliament as co-legislator (the co-decision procedure) and by the extension of qualified majority voting in the Council. EU action will be facilitated by the abolition of the existing separate policy areas – also known as pillars – that characterise today's institutional structure with regard to police and judicial cooperation in criminal matters.

Even if there is no question that a lot of progress has been made so far, the practice shows a lot of inconsistencies. To limit the analysis to the EU, the dilemma is this: can the idea of a criminal law area within Europe be considered as sufficiently implemented? Should we extend our reflection to the international and global level? The same question can be posed. Many international conventions have been adopted and ratified, upon input and on initiative of international organisations (*e.g.*, the UN), touching many fields of criminal law (organised crime, money laundering, corruption, cybercrime, terrorism). Do all these instruments work in practice? Is the level of international cooperation acceptable? Do the states practice a good standard of cooperation within their mutual relationships? Is there a sufficient level of connection and partnership among the EU, EU countries, and third countries? Which are the main factors that affect international cooperation on a global level? As you can see, many are questions that are not purely theoretical in nature, but have a great impact on the real lives of citizens all over the world.

From a practical point of view, on the basis of daily experience, the following observations can be made:

- There always seems to be a mix of both police and judicial cooperation. Within the EU, there is a certain inefficiency because many instruments have been created but are still to be implemented on a national level. In general, the quality of mutual cooperation is far from reaching an acceptable level. At the international level the situation is even more problematic due to the persisting difficulties of the states to become effectively and efficiently affiliated with each other in facing the growing threat posed by modern crime. Internal economic problems constitute the main focus of their actions, while political gaps and deficiencies which undermine the process for global cooperation is also a focus, as well as judicial authorities who still pay poor attention to the external dimension of their national proceedings. This produces a vicious circle. Because national authorities see limited concrete benefits from international cooperation – for example, being able to get hold of the proceeds of criminal activity – there incentives to engage in it is also limited. International organisations, despite their efforts, are also far from reaching their objectives. The necessary political compromises often jeopardise the level and quality of new international agreements and ultimately, the fight against modern crime.

- The balance is also not satisfactory when we pay attention to the other side of the problem. The question of civil rights and guarantees. The protection of rights in criminal investigations in the framework of the fight against cross border crime has been a topic of much discussion since the problem affects all forms of cooperation. Although several initiatives were launched and operated in order to establish procedural safeguards and minimum rights in criminal proceedings through Europe, they failed. The consistent past decisions of the European Court of Justice and of the Court of Strasburg have clearly recognised an obligation on the part of the Community to respect fundamental rights as they are guaranteed in the European Convention of Human Rights and as a general principle of Community law derived from the constitutional traditions common to member states. Behind these problems there is a common denominator. The tension between, the sovereignty of each State, which is particularly strong when it comes to criminal matters, on one hand, and the internationalisation of crime, on the other hand. There is an indisputable conflict between a national dimension of policies, proceedings and actions and the necessity for a coordinated approach to introduce an efficient, coherent and fair system of police and judicial cooperation.

3. The Possible Solutions: The Necessity of Shared Values on International Level

Our starting point, related to the crucial question that provides the grounds for any other consideration and comes first in any perspective analysis, is the question of values. Nothing was so difficult in the past as the identification of a collection of common values shared among the international community. Different traditions and economic conditions, various levels of development, ethnical and religious reasons and geographic distances were all factors that prevented the formation of a common basis of values on which an international community could find the pillars to coexist. When we speak about common values we are not speaking about the necessity to eliminate the vital and precious differences that will always characterise the populations of each country, but about the necessity to keep and to build an international community on the basis of shared values. These values can be easily found as written rules provided by international documents (mainly devoted to human rights) and in the national constitutions. The new problems and perspectives are basically there to enlarge the scope of these values from the individual side to the international dimension, involving the action of the states and furthermore, putting them into practice.

The enquiry for a new international foundation of the legal order starting from these values constitutes a prerequisite for any legal construction and is a condition for the effectiveness of any international agreement. Only in sharing basic principles can we assure the commitment of politicians and public and private authorities in the pursuit and achievement of high levels of international cooperation for the common progress of the whole of humanity.

If globalisation has often been analysed for its negative impact on the civil world, it can also represent a very important tool, capable of favouring this process, because it allows for the approximation of people, by reducing discrepancies and helping to elaborate a common culture based on respect for the human species and international solidarity. The latter can be identified as one of the basic foundations of the world community in the coming decades. After the end of the Cold War and the tension between East and West, the challenges affecting humanity are mainly local conflicts, poor and inhumane life conditions suffered by a huge section of the world population and the threats posed by crime. The international solidarity principle should lead any national and international policy, and should be able to involve the common efforts of legislators, the international community and states.

As far as judicial international cooperation is concerned, trust is another key element of any enduring future policy. Successful policy depends on trust, however mutual trust cannot be built with a decree. In order to move forward within Europe, and also beyond Europe, there must be a common foundation of trust. To build and maintain that foundation requires a sustained effort. Trust means to be confident in one another's legal systems and law enforcement capabilities, but this condition is not given. Trust should be continually reciprocated. This trust must also be present at different levels:

- At police and judicial levels all authorities concerned must trust each other if they are to cooperate across borders and they can count on the same level of commitment in fighting organised crime.

The good will of each partner is the only reliable condition for creating and building solid mutual trust.

- At national level, mutual trust first of all requires the correct and prompt implementation of many instruments already adopted. While Member States have made progress in the implementation and application of EU legislation, a persistent problem is the uncertain transposition of the legal instruments adopted. From a legal point of view it is essential that member states comply with their implementing obligations in a correct manner and within the set time limits. It is necessary to make the application of the instruments on mutual recognition more attractive for practitioners. Consideration should be paid to shortening and streamlining the certificates that are part of the instruments, in line with practitioners' needs. Following the experience of Eurojust on the practical application of the European Arrest Warrants (EAW), Eurojust is of the view, *inter alia*, that there is a need to consider some provisions, guidelines or other measures to be put in place at the EU level aimed at ensuring proportionate use in the issuing of EAW for the purpose of prosecution or execution. European citizens must trust that their rights are guaranteed, whether they are suspects, witnesses or victims and wherever in the EU they may find themselves;
- At a global level, trust must mean that policymakers and parliaments must make new efforts for effective action, taking care of the international implications of any initiative, in a way that is not subordinate to their national interest. But, on a global level, trust should mean trust in each other's rule of law. This trust can be increased through the sharing of knowledge and insight and also by simply meeting one another, an element that is also essential to strengthen practical cooperation in general. Common trust means continuing to work to create a common culture in which legal uniformity and the transparency of legal judgments are basic conditions for trust in one another's legal system and in the legal order of the international Community as a whole. By systematically sharing the key principles of different legal systems and, at the same time, being open to ideas from beyond our own borders, we will also increase transparency and build trust and accountability.

4. The Building of Harmonised National Legal Criminal Systems at a Global Level

If we look at the experience of the EU we can say that building mutual trust requires a certain degree of approximation and harmonisation of national laws. Experience very quickly showed that the cornerstone of judicial cooperation within the EU in practice, *i.e.*, the principle of mutual recognition, cannot be put in place without a high level of consistency and compatibility within national legal systems.

The principle of mutual recognition represents an important step in the evolution of mutual assistance in the European Union. The idea of mutual recognition comes from the following considerations. Each of the Member States of the European Union has its own unique criminal justice system, with its own criminal and procedural laws. As a result, the national definition of even the basic types of crime, and the rights enjoyed by suspects and defendants, can vary considerably and this can affect judicial cooperation. For example, many Member States have traditionally required double criminality as a condition for extradition on mutual assistance. The offence in question must be recognised as an offence in the member state requesting extradition or assistance and in the member state asked to extradite or to provide assistance. There are two ways to overcome these national differences in law; either require that all states have more or less the same laws (harmonisation), or that the states agree to enforce decision and judgments made in another state (mutual recognition). Those in favour of harmonisation argue that the laws defining the main forms of cross-border crime, as well as the basic elements of criminal procedure, should be the same in all the EU Member States. Those in favour of mutual recognition, in turn, argue that harmonisation is not necessary, as long as the courts and other authorities of each member state are prepared to enforce decisions taken in other Member States. Furthermore the proponents of said principle argue that the close ties among EU countries, and the fact that they are all signatories to the 1950 Convention for the Protection of Human Rights and Fundamental Freedoms, has led to a situation in which all member states should have full faith and confidence in the operation of the criminal justice system in one another's respective countries. In 1999, the European Union threw its weight on the side of mutual recognition. However, the European Union also decided that work should continue on the harmonisation of key areas of legislation, such as the prevention and control of money laundering.

As mentioned earlier, harmonisation turned out not to be an alternative to mutual recognition but an essential tool to better create mutual confidence in the differing legal systems and in doing so, it facilitated the correct implementation of the same principle of mutual recognition. As far as the EU dimension is concerned, the level of police and judicial co-operation will be enhanced only with the knowledge that certain norms and principles prevail in all member states and that judges, public prosecutors and legal professionals have a full working understanding of each other's legal systems.

The very close tie between the principle of mutual recognition and the approximation of penal law has also been underlined in the context of the Lisbon Treaty (Article 82), as far as the form of criminality having a transnational dimension is concerned.

The reasons behind these provisions are clear; they represent a structural condition for the proper functioning of the instruments, based on the principle of mutual recognition. Furthermore the presence of harmonised penal systems constitute the only legal framework that can discourage the so called criminal shopping forum, with gangs and criminal groups moving towards countries with less developed criminal standards in terms of legal provisions and sanctions and less effective prosecutions.

If the dimension of modern crime in the coming years will focus more on these current features, which are, as mentioned before, its international dimension and a more organised approach to the illegal activities, it would be more and more necessary to reach a good level of penal law harmonisation at a global level. The interconnections of different national environments will require a continuous effort to eliminate the discrepancies among different national legislations and the creation of common legal standards and principles.

Of course, it is possible that some areas of procedural law and some national provisions still keep themselves as differentiated entities. This sounds reasonable and responds to real needs due to some unavoidable differences among national systems. However, if progress must be achieved, it is vital to endeavour to reach a more harmonised criminal law system on a global level. That is why it is important to invest in meetings, discussions or joint training initiatives on an international level between politicians, judicial and law enforcement authorities, in the coming years. Whenever we meet one another, we automatically share knowledge and exchange best practices about different legal systems. This can lead to more effective cooperation on one hand, and on the other hand it can induce a reformation process to harmonise the system to the extent that seems to be necessary to face challenging threats posed by modern crime.

5. An International Coordination System for Prosecutions: The Necessity for new Global Players?

5.1. The Coordinating Function: The Example of Eurojust for the EU

There is little doubt that the direct contact between the competent judicial authorities and the support for their relationship is provided by many 'facilitators'. For the EU we can refer to the experience of the EJN and to the liaison magistrates, who can improve the level of judicial cooperation, in speeding up the execution of requests for judicial assistance and in providing essential legal information on the foreign legal system and the judicial authorities of the states concerned. Nevertheless, experience and practice shows that there is still a judicial necessity for an external authority to provide a special function, the coordination of investigations needed in proceedings against transnational crime. In the course of the 1990s the European legislator conceived a very innovative idea of setting up a separate entity that has gradually evolved, somewhat comparable to Europol in the law enforcement field, to coordinate national prosecuting authorities and support investigations of serious organised crime extending into two or more member states.

The idea for the establishment of such an entity received a considerable push at the special European Council held in Tampere, Finland in October 1999. The legal background of Eurojust can be found in the 46th Conclusion of the Tampere European Council:

> To reinforce the fight against serious organised crime, the European Council has agreed that a unit (Eurojust) should be set up, it is to be composed of national prosecutors, magistrates, or police officers of equivalent competence, detached from each Member State according to their legal system. Eurojust should have the task of facilitating the proper coordination of national prosecuting authorities and of supporting criminal investigations in organised crime cases, notably based on Europol's analysis, as well as of co-

operating closely with the European Judicial Network, in particular in order to simplify the execution of rogatory letters.

On the basis of personal experience we can say that stimulating and improving the coordination between the competent authorities of the member states dealing with investigations and prosecutions is one of the innovative and modern functions that make Eurojust stand out in respect of the traditional legal instruments of cooperation. This function will be more and more crucial in the coming years in light of the developments of transnational criminality described above. Should this function also become essential in a wider international context? Can the EU model be exported to wider international cooperation? Before trying to formulate a response, it is worth recalling what the coordinating functions means in practice. From an operational point of view, the coordinating function means that Eurojust is able to put in place:

- Collection and analysis of information coming from the Member States, in order to identify links and promote new investigation trails. From this point of view, Eurojust not only provides logistical support for the setup of meetings where the national authorities can get together and exchange information, but also analytical support as once information is introduced in the Case Management System, the case can be analysed providing further possibilities of investigation and connection with other cases at a national level unknown to the local authorities. In the framework of coordination, Eurojust stimulates spontaneous exchange of information during coordination meetings, and assures the contextual execution of several investigative measures.
- The coordinated execution of the activities contained in a request for international judicial assistance. This avoids the dispersion of the evidence and acquires useful elements for a trial. Eurojust in this context is a facilitator, providing best practices when drafting the request, identifying the correct authority and coordinating the timing among the countries involved. This feature of Eurojust's activities gains importance with the differences between the requesting and the requested states in the context of a request. For example, the different procedures needed for the authorisation and the execution of telephone interceptions.

- Identification of legal problems and the promotion of 'good practice' guidelines for harmonising the collection of evidence to be used abroad;
- Avoid duplicate investigations and prevent the conflict of jurisdiction and *ne bis in idem*. One of the principal objectives of the actions of the EU in the area of judicial cooperation in criminal matters regards the prevention of the conflict of jurisdiction among the member states. In the territory of the Union, the problem of the concurrence of jurisdictions and the possible duplications of criminal procedures have become so relevant that it has gained special attention in the negotiations for the draft of the constitutional convention. The drafter included the possibility of furnishing Eurojust, in collaboration with the European Judicial Network, with the task of compelling international cooperation in criminal matters by resolving conflicts of jurisdiction. This possibility has been considered again in the new Treaty of Lisbon.
- Facilitating the relationship with contact points in third countries in order to enhance judicial cooperation.
- Facilitating the setting of Joint Investigation Teams.

The adoption of the Decision on the strengthening of Eurojust and amending Decision 2002/187/JHA setting up Eurojust with a view to reinforcing the fight against organised crime by the Council of Ministers of the EU on 16 December has been a major step forward. The main innovations introduced are:

- Increasing the power of the College (see the decision that the College may give an opinion in order to settle conflicts of jurisdiction, whilst it would be non binding it would have a big impact in term of moral persuasion on the national authorities concerned, that would motivate their decision whether to follow the advice of the College);
- Increasing the exchange of information with national authorities and other European bodies, mainly Europol and the European Anti-Fraud Office (OLAF).

In order to ensure the effective application of the new Eurojust Decision, it is crucial that Member States implement it at a national level in a correct and coordinated manner and within the prescribed time limit, no later than two years after its publication in the Official Journal of the EU. It should be noted that with a view to stimulate a timely implementation in all Member States, coordinating common national approaches where possible, and harmonising the implementation at a national level, Eurojust together with the Trio made up of the EU Presidency, the Council Secretariat, and the Commission started working on the preparation of an Implementation Plan in the last quarter of 2008.

In particular, Member States shall ensure a correct and timely implementation in the following major areas:

- Amelioration of the operational capabilities of Eurojust.
- Strengthening of the powers of Eurojust (either acting thorough national members or as a College) and the powers of national members in their capacity as competent national authorities.
- Improvement of the exchange of information.
- Reinforcement of cooperation between national authorities and the EJN contact points, in particular by the setting up of the Eurojust National Coordination Systems.
- Enhancement of relations with privileged partners and third States.

As far as the international dimension of its activity, it is worth mentioning that although Eurojust primarily provides assistance to the competent authorities of the EU Member States, it should not be overlooked that since its establishment, Eurojust has striven to foster cooperation with third Countries and other international and European bodies active in the field of serious cross-border crimes, including human trafficking. Eurojust has legal personality and this has allowed it to conclude co-operation agreements with the United States, Norway, Iceland, and Switzerland.[1] Moreover, throughout last year, Eurojust continued to develop its relations with other countries in particular in the Western Balkans, Russia and Ukraine. Additionally, since its inception, Eurojust has developed a list of 31 contacts of which 23 are in non-EU Countries, including Argentina, Canada, Egypt, Israel, Japan, Moldova, Singapore, Thailand and Turkey. Additionally, under the new Eurojust Decision, Eurojust will have the

[1] Eurojust has also concluded co-operation agreements with Croatia and the Former Yugoslav Republic of Macedonia. These agreements, however, have not yet entered into force

possibility to second liaison magistrates to Third Countries.[2] Eurojust is further engaged in negotiations with international and European organisations, such as IberRed in order to intensify relations with the Countries of Central and Southern America. One should not forget that Eurojust and UNODC are themselves engaged in talks which might eventually lead to a Memorandum of Understanding.

6. The Creation of a European Public Prosecutor Office from Eurojust

The EU legislator should make use of the possibilities which will become available with the Lisbon Treaty in order to further strengthen Eurojust and put it in a position to play an even more effective and pro-active role in the fight against cross-border crime in the European Union. The latter is particularly relevant, especially in the context of the possible creation of the European Public Prosecutor's Office (EPPO) from Eurojust (see section 4 above).

On the basis of the Lisbon Treaty, it should be noticed that the creation of EPPO represents a last step, conceived in a bigger and more structured legal context and model. Indeed, before the creation of the new organism, according to Article 85.1 (a) TFEU, Eurojust should be given the power to initiate criminal investigations, particularly those relating to offences against the financial interests of the Union. Experience shows that in order to achieve a coherent and efficient action against cross-border crime, the decision to investigate should be made at European level. Logically, the College of Eurojust would play a fundamental role in this respect. This possibility is of great importance as to the future relations with the EPPO; in this context, it should be made clear that the initiation of investigations should be a task for Eurojust, not for the EPPO. Further consideration should be given to the nature of Eurojust's powers in the framework of the coordination of investigations and prosecutions (Article 85.1 (b)). The possibilities for future stronger powers of Eurojust, of a more binding nature, should be considered and a real harmonisation of powers between the national members achieved.

---

[2] Eurojust has initiated talks with the Russian Federation and Ukraine. In addition, study visits are being organised with Liechtenstein, Moldova, Montenegro, Israel, EULEX and Cape Verde. Serbia, Bosnia, Morocco and Azerbaijan have expressed interests in Eurojust as well.

The role of Eurojust in matters related to the conflicts of jurisdiction (Article 85.1 (c)) should be also strengthened. Consideration should be given to the possibility of establishing a resolution mechanism where Eurojust could play a more significant role. In this vein, Eurojust would support the mandatory referral to Eurojust of cases where the national authorities have failed to reach an agreement on the best placed jurisdiction.

Eurojust is willing to contribute in a positive and active way to the debate concerning the creation of a EPPO from Eurojust. At the same time, Eurojust would also like to stress that the possibilities which will become available with the Lisbon Treaty in order to further strengthen Eurojust as a coordination body and as a basis for future developments, should be used. The EPPO, being a logical development of Eurojust, should take into account both the legal framework and the practical experience of Eurojust. In this context, the following considerations seem to be relevant the future relations between the EPPO and Eurojust must take into account their different roles and powers and the need to optimise resources and exploit synergies between them. In particular, consideration should be given to the impact that the creation of the EPPO would have on practical issues such as budget, human resources and the housing situation. In relation to the rules on criminal procedure, including those relating to territorial competence and conflicts of jurisdiction, the operational experience of Eurojust should be considered.

The investigative capacity of the EPPO is an essential point to be addressed. The entities and authorities that must carry out the investigations and collect the evidence under the direction of the EPPO need to be identified in order to ensure the effectiveness of the EPPO powers:

- In this context, the use of joint investigation teams should be explored as much as possible;
- It will be also important to define the role of OLAF and Europol and their relations with the EPPO, and the strengthening of their competences in criminal investigations, taking into account the relations already established with Eurojust.
- Finally, there will be a need to consider the jurisdictional control of actions taken by the EPPO that may affect the fundamental rights of individuals. The question is not only to know which courts or judg-

es should be competent, but also how to ensure jurisdictional control.

7. One World Public Prosecutor or Several International Public Prosecutors for Different Homogeneous Areas?

Some time ago the Public Prosecutor of Palermo, Mr. Antonio Ingroia, speaking about the achievements reached with the Lisbon Treaty and the prospect of a European Public Prosecutor from Eurojust, said that nowadays the creation of such a prosecutor is already overcome by and superseded by the necessity of having a world public prosecutor. He added that due to the international dimension of modern crime the prevision and the functioning of such a Prosecutor would no longer be sufficient to face the threats posed by organised crime, which is swiftly able to act beyond any national boundary.

Can we share this statement? Is it correct to predict that the EU model of the EPPO will be exported to an international level? Furthermore, is it advisable to conceive a one world public prosecutor or more public prosecutors for different regional areas at an international level? And how can we balance such a concentration of public power that the creation of a world public prosecutor implies? I would like to end with a few short observations on this question, preceded by some closing observations regarding another key word for the coming two decades, the integrated approach.

At the international level it will be increasingly necessary for States to seek maximum cohesion between policy themes and their external dimension. Capacity building can play a crucial role in combating organised crime. Immigration and integration policy can have a major impact on delinquency as inadequate integration leads to social tension. Another example comes from the issue of human trafficking which must be considered not only at the level of immigration policy and the through implications of international cooperation, but also from the perspective of human rights and the victim's situation.

Coordinated policies at international level means building solid links not limited to EU countries but which consider all other countries as a vital part of the programme to combat serious crime in the context of shared security interests, values and also taking into account the protection of human rights. Should the national policies reach a good level of harmony in the field of criminal law and judicial cooperation, with an integrated approach that includes all the connected areas and issues, we estimate that the creation of more public prosecutors at an international level for the more homogeneous part of the world, meaning within a singular regional context, seems to be a realistic prospect for the coming years. Ruling out any reasonable plans to create a world public prosecutor because of the extremely high concentration of prerogatives this actor could have, the creation of a pluralistic model of international prosecutors, disseminated at crucial points on the planet, seem to be a more realistic prospect and it would indeed be a welcome one. The creation of such organs can assure the necessary coordinated approach, in the investigation against the organisation of transnational crime, which requires common efforts and a strategic vision that goes beyond a purely national perspective.

Of course, the launching of this idea should take some constraints, stemming from the taking of traditional common principle of criminal law into consideration, which are more or less, typical of all national systems. First of all the principle of legality and the national prerogatives in the field of the judiciary must be considered. However, the provisions and the experience of the EU could lead to finding shareable solutions. We need to turn to a clear and defined system of competences and to a proper balance of public prerogatives, in which the national competences are kept safe but at the same time, also coordinate an approach which could be followed by addressing international criminal networks in a specific crime area. The observance of the principle of subsidiarity is a key word for balancing these different needs and perspectives. According to the principle, the competence to prosecute should remain with the national judicial authorities, but when they are inactive or when they do not follow the coordinate perspective, there should be an external authority put in place, with binding powers, able to influence the due course of the investigations and able to connect and link to other prosecutors involved in the case. From a realistic prospective we can say that at present cross border fraud and other forms of transnational violations are not being pursued actively enough. Domestic prosecutions are seen as being slow, hesitant and even hampered in pursuing such complex cases. The missing link in the procedural chain could be an efficient European Public Prosecutor at the EU level who is equipped with the authority to direct and coordinate the work of all domestic judicial institutions and other European bodies such as

Olaf, Eurojust and Europol. In the long term and once the EPPO is established, its mandate can include many forms of crimes and not only those affecting the financial interest of the EU. Should the model work in practice, then why not consider the possibility of exporting it to a global level?

7.6

The Future of International and European Criminal Law

André Klip*

This think piece takes the readers on a journey into the future of European integration. In this particularly visionary contribution, critical remarks regarding today's challenges are mixed with fictive narrations of history as it would look in 2030. Based on the premise that what lies ahead is further integration, to an unprecedented and rather dramatic extent, various developments and novel features and institutions of the EU of the future are described. For instance, the establishment of the European Public Prosecutor's Office, the introduction of a European Penal Code and even the establishment of a European Criminal Court. A separate section of the think piece looks as the further development of the international criminal justice system, and in particular the ICC, in light of that court's not unproblematic first years. In that context, particular reference is made to the ICC's difficulty to treat leaders of world powers just as it treats, for instance, states in crisis in Africa. Also at stake here is the principle of complementarity which, looked at from 2030, is seen as failed to have achieved its objective. Overall, the core message conveyed by this think piece is that national criminal law will increasingly lose it position of primacy, giving way to more and more criminal law and institutions that transcend national borders.

1. Introduction

Predicting the future is a difficult task, especially when it concerns legal developments closely linked to political developments. What will happen between 2011 and 2030 in the field of criminal law? Looking back at the developments of the last 20 years, it is unbelievable what changes took place between 1990 and 2010. In Europe, during this period we have seen the evolution of European integration from a 10 Member State European Community (with a then still predominant focus on the internal market) to a 27 Member State European Union that has been able to extend its com-

* **André Klip** is Professor of Criminal Law, Criminal Procedure and Transnational Criminal Law at Maastricht University.

petencies dramatically, which now also includes criminal law. As regards international criminal law and tribunals, in 1990 it was reasonable to think that international criminal tribunals had only been a historical phenomenon and that it would not be possible to have tribunals like Nuremberg and Tokyo ever again. Since then, however, several *ad hoc* international criminal tribunals have been established, as well as a number of internationalised tribunals (national tribunals with international elements). In total, between 1993 (when the International Criminal Tribunal for the former Yugoslavia (ICTY) was established) and approximately 2015 (when the *ad hoc* tribunals will have completed their last cases), a total of some 1000-2000 cases will have been dealt with by the various tribunals (the ICTY, the International Criminal Tribunal for Rwanda (ICTR), the Special Court for Sierra Leone (SPSL), as well as the tribunals for East Timor, Lebanon and Cambodia), thus leading to a dramatic development of the law. The *ad hoc* tribunals also paved the way for the establishment of the International Criminal Court (ICC), the first ever *permanent* international criminal tribunal.

Are we going to see similarly unthinkable and revolutionary developments in these fields in the coming 20 years? The remainder of this think piece is a journey into the future, an attempt to describe some of what we might see in the next two decades.

2. A Glimpse into a Possible European Future: General Outlook of the Further Integration of the European Union

Our starting point is the entry into force of the Lisbon Treaty in December 2009. After that, the integration of Europe has taken new and important dimensions. The full implementation of the principle of mutual recognition in all areas of cooperation in criminal matters between the Member States of the EU has led to a situation in which Member States comply without objection to arrest warrants issued by other Member States.

After 2010, initial problems concerning a lack of mutual trust and differences in relevant standards have disappeared. With the adoption of a European Directive on the Rights of the Accused in Criminal Proceedings in the EU in 2011, some concerns with regard to respect for the rule of law could dissipate. By that time, the EU will have fully harmonised cooperation in criminal matters amongst the EU Member States as well as between the EU, Member States and third states.

Initially, it was difficult for the EU to balance the interests of the Member States as protected in the 'area of freedom, security and justice' with the interests of citizens, as protected in the regulation of the internal market, but eventually a good balance was found, whereby neither the freedom of citizens nor the interest of Member States to combat crime is absolute. This means that the disproportional use of the European Arrest Warrant (*e.g.*, for a minor theft case) comes to an end. On the basis of Articles 82 and 83 TFEU, the European Union will have gradually legislated in all areas of substantive criminal law and criminal procedure. The EU will enjoy primacy of legislation in all areas of criminal law. There is a directive specifically dealing with the allocation of criminal jurisdiction to national authorities in order to prevent conflicts of jurisdiction. Overlapping jurisdiction between Member States no longer exists.

Prosecutions are increasingly of a European nature. There is a common interest in jointly combating criminal activity that takes place within the territory of the EU. Given the fact that the internal borders have been abolished not only for market purposes but also for law enforcement agencies, there is no impediment whatsoever to conduct cross border investigations. In addition, multinational units have been established to combat certain serious forms of crime. After having obtained a clear picture of the criminal responsibilities of those involved, Member States divide amongst themselves the tasks for prosecution.

In 2030 a Turkish national is elected President of the EU for the first time. The EU now encompasses virtually the entire European continent, including Russia and excluding only the Vatican and Liechtenstein. Moreover, non-European states, such as Kazakhstan, Morocco and Israel, are candidates for EU membership. The EU still has no answer to the question of where and whether Europe ends, politically.

The European Court of Justice (ECJ) fulfils an ever more important and central role and has gradually taken over the position of the European Court of Human Rights as the main judicial authority on human rights issues in Europe. The causes for this are multifarious. First it was stipulated in the Treaty of Lisbon that the Charter of Fundamental Rights for the European Union has the same legal value as the Treaties. This meant that the Charter became an instrument that could be directly invoked in all criminal proceedings in the EU and obtained a status similar to a constitutional instrument. Due to the fact that the ECJ is the highest authority in all matters of Union law, many references were made to the Court by various national courts of the Member States. The second reason explaining the increased role of the ECJ in the area of human rights lies in the fact that the EU had acceded to the European Convention of Human Rights (ECHR). As a result, the local remedies that must be exhausted before an applicant may lodge a complaint with the European Court of Human Rights may now include a preliminary ruling by the ECJ. While accused persons were not entitled themselves to start proceedings at the ECJ, this was compensated for by preliminary references by national courts and by the Commission. The Commission has developed a practice of launching infringement proceedings against Member States that did not completely live up to the Charter and the ECHR.

3. Particular New Features and Institutions of Continued Integration of the European Union

3.1. The European Public Prosecutor's Office

The European Public Prosecutor's Office (EPPO) was established, as provided for in Article 86 TFEU, around 2015. On the day that the first European Public Prosecutor took office, the first European Penal Code, as well as the Code of European Criminal Procedure, was adopted. Whilst the European Penal Code initially dealt with a rather limited number of crimes related to subsidy fraud, fair competition and other crimes affecting the financial interest of the European Union, the catalogue of crimes has gradually expanded to cover all crimes that are likely to be committed in a transnational setting. The competences of the European Public Prosecutor have been extended also on the procedural level. Whereas, initially, the European Public Prosecutor needed the assistance of national law enforcement agencies to conduct investigations, subsequent revisions of the law enabled the European Public Prosecutor to send Europol officials directly to any state of the EU.

3.2. The European Criminal Court

In 2025, as a logical step following the establishment of a European Police Office in 1995 and the European Public Prosecutor's Office in 2015, the European Criminal Court (ECC) was set up as a special chamber of the ECJ. The absence of prison facilities at the Court of Justice in Luxembourg became problematic for the first time when, in early 2011, a national court of one of the Member States referred a criminal case for a preliminary ruling by the ECJ, and the accused in that case insisted that his right to be present had to be respected. Despite the fact that the new premises of the ECJ had been constructed for 500 million euro earlier, it did not provide for prison cells. With some difficulties and *ad hoc* agreement with Luxembourg, this human right of the accused person could be respected. Nevertheless, the ECJ and the EU understood the sign of the times and proposed the establishment of the ECC. However, this proposition was initially met with strong opposition from some Member States. Then, a wave of terrorist attacks in 2024 that included the bombing of a national parliament and the assassination of a head of state ended all objections and the ECC was created, with its own prison facilities as well as the EPPO for the execution of sentences it issues.

3.3. The Character of European Criminal Law

Similar to how international criminal law has been developed by the various international criminal tribunals, European criminal law has also become a field of law in its own right, with elements borrowed from both the common law and civil law traditions. The emergence of a separate European criminal justice system has led to further approximation of national criminal justice systems with the European system. In addition, the EU has entered a process of finding its own way in developing the European criminal justice system. Here, one can recognise a path of development similar to that which took place in the 1990s with the *ad hoc* tribunals (and later, also the ICC) developing their own legal system of international criminal law. Some elements are drawn from common law, others from civil law, but most of it is a wonderful new model of its own.

3.4. The Language of EU Law

Given the fact that both in Europe as elsewhere a process of integration and internationalisation takes place, it will become increasingly difficult to maintain the principle that all EU legislation and case law must be produced in all the languages of EU Member States. Rather, it will be necessary to considerably reduce the number of languages into which EU legal material must be translated. The dilemmas that arise concern the question of how to make choices here, and what this would entail for the principle that citizens must be able to read the law in the language it was written.

On the other hand, globalisation and the increased internationalisation of all areas of society have undoubtedly increased the dominance of English over other languages. More and more people speak English very well. In the end, the EU will inevitably abandon the principle that all languages in Europe are equally authentic and thus legally relevant. Apart from the problem that the EU will no longer be able to afford the enormous costs of translation, it will also have to realise that maintaining the unity of the EU and its interpretation when so many languages are involved is simply impossible.

4. The ICC's Bias Regarding International Crimes Related to World Powers

Leaving aside the evolution of a European criminal justice system, what can be said about the future of the international justice system that has been emerging since the 1990s, and in particular, the future of the ICC?

It has been relatively easy for international criminal tribunals to develop and even prosper in a period when the world powers of the time agreed on the establishment of these tribunals and so long as the leader of great powers did not run the risk of being judged by such tribunals themselves. The establishment of the ICC, with its permanent status and broad jurisdiction, was on the one hand a promising step towards the further development of the global justice system and ending impunity; but at the same time the risk it embodied even for great powers was an impediment to its potential success.

Thus, two decades from now we might be forced to admit that neither the first Prosecutor of the ICC nor any of the successive ICC Prosecutors have been able to get sufficient support to investigate and prosecute crimes committed by world or regional powers. In addition, the confidentiality restrictions have made it extremely difficult to continue criminal proceedings whilst respecting the right to a fair trial. This already came to the fore in the Lubanga case in 2010-2012, in which the ICC ordered a stay of the proceedings and eventually released the accused, because the prosecution was not able to lift the restrictions on the many pieces of evidence of which the origin was unknown to the defence and the trial chamber. This results from a situation in which the prosecution collects and uses only as much evidence and information as states and other providers allow.

To a large extent, proceedings before the ICC have been frustrated by its multiparty character and by confidentiality restrictions. Not only do the prosecution and the defence play a role in the proceedings, but also victims and witnesses, who occupy a procedural position equal to that of a party. All these developments came together at the proceedings of the ICC and lead to a situation in which there were multiparty proceedings and many more questions had to be dealt with rather than the simple cardinal question of whether the accused committed the offences in the indictment. Apart from what still is the main legal issue to be decided, there are all kinds of side issues where parties other than the prosecution and the defence have *locus standi* or have the power to influence whether and under which conditions a certain piece of evidence is admitted.

4.1. The Failure of Complementarity

By 2030, after almost thirty years of experience with the results of complementarity, the inevitable conclusion was reached that this principle has really proven its shortcomings. In practice, the existence of the principle often leads to inaction of states that, in theory, could prosecute. Many states do not want to become the policemen of the world and reserve their efforts to prosecute international crimes for foreigners that are found on their territory. It is now clear that complementarity has had an adverse effect in the sense that states have interpreted the establishment of the ICC as being the criminal court having primacy over all national courts. States therefore wait to see whether the ICC will take action, before they will do something. This attitude may be explained by various reasons. Politically, it is not an attractive task to investigate and prosecute international crimes, exactly because of the inherent political nature of such crimes. Whatever you will do as a state, you are messing with somebody else's business. It may result in a situation in which it is difficult to obtain assistance and may be damaging to international relations, which are relevant for other state interests. A second reason for the little activity on the side of national law enforcement authorities relates to costs and efficiency. By definition, international crimes relate to complex situations, in which an enormous effort must be made to obtain a good overall picture of the conflict, the parties involved and those responsible for atrocities.

The very fact that an overview of the conflict as a whole must first be made, makes the investigation an almost insurmountable task for small national law enforcement agencies. It takes quite some time before it is clear which individuals are responsible for international crimes. And if that is clear, the state must be lucky in that the person is to be found on its territory. If not, the whole effort was for nothing. Furthermore, the fact that all states might need to undertake the same exercise is not very efficient nor does it ensure coherence or consistency. Also the 'boomerang effect' does not stimulate prosecution. States with an active record on prosecution no longer find suspects and have managed to keep perpetrators out of the country. A handful of successful prosecutions will scare off other alleged criminals, which means that successful national prosecutions are the victim of their own successes.

Gradually the recognition emerges that universal jurisdiction might not be the single or best solution to impunity. Universal jurisdiction causes a 'bystander' effect. If every state in the world is competent to prosecute, why should we? Alternative modes of action might be advised here. How about, for example, assigning an individual state a specific conflict? Why do we not create a system in which one willing and able state assumes responsibility over a certain situation on behalf of the world community, specialises on that specific conflict and is thus able to become highly efficient in dealing with the criminal past of such a conflict? The ICC could remain in place for the prosecution of high ranking officials and persons carrying immunity under international law; it will also be the guardian of ICC Statute, entrusted with ensuring that trials are fair.

On evaluation, it seems that the added value of the ICC has been that it provides for a permanent *ad hoc tribunal*. This means that the ICC provides a permanent structure for an international criminal tribunal. Its advantage is that it does not need to reinvent the wheel and can be immediately operational as soon as a case is assigned to it. However, both complementarity and the reluctance of states in cooperating with the ICC have resulted in a situation in which the ICC can only operate effectively if the situation is not affected by world or regional powers' interests. As soon as nationals of world (or regional) powers face the risk of prosecution, the Office of the Prosecutor will not have access to all the relevant evidence and information.

5. Conclusion – The Decline of the Primacy of National Criminal Law

If we were to take only one message from the above 'journey into the future', it would be that national criminal law will increasingly give way to non-domestic criminal law. The European and international criminal justice systems will more and more determine the rules and structures of all criminal law, regardless of whether it concerns international or local crime. This development has already been visible for quite some years, both in European criminal law and in international criminal law. This is in fact a logical consequence of globalisation, as the latter makes the concept of territoriality less and less important. Especially in criminal law, where territoriality traditionally plays an important role. The basic rule for the application of criminal law is that the national criminal law applies on the territory of the State. Gradually, the principle of globality replaces the principle of territoriality.

7.7

Modern Penal Rationality Left Behind: A Call for Innovative Thinking and Practice in Criminal Law

Maíra Rocha Machado*

One of the main challenges for the development of law is the crystallisation of certain ideas concerning crime and punishment that have been acting as huge barriers to innovation. This think piece is, therefore, an effort to organise the results of my previous and ongoing research around the resistance surrounding innovative ideas that can be considered better equipped to deal with the complexity of contemporary social problems. To accomplish this goal, this piece will present a simplified sketch of these ideas concerning crime and punishment – the concept of 'modern penal rationality' as developed by Alvaro Pires (Ottawa University). It will also briefly introduce two problematic manifestations of the high level of sedimentation of these ideas: the widespread use of minimum punishments in national legal systems and the lack of space for restorative justice mechanisms in the international legal order.

1. Introduction

One of the main challenges for the development of law is the crystallisation of certain ideas concerning crime and punishment that have acted as huge barriers to innovation. This think piece is, therefore, an effort to organise the results of my previous and ongoing research around the resistance surrounding innovative ideas that can be considered better equipped to deal with the complexity of contemporary social problems.

To accomplish this goal, this piece will (i) present a simplified sketch of these ideas concerning crime and punishment – the concept of 'modern penal rationality' as developed by Alvaro Pires (Ottawa University). It will also briefly introduce two problematic manifestations of the high level of sedimentation of these ideas: (ii) the widespread use of min-

* **Maíra Rocha Machado** is a Professor at São Paulo Law School of Fundação Getulio Vargas (DIREITO GV).

imum punishments in national legal systems and (iii) the lack of space for restorative justice mechanisms in the international legal order.

2. Modern Penal Rationality as One of the Main Challenges to the Development of Law

The theory of the 'modern penal rationality' (MPR) is conceived in two axes.[1] The first relies on modern theories of punishment which constitute the foundation of modern criminal law itself: deterrence, retribution and rehabilitation in prison. In the mid-twentieth century, a fourth theory of punishment was added to these three: denunciation. According to Pires, these theories have played a decisive role in the formation of the modern criminal law as they have all addressed the core question of this emerging field: Why, who and how should we punish? At first sight, these theories have offered different answers – "to deter offenders and citizens from committing crimes", "to make the offender pay for what they did", "to rehabilitate offenders" and "to denounce the wrong behavior". They also seem to define and combine in different ways central legal concepts such as proportionality, moderation and seriousness of the offense. Besides these elements that might be observed as divergent, these theories also *converge* in several aspects. Focusing on the convergence, it is possible to

[1] This piece just provides a glimpse of the theory of the modern penal rationality as currently developed by Alvaro Pires. A sophisticated organization and discussion of this theory can be found at Margarida Garcia, "La Téorie de la Rationalité Penale Moderne: Un Cadre d'Observation, d'Organisation et de Description des Idées qui Habitent le Système de Droit Criminel", in Garcia Dube and Machado (eds.), *La Rationalité Pénale Moderne*, forthcoming. See also, in this regard, Alvaro Pires, "La Formation de la Rationalité Pénale Moderne au XVIIIe Siècle", in *Histoire des Savoirs sur le Crime et la Peine*, 1998, vol. 2; Digneffe Debuyst and Pires (eds.), *Bruxelles: Éditions Larcier*; Alvaro Pires, "La Rationalité Pénale Moderne, la Société du Risque et la Juridicisation de l'Opinion Publique", in *Sociologie et Société,* vol. 33, no. 1, 2001, pp. 179-204 ; Alvaro Pires, "La 'Ligne Maginot' en Droit Criminel: La Protection Contre le Crime Versus la Protection Contre le Prince", in *Revue de Droit Pénal et de Criminologie*, vol. 81, no. 2, 2001, p. 145-170; Alvaro Pires, "Une 'Utopie Juridique' et Politique pour le Droit Criminel Moderne?", in *Criminologie*, vol. 40, no. 2, 2007, pp. 9-18; Alvaro Pires and Jean-François Cauchie, "Un Cas d'Innovation 'Accidentelle' en Matière de Peines: Une Loi Brésilienne sur les Drogues", *Champ Pénal/Penal Field*, 2007, available at http://champpenal.revues.org/document 1541.html, last accessed 20 February 2011.

identify that these notions are all built upon the same cognitive tradition (or *system of ideas*).[2]

This system of ideas – called 'modern penal rationality' – has three fundamental features. First, it supports the 'obligation of punishment' instead of an 'authorisation' to punish in certain cases. Second, despite slightly different formulations regarding the goals to accomplish, this system of ideas provides a substantial definition of punishment as an *intentional infliction of suffering*. Third, the over appreciation of prison and the disregard of alternative methods of dispute resolution are the cornerstones of modern penal rationality: the *social exclusion* of the offender.

The modern penal rationality is therefore fostering a *hostile, abstract, negative* and *atomistic* form of justice. In Pires words, it is:

> ... hostile because it represents the offender as an enemy of the entire group and because it seeks to establish some sort of necessary (or ontological) equivalence between the value of the object protected by law and the level of suffering produced by the offender. *Abstract*, because the suffering (concrete) caused by punishment is recognized but conceived as likely to cause an intangible moral good ('restore justice by suffering,' 'strengthen the morality of honest people,' etc.) or even an invisible and future practical good (the deterrence). *Negative*, since these theories *exclude any other sanction* aiming to reaffirm the Law by positive action (as compensation) and stipulate that *only the concrete and immediate harm* caused to the offender may produce welfare for the group or reaffirm the Law. And finally, *atomistic*, because punishment – in the best case – is conceived not to be concerned about the concrete social links between people except in a very secondary and incidental way.[3]

The second part is not mainly descriptive as the first as it also includes an explanatory effort. It focuses on the issues regarding the evolu-

[2] Therefore, the theory of the modern penal rationality is organised on three levels of observation: the micro level of concepts and ideas (proportionality, moderation, etc), the medium level of the four theories of punishment and the macro level of this specific cognitive tradition (system of ideas) named "modern penal rationality". For a detailed description of the three levels of observation, see Garcia, forthcoming, *supra* note 1.

[3] Pires, 2001, p. 184, see *supra* note 1.

tion of criminal law and, specifically, the conditions under which innovative ideas can emerge and persist (or in other words, be selected and stabilised).[4] The working hypothesis in this regard is that modern penal rationality, as a system of ideas formed by modern theories of punishment, functions as a cognitive obstacle to the acceptance of non-prosecutorial forms of justice, to the reception and enforcement of non-prison sanctions and also to the reduction of the length of prison sentences and of the frequency of their use.

Notwithstanding the choice to focus on cognitive aspects of this challenge, specifically on the lack of opportunity to foster innovative thinking in the criminal sphere, this piece also highlights some of the very pragmatic outcomes of the sedimentation of these ideas. In this regard, the relative absence of public debate concerning the social exclusion of almost 10 million people on the planet is an issue of particular concern. According to the figures available for cross-country comparison, the Brazilian prison rate is 227 people per 100,000 of the national population, higher than its neighbours Argentina and Uruguay (whose rates stand at 154 and 193, respectively) and the median rate for southern and Western European countries which is 95. These figures are significantly lower than the United States of America, which is at the top of the world rankings with 756 people per 100,000.[5] The national figures for Brazil show that the prison population has increased substantially in the last two decades, even though legislative reforms were approved in this same period to allow forms of negotiation to avoid criminal procedure and non-prison sentences in minor criminal cases.[6] These reforms were too timid and there-

4 See, in this regard, Richard Dubé, "Éléments de Théorie sur les Commissions de Réforme du Droit et l'Innovation Cognitive en Matière de Justice Pénale: Contributions Conceptuelles de Michael Foucault et de Niklas Luhmann", in *Champ Pénal /Penal Field, Nouvelle Revue Internationale de Criminologie*, available at http://champpenal.revues.org/694, last accessed 28 February 2011; Garcia, forthcoming, see *supra* note 1 ; Pires and Cauchie, 2007, see *supra* note 1.

5 Roy Walmsley, "World Prison Population List", International Centre for Prison Studies, King's College, 2008. The authors of the report and I are fully aware that this information is collected from very different sources and the final results cannot be considered precise.

6 According to the statistics provided by the Brazilian Minister of Justice, Brazilian prison population increased 144% from 1995 to 2005, rising from 148 to 361 thousands of people. In 2009 the prison population reached 473,000. The same source also

fore unable to affect cases that are more likely to result in prison sentences. Furthermore their effects were countered by other laws that undermined or eliminated their potential to make any change in this scenario.

The lack of public debate about these figures warrants even more attention if we take into account the living conditions of the prison population in many countries, including Brazil. Overcrowding and poor living conditions are normally invisible issues in public debate. They only come to light as a human rights concern when the most tragic episodes, involving rebellion and death, occur.[7] Certainly, in the specialised public sphere, the terrible living conditions are denounced in human rights reports from national and international organisations.[8] The OAS Report on the Situation of Human Rights in Brazil, for example, dedicates a whole chapter to prison conditions.[9] The Report describes the shortage of resources, substandard hygienic issues, lack of opportunities to work, failure to divide the inmates according to the nature of the offense and age and several other aspects indicating non-compliance with international standards. The conclusion and recommendations of this Report illustrate the 'cognitive

informs that in 2009 Brazilian prison system was facing a deficit of 195,000 places. INFOPEN 2010, Minister of Justice, available at http://portal.mj.gov.br/data/Pages/MJD574E9CEITEMID364AC56ADE924046B46C6B9CC447B586PTBRIE.htm, last accessed 28 February 2011.

7 A study conducted at the ongoing master dissertation of Carolina Cutrupi Ferreira at Direito GV reveals that the most stories published at *Folha de Sao Paulo*, *Estado de São Paulo* and *O Globo,* the three most read Brazilian newspapers, concerning the prison system deals with rebellions and fights among prisoners. The other ones concern legislative reforms and some local efforts from public prosecutors to release inmates in excessively overcrowded prison.

8 Camara dos Deputados e Pastoral Carceraria, *Situação do Sistema Prisional no Brasil,* available at http://www.carceraria.org.br/fotos/fotos/admin/Sistema%20Penal/Sistema%20Penitenciario/RELATORIO%20DO%20SISTEMA%20PRISIONAL%20BRASILEIRO%20-%202006.pdf, last accessed 28 February 2011; *Global Justice Annual Report 2003: Human Rights in Brazil*, Rio de Janeiro, Justiça Global, 2004 (specifically chapter 1 "The Dreadful Situation of Prisons", pp. 17-26), available at http://www.observatorioseguranca.org/pdf/01%20(24).pdf, last accessed 28 February 2011. Also Human Rights Watch 1998, *Behind Bars in Brazil*. pp. 1-227, available at http://www.hrw.org/legacy/reports/reports98/brazil/index.htm, last accessed 28 February 2011.

9 Inter-American Commission on Human Rights, "Chapter 4 – Conditions of Detention", in *Report on the Situation of Human Rights in Brazil,* 2007, available at http://www.cidh.org/countryrep/brazil-eng/chaper%204.htm, last accessed 28 February 2011.

cage' discussed in this piece. Requiring "all of the political, technical and financial energy necessary", the Report recommends a "substantial increase of places in the prison system" and makes specific suggestions for improvements always taking for granted the continuing existence and widespread use of imprisonment.

3. First Problematic Manifestation: Minimum Punishment

The first problematic manifestation of the modern penal rationality discussed in this piece focuses on national legal systems. It concerns a legislative practice that can be described as a form of intervention of the political system in the legal system (more specifically in the criminal law system). To put it in very simple terms, the 'minimum punishment' is a political message stating that regardless of the characteristics of the concrete situation, the consequence cannot be defined 'less than' a certain amount of time. Due to the deeply rooted effect of modern penal rationality, this amount is, most frequently, a certain amount of time of imprisonment. Broadly speaking, the minimum punishment is a form of *de-construction of the alternatives* or *reduction of the field of alternatives*. When the legal sanction specifies what can be considered as an alternative (therefore excluding all other possibilities) it eliminates the judge's decision on punishment.

In other words, the minimum punishment eliminates the possibility of taking all peculiarities of the concrete case and defendant into account. Research with Brazilian and Canadian judges has shown that the political message sent through the minimum punishment ('not less than') either leads to the perception that their decision on a particular case 'was unfair but was following the legal rule' or to the creation of mechanisms to avoid the criminal conviction. Some of respondents reported that they might ignore part of the evidence, reread the files to change the terms of the accusation or even decide for acquittal.[10]

---

[10] A conceptual framework to observe empirical formulations of minimum punishments at Brazilian, Canadian and French criminal codes since the beginning of the nineteenth century is developed at Maira Machado and Alvaro Pires, "Intervention Politique dans la Sentence de Droit? Fondements Culturelles de la Peine Minimale", in *Criminologie*, 2011, vol. 43; And also Maira Machado *et al.*, *A Complexidade do problema e a Simplicidade da Solução: A Questão das Penas Mínimas*, Brasília, Secretaria de Assuntos Legislativos do Ministério da Justiça do Brasil, 2009, Vol. 17,

Even though minimum punishment can be identified in all Latin American countries, Brazilian criminal legislation has stabilised and generalised this practice in an extraordinary manner. According to SISPENAS' criminal legislation database, just 5 of 1,688 existing crimes do not have minimum punishments. Four of the five established non-prison penalties (loss of a public job and community services) and just one established a maximum term of imprisonment.[11] But minimum punishments are far from being a feature of developing countries' laws. In fact, even the distinction between the two main traditions of law – *common* and *civil law* – it is not a useful to explain differences as merely a distribution of tasks between the legislator and the judge regarding sentencing.

Since the emergence of this practice in the nineteenth century, it is possible to identify that the form and intensity of the minimum punishment varies significantly according to the legal system. The 1810 French Criminal Code establishes minimum punishments for *all crimes* while the 1892 Canadian Criminal Code establishes only 31 minimums (in which just 6 concern imprisonment and the other 25 are related to fines). This picture is quite different nowadays. Since 1976, it is possible to observe an intensive use of this practice in Canada where minimum punishments used to be marginal. At the same time, the 1992 French Criminal Code replaced this practice, without fully eliminating it, by maximum penalties only. However in 2007 a new law concerning the 'combat of recidivism', without completely eliminating some possibilities for the judge to decide otherwise, has reintroduced the minimum penalties in the French legal system.

In the US, Cavanagh and Teasely conclude that "since the enactment of a series of mandatory minimum sentencing statutes in the late 1980's, policymakers and researchers have debated their impact and ef-

available at http://portal.mj.gov.br/main.asp?View=%7B329D6EB2-8AB0-4606-B054-4 CAD3C53EE73, last accessed 28 February 2011.

11 SISPENAS is software developed to provide quantitative information on legal norms concerning crimes, penalties and alternatives to punishment. Marta Machado, Maira Machado and Fabio Andrade, *Sispenas: Sistema de Consulta Sobre Crimes, Penas e Alternativas à Prisão*, Brasília, Secretaria de Assuntos Legislativos do Ministério da Justiça do Brasil, 2009, vol. 6, available at http://portal.mj.gov.br/main.asp?View={329D6EB2-8AB0-4606-B054-4CAD3C53EE73}, last accessed 28 February 2011.

fectiveness. The recent publication of the U.S. Sentencing Commission's report on mandatory minimum penalties served to heighten the controversy, because the Commission suggested that these statues have tended to warp the guidelines system, led to inequities in the treatment of minorities, and caused first time offenders to receive longer sentences than those with extensive criminal records".[12] They also explain that even in the face of extensive and strong criticism, congressmen are likely to consider new legislation when adding minimum punishments. On the other hand, authors identified "a growing and increasingly vocal element, including Members of Congress, Federal judges and criminal justice professionals, who advocate the repeal of mandatory minimum penalties, in favour of greater emphasis on the use of guidelines or alternative sentencing".[13]

These different trajectories constitute the puzzle of how contemporary societies have come to accept, until recently, these forms of political intervention in the judicial sentence. In this regard, it is possible to argue that at the core of 'modern penal rationality', the modern theories of punishment provide the foundations of this legislative practice.[14] Certainly, these theories – overall deterrence and retribution – do not explicitly require minimum punishment (and no other specific form of punishment). They inspire the decision to create minimum punishment. Moreover, once these theories are mobilised to justify minimum punishment practices, its acceptance is much more likely to occur. "When a politician says: 'we have created minimum punishments to get more votes', this justification does not favour the acceptance of the practice. However, if he says 'we have created this punishment to protect society against criminality' and/or 'to make sure that punishment will be proportionate *vis-a-vis* the crime', these justifications raise the probability of acceptance of this punishment by the public and the criminal law system".[15]

---

12 Suzanne Cavanagh and David Teasley, "Mandatory Minimum Sentencing for Federal Crimes: Overview and Analysis", in L.V. Brinkley (ed.), *Mandatory Minimum Sentencing: Overview and Background*, Novinka Books, New York, 2003, p. 22.

13 Cavanagh and Teasley, 2003, see *supra* note 12.

14 Machado and Pires, 2011, see *supra* note 10. This article builds upon the distinction between foundations and supporting facts to organise and explain the different forms of justification of the practice of establishing flat or minimum punishments.

15 Machado and Pires, 2011, see *supra* note 10.

4. Second Problematic Manifestation: The Marginal Role of Restorative Justice Mechanisms

The second problematic manifestation of the modern penal rationality for contemporary societies refers to the international legal order. This piece will quickly refer to the marginal role of restorative justice mechanisms in the international arena, specifically in the Rome Statute of the International Criminal Court (ICC). The expression 'restorative justice' will be employed in extremely broad terms that encompass a rich and varied repertoire of alternatives to dealing with social problems, such as programs regarding victim's rehabilitation, mediation, restorative circles, truth and reconciliation commissions, peace agreements etc.

As is widely known, after years of negotiation, the international community has succeeded in approving the Rome Statute of the International Criminal Court. Presently, quite a significant number of countries (112) are State Parties. However Russia, India, China and the United States of America are not. Since the beginning of its activities in June 2002, the Prosecutor has received more than eight thousand communications of violations of human rights from 130 countries. The four cases that are being investigated at this moment concern African states: Uganda, Congo, Sudan and the Central African Republic.

For the purposes of this piece, it seems important to point out three aspects of this model of 'international criminal justice': the exclusive provision of 'suffering penalties' (imprisonment, life imprisonment and fine); the non-recognition of other forms of conflict resolution and the emphasis on the claim that only *criminal* justice must be considered sufficient and adequate to deal with the social problems under ICC competence.[16]

The Preamble of the Rome Statute very explicitly replaces the 'right to intervene' with 'the duty to trial': "Recalling that it is the duty of every State to exercise its criminal jurisdiction over those responsible for international crimes". In this context, the complementary principle, a core feature of the ICC's determination that the international court shall be complementary to national intervention, is conceived in very restrictive terms. According to the articles concerning the issues of admissibility of cases

[16] This argument is developed at Maira Machado, "Qu'Advient-Il de la Rationalité Pénale Moderne Quand on Parle de Problèmes Internationaux?", in Dubé, Garcia and Machado (eds.), *La Rationalité Pénale Moderne*, forthcoming.

and the *bis in idem* rule, it is quite clear that only the activities of national criminal jurisdictions are able to avoid the ICC's competence. Other possible solutions and mechanisms to deal with those extremely problematic situations are excluded.[17] Besides, recent discussion regarding the content of the 'principle of interest of justice' led the Office of the Prosecutor to publish a 'policy paper' stating, among other things, that "the exercise of the Prosecutor's discretion … is exceptional in its nature and that there is a presumption in favor of investigation or prosecution …". The document also states that "the criteria for its exercise will naturally be guided by the objects and purposes of the Statute – namely the prevention of serious crimes of concern to the international community through ending impunity". Finally, the policy paper affirms "that there is a difference between the concepts of the interests of justice and the interests of peace and that the latter falls within the mandate of institutions other than the Office of the Prosecutor".[18]

What is at stake here is the openness of the international legal order to accept ideas and experiences that are not part of modern penal rationality. International legal order could be fostering 'innovative thinking' and 'experiences' in this domain, instead of favouring the reproduction of semantics and practices of crime, criminals, blame and long term imprisonment.

5. To Conclude

> … the modern way to conceive criminal law has killed the legal utopia of the criminalists. We are unable to think a new criminal law different from the modern criminal law … Consequently we need to feel satisfied with … the theories of punishment that emphasizes negative mechanisms (death penalty, imprisonment, fine) because we simply don't have other ideas. Everything else is seen as threatening;

[17] Specifically Articles 1, 17 and 20 of the Rome Statute. See Rome Statute of the International Criminal Court, 17 July 1998, available at http://www.icc-cpi.int/NR/rdonlyres/EA9AEFF7-5752-4F84-BE94-0A655EB30E16/0/Rome_Statute_English.pdf, last accessed 28 February 2011.

[18] International Criminal Court Office of the Prosecutor, "Policy Paper on the Interests of Justice", 2007, available at www.icc-cpi.int/NR/rdonlyres/772C95C9-F54D-4321-BF09-73422BB23528/143640/ICCOTPInterestsOfJustice.pdf, last accessed 28 February 2011.

> everything else seems to intend to destroy or abolish the only criminal law that we are able to think of or imagine.[19]

This call for innovative thinking and practice in the criminal law field seems to be the most distinctive feature of the development of criminal law in the coming decades. It's definitely not clear to what extent and how contemporary societies (legal actors, social movements, politicians, social scientists, etc.) will react to innovative ideas in the criminal law field.

Certainly some of the specific issues discussed here are neither present, nor visible, to the same degree in all Western countries. To emphasise widespread theories and ideas does not make up for the necessity of developing local and comparative studies within the criminal law system in specific contexts. Moreover, the focus on the crystallised ideas helps us to avoid explanations for legal phenomena based only on local characteristics of the judicial or political system or on features of the prevailing legal tradition (common law vs. civil law).

According to this approach, when comparative or cross country studies illuminate different forms of concretisation of these ideas, we take these findings as evidence that, even in the presence of these consolidated and widespread ideas, *it is possible to conceive and construct the criminal law system otherwise*.

[19] Alvaro Pires, "Direito Penal e Orientação Punitiva: Um Problema só Externo ao Direito?", in Maria Lúcia Karam, *Globalização, Sistema Penal e Ameaças ao Estado Democrático de Direito*, Lúmen Júris, Rio de Janeiro, 2005, p. 194.

7.8

Alternative Futures of Crime and Prisons

Sohail Inayatullah*

While the rest of the world is undergoing dynamic change – genomics, democratisation in Southwest Asia, digitalisation, the rise of Chindia, the development of alternative energy such as solar – prisons are often considered static. They are hidden away from the eyes of the public unless there is a prison escape or if someone released on parole re-offends. However, prisons and policing are also in the process of radical restructuring. Generally the debate in this restructuring has been between rehabilitation, humanizing the prisons, and punishment, seeking stricter and longer punishment for offenders. But the external changes through the field of genomics, ecological design and through soft technologies such as meditation, yoga and biopsychology are changing prisons as well. Moreover, prisons themselves are being seen as organisations and thus in need of strategic planning, and indeed, some correctional facilities are attempting to become learning organisations, reflecting on their alternative futures and their desired visions. Based on literature regarding prisons and foresight workshops with correctional and police leaders, alternative futures of prisons are explored.

1. Popular Culture and the Futures of Crime and Prisons

What are the futures of crime and prisons? One way to understand the futures of crime and corrections is through popular movies. In the 1976 American movie Logan's Run, for example, living past the age of 30 was in effect a crime. Population and the consumption of resources are maintained at a steady state through policing. Demography is the primary issue. And as we rapidly age throughout the world, criminal activity toward the aging will likely increase and new crime categories, unthinkable today, will be created.

* **Sohail Inayatullah** is a Professor at the Graduate Institute of Futures Studies, Tamkang University, Taiwan; Centre for Policing, Intelligence and Counter Terrorism, Macquarie University, Sydney; and Faculty of Arts and Social Sciences, University of the Sunshine Coast, Sippy Downs.

In the 1982 Blade Runner, the criminals were replicants – biogenetically engineered individuals who performed tasks humans did not desire. They were banned from Earth, and if they secretly returned, they were hunted down and 'retired' (permanently turned off) by 'Blade Runners' (police specialists). Crime was associated with the undesirability of co-existing with a new species (one that, ironically, we created). As the science and technology revolution continues to explode, certainly new crimes associated with out-of-control robots and vicious digital viruses are likely to increase becoming far more serious threats than they are today.[1]

Not only are the dangers riskier but the science and technology revolution is giving new tools to address crime. For example, new forms of lie detection, based not on anxiety, but on brain scanning are likely to enhance the likelihood of apprehending criminals. Already a woman in India was found guilty of murder due to brain scan evidence in 2008.[2] The 2002 movie Minority Report takes this much further when a number of psychics gain the ability to predict crime. Police appear at a crime scene just before the criminal act is actually committed. However, and not surprisingly, mistakes are made. Eventually the program must be abandoned, but not before considerable harm is done. Increasingly, we can expect varied attempts to intervene earlier in the crime cycle. These will likely be in the form of enhanced surveillance technologies: from cameras in the sky to bio-monitoring cameras in the body.

---

[1] James Dator, Hawaii Research Center for Futures Studies, available at http://www.futures.hawaii.edu/, last accessed 1 April 2011; See also Sohail Inayatullah, "Futures Research in the Hawaii Judiciary: An Overview", in *World Future Society Bulletin*, 1983, vol. 17, no. 6; Sohail Inayatullah, "The Rights of Robot: Inclusion, Courts and Unexpected Futures", in *Journal of Futures Studies*, 2001, Vol. 6, no. 2, pp. 93-102.

[2] Steve Silberman, "Don't Even Think about Lying: How Brain Scans are Reinventing the Science of Lie Detection", available at http://www.wired.com/wired/archive/14.01/lying.html, last accessed 1 April 2011; Elizabeth Robinson, "Brain Scan Lie Detection", available at http://www.policyinnovations.org/ideas/briefings/data/000172, last accessed 1 April 2011. While the evidence remains mixed, certainly neuroscience information carries with it the allure of certainty: see Deena Skolnick Weisberg, *et al.*, "The Seductive Allure of Neuroscience Explanations", available at http://www.yale.edu/cogdevlab/aarticles/The%20Seductive%20Allure.pdf, last accessed 1 April 2011.

As climate change continues to disrupt the planet – creating droughts, floods, tidal waves, and typhoons, to begin with – the move toward sustainability will no longer be merely a feel good green option; rather, it will become mandatory and need to be policed. Environmental crime – crimes that make an ecosystem more vulnerable, at national, corporate and personal levels – will grow. As regulation thickens and expands, police and others branches of law enforcement will be called to ensure compliance. Unfortunately, given that policing tends to be reactive – waiting for legislatures and judiciaries at the nation-state jurisdictional level – they are unlikely to have the necessary skill sets to proactively and transparently police new arenas (ageing, environment, cyberspace, global, genomics, to begin with). While crimes keep on changing, the prison has strangely remained stable since the nineteenth century: walls and other barriers, to confine and restrict movement; wardens and guards to monitor and punish, and continued evidence that imprisonment does not reduce future offenses.

2. Futures of Crime

What then are the futures of crime? First we need to challenge how we define crime. Postmodernists, such as philosopher Michel Foucault, suggest we consider crime as a social constructed, historically defined, and not as an *a priori* universal.[3] Laws are invented. For example, thirty years ago in developed parts of the world, forecasts of water scarcity and water crimes were dismissed. However, already today because of water scarcity, watering lawns in many cities is a punishable activity. Will a water mafia develop in the near future? Already in poorer countries, electricity theft is common. Policing energy, however, is challenging as corruption ensures that offenders merely pay a personal fine to the local police officer or electric company. Energy 'thieves' are certainly not yet seen as criminals.

Or imagine a future vegetarian society where those who eat meat are sent to prison. What would our prisons look like then? What would be an appropriate sentence for a meat-eater? What would early intervention be like? Given the link between our diet choices and climate change, is

[3] Michel Foucault, *Discipline and Punish: The Birth of the Prison*, Vintage Books, New York, 1979; Sohail Inayatullah and Jennifer Fitzgerald, "Gene Discourses: Law, Politics, Culture, Future", in *Journal of Technological Forecasting and Social Change*, 1996, vol. 52, no. 2-3, pp. 161-183.

this really a far off scenario?[4] And if the meat industry becomes a criminal activity, how will those who skirt around meat prohibition be treated? And if environmental sustainability (how green are you?) is the emerging future, should the police of 2011 move toward carbon emission neutral police stations, cars? Should prisons become totally green? Should police and correction facilities engage in green audits? Become vegetarian? In what ways should police and prisons be representative of a changing society? As we continue to globalise, what is the appropriate jurisdiction for these types of questions?. While there are certainly some geographical distinctions, as we continue to move toward a fully globalised society (capital, technologies, climate and crime do not respect national boundaries!), can we create laws and policies around policing and prisons that are also shared at planetary levels?

As Foucault suggests, to understand the futures of prisons and the futures of crime we need to understand the nature of society: what is most important? What do we value today? What might we value tomorrow?

3. Rehabilitation

In the USA and most developed nations, the main debate as to the futures of justice is between rehabilitation and punishment. Those on the rehabilitation side believe crimes are generally committed because of social and economic reasons. They also argue that crime and criminality is socially constructed, and thus, not a 'god given' universal context but one that is created through historical practice.

The argument is: born into a poor family, or a single parent family, a person goes to a second-rate public school that labels them underachievers. Overtime, they see themselves as not very worthwhile. Eventually (and especially if there is a nominal increase in wealth) noticing their relative deprivation – that others are driving fancier cars, have more 'perfect' wives and girlfriends, live in beautiful estates – and accompanied by a trigger event, they steal, or commit other crimes.

Imprisoning someone like that merely adds to the problem. In jail, offenders rarely learn new skills, except how to be a more successful criminal. Their peer group consists of other prisoners, with similar stories.

[4] Robin Pagnamenta, "Climate Chief Lord Stern: Give up Meat to Save the Planet", The Times, 27 October 2009, available at http://www.timesonline.co.uk/tol/news/environment/article6891362.ece, last accessed 1 April 2011.

When they are released from prison, they stay within their learned behavior and thus are likely to commit crimes again.[5] For police, it becomes the story of arresting the 'usual suspects'.

If you believe in this perspective (rehabilitation), the reform interventions needed are multifold:

1) Remove class barriers. Ensure that the possibility to move from lower to middle class and even to the upper class is there for all. Society should be based on merit. Equity. Equity. Equity.
2) Help single parent families. By ensuring that children of single-parent families do not fall into the poverty trap, the chances of future crimes are reduced. Funding can come through various programs. Ensuring a nutritious breakfast for children (for body and brain development), housing allowance, unemployment insurance, counseling; indeed, any intervention that helps those outside of the merit system get the benefits that others are getting, and that increases the possibility of them feeling they are part of society is to be encouraged. And, it is crucial that a dependency trap not be created such that there is resentment on both parties – the state providing the benefits and the recipient who now becomes a welfare victim. Social justice should not be confused for psychological entitlement.
3) Promote finer peer groups. As children grow, and develop peer groups, intervention comes through job training, sports camps, and community clubs – again anything to ensure that children do not start on paths of crime, and that they remain integrated in the family and broader community.
4) Create learning and healing communities. Ultimately intervention is about healing communities, reweaving the fabric of friendship, helping peers see that we are all in this together.[6]
5) Rehabilitate through transforming the prison. The rehabilitation model in prisons as well works to ensure that when prisoners are released, they will leave behind previous behavior and start anew. Interventions go from the simple changing diet (research suggests that

[5] New Report Links Crime with Poverty, Honolulu Advertiser, 5 December 1999, A16.

[6] For more on this, see Sohail Inayatullah, "The Learning and Healing Organization", in *Executive Excellence*, 2003-2004, vol. 19, no. 12, p. 20.

diets rich in fruits and vegetables and low in refined sugar reduce prison violence), changing the colors of prison cells, giving prisoners meaningful work, prison gardens (so inmates can connect with nature), and work training.[7]

6) Use alternative sentencing. As much as possible, and where appropriate, keep those who have committed crimes out of prisons. Whether through electronic sentencing and half-way houses or recruiting volunteers to ensure that those sentenced find ways to reconnect, this allows prisoners to psychologically earn their way back into society.[8] European nations, especially, have had success with this approach.

In this model – aspects of what now are called in the social policy profession the 'what works' model – the goal is to ensure the prisoner (and victim, community) is healed, that connections between self, nature, god and community are remade, restored. Once balance is restored, the chances of the prisoner re-offending are diminished. The scientific evidence indicates that this model does work.[9]

---

7 Randall Atlas, "Changes in Prison Facilities as a Function of Correctional Philosophy", in Roger Dunham (ed.), *History of Prisons*, 1991, Chapter 3, available at http://cpted-security.com/atlas/index2.php?option=com_docman&task=doc_view&gid=19&Itemid=35, last accessed 1 April 2011; Andrew Coyle, *The Myth of Prison Work*, Kings College London International Centre for Prison Studies, 2011; Cathrine Sneed, "Seeds of Change: A prison Garden Program", in *Is It Time to Close the Prisons*, YES! Magazine, available at http://www.yesmagazine.org/issues/is-it-time-to-close-the-prisons/seeds-of-change, last accessed 1 April 2011.

8 See research publications at the Willem Pompe Institute for Criminal Law and Criminology, Utrecht University, December 1996. See also Newsletter of the European Society of Criminology, vol. 3, no. 2, available at http://www.esc-eurocrim.org/newsletter/July04ESCnewsletter.pdf, last accessed 1 April 2011.

9 Gene Stephens, "Preventing Crime: The Promising Road Ahead", in *The Futurist*, 1999, vol. 33, no. 9, pp. 29-34; Francis T. Cullen and Paul Gendreau, "From Nothing Works to What Works: Changing Professional Ideology in the twenty-first century", in *The Prison Journal*, 2001, vol. 81, no. 3, pp. 313-338; Jacinthe Allard, Carole Dolan and Pierre Cremer (eds.), *Reflections of a Canadian Prison Warden: The Visionary Legacy of Ron Wiebe: an Unfinished Conversation*, Correctional Service Canada, 2000, available at http://www.csc-scc.gc.ca/text/pblct/ronwiebe/2-eng.shtml, accessed 1 April 2011.

7) Finally, if the offender or the person on the margin is from a non-dominant ethnic background, there are many instances where culturally appropriate dispute resolution is important. Re-integrating back to the community may mean not using the dominant legal system but using restorative justice that is more culturally attuned. While this is not universally applicable, there are cases where culture is crucial in policing and sentencing.

4. Punishment

In contrast, is the punishment model. The argument is that all the rights are given to the offender and to the marginal, and the victim – who may have been raped or maimed – has none. In this approach, the best way to reduce present-day and future crimes is to keep serious offenders in jail. And there is evidence to back this up – twenty-five percent of criminal activity can be reduced by lengthy prison sentences.[10]

Underneath this approach is the view that if we do something wrong, we should be punished. We have sinned, whether against our community, ourselves, or our understanding of God. Merely focusing on rehabilitation sends a signal of weakness to potential criminals. It also frustrates police who tire of repeat offenders. Thus, the most extreme version of this is the death penalty. While most Western nations have eliminated it – seeing it as repugnant murder grievously committed by the State – the US continues this ancient practice, as do most traditional feudal nations (some of which would have an adulterous woman stoned to death, a sentence generally protested by certain other nations, including the US).

The punishment model as well supports (1) the war on drugs, (2) the transformation of the prison system through new surveillance technologies (making it safer for guards, in particular), (3) restorative justice for victims, and (4) privatizing prisons, to make them more efficient and cost-effective.

5. Genomics – A New Variable?

The debate between rehabilitation and punishment is being challenged on a multiple fronts, especially from revolutions in science and technology,

[10] Alfred Blumstein and Joel Wallman (eds.), *The Crime Drop in America*, Cambridge University Press, New York, 2000.

hard and soft. Three are pivotal: genomics, digital technologies and soft technology behavior modification methods such as meditation, yoga and diet.

The genetics revolution, for one, is searching for the roots of crime in our DNA. If certain individuals are more inclined toward committing crimes – as by their risk-taking proclivities – we should intervene to ensure they do not behave in this way in the future. This means mapping our genes and our theories of the factors of crime. Intervention could take the form of gene therapy (healing the damaged gene array) or germline intervention (ensuring the faulty gene is eliminated so that future generations do not inherit that fault).

Thus, the science of genetics joins criminology in a search for genetic solutions to crimes. These solutions can be done at various phases in the 'chain' of crime, even afterwards (in rape cases, judges have sentenced individuals to take castrations drugs).

As mapping the human genome becomes cheaper, from a million dollars to $50,000 per genome to $5,000[11] - and very soon less than a $1000 – every child in wealthy nations at birth will most likely be given a life diagnostic map with the main risks factors identified.[12] While currently the information of genome diagnostic sites is health focused – disease identification probabilities – we can well imagine 'tough-on-crime' parliaments suggesting that police use it to identify those at high-risk for offending, for example, young males who drive and are prone for alcohol abuse.[13]

There is already initial evidence for the aggression or warrior gene.[14] Biosocial criminologist Kevin Beaver of Florida State University's College of Criminology and Criminal Justice argues that young males

[11] Michio Kaku, "Personal Genome Sequencing Technology is Now Faster and Cheaper – And Fits on a Tabletop", Big Think, 2 January 2011, available at http://bigthink.com/ideas/26394, last accessed 1 April 2011.

[12] See Personal Health Monitor: Take Control of Your Health: Features, available at http://www.personalhealthmonitor.net/Features.html, last accessed 1 April 2011.

[13] A Gene for Alcoholism is Discovered, MedicineNet.com, available at http:// www.medicinenet.com/script/main/art.asp?articlekey=26119, last accessed 1 April 2011.

[14] 'Warrior Gene' Predicts Aggressive Behavior After Provocation, *Science Daily*, 23 January 2009, available at http://www.sciencedaily.com/releases/2009/01/090121 093343.htm, last accessed 1 April 2011.

who carry the MAOA gene are more likely to join gangs and engage in violence.[15]

"While gangs typically have been regarded as a sociological phenomenon, our investigation shows that variants of a specific MAOA gene, known as a 'low-activity 3-repeat allele', play a significant role". Previous research has linked low-activity MAOA variants to a wide range of antisocial, even violent, behavior, but our study confirms that these variants can predict gang membership", says Beaver. "Moreover, we found that variants of this gene could distinguish gang members who were markedly more likely to behave violently and use weapons from members who were less likely to do either".[16]

As the genome becomes cheaper to sequence (a map for all) and as the technology becomes more available (an application [an app] for all) not only will genomics be used after the fact (*i.e.*, forensics) but as part of social policy as well, as central to the rehabilitation and punishment debate. If we know that an offender is more likely to have the genetic variation that enhances his likelihood for criminal behavior, is more punishment warranted or does it behoove society to enhance rehabilitation…or is genetic modification the next route?

6. Digitalisation

Digitalisation is important largely to prevent current and future crimes. With increased video surveillance, poorly lit areas can be made safer. Child nabbing is far less likely as surveillance cameras will be able to capture a picture of the abductor. Over time, bio-digital devices linked to global positioning systems (GPS) can be fitted on most humans so that the capacity to prevent crimes is dramatically decreased (and new types of crime invented). Bio-devices are already being used in electronic sentencing. For crimes that do not hurt others – such as many drug crimes – home sentencing is already gaining in use.

Overtime, certain parts of the city could be seen as a digital no-go. A pedophile could have implanted in him a device that warns the local

15 Libby Fairhurst, "Florida State Study Links 'Warrior Gene' to Gang Membership, Weapon Use", *Florida State University News*, available at http://www.fsu.edu/news/2009/06/05/warrior.gene/, last accessed 1 April 2011.

16 Fairhurst, "Florida State Study Links 'Warrior Gene' to Gang Membership, Weapon Use", *Florida State University News*, see *supra* note 15.

prison/police center that he is nearing a primary school. In this sense the new technologies allow us to place the prisoner in limited exile. Instead of being sent far away, his capacity to move is limited. This enhances his chances of being rehabilitated as well his chances of not offending again. Of course, many fear with these 'all seeing eyes' the State could become too powerful, not only intervening in crime, but intervening in private non-criminal behavior. Corruption amongst the police could increase. The balance of individual civil liberties would certainly shift toward the needs of the State.

7. Soft Technologies

As important as hard technologies, such as bio-monitoring devices linked to GPS systems, are soft technologies. India, for example, has found prison violence is reduced and offenders rehabilitate far more effectively if meditation is used as an intervention method. Prisoners find themselves calming down, centering, having increased clarity on their present and futures. Yogic masters and social philosophers like P.R. Sarkar argue that there are four reasons for crime: (1) snap judgment – based on a single emotional event; (2) hormonal reasons – an imbalanced body-mind system; (3) genetic and (4) social and economic structures. For the first and second causes, he recommends yoga, meditation, dietary change – soft sciences. For the third, often prison is best at this stage (but with the goal to rehabilitate), and for the fourth, social and community intervention (economic opportunities, responsibility setting, peer pressure).[17]

The work of Kiran Bedi, former, director general of the Indian Bureau of Police Research and Development, is also worth noting. She has concluded and demonstrated that meditation in prisons reduces violence in prisons and reduces the probability that prisoners will commit further crimes when released.[18] Steven Landau has reported similar success for re-incarceration rates in North Carolina, USA.[19]

[17] Prabhat Rainjan Sarkar, *Prout in a Nutshell*, AMPS, Tiljila, India, 1987, Part 2, pp. 1-23.

[18] See "Vipassana Meditation Courses For Correction Facilities", available at http://www.prison.dhamma.org/, last accessed 1 April 2011; Kiran Bedi, "Vipasana Mediation in Prisons, available at http://www.kiranbedi.com/vipasanainprisons.htm, last accessed 1 April 2011; Mediation Changed Tihar's Face: Kiran Bedi, The Times of India, 5 July 2006, available at

8. Alternative Futures

What of the future? Will prisons remain stable? Even though we may know the drivers of the future – globalisation of law, dramatic revolutions through genomics and digitalisation, climate change and the quest for sustainability, an aging population in the developed world and a youth quake in Southwest Asia and Africa – their trajectory remains uncertain. Many unforeseen variables may impact the actual future that emerges. Indeed, the future is uncertain, created by complex dynamic and adaptive conditions, including the agency of humans desiring to create a better world – thus the need for alternative scenarios of prisons and criminal justice.

8.1. Prisons Forever

This scenario forecasts still more prisons, more overcrowding, more law and order, with only minor and occasional swings to rehabilitation. Generally the focus is on the victim, crime prevention through increased policing and incarceration. Police are expected to mediate less and use more force. Judiciaries are expected to increase the length of sentences. Legislatures are expected to pass tough laws and reduce the flexibility of both police and courts. The end result is possibly increased crime, as offenders are not effectively rehabilitated.

The drivers creating this future are the 'Law and Order' paradigm, the needs of the prison-industrial complex, and media and political rhetoric. Winning political power (at least in the short term) tends to require a peace through strength approach with a promise for more funding for security forces and a tougher stance on offenders.

8.2. Prisons Transformed

In this future, the intention is to achieve better outcomes within prisons (as well as after release) through (a) better prison design (for different types of offenses, better lighting, paint, environmentally sensitive), (b) cognitive and yoga therapy for inmates (c), a concern for the long term health, education and human rights of prisoners, and (d) other positive

---

http://timesofindia.indiatimes.com/NEWS/India/Meditation-changed-Tihars-face-Kiran-Bedi/articleshow/1708208.cms, last accessed 1 April 2011.

[19] See also Yoga Behind Bars: Benefits of our Program, available at http://www.yogabehindbars.com/index.php?pg=benefits, last accessed 1 April 2011.

interventions. Prisons are considered correctional facilities. The goal is to reintegrate, as much as possible, offenders into society. All stakeholders are consulted in this process from citizen groups, the judiciary, the police, nongovernmental organisations and victim groups.

The drivers creating this future include the failure of the current model (overcrowding in prisons, increased violence in prisons and increased cost of prisons), a rapidly aging society, the globalisation of human rights and human rights organisations, and the 'what works' prison policy approach.

8.3. Community Alternatives

A third scenario focuses on community alternatives, including restorative justice and community building. Electronic monitoring and bio-monitoring allow increased mobility and surveillance. Through the use of digital tagging, safe zones are created. Surveillance comes from neighborhood residents and police. As much as possible, community reintegration is practiced. This occurs as the worldview has shifted from punishment to correction. A small percentage of highly violent offenders still end up in prison. But generally, the expectation is that the 'punishment' model of justice is too costly and ultimately ineffective especially in an aging society. The prison ceases to be a physical bound and becomes more and more a digital space.

The drivers here include the impact of pro-rehabilitation criminologists; the rise of East Asian collectivism; the professional ideology of 'what works'; the search for 'community' in a increasingly fragmented world; the need for cost savings; demographic changes, and new technologies. While the 'prisons transformed' scenario changes the nature of prisons, in this scenario, pre-prison and post-prison are where interventions occur.

8.4. Prevention

A fourth scenario ensures societal conditions are changed so that imprisonment is a rarity. Prevention has numerous dimensions, such as keeping families together, counseling for abused adolescents, better policing and digital surveillance (reducing the opportunities of crime), transforming prisons using bioscience intervention by identifying high risk individuals, and creating a more equitable society. Finally, the number of individuals in prison is seen a sign of societal mal-development. Prevention is rigorously measured in policing and in prisons.

The drivers here include a swing away from punishment, evidence-based criminology, a social welfare state, the human genome project, and other scientific breakthroughs in the life sciences.

8.5. Punishment Plus

Along with these four divergent scenarios there are other possibilities such as the integrated 'punishment plus'. In this future, the correctional system has elements of punishment and strong dimensions of rehabilitation. In this system, instead of being swayed by politicians, scientific policy studies inform prison design and correctional policies. Thus, along with the prison, the system focuses on cognitive skills and a rehabilitative behavioral program. It is restorative and yet also preventative. It is punishment focused enough so that the rhetoric of political leaders allows professionals in policing and corrections to 'get on with their job'.

8.6. Prisons and the Justice System as a Learning Organisation

While the previous scenarios are based on external conditions, it is important for organisations to consider futures where they have enhanced agency. One could thus imagine a corrections system or policing or an entire justice system that was smart, adaptive, and learning based, working to not only ensure that crime was prevented but also restoring persons and communities. In this proactive future, the Department of Justice will make use of extensive stakeholder consultation (citizens, all sub-systems, the clients and media) rather than being the recipient of external change to create its desired future. The challenge would be ensure that humane and ethical innovation are central to prisons and policing, instead of tolerating a laggard institution stuck in the medieval and industrial era. Prisons and correctional facilities thus transform into learning organisations instead of being walled-off cities for the least desirable. For this to occur, prisons need to adapt to the changing world, instead of confining those who are unadaptive themselves.

9. Crime and Its Futures Based on Our Views of Justice

Crime and corrections are based on our deeply held, unconscious view of criminality.[20] While science and technology, hard and soft, race ahead, many penal institutions remain lost in time. The ideas that govern them remain based on traditional notions of crime and punishment (sin and hell) and traditional notions of imprisonment (the prison, the cell, the jailor, the watchful eye).

If we wish to transform these places, we need to ask: what is our preferred view of justice and policing, crime and corrections? Which would be the most serious crimes? Which less serious? Would you still have prisons? If so, how would they be designed? What are the appropriate roles of other stakeholders such as police, courts, communities and others in the Department or Ministry of Justice? Seen this way, the futures of crime and corrections are less about forecasting new technologies, climate change, levels of globalisation, demographic shifts, or social movements, and more about asking what type of world we really want to live in and what steps can we take today to help create that world.

[20] Crime and punishment is also based on the type of society. In a warrior dominated society, where issues of loyalty, honor and courage are foremost, punishment can be extreme. In warrior societies, as in Saudi Arabia or Afghanistan, hands are cut off for certain offenses. In modern societies, where bureaucratic rules are foremost, the process of law has become most important. While we can never know for sure if someone committed a crime, we do our best to ensure that the process of justice is fair. Thus, the rights of a possible criminal are read. To those who can't afford an attorney, the State provides a lawyer and a group of peer judges. The reasoning here is that it is far worse to punish an innocent than let the guilty go.

LIST OF CONTRIBUTORS

Marc Amstutz is Professor of Commercial Law, Legal Theory and Sociology of Law at the University of Freiburg. He has studied in Bern, Zurich and Harvard and has taught as a visiting professor in several European Universities. He is a member of the executive board of the German Association for Law and Society *(Vereinigung für Recht und Gesellschaf)* and co-founder of the *Institut für Recht und Wirtschaft* (IDÉ) at the University of Freiburg where he is executive director.
His publications in English include: *In-Between Worlds: Marleasing and the Emergence of Interlegality in Legal Reasoning*, European Law Journal 11 (2005), 766-784; *Civil Society Constitutionalism: The Power of Contract Law*, Indiana Journal of Global Legal Studies 14 (2007) (together with Vaios Karavas); *Global (Non-) Law: The Perspective of Evolutionary Jurisprudence*, German Law Journal 2008, 235-258; *Networks: Legal Issues of Multilateral Co-operation*, Hart Publishing 2008 (ed. together with Gunther Teubner); *The Mutation of Law: On the Genesis and Evolution of Transnational Law*, in: Peer Zumbansen/Gralf Calliess (eds.), Law, Economics and Evolutionary Theory (in print, Edward Elgar 2010) (together with Vaios Karavas); *Globalizing Speenhamland: On the Transnational Metamorphosis of Corporate Social Responsibility*, in: Christian Joerges/Josef Falke (eds.), Karl Polanyi, Globalisation and the Potential of Law in Transnational Markets (in print, Hart 2010).

Norberto Nuno Gomes de Andrade is a scientific officer at the Information Society Unit of the Institute for Prospective Technological Studies (IPTS), Joint Research Centre (JRC) – European Commission. Norberto is also a legal researcher and PhD candidate at the Law Department of the European University Institute (EUI, Italy). He graduated in Law at the Faculty of Law of the University of Lisbon, and he holds a Master of Arts in International Relations and European Studies from Central European University (CEU, Hungary), as well as a Master of Research from the European University Institute. He has previously worked as a legal expert at the External Relations Department of the Portuguese Regulatory Authority for Communications (ANACOM, Portugal). His research interests are focused on law and technology (including biotechnology, neuroscience, artificial intelligence, genetics and genomics, digital environments, ambient intelligence), data protection and privacy law, intellectual property, philosophy of law and legal theory. In 2009 Norberto co-edited and published *Law and Technology: Looking into the Future – Selected Es-*

says. A sample of his scholarly published papers are listed on the Social Science Research Network (SSRN) at: http://ssrn.com/author=715910.

Jean-Bernard Auby is Professor of Public Law and Director of Governance and Public Law Center at Sciences Po since 2006. His teaching fields are administrative law (French and comparative), planning law, local government law, law and globalisation. He has been Dean of the Faculty of Law at the University of Paris XII and professor of law at University Paris II-Assas, from 1994 to 2006. From 1998 up to 2000, he was a visiting professor at Oxford University and Deputy Director of the Institute of European and Comparative Law. He has also been a visiting professor at the University Pompeu Fabra in Barcelona (2006), University of Rome-La Sapienza (2007), the University of Pennsylvania (2009), the Academy of European Public Law in Athens (2009) Bocconi University of Milan (2009) and Zhengfa University of Beijing (2010). Since 1998, he is the Director of the "Juris-Classeur Administratif" (administrative legal encyclopedia) and of the periodical "Droit administratif" ("Juris-Classeur Administratif" monthly joint review). He is also Former President of the French Local Government Law Association. Some of his important publications include;
- *The Public Law/ Private Law Divide; Une entente assez cordiale?* (edited by Mark Freedland and Jean-Bernard Auby), Hart Publishing, 2006
- *Tortious liability of Statutory Bodies. A Comparative and Economic Analysis of Five English Cases* (with B.S. Markesinis, D. Coester-Waltjen & S.F. Deakin), Oxford, Hart Publishing, 1999
-*Values in Global Administrative Law*, (edited by Gordon Anthony, Jean-Bernard Auby, John Morison and Tom Zwart), Hart Publishing, 2011

Larry Catá Backer joined the faculty at the Pennsylvania State University in 2001, where he splits his teaching between the law school and the school of international affairs. He came to Penn State after having served as Professor of Law and Executive Director of the Comparative and International Law Center at the University of Tulsa College of Law. He has lectured in schools in Brazil and Turkey, and taught in the overseas programs of several American Law Schools in Argentina, Belgium, Italy, Ireland, Spain, Slovakia and the United Kingdom. The courses he has taught include: Actors, Institutions, and Legal Frameworks in International Affairs; Elements of Law; Comparative Constitutional Law; Comparative Corporate Law; European Union Law (Constitutional, Legal and Institutional Framework); European Union Law (Substantive Law and International Relations); Commercial Law of the European Union; Constitutional Law Seminar (Personal Autonomy, 14th Amendment, Morality Legislation, and Religion); Comparative Law; Civil Procedure; International Civil Litigation in U.S. Courts; and International Business Transactions. In 2006 he started blogging *Law at the End of the Day*, which consist of short essays and commentaries. He joined with a number of people to form a non-profit organisation, the Consortium for Peace and Ethics (CPE); it is to provide an institutional space for an ideology free, non-partisan and independent investigation, analysis, scrutiny, research, inquiry and examination of peace and ethics. Therefore, it will encourage and support boundary-pushing, multi- and interdisciplinary research that advances an understanding of issues relating to peace and ethics studies. CPE will be serving as an informational clearinghouse and as a forum for the discussion of issues of peace and ethics as they affect individuals, governments, religion, business, and other organisations.

Thorsten Beck is Professor of Economics and Chairman of the European Banking Center. Before joining Tilburg University and the CentER, he worked at the Development Research Group of the World Bank. His research and policy work has focused on two main questions: What is the effect of financial sector development on economic growth and poverty alleviation? What are the determinants of a sound and effective financial sector? Recently, his research has focused on access to financial services by small and medium-sized enterprises and households. He is co-author of *Making Finance Work for Africa* and *Finance for All? Policies and Pitfalls in Expanding Access*. His country experience in both research and policy work includes Bangladesh, Bolivia, Brazil, China, Colombia, Mexico, Peru, Russia and several sub-Saharan African countries.

John Bell is Professor of Law at the University of Cambridge since 2001. He previously has been Professor of Law at the University of Leeds (1989-2001) and Fellow and Tutor in Law at Wadham College, Oxford (1979-1989). He held the position of Chair of the Council of the School of Humanities and Social Sciences from 2005 to 2009. He is the Editor of *Cambridge Law Journal*.

Dr. Gralf-Peter Calliess is Professor for International Commercial Law at the Law Department of the University of Bremen. From 1989 he studied at the University of Göttingen where he graduated in law in 1993. The Academic Year 1993/94 he spent as a researcher in the PhD-program of the Law Department at the European University Institute in Florence. After a two years clerkship at the District Court of Constance he was admitted to the Bar in Frankfurt/Main where he worked as an associate of the law firm Hengeler Mueller. In 1998 he received his PhD in law from the University of Göttingen and worked as a research associate at the Freie Universität Berlin and at the University in Frankfurt/Main, where he earned the Habilitation (second book requirement) in 2005. After visiting professorships at the University of Osaka and the University of Heidelberg he was appointed Professor of European and international Private Law at the LMU Munich in 2006, from where he moved to Bremen in 2007. Professor Calliess is author of the book *Rough Consensus and Running Code. A Theory of Transnational Private Law* (Hart: Oxford 2010, together with Peer Zumbansen) and editor of *Rome Regulations. Commentary on the European Rules of the Conflict of Laws* (Kluwer Law International: Alphen aan den Rijn 2011). He is chair of the German Association for Law and Society (*Vereinigung für Recht und Gesellschaft*).

Hugh Collins is Professor at the London School of Economics (LSE), Department of Law. He joined LSE in 1991 when he was appointed to the chair of English Law. He studied law at Oxford and Harvard. Previously he was a Fellow of Brasenose College, Oxford University. He has also visited and taught in several American law schools including as a Visiting Professor at Boston University and NYU Law School, and has spent extended periods of research at Harvard and the University of Virginia. He serves as General Editor of The Modern Law Review and is co-founder of the European Review of Contract Law and operates as editor of its Articles. He was rapporteur for the Study Group on Social Justice in European Law, and a founder of the Society for European Contract Law (with Profs. Grundmann and Bianca). He participated in invited lectures in recent years at the universities of Helsinki, Rome-Sapienza, Paris Sorbonne, Amsterdam, Genoa, Catania, Harvard, Oxford, Cambridge, and Waseda.

Hans Corell is a former Judge and Ambassador. He served as Under-Secretary-General for Legal Affairs and Legal Counsel of the United Nations from 1994 to 2004. From 1962 to 1972, he served in the Swedish judiciary. In 1972, he joined the Ministry of Justice where he became Director of the Division for Administrative and Constitutional Law in 1979. In 1981, he was appointed Chief Legal Officer of the Ministry. He was Ambassador and Under-Secretary for Legal and Consular Affairs in the Ministry for Foreign Affairs from 1984 to 1994. Since his retirement from public service in 2004 he is engaged in many different activities in the legal field, *inter alia* as legal adviser, lecturer, and member of different boards. Among other, he is involved in the work of the International Bar Association, the International Center for Ethics, Justice and Public Life at Brandeis University and HiiL. He is Chairman of the Board of Trustees of the

Raoul Wallenberg Institute of Human Rights and Humanitarian Law at Lund University, Sweden.

Jan Eijsbouts is Extraordinary Professor Corporate Social Responsibility (CSR) and Professorial Fellow of the Institute of Corporate Law, Governance and Innovation Policies at the Law Faculty of Maastricht University. He is responsible with Prof Sybren de Hoo for the development of and teaching in the core course Corporate Social Responsibility in the International Master programme Globalisation and Law. Jan Eijsbouts studied Dutch Law at Groningen University (master's degree 1969, with optional course Anglo American Law). After having acted as in-house counsel at Royal Philips Electronics (1971-1975) and at Royal DSM (1976-1988) he retired mid 2007 from Akzo Nobel as Group General Counsel and Corporate Director Legal Affairs, a position he had held since 1999. From 2001 till 2008 he was also member of the Dutch Bar. He was Co-Chair of the Corporate counsel Forum (2004-2006) and of the CSR Committee (2007-2008) of the International Bar Association. In 2010 he delivered his pre-advice to the Dutch Association of Jurists NJV on the general civil and corporate law aspects of CSR. As adviser on corporate law and conflict management at the Gaemo Group he contributed to the work of Prof. John Ruggie (Harvard Kennedy School of Government), Special Representative of the UN Secretary General on the subject of business and human rights. Jan Eijsbouts also acted as legal adviser to the Business and Human Rights Initiative of the UN Global Compact Network Netherlands. Jan Eijsbouts is mediator at Nederlands Mediation Instituut (NMI), ACB Foundation and The Centre for Effective Dispute Resolution (CEDR). He is member of the International Advisory Boards of the Mentor Group (Boston, US) and the CEELI Institute (Prague) and Chairman of the Board of the World Legal Forum Foundation (The Hague). He is member of the Public Private Network of HiiL.

Tom Ginsburg is Professor of Law at University of Chicago Law School. He focuses on comparative and international law from an interdisciplinary perspective. He holds BA, JD, and PhD degrees from the University of California at Berkeley. He is the author of several books, including the award-winning *Judicial Review in New Democracies* (2003) and *The Endurance of National Constitutions* (2009). He has served as a visiting professor at the University of Tokyo, Kyushu University, Seoul National University, the Interdisciplinary Center Herzliya, the University of Pennsylvania, and the University of Trento. He currently co-directs the Comparative Constitutions Project, an effort funded by the National Science Foundation to gather and analyse the constitutions of all independent nation-states since 1789. Before entering law teaching, he served as a legal adviser at the Iran-U.S. Claims Tribunal, The Hague, Netherlands, and consulted with numerous international development agencies and foreign governments on legal and constitutional reform.

H. Patrick Glenn is the Peter M. Laing Professor of Law at McGill University and a Member of the International Academy of Comparative Law. Professor Glenn teaches and has research interests in the areas of comparative law, private international law, civil procedure and the legal professions. His book *Legal Traditions of the World* (4th ed., Oxford Univ. Press, 2010) received the Grand Prize of the International Academy of Comparative Law and he has also published *On Common Laws* (Oxford University Press, 2007). He is a former Director of the Institute of Comparative Law, McGill University, and in that capacity worked on projects on the reform of the Russian Civil Code and judicial education in China. He is a member of the Royal Society of Canada and the International Academy of Comparative Law and has been a Bora Laskin National Fellow in Human Rights Law, a Killam Research Fellow, and a Visiting Fellow of All Souls College, Oxford. Professor Glenn is the 2010-11 Henry G. Schermers Fellow of the Hague Institute for the Internationalisation of Law and the Netherlands Institute of Advanced Studies.

Richard J. Goldstone was born on the 26th October 1938. Since 1962 he practised as an Advocate at the Johannesburg Bar. From 1980 he served in various judicial positions, including as a Justice of the Constitutional Court of South Africa, from 1994 to 2003. From 1991 to 1994, he served as Chairperson of the Commission of Inquiry regarding Public Violence and Intimidation that came to be known as the Goldstone Commission. From 15 August 1994 to September 1996 he served as the Chief Prosecutor of the United Nations International Criminal Tribunals for the former Yugoslavia and Rwanda. His international legal career also included appointments to a range of UN committees, most recently as the head of a Fact Finding Mission on possible war crimes and international human rights violations committed by any party in the context of the military action in Gaza in December 2008 and January 2009. Justice Goldstone received numerous awards locally and internationally. Since 2004, he has been teaching law as a visiting professor at Harvard, NYU, Fordham, Georgetown University, Central European University in Budapest and at Yale University. He is the author of *For Humanity: Reflections of a War Crimes Investigator*, (2001) Yale University Press, and the co-author of *International Judicial Institutions: the Architecture of International Justice at Home and Abroad* (2008) Routledge. Justice Goldstone presently chairs several advisory boards and he is a member of the boards of several other NGOs and academic institutions and is a visiting professor at Stanford Law School.

James Gordley came to Tulane Law School in 2007 from Boalt Hall, University of California, Berkeley, where he served on the faculty beginning in 1978. He was a fellow at the Institute of Comparative Law at the University of Florence and an Ezra Ripley Thayer Fellow at Harvard Law School before beginning his teaching career. He is a fellow of the American Academy of Arts and Sciences, a Corresponding Fellow of the British Academy, and a titulary member of the International Academy of Comparative Law. He has been a Guggenheim Fellow, a Fulbright Fellow, a Senior NATO Fellow and a fellow of the Deutscheforschungsgemeinshaft. He has been Jean Monnet Distinguished Professor in Comparative Law at the University of Trent, a visiting professor at the Universities of Fribourg, Regensburg, Munich, Milan, and the Università Commerciale Luigi Bocconi; and a visiting scholar at the Max Planck Institute for Comparative Law in Hamburg, the European University Institute in Fiesole, and the University of Cologne. He was awarded the Felix Frankfurter Award for Distinguished Teaching in 2010, Rutter Award for Teaching Distinction in 2001, and the UC Berkeley Distinguished Teaching Award in 1984. He is the author of several books, including: James Gordley and Arthur von Mehren, *Foundations of Private Law: An Introduction to the Comparative Study of Private Law*, Cambridge University Press, 2006; James Gordley, *The Enforceability of Promises in European Contract Law,* Cambridge University Press 2006; Gratian, Augustine Thompson, James Gordley, *The Treatise on Laws with the Ordinary Gloss*, Catholic University of America Press, 1994; and James Gordley, *The Philosophical Origins of Modern Contract Doctrine*, Oxford University, 1993. Recent publications include: James Gordley, "Ius Quaerens Intellectum: The Method of the Medieval Civilians", in P.J. du Plessis & J.W. Cairns (eds.), *The Creation of the Ius Commune: From Casus to Regula*, Edinburg University Press, 2010; James Gordley, "The Origins of Sale: Some Lessons from the Romans", in *Tulane Law Review*, vol. 84, 2010; James Gordley, "Disturbances among Neighbours in French Law", in J. Gordley (ed.), *The Development of Liability between Neighbours*, Cambridge University Press, 2010; and James Gordley, Louisa Antoniolli, and Francesca Fiorentini "A Case-Based Assessment of the Draft Common Frame of Reference", in *American Journal of Comparative Law*, vol. 58, 2010.

Stefan Grundmann, Prof. Dr. Dr., LL.M., has been Professor at Humboldt-University, Berlin, for German, European and International Private and

Business Law since 2004. He heads the Institute for banking and capital market law. He is currently the deputy of the faculty within the steering committee of the European Law School. From 2001 to 2004 he had been professor for the same subjects in Erlangen, where he also headed the interdisciplinary Institute for European Business Law. From 1995 he held a Professorship at the Martin-Luther-University in Halle-Wittenberg, where he founded the Institute for Business Law.
He studied in Munich, Aix-en-Provence, Lausanne, Lisbon and Berkeley. He specialises in three areas: his book *Fiduciary Duties and Trust relationships* (1997) deals with the central themes in the area of foreign businesses management, including asset management services on a professional level. Civil law and business law are both covered in Bank and Capital Market Law (Financial Law), his second research specialisation. His book *European Bank Supervisory Law* (1990), includes numerous papers and commentaries about half of the Bank Laws for the major Commentary Ebenroth/Boujong/Joost (2001, 2009). European Private Law is also comprehensively covered with his research into organisation and business management. His last specialisation is in the area of European Contract Law (as per the *ZGR* special publication *European Contract Law* (1999, 2nd ed. 2011).
Prof. Grundmann has also organised several conferences for the discussion of key topics and founded the Society of European Contract Law (SECOLA). Since 2005 he is editor-in-chief of the European Review of Contract Law. In 2004 Prof. Grundmann published *European Company Law" including Capital Market Law (2nd ed. 2007)*, of 10 text books in a series on Law in the Common Market, called IUS COMMUNITATIS.
Stefan Grundmann also studied philosophy and the history of art. He has written books on the paintings of Titian (1987), modern and postmodernist architecture (1995) and the architecture of the city of Rome (1997, 2007).

Deborah R. Hensler is the Judge John W. Ford Professor of Dispute Resolution and Associate Dean for Graduate Studies at Stanford Law School. She teaches courses on complex litigation, the legal profession, the use of policy analysis in the law and empirical research methods for socio-legal studies, and leads the law school's doctoral program. Prior to joining the Stanford faculty, Prof. Hensler was Director of the RAND Institute for Civil Justice (ICJ), which she helped found, and a faculty member of the University of Southern California Law School. She received her Ph.D. in Political Science from the Massachusetts Institute of Technology and is a fellow of the American Academy of Political and Social Science and the American Academy of Arts and Sciences.

Prof. Hensler's research focuses on dispute resolution in complex multi-party, multi-forum litigation, typically involving mass harms. She is the lead author of *Class Action Dilemmas: Pursuing Public Goals for Private Gain* (2000), and the co-editor of *The Globalization of Class Actions* (2009). She is currently co-leading, with Christopher Hodges (Oxford University) and Ianika Tzankova (University of Tilburg), an international research collaborative that is conducting comparative research on class and non-class group litigation in a dozen countries in North and South America, Europe, and Asia. She and Tzankova are conducting research on the Netherlands collective settlement procedure, with a grant from the Royal Netherlands Academy of Sciences.

Prof. Hensler has written extensively about asbestos litigation, mass torts, and compensation for personal injury in the U.S. In 2002, she received the Robert McKay Law Professor Award from the Torts and Insurance Practice Section of the American Bar Association.

Aalt Willem Heringa is Professor of Comparative constitutional and administrative law at Maatricht University. He graduated from the Rijksuniversiteit Leiden in 1978, where he worked until 1987 as an assistant professor. He was a visiting researcher at the Centre of European Governmental Studies of the University of Edinburgh (1986) and at the European Research Center of the Harvard Law School (1996). In 1989 he completed his Ph.D. thesis 'Sociale Grondrechten' (Social Rights). He has been working at Maastricht University, the Faculty of Law, since 1987; he was appointed full professor of comparative constitutional and administrative law in 1995. He is an author and editor of numerous books and articles on Dutch Constitutional law, the European Convention of Human Rights, the European Social Charter, comparative constitutional law, US constitutional law and Human Rights. He has served for many years as a Member of the Netherlands Commission on Equal Treatment. He is one of the founding editors of *het NJCM Bulletin* (the Dutch Human Rights Journal); of *EHRC* (European Human Rights Cases) and of *EVRM Rechtspraak & Commentaar* (a loose leaf commentary on the European Convention of Human Rights). He served on the supervisory board of Hiil and on the Supervisory Board of LVO (a major Limburg based school board for secondary education; from 1999 until 2010). He is since 2010, a member of the supervisory board of Orbis Medical Center. Since 2003 he is Dean of the Law Faculty and member of the Mangement Team of Maastricht University. Since 2006 he is president of the Council of Law School Deans and of the Association of Law Faculties. Furthermore, he is a member of the Board of the International Association of Law Schools (IALS), academic director of Maastricht University's Campus Brussels, and a substitute judge in the

District Court of Roermond. He also sits on the Board of the China-EU School of Law (CESL). In the Faculty of Law of Maastricht University he was one of the founders of the LLM program, Magister Iuris Communis (master in comparative, European and international law, which was the predecessor of the present master on International and European Economic Law) and of the original and innovative European Law School LLB and LLM: the only programme to train European lawyers in an English taught program in European law, international law and comparative law. Recently he was a member of groups of experts accrediting law schools in Estonia (2006 and 2008) and assessing the organisation of teaching in Helsinki University (2008). His most recent book is *Constitutions Compared* (Intersentia 2009, second edition), *An Introduction to Comparative Constitutional Law*, with co-author Philipp Kiiver.

Ewoud Hondius (1942) read law in Leiden and New York (Columbia University). From 1966-1980 he was Assistant Professor and later Professor of Civil Law at Leiden University. From 1980 until the present he has held a similar position at the University of Utrecht. He has published books and law review articles on European private law, consumer law and the law of obligations. He is the co-editor in chief of the trilingual *European Review of Private Law* and served as editor in chief of the *Nederlands Tijdschrift voor Burgerlijk Recht* for some twenty years. He is a member of the Royal Netherlands Academy of Sciences and a justice surrogate in the Court of Appeal in Amsterdam. He was a Visiting Professor in Baton Rouge (Louisiana State University), Cambridge (Trinity College), Gent, Hamburg (Bucerius), Kyoto (Ritsumeikan), London (Queen Mary), Münster, Paris I, Stellenbosch and Sydney. He is a member of the Programmatic Steering Board van het Hague Institute for the Internationalisation of Law and vice-president of the national committee on scientific ethics. In 2003 he was awarded an honorary doctorate by the Catholic University of Leuven.

Peter J. Hustinx (1945) has been European Data Protection Supervisor since January 2004. He was appointed by a joint decision of the European Parliament and of the Council of 22 December 2003, and reappointed on 14 January 2009 for a second term of five years. The European Data Protection Supervisor is entrusted with monitoring and applying the provisions of Regulation (EC) No. 45/2001 to the processing of personal data carried out by the EU institutions and bodies. He is also responsible for advising those institutions and bodies on all matters concerning the processing of personal data, and has a duty to cooperate with national supervisory authorities and supervisory bodies established under the former "third pillar" of the European Union.

Mr. Hustinx has been closely involved in the development of data protection legislation from the start, both at the national and at the international level. Before entering his office, he was President of the Dutch Data Protection Authority for a period of more than twelve years. He received law degrees at the University of Nijmegen, the Netherlands (LLM 1970), and at the University of Michigan Law School in Ann Arbor, U.S.A. (MCL 1971).

In 1971 he joined the Dutch Ministry of Justice and worked in the field of constitutional and criminal law and in the preparation of legislation. As a member of the Committee of Experts on Data Protection of the Council of Europe he took part in the preparation of the 1981 Convention on Data Protection and of several recommendations in this field. From 1985 until 1988 he was Chairman of this committee. In 1991 he was appointed and in 1997 reappointed as President of the Dutch Data Protection Authority (*Registratiekamer*). In September 2001 he continued as President of the Data Protection Authority (*CBP*) established by the new Data Protection Act which entered into force then. In 2003 he was reappointed for a third term of six years. In 1994 he was Chairman of the International Conference of Data Protection Commissioners. From 1996 until 2000 he was Chairman of the Article 29 Working Party (established under Directive 95/46/EC). From 1998 until 2001 he was Chairman of the Appeals Committee of the Joint Supervisory Board of Europol (established under Article 24 of the Europol Convention). From 2002 until 2009 he was Chairman of the Commission for the Control of Interpol's Files. Since 1986 he has also been deputy judge in the Court of Appeal in Amsterdam.

Professor Sohail Inayatullah is a political scientist/futurist at the Graduate Institute of Futures Studies, Tamkang University, Taiwan; the Centre of Policing, Intelligence and Counter Terrorism, Macquarie University, Sydney; and the Faculty of Arts and Social Sciences, the University of the Sunshine Coast, Sippy Downs. He also co-teaches an annual course titled, "Futures thinking and strategy development" at Mt Eliza Executive Education, Melbourne Business School. In 1999 he held the Unesco Chair at the University of Trier, Germany and the David Sutton Fellowship with the International Management Centres. He is one the 2010 Laurel award winner for all time best futurists as voted by the Foresight network. In 2011, he received an honorary doctorate from Universiti Sains Malaysia in Penang.

In the past year, he has addressed or conducted many foresight workshops for different organsations in many countries. Professor Inayatullah has authored/edited thirty books (with titles such as Questioning the Future; the University in Transformation; Macrohistory and Macrohistorians; Alternative Educational Futures), journal special issues and cdroms and over 350 journal articles and book chapters as well contributed to the Oxford Encyclopedia of Peace, the Routledge Encyclopedia of Philosophy, The Macmillan Encyclopedia of the Future and the Unesco Encyclopedia of Life Support Systems.

Sébastien Jodoin is a lawyer, expert, and advocate specialising in international law, human rights, environment, sustainable development, trade, climate change, and international criminal justice. He is the Director of the One Justice Project, a Lead Counsel at the Centre for International Sustainable Development Law and holds Fellowships at the Canadian Centre for International Justice and the McGill Centre for Human Rights and Legal Pluralism. He has lectured widely in universities and conferences in Europe, Asia, Africa, and North America, has published in leading academic journals and has been interviewed by a number of media outlets in Canada and Africa. He has worked at Amnesty International Canada, the United Nations, and the McGill International Criminal Law Clinic. He holds degrees in law, international law, and international relations from McGill University, the London School of Economics, and the University of Cambridge. He is best known for his research on the links between human rights and climate change and his work advocating for the recognition of a new international crime: crimes against present and future generations.

J.M. (Matthijs) de Jongh (1974) is working as a law clerk at the Supreme Court of the Netherlands since 2005. From 1999 through 2005, he practised as a corporate lawyer in Amsterdam. Since 2007, he is writing a PhD on the history of shareholder control rights in listed companies. Together with Vino Timmerman and Alexander Schild, he presented a paper on a community interest company in the Netherlands at the 2010 annual meeting of the Dutch Lawyers Association. The Dutch Lawyers Association endorsed their plea for a separate legal entity for social enterprises.

Philipp Kiiver is Associate Professor of European and Comparative Constitutional Law at Maastricht University. He obtained his law degree (2003) and his PhD (2005) from Maastricht. He is a fellow at the Montesquieu Institute Maastricht and a member of the editorial committee of the Maastricht Journal of European and Comparative Law. From 2008 to 2010 he served as Associate Dean of the Maastricht Law Faculty. He is the co-author of an introduction to comparative constitutional law (*Constitutions Compared*, Intersentia, 2nd edition 2009) and he gives lectures and co-supervises PhD theses in that field of expertise. In 2008 he was awarded a Veni grant from the Netherlands Organisation for Scientific Research

(NWO) to carry out a three-year research project into different forms of parliamentary accountability. His research interests include EU institutional law and comparative constitutional law, in particular parliamentary studies.

Benedict Kingsbury is Murry and Ida Becker Professor of Law and Director of the Institute for International Law and Justice at New York University School of Law (iilj.org). With Richard Stewart, Kingsbury initiated and directs the IILJ's Global Administrative Law Research Project, a pioneering approach to issues of accountability, transparency, participation and review in global governance, focused especially on developing countries. His recent co-edited volumes in that project include *Climate Finance: Regulatory and Funding Strategies for Climate Change and Global Development* (NYU Press, 2009); and *El nuevo derecho administrativo global en América Latina* (Buenos Aires: Rap, 2009). With Kevin Davis and Sally Merry, Kingsbury leads an IILJ project on Indicators as a Technology of Global Governance, including a forthcoming book on *Governance by Indicators: Global Power Through Quantification and Rankings*. Kingsbury works also on the history and theory of international law, and co-edited (with Benjamin Straumann) *The Roman Foundations of the Law of Nations: Alberico Gentili and the Justice of Empire* (OUP, 2010), and a Latin-English critical edition of Alberico Gentili's *The Wars of the Romans (1599)* (OUP, 2011). He has been a visiting professor at Harvard Law School, the University of Tokyo Law Faculty, the University of Padua, and the University of Paris-I (Pantheon-Sorbonne).

Jan Klabbers was educated in international law and political science at the University of Amsterdam, and obtained a doctorate from the same university in 1996 (with distinction). Since 1996, he has been teaching at Helsinki University, most recently as professor of international law. He also directs the Academy of Finland Centre of Excellence in Global Governance Research. Main publications include *The Concept of Treaty in International Law* (The Hague: Kluwer, 1996) and *An Introduction to International Institutional Law* (Cambridge University Press, 2002, second edition 2009). His monograph is titled *Treaty Conflict and the European Union* (Cambridge University Press, 2009). He has held visiting professorships at Hofstra Law School (2007) and at the Graduate Institute of International Studies and Development (2008).

André Klip is Professor of criminal law, criminal procedure and international criminal law at Maastricht University since 2001. He is the author of *European Criminal Law*, the first book using an integrative approach on criminal law in the European Union, published by Intersentia Publishers Antwerp 2009. Professor Klip is Member of the Board of Directors of the International Association of Penal Law. He has been a part-time judge at the 's-Hertogenbosch Court of Appeal (criminal division). Member of the Standing Committee of Experts on International Immigration, Refugee and Criminal Law, member of the Editorial Board of the Netherlands Journal on Criminal Law (Delikt en Delinkwent) co-editor of the Commentary on Dutch law on International Co-operation in Criminal Matters. He is founder and co-editor of the series *Annotated Leading Cases of International Criminal Tribunals* of which 26 volumes appeared since 1999. The series Annotated Leading Cases of International Criminal Tribunals covers decisions of the ICTY, the ICTR, the Special Court for Sierra Leone, the ICC and the East Timor Special Panels. He has published a number of other books, including European Cooperation between Tax, Customs and Judicial Authorities (2002); Investigation into war crimes/ Opsporing van oorlogsmisdrijven (2002), Criminal Law in the European Union (2005), European Integration and Law (2006), An additional Evaluation Mechanism in the field of EU Judicial Cooperation (2009), as well as many articles on criminal law, European criminal law, international cooperation, war crimes, human rights and comparative law.

David Koepsell is an author, philosopher, and attorney whose recent research focuses on the nexus of science, technology, ethics and public policy. He obtained his PhD in Philosophy as well as his law degree from the University of Buffalo. He has authored numerous articles as well as authored and edited several books, including *Searle on the Institutions of Social Reality*, co-edited with Laurence Moss, (Oxford UK: Blackwell 2003), *Reboot World*, (New York: Writer's Club Press 2003) (fiction), and *The Ontology of Cyberspace*: *Law, Philosophy, and the Future of Intellectual Property*. He has lectured worldwide on issues ranging from civil rights, philosophy, science, ontology, intellectual property theory, society, and religion. Koepsell has practiced law, worked for Bowstreet, Inc. as an ontologist in Portsmouth, New Hampshire, and taught at SUNY Buffalo. He was appointed Assistant Professor of Philosophy at TU Delft in 2008. He is an associate editor of *Free Inquiry* magazine. He is the co-founder, with Edward Summer, of Carefully Considered Productions, an educational media not-for-profit corporation.

Tineke Lambooy, PhD LLM, advises HiiL as theme coordinator on the HiiL theme 'Private Actors' and their influence on the development of law. Lambooy is associate professor at the Law School of Utrecht University, the Netherlands. Since 2007, she lectures on Legal Aspects of Globalisa-

tion I – Corporate Social Responsibility (CSR) and Mergers & Acquisitions (Corporate Law), which courses are part of the LLM programme International Business Law and Globalisation.
Lambooy is also a senior researcher in the field of CSR at the Centre for Sustainability of Nyenrode Business University, the Netherlands, where she conducts research on the implementation of CSR and on Business and Biodiversity.
Her career started with practising commercial and corporate law in a Netherlands-based international law firm, Loyens & Loeff, Attorneys, Tax Lawyers and Civil Law Notaries in Amsterdam, the Netherlands. She specialised in international transactions (privatisations, mergers and acquisitions) and in due diligence research.
Lambooy obtained a PhD on a study *'Corporate Social Responsibility. Legal and semi-legal frameworks supporting CSR'* (Kluwer: Deventer, The Netherlands, 2010). She also publishes articles on various subjects including corporate law, corporate governance, CSR, public reporting, private regulation, business and human rights, and business and biodiversity.
In 2008, together with Ruud Lubbers and Willem van Genugten, she published the book *Inspiration for Global Governance - The Universal Declaration of Human Rights and the Earth Charter* (Kluwer: Deventer, 2008). This book has been translated into Italian, Spanish and Chinese.

Pierre Larouche is Professor of Competition Law at Tilburg University and Co-Director of the Tilburg Law and Economics Center (TILEC), as well as Professor at the College of Europe (Bruges). Before starting his academic career in 1996 at the University of Maastricht, he clerked at the Supreme Court of Canada in 1991-1992 and practised law for three years in the EU law unit of Stibbe Simont Monahan Duhot in Brussels. His teaching and research interests include competition law, telecommunications law, media law, basic community law and the common European law of torts. He received a number of research grants from Dutch and European funding organisations as well as from private sources. He has been a guest professor at McGill University (2002) and National University of Singapore (2004, 2006, 2008, 2011) and a Searle fellow at Chicago's Northwestern University (2009-10). Professor Pierre Larouche is the author of more than fifty scientific papers published in reputable law journals.

Hans Lindahl is Professor of philosophy at Tilburg University. His research and teaching focus is on legal and political philosophy, with a special emphasis on issues pertaining to political representation, sovereignty and (collective) identity, in particular in the context of the EU legal order. A subtheme within this general line of research is the structuring of politico-legal space and time from the first-person plural perspective of a 'we'. In dealing with these issues he draws on both phenomenology and analytical philosophy. Hans Lindahl obtained his law degree with a minor in economics at Universidad Javeriana (Bogotá, Colombia), 1981; M. Phil. in Philosophy, Universidad Javeriana, 1988; and his Ph.D in Philosophy, at Higher Institute of Philosophy of the Catholic University of Louvain (Leuven, Belgium), 1994. He has operated as lecturer in law at the Universidad de los Andes, Bogotá (1987-1988). He has been a legal practitioner in Colombia (1982-1988). In 1994 he was a post-doc researcher in philosophy at Tilburg University and later became associate professor of philosophy at Tilburg University. He now holds the chair of legal philosophy at Tilburg.

Yan Ling is Professor at China University of Political Science and Law. She operates as Director at the Research Center for International Criminal Law and International Humanitarian Law and as Deputy Director at Research Center for Air and Space Law of the University. She is also editor-in-chief of the Chinese Yearbook of International Law. In the past, she has been active as a visiting professional at International Criminal Court (2009). She has been working as a legal officer at the International Criminal Tribunal for Rwanda (ICTR) from 1998 until 2004. Furthermore, she has been a visiting scholar at the International Institute of air and space law at Leiden University for a year (1990-1991). She studied international law and organisations from 1991 until 1992 at the Institute of Social Studies in The Hague, Netherlands and at China University of Political Science and Law she studied international law. She has published numerous articles and several books including *The Theory and Practice of the International Criminal Tribunal for Rwanda*; *Making Peace through Justice; International Criminal Law*; *New Legal Issues of Space Law*; *A Commentary on the Rome Statute*; *Cases on International Law*; *The Hague Trial - International Criminal Tribunal for the Former Yugoslavia* and *International Law etc.*

Maíra Rocha Machado joined São Paulo Law School of Fundação Getulio Vargas (DIREITO GV) as Professor of Law in 2004. She was formerly a full time researcher at the same institution. She teaches courses on Criminal Law, Criminology and Sociology of Law, as well as seminars on the interaction among criminal, administrative and international law. She graduated in Law from the University of São Paulo (1997) and obtained her Ph.D. in Philosophy and Theory of Law at the University of São Paulo (2003). Her current research focuses on sentencing and theoretical aspects of punishment, economic crimes and corruption and transnational organisations. She has recently completed a post-doctorate program at Ottawa University, where she researched minimum punishment as a form of political intervention at the judicial sentence. She is the author of *The Internationalization of Criminal Law* (2004) and co-editor of *Money Laundering and Asset Recovery: Brazil, Nigeria, the United Kingdom and Switzerland* (2006), *New Directions in the Governance of Justice and Security* (2006) (all in Portuguese) and *La rationalité pénale moderne : réflexions conceptuelles et explorations empiriques* (2011, forthcoming).

Ralf Michaels, a professor of law at Duke Law, is an expert in comparative law and conflict of laws. His current research focuses mainly on three issues: the role of domestic courts in globalisation, the potential of conflict of laws as a theory of global legal fragmentation, and the status and relevance of non-state law. He is the editor or co-editor of two special volumes of the *American Journal of Comparative Law* (Beyond the State? Rethinking Private Law, 2008, also published as a book with Mohr Siebeck; and Legal Origins, 2009), as well as a book and a journal issue on conflict of laws (*Conflict of Laws in a Globalized World*, Cambridge Univ. Press, 2007; and "Transdisciplinary Conflicts", in *Law and Contemporary Problems*, 2008. In addition, he has authored numerous articles and lectured widely on all three topics. Michaels studied law at the Universities of Passau and Cambridge, UK. While at Duke, he has been a visiting professor at the Universities of Panthéon/Assas (Paris 2), Princeton, Pennsylvania, and Toronto; he has also held senior research fellowships at Harvard and Princeton, as well as the American Academy in Berlin and the Max Planck Institute for Private Law in Hamburg.

David Nelken is professor at Cardiff Law School. He received a PhD in Criminology from the Cambridge Institute of Criminology and then taught in the law departments at Edinburgh 1976-1984 (where he was also a panel member of the Scottish juvenile justice Childrens' Hearings system) and University College London 1984-1990. In 1990 he moved to Italy where he is Distinguished Professor of Sociology at the University of Macerata (and was also involved in crime policy committees). He maintains a strong connection with the UK as Distinguished Professor of Law at Cardiff Law School and Honorary Professor of law at the London School of Economics (LSE). He has been a visiting professor in a number of different countries, including teaching courses on comparative criminal justice at Berkeley, NYU and Sydney. Most recently, in 2008, he was appointed 'Wiarda' visiting professor at The Willem Pompe Institute at Utrecht University, and in 2009 was elected the S.T. Lee Professorial fellow at London University's Institute of Advanced Studies. David is an academician of the UK Academy of Social Sciences, and was a recipient of an American Sociological Association distinguished scholar award in 1985 and the American Criminology Society's Sellin-Glueck award in 2009. Widely published, David's criminological work mainly focuses on white collar crime and comparative criminal justice (overlapping with sociology of law and comparative law).

Janne Nijman is an associate professor of public international law at the Department of European and International Law and a senior research fellow of the Amsterdam Center for International Law (ACIL). She participates in The International Rule of Law research program. She is one of two Deans for PhD students of the Law School. Currently, Janne Nijman is a member on the ILA International Committee on Non-State Actors. She is an editor on the board of the Netherlands Yearbook of International Law as well as editor on the board of the Grotiana Journal. Nijman is a member of the executive board of Oikos, a NGO focused on fair and sustainable globalisation, and Research advisor on Global Justice to The Broker, a bimonthly magazine that aims to 'bridge the gap' between academics and development policy makers. She is also on the board of the Nederlandse Vereniging voor Internationaal Recht (NVIR, the Dutch branch of the International Law Association). She acts as a guest lecturer at the Netherlands Institute of International Relations "Clingendael" and at the Institute of Interdisciplinary Studies (UvA).
Previously, she has been a post-doc researcher in the ACIL-based NWO Pioneer Project "The Divide and Interaction between National law and International Law". Janne Nijman has been a Global Research Fellow of New York University School of Law (2003-04), affiliated to the History and Theory of International Law Program of the Institute for International Law and Justice, and a Visiting Fellow at Queen Mary College School of Law, University of London (summer 2006). Nijman is founder and director of N.I.L.O. (www.nilaw.eu).

André Nollkaemper is Professor of Public International Law and Vice-Dean for Research at the Faculty of Law at the University of Amsterdam, and Academic Director at the Amsterdam Center for International Law (ACIL). He is also Member of the Advisory Committee for Public International Law of the Government of the Netherlands; and of-counsel for international law with Böhler, an Amsterdam-based law-firm specialising in transnational and international litigation. He has given legal advice on cases before the European Court of Human Rights, the Special Court for Sierra Leone, the International Criminal Tribunal for the Former Yugoslavia, the Extraordinary Chamber for the Courts of Cambodia and courts of the Netherlands. He is Editor-in-Chief of International Law in Domestic Courts and author of many publications on the relationship between international law and national law (including National Courts and the International Rule of Law, OUP, forthcoming 2011) and international responsibility. In 2010, he received a 5-year Advanced Investigator Grant by the European Research Council (ESR) for a project on Shared Responsibility in International Law. He is member of the Board of ESIL. He co-directs the research project; The Internationalisation of the Rule of Law of the Hague Institute for the Internationalisation of Law (HiiL).

Mark Osiel's writings have inspired several conferences and are assigned at many leading universities in North America and Europe, in a number of fields. His scholarship seeks to show how legal responses to mass atrocity can be improved by better understanding its organisational dynamics, revealed through comparison of historical and contemporary cases. This research also explores the relation of empirical social explanation to liberal normative judgment of leaders, followers, and bystanders. Osiel's six volumes include *Mass Atrocity, Collective Memory and the Law* (1997), *Obeying Orders: Atrocity, Military Discipline, and the Law of War* (1999), *Mass Atrocity, Ordinary Evil, and Hannah Arendt: Criminal Consciousness in Argentina's Dirty War* (Yale Univ. Press, 2002), *Making Sense of Mass Atrocity* (Cambridge Univ. Press, 2009), *The End of Reciprocity: Terror, Torture and the Law of War* (Cambridge Univ. Press, 2009); and *After Atrocity: New Approaches to the Restraint and Redress of Mass Killing* (Cambridge Univ. Press, forthcoming).

Efthimios Parasidis is Assistant Professor of Law at the Center for Health Law Studies, Saint Louis University School of Law. His scholarship explores topics at the crossroads of health law and intellectual property, with a focus on emerging issues in biotechnology law and policy. He is a member of the Law and Policy Workgroup of the Missouri Health Information Organization, the entity responsible for creating Missouri's health information exchange. He was recently selected as a Health Law Scholar by the American Society of Law, Medicine and Ethics, and is a consultant to the American College of Physicians. As a Fulbright Fellow, Prof. Parasidis researched legal and ethical issues related to medical informed consent policies and practices in Greece. In addition to his scholarly work, he served as an Assistant Attorney General for the State of New York, under Eliot Spitzer and Andrew M. Cuomo, where he was lead counsel for more than 300 cases in state and federal courts at both the trial and appellate levels. He worked as an associate in the Litigation group of Jones Day and the Intellectual Property group of Dickstein Shapiro. At these law firms, he focused his practice on intellectual property counseling and litigation, as well as mass tort and commercial litigation. He has counseled biotechnology companies on corporate and intellectual property matters, is a co-founder of a biotechnology start-up company, and is a co-inventor on a patent application related to health information technology and comparative effectiveness research.

Joost Pauwelyn is Professor of International Law at the Graduate Institute of International and Development Studies (IHEID) in Geneva, Switzerland and Co-Director of the Institute's Centre for Trade and Economic Integration (CTEI). He is also Senior Advisor with the law firm of King & Spalding LLC. His area of expertise is international economic law, in particular, the law of international trade and investment. Before joining the Graduate Institute in 2007, Pauwelyn was a tenured professor at Duke Law School, USA. He also served as legal officer at the World Trade Organization from 1996 to 2002 and practiced law at a major Brussels law firm. Pauwelyn received degrees from the Universities of Namur and Leuven, Belgium as well as Oxford University and holds a doctorate from the University of Neuchâtel. He is the author of, amongst other works, *International Trade Law* (2009, with A. Guzman), *Conflict of Norms in Public International Law* (2003, winner of the Guggenheim Prize), *The Transformation of World Trade* (Michigan Law Review, 2005) and *Optimal Protection of International Law: Navigating between European Absolutism and American Voluntarism* (2008).

Randall Peerenboom is a law professor at La Trobe University and an associate fellow of the Oxford University Center for Socio-Legal Studies. He was a professor at UCLA Law School from 1998 to 2007 and director of the Oxford Foundation for Law, Justice and Society Rule of Law in China Programme. He has been a consultant to the Asian Development Bank, Ford Foundation, EU-China, UNDP and other international organisations on legal reforms and rule of law in China and Asia, and is the Co-Editor in Chief of *The Hague Journal of Rule of Law*. He is also a CIETAC arbitrator, and frequently serves as expert witness on PRC legal issues. His recent sole-authored and edited books include *Judicial Independence in China* (2010); *Regulation in Asia* (2009); *China Modernizes: Threat to the West or Model for the Rest?* (2007); *Human Rights in Asia* (2006); *Asian Discourses of Rule of Law* (2004); and *China's Long March toward Rule of Law* (2002).

Thomas Pogge is currently Leitner Professor of Philosophy and International Affairs at Yale University. He is also Professorial Fellow at the ANU Centre for Applied Philosophy and Public Ethics and Research Director at the Centre for Study of Mind in Nature, University of Oslo. He received his Ph.D. from Harvard University. He is a prolific writer and lecturer, who has written extensively on moral and political philosophy, including books on cosmopolitanism, global justice and extreme poverty. His book *World Poverty and Human Rights* is regarded as one of the leading works on global justice. Pogge also heads a team that is working towards developing a complement to the pharmaceutical patent regime that would improve access to advanced medicines for the poor worldwide. His work on global justice and eradication of world poverty is marked by an emphasis on negative duties. He has argued that the massive persistence of severe poverty reflects not merely a breach by the global rich of their positive duty to assist people in great need but also a violation of their negative duty not to contribute to the imposition of a global institutional order that foreseeably and avoidably renders the basic socioeconomic human rights of millions unfulfilled.

Jo Ritzen is Professor at the Maastricht School of Governance/MERIT/UNU. He retired in February 2011 from the Presidency of Maastricht University. During his 8 year tenure Maastricht University became one of the most international research universities worldwide (almost 50% students from abroad) renowned for its problem based learning approach in all degree courses. Before assuming the Presidency of Maastricht University Mr. Ritzen was Vice President of the World Bank's Development Economics Department. He assumed this position in August 1999. In July 2001 he assumed the position Vice President of the World Bank's Human Development Network, which advises the institution and its client countries on innovative approaches to improving health, education and social protection. Mr. Ritzen joined the Bank as Special Adviser to the Human Development Network in September 1998. Prior to coming to the Bank, he was Minister of Education, Culture, and Science of The Netherlands, one of the longest-serving Ministers of Education in the world. During his term, he enacted a series of major reforms throughout the Dutch education system. Mr. Ritzen has also made significant contributions to agencies such as UNESCO and OECD, especially in the field of education and social cohesion. Prior to his appointment as Minister in 1989, Mr. Ritzen held academic appointments with Nijmegen University and Erasmus University in The Netherlands, and the University of California-Berkeley and the Robert M. LaFollette Institute of Public Affairs at the University of Wisconsin-Madison in the United States. Mr. Ritzen obtained a master's degree in physical engineering in 1970 from the University of Technology in Delft, and a PhD in economics in 1977 from Erasmus University in Rotterdam. His dissertation on education, economic growth, and income distribution earned him the Winkler Prins prize.

Michel Rosenfeld is Justice Sydney L. Robins Professor of Human Rights and Director for the Programme on Global and Comparative Constitutional Theory at Benjamin N. Cardozo School of Law, Yeshiva University, New York. He has been teaching there since 1988. His specialties are: constitutional law, comparative constitutional law and jurisprudence. Professor Rosenfeld has lectured widely in the United States, and internationally. He is the author of several books, including *Affirmative Action and Justice: A Philosophical and Constitutional Inquiry*, which in 1992 was named outstanding book on the subject of human rights in the US by the Gustave Meyers Center, *Just Interpretations: Law Between Ethics and Politics* (1998),*Comparative Constitutionalism: Cases and Materials* (with Baer, Dorsen, and Sajo.) (2d ed., 2010), and *The Identity of the Constitutional Subject: Selfhood, Citizenship, Culture and Community* (2010 0. He is the co-editor of *the Oxford Handbook of Comparative Constitutional Law* (2012 (forthcoming) ,*The Longest Night: Perspectives and Polemics on Election 2000*; *Hegel and Legal Theory*; *Habermas on Law and Democracy: Critical Exchanges, Deconstruction and the Possibility of Justice*; and editor of *Constitutionalism, Identity, Difference and Legitimacy: Theoretical Perspectives*. Professor Rosenfeld is an affiliated member of the graduate faculty of the New School University. He is a founding member and president of the United States Association of Constitutional Law (since 2004), editor-in-chief of the International Journal of Constitutional Law (I•CON), and was president of the International Association of Constitutional Law (1999-2004). Among his many honors, he received the French government's highest and most prestigious award, the Legion of Honor. In 2007, Professor Rosenfeld was appointed to an International Blaise Pascal Research Chair.

Alexander J.P. Schild (1972) is working as a law clerk at the Supreme Court of the Netherlands since 2005. Before that, he practised law in Amsterdam and The Hague. Since 2008, he is writing a PhD on the impact of fundamental righs on Dutch company law. Together with Vino Timmerman and Matthijs de Jongh, he presented a paper on a community interest company in the Netherlands at the 2010 annual meeting of the Dutch Lawyers Association. The Dutch Lawyers Association endorsed their plea for a separate legal entity for social enterprises.

Dr. Ruth Sefton-Green, literae humaniores M.A. Oxon, is qualified as a solicitor in England and an avocat in France. She is now a Maître de conférences of comparative private law at the Ecole de droit de la Sorbonne (Université Paris 1 - Panthéon-Sorbonne) where she obtained her doctorate (PhD, 1997) and attached to the comparative law research centre UMR de droit comparé de Paris. She teaches mainly the comparative law of obligations and introduction courses to another legal system involving comparative law methodology. Her thesis La notion d'obligation fondamentale: comparaison franco-anglaise (LGDJ, 2000) was awarded the Lévy-Ullmann prize for comparative law. She has given conferences at several universities in Europe, as well as participating in many international colloquia in Europe, U.S.A and Canada. Her extensive publications include, as editor, a book in the Common Core of European Private Law series, "Mistake, Fraud and Duties to Inform in European Contract Law (Cambridge University Press, 2005) republished in paperback (Cambridge University Press, 2008). She has participated as a reporter in other Common Core of European Private Law volumes and is an active member of the Study Group for Social Justice in European Private Law. She has also published numerous articles, singly and collectively, in French and English law books and periodicals on themes and issues relating to the comparative law of obligations, European contract law and comparative law in general.

Göran Sluiter is Professor of International Criminal Law, in particular the Law of International Criminal Procedure at the University of Amsterdam and lawyer at Bohler Advocaten (Amsterdam). As an ad-litem judge, Sluiter sat on the Van Anraat case, the first genocide case in the Netherlands. Previously, he worked as a Senior Lecturer in Criminal Law at the University of Amsterdam and a Lecturer in International Law at Utrecht University. He is the co-founder and co-editor (with Prof. André Klip) of the series *Annotated Leading Cases of International Criminal Tribunals*, the co-editor (with C. Stahn) of *The Emerging Practice of the International Criminal Court* (Brill, forthcoming 2008) and the co-editor (with S. Vasiliev) of *International Criminal Procedure: Towards a Coherent Body of Law* (CMP, 2009). He is also the author of *International Criminal Adjudication and the Collection of Evidence: Obligations of States* (Intersentia, 2003), the co-author (with Alexander Zahar) of *International Criminal Law: A Critical Introduction* (Oxford University Press, 2008). He has published an extensive number of articles in journals, including the *Journal of International Criminal Justice* and *International Criminal Law Review*.

Jan M. Smits holds the Chair of European Private Law at Maastricht University and is the academic director of the Maastricht European Private Law Institute (*M*-EPLI). He is also research professor of Comparative Legal Studies in the University of Helsinki. After his study of law at the universities of Leiden and Poitiers (1986-1991), Jan Smits defended his PhD at the University of Leiden (1995), developing a theory of how contractual liability can best be explained. In 1995 and 1996 he taught at the universities of Stellenbosch and Tilburg. He then was appointed at Maastricht University, first (1996-1999) as an associate professor and then (1999) to the Chair of European Private Law (the first chair for this field worldwide). At Maastricht, Jan Smits led the private law research group of the Ius Commune Research School. From 2008 to 2010, he was distinguished professor of European Private Law and Comparative Law at Tilburg University, a post he gave up in late 2010 to return to Maastricht and found the Maastricht European Private Law Institute. He held visiting positions at a number of foreign institutions, including Tulane Law School, Leuven University, the University of Liège, Louisiana State University and the Penn State Dickinson School of Law. In 2010-2011, he holds the UM-HIIL Visiting Chair on the Internationalisation of Law. Jan Smits is an elected member of the Royal Dutch Academy of Arts and Sciences (KNAW).

Filippo Spiezia is Deputy National Member for Italy of the European Union's Judicial Cooperation Unit. He has worked as a Public Prosecutor since 1991 and as an Antimafia Public Prosecutor since 2003. He also worked in the Italian Justice Superior Council as a member of the Scientific Committee, dealing with judicial training for judges and prosecutors. He is the author of several books on the fight against transnational crime, including on traffic of human beings and corruption.
In his professional experience He was in charge of many investigations for transnational crimes. He also gave several lectures in the same field of law, in the framework of international conferences and national and international academies. In the 2003 he was awarded eawarded the Falcone and Borsellino International Prize after the publication of his article entitled *The trafficking and exploitation of human beings*, edited by Giuffrè. He has authored several other books in the fields of criminal law and judicial co-operation; the latest book, entitled *Judicial co-operation before and after the Lisbon Treaty*, was released in 2009.

Levinus Timmermans is a lawyer, professor and Advocate General at the Hoge Raad der Nederlanden. He studied at the Dutch School of Economics in Rotterdam. In 1988 he obtained his doctorate on employee participation and multinational corporations at the University of Utrecht . Since 2003

Levinus has worked as Advocate General at the Supreme Court. In 2004 he became professor of Business Law at the University of Leiden . In 2006 he was appointed Professor of Foundations of Corporate Law at the Erasmus University Rotterdam.

Nicole Vincent conducts research into theories of responsibility, and she studies how these theories inform ethical, political and legal debate. Her current research project in the Department of Philosophy at Macquarie University in Sydney, Australia, is entitled "Reappraising the Capacitarian Foundation of Neurolaw". This project investigates whether capacitarian intuitions about the relationship between mental capacity and responsibility still obtain in contexts where mental capacity has been increased (*e.g.*, restored or enhanced). She is also working on constructing an Australasian Neurolaw Database that will provide the first glimpse of how neuroscience and behavioural genetics are used within legal settings in the Antipodes where questions of responsibility are at issue. Nicole also works in the Philosophy Department at Delft University of Technology, conducting research into theories of responsibility, and studying how these theories inform ethical, political and legal debate. She previously worked at the 3TU Centre for Ethics and Technology in The Netherlands on another neurolaw research project entitled "The Brain and The Law". That project aimed to develop a philosophically informed and legally useful account of responsibility – an account which accommodates neuroscientific and behavioural genetic discoveries about the nature of human agency and related empirical contributions in a way that explains rather than explaining away responsibility.

Stavros Zouridis is connected to Tilburg University as professor of Public Administration. Within this context he regularly lectures at the Nederlandse School voor Openbaar Bestuur (NSOB) and fulfils the role of co-dean of the Master Public Administration (MPA). After completing his study Legal Public Administrative Science in 1993, Zouridis combined his work at Tilburg University with a job at Publiek Domein BV (Public Domain Inc.). At Tilburg University, his research focused primarily on the interplay of law, public organisation, and informatisation. At Publiek Domein he was responsible for the educational programmes offered to aldermen, majors and city councils. From 2005-2010 he was director of Strategy department of the Ministry of Justice. Currently he combines his prime function as professor in Public Administration with an advisory role at WagenaarHoes Organisatie advies. His research focuses on the impact of the rule of law on public decision making, public organisation, and the actions of administrators, regulators, prosecutors, and judges.

Peer Zumbansen holds the Canada Research Chair in Transnational Economic Governance and Legal Theory at Osgoode Hall Law School in Toronto. Prior to joining Osgoode, he researched and taught at the University of Frankfurt and spent the academic year 2001-02 as a Jean Monnet Fellow at the European University Institute in Florence, Italy. He held Visiting Professorships at the University of Idaho College of Law, at Osgoode, at Melbourne Law School, Lucerne, and at the International Institute of Legal Sociology in Onati. His current research in private law focuses on corporate governance, comparative company law and the implications of different political economies in shaping the 'constitution of the firm'. He is Founder of the interdisciplinary Comparative Research in Law and Political Economy (CLPE) Research Network at Osgoode and the founding Editor of the *CLPE Research Paper Series*, together with Osgoode professors Shelley Gavigan and Lisa Philipps. He is a Member of the Executive Board of the Canadian Centre for German and European Studies at York University and Université de Montréal. Together with Professor Russell Miller of the University of Idaho College of Law, Professor Zumbansen is the Co-Founder and Co-Editor in Chief of the monthly English-language, peer-reviewed legal periodical *German Law Journal – Review of Developments in German, European and International Jurisprudence*, and of the Annual of German and European Law, a hardbound collection of articles and book reviews. He is also Co-Editor of the German legal quarterly, *Kritische Justiz* as well of *Transnational Legal Theory*, a magazine published monthly. In 2007 Professor Zumbansen founded the Critical Research Laboratory for multimedia projects on global cities (CRL), funded by the Canada Foundation for Innovation.

In 2010-2011, he is spending his sabbatical at Massey College in downtown Toronto, where he is working on a short study on the 'Rule of Law'. His areas of interest are: Corporate/Commercial Law, International Law, Legal Theory, Comparative Law, Urban Planning, and European Studies.

INDEX

D

E

F

G

H

I

J

L

M

N

O

P

R

S

T

U

V

W

FICHL PUBLICATION SERIES

Judge Advocate General Arne Willy Dahl, Norway
Professor Emeritus Yoram Dinstein, Tel Aviv University
Professor Jon Elster, Columbia University and Collège de France
Mr. James A. Goldston, Open Society Institute Justice Initiative
Mr. Richard Goldstone, former Chief Prosecutor,
International Criminal Tribunal for the former Yugoslavia
Judge Hanne Sophie Greve, Gulating Court of Appeal, formerly
European Court of Human Rights
Dr. Fabricio Guarigli, Senior Appeals Counsel, Office of the Prosecutor,
International Criminal Court
Dr. Franz Guenthner, Ludwig-Maximilians-Universität
Mr. Christopher Keith Hall, Amnesty International
Professor Emeritus Frits Kalshoven, Leiden University
Judge Hans-Peter Kaul, International Criminal Court
Judge Erkki Kourula, International Criminal Court
Dr. Claus Kress, Director of the Institute for Criminal Law and Criminal Procedure,
Cologne University
Professor David Luban, Georgetown University
Mr. Juan E. Méndez, Special Adviser to the ICC Prosecutor on Crime Prevention, former
President, ICTJ
Dr. Alexander Muller, Director, The Hague Institute for the Internationalisation of Law
Judge Erik Møse, Norwegian Supreme Court, former President,
International Criminal Tribunal for Rwanda
Dr. Gro Nystuen, University of Oslo and Norwegian Defence Command and Staff College
Mr. William Pace, Convener, Coalition for the International Criminal Court
Ms. Jelena Pejić, International Committee of the Red Cross
Mr. Robert Petit, former International Co-Prosecutor,
Extraordinary Chambers in the Courts of Cambodia
Maj-Gen (ret'd) Anthony P.V. Rogers, Cambridge University
Professor William A. Schabas, National University of Ireland, Galway
Professor James Silk, Yale Law School
Professor Emeritus Otto Triffterer, Salzburg University
Professor Marcos Zilli, University of Sao Paulo

OTHER VOLUMES IN THE FICHL PUBLICATION SERIES

Morten Bergsmo, Mads Harlem and Nobuo Hayashi (editors):
Importing Core International Crimes into National Law
Torkel Opsahl Academic EPublisher
Oslo, 2010
FICHL Publication Series No. 1 (Second Edition, 2010)
ISBN 978-82-93081-00-5

Nobuo Hayashi (editor):
National Military Manuals on the Law of Armed Conflict
Torkel Opsahl Academic EPublisher
Oslo, 2010
FICHL Publication Series No. 2 (Second Edition, 2010)
ISBN 978-82-93081-02-9

Morten Bergsmo, Kjetil Helvig, Ilia Utmelidze and Gorana Žagovec:
The Backlog of Core International Crimes Case Files in Bosnia and Herzegovina
Torkel Opsahl Academic EPublisher
Oslo, 2010
FICHL Publication Series No. 3 (Second Edition, 2010)
ISBN 978-82-93081-04-3

Morten Bergsmo (editor):
Criteria for Prioritizing and Selecting Core International Crimes Cases
Torkel Opsahl Academic EPublisher
Oslo, 2010
FICHL Publication Series No. 4 (Second Edition, 2010)
ISBN 978-82-93081-06-7

Morten Bergsmo and Pablo Kalmanovitz (editors):
Law in Peace Negotiations
Torkel Opsahl Academic EPublisher
Oslo, 2010
FICHL Publication Series No. 5 (Second Edition, 2010)
ISBN 978-82-93081-08-1

Morten Bergsmo, César Rodríguez Garavito, Pablo Kalmanovitz and Maria Paula Saffon (editors):
Distributive Justice in Transitions
Torkel Opsahl Academic EPublisher
Oslo, 2010
FICHL Publication Series No. 6 (2010)
ISBN 978-82-93081-12-8

Morten Bergsmo (editor):
Complementarity and the Exercise of Universal Jurisdiction for Core International Crimes
Torkel Opsahl Academic EPublisher
Oslo, 2010
FICHL Publication Series No. 7 (2010)
ISBN 978-82-93081-14-2

All volumes are freely available as e-books on the FICHL homepage www.fichl.org/toaep. Printed copies may be ordered online at www.amazon.co.uk.

www.ingramcontent.com/pod-product-compliance
Lightning Source LLC
Chambersburg PA
CBHW071338230926
51849CB00006B/512/J
* 9 7 8 8 2 9 3 0 8 1 2 7 2 *